ISBN 978-1-5283-3897-4
PIBN 10931179

1 MONTH OF
FREE
READING

at
www.ForgottenBooks.com

By purchasing this book you are eligible for one month membership to ForgottenBooks.com, giving you unlimited access to our entire collection of over 1,000,000 titles via our web site and mobile apps.

To claim your free month visit:
www.forgottenbooks.com/free931179

Richmond, Virginia

Report on a Survey of the City Government

Prepared for the

Civic Association of Richmond

by the

Bureau of Municipal Research

New York City

1917

CONTENTS

Richmond, Virginia

Report on a Survey of
the City Government

Prepared for the

Civic Association of Richmond

by the

Bureau of Municipal Research

New York City

1917

November 5, 1917.

BEN T. AUGUST, Esq.,
  City Clerk of the City of Richmond, Virginia.

DEAR SIR:
  In accordance with the terms of a contract dated July 7
1917, between the City of Richmond, certain officers of the Civi
Association and the Bureau of Municipal Research, the latter ha
completed the survey required by said contract, and begs to sub
mit herewith the final report thereon.

Respectfully submitted,
HERBERT R. SANDS,
Director of Field Work.

Received by the City Clerk.

Transmitted to the Board of Aldermen November 13th, 1917
and referred to the Special Joint Committee on Charter Amend
ments, with authority to report to either branch, and with th
request that they have 100 copies printed for distribution to mem
bers of the City Council and Heads of the City Departments.

BEN T. AUGUST,
Clerk Board of Aldermen.

SUMMARY OF RECOMMENDATIONS.

(Recommendations marked with a star require statutory or charter changes).

The Mayor.

So far as the executive management of the public business of Richmond is concerned the city corporation is headless. Or it may be argued that it is triple headed. At least there is no centralization of executive authority. That the mayor is mayor in name only is sufficiently discriptive of that office.

His appointive power practically limited to the head of the police department, his power of removal of administrative heads more apparent than real, his power of investigation little more than that possessed by all taxpayers, the mayoralty of the city of Richmond is little more than a figure head.

Nor is any other office of the government vested with authority and responsibility for leadership. Appointive and reporting power is diffused, not only as between the mayor and administrative board, but among the entire legislative, executive and judicial branches of the government.

It is the experience of government throughout the world and also of commercial enterprises that progress and success demand the centralization of executive authority in a single official.

*Therefore, it is recommended that the entire structural organization of the ctiy government of Richmond be revamped by amending the charter or preparing a new one so as to centralize in the mayor both authority and responsibility for the management of all of the administrative departments.

The City Council.

Originally established on a bicameral plan as required by the state constitution, time has abundantly demonstrated that as the city's legislative machine the organization of the city council is unnecessarily complicated and hence not well adapted to the city's needs. The dual plan contributes more to deterring and confusing legislative action than to expediting and simplifying it.

*Therefore it is recommended that in revising the charter the city council be limited to a single body.

*Inasmuch as a small group can proceed with better facility and understanding than a large group, it is recommended that the council be limited to nine members. Throughout the large corporations of the commercial world the present tendency is in favor of small boards of directors. To preclude the possibility of "log rolling," ward legislation and other evils of the ward system, the majority of the members, say five, should be elected at large. Each standing committee should consist of the entire council membership.

*The charter should limit the council strictly to matters of legislation and thus prevent a recurrence of the former practice of usurping administrative functions.

As an alternative to the mayor and small council plan, the city manager and commission plans are suggested.

The Administrative Board.

*Created originally to meet an imaginary need, this board should be abolished at the earliest opportunity. As a means of relieving the city council of the burdens of administrative business it was quite unnecessary. The $36,000 annual cost of maintaining the board and its staff can be better used for other purposes. Whatever advantages there may be in having the judgment of a group of minds on administrative problems can easily be secured through constituting as an administrative board or cabinet, the heads of the four or five largest departments of the government, as subsequently described in this report.

City Clerk and Clerk of Committees.

These offices should be consolidated. The present clerk of committees could readily do the work of both offices.

The City Auditor.

*When revising the charter the auditing and accounting functions of this office should be separated. The auditor should be appointed by the city council as an independent check on the administrative department of government. but the mayor should appoint a city accountant who would co-ordinate with such administrative departments, keep all the central financial records, assist the mayor in preparing the annual budget, and currently inform him throughout the year relative to operating costs.

Accounting and Reporting.

The accounting and reporting system now in use, although needing considerable further development, is not deserving of any serious criticism. The greatest need is to re-adjust it so as to show separately and readily at all times what portion of the cash balance at the end of any given period belongs to bond funds, what amount belongs to the general funds of the city, and what amount to special and trust funds.

It is also important that the excellent beginning already made to record contingent liabilities as encumbrances on the respective appropriations should be followed out to its logical conclusion. Balance sheets which will be really informative as to the city's financial condition cannot be prepared until the two foregoing recommendations are made effective.

Each appropriation account should be closed at the end of the year. This has not been done in the case of appropriations against which contract encumbrances continue from year to year.

Both the monthly and annual reports showing the city's financial condition should be made more informative as described in detail in the text of this report.

Audit and Payment of Claims Other Than Payrolls.

There is need of better evidence as to the receipt of deliveries from vendors in the quantity and quality as prescribed in the contracts. This involves a revision of the invoice and voucher forms so as to include certificates which will really fix responsibility. Better certification by the Auditor's office as to the integrity of the claims is also needed.

The practice of having claimants call at the auditor's office for their payment warrants should be discontinued. It seriously interferes with the regular business of the office and is entirely unnecessary. As soon as the claim has been audited and a warrant signed by the auditor, the documents should be transmitted in groups each day to the treasurer and claimants should be required to call only at the latter office. At the present time they are compelled to visit both offices. A still better plan would be for the treasurer to mail the warrants to the payees.

The clerk to the auditor appointed by council should no longer be required to countersign the payment warrants. The signature of the auditor when countersigned by the treasurer and supported by the proper certification on the voucher should be adequate.

Auditing and Payment of Payrolls.

What is said in the report with respect to need for better certification and fixing of responsibility with respect to claims other than payrolls, applies with equal force to the payroll system.

The establishment of a separate paymaster system for the departments under the administrative board does much to strengthen the procedure, but the advantage derived from having a separate paymaster should be extended to the entire government.

With the abolition of the administrative board the treasurer or an employee in his office should be appointed as city paymaster.

Audit of Revenues.

*The procedure incident to paying moneys into the city treasury should be simplified. This does not apply to taxes nor to water and gas bills. Strange as it may seem, however, there is altogether too much "red tape involved in paying certain other miscellaneous revenues into the treasury and getting a receipt therefor.

As a whole, the central auditing control over revenue accruals and collections is adequate.

Management of Sinking Funds.

Much care and attention has been given in recent years to properly maintaining the sinking funds of the city. Detailed actuarial computation of the entire city debt was made as a part of this survey. Based on the amount of the debt now existing it showed that if the present sinking fund policy of the city is continued an amount will be produced sufficient to redeem all outstanding bonds at their respective dates of maturity with the exception of the $2,000,000 maturing in 1950 which, if redeemed from the sinking fund will produce a deficit of about $266,000. All other bonds maturing to 1950 can be redeemed and there will be $1,734.000 available for the redemption of the $2,000,000 issue. In order to produce an amount to amortize the deficiency of $266.000, which will otherwise exist in 1950, it will be necessary to set aside semi-annually henceforth the additional sum of $2,032.

The Budget.

*Instead of postponing the adoption of the annual appropriation ordinance until nearly two months after the year has begun, is under the existing practice, it should be adopted prior to the beginning of the fiscal year. To insure conformity with this recommendation, the revised charter should specify definitely the dates for the successive steps in the development of the annual budget.

Instead of obtaining appropriation requests from department heads without uniformity of classification, they should be obtained on uniform blanks which would contain instructions and rulings for a standarization of all items. Thus it will be possible to make better comparisons not only with preceding years but also as between departments.

Centralization of executive responsibility in the city's government should be accompanied by the establishing of an executive budget system whereby the mayor would prepare the budget with the assistance of his department heads and the city accountant, submit it to the council and be required to defend it in that body.

The present procedure provides adequately for budget hearings and publicity.

The restriction in the appropriation ordinance relative to restricting department heads to the amounts appropriated should be enforced.

The City's Finances.

Approximately $80,000 should be deducted from next year's appropriations. The details supporting this recommendation are shown in the chapter of this report relating to "The City's Finances." This reduction should be effected not only because it is good business, but also to show the good faith of the latter before any steps are taken in revising the tax rate. The report points out certain additional economies which, if conditions become acute, can be adopted temporarily as war measures; also further economies which can be effected just as soon as the requisite statutory and charter revision is obtained.

With respect to revenues the gas rates must be increased if this municipal enterprise is to continue self-supporting. The report also cites certain minor sources of additional revenues which should be immediately developed. But on the whole, if additional revenues are found necessary, pending revision of the constitution to permit the levying of special assessments, they must come through the general tax levy.

Among the eight cities of the United States which have a population of 145,000 to 185,000, two have a higher and six a lower

per capita net debt. A detailed study of the financial statistics
of that group and also of twenty-six southern cities shows that
as a rule the tax rate is comparatively low in those cities which
levy special assessments for local improvements, and vice versa.
Also that those cities which have large collections from business
licenses show a tendency to low tax rates.

The borrowing margin of the city is ample, and care should
be taken to continue it in the same condition. As above cited,
the sinking funds have been well administered and if the policy
is continued, will be sufficient to pay the city's debt as it matures.

In issuing future bonds, preference should be given to the
serial bond plan which precludes the necessity for providing any
sinking funds. The terms of future issues should be made to conform more nearly with the life of the assets to be acquired from
the proceeds of the bonds.

Purchasing Methods.

The city is deserving of considerable credit for its purchasing
methods. All purchases for departments coming under the jurisdiction of the administrative board are required to be made
through the board. The contract method is extensively used and
to some extent blanket contracts are made for all departments.
With occasional exceptions awards are made to the lowest bidder
and there is fairly good competition for the city's business. In
thus giving credit for progress made to date, it should not be
assumed that the city is buying as economically as it should. To
accomplish the latter object the purchasing methods should be
further developed and improved as follows:

1. There must be complete centralization of the city's purchasing power.
2. Written specifications must be prepared for the principal items
   of supplies, materials and equipment and adopted as standard for all departments.
3. There must be more publicity relative to all purchasing proposals both on contract and open market order, so as to
   secure more competition in bidding.
4. Many of the commodities now purchased in small amounts
   should be obtained under contract.
5. Supplementing the inspection by departmental employees made
   at the various receiving points, there should be inaugurated

*Instead of appointing three special assessors every five years to re-assess real estate, the assessment of lands and buildings should be a continuing process from year to year by the commissioner of revenue. With respect to experience, staff and equipment, that official is in a position to do the work better than is possible for any assessing board which is of mushroom growth every five years. The commissioner should adopt the Hoffman-Neill or similar scientific tables for the assessment of land as have those cities which have made the most progress in their assessment work. For the same reason he should also adopt a scientific classification of buildings, definite factor values and depreciation tables.

To secure a more equitable valuation as between various properties in the city, the policy of the assessing office should be to assess as nearly as possible the "fair market value" as required by the constitution. At the present time it is believed that property is being assessed at only 75 to 80 per cent. thereof.

*The fifty-cent poll tax should be abolished because the work incident to the collection is not justified by the amount received.

In preparing the city's personal property book the commissioner should use forms which will meet the requirements of the city collector's office when the book is turned over to that official, as a basis for billing and collecting instead of using forms which require the collector to copy the entire contents of the books before he can proceed with his work.

Fewer copies of the real estate rolls should be prepared. If authority cannot be secured to reduce the number of copies of the tax books now required, they should at least be simplified so that all copies and also the tax bills, if possible, can be made at a single writing on a wide carriage typewriter by carbon process.

Collector of City Taxes.

This office should be consolidated with that of the city treasurer. Thereby a saving of several thousand dollars would be effected and the convenience of the general public facilitated. In making this recommendation not the slightest reflection is intended upon the present collector or his staff because there was evidence of a conscientious desire to administer the office efficiently. In fact it is being well conducted.

*The branch collection office on the south side of the river should be abolished irrespective of whether the entire plant be consolidated with the treasurer's office or not.

There is need for improving the form of tax bills in use so as to provide a carbon copy or coupon for posting purposes when crediting the payments on the tax books and in establishing the correctness of the amount of cash received each day.

Collector of Delinquent Taxes.

If the office of collector of city taxes is continued the collection of delinquent taxes should be made a function thereof instead of council appointing a special official for that purpose who is co-ordinate in salary with the tax collector.

*If the collecting function is transferred to the treasurer's office the collection of delinquent taxes should, of course, be included.

The Treasurer.

The treasurer should distribute all payment warrants instead of payees being required to go first to the auditor and then to the treasurer.

*The branch office on the south side of the river should be abolished and that district covered by sub-stations, the same as other outlying sections of the city.

City funds are scattered in too many depositories. There is little doubt but that a higher rate of interest could be obtained if fewer banks were selected. This could be done without lessening in any degree the city's security.

The treasurer, or one of his assistants should be designated as paymaster for the entire city. As already pointed out in connection with the collector's office, the city treasurer should collect all city taxes, similarly as he now collects water and gas bills and miscellaneous revenues.

Police Department.

Appointments, Promotion and Discipline.
*In some ways, the control over appointments and promotions appears to be the most important matter in connection with the

management of the police department. It will be placed first in this summary of recommendations. All appointments to the police and fire departments should be made only as the result of a competitive civil service examination. The chief should be selected as a result of a competitive civil service promotional examination and, in order to protect him against arbitrary removal, he should be given the right of an appeal to a court of record upon dismissal.

The police force appears to be large enough at present, and by a re-arrangement of patrol posts and the abolishment of special details, the number of men available for patrol can be increased materially.

*All promotions in the police and fire departments should be made only from one rank to the next as a result of competitive civil service promotional tests.

*The mayor should be given power to drop from the roll any member of the police department who, after serving a probationary period of six months, is deemed unfit for the service and no appeal should be allowed to dismissed probationary policemen.

Instead of having a physician employed on a fee basis, the position of salaried medical officer to the police and fire departments should be established and the law should require that appointment to this position be made only as a result of competitive civil service examination.

The medical officer would conduct a physical examination of all policemen and firemen prior to their appointment and also at end of their probationary period. An annual physical examination of all the members would be an excellent innovation that would tend to keep the men in good condition.

All applicants for appointment to the police force should be required to furnish corroborative proof of age, instead of taking their statements without question. A probationary period of six months for newly appointed policemen should be fixed and final appointment at the end of this period made dependent upon their efficiency and physical condition. The captains and sergeants should be required to furnish written reports concerning the work performed by probationers in their districts. The probationers should be assigned to duty at first with policemen selected especially for experience, intelligence and character.

The discipline among patrolmen is poor. This is a matter for the sergeants to correct under the supervision of the captains.

There are not enough sergeants to supervise the patrolmen, and three additional sergeants should be appointed from the ranks of the patrolmen. The number of sergeants on patrol should be increased also by transferring the plain-clothes sergeants in the third district to active patrol duty. A rule should be adopted requiring uniforms to be completely buttoned when worn, and prohibiting smoking while in uniform.

One of the most effective ways of obtaining better service and increasing the interest of the members of the force in their work is through a board of honor. Such a board should be established and should award annually, medals to the policeman and firemen performing the most notable acts of bravery, and to those as well you have made the best suggestion during the year for the improvement of the departments. The members of the force should be graded on the basis of efficiency according to a system of merits and demerits, and those having the greatest number of merits should be marked accordingly in promotional examinations.

*As a disciplinary officer, the department physician should not have any business relations whatever with members of the police or fire department or their families, and the members of the force should not be required to make any contribution towards his salary.

*The maintenance of a separate police station in the annexed section known as the south-side, was required for five years by the annexation agreement. Twenty-four members of the department are detailed thereto. It is questioned whether the law requires that this separate force be maintained for longer than five years after annexation. Whether the law requires this or not, it should not be continued and the law should be amended if an amendment is necessary. The territory now included in this district should be made a part of the first police district.

A peculiar practice is followed in the police court of allowing policemen to request the dismissal of their cases and the discharge of prisoners. This practice has been abused, to judge from the record of the past year, and is one that opens the way to the most serious irregularity. The mayor and the chief should exercise the greatest care in reviewing the results obtained by the policemen in the prosecution of their cases and the mayor should strictly prohibit the members of the force from requesting a dismissal of the complaints they have made.

Police School of Instruction Recommended.

That the members of the force be given proper training for their work, and that for this purpose there be established a police school of instruction.

That the school be used to determine fitness for police duty as well as for instruction of the force, and that the course of instruction include training for detective service.

That members of the force be provided with printed instructions as to procedure in homicide cases.

Uniforms.

That the shield worn by sergeants be of a different design from those worn by patrolmen.

That as soon as the city is financially able, all uniforms and equipment of policemen and firemen be furnished without cost to the men, and that provision be made for the purchase of cniforms and equipment under contract.

That all revolvers be carried in a holster in the blouse instead of the hip pocket.

Special Details to be Revoked.

*That at such time as the statute is amended, all details to courts be revoked.

That the details of the telephone operators and the policemen now serving as clerks be revoked and civilians employed in their place.

That the third district be placed under the command of a sergeant and the force reduced to thirteen, pending the amendment of the law permitting the abolition of this district.

That the captain in charge of the third district be assigned to headquarters as night captain.

That the practice of detailing a policeman to Forest Hill Park be discontinued and that the owners of the park be required to furnish their own policemen.

Re-apportionment of Patrol Posts.

That the chief be required to make a complete census and study of every block in the city and that as a result of this study a re-apportionment of the patrol posts be made.

That circular patrol posts be abandoned and straight avenue and side street posts be substituted.

That police patrol booths be established in the suburban and residential sections and that mounted and foot patrols be abandoned.

That an immediate re-apportionment of the patrol posts on Broad Street be made and the new posts established on a straight way basis.

That the number of men assigned to patrol Broad Street be greatly reduced.

That the superintendent of the signal service be instructed to plan for and furnish an estimate as to the cost of installing flashlight signals throughout the city.

Special Patrolmen.

That the method of appointing special patrolmen be revised so as to provide that they will be required to furnish a bond to the city, wear a uniform of a design established by the department which should be different from that of the regular service, report regularly to the chief of police, be under his supervision and appointed only upon his recommendation.

Traffic Control.

That the officer in charge of traffic be regularly promoted to the rank of sergeant and paid the salary of the sergeant.

That the sergeant in charge of traffic be permitted to visit New York and Philadelphia and there to study methods employed in regulation of traffic.

That upon his return he conduct a course of training for the traffic men.

That the traffic booth, if continued in use, be of an ornamental design.

That the patrolmen in charge of traffic duty be prohibited from sitting down while on duty; that all chairs and seats be removed from their shelter houses, and that as soon as possible these shelter houses be equipped with telephones connected with the police department switchboard.

Arrests.

That the practice of including as an arrest each complaint made against the prisoner be discontinued at once and that in tabulating arrests only the number of persons arrested be included.

That in all cases of arrests the records show clearly upon whose initiation the warrant was issued and the arrest made, and in tabulating the arrests care be taken to indicate the number of arrests made upon warrants issued by magistrates upon citizens' complaints, and those made upon the initiative of the police or as the result of police investigation.

That the records of arrests include a more detailed history of the prisoner and that care be taken to indicate in the records of arrest any wounds, bruises or marks appearing upon the prisoner at the time of arraignment before the desk sergeant.

That the procedure for maintaining the record of arrests be revised in accordance with the suggestions contained in this report.

That all women prisoners, whether black or white, be detained at the first precinct in charge of the matron who should make ample provision for segregation.

That the procedure for receiving women prisoners be revised so as to require that all women prisoners be delivered to the matron at the sergeant's desk, regardless of the time, day or night, they are received.

That no male member of the department be permitted in the female detention cell or the matron's quarters, except superior officers, when making inspection or when rendering aid to the matron in restraining disorderly prisoners.

That, when searched, all property be taken from the prisoner and retained by the desk sergeant until the case is disposed of.

Detectives.

That the method of selecting detectives be revised so as to provide that all detectives be selected upon the recommendation of the captain of detectives from the list of those who passed as the result of a civil service examination.

That assignment to detective service carry with it no definite tenure and that the length of the service of a detective be dependent wholly upon the efficiency of the service rendered.

That the captain of detectives be empowered by the chief to remand to patrol service such members of his force as he may deem inefficient.

That the mayor make every effort possible, at once, to produce harmony between the captain of detectives and the uniformed officers, even to the extent of making a change in the personnel.

That the detective bureau be reorganized in accordance with the plan outlined in the report.

That the detective staff be increased from eight to twelve.

That provision be made at once for the training of the detectives.

That the system of recording complaints be completely revised so as to provide for a detailed history of cases, the action taken upon them and a proper review of the progress made.

That detectives be required to file written reports upon all cases assigned to them, that these reports show in detail the service rendered by the detective and the results of investigation of the case.

That the detectives' daily report be revised, that the captain of detectives be required to furnish the chief and the mayor a detailed daily report and a monthly report upon a comparative basis.

That the procedure for checking pawnshop lists be improved and what is known as the "Boston System" be installed.

That the ordinance requiring the installation of buzzers in the pawnshops be enforced.

That the Bertillon operator be permitted to visit the New York police department's school of instructions to study the methods of taking, photographing, recording and classifying finger prints, as well as the advanced methods of criminal identification.

That the plain clothes men now assigned to captains, operate under the supervision of the captain of detectives, as junior detectives.

Care of Property.

That in connection with the care of property there be maintained a standard property register and that regulation property sacks, properly marked, be used in storing property.

That as such times as the law is amended, council change the title of the secretary and purchasing agent to that of chief clerk of the police department and that he be placed in direct charge of all of the records of the department, and directly responsible to the chief of police.

Vice.

That the mayor and chief of police conduct a vigorous campaign against the use of motor vehicles in connection with commercialized vice.

That a police woman be appointed as a result of competitive civil service examination.

Surgical Division.

That the surgeon be required to respond, with the fire appa--ratus, to every second alarm of fire.

That the surgeon be required to maintain complete medical records of the police and firemen.

That a free clinic be established by the surgeon for the services of policemen or firemen.

That the surgical division be provided with a complete equipment with which to conduct examinations and treatments.

General Administration.

That the city be permitted to abolish the third district station.

That the position of secretary and purchasing agent be abolished and the position of chief clerk established.

That the moneys collected as costs in the police and juvenile courts, pending the abolition of the cost system, revert to the general city funds and not to the police department, as as present.

That the mayor direct at once the discontinuance of the monthly payment to the secretary of the department out of the police department's special fund.

That an improved system of records and reports be installed in accordance with the recommendation in the text of this report.

Fire Department.

While a careful examination of the records of the board of fire commissioners indicate that the members are faithful in their attendance at meetings and interested in their work, the weight of experience in other communities is against the administration of a highly technical service like a fire department, by a board of commissioners. The powers conferred, by charter, upon the board tend to remove the department from the remainder of the government and thus to prevent close co-operative relation.

The work of the board itself into two main parts: one, the purchase of supplies, and the other, control over appointments, promotions, transfers and dismissals. The making of purchases is a function which belongs to a central purchasing agent, a position the establishment of which is recommended elsewhere in this report. appointments and promotions should be made as the result of competitive civil service examination, while the transferring of firemen and their officers is a function which should be exercised by the chief of the department. The main operations of the fire department should be under the direction of the chief, who should be selected because of expert technical training and experience. Consequently, the department could best be administered if placed under the supervision of the mayor or central executive to whom the chief would be directly responsible.

*Therefore, it is recommended that the charter be amended so as to abolish the board of fire commissioners.

The absence of scientific training is perhaps the chief defect of Richmond's fire department, aside from civil service regulations. Special training is required at every step in a fireman's work, and since principles of fire extinguishment have practically been standardized, the training of men to put out fires is no longer a difficult matter and its need is no longer questioned. But the ability to put out fires with the minimum loss is no longer all that is necessary to make an efficient fireman. He should be trained to prevent fires through careful inspection, and he should be familiar with every modern development for fire prevention. Therefore, it is recommended that a training school for fire service be established in accordance with the suggestions as to equipment and course of instruction that are contained in the text of this report. A fireman should not be confined to one company, but should be trained by being attached successively to companies in all parts of the city, truck companies as well as engine companies. All firemen should be instructed in the operation of the steam or gasoline fire engines and elevators in buildings. The drivers of the motor vehicles should receive special training, because the number of accidents resulting in damage to apparatus is high, and most of the drivers do not know how to make repairs of the most ordinary character. Setting up exercises, frequent drills and tests should be regularly conducted under the supervision of the officers.

*In general, the recommendations relating to appointments, promotions and dismissals in the police department apply also to the fire department, and the charter should be changed accordingly.

The chief's control over the force is somewhat weakened because promotions are made by the board of commissioners and not always in accordance with the recommendations of the chief. Pending the introduction of the merit system for promotions, the board could strengthen the chief's authority considerably by acting solely upon his recommendations. While the charter aims to protect the chief against arbitrary removal without cause, the method of appointing him is not in accordance with the best practice. Nothing in the charter prevents the appointment of a chief from outside of the force. The charter should be amended in this particular, so as to provide that the chief could be appointed only as the result of a competitive civil service examination, which would be open to the assistant chiefs only. The chief should be given the right of appeal to a court of record for a review of the findings in case of dismissal.

An additional assistant chief should be appointed because of the size of the city and the way in which the important risks are distributed. Under present conditions, in the absence of one of the two assistant chiefs, it is necessary to detail a captain as acting assistant chief, which is contrary to good practice. It is recommended elsewhere that the secretary, who is now given the rank of assistant chief, be made a civilian employee and relieved of the title of third assistant chief. The city should be divided into three districts, with one active assistant in charge of each district. In the absence of one of the assistants, another could assume charge of two districts temporarily. The assistant chiefs should be selected from among the captains as the result of competitive civil service examination.

Under the present procedure, it is possible for a fireman who has been in the service but a very short time to be appointed to the rank of captain. Captains should be selected only as the result of competitive civil service examination to which only the lieutenants should be admitted. At least two years of service should be required of a candidate for appointment as captain.

The lieutenants, in turn, should be elected only as the result of competitive civil service examination for promotion, to which firemen and enginemen should be admitted. There is no regularly established rank of lieutenant at present, and the city council should establish that grade. In the absence of an ordinance definitely fixing their status, the firemen do not show the proper respect for the men designated to act as lieutenants. Some of the firemen even receive more pay than the men who act as lieutenants. The lieutenants should certainly receive more pay than the salary paid firemen of any grade or engineers. Most of the engineers showed a thorough understanding of their duties, but some did not. They are appointed without any examination to ascertain their fitness for this most important position. They should receive higher pay than firemen, and should be required to instruct all members of engine companies in the operation and maintenance of the engines.

The department has made thousands of inspections during the past year to discover and correct conditions that may result in fires. These inspections were made by officers of the department. Uniformed firemen should also be assigned to this work in order to obtain experience and familiarize themselves with conditions in their districts. The laws do not give the chief or the board of fire commissioners broad enough powers to require property owners to correct dangerous conditions.

*It is recommended that a law be enacted creating a fire prevention commission with broad powers. The commission should consist of the mayor, the superintendent of buildings or building inspector, the chief of the fire department and one citizen appointed by the mayor to serve without pay. The chief of the fire department should be the executice officer of the commission. The commission should have full power to make rules and regulations and to issue orders which should have the force and effect of law, and the commission should have jurisdiction over buildings of all kinds. The need for the inspection and regulation of conditions in dwellings is important, because in most of the cities in the United States the largest number of fires occur in dwelling houses.

Among the other recommendations in the report on the fire department, the more important are:

That the administrative head be currently advised of all activities of the department through a proper reporting system.

That the chief be required to furnish the administrative heads with a complete and detailed fire service report within twenty-four hours after the fire.

That the board of commissioners adopt a revised procedure for the purchasing of supplies and equipment, pending the establishment of a central purchasing division for the city, and that all purchases be made upon requisition through the secretary of the board, who should exercise complete control over the purchasing procedure.

That at such time as the city is financially able, new quarters be provided for engine company "seven" and truck company "two."

That the schedule of furlough be revised so as to provide for each member being allowed one day off in five.

That sufficient funds be provided as promptly as possible for the erection of a fire station at the corner of Kensington avenue and Cleveland street, and that this company be furnished with a motor driven combination chemical and hose wagon.

. That council request the co-operation of the street car companies in the installation of a signal service which will provide for bells and red signal lights along the lines of the railway system at points near fire stations.

That the board of commissioners direct the chief and his two assistants to make as promptly as possible a complete examination of the distribution of the apparatus with a view of bringing into active service such apparatus as is now assigned to outlying territories.

That every effort be made to effect a complete motorization of the apparatus of the department as promptly as possible.

That all hose of the department be tested annually and redistributed in accordance with its condition.

. That as rapidly as the finances of the city will permit, additional fire alarm boxes be installed, so that there will be a fire alarm box within 500 feet of every building in the mercantile and manufacturing section, and within 800 feet of every valuable group of buildings.

That all fire alarm boxes be equipped with a red light, to be used during the night, so as to indicate the location of the box.

That all fire alarm boxes located in and immediately outside the fire houses be removed and placed at points in need of boxes.

That provision be made for having two alarm operators on duty during the night.

That the practice of allowing alarm operators discretion in a matter of dispatching apparatus in response to silent or still alarms be discontinued, and that all alarms be treated in precisely the same manner as box alarms.

That the running card be rearranged so as to provide for the automatic "filling in" of companies in the event of two or more alarms.

That the use of the tower bells be discontinued at once, as it only tends to draw a crowd to a fire, which handicaps the work of the firemen.

That there be reserved one trunk line at each of the telephone exchanges over which fire alarms may be dispatched.

That private telephones be removed from the fire houses.

That "tappers" be removed from the firemen's homes, since the schedules should be so arranged that a fireman on regular leave should not be called out on every alarm, and the "tappers" only make much extra work for the signal men.

That the superintendent of the signal service cause to be installed in connection with the police switchboard at headquarters exchanges from trunk lines, so that the police department will have one telephone number, all calls being received at the switchboard and transmitted to the person for whom they are intended.

That an ordinance be adopted requiring the owners of theaters to pay for the services of firemen detailed to the theaters during performances.

That firemen detailed to theaters be equipped with electric torches.

That the practice of detailing the same firemen contiuously to theater duty be discontinued, and that all the firemen be given equal opportunity in inspecting and observing theater conditions.

That there be installed as promptly as possible an improved reporting system for reporting fire prevention inspection.

That each captain be required to carry with him upon the apparatus a card record of the structural conditions of the buildings within his district, such record to be compiled from the information contained in the fire prevention inspection report.

Police Benefit Association.

An examination of many pension and relief associations in this country which has been made by the Bureau of Municipal Research has shown that a neglect of actuarial principles in the establishment and operation of these systems is widespread, with the result that costly reorganization is required or complete bankruptcy is imminent or has occurred. The twenty men who compose the trustees of the Richmond fund have not the information which would be required by the board of directors of a regular insurance company, and yet they are actually conducting an insurance business. While the reports of this fund show that for each of the five years ending November 2, 1916, the fund had received more than it has disbursed for benefits and expenses, no statement has been prepared showing the prospective benefits which the fund will ultimately be called upon to pay and the prospective assets.

It is recommended that the board of trustees of the fund have an actuarial investigation made to determine whether the revenues are sufficient to meet the anticipated benefits, whether they are excessive or whether they are insufficient, and that the board then devise means to meet the situation on a sound financial basis with full knowledge of the prospective liabilities and assets. An outline of the information necessary to be obtained and the calculations to be made is contained in the text of this report.

Firemen's Mutual Aid Association.

The same situation relatively exists and the same recommendations are made in the case of the Firemen's Mutual Aid Association as in the case of the Police Benefit Association.

Police Court.

The atmosphere of the court, the lack of order, the mingling of persons of all kinds, the "comedy" of the police court judge often at the expense of unfortunate and helpless men and women, the antiquated cost system, are all reminiscent of days and methods that have passed in most other English-speaking communities. Many of the people of Richmond look upon the proceedings in this court as one of the best shows in town, and a well-known vaudeville actor has copied the mannerisms and the language of the court and appeared in all parts of the country with success as an entertainer. The possibility of using the court as a correctional institution seems to be overlooked in the eagerness to amass a large total of fines, and it is even possible for a defendant to avoid appearance in court at all, provided he sends in the "standard" fine for his offense to the court clerk by messenger.

The methods of this court add nothing to the reputation for jurisprudence of the State of Virginia, and the members of the bar and the public should not rest until the procedure is improved and its dignity of the court asserted and maintained. One of the most serious features of the practice in this court is the toleration by the judge of requests from police officers that the complaints they have brought against law-breakers be withdrawn and the cases dismissed. This is a matter for both the mayor and the public to investigate. A list of the cases in which such requests were granted by the judge may be found in the text of this report relating to the police department.

The terms of the act of annexation of the city of Manchester have been construed to require the continued employment of a police court judge for that section, known as Part II of the police court. Despite this duplication, when the police court judge of the old court takes a vacation a magistrate is designated to sit in place of the judge, and his salary is paid out of the funds of the police department. This is an unjustifiable practice, and should be changed so that the judge of Part II shall be required to sit instead of a magistrate in case of the absence of the judge in Part I, until such time as Part II is abolished.

*It is recommended that Part II of the police court be abolished, even though an act of the general assembly of Virginia may be required to do it, although it is not settled in the minds of attorneys that such an act will be required. There is no justification for having two police courts in Richmond, particularly when the court now ends its sessions at 11 or 11:30 A. M.

It is recommended that the police court remain in session until at least 4 P. M. The judge of Part II frequently holds afternoon and evening sessions for the relief of persons who may be arrested and who might otherwise be detained illegally over night, and he is to be commended for this practice.

Other recommendations regarding the police court are:

*That the police justice be appointed by the mayor for a term of not less than ten years, and that his salary be paid out of city funds; that he be removable only through impeachment proceedings brought before a court of higher jurisdiction.

*That the cost of operating and maintaining this court be borne by the city.

*That the cost and fee system in connection with this court be abolished.

*That all fines collected in this court be paid into the city treasury.

*That the laws be amended so as to permit of a Sunday session of the police court.

*That the laws be amended so as to provide for the inauguration of the probation system, the granting of suspended sentences by the court and the appointment of probation officers.

*That the laws be amended so as to provide for the establishment of a summons procedure similar to the statute now in effect in the city of New York.

*That the laws be amended so as to provide that in all felony cases the approval of the commonwealth attorney be required before a bond is accepted by the court, and that he be given forty-eight hours in which to investigate the securities offered.

*That the clerk and all attaches of the court be appointed by the mayor as a result of competitive civil service examination; that the clerk be required to qualify as a stenographer and typewriter; and that the detail of a policeman for this service be discontinued.

*That the procedure and records of the court be simplified, and that the Inferior Courts Act of the City of New York be adopted as a guide in revising the procedure and the court records.

*That for the guidance of council, the administrative officials of the city of Richmond and the Legislature, the police court justice be required by statute to prepare and file officially a complete and detailed annual statement of the business carried on in the court. ·

That the practice of delegating judicial powers to the cashier of the court and trial powers to the magistrates be discontinued at once.

That, as a convenience to the citizens and the city departments, there be held special sessions of the police court for the hearing of cases involving violation of the traffic ordinances and departmental regulation.

That the cases in which women are defendants be heard either in private chambers or after the cases of the male prisoners have been completely disposed of.

That no spectators be admitted to hearings in cases where the defendants are women, and that only the police officers and newspaper representatives be admitted.

That the procedure for the acceptance of bail bonds be revised so as to provide that all bondsmen be required to make a complete and detailed statement of property holdings in affidavit form, and that they furnish the court with the location of their residence, their occupation and the location of the place of their business.

That a stenographic record be made of all examinations in felony cases and in such cases as are held for trial in the higher courts or for the grand jury, the testimony to be transcribed and a copy furnished the commonwealth attorney.

That fines be collected in the inside office and not in the open court-room, and that the procedure be changed so as to make this reform possible.

That police officers awaiting the trial of their cases be required to remain seated in a part of the court-room specially set aside for them. and that no smoking be permitted in the court-room.

That policemen when testifying appear properly uniformed, and that detectives and policemen performing duty in plainclothes display their shields on the lapels of their coat when in attendance at court.

That no person other than counsel, police officers and witnesses in the specific case being heard be admitted within the enclosure immediately before the judge's desk, and that no persons be permitted to stand about or loiter back of the judge's desk, or in the doorway immediately back of the judge.

That all warrants in criminal matters be issued by the judge of the police court.

That there be maintained a register of warrants, and that the court require a written return upon all warrants issued, within a reasonable time after their issuance.

Sealer of Weights and Measures.

The sealer of weights and measures is required by law to perform so many duties and act in so many different capacities that he cannot give the purchasing public and the honest merchants the protection that is needed against fraud in weighing and measuring devices. The sealer is also the city gauger and the city weighmaster. He receives a small allowance from the city as sealer, but his income depends mainly upon fees for acting as gauger and weighmaster. He is frequently required to weigh coal for the city at the point of delivery for as much as a day at a time. He cannot, therefore, conduct the inspections necessary to detect fraudulent weighing and measuring devices. Of 156 scales tested during the present survey, seventy (45 per cent) were found to be incorrect. The shortages in package goods were even more serious.

*It is recommended that the law be amended so as to require the sealer to devote his entire time to weights and measures work. The fee system should be abolished and he should be paid a salary commensurate with his services. He should be appointed by the mayor as the result of a competitive civil service examination and should be given the title of inspector instead of sealer, because of the misleading impression created by the term "sealer" and "sealed."

*Since the laws governing the use of weighing and measuring devices are inadequate, it is recommended that they be amended so as to provide for control over the manufacture and sale of devices and for the sale of package goods by net weight, the weight to be indicated on the outside of the package. The inspector should be empowered to prohibit the use of inferior and defective types of "tricky" weighing and measuring devices.

The sealer should be empowered to employ women shoppers from time to time to conduct secret investigations.

Deliveries of coal and other supplies purchased by the city should be weighed under the supervision of an official of the department purchasing them, and not by the sealer. The sealer should devote more time to sporadic inspections and detective work than to routine inspections.

The sealer should conduct a vigorous campaign against short-weighting, and in connection with it he should secure the co-operation of the newspapers in an effort to educate the purchasing public against fraudulent practices.

Provision should be made for the appointment of an assistant inspector of weights and measures, whose salary shall be less than that the sealer. The assistant should be selected as the result of a competitive civil service test.

An ordinance should be adopted requiring peddlers and hucksters to secure a certificate of inspection from the inspector of weights and measures as to the accuracy of their weighing and measuring devices before a license is issued to them.

The council should make provision in the next budget for furnishing the sealer with a complete new testing outfit, and ample provision should be made in one of the public markets for an office and quarters for the inspector and his assistant. Signs should be conspicuously displayed in all of the public markets calling attention to the office of the inspector and advising the purchasing public to have their purchases reweighed from time to time.

All the public scales and public weighmasters of the city should be placed under the immediate supervision of the inspector of weights and measures.

The inspector of weights and measures should be required to install and maintain a system of records and reports, such as is recommended in this report.

Public Welfare Functions.

*In view of the need for closer co-ordination of the public health and social welfare work of the city, it is recommended that a department of social welfare be created under a commissioner of public welfare appointed by the mayor. In this department there should be the following bureaus:

1.—**A** bureau of health.
2.—**A** bureau of charities (City Home, Virginia Hospital and Pine Camp Hospital).
3.—**A** bureau of markets.
4.—**A** bureau of public employment.

The chief health officer should be made the director of the bureau of health, and the commissioner of the department of public welfare should act *ex-officio* as director of the bureau of charities. A director of the bureau of markets should be appointed, and the manager of the present public employment bureau should be the director of the bureau of public employment of the proposed department.

Juvenile and Domestic Relations Court.

The city of Richmond in establishing a juvenile and domestic relations court indicated its desire to surround the delinquent or unfortunate child with protection such as can be given only by a well-managed juvenile court. But in failing to make this a court of record, the State has failed to afford protection to the child who has been wronged through no fault of its own, and it still leaves such a child exposed to the atmosphere and surroundings of the criminal courts in serious cases. If the judge of the juvenile court is to offer the kind of protection which the community evidently believes the child should have, he should be provided with broad powers of inquiry into the causes of delinquency and into crimes committed by adults that affect the child. He should be vested with power also to punish persons guilty of contributing to the delinquency of the child.

*Therefore, it is recommended that a law be enacted establishing the juvenile and domestic relations court as a court of record, and providing for the selection of the judge of the court in the same manner as judges are selected for other courts of record. In this act, the procedure might also be set forth to require that cases against children be conducted in chancery, so that the child would not be the defendant, but be the ward of the State and the proceeding be to determine the cause of the child's delinquency. In this connection, it might be possible, and it would certainly be advisable, to allow the appointment of a woman as master in chancery, particularly for cases involving girls. The constitutional provision against women in public office might not hold in this instance if it were interpreted to mean that a master in chancery is not a public officer within the meaning of the Constitution.

The court requires the services of two additional probation officers, as the present probation officers have entirely too many cases to handle, and it is recommended that one male and one female probation officer be appointed. The services of a competent physician qualified to attend and examine children should also be retained on a part-time basis. The three police officers who are assigned as probation officers in connection with domestic relations cases should be returned to active police duty and their places taken by three civilian probation officers.

The business methods of the court in connection with records, filing and control over collections need to be revised, and it is recommended that this be done as outlined in the text of the report.

Detention Homes.

There are two detention homes, one for white and one for colored children, which are subject to control by the judge of the juvenile court and the mayor. The mayor appoints the employees and directs the management, but the court is held responsible for the care of the children. This division of responsibility should be ended by giving complete control of the homes to the judge of the juvenile court.

Conditions in the home for white children were not of the best. It evidently required more care and soap and water. An effort should be made to make them more attractive, and the so-called "strong rooms" should be given up. The emphasis should be on the idea of "home" rather than on "detention." The home for colored children was found to be scrupulously clean, but otherwise just as bare and unattractive as the home for white children. More attention should be given to the meals furnished the children and the system of furnishing meals for a fixed charge per day should be abandoned.

Justices of the Peace, or Magistrates.

Richmond has a civil court for the trial of civil suits of a minor character, a police court for the hearing of criminal cases, and a juvenile and domestic relations court. There appears to be no logical reason for the continuance of twelve justices of the peace or magistrates. In connection with civil warrants, the magistrates

retain the fees which should be turned into the city treasury and
go towards the support of the civil court. The ease with which
warrants may be obtained from justices of the peace in police and
criminal cases, because the magistrates depend on these fees for
their remuneration, indicates but a slight regard for the right of
liberty of persons. The magistrates exercise powers not vested in
them by law in what they term minor cases by imposing the fine
that they believe is usually imposed by the judge of the police
court and discharging the prisoner on payment of the fine. The
magistrates accept bail, and the record of uncollected forfeited
bail bonds indicates that the magistrates are not very careful about
the quality of the surety offered in many cases. The police captains and sergeants on desk duty could do at least as well in
accepting bail.

*Therefore, it is recommended that the position of magistrate
or justice of the peace be abolished, that civil warrants be issued
by the clerk of the civil court, criminal warrants by the police
justice at the police court, and police captains and sergeants empowered to accept bail.

Civil Court.

*As already recommended, the law should be amended so as
to provide that all warrants in civil cases be issued by the clerk
of the civil cases be issued by the clerk of the civil court and
the fees therefore be turned into the city treasury. The amount
collected by the magistrates for the issuance of these warrants
during 1916 was estimated to be in the neighborhood of $8,000
which, if paid into the city treasury would more than pay for
the maintenance of the civil court. The procedure followed in the
court and the records kept are in accordance with good practice,
but the clerk should make a more detailed annual report as suggested in the text.

Commonwealth Attorney.

The commonwealth attorney is an important officer of the
state, whose compensation should not be dependent upon fees or
upon his success in securing convictions. He is limited to a maximum of $2,250 a year in fees from criminal cases and is allowed
to collect fees from delinquent taxpayers but refuses to do so.

In addition, the city pays him $1,000 a year. The fee system has long since been condemned in many communities as against public policy.

*The statute should be amended so as to provide for the payment of an annual salary to the commonwealth attorney by the state. The city should make no payment towards the compensation of this official, since he is a state officer and not a city employee. Any fees collected by his office should be paid into the public treasury of the state. It should further be enacted that the commonwealth attorney should not engage in private practice since although the present incumbent voluntarily refrains from doing so, his successors might not view the matter with such scrupulous care.

*The commonwealth attorney requires assistance. He needs an assistant and a stenographer. His records should be carefully kept and he should be required by law to file a report with the judge of the Hustings court which shall accurately describe all the services performed by him during the year. It is recommended that the law be amended in these respects.

In many communities, it has been found most profitable from the point of view of protecting the public and punishing offenders to have the prosecuting attorney notified at once by the police when any particularly serious crime such a murder is discovered. It is recommended that the commonwealth attorney obtain the co-operation of the police in accordance with this suggestion.

The City Jail.

The city jail is dirty and insanitary. The cells are infested with vermin and many of them are used as storage places by the prisoners for old clothing, etc. The utility corridors showed that they had not been inspected. No towels are supplied for the use of the prisoners, even for their daily washing of face and hands. The prisoners are not given work to do, but are allowed to congregate in the corridors promiscuously so that the jail is in many respects a school of crime. Women prisoners are left in the custody of male guards for seventeen hours out of the twenty-four The jail is without fire buckets, not to speak of fire extinguishers or fire hose. The number of guards is entirely inadequate and they are required to remain on duty from eleven to twelve hours a day, seven days a week. Visitors are permitted to enter the jail any day during the week and as often as desired, and they are not inspected to see that contraband is not delivered to the prisoners. Lawyers are permitted to solicit business from prisoners in the jail, a custom that is open to grave abuses.

The defects in the management of the jail that have been pointed out and others that are mentioned in the report, should be corrected through a complete change in methods, organization and regulations, as outlined in the report.

Since the jail is under the supervision of the city sergeant who receives no salary, but depends entirely upon fees at the rate fixed by law, and who pays his subordinates out of his fees, (although some of the subordinates are paid small salaries in addition, by the city or state), many of the features that were observed in the conduct of the jail can be readily understood. In order to make a living, the city sergeant must make the jail pay.

*The fee system of reimbursing the city sergeant should be abolished and the jail should be conducted, supervised and financed by the city of Richmond through a warden, with guards and matrons. All these employees should be placed on the city payroll and controlled through the budget. The jail should not be conducted on a fee basis. The position of city sergeant should be abolished and the functions he now exercises in connection with the Hustings court be exercised by the sheriff. The old and inadequate device of allowing a fixed sum per day for food and maintenance of each inmate should be abandoned and the prisoners treated in the same way regarding food as inmates of other city institutions, although the menu should not be elaborate.

It is also recommended:

*That all employees of the jail be selected by the mayor as a result of competitive civil service examination.

*That the salaries of all employees of the jail be fixed by council and paid out of city funds.

*That the indeterminate sentence law of the State of New York be adopted and a board of parole for the city of Richmond be appointed.

*That a farm colony be established and that provision be made by law for permitting the prisoners to share in the profits accruing out of their labor at industries which should be established.

*That but one physician be employed instead of two, and that the physician be required to reside at the jail, as at present, and that he maintain complete and detailed records of the services rendered by him.

That all prisoners on admission be searched by an officer of the jail and all property in their possession removed, including money; that a proper record of such property be maintained and that two guards be present when prisoners are searched.

That all prisoners on admission be detained in the unused cell and not assigned to regular cells until they have been given a thorough physical examination.

That all prisoners be required to bathe upon admission.

That all convicted prisoners have their clothing removed and be furnished with a suit of underwear and lightweight prison clothes; that their personal clothing be fumigated and for this purpose there be installed in the jail the necessary apparatus for sterilizing.

That the prisoner's personal clothing be put into good condition by prisoners detailed as "trusties" so that upon discharge the prisoners will not be at a disadvantage.

That a complete and detailed pedigree of all prisoners be taken and that sufficient inquiry be conducted by the officials to ascertain the number of previous commitments of the prisoner to the jail.

That in so far as the structural conditions of the jail will permit, prisoners be segregated so as to prevent prisoners of the hardened criminal type associating or coming into close daily contact with the younger and less serious offenders.

That the rules of the jail provide for a routine daily inspection of the cells.

That once in each week the city sergeant conduct a cell inspection in order to see that the guards have complied with the regulations as to the daily inspection of cells.

That the prisoners be served three meals a day.

That no food be permitted to be retained in the cells and that the prisoners be prohibited from storing any materials in any part of their cells.

That the large room now used for storage in the basement be equipped as a mess hall and that all meals be served in this room.

That definite hours be fixed for exercising prisoners.

That a matron be employed who will live at the jail and be available for service and in charge of the woman's prison at all hours.

That better bathing facilities be afforded both male and female prisoners and that towels be furnished.

That discipline be maintained to the extent of preventing, as far as possible, prisoners congregating in groups about the jail.

That all of the mattresses now in use be condemned and that new mattresses be provided; the new mattresses should be equipped with an outer covering which can be removed and washed at intervals.

That each prisoner, upon admission, be given a clean mattress cover.

That all cells be thoroughly cleaned at once.

That a committee of council be appointed to make a study of jail industries for the purpose of establishing at the city jail industries which will be profitable both to the city and the prisoners.

That convicted prisoners be prohibited from securing at their own expense foods from outside of the jail.

That more nutritious food in greater variety be fed the prisoners.

That the practice of allowing lawyers to visit the jail for the purpose of soliciting business be discontinued, and that lawyers only be permitted to visit prisoners at the prisoner's request.

That a record of all visits of lawyers to the prison be maintained.

That convicted prisoners be restricted as to the number of visitors they may receive and that definite days and hours be set aside as visiting times.

That in order to prevent contraband materials entering the jail, all prisoners be properly inspected upon admission.

That no prisoners be delivered to any persons for any reason except upon the written order of the committing judge, which order should be filed in the office of the city sergeant and a detailed record of the prisoners leaving and returned to the jail, be maintained.

That the practice of performing major surgical operations in the prison hospital be discontinued, and that all prisoners requiring such operations be transferred to the city hospital.

That the jail be equipped with the necessary auxiliary fire fighting apparatus to afford ample protection.

Coroner.

The direct cost of coroner to the city is about $3,500 a year. The work requires only a small part of the coroner's time, and it could be performed easily and more satisfactorily by two medical examiners on part time at $1,000 a year each or less, having the medical examiners attached to the office of the commonwealth attorney. This would not only save about $1,500 a year, but it would be in accordance with the tendency of the times which is to abolish coroners and coroners' courts with their record of irregularities in many communities. The very nature of the quasi-judicial proceedings held by coroners, who are usually not well versed in the conduct of legal investigations, opens the way to irregularities even with the best intentioned coroners. The coroner's status in Richmond is uncertain as he claims to be a state officer, while at the same time he is paid out of the city treasury.

*It is recommended that the position of coroner be abolished and that two medical examiners, one for each side of the river, be appointed preferably by the commonwealth attorney.

Sheriff and High Constable. .

The sheriff and the high constable duplicate each other's functions. Both are fee officers and are limited to maximum incomes (from fees) of $6,500 per annum. after January, 1918. Fees collected in excess of this amount will be turned over to the state. The anxiety of the high constable to collect fees, a natural result of the fee system of compensation, has led him to the use of "dunning" notices that are almost in the nature of threats. Since his attention was caled to these forms during the survey he has ordered them discontinued, but their use would never have been tolerated except for the pernicious fee system.

*It is rcommended that the offices of sheriff and of high constable be consolidated and that the business of these two offices be placed under the supervision of one official. A salary should be provided for this official and all of the fees collected should be turned into the public treasury.

Department of Health.

While the health department as managed at present, and under the previous heath officer, has done a great deal towards improving conditions. there are several matters of serious importance that require attention. Practically all of these call for changes in the laws but if facts are collected and presented in a way that will arouse public interest the securing of such amendments should not be difficult.

Richmond has a high typhoid fever rate. Typhoid is a preventable disease, and its prevalence is a blot upon the record of any city in these days. The origin of typhoid is sometimes difficult to trace and it would be almost impossible to lay the blame at any particular condition in the city. For one thing, the milk supply which is so often suspected in other communities would, it seems, almost be disregarded in an investigation into the causes of this disease in Richmond, because of the high standards of dairy inspection and milk requirements that have been developed by the health department. The fight against mosquitoes which has been waged incessantly has also reduced the possibility of infection through that means as well as practically eliminating malaria. But the sanitary conditions owing to the absence of sewer connections with a large number of dwelling houses, the presence of bacillus coli in the water supply, the use of numerous wells, springs and other sources of water supply apart from the city system, and the criminal carelessness and insanitary surroundings at the public markets may furnish the reasons for the presence of typhoid in Richmond. It is recommended that an exhaustive study of the origin of cases and of sanitary conditions be inaugurated immediately with a view to eliminating the points of infection.

The housing conditions also, particularly in the negro sections, should be radically improved. Many old disease-producing dwellings should be torn down. It is well known to the citizens of Richmond that many of the houses are unfit for human habitation. Other cities have removed such pest spots and Richmond can do it if the public so wills. This situation is closely related not only to the health of the large negro population, but to the industrial effectiveness of the city as well. A growing tendency on the part of the negro to move away from communities with poor housing and living conditions to communities where better conditions prevail has been noted of late throughout the south. Unless inducements in the form of improved conditions are offered, Richmond may suffer from the same tendency in the near future.

*It is recommended that laws be secured from the legislature empowering the health department to investigate the housing conditions and enforce remedies. The department should have the power to condemn as unfit for habitation, and to order the destruction of houses that are a menace to the health of occupants and to the community, to exercise control over building plans, and to compel owners to improve conditions.

The inspection of food is crippled because of defects and omissions in the city ordinances. The ordinances definitely except the public markets from the jurisdiction of the food inspections and confine the inspection to dealers selling meat, butter, fish, fruit or vegetables. The ordinance has been construed to mean that restaurants, eating houses and soda fountains, for example, are excepted from the regulations of the food inspection division. All establishments manufacturing, handling, storing, selling or exposing for sale, food or drink, intended for human consumption, should be placed under the supervision of the food inspection division of the department of health. Improved methods of inspection, as described in the text of the report should be followed. Tuberculous cattle are unquestionably slaughtered for food in the city and the health department is powerless to prevent it because it does not see the animals at slaughter. This condition should not be ignored. It is an established fact that human tuberculosis may develop from bovine tubercle bacilli, particularly in children. All meat for sale in Richmond should be inspected at the slaughter houses and the method preferred is to have a municipal slaughter house established, as recommended many times by the chief food inspector. Such an establishment could be conducted without any cost to the city by imposing a fee for its use.

From the point of view of decency as well as of public health, the public markets require drastic action. At present the markets are not under the control of the health department, but are supervised by clerks who are responsible directly to the administrative board. The markets are filthy and constitute a menace to the community. The nauseating conditions are fully described in the text of the report and need not be summarized here.

There are many other important features of the public health service in Richmond that should be improved. It is desired to give special emphasis here to two more points, one the neglect of health conditions among negroes, and the other the need for more stringent control over contagious and infectious diseases. The mortality of the colored race is higher than that of whites. The negro is made the prey of quacks and fakers, who are allowed to advertise extensively and to practice almost unhindered among them. The city does not provide proper facilities and care either for the entrance of colored babies into the world, or for the care of colored children. It provides no public baths for its colored population. It does not provide as good facilities for the care of the colored adult sick as for the white adult sick, nor adequate means for diagnosis and treatment of venereal diseases.

The vigor and intelligence manifested in combatting epidemics in Richmond has been commendable. But there is one serious weakness in the method of dealing with contagious diseases. The code now provides that the physicians shall report contagious diseases within twenty-four hours "after making diagnosis." The physician may not be able to make a diagnosis for several days after his first visit and yet the case may be one of which the department should receive immediate information owing to the likelihood of the development of one of the common contagious diseases. In the infantile paralysis epidemic last year the physicians were required to report all suspected cases, even before actual diagnosis was made and the department was highly successful in handling the epidemic and kept the number of cases well within bounds. This requirement of reporting all suspected cases immediately should be extended to all suspected cases of contagious disease and the department should also add a number of diseases to its list of reportable cases, as suggested in the report.

General Administrative Changes Recommended.

Among the general administrative changes recommended are.

That the department of health be re-organized to include only the following divisions, each under the supervision of a chief—

1—A division of records
2—A division of preventable diseases
3—A division of food inspection
4—A division of sanitary inspection
5—A division of public health nursing
6—A division of laboratory
7—A division of public health education.

That an advisory public health council be created by the health officer, such council to comprise representatives of the various public health and social agencies of the city.

That if extension of public health service is desired by the city of Richmond its citizens give proper consideration to the necessity of adequately financing such extension of service.

That the chief executive of the health department be required periodically (preferably monthly) to submit complete and detailed written reports to the administrative head of the welfare work of the city, relative to the work performed, work on hand, and work proposed.

That in the event of the continuation of the administrative board as the administrative head of the department of health, more consideration be given by this board to the recommendations of the health officer, relative to the appointment of health department empoyees.

That offices of the department be re-arranged so as better to economize spuce, promote efficiency of office work and permit more satisfactory handling of visitors to the department.

Preventable Diseases.

Additional recommendations regarding the control over preventable diseases are—

That a division of preventable diseases be created under the supervision of a chief, who should be the medical inspector of the department. He should be charged with the investigation, supervision and control of preventable diseases in their homes and in the institutions of the city, including the contagious disease pavilion of the City Home and the Smallpox and Leper Isolation Hospitals.

. That following the termination of cases of communicable disease which ordinarily confer immunity, the health department issue to the discharged patient, whether child or adult, a certificate to the effect that he has had the disease and been properly discharged.

That effort be made to secure reports from physicians and midwives, relative to the prevalence of opthalmia neonatorum (infective conjunctivitis of infants). and that the co-operation of the state health authorities be solicited in requiring physicians and midwives to certify upon birth certificates that they have used proper measures to prevent this disease.

That effort be made to secure better control of venereal diseases by —

1—Reports of venereal disease from physicians
2—The provision of evening clinics for venereal disease patients

3—An educational program on the prevention of venereal
disease

4—The elimination of venereal disease quacks, fakirs and
patent medicines

That for the further prevention of typhoid fever in Richmond,
active efforts be made to—

1—Eliminate flies

2—Eliminate dry closets

3—Eliminate private wells

4—Improve the water supply by an adequate distributing
and purification system.

That in view of the periodic nature of epidemics of measles
in Richmond, as shown by previous experience, a campaign of
education be immediately begun to educate the public as to the
serious nature of this disease, and the measures which they should
take to assist the health department in preventing a possible epidemic in 1919 or 1920.

That in view of the severity of whooping cough in Richmond
(the total deaths from this one disease equalling the combined
deaths from scaret fever, measles and diphtheria), systematic
effort be made by educational publicity to inform the public as
to method of spread of the disease, methods of prevention, signs
and symptoms, and treatment.

Industrial Hygiene.

A beginning shoud be made in efforts to prevent industrial
diseases by requiring reporting of industrial diseases by physicians,
by investigation of conditions responsible for such diseases and
the correction of these conditions through the co-operation of employers or by mandatory regulation.

Effort should be made by the chief health officer to secure the
co-operation of the courts in granting work permits to children
under fourteen, to the end that no permits shall be issued by the
court until the physical and mental ability of the child to work
shall be certified by the health department.

Smallpox Hospital.

The smallpox hospital should be put in better condition of
repair and better equipped or else abandoned. The fly menace

at the hospital should be eliminated by proper screening of rooms, the use of ·fly traps and the improvement of the horse stable so as to prevent fly breeding. The use of a common drinking cup at the hospital should be prohibited.

A survey of the farm at the Smallpox Hospital should be made by the agricultural experts of the state agricultural school to determine the practicability of considerably increasing the extent of farm operations.

Consideration could profitably be given to the matter of establishing in the city farm a municipal dairy under the supervision of the chief dairy inspector of the health department to supply milk to the City Home, the Virginia Hospital and the Pine Camp Hospital.

City Bacteriologist.

Owing to the resignation of the full-time bacteriologist and the difficulty at this time of filling this position satisfactorily, it is recommended that the present technician be given an increase of salary and permitted to perform such routine laboratory work as may be required under the supervision of a bacteriologist on part time from the medical school or the state health laboratory.

As soon as practicable the health department should make available to physicians, the services of this laboratory, in the making of Wasserman tests for syphilis. The equipment of the laboratory should be improved, as suggested in the report.

City Physicians.

It is recommended that city physicians discontinue the visiting of schools for the purpose of examining suspected cases of contagious disease, and that this function devolve upon the medical inspection staff of the board of education.

*The city physicians should be transferred to the bureau of charities of the proposed department of public welfare and made a staff agency of that bureau.

Public Health Nursing.

An effort should be made to bring about a centralization of all public and private agencies engaged in nursing work, so that cost may be reduced, overlapping and duplication eliminated, and a uniform and effective program carried out. A colored nurse should be employed who may work exclusively in the colored districts of the city.

Food and Dairy Inspection.

A division of food inspection should be created and placed under the direction of the present chief dairy inspector, this division to include all of the functions of the two existing divisions of dairy inspection and food inspection.

Dairy permits should be issued for a period of one year instead of for an indefinite period and the annual permit fee should be made $1. It would lead to economy and better service to furnish an additional automobile for the use of dairy inspectors in place of the horse and buggy now used.

The food ordinance should be revised so as to include under permit from and supervision by the health department all places producing, manufacturing, handling, storing or selling foods and drinks, and that the ordinance require such places to pay $1 per year for such permit which must be renewed annually.

All food establishments should continue to be graded according to the scoring methods now used and a certificate of merit should be issued to each establishment with a standing of "excellent," this certificate of merit to be displayed conspicuously by the proprietor of the establishment.

The meat inspection service of the city should be improved by requiring that all meat sold in the city of Richmond, bear either the stamp of the federal inspection service or the local health department. To require this means, however, either that slaughter house men must agree to slaughter in one or two of the existing abbatoirs or that a municipal abbatoir must be established.

Sanitary Inspection.

An effort should be made to induce the former chief sanitary inspector (recently resigned) to return to this position at increased salary.

The position of fumigator of the department should be discontinued and this officer, who is now assigned to the sanitary division be dropped from the payroll. If two additional automobiles were purchased for the use of sanitary inspectors, it would be possible to reduce the force of sanitary inspectors by two or three men.

The health department should furnish the uniforms for sanitary inspectors, instead of requiring these officers to purchase their own uniforms from their meagre salaries.

An effort should be made to reduce the time spent by field inspectors in office clerical work. The clerk of the department should be required to keep records of the time spent by inspectors in the office and in the field, or as an alternative a time clock should be installed. The investigation and prosecution of complaints regarding weeds could well be discontinued as not being of direct health benefit.

A program of co-operation in sanitary inspection could be worked out with the police department and other city departments as well as private agencies, and a uniform reporting form be devised for use by such co-operating agencies.

The regulations of the department governing the construction and maintenance of stables should be completely revised, and a license to construct and operate a stable should be required of all stable owners. The regulations of the department should provide for a uniform type of stable construction and for uniform procedure in handling and disposing of stable manure.

Immediate consideration should be given to the construction by the city, of public comfort stations which may be made self-supporting through the provision of pay toilets. Street trash cans should be provided, either through appropriation by the city or through the co-operation of private civic agencies.

Richmond is certainly a smoky city. This, unquestionably, has ill effects on the health of citizens and in addition it means a loss of money through more rapid deterioration of buildings, etc.

Steps should be taken to secure the passage of a smoke prevention ordinance.

The regulations regarding the removal of night soil should be revised to require the removal of night soil more frequently than once a month. and to permit the removal of night soil in the daytime when the procedure can be better controlled.

Vital Statistics.

It is recommended—

That a division of records be created in the charge of the register of vital statistics. Such division should include the present office of the registrar, and the office of the clerk should be charged with the handling of all records and statistical work of the department.

That a fee of fifty cents be charged for each certified copy of birth or death records issued by the registrar. the receipts from this source to be turned into the general funds of the city.

That efforts be made to improve further the reporting of births by the publication of birth notices in the daily papers, the examination of the baptismal records of churches, and a general educational program of publicity regarding the importance of birth reporting.

Public Health Education.

A division of public health education should be created for the purpose of correlating and disseminating public health information, the chief of this division to be designated from among the officers of the health department in rotation. The initial purpose of this division should be to work out a program of public health education as far as that is possible, through the existing force and without additional cost. Effort should be made to get together all material possible for health exhibit purposes. This material might be used as a permanent exhibit or exhibits on the basement floor of the city hall. Public bulletin boards should be used for special public health notices, and the co-operation of advertising companies in printing and displaying public health advertisements might be obtained. A lecture program should be prepared, lectures to be given before private organizations and associations by heatlh department officers on special phases of health service.

The sanitary code should be completely revised and brought up to date for printing in compact pocket size form for the information of inspectors, nurses, policemen, and the general public.

An educational program for the elimination of advertising medical quacks and fakirs should be begun, and the co-operation of the newspapers be sought for the elimination of patent medicine advertising from their columns.

Plumbing Inspection.

The division of plumbing inspection of the health department is doing satisfactory work. But this is not a health function and it should be transferred to the building department.

In view of the fact that the chief benefit of plumbing inspection is derived by the householder, it is recommended that fees be required for plumbing inspection depending upon the number and character of fixtures installed, such fees to be paid by the plumber.

City Chemist.

The present arrangement for the services of a city chemist has been analyzed in the report. It should be continued as being the most satisfactory arrangement possible under existing conditions.

Virginia Hospital.

The visiting medical staff of the Virginia Hospital should be increased by the creation of an adjunct or assistant visiting staff made up of the young physicians of the community, who need such experience and training and who may be counted on to give generously of their time and effort. The recently created position of medical director for the Virginia Hospital should be abolished and a trained and experienced superintendent for the Virginia Hospital should be secured as soon as practicable.

A visiting pathologist should be employed at the Virginia Hospital. preferably a member of the staff of the medical college, who may act also as visiting pathologist to the City Home and efforts made to increase the autopsy work of the hospital for the benefit of attending physicians and internes.

As soon as practicable graduate internes should be secured in place of the present undergraduate internes, and a definite rotation of interne service through all branches of hospital work be established. The internes should be given instruction in anaesthesia on the basis of definite assignment by the paid anaesthetist. It is possible by re-arranging the internes' quarters to provide space for a reading and recreation room for internes and this should be done.

An X-Ray laboratory should be provided and equipped within the hospital so that X-Ray plates may become the property of the hospital and may be utilized more effectively for the information and instruction of the medical staff.

At least three additional trained nurses should be employed to take charge, under the direction of the superintendent of nurses, of the various hospital floors, and if living quarters can be provided the number of pupil nurses should be increased to the maximum.

Better supervision of ambulance bags and other equipment is required and only those articles authorized by the chief house officer should be carried. Lists of ambulance supplies and equipment should be prepared and the contents of the ambulance bags and lockers should be daily checked against this list and kept in complete and proper order. The admitting room of the hospital should be equipped as a first aid for emergency surgery.

In view of the need for better accommodations for children, consideration should be given to the establishment of a summer baby camp at the Pine Camp Hospital, which may be utilized as an adjunct to the Virginia Hospital service. (See report on Pine Camp Hospital).

Other recommendations are:

That as soon as practicable a social service department be established at the hospital, which may be conducted in co-operation with the dispensary of the medical college.

That better provision for the care of patients' clothing be made so that discharged patients may go from the hospital with their clothing clean and in good order.

That in the dispensing of drugs a formulary be used such as is recommended for use at the City Home. A standard formulary for the two institutions should be adopted.

That more adequate fire preventive and protective equipment be provided at the Virginia Hospital by the installation of fire hose and water buckets, improved fire escapes, fire drills by employees and the thorough instruction of employees in the most effective methods of fire fighting and rescue of patients.

That common drinking cups be abolished throughout the hospital.

That a trained dietitian be employed to take charge of the purchase, preparation and serving of food, the inspection of food supplies, the reduction of food wastes, and the instruction of nurses and other employees in the handling of foodstuffs.

That all costs of Virginia Hospital service, as for example, the cost of ambulance service now charged against the City Home, be included in the financial statements of the Virginia Hospital, and that the accounting procedure be made uniform with that of the City Home and Pine Camp Hospital.

That the annual report of the hospital be improved so that it may show more clearly the results and costs of hospital service, eliminating information of little or no statistical value to which at present considerable space is given.

City Home.

It is recommended—

That in view of the need for more efficient management of the City Home, a superintendent with training and experience in institutional management be appointed at an increased salary, if necessary.

That greater economy be observed in the provision of food for the officers' table, and that accounts be kept which will show separately the cost of feeding officers and employees and the cost of feeding inmates.

That the system of record keeping of facts relative to inmates be completely revised so as to include all data regarding their admission, physical and mental condition on admission, subsequent illnesses, condition on discharge and reason for discharge.

That each inmate be given a compete physical and mental examination on admission by a medical officer and that his physical and mental ability to work be certified to from such examination.

That effort be made to provide a more satisfactory diet for inmates, through the employment of a skilled dietitian.

That a resident graduate physician be employed who may assume responsibility for and direct the work of internes who are undergraduates.

That as soon as practicable two graduate internes, on full time, be appointed to replace the three undergraduate internes now employed, such graduate internes to be paid nominal salaries.

That effort be made to improve the pathological service of the hospital by better utilization of the laboratory, better training of internes in pathological work and by providing for a visiting pathologist from the medical college.

That the colored tuberculosis pavilion be transferred from the City Home to the Pine Camp Hospital in order that these colored patients may have the same advantage as white patients.

That at least two additional trained nurses be employed, one for the infirmary at the white home, and one for the infirmary at the colored home.

That special wards for children be provided at the City Home in order that they may be given more satisfactory care and kept apart from the older inmates, many of whom are not fit to associate with children.

That the prison cells now used as isolation rooms for patients with venereal disease be abolished, and that isolation ward rooms be provided for these patients.

That owing to the lack of adequate facilities for the isolation of patients afflicted with contagious disease at the City Home, consideration be given to the erection of a contagious disease hospital conveniently located within the city but not upon City Home grounds.

That the physicians in charge of the various medical services of the City Home be required to submit more complete reports of work performed and results obtained in the treatment of patients.

That non-removable full length fly screens be provided for all windows and that the other usual measures for fly elimination be carried out.

That common drinking cups and common towels be abolished.

That in view of the need for economy in the dispensing of drugs, a formulary be devised by the medical staff for the use of attending physicians and house officers, and that prescriptions be filled as far as possible from the number of those authorized in the formulary.

That the records of the dispensing of narcotics, as required by the federal law, be properly kept and that hereafter house officers be furnished narcotics only upon proper prescriptions by a graduate physician and with full and complete record of all facts in the matter.

That improved stores records be devised and a card index substituted for the very cumbersome book records now in use.

That a system of stores records which will be uniform with that of the City Home, be adopted for use also in the Virginia Hospital and Pine Camp Hospital, so that it will be possible to compare consumption and costs in these institutions.

That hereafter persons requisitioning new articles from the stores at the City Home, be required to turn in the worn or used articles to the storeroom in order that such articles may be salvaged, and in order to check extravagance in the use of supplies and equipment.

That effort be made to provide some form of employment for more of the inmates.

That the laundry service of the City Home be extended and the laundry quarters enlarged so as to perform all laundry work for the City Home, the Virginia Hospital and the Pine Camp Hospital.

That consideration be given to the matter of establishing an ice plant at the City Home with a capacity sufficient to provide the ice required at the City Home, the Virginia Hospital and the Pine Camp Hospital.

That fire preventive and fire protective equipment at the City Home be increased by the addition of fire extinguishers, fire hose and water buckets; that proper iron fire escapes be provided with exits adequately illuminated at night, and that regular fire drills be inaugurated.

That hereafter no expenditures be charged against funds for the outdoor relief of the poor, except such as may be properly charged against those funds.

That outdoor relief by the city be discontinued, as soon as practicable, and that effort be made to make an arrangement with the associated charities whereby that organization will conduct all investigations and provide all material relief of proper city charges, the city paying for such service on the basis of statements rendered by the associated charities and approved by the proper municipal authority.

Regarding other public welfare activities, the report makes the following recommendations:

Public Employment Bureau.

That city departments make more use of the public employment bureau in the selection of their employees.

Payment to Private Institutions.

That payments of annual lump sums to private institutions be discontinued, and that hereafter payments to such institutions be made only on the basis of actual service rendered and approved by the proper city authority. In the event that a department of public welfare is created, the commissioner of public welfare should constitute such authority.

That unless the above recommendation is made effective, appropriations to institutions be made only on the basis of complete reports of finances and service rendered, submitted by the various institutions to the council each year prior to the passage of the appropriation ordinances. (The city appropriates annually $13,200 to institutions and charitable agencies without control of this expenditure, and even without knowledge of the institutions' needs).

Public Baths.

That future appropriations for the Branch public baths be based upon the actual needs of the baths rather than upon precedent.

That in view of the unsatisfactory experience of the present public baths, consideration be given to the establishment of a public bath for negroes.

Public Markets and City Weighmaster.

That the clerk of the first market be required to have his office in the market building, instead of in the scale house, which is at a considerable distance from the market building.

That the present method of leasing stalls at fixed rates be discontinued, and that all stalls be auctioned annually to the highest bidders.

That the terms of the lease be strictly enforced, particularly with reference to the sanitation of market stalls.

That in view of the filthy condition of public markets, immediate steps be taken to require, by regulation, uniform equipment and methods of handling food by stallholders and their assistants.

That uncovered refuse piles at the markets be eliminated and that covered wagons be provided at each market, which may be filled with refuse and hauled away, without exposure of the refuse to flies.

That the public toilets used by workers at the markets be put in sanitary condition, and provided with proper facilities for the cleansing of the hands of users of the toilets, to prevent food contamination and the menace to the health of the public resulting therefrom.

That the armory building, now little used at the second market, be abandoned as a market building.

That hot water plants and refrigerating plants be installed as soon as possible in market buildings.

That the effort of the health department be directed toward the public markets as a first step in improved food control. Proper inspection of the public markets is more important than the inspection of isolated retail stores.

That market stallholders be required to secure food permits from the health department, such permits to continue in force only through maintenance of proper sanitary conditions, regarding the covering of foodstuffs, the cleanliness of workers, premises and utensils, and the character of food sold or exposed for sale.

That a uniform accounting procedure be worked out for use by market clerks so that their reports may be uniform in method of statement and adapted to proper comparison, and that the methods of record-keeping be revised so as to be readily subject to interpretation by the responsible officer or officers.

That effort be made to keep the streets in the market area in better condition of repair so as to render cleaning of the market area easier and more satisfactory.

That the office of city weighmaster be placed under the supervision of the sealer of weights and measures, or his successor, by whatever title he may be known, and not hereafter considered as a part of the public market organization.

Pine Camp Hospital.

That the newly created office of medical director of the Pine Camp and Virginia Hospitals be abolished as unnecessary. (See Virginia Hospital recommendations).

That all patients admitted to Pine Camp Hospital be first admitted to the Virginia Hospital where they may be carefully examined and kept under observation for a sufficient length of time to establish proper diagnosis of their condition.

That as soon as practicable a full-time graduate interne be secured at the Pine Camp Hospital at a nominal salary in place of the present undergraduate interne.

That in view of the need for more adequate care for infants, it is urged that consideration be given to the establishment of an infants' summer hospital at the Pine Camp Hospital. (See Virginia Hospital recommendations.)

That the tuberculosis pavilions for colored patients now at the City Home be transferred to the Pine Camp Hospital. (See report on City Home.)

That the nurses' home be altered so as to provide better accommodations for nurses. This can readily be done by slight changes which will permit the utilization of a large storeroom, now little used. as a nurses' bedroom.

That the bathrooms of the infirmary be enlarged so as to minimize the dangers to patients from the stoves which now take up a great deal of floor space in the present very small bathrooms.

An adequate heating plant to take the place of these stoves is of course desirable. If stoves are continued the walls around them should be sheathed with fire-resisting material.

That additional fire preventive and protective equipment be provided, namely, larger chemical fire extinguishers, additional lengths of hose and water buckets. In addition, regular fire drills should be held and employees instructed in their duties in the event of fire.

That a small morgue building be erected, so that the dead may be removed immediately from the infirmary buildings.

That an annual report be prepared showing the results of work performed and the costs of service. Accounting records should be, as far as possible, uniform with those of the Virginia Hospital and the City Home, so that proper comparisons may be made.

That all laundry work of the Pine Camp be done at the City Home if the laundry service at that institution is enlarged as recommended in the report on the City Home.

That the poultry farm at the Pine Camp be enlarged so as to produce sufficient poultry and eggs for the Pine Camp at least, and if possible, for the City Home and the Virginia Hospital.

That proper steps be taken to eliminate the fly nuisance at the Pine Camp by better screening of windows and also by the improvement of the horse stable, so as to abolish fly-breeding places.

That an improved ice house be constructed at the Pine Camp so that ice may be purchased and stored in larger quantities. If an ice plant is installed at the City Home, as recommended in the report on that institution, all ice for the Pine Camp should be secured from the City Home.

That proper basins and drains be installed beneath the leaders of the nurses' home so that the walks may be adequately drained.

That a pathway or walk be built from the dirt road in front of the Pine Camp across the adjacent field to the macadam highway, so that nurses and visitors may reach the car line readily.

Department of Engineering.

The policy relating to public improvements followed by the administrative board is criticized in the survey report. In the first place, the city engineer is given practically no voice in the determination of the character of any public improvement. He is occasionally consulted, but the administrative board is in no way bound by his advice or recommendations.

The condition of the street paving as well as the types of pavement afford evidence of the pernicious nature of this policy. The board has established a separate engineering organization to carry on a street and drainage survey of those sections of the city recently acquired by annexation. The street repair and maintenance forces have been transferred from the jurisdiction of the city engineer to the superintendent of street cleaning. Responsibility for this work, which is essentially an engineering problem, should be vested in the city engineer's office. Very important public improvements, the plans of which were opposed by the city engineer, have been approved by the administrative board and the council, resulting in a loss of public funds, particularly in connection with the boulevard along Chamberlayne avenue.

Another restriction on the work of the city engineer results from the financial policy of the council. No bond issues for public improvements have been issued since 1914, and the annual appropriations have been markedly decreased from 1913 to 1917. The results of such a policy are apparent in the condition of most of the streets. Another restriction of public improvement work is the cancellation of appropriations that are not expended within the fiscal year. Funds for public improvements are not available until about the middle of March. The award of contracts has to be deferred beyond the ordinary season for such work, and the result is the work costs more.

*The authorities of the city should do all in their power to secure the enactment of legislation which will relieve the city of its present limitations on assessments for public improvements. Under the present law, local improvement work which is generally paid for in other cities by local assessment on the property benefited, is paid for out of the general funds of the city. This naturally restricts the amount which the city can pay for in any one year.

The restrictions on the authority of the city engineer have tended undoubtedly to break down the effectiveness of the department. It is recommended that the department be completely reorganized along the lines indicated in the text of this report.

The report shows that the repair work on street pavements has been extremely restricted. The amount spent on contract repair has been gradually reduced during the past three years. The repair force employed by the city has been transferred to the street cleaning department, and only a fraction of the amount required has been made available.

*The cost of sewer construction for other than trunk sewers is a legitimate charge on the property directly benefited and should be assessed on the property.

The care of bridges is purely a maintenance function and should be transferred to the bureau of maintenance and operation of the city engineer's department from the bureau of sewers.

Contractors erecting buildings should not be allowed to store building materials on the streets except under restrictions that will protect the interests of the city. A fee should be charged to cover the expenses of controlling such work, and where the pavement is damaged the contractor should be obliged to pay for the damage.

The city engineers make surveys to establish line and grade data for for the construction of buildings. This service should be paid for by the property owners. In order to arrive at the cost of this and similar work each member of the staff of the city engineer should be obliged to keep a daily time record.

Street Cleaning Department.

In addition to street cleaning, the department of street cleaning attends to refuse collections, refuse disposal, the operation of the dog pound and the repair of streets. In order to create a title for the department which will be fairly descriptive it is recommended that the title "department of sanitation" be employed. The present organization of the department is good, and a general reorganization is not required.

Garbage collection should be improved by the enforcement of regulations requiring the use of standard receptacles and through obtaining the co-operation of the public.

The collection of ashes and rubbish should be improved by requiring that ashes be separated from rubbish so that carts of large capacity may be used for rubbish, thus reducing the number of trips to be made.

It is recommended that the position of foreman of garbage collection in the east district be abolished. The east end assistant superintendent should be provided with motor transportation similar to that used in the west district.

It is apparent that a careful study of the routes followed by the street cleaning gangs will save a great deal of time between stopping and starting points and will permit either reducing the number of men and carts employed or increasing the area covered by the present force. It is recommended that the suggestions made in the report for changing the routes and work methods be followed.

The use of machine broom cleaning on the granite pavements and on the smooth pavements is ineffective and uneconomical. Such streets should be dropped from the machine broom routes and hand patrol cleaning and squee-gee cleaning methods used instead. The equipment of the hand patrol cleaners should be improved and their methods changed, as outlined in detail in this report.

There are fourteen gangs employed in the collection of ashes and rubbish and thirty helpers or lifters are employed in these gangs. The helpers are not needed except in winter on routes where there are large collections of ashes. It is recommended that the number of lifters and helpers be reduced to what is actually needed. A saving of $13,750 a year will result.

A new stable is required in the west end district because the present stable is unsafe. A lack of care in cleaning the horses and mules was evident at the west end stable. More efficient supervision should be exercised over the care of the animals.

Not one of the four motor trucks owned by the department was in operation at the time of the survey. They should either be used or sold.

The street cleaning department is required to carry seventeen superannuated and incapacitated city employees, of whom only ten were ever employed by the department. Money paid to these men is in the nature of a pension and should not be made a charge on the street cleaning department. If a pension system is desired, it should be regularly established and the present practice discontinued.

Work for other departments, such as carting coal, trimming trees and spraying ponds is charged to the street cleaning department. These are improper charges and should be located elsewhere.

It is recommended that this department be required to keep the maps, records and reports outlined in the text of the report, so that it may be directed more understandingly and efficiently.

Building Department.

In general, the building department appears to be very well managed. A number of recommendations are set forth in the text of the report which are designed to produce a higher degree of efficiency.

In one particular the procedure of the building department should be radically changed. All permits issued by the department are obtained by the applicant without the payment of any fees. The approximate salary expenditures for building inspection amount to $8,900, and in return the city receives no payment. It is recommended that all applicants for permits be required to pay a fee to the department, and that a sliding scale of fees be established in proportion to the value of the work comprehended under the permit. An annual inspection charge also should be made for billboards.

The operation of the city auditorium for the year 1916 produced a deficit of more than $400. It is recommended that the charge for the use of the auditorium be increased in order to make this building self-sustaining.

Park Department.

Under the charter responsibility for the care of parks and city-owned cemeteries is vested in the city engineer. The administrative board has appointed an assistant superintendent of parks and relieved the city engineer of all except nominal responsibility. The administrative board on occasion has also retained outside engineering service in connection with the parks—a policy that has frequently resulted in waste of the city's money due to imperfect construction and other causes. It is recommended that the city engineer be restored to authority over construction work in the parks. The maintenance and repair of roads should also be centered in the proposed division of maintenance in the city engineer's office.

*It is recommended that a department having jurisdiction over the recreational activity to be known as the department of parks and recreations be established.

The present distribution of park workers is open to criticism. The park keepers should be required to assist in the maintenance of the areas under their supervision. The force now distributed among the various parks should be organized into one gang under a competent foreman. This would reduce the payroll by $4,000 a year.

The tree nursery is mismanaged owing to incompetent help. Either competent help should be employed or the nursery abandoned. It appears necessary to provide additional funds so that the city's nurserymen may be able to employ an adequate and competent force.

The condition of the cemeteries appears to be satisfactory and the force employed to be adequate and not excessive. But the revenues derived from the cemeteries through the sale of burial lots and through the present scale of charges is not sufficient to make them self-supporting. The city should adopt a definite policy in establishing equitable charges for the maintenance of burial plots.

The playgrounds appear to be well managed, but additional playgrounds and other facilities for the colored children are very much needed.

It is urged that steps be taken to bring about co-ordination between the public recreational activities and similar activities provided by private organizations.

Municipally Owned Public Utilities.

Organization.

The city of Richmond maintains three distinct departments, one for each of its public utility services. Wherever the nature of the services of any of these departments are similar, the departmental organization and the duties of the employees are also similar. An analysis of the organization and duties of the employees of the water, gas and electricity departments indicates that by consolidating the three into one department substantial economy would result as well as greatly improved service.

*It is recommended that the water, gas and electricity departments be consolidated under the direction of a single commissioner responsible directly to the mayor.

Under a single executive it would be possible to carry out campaigns for the promotion of business along uniform lines and to correct inconsistencies in the development of the service. The inconsistencies are numerous. For example, the water department collects its rates in advance, while the gas department collects after service has been rendered. The public in its dealings with the three departments is now subjected to many delays and inconveniences, such as visiting two offices in order to adjust a complaint, a waste of time which would be eliminated by a consolidation of the departments.

The city ordinances affecting the management of the three departments should be extensively revised. The practice of prescribing by ordinance the office duties and routine and fixing the number of employees interferes with the management of the property by removing from the executive an opportunity for the exercise of judgment.

Duties of Employees and Office Methods.

A revision should be made in the present system of handling applications for water service, in order that the unnecessary work now being carried on may be discontinued. The practice of reading water meters monthly should also be discontinued, such reading being made quarterly, in conformity with the present practice of quarterly billing. Instead of the monthly inspection service now furnished by water meter readers, there should be a periodical and more thorough inspection by qualified inspectors at intervals of approximately one year. The use of the present meter readers' books should be discontinued and the employees furnished instead with a list of the meters and their location, such lists to have no reference to previous readings of the meters. Bills for water service should be rendered without recording the data now carried in the "listing book." The form of water service bill now used should be so changed as to make possible and encourage payment by checks.

The office of bookkeeper in the gas division should be abolished and the work now performed by that employee assigned to a clerk. All payments received by the gas division from the sale of residuals should be handled in accordance with the general rules governing sales and collections in other city departments. The recommendations made above with respect to reading meters and billing consumers for water service apply with equal force to the meter reading and billing for gas service.

A record should be made showing in detail by months the amount of energy delivered by the electric utility to the various municipal departments, making a demand on that service in the same form as if such municipal departments were private or commercial consumers.

Accounts.

No attempt has been made in either the water or electricity department to keep adequate records in accordance with a standard classification of accounts. Two of the utilities, the water and gas properties, have been in service for over sixty-five years, and yet there are no adequate records on their costs. The records and reports of the water department do not show the details or classify the expenses of operation.

An analysis of the operations of the water department indicated that the net income was approximately $62,800. In addition to the interest on the bonds the calculations included a further charge of 4 per cent. to cover interest on the amount invested in the property in excess of the value of the existing bond issues. This interest charge for the year amounts to $68,666.97, and when deducted from the net income shows a deficit from operation of the water department of $5,843.02. It is evident that economies are required in the operation of the water department.

An analysis of the accounts of the gas department showed a surplus for the year's operation amounting to $139,790.22. On the basis of advancing prices of oil, gas coal, and steam coal, the accountants estimate that the total increase in gas manufacturing cost for the present year will amount to $139,080.84, absorbing the entire surplus remaining from operations in 1916. If this outcome is to be avoided, economies must be secured in the gas departments.

One method of reducing the cost of production is to permit a reduction in the heating value of the gas below the standard generally adopted ten years ago. With the use of mantles in place of flat flame burners the lighting efficiency of the gas is not impaired. Such a reduction in the heating quality of the gas would be in conformity with present tendencies in many large cities throughout the country.

An analysis of the costs of operation of the electric plant shows that the unit cost of energy production and distribution for the year 1916 compares favorably with the average electric plant in other cities. In case the city of Richmond desires to extend its use of electrical energy to a degree that would require an increased investment in the municipal plant, careful study should be made to determine whether it would not be cheaper to purchase the electricity from private commercial stations. Further investments from the city's plant should be made only in the event that energy cannot be obtained elsewhere on a more economical basis.

The detailed accounting for revenues and expenses now carried on by the several present utility departments should be discontinued and this work performed in the office of the city auditor, the details for such work to be furnished that office by the proposed utility department. Classifications of accounts similar to those prescribed by public utility commissions should be adopted for the accounting work applying to each utility service, and these records should be so kept that the earning and expenses of each service may be shown separately. The present office practice with respect to the "listing book" should be discontinued and replaced by a system providing for the totalling of bills on adding machines and for the forwarding of the results of such tabulations by memorandum to the auditor, who should use such memoranda as the basis of his accounts. Under this plan bills would be paid to the city treasurer in the usual manner, and this official would list his receipts daily from the stubs of bills paid, showing the number of the bills or other identification and the amounts paid, which listing would constitute his daily cash record and could be posted to the consumers' register in both the gas and water divisions. Provision should be made for interdepartmental billings wherever service is furnished by one utility to another or to other departments of the city government.

Rates.

The employment of flat rates for water service is undesirable. Flat rates lead to waste of water, especially among domestic consumers, and there is yet to be found a reliable basis for estimating the maximum consumption upon which a reasonable flat rate can be based for commercial consumers. A systematic policy of elimination of all flat rate service should be adopted by the department. Meter service should first be extended to commercial consumers and then to domestic consumers.

The present meter rates for water are not only too numerous, but they are discriminatory and obsolete. There are at the present time sixty-four meter rates in force. A number of the schedules to which exception has been taken are rapidly being discontinued by the water department. It is recommended that a schedule of the increment type should be adopted, as suggested in the text of the report.

The practice of collecting the minimum bill in advance should be discontinued. The credit which the water department now receives for fire protection does not cover the cost of such service, and the utility should therefore receive the benefit of an increased credit from the city.

The present minimum bill policy of the gas department should be changed from an annual to a monthly basis. Under the present conditions a consumer paying the minimum bill secures considerable service for less than its cost to the department. A statement should be rendered to each consumer monthly, whether the consumer uses less than the minimum allowance or more than this allowance. A minimum bill of fifty cents per consumer per month would increase the revenue of the department it is estimated from $7,000 to $10,000 a year.

The electric department has no schedule of rates, since it does not sell energy to private consumers. The charge of three cents per k. w. hour to the various city departments is more in the nature of an insurance against waste than a measure of the cost of service rendered. No rate has been established for service to the water department or for street lighting. In order to furnish an index to the efficiency of the plant it would be advisable to fix rates to be charged for all services.

Engineering—Water Department.

Since the annexation of South Richmond the city has maintained an independent office of the water department which is not required. The needs of the community do not justify the employment of the staff in this office.

*It is recommended that the South Richmond office of the water department be discontinued and the position of second assistant superintendent abolished.

The conditions at the intake of the water supply on the James river are not satisfactory. Currents in the river at that point tend to form sandbars and obstruct the flow of the water, resulting in a considerable growth of algae. The water has a distinctly unpleasant taste, which can be attributed largely to this condition. Apparently the only means of correcting this situation is to secure a supply from a point farther upstream, and it is recommended that as soon as funds can be provided this improvement be made.

The coagulation basins at the treatment works require cleaning at least once every three months. They have not been cleaned as often as required in the past, owing to the lack of appropriations. This should not be allowed to continue. The gatemen at the treatment works are employed on straight twenty-four hour shifts on alternate days. This is a highly undesirable practice and should be discontinued.

The presence of bacillus coli in the river water is a menace to health, and steps should be taken to provide funds for the construction of a mechanical filtration plant, which is the most satisfactory method of removing this contamination.

The concrete conduit between the treatment works and the pumping station is largely without protective covering of any kind. It is urged that the conduit be guarded against injury by the railroad near by and from other causes by a protective covering.

At the pumping plant five men are on duty daily on twenty-four hour shifts. It is recommended that the employment of men on these excessively long shifts be discontinued, and that the plant be operated on two ten-hour shifts. By a reorganization of the pumping station a saving of approximately $4,500 annually could be obtained without impairing the service.

Complete records of the operation of the plant and of the cost of repairs should be kept.

It is recommended that the entire operation of the pumping plant be placed under the supervision of the superintendent of the electric department. In view of the inadequacy of the water distribution system, it is recommended that the city prepare plans and estimates for an adequate water distribution system and lay out a work program, indicating the amount that is to be expended annually until the distribution system has been enlarged to meet the requirements.

The three present methods of defraying the cost of making house connections, desribed in the report, are not scientific and in many cases are unfair. It is recommended that a new procedure be adopted so as to apportion the expense equitably in accordance with the character of the service performed.

Decided laxity is manifested in the control over the withdrawal of supplies from the store yard for repair work. There is a marked need for stores control over the entire maintenance and repair work of the water department.

The administration of the repair work is open to criticism with regard to the distribution of men and the number employed and the inadequacy of transportation equipment. It is believed that the needs of the city can be met by a smaller repair force, and it is therefore recommended that if the water department is to be retained as a separate department the force be reorganized in accordance with the recommendations contained in the text of the report. If the water department is to be consolidated with the two other utilities departments, a reorganization, such as is recommended in the discussion of the proposed department of public utilities, should be effected.

Gas Department.

The general condition of the gas plant is excellent. Attention should be given, however, to the need for increasing the capacity of the plant to meet the increasing consumption. Consideration should be given to the recommendation of the superintendent in favor of the installation of an improved type of coal gas plant with vertical benches. The present coal handling and coal storage facilities at the gas works should be improved and extended.

The same criticisms that were expressed regarding the repair and construction forces in the water department apply to the repair and construction forces in the gas department.

The use of push carts by repair gangs should be discontinued, and these gangs should be provided with motor transportation. The force employed in making connections for meters should be supplied with motor transportation.

The organization of the repair gangs and the stove setters or helpers in the gas department should be reorganized as suggested in the report, provided the gas department is to be maintained as a separate unit. If the department is consolidated with the water and electricity departments as recommended, still further economy can be effected, as indicated in the report on the proposed department of public utilities.

The general condition of the store yard of the gas department is good, but the control over supplies should be more carefully supervised. What the city needs is a central store yard for the three utilities departments.

Many of the services performed by the gas department are rendered without any expense to the consumer. Since the results are for the benefit of the consumer as well as the city it appears only fair that the consumer should be obliged to pay a certain proportion of the expense involved. The labor cost alone of certain of these services approximated $16,200 for the year 1916, of which $5,000 represented the work of the gasfitters and complaint men on small repairs. It is recommended that the superintendent of the gas department be empowered to charge a reasonable fee for making changes in the gas piping system or connections in private buildings.

Electrical Department.

The electrical plant is kept in good condition, but the control over supplies is rather loose. This is another argument for the consolidation of the stores and supplies of the three departments of water, gas and electricity in a single storehouse under a competent storekeeper.

The force employed in the electrical inspection is inadequate. The department should inspect outdoor electrical construction as well as interior installations.

No fees are charged for electrical inspections made by the department. The expense involved in making the electrical inspection constitutes a legitimate charge against the property inspected and it is recommended that the city establish a scale of charges for this service similar to the scale prevailing in Chicago and Detroit. If this were done it would increase the city's revenues by approximately $6,000 annually and make the division of inspection practically self-supporting.

The city government has consented to the construction of a high-voltage feed line within the city limits despite the protest of the superintendent of the electrical plant. This action is open to criticism.

In general, the lighting of streets in Richmond is adequate, but on Monument avenue and Franklin street, which are subject to heavy traffic, the lighting is decidedly inadequate. This has resulted from a policy of complying with the requests of owners and residents along these streets regarding the location and intensity of the street lights. This policy has been objected to by the superintendent of the electrical department. It is recommended that it be abandoned, and that the city install adequate lighting facilities along these streets without reference to the personal preference of the residents.

Standardization of Salaries and Wages.

The methods of appointment to employment in the service of the city of Richmond are defective when judged by conditions prevailing in other cities which enjoy the benefit of a system of civil service control. It is desirable that there should be an agency of the government for the recruiting of employees, and that there should be uniformity in methods of advancing and promoting employees. Such uniformity can only be secured through a central employment agency. By extending the functions of an existing department of the government—the public employment bureau— to include the recruiting, promotion and record keeping of municipal employees, Richmond can obtain the benefit of a civil service system. It is recommended that this bureau be given the powers listed in detail in the text of the report.

Inquiries were made during the course of the survey to ascertain the prevailing rates of compensation in the city of Richmond and in similar communities as a basis for recommending rates to be paid for city employment. Other factors, such as long hours, unpleasant surroundings in certain institutions, as well as some of the more advantageous features of public employment were considered in framing the schedules recommended in the report.

police department must be satisfactory to him, but the fact remains that of the various heads of administrative departments, the mayor appoints only one. He can suspend city employees for thirty days or remove them, but in event of removal they may appeal to the judge of the Hustings Court whose judgment in the matter is final. The result is that in case of an appeal, the mayor's position is at once shifted to that of defendant. Furthermore, even if his action is upheld by the court, there is nothing to prevent the appointive authority—the city council or the administrative board, from immediately re-appointing the person who has just been remooved. Thus it is that this removal power of the Mayor is almost useless in its operation.

Similarly, the charter gives other minor powers to the mayor which are more apparent than real. For example, it provides that he "shall have access to all books and documents in the offices of the various offices or boards." The fact is that the books and documents of the city are public records and as such are open to inspection by any taxpayer.

The heads of most of the large administrative departments are appointed by the administrative board. To expect leadership from a board or organization is to expect the impossible. Executive leadership is an individual attribute, and even if an individual member of the administrative board endeavored to assume leadership, he would soon have to contend with jealousies and lack of co-operation in his own board. Moreover, he could not protect his leadership.

It was unfortunate that, at the time the charter was revised to provide for an administrative board, membership therein was not made appointive by the mayor instead of elective by the people. Experience everywhere shows conclusively that popular elections, however democratic the plan may be, cannot be depended upon as a means of selecting properly qualified executives. Particularly is this true when the alluring attraction of a $5,000 salary is included. Irrespective of the personnel of the existing board, leaving it entirely out of consideration, and irrespective of occasional notable exceptions, the fact must be recognized that efficient business executives are loath to stand for election. It is far easier to secure a competent executive by appointment than by popular election.

A city council cannot exercise executive leadership for the same reasons cited concerning the administrative board. As a legislative body the city council of Richmond is given the appointive power of altogether too many administrative offices. It should be required by charter to adhere to its proper functions as the representative branch of the government in serving as a check on the executive branch and as the local legislature.

The Organization Is Too Complicated.

The organization of the city's government is so complicated that it is difficult to understand, unless set forth graphically on a chart. Complexity in governmental organization is always synonymous with red tape, waste, duplication, lost time and general inefficiency. Instead of being constructed on a simple plan, which could be readily understood, not only by the average voter, but also by the children in the city schools, the plan has been revised and readjusted until comparatively few persons outside of the city government really understand it. For this reason a graphic chart thereof has been prepared and is included herewith (Chart A). Reference to this chart will afford a better knowledge of the existing conditions than can be obtained by any written description.

Insufficient Correlation of Related Functions.

Practically no correlation of related functions is provided for in the present charter, except to the extent that a large group of departments are placed under the supervision of the administrative board. The public works functions thereunder are not only divided as between the city engineer, the superintendent of street cleaning and the park-keepers, but the lack of correllation extends to the building inspector, city hall engineers, cemetery keepers, etc. Although the city has developed three large public utility plants, each is still operating independent of the others. Similarly, although it is generally recognized that there is a close relation between the uniformed forces of the police and fire departments—the public safety branch of the government—the police department is assigned to the mayor and the fire department to a board appointed by the city council. The city council also appoints the clerk of police court, collector of delinquent taxes. etc. The confusion in organization is further enhanced by the fact that not content with appointing the city auditor as a check upon the financial transactions of the executive departments, it also appoints a "clerk to the auditor" as an additional check on the auditor himself. For similar reasons it appoints a "clerk to the treasurer" as an additional check upon that official. If such appointments are based on sound reasoning, then it would be equally good logic to appoint additional clerks to act as a check upon already appointed, and so continue and infinitum.

Although the collector of taxes is also elected by the people, the collector of delinquent taxes. who jointly occupies the same office with the collector. is appointed by the city council.

Not content with distributing administrative responsibility between the mayor. the administrative board and the city council. the positions of special accountant and the clerk of special assessments are made subordinate to the finance committee of council. Supplementing all of this confusion in organization and lack of correlation, various important administrative officers, such as the high constable, sheriff. city sergeant, city treasurer, commissioner of revenue, etc., by constitutional requirements, are elected directly by the people.

The coroners are appointed by the judge of the Hustings Court although their duties might better be distributed between the commonwealth attorney and medical inspector of the health department.

The school trustees are appointed by the city council, but the superintendent of schools is appointed by the state board of education.

Three Alternative Plans Recommended.

The Bureau of Municipal Research suggests three different plans of organization of the city's government, any one of which should be conducive to better government than can be obtained under the existing plan. None of the plans proposed is designed exactly as it should be because of the restrictions in the state constitution. Instead of recommending a plan which would require constitutional amendment, the Bureau believes it more practicable to suggest corrective measures which conform with the constitution. If subsequently constitutional revision can be secured so as to reduce the number of elective offices by making them appointive by the central executive officer of the city, so much the better. Thereby the full advantage of what is commonly known as the "short ballot" can be obtained. Meanwhile, instead of marking time until such revision is secured, it behooves the voters of the city to adopt such remedy as is available, through legislative revision of the city charter.

The three plans herein recommended are set forth in what is believed to be the sequence of their individual merit and their relative fitness to local conditions in the city of Richmond. They provide, respectively, for a plan of government by—

1.—Mayor and small council
2—Commission-manager
3—Commission.

Mayor and Small Council Plan.

This plan, as proposed for Richmond is shown graphically on chart B herewith. It centralizes executive authority and thereby fixes responsibility in the mayor except in so far as the constitutional officers must be retained. In the latter connection it is recommended that the office of city tax collector be abolished, and the duties thereof transferred to the city treasurer.

The city council would be reduced to a single body of nine members. That is enough to insure adequate representation in a city the size of Richmond, and still keep the council small enough to enable it to act as a unit. Every standing committee should consist of the entire membership of council. This would not only facilitate a thorough understanding by every member, of all business coming before the committees, but it would greatly expedite committee work in general. Under such a method all committees could meet on the same evening and transact their business at a single sitting by the simple process of having the various chairmen succeed one another at the head of the council table as the respective committees adjourned.

The revised or new charter should stipulate that neither the council nor any of its committees may perform any administrative functions. This was the most serious defect in the government prior to the establishment of the administrative board, and in fact was the reason for bringing the latter into existence. The charter should restrict the work of council to legislation and the incidents thereof, and assign all administrative work to the executive departments. The duties of council will thereby be no more onerous than at present and the salaries of the councilmen, if any, can be nominal.

The offices of clerk of committees and sergeant-at-arms should be consolidated in the city clerk's office, and the auditor should be ex-officio city clerk. This would be mutually advantageous because the auditor has much information of our rent value to council which would be readily available to that body if he acted as city clerk. It would also keep the auditor informed as to council action and matters pending before that body. The fact is that in most cities the city council and auditor each recognize the need for the latter's presence at council meetings to such an extent that he usually attends anyway. In so large a city as Portland, Oregon (population 273,000), the charter provides that the city auditor shall act as city clerk.

It is suggested that the departmental organization comprise seven groups with an administrative head over each. If desired, it might be reduced to five groups. For example, the department of public works might with some advantage be expanded to include the department of sanitation (street cleaning department). Similarly, if desired, department of parks and recreation could be placed under the department of public welfare, with the department of public works doing the park, road and other construction work, and still preserve a good working organization. As the city grows the police and fire departments might well be correlated in a department of public safety under a single commissioner. It is not believed that the need is sufficient to justify creating the additional position at this time.

Irrespective of whether there be seven, five or four administrative heads, they should be appointed and removable by the mayor without any reference to council and without appeal in case of removal. It is to be noted that these administrative heads would constitute in effect an administrative board. In fact, they might organize and hold meetings as such. Thus the advantages of the administrative board would be obtained without any of its disadvantages.

In order that the mayor may at all times be kept informed as to the city's financial condition and have complete access to the accounts at budget-making time, the central accounting and book-keeping office of the city should be under his supervision, i. e., he should appoint a city accountant to have charge thereof. Whereas the mayor should at all times have the fullest co-operation and assistance of the city accountant, the city auditor should be entirely independent of the mayor and of the executive offices, so that he can act as an independent check thereon. Hence the auditor should be appointed by the council.

Inasmuch as close co-operation is essential between the police force and the police courts, the judges of the latter should also be appointed by the mayor. He should be given power to select the city attorney and, if the constitution permits, also appoint the school trustees. Throughout the country, it is now generally recognized that better men can be secured by appointment for members of school boards than by election, even though such election be by a councilmanic body. Moreover, when a single official, such as the mayor, is charged with responsibility for selecting competent school trustees, and the eyes of the entire community are on him, he is more liable to make good appointments than if responsibility is diffused over the membership of council or any other appointing group.

Under the proposed plan the inspection of weights and measures should be placed in the department of welfare and the other minor departments distributed to the large groups according to the nature of their duties.

The Commission-Manager Plan.

This plan is shown graphically on Chart C. It should need little explanation because it is practically the same form of organization as is used by every large successful private corporation in the country. The five commissioners who would be elected by the people are comparable to the directors of a private corporation, and the city manager who would be employed by this board of five commissioners is comparable to the general manager or other central executive head employed by the directors of the private corporation. The commission-manager plan is now in successful operation in more than fifty cities in the United States, and the number and size of the cities is constantly increasing.

The five commissioners should be elected at large and receive but a nominal salary. They should have power to select as city manager the best man available for the salary that is offered irrespective of his place of residence. The departmental organization herein suggested is the same as that outlined under plan No. 1, and could, if it seemed desirable, be readjusted, as suggested therein. The administrative head of each department should be appointed by and directly responsible to the city manager. The latter would be charged with the preparation and submittal of the annual budget to the commission.

The same consolidation of the offices of the city clerk and auditor is recommended as under plan No. 1. In addition, such office might function as the central accounting office, because the reasons which exist in plan No. 1 for separating these functions would be less important.

The commission-manager plan has almost the same advantage of keeping a separation between the legislative branch of the government (the commission) and the executive branch as has plan No. 1.

The Commission Plan.

The third alternative is shown graphically in Chart D. The commission form of government has been developed generally throughout the United States since the establishment of the original commission in Galveston, Texas. At the present time over 400 cities are operating under this plan. It is to be noted, however, that it possesses certain fundamental defects, such as vesting legislative and administrative authority in the same man. Also that the administrative heads of the various departments are elected instead of being appointed, thereby laying it open to the objections already noted herein concerning the selection of administrative officials by popular election.

It is well to realize that many of the cities now under the commission-manager plan of government at first tried commission plan. Finding it unsatisfactory, they decided to take the next logical step—confine the functions of the commission to legislative matters and have the commission employ a trained executive to administer the city's business affairs. It should also be noted that the cities of Denver, Colorado, and Salem, Massachusetts, after trying commission plan of government reverted to the mayor and council plan.

In connection with a commission plan it is also well to remember that the departments of Richmond's government fall logically into only four groups:

> Utilities,
> Public works,
> Public safety,
> Public welfare.

A commission of four members would have difficulty in maintaining a majority. Three is not enough, and hence five has come to be the generally accepted number for this form of government. In event it be decided to adopt commission government, it is recommended that the fifth commissioner be placed at the head of a department known as the department of commerce. In fact, such a department might with advantage be included in either plan No.

1 or plan No. 2. This suggestion is based on the theory that the development of the commercial industries now in the city of Richmond and the securing of additional industries is important to the welfare of the people, and hence logical undertaking for the government. The duties of a commissioner of commerce would be to effect and maintain a closer relation between the government and the commercial organization of the city. The department would function somewhat as a chamber of commerce, but without the club and social features. The principle underlying this suggestion is incorporated in the present charter of the city of Denver, Colorado.

Representative Government.

When revising the city charter serious consideration should be given to making the local government more truly representative. Under the present plan of electing members of the local legislature by wards, the minority in each ward has in point of fact no representation. Such conditions are undemocratic and un-American. They breed apathy and discouragement in the hearts of the minority voters. The ideal in civic progress, civic interest and loyalty cannot be attained under such conditions. Ashtabula, Ohio, has led the way to real representative government in this country by adopting in its new charter what is commonly known as proportional representation. That the plan is entirely practicable has already been demonstrated by cities and nations in various parts of the world. It is unnecessary to describe it in this report because abundant literature thereon may be secured from the Proportional Representation League (802 Franklin Bank Building, Philadelphia, Pa.) which numbers among its members many of the leading statesmen and economists of the United States. It is recognized that the adoption of proportional representation by the city of Richmond might require a constitutional amendment, but the subject is of sufficient importance to justify its inclusion among the recommendations of this survey.

If the ward system is continued in Richmond, then charter revision should provide for the election of such a number of councilmen at large as will exceed the number elected by wards. For example, if four wards are retained, then five councilmen should be elected at large.

If proportional representation is not adopted, the revised charter should at least provide for voting on what is known as the "preferential method." Under such a plan each voter indicates a first, second and third choice for each candidate.

Moreover, provision should be made for rotation of names on the ballots so that the same name will not appear first on all ballots simply because it begins with "A", or because a particular person was fortunate in getting his petition filed first.

There should be no overlapping of terms in any ordinance-making body. The city's government should come back to the people at least every four years and afford opportunity for them to make a clean sweep if they so desire. The only argument in favor of overlapping terms is to preserve a continuity of policy. The fact is, however, that it is liable to be the wrong policy which is continued. With respect to the continuation of policies which are for the public good, it is usually possible to re-elect the persons who support them and thus preserve all essential continuity. Overlapping terms are unnecessary.

Although it is believed that sentiment in Richmond would not yet favor adopting such a plan, the Bureau of Municipal Research would call attention at this point to its belief that a city charter should enable either the mayor or the city council "to go to the people" at any time a deadlock arises on an important issue between these two branches of the government. The practical result of such a plan would be a "recall" on public policies instead of merely a recall of man.

The City's Finances

THE CITY'S FINANCES.

Confronted with a large mileage of streets in need of new pavements, or repairs of existing pavements, by a demand for the extension of sewers and other public utility service, by a large increase in the cost of supplies, materials and equipment, by the demands of the city employees for increased compensation whereby they may meet the advance in cost of living, the present financial difficulty of the city of Richmond is obvious. To meet the situation the government should both decrease its expenditures and increase its revenues. To take the latter step without taking the first, could not be justified in the light of the present survey. On the other hand, the survey has demonstrated that it may not be practicable to reduce expenditures sufficiently to keep the necessary budget appropriations within the limitations of existing revenues. Reduction in expenditures may have to be supplemented by some increase on the credit side of the city's account.

It is believed unnecessary in this report to go into the reasons which are responsible for the present situation. The large demands for increased expenditures without adequate compensating revenues resulting from the annexations of adjacent territory must have been unforeseen at the time by a considerable proportion of the population. The recent reduction in the city's annual income caused by legislative readjustment of the entire revenue system of the State was beyond local control. Similarly, the financial trouble which would be caused by amending the State constitution so as to preclude the levying of special assessments for local improvements was both beyond local control and probably not fully appreciated at the time by those responsible for its adoption. The other factors entering into Richmond's problem on both the expenditure and revenue side are not uncommon today in other cities throughout the country. In discussing the city's finances one naturally considers first the subject of the existing debt.

*Indebtedness.**

Amount Outstanding.

The total debt of the city on January 31st, the end of the last fiscal year, was as follows:

---

*For discussion of sinking funds see chapter on City Auditor.

Bonded Debt.

Bonds originally issued by city of Richmond $16,122,525
Bonds of other communities assumed by the city of Richmond by annexation.   925,530
                                                                                        $17,048,055

Floating Debt.

Notes due for improvements and in anticipation of taxes ....$ 465,000
Notes due for school property acquired by annexation   67,420
                                                                                         532,420
                                                                                        $17,580,475

Net Debt.

Bonded debt $17,048,055
Less: Sinking fund ....$ 4,018,276
      Water bonds 2,148,000
                                                        6,166,276

Net bonded debt ....$10,881,779   =.086 of the assessed valuation of real estate
Add: Floating debt   532,420

                                                    $11,414,199   = 09 " "

Borrowing Margin.

The charter (section 67) provides: "the bonds or interest bearing debt of the city of Richmond shall not, in the aggregate exceed 18 per cent. of the assessed value of the taxable real estate on said city."

In 1916 the assessed value of real estate in the city was $125,631,487.

18 per cent. of above valuation.......................$22,613,668
Less: Interest bearing debt 17,580,475

Net margin ....$ 5,033,193
Add: Amounts not deducted from total debt:
    Sinking funds   4,018,276
    Water bonds   2,148,000

Gross margin $11,199,469

Note that if the floating debt of $532,420 were excluded from the $17,580,475 of interest bearing debt shown above, the net margin would be $5,565,613 and the gross margin $11,731,889.

The charter seems to be specific, however, that in computing the borrowing margin, all interest bearing debt of the city must be included. This report would point out that simply because there exists a comparatively wide borrowing margin, it does not follow that the city can, with justification, and in conformity with sound financial policy, continue to issue bonds so long as it remains within the 18 per cent. limitation. The reason for this is that 18 per cent. is an unusually high allowance as compared with the debt limitations in other states, hence, conservative administration demands that there should always be a considerable balance of borrowing power remaining unencumbered.

Debt of Other Cities.

Compared with the net per capita debt of the other seven cities of the United States which have a population of from 145,000 to 185,000, Richmond ranks third, i. e., only two cities in that population group have a larger per capita debt. These figures are based on the 1916 report of the United States Census Bureau which in computing net debt places all cities on the same basis and simply deducts the existing sinking fund assets from the aggregate funded and floating debt. Both the amounts and per capita of the gross and net debt of the eight cities in the group are shown in the following table:

CITY	GROSS DEBT		NET DEBT	
	Total	Per Capita	Total	Per Capita
Omaha	$ 21.656,357 00	$ 132 70	$ 17 420,841 00	$ 106 75
Memphis	13,975,908 00	95 65	12,071,489 00	82 62
Richmond	16,280,405 00	105 14	11,468,407 00	73 07
Syracuse	12,334.306 00	80 86	9,869,236 00	64 70
Worcester	14,598,644 00	91 07	7,954,591 00	49 63
Birmingham	8,954 088 00	52 02	6,812,466 00	39 58
New Haven	5 059,950 00	34 40	4,499,638 00	30 59
Atlanta	6,243,689 00	33 77	4,728,500 00	25 56

A comparison of the twenty-six southern cities subsequently discussed in detail herein shows Richmond ranking sixth, with only five of the twenty-six having a larger per capita debt:

Total and Per Capita of all Debt of 26 Southern Cities Having Population of 40,000 to 200,000

CITY	GROSS DEBT		NET DEBT (a)	
	Total	Per Capita	Total	Per Capita
Atlanta	$ 6,243,689 00	$ 33 77	$ 4,728,500 00	$ 25 58
Birmingham	8,954,088 00	52 02	6,812 466 00	39 58
Richmond	16 280,405 00	105 14	11 468,407 00	74 07
Memphis	13,975,903 00	95 65	12 071,489 00	82 62
Dallas	7,332,969 00	60 46	5,991,356 00	49 40
San Antonio	7,688 293 00	63 40	6,149,773 00	50 71
Nashville	9,009,372 00	77 68	7,737,030 00	66 71
Houston..........	13,748,038 00	127 09	11,731,720 00	98 45
Fort Worth......	6 202,824 00	62 32	5,245,710 00	52 71
Oklahoma City..	6,223,294 00	68 68	4,619,024 00	50 97
Norfolk	10 077,597 00	113 43	8 098,844 00	91 16
Jacksonville	4,524,749 00	61 87	3,840 507 00	52 51
Savannah	3,922,105 00	57 37	3 369 605 00	49 29
El Paso	4,001,313 00	55 86	3,231,849 00	53 20
Charleston	4,219,150 00	69 82	4,106 892 00	67 96
Chattanooga.....	3,911,700 00	67 21	3,498,144 00	60 10
Covington........	3,046,067 00	53 89	2,542,910 00	44 99
Mobile	3,837,992 00	68 18	3,045,548 00	54 10
Little Rock	1,417,131 00	25 69	871,274 00	15 80
Tampa	3,497,747 00	66 62	3,111,297 00	59 26
Augusta	4,424,402 00	88 76	3,703,903 00	74 30
Macon	1,903,569 00	41 91	1,582,952 00	34 86
Montgomery.....	3 855,782 00	89 86	2,906,963 00	67 75
Muskogee	3,206,142 00	75 02	2,248 939 00	52 62
Roanoke	2,072,799 00	49 44	1,826,956 00	43 57
Galveston	5 683,387 00	137 92	4,864,899 00	118 06

(a) Funded and floating debt less sinking fund assets.

Serial Versus Long-Term Bonds.

An examination of the state constitution and the city charter indicates that there is nothing to prevent the issue of serial bonds in lieu of the customary thirty-four year bonds. In issuing the latter class of bonds, it becomes necessary to establish and maintain sinking funds for their redemption. Throughout the country sinking funds are becoming obsolete as a method of paying bonded debt, because, however well they may be administered, it is a cumbersome method of accomplishing the desired result. Not only is there the initial obligation to keep the funds properly invested, but equitable assessments upon the taxpayers during the period of the loan involve complicated mathematical computations if the debt is to be paid at maturity.

Evidence is abundant in cities, counties and states, of sinking funds to which contributions in the right amounts have not been made from year to year, with the result that at maturity of the loans these funds were found to be short of the amounts necessary to pay the debts for which they were created. The city of Richmond, in recent years has been fortunate in having as administrators of the sinking fund, men who realized the necessity of great care in setting aside each year amounts which, together with the increment thereon, would be adequate at maturity of the bonds. There is no assurance, however, that the city will always be so fortunate in its sinking fund administrators.

The serial method of paying debt not only obviates the administrative requirements of the sinking fund method, but it is aso cheaper and imposes a limited burden upon the taxpayers. Moreover, its operation is so simple that it is usually understood by the average citizen.

Term of Bonds.

When revising the city charter, provision should be made so far as practicable that no bonds may be issued for a period existing beyond the life of the property to be acquired. The maximum bond limitation in the present charter is thirty-four years. Among the reasons for adopting this arbitrary period was probably the fact that originally money rates justified computing debt amortization on a 6 per cent. base, and thus in thirty-four years, by paying 50 cents into the sinking fund every six months for each $100 of debt, an amount equalling the principal would be produced in thirty-four years. Conditions have changed greatly since then and will no doubt continue to change, and hence the life of bonds should not be made arbitrarily to conform to any predetermined basis of amortization. There should be incorporated in the charter a brief schedule setting forth the various classes of properties for which ten-year bonds, fifteen-year bonds, twenty-year bonds, etc., may, respectively, be issued up to, say, thirty years. It is to be noted in this connection that the state legislatures in both Massachusetts and New Jersey have not only limited all civil divisions of government within those states to the serial method of issuing bonds, but also have incorporated in the state law schedules similar to those here suggested for the city of Richmond.

Temporary Loans and Flow of Cash.

The city formerly received its liquor license revenues and also the income from certain other business licenses early in the year. Now, however, it no longer receives the former and does not get the business licenses until about May. About $100,000 a month is received from general sources—principally on gas and water bills—but the operating expenses of the government are approximately $300,000 a month. Property taxes are not received until June and hence there is a deficit of over $200,000 a month from February until June. One-half of the real estate taxes are received then, but the other half, and also the personal property tax is not received until November. Hence, there is a deficit again from August to October. These deficits are necessarily met by the issuance of temporary loans (notes).

How much it costs the city in interest each year for money borrowed to meet its expenses pending the collection of the year's revenues, it would be difficult to determine, because the money needed currently to pay for construction and other purposes is also obtained to a considerable extent, by issuing temporary loans (notes). These latter are funded from time to time by the issuance of bonds. Owing to the fact that the central accounts of the city do not maintain a clear distinction between the cash of the various funds, it would require much analysis work to determine the amount of interest on temporary loans issued in anticipation of revenue collections as distinguished from the temporary loans which are subsequently funded.

It is always desirable to keep at an absolute minimum, the amount which a city pays for interest on temporary loans because such money could be used to much greater advantage elsewhere in the annual budget. The corrective remedy usually consists in moving forward the collection date of the first installment of property taxes. Owing to the complicated condition of the revenue laws in Virginia, it is not possible for Richmond or any other city to do this alone.

Comparison of Revenues and Expenditures of the Eight Cities In the United States Having a Population of 145,000 to 185,000.

Supplementing the statistics shown throughout this report, it is important that the citizens of Richmond should study their government costs in comparison with other cities of similar size. Unless the data for such comparisons is on the same basis they are liable to be misleading. The only comparative data available is that contained in the United States Census Bureau publications, and for that reason the bulletin of December, 1916, has been used as the basis for special tables prepared for this report. Even though experienced census examiners spend several weeks each year in every city of over 30,000 population, it is to be remembered that the accounting and business systems vary as between cities. Hence the reader of this survey report is cautioned that some of the figures may lead to erroneous conclusions unless interpreted with great care.

Referring to Table II, columnar heading "rate of levy" it will be noticed that there exist wide variations between the rates of levy of the cities considered. As regards the rates based on the "assessed valuation" it must be remembered that the reported percentages which the assessed valuations form of the true value are only estimates, and that the figures for each city were estimated by a different official. For this reason, if there were any errors made in determining the basis of the assessed valuations, the same errors were naturally perpetuated in adjusting the valuations and tax rates from the "assessed" to the "true" or 100 per cent. basis.

In assembling these tables the Bureau of Municipal Research has excluded the rates of levy for state and county purposes, which were as follows per $1,000 on general property:

CITY	STATE		COUNTY	
	On Assessed Value	On Estimated True Value	On Assessed Value,	On Estimated True Value
Atlanta	$ 4 80	$ 2 94	$ 7 50	$4 62
Birmingham	6 50	3 90	7 00	4 20
Omaha	6 80	1 10	16 60	2 68
Worcester	2 05	2 05	93	93
Richmond	2 58 (a)	1 94 (a)	....	....
Syracuse	2 10	2 10	6 20	6 21
New Haven......	2 00	2 00	50	50
Memphis	3 50	1 72	10 40	5 12

(a) Average rate.

Worcester and New Haven claim to assess both real and personal property on a basis of 100 per cent. of the true value, thus making the rate of levy on the general property tax per $1,000 of assessed valuation identical with the rate per $1,000 of estimated true value. Omaha is reported as assessing both real and personal property on a basis of only 16 per cent. of its true value, thus throwing the rate of levy per $1,000 of assessed valuation very high. Atlanta, Birmingham and Memphis, the cities showing the lowest tax rates, all claim to assess on a basis of 60 per cent. of the true value. Assuming that these cities have reported the facts with respect to the basis actually used, there are several explanations as to why the rates should vary so much in cities of the same population group. The following are specially significant:

1—Some cities derive extra returns from business licenses, as Atlanta and Birmingham.

2—Some cities derive especially large returns from special assessments and special charges for outlays, as Birmingham, Omaha and Syracuse.

3—Some cities derive proportionately heavy revenues from fines, forfeits and escheats, as Atlanta, Birmingham and Memphis.

4—Some cities derive especially large revenues from subventions and grants, as Atlanta, Birmingham and Memphis.

The average tax rate on general property in these eight cities is $12.73 per $1,000 of estimated true value. For convenience, the following table is reproduced from Table II, re-arranged as regards lowness of rate:

Rank	City	General Property Tax Per $1,000 of Estimated True Value (a)
1st	Birmingham.........	$ 6 00
2nd	Atlanta	7 66
3rd	Memphis	9 06
4th	Richmond	10 24
5th	Omaha	12 33
6th	Worcester...........	17 42
7th	Syracuse	19 46
8th	New Haven	19 73

(a) Combined city corporation and school district rates.

From the above it will be seen that the city of Richmond ranks fourth in having a low tax rate, being led by Memphis, Atlanta and Birmingham, respectively. As to why these three cities have a lower tax rate than Richmond, it may be said that it is due in large part to the different methods of financing the expenditures for outlays, and in small part to the differences in several minor classes of revenue received. As to the latter, the following table is suggestive:

City	Revenue From Business Licenses	Revenue From Fines, Forfeits and Escheats	Revenue From Subventions and Grants
Birmingham	$ 407,034	$ 46,974	$ 289 436
Atlanta	315,742	50,599	176,917
Memphis	90,624	68,653	271,366
Richmond	186,924	30,848	80,517

As regards expenditures for outlays, the following table shows the payments of each of the four cities:

City	Total Payments for Outlays	Per Capita Payments for Outlays	Receipts From Assessments for Outlays	Per Capita Receipts From Special Assessments for Outlays
Birmingham.....	$ 264,360 00	$ 1 53	$ 339,356 00	$ 1 97
Atlanta	859,710 00	4 65	141,536 00	76
Memphis	967,613 00	6 62	219,288 00	1 50
Richmond	2,251,833 00	14 54	29,879 00	19

While there is rarely a direct relation in any one year between the total amount expended for local improvements and the total amount of special assessments actually collected during that same year, the following figures are nevertheless significant. Reduced to a dollar basis it appears that during the year under review, for every dollar paid for outlays, the following revenue was collected from special assessments:

Birmingham $1.287
Atlanta .... .163
Memphis .... .226
Richmond .... .013

Birmingham, by virtue of its high rate of special assessments for outlays and its comparatively low per capita expenditures for expenses of the general departments, is able to maintain the very low tax rate of $6.00. The following table presenting the per capita expenditures of the largest departments in those cities having a lower tax rate than Richmond helps to account for the difference in rates:

CITY	Per Capita Payments for				
	General Government (a)	Police Department	Fire Department	Sanitation (b)	Education
Birmingham..........................	$0 60	$1 01	$1 36	$0 71	$3 16
Atlanta	0 86	1 61	1 48	1 69	3 66
Memphis	0 63	1 61	1 45	1 11	3 95
Richmond	1 72	1 51	1 64	1 50	4 02

(a) Includes legislative, executive, judicial, elections and general government buildings,
(b) Includes sewage disposal and refuse collection.

For all the expenses of the general departments, Birmingham shows a per capita expenditure of only $8.63, as against $13.98 for Richmond; $13.52 for Atlanta; and $13.46 for Memphis. Another very probable cause of difference in tax rates lies in the aggregate of debts and interest payments, as per the following table:

CITY	Gross Debt	Per Capita Gross Debt	Net Debt (a)	Per Capita Net Debt	Total Payments for Interest	Per Capita Payments for Interest
Birmingham.	$ 8,954,088 00	$ 52 02	$ 6,812,466 00	$ 39 58	$ 436,638 00	$ 2 54
Atlanta	6,243,689 00	33 77	4,728,500 00	25 58	210,656 00	1 14
Memphis	13,975,908 00	95 65	12,071,489 00	74 07	628,178 00	4 30
Richmond _..	16,280,405 00	105 14	11,468,407 00	82 62	649,504 00	4 19

(a) Funded and floating debt less sinking fund assets.

As to why the tax rates in the remaining four cities are higher than the corresponding rate in Richmond, it is believed that a study of the "summary table" presented herewith will throw much light on the subject. So far as this survey is concerned, it seemed only necessary to analyze the rates and figures of those cities in the same population group which appeared to have a lower tax rate than that of Richmond.

The fact may or may not be significant that the commission-governed cities included in the study, three in number, have an average tax rate of $9.13, while the five other cities considered have an average rate of $14.90, a difference of $5.77 in favor of the former. It will also be noticed from Table I that the four cities showing the lowest tax rates are all southern cities, with an average of 35.3 per cent. of their total population colored.

EXPLANATION OF CODE SYMBOLS:

Richmond	—A	Worcester	—E
Atlanta	—B	Syracuse	—F
Birmingham	—C	New Haven	—G
Omaha	—D	Memphis	—H

Summary Table

	RANK							
	1st	2nd	3rd	4th	5th	6th	7th	8th
Population	B	C	D	E	A	F	G	H
Per capita wealth based on assessed valuation	E	G	A	F	B	H	C	D
Per capita wealth based on estimated true value	D	B	A	H	E	G	F	C
Lowest tax rate (a)								
Based on assessed valuation	C	B	A	H	E	F	G	D
Based on estimated true value	C	B	H	A	D	E	F	G
Lowest per capita gross debt	B	F	C	F	E	H	A	D
Lowest per capita net debt	B	G	C	C	F	A	H	D
Lowest per capita payments for interest	B	G	C	C	F	E	A	H
Highest per capita revenue from taxes (b)	E	F	G	A	D	H	H	A
Highest per capita revenue from licenses (c)	C	D	G	B	G	E	A	H
Highest per capita revenue from business licenses exclusive of liquor	C	B	H	A	F	D	B	G
Amount of revenue from taxes (b)	E	F	A	G	B	D	H	C
Amount of revenue from licenses (c)	C	B	B	G	G	A	F	H
Amount of revenue from business licenses exclusive of liquor	C	B	H	A	F	D	E	G
Highest per capita payments for expenses of police department	E	G	B	H	F	A	D	C
Highest per capita payments for expenses of fire department	D	E	G	F	A	B	H	C
Highest per capita payments for expenses of highways (d)	E	H	F	G	D	B	A	C
Highest per capita payments for education (e)	E	G	D	F	A	H	B	C

(a) Based on city government figures and showing general property tax rate per $1,000.
(b) Includes general property, special property and poll taxes.
(c) Includes business and non-business licenses.
(d) Includes general expenses and repair and construction for compensation.
(e) Includes both schools and libraries.

Comparison of the Revenues and Expenditures of the Twenty-six Southern Cities Having a Population of 40,000 to 200,000.

While the foregoing comparisons of Richmond with the seven other cities of the United States most nearly approaching it in population sheds much light on the local situation, there are certain factors which make conditions in southern cities very much alike as among themselves, and very different when compared with northern cities. The main point of difference in this respect is the large percentage of negro population in the southern cities. This single fact affects very materially the value of any comparisons of municipal finances. Particularly is this true of general statistics on a per capita basis. For example, in Richmond applying the last population figures of the United States Census—99,156 white population to $117,030,740, the 1916 assessed valuation of real estate owned by whites, gives an average white per capita ownership of $1,180. As compared with this the reported 55,518

TABLE I

GENERAL STATISTICS, EMBRACING ALL CITIES IN THE UNITED STATES HAVING AN ESTIMATED POPULATION BETWEEN 145,000 AND 185,000

City	State	Estimated Population (a)	Form of Government	Assessed Valuation of Taxable Property (b)	Estimated Population July 1, 1915		Per Cent. Colored	Fiscal Year Covered by These Tables
					White	Colored		
Atlanta	Ga.	184,373	Mayor and upper and lower houses	$182,512,586	126,969	57,983	31.3	Jan. 1, 1915—Dec. 31, 1915
Birmingham	Ala.	172,119	Commission	98,531,525	108,679 (c)	65,429	37.5	Sept. 30, 1914—Sept. 30, 1915
Omaha	Nebr.	163,200	Commission	44,607,464	119,670 (c)	4,426	3.6	Jan. 1, 1915—Dec. 31, 1915
Worchester	Mass	160,291	Mayor and upper and lower houses	180,061,080	144,746 (c)	1,941	0.9	Nov. 30, 1914—Nov. 30, 1915
Richmond	Va	154,841	Mayor and upper and lower houses	165,861,756	99,156	55,518	35.8	Jan. 31, 1915—Jan. 31, 1916
Syracuse	N.Y.	152,534	Mayor and single house	157,902,920	136,126 (c)	1,124	0.8	Jan. 1, 1915—Dec. 31, 1914
New Haven	Conn	147,095	Mayor and single house	161,750,542	130,044 (o)	3,561	2.7	Jan. 1, 1915—Dec. 31, 1915
Memphis	Tenn	146,113	Commission	117,914,490	92,252	53,861	36.8	Jan. 1, 1915—Dec. 31, 1915

(a) Estimated by United States census as of middle of fiscal year shown in last column.
(b) As ruled by the city corporation.
(c) 1910 figures, United States census.

TABLE II

ASSESSED VALUATION, REPORTED BASIS OF ASSESSMENT, AND RATE OF LEVY

(For Period Covered. See Table I)

City	Assessed Valuation of Property					Reported Basis of Assessment In Practice (Per Cent of Estimated True Value) (a)			Rate of Levy (d)			Of Poll Taxes
	Total	Subject to the General Property Tax			Subject to Special Property Taxes	Real	Personal	Other	Of General Property Tax Per $1,000 of		Of Poll Taxes	
		Real	Personal	Other					Assessed Valuation	Estimated True Value		
Atlanta	$182,812,883	$132,770,618	$30,876,452	$19,165,798		60	60	75	$12.50	$ 7.66		$1.00
Birmingham	93,531,525	66,422,976	27,103,549			60	60		10.00	6.00		(a)
Omaha	44,607,494	28,465,495	16,141,969		$ 895,030 (e)	16	16 (b)		75.80	12.33		2.00
Worcester	180,061,040	139,822,850	39,343,200			100	100		17.42	17.42		1.00
Richmond	165,881,756	105,035,792	60,905,964			75	75		13.66 (f)	10.24 (g)		
Syracuse	157,992,920	138,450,848	4,660,868			102	102		1909 (f)	19.46 (h)		
New Haven	161,750,542	134,498,039	21,178,207		13,791,264 (c)	100	100		19.73 (i)	19.73 (i)		2.00
Memphis	117,914,498	93,846,005	13,144,399	10,924,092	6,074,296 (c)	60	60	40	15.80	9.06		

(a) For property subject to the general property tax.
(b) Basis for all personal property except railroad property which is assessed on a basis of 20 per cent
(c) In calculating the estimated true value, these valuations are assumed to have been assessed on a 100 per cent basis.
(d) ding both city corporation and school district, where these are constituted as independent taxing divisions and exclu-

sive of ot   state, county, etc.

(e) tangible $16.50; bank stock $14.00; and bonds, stocks, etc. $3.00; average $13.66.
     2.38; bank stock $10.50; and bonds, stocks, etc. $2.25; average $10.24.
(f)   fund.
(g)
(h)   9.29 and school district tax if $9.61; city corporation tax made up of following rates: wards 1 to 12, $20.00; ward
       2.00; average $19.39; school district tax made up as follows: ward 13, $10.00, Westville school district $8.00;

13, $6.00;
average $9.61; average for city   district $19.73.

TABLE III

SUMMARY OF REVENUE RECEIPTS

(For Period Covered. See Table I)

City and Division of City's Government	Total	From Taxes						From Special Assessments and Charges for Outlays	From Fines, Forfeits and Escheats	From Earnings of Public Service Enterprises	From Other Sources (a)
		General Property	Special Property	Poll	On Liquor Traffic	Other Than On Liquor Traffic	Non-Business Licenses				
Atlanta	$3,818,864.00	$2,398,522.00		$15,572.00				$250,620.00	$50,699.00	$506,306.00	$311,444.00
Birmingham	2,223,716.00	935,939.00			65,214.00	341,520.00	31,734.00	339,356.00	46,974.00	40,023.00	419,656.00
Omaha	4,404,378.00	2,202,113.00			266,160.00	19,800.00	8,596.00	552,100.00	22,532.00	880,505.00	528,142.00
City corporation	2,340,572.00	1,459,343.00						501,456.00	14,675.00	4,470.00	347,085.00
School district	1,098,462.00	742,810.00							7,854.00		66,992.00
Water district	969,044.00									876,335.00	2,065.00
Rochester	5,192,798.00	3,180,127.00	406,683.00	95,676.00	183,005.00	18,454.00	4,121.00	50,644.00	6,461.00	500,569.00	607,123.00
Richmond	4,997,599.00	2,455,537.00		32,492.00	110,248.00	76,674.00	7,994.00	184,459.00	30,948.00	914,491.00	425,991.00
Syracuse	4,045,325.00	2,702,492.00	73,795.00		148,509.00	29,274.00	9,318.00	567,532.00	9,190.00	390,194.00	168,532.00
City corporation	4,009,280.00	2,640,034.00	49,277.00					567,532.00	6,190.00	390,194.00	168,522.00
County supervisor's fund	86,946.00	62,498.00	24,518.00								
New Haven	3,087,639.00	2,380,838.00	33,115.00	33,301.00	196,424.00	8,684.00	15,817.00	100,285.00	31,149.00	2,170.00	255,867.00
City corporation	3,023,046.00	2,319,695.00	58,115.00	33,301.00	196,424.00		15,817.00	100,285.00	31,149.00	2,170.00	252,417.00
Westville school district	54,945.00	51,797.00									3,158.00
Borough of Fairhaven, East	9,648.00	9,356.00									292.00
Memphis	3,179,446.00	1,901,574.00			90,624.00		12,236.00	226,468.00	68,653.00	453,601.00	426,090.00

(a) Includes receipts from: subventions and grants; donations and gifts; pension assessments; earnings of general department; highway privileges; rents; interest.

TABLE IV

EXPENSES OF GENERAL DEPARTMENTS

(For Period Covered, See Table I)

(For Per Capita Costs of Same, See Table IX)

City	Total	General Government (a)	Protection to Person and Property	Conservation of Health	Sanitation (b)	Highways	Charities, Hospitals and Corrections	Education	Recreation	Miscellaneous and General
Atlanta	$2,493,674.00	$188,412.00	$602,671.00	$93,937.00	$313,134.00	$300,955.00	$223,141.00	$676,658.00	$72,605.00	$57,160.00
Birmingham	1,435,090.00	103,663.00	436,656.00	15,970.00	122,104.00	157,889.00	42,757.00	543,520.00	24,625.00	37,922.00
Omaha	2,329,378.00	185,809.00	658,573.00	41,948.00	147,766.00	275,849.00	1,479.00	881,197.00	87,533.00	39,382.00
Worcester	3,244,045.00	135,815.00	595,017.00	93,524.00	224,540.00	466,501.00	315,672.00	1,217,627.00	106,899.00	70,637.00
Richmond	2,164,509.00	266,976.00	540,208.00	40.99 .00	233,571.00	135,821.00	155,591.00	622,491.00	92,648.00	27,326.00
Syracuse	2,588,673.00	236,154.00	509,990.00	70.46 .00	251,765.00	337,417.00	288,620.00	704,281.00	74,180.00	83,990.00
New Haven	2,388,926.00	160,030.00	525,701.00	47.43 .00	120,989.00	271,170.00	128,071.00	952,249.00	92,241.00	89,382.00
Memphis	1,906,289.00	91,541.00	471,180.00	66. .00	162,072.00	350,161.00	199,623.00	577,669.00	120,758.00	11,899.00

(a) Embraces legislative, executive and judicial branches, elections, and general governmental buildings.
(b) Includes sewage disposal and refuse collection.

TABLE V
PAYMENTS FOR INTEREST (a)
(For Period Covered, See Table I)

City	Total Payments for Interest	Payments for Interest on Funded and Floating Debt			Paid for Interest On Special Assessment Debt	Payments for Interest on Other Debt		
		Of City Corporation	Of School District	Other Governmental Units	Of City Corporation	Of City Corporation	Of School District	Other Governmental Units
Atlanta	$210,656.00	$208,017.00			$104,103.00	$ 2,639.00		
Birmingham	436,658.00	311,884.00		$338,056.00	116,906.00	20,671.00		
Omaha	342,797.00	318,388.00	$95,092.00			147.00	$3,208.00	
Worcester	551,373.00	517,729.00				33,544.00		
Richmond	649,504.00	616,064.00			73,861.00	33,450.00		
Syracuse	490,861.00	348,138.00				38,962.00		
New Haven	170,730.00	162,625.00	3,600.00			3,034.00	1,418.00	
Memphis	628,178.00	540,434.00			79,543.00	8,201.00		$53.00

(a) Represents gross payments for interest on city debts less—(1) Amounts paid in error, and

TABLE VI

PER CENT DISTRIBUTION, BY PRINCIPAL CLASSES, OF REVENUE RECEIPTS AND GOVERNMENTAL COST PAYMENTS

(For Period Covered, See Table I)

City	Revenue Receipts												Percent of Governmental Cost Payments Represented By Payments for			
	Percent Obtained From								Percent Required for Meeting						
	Taxes		Business and Non-Business Licenses	Special Assessments and Special Charges for Outlays	Fines, Forfeits and Escheats	Subventions, Grants, Gifts, Donations and Pension Assessments	Earnings of General Departments	Highway Privileges, Rents and Interest	Earnings of Public Service Enterprises	Expenses	Interest	Per Cent Available for Outlays and Other Purposes	Expenses of General Departments (a)	Expenses of Public Service Enterprise	Interest	Outlays
	Property	Poll														
Atlanta	62.0	0.4	8.3	6.6	1.3	4.7	2.2	1.3	13.2	71.2	5.5	23.3	66.0	5.8	5.6	22.7
Birmingham	42.2	....	19.7	15.3	2.1	13.2	3.9	1.8	1.8	68.1	19.6	12.3	67.1	1.3	19.7	11.9
Omaha	50.0	....	6.7	12.5	0.5	1.7	1.3	7.3	20.0	59.0	19.1	21.9	54.1	4.3	19.6	26.0
Worcester	69.1	1.8	4.0	3.6	0.1	0.9	5.6	5.2	9.8	64.7	10.6	24.7	63.7	2.2	10.8	23.2
Richmond	59.9	0.8	4.8	1.0	0.8	2.2	1.7	6.6	22.3	63.5	15.9	20.6	39.3	7.9	11.8	40.9
Syracuse	67.8	....	4.6	13.9	0.2	1.9	0.9	1.3	9.5	66.2	11.3	22.5	54.9	2.0	9.9	32.7
New Haven	70.0	1.2	7.2	3.3	1.0	3.6	3.4	1.3	0.1	77.4	5.5	17.1	69.2	0.1	4.9	25.8
Memphis	59.9	....	3.2	7.1	2.2	8.5	3.7	1.2	14.3	69.3	19.8	10.7	51.7	6.4	16.5	25.4

(a) For per cent. distribution of same, see Table VII.

TABLE VII

PER CENT DISTRIBUTION OF THE GENERAL DEPARTMENTS, BY PRINCIPAL DIVISIONS OF GENERAL DEPARTMENTAL SERVICE

(For Period Covered, See Table I)

City	General Government				Protection to Person and Property			Conservation of Health	Sanitation	Highways		Charities Hospitals and Corrections	Education		Recreation	Miscellaneous and General
	Legislative Branch	Executive Branch	Judicial Branch	Elections and General Government Buildings	Police	Fire	All Other			General Expense	Repair and Construction for Compensation		Schools	Libraries		
Atlanta	1.2	4.4	0.2	0.6	11.9	10.9	1.3	3.8	12.5	11.6	0.6	8.9	26.1	1.0	2.9	2.3
Birmingham		5.8	-0.4	0.8	11.6	15.8	1.9	1.1	8.2	10.1	0.5	2.9	36.6	1.0	1.7	2.5
Omaha		5.8	0.3	1.9	9.0	8.7	1.7	1.8	6.3	11.8	(a)	0.1	37.1	1.2	3.8	1.7
Worchester	0.2	3.1		1.5	10.8	11.7	0.6	2.9	6.9	14.3		9.7	35.3	0.2	3.3	2.2
Richmond	0.7	6.8	2.5	2.3	9.3	9.7	2.4	1.9	10.7	8.6		7.2	28.7	0.1	4.3	1.3
Syracuse	0.8	8.5	0.9	1.9	10.4	10.4	0.7	2.7	9.7	13.0		10.0	28.1	1.0	2.9	3.3
New Haven	0.1	3.3	1.9	1.4	10.4	10.8	1.2	2.0	5.1	11.2	0.1	5.4	38.3	1.6	3.9	3.7
Memphis		4.1	0.4	0.2	11.9			2.1	8.2	17.8		7.1	27.8		6.1	0.6

(a) Less than 1-20 of 1 per cent.

TABLE VIII

PER CAPITA REVENUE RECEIPTS FROM TAXES AND LICENSES AND PAYMENTS FOR EXPENSES, INTEREST AND OUTLAYS

(For Period Covered, See Table I)

City	Per Capita Revenue Receipts From		Per Capita Governmental Cost Payments For			
	All Property Taxes	Business and Non-Business License	Expenses and Interest			Outlays
			All Expenses	Expenses of General	Expenses of Public	

TABLE IX

PER CAPITA PAYMENTS FOR EXPENSES OF GENERAL DEPARTMENTS, BY PRINCIPAL DIVISIONS OF GENERAL DEPARTMENTAL SERVICE

(For Period Covered, See Table I)

City	Police	Fire	Conservation of Health	Sanitation	Highways	Charities, Hospitals and Corrections	Education	Recreation
Atlanta	1.61	1.48	0.51	1.69	1.63	1.21	3.66	0.39
Birmingham	1.01	1.36	0.09	0.71	0.91	0.25	3.16	0.14
Omaha	1.28	2.50	0.26	0.91	1.69	0.01	5.45	0.54
Worchester	1.82	1.77	0.58	1.40	2.91	1.97	7.60	0.66
Richmond	1.61	1.64	0.26	1.80	1.30	1.00	4.02	0.60
Syracuse	1.58	1.64	0.46	1.65	2.21	1.70	5.01	0.49
New Haven	1.68	1.69	0.32	0.32	1.84	0.87	6.48	0.68
Memphis	1.61	1.45	0.78	1.11	2.40	0.96	3.95	0.83

of colored population owned real estate in 1916 assessed at $2,-817.741, which gives an average colored per capita ownership of about $50, thus it is apparent that in making comparisons on a per capita basis southern cities should be considered in a separate group.

For this reason there has been prepared for this report, a grouping of twenty-six exclusively southern cities with the possible exceptions of El Paso, Texas, and Covington, Ky., which cities, in character, are rather western and northern, respectively, possessing as they do a considerable percentage of foreign-born population. The group includes all southern cities having a reported population of 40.000 to 200,000. It was thought best not to include Louisville because of the wide variance between its 236,379 population and the 184,873 of Atlanta, the largest in the group. For similar reasons New Orleans was excluded. The bulletin of December, 1916. United States Census publications, has been made the basis of this study.

Of the twenty-six cities, two, El Paso and Covington, have less than 10 per cent of their population composed of negroes; four have between 10 and 20 per cent.; five between 20 and 30 per cent.; eight between 30 and 40 per cent.; five between 40 and 50 per cent.; while two cities have a trifle over 50 per cent. The average per cent. of colored population, excluding El Paso and Covington is 33.2, practically one-third.

It is also to be noted that of the twenty-six cities, fifteen are commision-governed, six of these being in Texas alone, two in Oklahoma, three in Tennessee. three in Alabama, and one in Kentucky.

In examining the following table showing the reported basis of assessment and rate of levy, it should be borne in mind that what was said concerning the reliability of the reported basis of assessment of the eight city group, is equally true with respect to the figures of the twenty-six cities here presented. It should also be remembered that the figures given do not include the rates of levy for state and county purposes:

CITIES (Arranged in sequence of population beginning with the largest)	Reported basis of assessment in practice (Per cent. of estimated true value) (a)			Rate of Levy (b)		
	Real	Personal	Other	Of the general property tax per $1,000 of Assessed Valuation	Estimated true value	Of Poll Taxes
Atlanta	80	80	75	$ 12 50	$ 7 66	$ 1 00
Birmingham	80	80	....	10 00	6 00	....
Richmond	75	75	....	13 66 (c)	10 24 (d)	1 00
Memphis	80	80	40	15 80	9 06	....
Dallas	80	60	....	19 00	11 40	....
San Antonio	68	75	....	19 37 (e)	13 44 (f)	....
Nashville	75	75	40	15 00	10 43	....
Houston	77 (h)	50	....	18 00	11 53	....
Fort Worth	65	65	....	19 00	12 35	....
Oklahoma City	55	55	100	15 00	9 62	....
Norfolk	66	40 (k)	....	15 66 (l)	9 14 (m)	1 00
Jacksonville	65	65	....	12 73 (r)	8 28 (s)	....
Savannah	67	67	75	13 90	9 43	....
El Paso	60	60	....	18 31 (g)	10 98 (g)	....
Charleston	42	60	....	38 50 (p)	16 31 (q)	....
Chattanooga	50	50	40	16 50	8 07	....
Covington	75	75	80	17 50	13 20	....
Mobile	60	60	....	11 00	6 60	....
Little Rock	40	40	....	12 00	4 91	....
Tampa	65	65	....	24 36 (t)	15 83 (u)	....
Augusta	67	67	75	15 00	10 10	....
Macon	67	67	75	12 50	8 45	....
Montgomery	60	60	....	11 25	6 75	....
Muskogee	75	75	100	17 20	13 19	....
Roanoke	50	50	....	13 21 (n)	6 60 (o)	1 00
Galveston	70 (h)	60	....	17 30 (i)	10 41 (j)	....

(a) For property subject to the general property tax.

(b) The above figures do not include tax rates for civil divisions other than the city corporation (or city corporation and school district where the latter is constituted as an independent taxing division), such as county, State, etc.

(c) Average rate, composed of real and personal tangible, $16.50; bank stock, $14.00; and bonds, stocks, etc., $3.00; average, $13.66.

(d) Average rate, composed of real and personal tangible, $12.38; bank stock, $10.50; and bonds, stocks, etc., $2.25; average, $10.24.

(e) Composed of city corporation tax of $15.37 (average rate) and school district rate of $4.00.

(f) Composed of city corporation tax of $10.66 (average rate) and school district rate of $2.78.

(g) Average rate, composed of general city and paving district rates, general city rates $18 00 and $10.80, respectively, and paving district No. 1 rates $0.90 and $0.54, respectively.

(h) Basis for land; improvements are assessed on a basis of 50 per cent.

(i) Composed of city corporation tax of $14.80 and school district tax of $2.50.

(j) Composed of city corporation tax of $8.91 and school district tax of $1.50.

(k) Basis for all personal property except intangible, which is assessed on a 50 per cent. basis.

(l) Average rate, composed of following rates: real estate, except Seventh ward, $19.00, personal tangible, except seventh ward, $19.00, real estate, seventh ward, and personal tangible, seventh ward, $19.50; personal tangible: bonds, stocks, etc. $3.00; personal intangible: bank stock $8.00; average $15.66.

(m) Average rate, composed of real estate except seventh ward $12.54, personal tangible, except seventh ward $7.60, real estate, seventh ward, $12.87, personal tangible, seventh ward, $7 80, personal intangible: bank stock $4.00, personal intangible: bonds, stocks, etc. $1.50; average $9.14.

(n) Average rate, composed of real and personal tangible $15.00, personal intangible: bank stock $12.50, bonds, stocks, etc. $3.00; average $13.21.

(o) Average rate, composed of real and personal tangible $7.50, personal intangible: bank stock $6.25, bonds, stock, etc. $1.50; average rate $6.60.

(p) Composed of city corporation rate of $34.50, and school district rate of $4 00.

(q) Composed of city corporation rate of $14.62, and school district rate of $1.69.

(r) Average rate, composed of tax on property inside fire limits at $12.80, on property outside fire limits at $10.80; average rate $12.73.

(s) Average rate, composed of tax on property inside fire limits at $8.32, on property outside fire limits at $7.02; average rate $8.28.

(t) Average rate, composed of original city $25.00, annexations $22.00; average $24.36.

(u) Average rate, composed of original city $16.25, annexations $14.30; average $15.83.

There is noticeable a very wide difference in the several rates of levy of the general property tax per $1,000 of estimated true value. The rate varies from $4.91 in Little Rock to $16.31 in Charleston. The average tax rate for the twenty-six cities is $9.96 per $1,000, with thirteen cities under the average. For convenience of analysis and study, this difference in rates has been divided into four divisions as follows:

Group 1, including all cities whose tax rate is from $4.91 to $7.76.

Group 2, including all cities whose tax rate is from $7.76 to $9.96.

Group 3, including all cities whose tax rate is from $9.96 to $12.35.

Group 4, including all cities whose tax rate is from $12.35 to $16.31.

The cities included in each group are as follows:

GROUP 1		GROUP 2		GROUP 3		GROUP 4	
Tax Rate of From $4 91 to $7.76		Tax Rate of From $7.76 to $9.96		Tax Rate of From $9 96 to $12 35		Tax Rate of From $12.35 to $16 31	
City	Rate	City	Rate	City	Rate	City	Rate
Little Rock	$4 91	Chattanooga ..	$8 07	Augusta	$10 10	Muskogee	$13 19
Birmingham...	6 00	Jacksonville ..	8 28	Richmond.....	10 24	Covington ...	13 20
Mobile..........	6 60	Macon	8 45	Galveston	10 41	San Antonio ..	13 44
Roanoke	6 90	OklahomaCity	8 62	Nashville......	10 43	Tampa........	15 83
Montgomery ..	6 75	Memphis	9 06	El Paso	10 98	Charleston	16 31
Atlanta	7 66	Norfolk	9 14	Dallas..........	11 40		
		Savannah	9 43	Houston	11 58		
				Fort Worth....	12 35		
Average	$6 42	Average	$8 72	Average	$10 93	Average	$14 39

The average per capita revenues from business and non-business licenses in the cities of group 1 is $2.21, in those of group 2 is $1.75, in those of group 3 is $1.24, while in those of group 4 is $1.15. This indicates that business is taxed at a higher rate in the cities of group 1, resulting in a proportionate lowering of the tax rate, and so on throughout the four group classifications. Muskogee (group 4) for instance, has the high tax rate $13.19, but its per capita receipts from its licenses is very low, only .16.

The following table is presented to show the average per capita expenditures of each group for the eight general departments:

Group	Police	Fire	Conserva-tion of Health	Sanita-tion (a)	High-ways	Charities, Hospitals & Correc-tions	Educa-tion (b)	Recrea-tion
Group 1...	$1 28	$1 40	0 31	$ 81	$1 26	0 49	$3 07	0 18
Group 2...	1 69	1 70	0 28	1 57	1 53	0 73	3 27	0 44
Group 3...	1 58	1 58	0 24	1 56	1 95	0 92	3 96	0 44
Group 4 ..	1 43	1 52	0 21	1 35	1 49	0 77	3 22	0 33

(a) Includes sewage disposal and refuse collection.
(b) Includes schools and libraries.

As regards group 1, it is evident that those cities which have the lowest tax rates (that is, between $4.91 and $7.76; average $6.42) spend the least amounts per capita for each of the several general departments as enumerated above or stated inversely, that they are able to maintain a low tax rate by virtue of their com-paratively low expenditures.

Group 2 presents a distinct increase in per capita expenses for every department save that of conservation of health, which shows an average per capita decrease of .03 for this function. The same general conclusion is true of group 2 as of group 1.

Group 3 presents apparently some very significant changes. As against group 2, there is an average per capita decrease of .11 in expenses of the police department, .12 in the fire depart-ment, .04 in expenses for conservation of health, and .01 in expendi-tures for sanitation. They each expend a per capita average of .44 for recreation. There is an average per capita increase of .42 for highways, .19 for charities, hospitals and corrections, and .69 for education, which over-balances the decreases noted and results in a higher average per capita for the eight departments as per the following table:

Average Per Capita

Group 1 .... $ 8.80
Group 2 .... 11.21
Group 3 .... 12.23
Group 4 .... 10.32

Group 4 shows a decrease in the total average per capita ex-penditures of the eight general departments, due in large part to the very low expenditures of the city of Muskogee for its police, fire, health, sanitation, and highways departments, in all of which it stands lowest in its respective group, and its correspondingly high per capita payments for interest necessitating of course the high tax rate. Charleston also spends a proportionately low amount for highways and education and helps to bring down the general average. But San Antonio ranks third in the entire twenty-six cities in high per capita expenditures for education and first in high per capita payments for outlays, thus accounting for its presence in group 4. A number of other striking exceptions might be noted, but it is sufficient to say from the illustrations given above, that the comparatively lower total average per capita expenditures of group 4 is accounted for in considerable degree on the basis of these exceptions.

The following table is presented to show the average per capita payments of each group for interest and outlays:

| | Average Per Capita Payments for | |
	Interest	Outlays
Group 1	$2 34	$ 2 76
" 2	3 23	· 6 88
" 3	· 3 74*	11 16**
" 4	2 86	6 82

*Richmond $ 4 19.
** " 14.54.

The same general relation between groups 1 and 2, and 2 and 3 is noticed here as in the table showing the per capita payments for the eight general departments. Both in the interest and outlay columns there is noted an increase in each group as over the corresponding figure of the preceding group, the figures reaching their maximum in group 3. As regards the last figure in the table, the average per capita expenditures of the cities of group 4 for outlays, it may be said that San Antonio and Tampa spent respectively $15.36 and $10.24 for this purpose, while Covington, Muskogee and Charleston spent respectively only $2.19, $3.01 and $3.30, thus bringing the average very low.

With respect to the relative percentage of revenue derived respectively from general property taxes and from special assessments, it is specially significant that while each group shows a successively higher percentage derived from taxes (just as they showed successively higher tax rates), with slight exceptions between groups 2 and 3, they show successively lower percentages derived

from special assessments. Inasmuch as this relation of the general
tax rate to the levying of special assessments is of much importance in determining the future financial policy of Richmond, the
figures are set forth below not only by groups, but for each of the
twenty-six cities. Such a presentation is also desirable because
there are certain notable variations between some of the cities in
each group:

(For table see next page.)

As to any further reasons why the tax rates of the twenty-
six cities should vary so it is believed that a careful study of the
"summary" table herewith will serve to explain the causes.

Percentage of Revenue Receipts Derived from Taxes on General Property and from Special Assessment.

GROUP 1			GROUP 2			GROUP 3			GROUP 4		
City	Taxes	Spec. As-ts.	City	Taxes	Spec. Asts.	City	Taxes	Spec. Asts.	City	Taxes	Spec. Asts.
Little Rock	45.1	23.8	Chattanooga	65.1	5.6	Augusta	47.0	1.1	Muskogee	73.4	.....
Birmingham	42.2	15.3	Jacksonville	39.1	4.7	Richmond	59.9	1.0	Covington	57.3	6.9
Mobile	41.1	13.4	Macon	34.9	9.0	Galveston	49.5	3.1	San Antonio	86.8	.....
Roanoke	64.0	3.4	Oklahoma City	76.3	1.1	Nashville	50.8	4.5	Tampa	61.7	6.6
Montgomery	38.8	17.6	Memphis	59.9	7.1	El Paso	60.4	4.5	Charleston	71.1	1.9
Atlanta	62.0	6.6	Norfolk	62.2		Dallas	63.3	12.6			
			Savannah	48.2	3.6	Houston	70.1	.2			
						Ft. Worth	66.2	10.1			
Average	48.8	13.3	Average	54.9	4.4	Average	58.4	4.6	Average	69.8	3.1

As to any further reasons why the tax rates of the twenty-six cities should vary so it is believed that a careful study of the "Summary" table herewith will serve to explain the causes.

Summary Table

	RANK									
	1	2	3	4	5	6	7	8	9	10
Population (a)	A	B	C	D	E	F	G	H	I	J
Lowest tax rate (b)										
Based on assessed valuation......	B	R	W	S	A	V	L	Y	C	M
" " estimated true value..	S	B	R	B	W	A	P	L	V	J
Lowest per capita gross debt......	S	A	V	Y	W	B	M	E	L	I
" " " net debt (c).....	S	A	V	B	Y	Q	M	E	F	J
" " " payments for interest...	A	S	V	Y	Q	N	B	M	E	F
Highest per capita revenue from all property taxes.............	H	E	F	Z	C	K	N	T	I	D
Highest per capita revenue receipts from business and non-business licenses.............	K	U	M	W	B	Y	R	V	O	A
Highest per capita payments for expenses of police department ..	O	L	Z	M	U	V	K	A	D	H
Highest per capita payments for expenses of fire department	Z	V	O	L	M	P	F	T	C	E
Highest per capita payments for conservation of health............	A	R	W	M	K	Z	O	P	U	N
Highest per capita payments for expenses of highways (d).........	Z	U	T	D	L	E	G	H	Q	A
Highest per capita payments for expenses of schools, libraries, etc. (education)	H	E	F	K	C	J	D	G	N	S
Highest per cent of colored population July 1, 1915.............	O	M	L	W	U	R	V	P	B	K
Highest per cent of revenue receipts obtained from taxes (property)...........	F	J	X	O	H	I	P	Y	E	K
Highest per cent of revenue receipts obtained from business and non-business licenses.........	B	Y	W	U	K	R	M	O	S	Q
Highest per cent of revenue receipts obtained from special assessments and special charges for outlays (f)	S	W	B	R	E	I	V	D	Q	A
Highest per cent of revenue receipts obtained from subventions, grants, gifts, donations and pension assessments	V	M	Z	P	G	T	B	H	U	L
Highest per cent of revenue receipts obtained from earnings of public service enterprises	L	C	R	N	W	V	U	Q	G	D
Lowest per cent of revenue receipts required for meeting interest charges...................	A	V	S	E	N	L	M	F	Q	T
Highest per capita payments for expenses of public service enterprises	L	Z	C	V	N	I	D	M	R	E
Highest per capita payments for outlays	F	E	C	H	Z	M	U	L	T	V

(a) Estimated by United States Census as of middle of fiscal year shown in last column of Table 1.
(b) Based on city government figures, and showing general property tax rate per $1,000.
(c) Net debt is funded and floating debt less sinking fund assets.
(d) Includes general expenses and repair and construction for compensation.
(e) 191 figures.
(f) San Antonio, Muskogee and Norfolk received no revenue from this source, hence only 23 cities appear in ranking columns

Explanation of Code Symbols

Atlanta.........A   Oklahoma City J   Little Rock ...S
Birmingham .. B   Norfolk ....K   Tampa ....T
Richmond C   Jacksonville ...L   Augusta ....U
Memphis ......D   Savannah.....M   Macon V
Dallas ....E   El Paso ....N   Montgomery...W
San Antonio....F   Charleston....O   Muskogee X
Nashville.......G   Chattanooga...P   Roanoke ...... Y
Houston ....H   Covington......Q   Galveston ....Z
Fort Worth I   Mobile..........R

Summary Table—Continued

							RANK								
11	12	13	14	15	16	17	18	19	20	21	22	23	24	25	26
K	L	M	N	O	P	Q	R	S	T	U	V	W	X	Y	Z
G	J	U	K	D	P	X	Z	Q	H	N	R	I	F	T	O
D	K	M	U	C	Z	G	N	E	F	H	I	X	Q	T	O
P	N	T	P	R	J	O	X	G	U	W	D	C	R	T	Z
L	X	I	N	R	T	P	G	W	O	C	U	D	K	H	Z
O	P	L	G	I	T	R	U	X	J	W	C	D	K	H	Z
A	O	J	M	L	U	G	X	P	Q	V	Y	S	W	R	B
L	T	Q	S	G	C	N	Z	P	D	E	H	F	I	J	X
F	C	W	G	E	R	T	N	Q	P		I	B	S	J	X
H	U	K	S	A	D	W	B	Y	G		R	Q	1	J	X
D	L	C	G	F	S	T	J	Y	H		E	V	X	B	I
S	R	M	F	P	K	C	V	Y	I	Y	W	B	J	X	N
A	Q	Z	I	U	B	Y	X	V	M	P	T	W	O	R	L
D	C	X	A	G	H	S	T	Z	Y	E	I	F	J	Q(e)	N(e)
A	T	N	C	D	Q	G	Z	M	U	S	B	R	L	W	V
A	V	G	T	L	P	N	C	Z	D	F	E	I	J	H	X
T	P	L	G	N	M	Y	Z	O	J	U	C	H	(f)	(f)	(f)
S	D	Q	F	N	E	1	W	A	R	O	Y	J	X	K	C
X	A	Z	1	M	K	J	E	H	O	B	Y	S	P	F	T
Y	G	U	I	O	C	H	Z	P	B	D	J	K	R	W	X
K	W	Q	A	U	G	H	X	J	S	B	O	P	F	Y	T
N	D	G	Y	A	I	O	P	K	X	Q	R	S	B	W	J

TABLE 1—*Embracing all Southern Cities in the United States having an Estimated Population Between 40,000 and 200,000.*

CITY	STATE	Estimated Population (a)	Assessed Valuation of Taxable Property (b)	White	Colored	Per Cent Colored	FORM OF GOVERNMENT	FISCAL YEAR COVERED BY THESE TABLES
Atlan m...	Georgia	181,873	$182,812,898	126,989	57,983	31.3	Mayor and two chambers	January 1, 1915—December 31, 1915
Birmi...	Alabama	172,119	93,331,325	108,679	65,429	37.6	Commission	October 1, 1914—September 30, 1915
Ri...	Virginia	154,841	165,861,756	99,156	55,518	3,.8	Mayor and two chambers	February 1, 1915—January 31, 1916
Memp...	Tennessee	146,113	117,914,496	93,232	53,861	36.9	Commission	January 1, 1915—December 31, 1915
Dallas...	Texas	121,277	119,102,525	95,384	22,898	19.3	"	May 1, 1915—April 30, 1916
San A lo...	Texas	121,274	107,996,466	106,938	12,509	10.5	"	June 1, 1915—May 31 1916
Nashv...	Tennessee	1 5,978	7,9 7,710	79,857	36,121	31.1	"	January 1, 1915—December 31, 1915
Houst th...	Texas	108,172	135,805,000	75,978	32,194	29.8	"	January 1, 1915—December 31, 1916
Forth...	Texas	99,528	67,046,941	80,714	18,794	18.9	"	January 1, 1915—December 31, 1915
Oklah City...	Oklahoma	90,620	61,731,938	79,162	9,196	10.3	Mayor and two chambers	July 1, 1915—June 30 1916
Norf...	Virginia	88,844	83,298,450	51,920	33,1?6	37.6	Mayor and single chamber	July 1, 1915—June 30 1916
Jacksonville...	Florida	73,137	59,723,460	33,622	38,285	49.6	" "	January 1, 1915—December 31, 1915
N...	Georgia	64,361	38,063 92	37,827(c)	34.7-9	50.8	Commission	January 1, 1915—December 31, 1915
El...	Texas	60,754	46,707,670	29,623	1,452(c)	3.7(c)	Mayor and single chamber	April 1, 1915—May 31 1916
Chatt a...	Tennessee	60,427	20,787,105	35,667	30,804	50.9	Commission	January 1, 1915—December 31, 1915
Covin ga...	Kentucky	56,520	35,728,431	50,371(c)	22,911	39.1	"	October 1, 1914—September 30 1915
Mobil...	Alabama	38,201	30,185,085	31,565	2,899(c)	5.4(c)	Mayor and single chamber	January 1, 1915 December 31, 1915
Little k...	Arkansas	6,295	33,360,761	38,748(c)	16,410	44.2	" "	January 1, 1911—September 30, 1915
Tampa...	Florida	55,158	34,116,850	39,791	11,730	29.8	Mayor and single chamber	January 1, 1915—December 31, 1915
Augu...	Georgia	52,506	31,010,715	27,306	22,542	45.2	" "	June 1 1915 916
Maco ry...	Georgia	49,848	30,892,983	21,845	19,642	43.3	" "	January 1, 1915—mber 31, 191?
Mont...	Alabama	45,415	24,341,745	28,2.3	20,666	48.6	Commission	January 1, 1915—December 31, 1915
Musk...	Oklahoma	42,908	21,077,569	21,810	13,010	31.5	"	July 1, 1915 June 30, 1916
Roano...	Virginia	4?,740	27,028,410	32,886	9,082	21.5	Mayor and two chambers	January 1, 1915—December 31, 1915
Galves...	Texas	41,207	40,631,452	32,095	8,981	21.8	Commission	March 1, 1915—February 29, 1915

(a) Estimated by United States census as of middle of fiscal year shown in last column.
(b) As rated by the city c rporation.
(c) Figures of 1910 census.

TABLE 2.—*Per Cent. Distribution, by Principal Classes, of Revenue Receipts.*
(For Period Covered, See Table 1.)

CITY	TAXES — Property	Poll	Non-Business and Business License	Special Assessments and Special Charges for Outlays	Fines, Forfeits and Escheats	Subventions, Grants, Gifts, Donations, and Pension Assessments	Earnings of General Departments	Highway Privileges, Rents and Interest	Earnings of Public-service Enterprises	Expenses	Interest	Per Cent. Available for Outlays and Other Purposes
Atlanta	62.0	0.4	8.3	6.6	1.3	4.7	2.2	1.3	13.2	71.2	6.5	22.3
Birmingham	42.2	0.8	19.7	15.3	2.1	13.2	3.9	1.8	1.8	68.1	19.6	12.3
Richmond	59.9		4.8	1.0	0.8	2.5	1.7	6.6	22.3	68.5	15.9	20.6
Memphis	59.8		5.2	7.1	2.4	6.1	8.7	1.2	14.3	69.5	19.8	10.7
Dallas	63.3		2.3	12.6	0.5	5.1	2.0	3.4	9.8	62.7	8.9	28.4
San Antonio	86.8		2.4		0.6	15.3	1.4	1.8	0.5	58.2	12.3	29.5
Nashville	50.8		7.5	4.5	0.6	12.9	2.7	4.7	14.7	67.4	15.0	17.6
Houston	70.1		1.7	10.1	1.3	4.8	1.4	6.9	6.9	40.7	16.8	33.5
Fort Worth	86.2		2.2	1.1	0.2	3.1	8.4	1.8	12.9	55.1	16.5	29.4
Oklahoma City	75.3	0.3	2.0		1.2	2.8	1.7	3.9	9.9	67.2	20.0	24.2
Norfolk	62.2		15.1	4.7	1.0	9.7	2.2	5.8	11.8	66.5	21.1	11.7
Jacksonville	39.1		6.3	3.6	1.4	17.4	1.0	2.2	34.1	69.6	10.8	19.7
Savannah	48.2		5.4	4.5	1.6	6.3	1.9	2.2	12.5	68.1	10.7	18.7
El Paso	60.4	0.4	10.6	1.9	0.3	3.8	1.1	3.8	19.0	73.9	10.2	10.5
Charleston	71.1		6.1	5.6	0.8	16.0	8.2	2.4	6.2	73.0	15.6	8.1
Chattanooga	65.1		9.5	6.9	0.3	7.5	0.6	2.1	16.8	78.5	18.4	13.1
Covington	57.3		14.8	13.4	1.7	4.1	2.1	2.1	20.6	66.7	13.4	11.8
Mobile	41.1		9.8	23.8	1.7	9.7	5.1	4.4	0.2	65.0	21.5	27.5
Little Rock	45.1		7.0	1.1	0.4	14.2	6.1	1.8	17.2	60.8	7.5	25.0
Tampa	60.7		8.1	9.0	1.4	12.2	4.5	2.7	17.6	71.5	14.2	13.4
Augusta	47.0		5.3	1.1	2.1	23.6	3.0	1.2	16.7	60.9	15.1	32.3
Macon	34.9		8.1	9.0	1.4	4.8	0.9	3.5	14.3	63.4	6.8	14.1
Montgomery	38.8		16.0	17.6	3.0	3.1	2.7	4.9	1.3	62.1	2.5	12.9
Muskogee	73.4		16.2	3.4	1.8	8.5	1.9			71.4	25.0	13.7
Roanoke	64.0		18.1		3.0	3.1		3.5	14.3		14.9	13.5
Galveston	49.5	1.4	3.2	3.1	0.2	16.8	9.0	4.9	13.0	68.0	18.5	

Table 3—Per Cent. Distribution of Expenses of the General Departments By Principal Divisions of the Departmental Service.
(For Period Covered See Table 1.)

City	General Government				Protection to Person and Property			Conservation of Health	Sanitation	Highways		Charities, Hospitals & Corrections	Education		Recreation	Miscellaneous and General
	Legislative Branch	Executive Branch	Judicial Branch	Elections and Gen'l Gov't, Buildings	Police Dept.	Fire Dept.	All Other			General Expense	Repair & Construction Compensation		Schools	Libraries		
Atlanta	1.2	4.4	0.2	0.5	11.9	10.9	1.9	3.8	12.5	11.6	0.5	8.9	28.1	1.0	2.9	2.3
Birmingham	0.7	5.8	0.4	0.8	11.8	15.8	1.9	1.9	8.2	10.1	0.5	2.9	35.6	1.0	1.7	2.5
Richmond	....	6.8	2.5	2.3	10.8	11.7	2.4	2.1	10.7	8.6	....	7.2	29.7	0.1	4.8	1.3
Memphis	....	4.1	0.4	0.2	11.9	10.8	3.1	2.1	11.6	17.8	....	7.1	27.8	1.6	6.1	0.6
Dallas	....	5.2	0.3	1.2	10.2	11.4	8.1	1.8	11.5	14.3	0.5	4.1	32.6	0.6	8.8	0.8
San Antonio	....	6.0	0.8	0.7	12.2	18.3	1.4	2.0	6.5	10.4	0.5	4.7	28.6	0.1	8.8	0.8
Nashville	....	9.0	0.3	0.8	11.1	10.6	1.5	1.8	3.7	15.5	0.9	2.1	29.8	1.1	5.1	1.7
Houston	....	7.0	0.3	1.6	11.1	11.1	2.4	1.3	6.0	13.6	0.2	2.6	36.5	0.6	2.0	0.9(a)
Fort Worth	1.0	8.1	0.4	0.7	11.4	12.6	1.3	1.0	8.7	11.8	....	2.0	36.0	1.1	4.8	1.7
Oklahoma City	1.0	7.8	0.2	1.1	9.0	12.8	0.8	2.1	6.8	9.3	0.8	4.1	44.3	0.8	2.4	5.3
Norfolk	1.6	6.8	0.2	1.1	18.0	11.0	2.1	2.5	14.7	7.9	0.7	4.1	29.7	0.9	3.3	0.3
Jacksonville	1.1	4.9	0.2	1.4	16.6	12.8	1.1	1.9	6.9	16.1	....	3.8	14.6	0.5	4.0	0.9
Savannah	....	4.9	0.5	1.0	15.9	12.5	2.1	2.4	18.5	10.0	0.1	8.8	20.0	1.2	5.2	2.4
El Paso	0.7	8.2	0.2	1.0	11.2	18.1	1.1	2.4	17.2	11.1	0.2	3.8	11.1	0.8	8.3	2.8
Charleston	....	6.6	0.4	1.0	10.6	10.6	0.7	2.9	8.9	10.6	(*)	8.8	18.3	(b)	5.2	0.9
Chattanooga	....	6.3	0.8	1.5	10.9	16.0	0.7	2.3	8.9	6.9	0.4	12.2	22.5	1.8	8.3	3.2
Covington	....	7.0	1.4	2.6	11.8	11.0	0.3	1.7	12.4	11.7	0.1	10.6	29.4	2.0	1.4	4.1
Mobile	1.5	6.8	0.4	0.5	16.3	14.0	1.7	4.7	8.5	15.2	0.3	2.6	25.4	....	2.5	0.8
Little Rock	0.8	6.8	0.3	1.0	9.7	15.0	0.9	2.1	5.5	16.5	0.3	8.4	38.0	0.9	0.7	0.8
Tampa	0.7	4.4	0.3	0.9	10.2	10.8	0.7	2.6	18.8	19.0	....	14.3	18.9	0.1	2.5	0.9
Augusta	0.7	4.2	0.2	0.3	18.1	10.8	1.2	2.1	6.1	20.9	....	14.3	22.1	(b)	1.5	1.9(a)
Macon	1.0	4.2	0.3	1.0	15.1	19.1	1.7	1.1	7.8	8.8	....	8.6	23.1	0.2	8.0	1.0
Montgomery	....	9.7	0.1	1.7	15.9	15.1	2.6	4.3	9.8	8.8	0.4	4.8	24.7	1.3	8.0	2.0
Muskogee	....	11.8	0.8	1.6	8.1	12.3	1.5	1.7	8.3	11.0	0.1	4.6	38.9	1.8	3.0	1.7
Roanoke	1.0	7.6	0.8	1.3	11.9	14.3	0.6	2.0	6.1	10.8	0.8	4.7	32.1	1.8	1.4	8.4(a)
Galveston	....	4.0	0.3	0.6	11.8	12.8	1.0	1.9	18.6	17.4	0.8	11.7	18.0	....	1.3	0.7

(a) General only—miscellaneous being less than 1-20 of 1 per cent.
(b) Less than 1-20 of 1 per cent.

Table 4—*Per Capita Revenue Receipts From All Property Taxes and Business Licenses, and Payments for Expenses, Interest and Outlays.*
(For Period Covered See Table 1.)

City	Per Capita Revenue Receipts From		Per Capita Governmental Cost Payments For					
	All Property Taxes	Business and Non-Business Licenses	All Expenses and Interest	Expenses and Interest				Outlays
				Expenses of General Departments	Expenses of Public Service Enterprises	Interest		
Atlanta	12.81	1.71	15.84	13.52	1.18	1.14		4.65
Birmingham	5.46	2.55	11.38	8.68	0.17	2.54		1.54
Richmond	15.96	1.26	21.00	13.98	2.82	4.19		14.54
Memphis	13.01	0.70	19.42	18.46	1.65	4.30		6.68
Dallas	18.67	0.83	18.85	14.29	1.41	2.66		15.25
San Antonio	18.88	1.51	15.27	12.02	0.09	2.66		13.38
Nashville	10.31	0.54	16.70	12.66	1.00	3.04		6.49
Houston	21.76	0.43	20.66	14.46	0.97	5.23		14.44
Fort Wth.	13.10	0.34	13.97	0.94	0.69	3.07		8.67
Oklahoma City	12.77		12.86	8.78	1.39	3.39		0.71
Norfolk	14.61	3.05	20.74	14.39	4.10	0.69		9.18
Jacksonville	10.49	1.69	21.53	14.03	1.47	2.96		11.42
Savannah	10.50	3.04	17.71	18.70	2.40	2.91		12.70
El Paso	13.96	1.24	16.94	12.18	0.12	2.56		9.57
Charleston	12.90	1.91	16.11	13.18	0.10	2.36		8.30
Chattanooga	9.78	0.92	13.81	10.67	1.19	2.90		8.29
Covington	9.52	1.98	14.42	11.00	1.42	2.84		2.19
Mobile	6.81	2.27	18.58	8.81	0.24	2.23		1.99
Little Rock	18.92	1.08	11.76	10.81	0.07	3.29		1.77
Tampa	10.41	1.60	17.20	13.69	1.13	1.71		10.24
Augusta	8.72	3.59	19.17	12.70	2.51	3.25		12.49
Macon	6.62	2.02	16.91	9.48	1.34	3.35		10.14
Montgomery	9.91	2.73	14.67	7.51	0.88	1.69		1.07
Muskogee	8.57	0.16	11.77	9.48	0.06	3.84		3.01
Roanoke		2.42	11.56			3.88		5.54
Galveston	16.25	1.12	28.38*	19.00	3.23	6.06		12.94

TABLE 5

Per Capita Payments for Expenses of the General Departments by Principal Divisions
(For Period Covered see Table 1)

CITY	Police	Fire	Conservation of health	Sanitation	Highways	Charities' Hospitals and Corrections	Education (Schools and Libraries)	Recreation
Atlanta	1 61	1 48	0 51	1 69	1 63	1 21	3 66	0 39
Birmingham	1 04	1 36	0 09	0 71	0 91	0 25	3 16	0 14
Richmond	1 51	1 64	0 26	1 50	1 20	1 00	4 02	0 60
Memphis	1 61	1 45	0 28	1 11	2 40	0 96	3 95	0 83
Dallas	1 45	1 63	0 17	1 66	2 11	0 59	4 70	0 44
San Antonio	1 53	1 66	0 23	1 31	1 32	0 29	4 56	0 47
Nashville	1 48	1 34	0 25	0 82	2 02	0 59	3 92	0 65
Houston	1 60	1 61	0 18	1 40	2 00	0 38	5 13	0 29
Fort Worth	1 02	1 13	0 08	0 53	1 01	0 18	3 31	0 43
Oklahoma City	0 79	1 13	0 19	0 60	0 89	0 18	3 96	0 21
Norfolk	1 88	1 57	0 87	2 11	1 24	0 59	4 19	0 47
Jacksonville	2 27	1 82	0 28	2 59	2 34	0 56	2 26	0 58
Savannah	2 18	1 80	0 39	2 53	1 40	0 52	2 90	0 45
El Paso	1 87	1 28	0 90	2 09	0 83	0 28	3 87	0 64
Charleston	2 32	2 16	0 31	1 80	0 96	1 61	2 42	0 43
Chattanooga	1 18	1 74	0 31	0 97	1 27	1 15	2 65	0 15
Covington	1 29	1 21	0 18	1 37	1 68	0 29	3 46	0 18
Mobile	1 43	1 24	0 41	0 44	1 48	0 32	2 28	0 22
Little Rock	1 00	1 54	0 22	0 57	1 52	0 35	3 81	0 07
Tampa	1 42	1 66	0 22	2 53	2 64	1 29	2 63	0 35
Augusta	1 94	1 59	0 31	0 90	3 08	2 09	3 25	0 22
Macon	1 92	2 42	0 14	0 99	1 17	1 16	2 96	0 38
Montgomery	1 50	1 43	0 41	0 89	0 94	0 34	2 46	0 10
Muskogee	0 61	0 93	0 18	0 25	0 84	0 38	3 02	0 22
Roanoke	1 12	1 35	0 19	0 58	1 05	0 44	3 05	0 13
Galveston	2 25	2 44	9 37	3 56	3 33	2 23	3 43	0 24

Conclusions.

Reductions in Expenditures.

It is submitted that the city officials in their duty to the tax-payers should reduce the appropriations in next year's budget so far as it is possible to do so without decreasing the value of the city's service. To assist in making such reductions, this survey has carefully listed such expenditures as may properly be eliminated at this time; also expenditures which should be eliminated but which on account of existing charter or statutory provisions must be continued temporarily until necessary changes in the laws can be obtained.

Reductions in Expenditures Which Can Be Made Effective Without Charter or Statutory Change.

Street Cleaning Department:

By abolishing during the dull season the position of "helpers" on the majority of routes in the collection of ashes and rubbish ....$ 13,700

Park Department:
By re-organization of the labor forces............... 4,000
City Engineering Department:
By abolishing the position of 3 watchmen on 2 bridges. 2,300.
By abolishing the position of title examiner on annex-
ation survey and having all this work done by the
chief clerk 1,800
By reducing the force on the annexation survey through
the abolishment of at least two positions, that of as-
sistant engineer and the chief of surveying party.. 3,300
Muncipally Operated Public Utilities:
By consolidation of the repair forces and miscellaneous
service forces of the water, gas and electricity departments ....$ 10,350
By economies in accounting, clerical and office work
through consolidation of the departments of water,
gas and electricity into one department of public
utilities 12,300
Water Department:
By combining present positions of superintendent and
assistant superintendent of the water department in
a single head of the bureau of water collection, storage and distribution, and eliminating the present
office staff of the superintendent 4,000
By abolishing position of second assistant superintendent at South Richmond 1,500
By re-organization of the pumping station employees.. 4,500
Collector of City Taxes:
By abolishing this office and having the city treasurer
collect the taxes. Present salary cost of
office $10,000
less estimated increase in treasurer's staff. 5,000
                                                        ─────
                                                        5,000
City Clerk and Clerk of Committees:
By consolidating these offices as described in this report. 2,600
Health Department and Hospital Service:
By abolishing six city physicians at $900, and by having
the assistant bacteriologist do the work of that office
a reduction of about $7,500 can be effected, which
will offset the salary increases recommended.

Improvement of Purchasing Methods:

By adoption of the five principal recommendations of
this report, with respect to purchasing, it is con-
servatively estimated that a saving of from 3 to 5
per cent. could be effected on the $550,000 annual
expenditure for supplies, material and equipment,
say $20,000
less estimated cost of a central purchasing
office 5,000
                                        ——————   15,000
                                                 ————————
    Total ....$ 80,350

In addition to these direct net savings, there are numerous and
extensive economies that may be effected by carrying out the suggestions and recommendations contained in the report. It is difficult to estimate the amount thereof, but as a single example may
be cited the intensive development of the city's farm, the doing of
the city's laundry work at the City Home, a central ice plant
for institutions, etc.

In recommending the foregoing reductions in the next budget
appropriation, it is fully appreciated that throughout this report
need is shown for increased appropriations if better service, and
in some cases even a continuation of the same service, is to be
obtained. The reductions listed will help to offset such increases
and secure a more effective use of the limited funds available.

Reductions in Expenditures Which Should Be Made As Soon As
Statutory or Charter Revision Can Be Secured.

Administrative Board:

By abolishing the board and its entire staff.........$ 36,000

Commissioner of Revenue and Real Estate Assessors:

By statutory revision abolishing the quinquennial assessment of real estate by special assessors and requiring the commissioner of revenue to asses it all
annually   2,250

Commonwealth Attorney:

By discontinuing the payment by the city of $1,000 to
the commonwealth attorney, who should be paid by
the state   1,000

Coroner:

By abolishing the office of coroner which costs $3,500
with its assistants, and appointing two medical examiners on part time at $1,000 each, making a net
saving of 1,500

Collector of Delinquent Taxes:

By abolishing this office and transferring the duties to
the city treasurer. Present salary cost of
office ....$ 5,400
less estimated increase in treasurer's staff.. 1,500
——————
3,900

Treasurer:

By abolishing the south side office of the treasurer and
tax collector. Rental to be saved............... 600

Police Court:

By abolishing Part II on the south side, salaries of
judge and bailiff 2,500
——————
Total ....$ 447,150

Increase of Revenue.

It is unnecessary to discuss in this survey report on the city
of Richmond, changes which affect the revenue system of the
entire state and which cannot be had without favorable action of
the general assembly. That there is crying need for further revision of the state revenue laws so as to make them equitable to
cities, counties and state alike, must be apparent to all. Therefore,
it is suggested that in undertaking any further revision it should
be made jointly by representatives of each of these three branches
of government in the commonwealth. A practicable method would
be to secure the appointment of a commission composed of those
representatives of the state and of each class of cities and counties within the state who, by virtue of their experience, are best
qualified to draft an equitable revenue law. Perhaps no more
practical method is available than for the League of Virginia
Municipalities to undertake the conducting such propaganda
as its definite program until the desired result is obtained.

An examination of the fees now assessed for licenses and business taxes indicates that practically everything is already licensed
or taxed where such an impost would be justifiable and also that
the scale of fees is about as high as could reasonably be levied.
The present dual system of taxing merchants should be re-adjusted

at the time the state revenue laws are again considered so that the merchants will pay but a single tax on their business.

With respect to the revenue derived from the municipally owned public utilities, it is pointed out elsewhere in this report that the local rate for gas service must be increased immediately if the plant is to continue self-supporting.

As relates to fees received by public officers, state legislation in 1914 and 1916 has already placed such offices on practically a salary basis and required that the excess earnings shall be turned into the state treasury. Whether the city could equitably claim a portion of such excess is extremely doubtful.

With respect to the miscellaneous revenues of the city the following recommendations are made:

Revenue Increases Available Immediately and for Which It Is Possible to Estimate the Amounts.

Department of Electricity:
By charging for electrical inspection work on private
buildings ....$ 6,000
Gas Department:
By establishing a minimum bill of 50 cents a consumer
per month, at least   7,000
City Engineering Department:
By charging a fee for furnishing line and grade data
to owners of private property for the construction
of buildings, approximately   400
Health Department:
By charging fees for plumbing inspection so as to put
this work on a self-supporting basis 2,800
By charging fees for transcripts of vital statistics, ap-
proximately   500
By requiring the payment of an annual fee for food
permits and dairy permits, approximately........   650

Revenue Sources Available Immediately But for Which It Is Difficult to Estimate the Amounts Derivable Therefrom.

Parks and Cemeteries:
By making an increased charge for maintenance of
burial plots in order that the cemeteries will be self-
supporting.

Building Department:

By charging fees for building permits, electric signs and bill-boards and making an annual inspection charge for signs and bill-boards to reduce the cost to the city for inspection.

City Council:

By reducing the number of city depositories and thereby obtaining a higher rate of interest on city deposits in bank.

City Engineer's Department:

By charging fees for the privilege of storing material on the street, particularly to cover the cost of damage to pavements thereby.

Gas Plant:

By increasing the service rates.

There are also increases practicable but which require change of statutes, as for example, city magistrates or justices of the peace should be abolished and the fees for the issuance of certain processes turned into the city treasury.

It is submitted that the facts shown by this survey and also the foregoing comparison with other cities, proves conclusively that the city should obtain authority to levy special assessments for local improvements. The shortage in revenues caused by its present inability to do so may be met by an increase in the general tax rate, but that is undesirable and may have to be followed by other increases. Ultimately the situation will be reflected on the tax bills of every property owner as to force the repeal of that amendment to the state constitution which prohibits such assessments. It should be remembered that Norfolk, Roanoke and other cities in Virginia are having and will continue to have similar financial trouble until state-wide relief is obtained. Instead of deferring action until conditions become further complicated and hence more difficult of equitable adjustment, a campaign for revision of the constitution should be launched immediately and all civic and commercial organizations throughout the state enlisted in active and aggressive support thereof.

Although local sentiment in Richmond or in Virginia may not as yet favor the adoption of a tax upon unearned increment of land value, it is nevertheless one of the important revenue sources of European cities and can be adopted with much advantage by any state in this country. Taking as a basis the assessed valuation of a parcel of property at the time the tax becomes effective (or an average of years of assessments), the system provides that each year thereafter a dual tax shall be levied, one part at the regular rate on the assessed value of the property and a second part at a fractional rate on the amount by which the assessed valuation has increased within the year on account of other causes than for improvements made by the owner, or for which he is required to pay in the form of special assessments. Such a tax would be eminently fair, and as a means of reaching community values otherwise not assessed, it is worthy of serious consideration. The main point would seem to be whether it violates the requirements of uniformity in taxation of property as provided in the constitution of Virginia.

Whether the general tax rate should be increased next year or not, or whether certain divisions thereof should be made, as for example, the setting aside of a separate rate sufficient to meet the expenditures of the city's schools, is beyond the province of this report. At the time the survey was made, neither the appropriation requests nor the revenue estimates for 1918 were available. The survey report submits the facts, endeavors to interpret them, and in addition to pointing out certain opportunities for decreasing the expenditures and increasing the revenues, makes many recommendations whereby the city may obtain more and better service from its government without increasing the tax rate whatsoever.

War-Time Retrenchments.

It is desirable at this point to call attention to special retrenchments, which, if later found necessary, may be made for a temporary period as war-time measures.

This subject can best be considered under two main heads (1) capital expenditure, and (2) expenditures for operation and maintenance.

With respect to the former, no bonds should be issued unless absolutely necessary, because the interest rates at which they must be floated, will probably continue high during the war, and the interest and sinking fund charges will immediately increase the city's tax budget.

The Local Government Board of England early in the war requested English cities to postpone all public works not necessary for (1) reasons of public health, or (2) on account of war requirements. It is urged that all borrowing be restricted to the narrowest possible limits, and that the time of completing construction contracts be extended. Where pipe fittings, etc., has been purchased, the Local Government Board was able to sell them through the war office or ministry of munitions, regard being had of course for the importance of the work and its effect on the labor market.

In considering the opportunities for reducing, operating and maintenance costs, a city government should be likened to the human body. It contains certains organs which are vital to its existence. They cannot withstand an amputation either in whole or in part. Departments of health, police, fire, etc., constitute such organs in a city government. On the other hand there are in the human body various non-vital organs which can be successfully amputated without curtailing its normal functions. It is in corresponding branches of the city government that opportunities for war-time retrenchment must be found.

One of the largest items of expenditure is for street purposes. Although it is always false economy to postpone the repair of permanent pavements, Richmond may be able to reduce its present expenditures for street lighting and street cleaning. That the reduction in lighting would not result in an increase of street accidents is indicated by the experience of London which has been darkened since early in the war. The Local Government Board of England gives the following statistics for the metropolitan district of London:

YEAR	Total Number of Accidents		Total Number of Persons Killed or Injured	
	Day	Night	Day	Night
1913	50,324	6 210	20,898	3 475
1914	49,151	6,576	22 077	4 032
1915	47,798	6 234	22,450	4,268
1916	41,500	4,699	19,523	3,401

It is stated that the increase of persons killed or injured during 1914-15 is attributable mainly to the fact that the calls for military service rendered necessary the employment of less experienced drivers. That the restricted lighting was not a primary factor is indicated by the fact that the accidents during 1916 were less than during 1913.

That the restricted lighting has not caused an increase in crime is evident from the following figures:

YEAR	Number of Criminal Offences Reported to Police	Number of Apprehensions for Criminal Offences	Number of Apprehensions for Other Offences.
1913......................	17,952	14,760	118 216
1914......................	15,167	13,165	118,676
1915......................	12 214	11.526	102,733
1916 (approximately)......	12 879	12,959	74,669

While there has been a decrease in the number of criminal offences reported to the police, there has been some increase in juvenile crime as the result of less parental influence because of the war.

Street cleaning beyond a certain point may, if necessary, be curtailed during the war. This suggestion should not be interpreted as counter to suggestions already set forth herein for securing cleaner streets. The present suggestion is only for a contingency which may not develop.

The amount of park department appropriations which will be used for flower gardens. planting new shrubbery, etc., should also be queried. Granting the desirability of playground instructors, the extension of such service might be temporarily postponed.

All stationery forms should be standardized, in most cases it will be found that smaller sizes. and cheaper grades of paper can be used. Throughout the departments all paper should be used on both sides. Carbon copies of replies to letters should at least be made on the reverse side of the original communication. Colored paper in bookkeeping forms, etc.. should be eliminated, the printing of minutes should be minimized and one insertion of advertising be made to suffice.

With respect to several of the items already noted herein, the statements of the editor of Municipal Engineering (London) are of value: He says, "Street cleaning has been curtailed and the work is only done sufficient for public health purposes. Borough libraries and museums have been closed in many towns, and in the principal libraries women have been employed. All public works have been stopped. Only necessary work to keep the roads in safe condition for traffic is undertaken. The dinner hour for schools has been curtailed and taken off the end of the day. Ornamental public gardens have been converted in a large number of cases into food production plots, and less labor is employed in parks and ornamental grounds, etc."

It is already evident that most American cities will follow the cities of England in paying to their own employees who go to the colors, or to their families, the difference between their military pay and the salaries they received from the city. The vacancies caused by such withdrawals will, of course, in most instances, need to be filled, but so far as possible the duties thereof should be distributed to employees who remain. In making new appointments, women should receive the preference. In any event no men should be appointed, whose age may cause them to be drafted for military service. The excellent result secured by English cities is stated as follows by Sir Horace Monroe of the Local Government Board of England:

"While it has not been found possible, in most municipalities, to effect any material decrease in the (tax) rates, the fact that, generally speaking, rates have not increased to any considerable extent must be regarded as satisfactory in view of the general increase of wages and cost of food and material of all kinds, and the large sums paid to employees with the colors. The maintenance of rates at approximately pre-war levels points, in the circumstances, to a series of successful efforts to economize."

The Budget

The Bridge

THE BUDGET.

Budget Calendar Should Be Specified In Charter.

Every city should adopt its annual appropriation ordinance prior to the beginning of the fiscal year. Only in that way can department heads arrange their work programs and plan definitely and with understanding for the year's work. Only in that way can the various appropriation accounts be opened in the financial records of the accounting offices and be ready for operation on the first day of the year when expenditures are made. Moreover, no money should be expended until it has been formally appropriated.

To insure the preparation of the budget estimates and final adoption of an appropriation ordinance prior to the beginning of the year, the dates of the various successive steps to be taken in the budget-making process should be definitely set forth in the charter. The present charter says nothing concerning budget dates. Its only requirement in this respect is that:

"The auditor shall annually submit to the administrative board during the month of January a report of the estimates necessary, as nearly as may be, to defray the expenses of the city government during the succeeding fiscal year."

Nothing is said as to when the budget shall be submitted to the council, when it shall be adopted, etc. In the absence of adequate charter requirements for earlier dates, the following practice has grown up:

Early in December the auditor requests the department heads to submit estimates of appropriations needed for the ensuing year (such request was sent out December 8th, in 1915, and December 5th in 1916).

At the first meeting of the city council in January, the auditor submits to council a summary of the estimates.

Council then refers the summarized estimates to the finance committee. which proceeds to hold hearings thereon, and having agreed upon amounts to be recommended, it reports back to council (in 1915 and 1916 the committee reported in February, and in 1917 it did not report until March). There is no time limit.

Council then proceeds to adopt the committee's report and the ordinance is submitted to the mayor for signature. (In 1917 it was signed March 15th.)

The fiscal year of the city begins February 1st. Thus, when the appropriation ordinance does not become effective until March 15th, as in 1917, one and one-half months of the year have already elapsed. There is nothing whatever in the charter to prevent the lapse of two, three or six months, or even a longer period. To bridge over the interim between the beginning of the year and the adoption of the appropriation ordinance, it is customary for council to adopt a resolution authorizing the payment of salaries on the same basis as for the previous year. The charter seems to be silent with respect to the authority of council to cover such expenditures by resolution. Moreover, the resolution does not include the payment of any claims except salaries, and hence all invoices of vendors doing business with the city remain unpaid until the final adoption of the appropriation ordinance.

If charter provision fails to provide for moving the budget dates forward and definitizing them so that the appropriations will be adopted prior to the beginning of the fiscal year, it should authorize the department pending the adoption of the annual appropriation ordinance each year, to continue their expenditures on the monthly basis of one-twelfth of the amount appropriated to the respective departments the preceding year. Such a clause is desirable as a safety measure to prevent the legislative branch of the government from tying the hands of the executive branch by not authorizing the annual budget appropriations until late in the year.

Preparation of Appropriation Requests.

In his capacity as both auditor and clerk of the finance committee, it is customary for the auditor each December to send to the head of each department asking for an estimate of its appropriation need for the ensuing year. The letter sent out in December, 1916, also asked them to "prepare and submit at the time fixed for hearing the needs of your department an itemized statement of the expenditures of 1916." It further requested each department head to make ten copies of both "budget of wants" and the "itemized statement of expenditures."

The request said nothing as to submitting the estimates on uniform blanks nor adhering to any standard classification of appropriations or expenditure titles.

Having received from the departments the estimates, as requested, the auditor prepares a summary thereof on a large printed sheet, of which he makes ten copies—one for each member of the finance committee and one for himself. Early in January (January 9 in 1917) the auditor submits to the city council his estimate of receipts, together with the summarized requests for appropriations. The entire matter is then referred to the finance committee of the council.

To facilitate consideration of the various departmental estimates by the council and its finance committee, by the chief executive of the city and by the public at large, uniform blanks should be printed and a supply thereof distributed to the department heads for use by them in preparing their estimates. Such forms should be standard for all departments and include detailed instructions for their preparation. They should provide for showing separately for each class of expenditure: (1) expense incurred each year during the preceding two years; (2) appropriations for and expenses incurred to date during the current year or estimated amount for the entire current year; (3) estimated expenses for the ensuing year; (4) increases and decreases between preceding year's, current year's, and next year's estimates. All increases for personal services should show clearly whether caused by new positions, or by increases in salaries of present incumbents. Such forms are in use by many cities throughout the country and copies thereof may readily be obtained as a guide.

The Bureau of Municipal Research advocates an executive budget system as a necessary part of providing leadership in the city's government. It is therefore recommended that in revising the charter, provision shall be made whereby all departmental estimates shall be submitted to the mavor by the various executive departments and be thoroughly considered by him and revised, if desired, before submitted to the city council. In this work he should of course have the assistance of the central accounting officer of the city. Being a principal part of his administrative policy for the ensuing year, he should be prepared to defend it on the floor of the council. His should be the responsibility for preparing the work plans and the appropriation requests and administrative policies in support thereof. It should remain for the representative branch of the government (the council) to pass judgment on the proposals and requests of the executive branch.

Budget Hearings and Publicity.

Public hearings on the appropriation requests are held by the finance committee, after which the committee embodies in report form the appropriations it recommends for adoption. At the committee meeting of February 28, 1917, it was ordered that 300 copies of this report be printed immediately and 700 more after its adoption by council and approval by the mayor. The opportunity for local taxpayers to become informed with respect to the proposed appropriations and to have a hearing before final adoption of the annual budget therefore appears to be ample.

Classification of Appropriations.

Appropriation requests submitted to the auditor by the various department heads are on various kinds and sizes of stationery and are assembled in sundry kinds of classifications and arrangements. Examination thereof shows that they are all typewritten in the ten copies as requested, and that it is customary to follow about the same classification as was set forth in the appropriation ordinance the preceding year. It is to be noted that there are practically only two divisions of appropriation items—"salaries" and "expenses." The estimates show considerable detail with respect to salary items, but requests for expense appropriations are bunched in lump-sum amounts. These latter are frequently very large— for example, the following lump-sum expense items were taken at random from the 1917 appropriation estimates:

Street cleaning—expenses and improvements: feed and supplies and purchase of machines, mules, etc. $50,000
City Home—expenses: repairs and maintenance, fuel, etc. 80,000
Virginia Hospital—expenses: maintenance and hospital supplies 35,000
Pine Camp Hospital—expenses: maintenance, hospital supplies, etc. 10,700
Grounds and parks—expenses: including nursery, feed, machines, etc........................... 10,000
Electric plant—expenses: supplies, fuel, wires, poles, etc. 27,500

No criticism should be made of the practice of appropriating in lump-sum amounts as above indicated, but it is very essential that a detailed classification be maintained in recording the expenditure of such appropriations. Also that the results of such detailed expenditure distribution be made available at budget-making time and fully set forth on the appropriation requests of the several departments. Only in that way can the council, finance committee and the chief executive of the city have an adequate basis for judgment in determining upon the amounts which should be appropriated for the ensuing year.

The auditor does not maintain such a detailed distribution of expenditures. He simply records them according to appropriation titles and depends on the departments to segregate the expenditures in their financial records. Some of the departments do this fairly well, especially the central accounting (paymaster's office) of the administrative board. However, insufficient use is made in the departmental estimates of such detailed information. The accountants of the administrative board, who have taken much pains not only to prepare a segregated classification and to record the expenditures of their various departments thereunder, but have also submitted typewritten reports of the expenditures thus segregated and classified, naturally feel rather discouraged that greater use is not made of the results.

It is urged that a standard classification be adopted for all expenditures of the government and that the various departments be required to keep their expenditure records in accordance therewith. If it be decided to centralize all expenditure accounting in the central accounting office, the same detail should be observed. It is especially important that the results of such expenditure analysis be fully set forth on the annual appropriation estimates for use of the finance committee and council.

Not only would such a plan facilitate a better understanding of the budget estimates, but it would be of much use in placing the city on a better trading basis by furnishing automatically to the central purchasing agent for all departments the aggregate cost of the various commodities purchased. For example, before letting contracts for the purchase of forage, fuel, oil, etc., the purchasing agent could have readily available the total cost thereof for the entire city government during the preceding month, quarter or year, and thus be in position to obtain lower prices by letting a single blanket contract.

Restrictions on Spending.

Several paragraphs are inserted in the appropriation ordinance relative to how the appropriations may and may not be administered. Taking the appropriation ordinance of 1917 as an illustration, the following points are to be noted:

Paragraph 1 directs the auditor and treasurer to place to the credit of all appropriation accounts which show an overdraft for the fiscal year 1916, the amount necessary to balance same and to close all such accounts for the fiscal year 1916. Such a direction should have been unnecessary, because the charter not only prohibits the exceeding of all appropriations, but the appropriation ordinance of the preceding year had contained the following clause:

> "That the amounts herein shall be deemed to be the limit of amounts to be expended by any committee, administrative board, or head of department, respectively, except by transfers authorized by the council. and that for any debt created by any committee, administrative board or head of department in excess of any appropriation herein, unless authorized by the city council, the city of Richmond shall be held in no wise responsible."

Paragraph 2 relative to payments in quarterly installments, restricting the expenditures of the first six months to one-half of the total appropriations, restrictions against salary increases, prohibiting the use of "expense" appropriations for salaries, wages, etc., is highly commendable. However, the city council practically nullified the latter important provision relative to the use of "expense" appropriations for payroll purposes, and made it farcical by adding the following words. "except that this paragraph shall not be applicable to departments under the administrative board." Most of the departments of the government are under this board, and it had been the worst offender in using expense money for payroll purposes. The clause should be stricken out of the next appropriation ordinance.

Paragraph 3 is practically the same as that cited above as having been included in the 1916 ordinance. It is important and should not only be retained but enforced.

The recent charter revision which restricts appropriations to 95 per cent. of the estimated receipts, thus making the other 5 per cent. available as a contingent fund, was well-advised.

Although not required by the charter, the auditor has also adopted the wise policy of deducting from the estimated receipts, and excluding the same from the appropriations, the average unpaid delinquent personal property taxes of the preceding five years.

Unless such policy be continued, the city is liable to find that it has over-appropriated or made what are sometimes called "wind" appropriations. The present plan is the equivalent of setting up on the auditor's ledger a "reserve" to offset uncollectible taxes.

The fact that the collection of miscellaneous revenues usually exceeds the amount estimated and appropriated at the beginning of the year is quite another matter and should not be permitted to affect the practice above described, because it may happen any year that the collections of miscellaneous revenues will be less instead of more than was estimated. In this connection the State of New Jersey has recently adopted a law which requires each city of that State to transfer its excess collections of miscellaneous revenues to a surplus reserve and use the latter in reduction of the next year's tax levy.

Purchasing Methods

PURCHASING METHODS.

If Richmond is to obtain all the advantages of economic buying the present methods must be revised in five important particulars:

1—There must be complete centralization of the city's purchasing power.

2—Written specifications must be prepared for the principal items of supplies, materials and equipment and adopted as standard for all departments.

3—There must be more publicity of all purchasing proposals, so as to obtain wider competition for the city's business.

4—More purchases should be made in quantities and the system of blanket contracts covering all departments should be extended.

5—Adequate inspection of deliveries and physical or chemical tests of samples taken therefrom must be made so as to insure the delivery of the same kind and grade of commodities as ordered.

Centralization of Purchasing Power.

The administrative board does the buying for all departments under its jurisdiction. There is a central blanket contract for printing and stationery, but otherwise each department does practically all of its own buying. Even with respect to centralization in the administrative board of the purchases for the various departments thereof, no purchasing agent has been appointed nor have the duties of such an official been delegated to any particular employee. The board handles the matter of purchasing just the same as it does other routine business. It clears through the book-keeping office, the main clerical office and the board meetings, and receives the attention of various clerks and officials without any one person being charged with responsibility for results.

It is estimated by the auditor that the city spends about $550,-000 a year for supplies and materials exclusive of about $50,000 paid out by the schools for similar purposes. There should be no need to discuss in this survey report the advantages to be derived from centralization of the city's entire purchasing power. The advantages are well known to every business man. The aggregate amount paid out by the city each year for supplies and materials is sufficient to justify the appointment of a full-time purchasing agent. In making such appointment, however, great care should be had to select a man thoroughly experienced in such work, as for example, a man who has had experience in the central purchasing office of a large railroad system. Having appointed a properly qualified purchasing agent, an adequate plant of trade catalogues, card indices of prices current, etc., should be established and kept up to date.

With the abolition of the administrative board, as elsewhere recommended herein, complete centralization of the city's purchasing authority would be a simple matter. Such an office should be appointive by the mayor. Meanwhile, irrespective of charter mandates, but through a spirit of co-operation, an arrangement should be perfected whereby all outside departments will do their buying through the administrative board—at least the commodities of which they purchase large quantities. In various cities throughout the country where it has thus far been impossible to secure legal action for establishing a central purchasing agency—including New York City, Indianapolis, etc.—the purchasing of all city departments has been centralized simply by a "getting together" of the various department heads in friendly co-operation for the good of the city.

The purchasing procedure of the administrative board should be centralized with one of the clerks in' the paymaster's office, either of whom, if properly supported by the board, should be able to effect marked economies in buying compared with the present methods.

In this connection it is recommended that the position known as city printer be abolished. There is nothing so technical about the duties of the office that could not be quickly learned by the person who does all the other buying for the city. For many years the city has paid a local printer $600 a year to supervise its purchases of stationery and printing. He prepares the specifications (such as they are), vises requisitions and invoices, and measures the city's advertisements in the local newspapers. The contention that he more than saves his salary each year by keeping down the printing cost is not only open to argument as shown by the defects of the specifications subsequently cited herein, but also by the lack of adequate competition for this part of the city's business. Whatever economies have resulted from the employment of the city printer can just as well be obtained by a regular purchasing agent. In fact, the saving would probably be greater.

Standardization of Specifications.

Most commercial organizations and some cities have awakened
to the savings which are possible through standardizing supplies,
materials and equipment and describing such standards in detailed
written specifications. Richmond should get in line with this policy. A beginning has already been made—such, for example, as
the use of standard specifications for steam coal. But it is only a
beginning. The so-called standard specifications for stationery
supplies cannot in their present state be called proper standardization. For example. departments are allowed to requisition—in
fact, last year the proposal actually asked for bids on twenty-one
different kinds of lead pencils. nine different kinds of penholders,
thirty different kinds of steel pens, etc. Even then the specifications did not include certain well known brands of lead pencils
which are widely used. There are various commodities on which
it should be possible to effect large savings if scientific specifications
were adopted. The matter is of sufficient importance to justify
taking it up systematically, starting with a list of commodities
which are purchased in the largest quantities, proceeding in logical
order to standardize each. and having determined upon the best
kinds. grades. etc., adapted to the particular uses of the city, to
reduce them to written specifications. Only in that way can the departments obtain an adequate basis for preparing their purchase
estimates and budget specifications. Only in that way can local
merchants and dealers be given an adequate basis on which to bid
for city business. Only in that way can an adequate basis be obtained for the making of physical and chemical tests to determine
whether deliveries conform to what is ordered, and only in that
way can the city auditor obtain a real basis for audit.

This work of standardization should be begun without delay,
and the administrative board is an excellent agency for its accomplishment. The board members now have plenty of leisure time
which might better be devoted to some constructive undertaking,
such as standardization herein recommended. In determining the
standards and in preparing specifications, the board should advise
freely with department heads. local dealers, manufacturers and en-

Advertising for Bids.

Centralization of purchasing power and standardization of
specifications will be of little avail unless the city has real competi-

tive bidding. Advertising should be conducted economically, but the advertisements should be sufficiently full to interest prospective bidders. There has been some complaint in Richmond that the advertisements of the administrative board did not contain sufficient information relative to the size of the contract, the location of the work, and in general whether it was worth bidding for. Although there is no occasion to include plans and specifications in an advertisement, it being sufficient to state where they can be obtained or consulted, the advertisement should contain sufficient information to enable contractors to determine whether or not it is to their interest to seek further information.

If it be found in connection with any particular kind of commodity that vendors are not responding to the advertisement in sufficient number, the purchasing agent should send special letters to dealers, enclose copies of the advertisement, and urge them to submit bids.

In respect to those supplies, materials and equipment which are needed only in small quantities and intermittently by the departments, and which cannot be bought to advantage under contract. the blackboard system of notification should be adopted. This consists in posting on a blackboard in the purchasing agent's office each day a list of the kinds and quantities of such commodities as are desired. The city salesmen of the various houses soon get in the habit of dropping in daily and looking at such lists and submitting bids thereon.

A policy should be adopted whereby at least three informal bids are secured on each open market purchase of say. $20, or even $15. With proper methods. the obtaining of such bids is a simple matter, and the financial saving made possible thereby is well worth the small effort needed.

An essential that is often overlooked in municipal buying is the spirit and point of view of local vendors with respect to the city's business. They must be made to feel that they will get a square deal. In this respect municipal buying should be on even a higher plane than the buying of private corporations.

The charter does not require the administrative board to award its contracts to the lowest bidders. but an examination of the bids and awards shows that in the majority of instances the awards have been to the lowest bidders. When adequate restrictions surround the letting and administration of contracts. it is well enough to permit awards to other than low bidders. It was not apparent in Richmond that the privilege had been abused.

At this point it is desirable to mention the procedure followed by the board in opening and awarding the bids. They are opened publicly in board meeting, and in practically every instance are then referred for tabulation and recommendation to the head of the department where the requisition originated. The official minutes of the administrative board in every case contained practically the same pro forma phraseology:

> "Bids for ———— were opened and read, and on motion of Mr. ———— were referred to ———— (head of department) for tabulation, report and recommendation."

At a subsequent meeting of the board, when the department head to whom the bids were referred has submitted his report, the minutes usually read as follows:

> "Mr. ———— moved that the contract for ———— for the year ———— be awarded to ———— at the prices named in their proposal dated ————."

It is to be noted that the board retains no copy of the bids, but that they are delivered to the department head immediately after being opened. This at once opens up various opportunities for collusions in the changing of bids, substitution, etc. The agency which assumes responsibility for opening bids should forthwith proceed to tabulate them. If it is desired to obtain the judgment of the department head, a copy of the tabulation should then be furnished him.

Purchasing in Quantities.

Examination of the records showed that it is a fixed policy of the administrative board and of the city as a whole to take advantage of quantity buying. It was also noted that discretion is used in the matter of letting contracts. This is desirable, particularly in the present unsettled condition of the markets, because while it may have been good economy to buy on an annual contract last year or two years ago, such a procedure might now be more costly than in buying in the open market, and vice versa. Similarly, there may be instances where commodities previously bought on an annual contract should now be bought on quarterly or monthly contract. No definite rule can be laid down. It is an illustration of the need for adequate training and mature judgment on the part of the purchasing agent. Although most of the Richmond contracts are on an annual basis, it was noted that in certain instances, such for example, as provision for the charitable institutions, the purchases were on a quarterly contract. Also that whereas forage was formerly bought quarterly, it is now bought in the open market because of fluctuating prices. These methods are to be commended. The purchase of steam coal on standard specifications has already been referred to. It is one of the items contracted for in large quantities. Other items similarly purchased are gas oil, alum, clorine, water meters, iron pipe, cement, milk, etc. The board is also to be commended for centralizing all trench digging work in one contract for the water, sewer, and other departments. Fire hose is purchased by the fire department, and with good economy.

While credit is thus due for making a large proportion of the purchases on a quantity basis, there is still abundant opportunity for expansion thereof, and hence the securing of further economies in this particular direction. For example, there are frequent requisitions for small quantities in one barrel lots of various kinds and brands of lubricating oil. Also small quantities of many varieties of supplies and equipment, such as hammers, hoes, trowels, oil cans, wrenches, pruning shears, etc., are ordered one or two at a time. Turpentine, paint, etc., appear on many requisitions in very small quantities. An illustration of the opportunity for further standardization and purchasing in quantities is shown by the following requisitions taken at random from the files:

Requisition No. 381, dated April 9, 1917, engineering department—for grounds and parks:

Wheelbarrow	$4.25	
Files	.60	
Stillson wrench	1.10	
Water cooler	2.50	
1 pound nails 8d	.25	
Hammer	.75	$9.45

Requisition No. 378, dated April 7, 1917, engineering department—for streets:

Hickory pick handles at 25c.	.75	
Pad for mule	.25	$1.00

Requisition No. 122, dated May 2, 1917, electric plant:

2 gallons kerosene oil	$ .26	
1 quart enamel	.50	
6 R. O. files	.75	
1 taper file	.20	
2 axe handles	.30	$2.01

Requisition No. 269, dated June 25, 1917, gas works:
1 barrel Delaware valve oil at 48c.
1 barrel red engine oil, 24.1-2c.
1 barrel crown safety oil.

(In connection with the above, it was noted that the engineering department also bought a barrel of red engine oil June 11 at 23 cents.)

Requisition No. 243, dated April 17, 1917, gas works:
1 barrel Delaware valve oil, 45c.
1 barrel red engine oil, 21 1-2c.

(It was noted that the above order was repeated on May 17th, and on May 21st one barrel of lubricating air cylinder oil at 40 cents was purchased.)

During the same period the water department bought lubricating oil as follows:

Req. No.	Date.
263	April 6—1 bbl. crown safety oil, 12c.
307	April 23—1 bbl. crown safety oil, 11c.
373	May 7—1 bbl. crown safety oil, 12c.
403	May 18—1 bbl. crown safety oil, 12c.
413	May 22—1 bbl. engine oil, 29c.
429	May 29—1 bbl. extra heavy motorcycle oil, 63c.
460	June 6—1 bbl. crown safety oil, 11c.
489	June 19—1 bbl. crown safety oil, 11c.
501	June 22—1 bbl. crown safety oil, 11c.

It is apparent that more attention should be given to securing from all departments at least annually, and preferably every three months, a complete estimate of all of the supplies and materials they will respectively require during the ensuing period. In the securing of such estimates, blank forms specially designed for the purpose should be provided. This will not only facilitate preparation, but will make for accuracy in their tabulation in the central office and in the drafting of proposals for contracts, etc.

There has been so much discussion relative to the purchase of stationery and printing as to make it desirable to refer thereto in this report. The Southern Stamp and Stationery Company for many years had the contract for furnishing stationery. No register of bids was available, but the city printer frankly stated that while occasionally there were two bidders, and once three bidders, there was usually only one, i. e., the Southern Stamp and Stationery Company. The 1916 contract was let to Everett Waddey & Company, who submitted a radically unbalanced bid; for example, they bid one cent each on automatic numbering machines, postal scales, large yellow pads, etc. Naturally, they lost money on the contract, and in 1917 the former contractors were again successful. The quantity estimates contained in the printed proposal have mostly been carried forward from year to year. As a result the bidder who has had the contract for a year or two is given a great advantage. because he has inside information as to the actual quantities of each line item which will be purchased. The specifications and proposals should be carefully standardized and brought up to date, and extra effort made to obtain real competition of local dealers by assuring them of fair treatment throughout.

There is no doubt but that considerable economy could be effected in printing the annual reports of the departments. The administrative board itself has been the worst offender. The grade of paper in both cover and contents and the general workmanship of the board's annual report, while highly artistic, is not a good commentary on the business methods. For example, voucher No. 2349, paid April 14, 1917, shows that $275 was paid the Wm. Byrd Press for 1,000 copies of a small paper-covered pamphlet report. This is an average of 27 1-2 cents per copy.

Inspection and Tests.

To obtain real benefit from the adoption of standard specifications, there must be adequate inspection of deliveries. Departmental inspection by employees who happen to receive the deliveries is insufficient because frequently they are not familiar with the specifications of what was ordered and therefore have nothing with which to make a comparison. However, such employees are prone to make the inspection perfunctory or not at all. The delivery of commodities is usually accompanied by the driver presenting to the receiving clerk a delivery slip with a request that it be signed. The receiving clerk asks where he shall sign, and after attaching his signature or initials, the inspection is ended. Thus it is that there should be provided a certain amount of independent inspection by the central auditing office of the city because it is, in fact, a field audit and a proper function of that office. It is unnecessary to inspect every delivery because the same moral effect can be had if only a small proportion of the deliveries is inspected, so long as the inspection is made at unexpected times. The adoption of the "blind tally" forms of receipt recommended herein would serve automatically as notice to the auditor that supplies had been received at a certain point and were ready for inspection.

With respect to the chemical or physical tests of samples taken from deliveries, it is already the practice to make tests of coal, cement, and certain other commodities. This excellent practice should be expanded accordingly as additional specifications are prepared and used as a purchasing basis.

Payment to Vendors.

Prompt payment to vendors is fully as important to efficient buying as are various other essentials hereinbefore discussed. Although no audit was made, the survey indicated that the vendor's claims in Richmond were not being unduly delayed in payment. When there is delay it is usually attributable to the department heads. It means that the invoices have been held up there instead of being transmitted promptly to the auditor. The latter official has adopted a definite schedule on which he pays claims of the various departments each month. The re-adjustment of the invoice procedure, as recommended herein would furnish the auditor automatically with notice of delivery and enable him to follow up and expedite the transmittal of claims from the departments. Everything should be done to facilitate the prompt payment of vendors in every instance, because if vendors know their money may be tied up for several weeks by the city, they will naturally make their estimates higher in submitting bids, or they will discontinue soliciting city business.

With respect to the preparation of purchase requisitions, it was noted that the detail shown thereon in most instances did not conform to the accounting and auditing procedure. For ex-

entitled "extension."

Automobile Costs.

The accountants in the paymaster's office of the administrative board are to be particularly commended for installing a system whereby they can, at any time, state the operating cost of every automobile in the city's service, separately for gasoline, tires, repairs and storage. However, the real value of this data is negatived by failure of the administrative board and other department heads to require that a record be kept of the mileage of each car. Figures concerning the cost of operating any particular car are of little significance, unless they can be accompanied by the car's mileage during the same period. The board should require that a record of the mileage of each car be reported at least monthly to its central accounting office. The importance of this recommendation may be appreciated by referring to the following list of the city's automobiles. Exclusive of the motor equipment of the fire and police departments, there are—

1 Stevens—seven passenger	Administrative board
1 Runabout	Chairman of the board
3 Runabouts	Board of health
1 Runabout	Building department
3 Ambulances	Virginia Hospital and City Home
2 Three-passenger cars	Electric plant
2 Trucks	Electric plant
1 Ford Wagon	Electric plant
2 Runabouts	Gas works
1 Truck	Playgrounds
1 Runabout	Street cleaning department
2 Runabouts*	Street cleaning department
2 Trucks	Water department
2 Runabouts	Water department
1 Truck	Sealer of weights and measures
1 Runabout	Mayor and chief of police
1 Car	Department of engineering

*This department also has an Elgin Motor Sweeper.

It is worthy of notice that economy seems to have been exercised in purchasing automobiles for city use. Instead of buying large touring cars, the departments, with the exception of the administrative's board's car, have been content to use runabouts.

The Auditor

THE AUDITOR.

Accounting and Reporting.

In General.

With the exceptions noted subsequently herein, the accounting system in the auditor's office meets the city's needs adequately. It is largely the development of recent years and may be said to be somewhat above the average of accounts maintained by cities throughout the country. As the city grows it will be found desirable to install certain other records and to complete some of those now in partial operation. For example, expense accounting on a consumptive basis has not yet been attempted, nor has any vendors' ledger been installed. A contract ledger in card form has been established, but is not under general ledger control. At the time of the survey the records maintained were found posted to date. The auditor and his entire office force manifested much intelligent interest in the system as it now exists, and in its further development. The features of the accounting system specially suggested for further improvement follow:

Contingent Liabilities.

An excellent beginning has been made to safeguard the appropriations by making it possible to ascertain at all times not merely the unexpended balances but also the unencumbered balances of appropriations. However, such result has not yet been attained. The office has progressed only so far as posting the contingent liabilities (purchase orders and contracts) as encumbrances against the respective appropriations. These contingent liabilities are not liquidated except by the posting of voucher payments. Inasmuch as the amount of the latter is frequently different from the amount of the purchase order, there is need to adjust the amount of variation between the two. Such adjustment is rarely made. The amount of the original order is not liquidated by again posting the amount of the order simultaneously with the posting of the voucher, nor is any debit or credit entry made of the difference between the order and the voucher. It was stated that the entry showing the amount of the order is sometimes changed to agree with the voucher when there is a wide variation.

This failure to follow out the system to its logical conclusion largely destroys the value of appropriation accounting on a contingent liability or encumbered balance basis. The method used in collating purchase orders so as to reduce the number of contingent liability postings and also the collating of voucher payments so as to reduce the number of postings thereof is commendable. But the fact remains that the system is not yet being operated so as to furnish the auditor, the finance committee or department heads currently with information as to unencumbered balances of appropriations, nor will it furnish statements of contingent liabilities and unencumbered balances of appropriations for use in the preparation of a complete balance sheet of the city's assets and liabilities. It should go without saying, that the excellent beginning already made should be followed up with the operation of the complete system.

Accounts Should be Closed at End of Year.

An examination of the appropriation ledger containing the accounts for 1916 and 1917 showed that in most of the 1916 accounts the aggregate amount of contingent liability postings (contracts and purchase orders) at the end of the year had been carried right forward into 1917. It was stated that this has been done to insure a continuity of the liability postings on contracts remaining incomplete. The practice is most confusing and unbusinesslike. Each account should be closed at the end of the fiscal year and the uncomplete balances of contracts, if any, should be estimated and set up anew as liabilities against the appropriations of the ensuing year.

Fund Accounting.

No adequate fund separation is maintained of the cash collected by the city. It becomes a part of one general cash record irrespective of whether it is derived from taxes and other tax budget sources, whether it comes from the issuance of long-term bonds, issuance of temporary loans, or other sources. Irrespective of whether cash is received for operating purposes or capital purposes, it is immediately merged with what is on hand. For example, it would take a most exhaustive analysis, going back several years, to determine how much of the money derived from temporary loans has been used for operating purposes pending the collection of taxes as distinguished from the amount of such loans which have been issued for capital purposes pending the sale of bonds. Thus at the end of some years a cash balance appears in the report of the auditor and treasurer, but an audit and analysis might show that it was comprised mostly of money derived from the sale of bonds and hence applicable only for capital purposes. Although no audit was included in this survey, an inspection of the accounts indicates that some years the city's borrowing on temporary loans has been kept at a minimum by temporary using bond money for operating purposes. That there was no misappropriation of funds in such cases is evidenced by the fact that the amounts of bond funds ultimately expended for capital purposes equalled the amount authorized. When short of money for operating purposes, pending the collection of taxes or other revenues, it is economical and hence good business policy for the city to borrow from other funds which it may have in the treasury, i. e., to borrow from itself instead of from outsiders. Thereby the city is able to save interest charges. It is submitted, however, that a clear-cut line of demarcation in the city's cash account should be maintained as between (1) the general fund accounts (including revenues from public utilities as well as from taxes and other revenue sources), (2) bond fund accounts, (3) special and trust fund accounts, and (4) sinking fund accounts. Otherwise it will continue to be impossible for the city to produce any kind of a balance sheet except a general consolidated statement such as appears at the beginning of the auditor's report.

The city's books should at all times reflect the amount of cash advanced from each fund group to the other fund groups because they constitute assets or liabilities of such funds according as the money has been advanced or borrowed.

It is not intended to over-stress this criticism because the excellent work of the auditor and his staff in developing the accounting system thus far is fully realized. The desirability of making the necessary analysis and setting up separate fund accounts is cited more as a suggestion for the future constructive work of the office than as a criticism of what is past or present.

The general ledger accounts should be expanded and arranged in fund groups so that an operating statement and balance sheet of each group may be produced from that particular part of the ledger. It should be able to produce therefrom the figures for financial statements I to IV, inclusive, subsequently set forth herein.

Financial Reporting.

The ideal to be observed in financial reporting is to include enough data but not too much. This ideal has evidently been kept in mind by the auditor of Richmond. There is, however, still opportunity for considerable improvement in his reports—principally with respect to the character of the content rather than the quantity.

The monthly reports which are published as required by charter would be far more useful if they showed unencumbered balances of appropriations. This can readily be done as soon as the appropriation ledger is operated as recommended herein. Statement No. 1 herewith suggestive for the preparation of monthly statements.

With respect to the annual report, reference has already been made to the need for developing and expending the city's balance sheet. A summary or consolidated balance sheet is of course desirable, but it should be accompanied by a balance sheet of each of the fund groups similar to statement No. 2 herewith. Similarly, in preparing an operation statement of the year's transactions, each fund group should be kept separate instead of practically bunching them together as is done in the annual reports thus far published by the auditor. For example, in the published statement of a year's operations, the cash balances at the beginning and end of the year include all cash irrespective of whether it belongs to the general fund, bond funds, or special and trust funds. The present condition of the general ledger accounts makes it impossible to present any other kind of a statement. In statement No. 3, herewith, the fund groups might be arranged in sequence instead of in columns.

1.—*Statement of Appropriation Balances.*

Fund................Department...........................Month Ending................19.....

Title of Appropriation	Net Amount Available (including Transfers)	Amount Expended	Unexpended Balance	Contingent Liabilities Outstanding	Unencumbered Balance

11.—*Balance Sheet.*

Fund* _____ Conditioned as at _____ 19____

	Amt.		Amt.

CORRECT ASSETS

Cash:
In bank ....
In hand ....
Amount due the city:
Revenue receivable ....
Accounts receivable ....
Stores:
Advances:
To other accounts ....
Miscellaneous ....

CAPITAL ASSETS

Cash in reserve ....
Amount due the capital accounts ....
Work in progress ....
Lands ....
Structures and other improvements ....
Equipment ....

SINKING FUNDS ASSETS

Cash in reserve ....
Amounts due the sinking funds ....
Investments ....

SPECIAL AND TRUST FUND ASSETS

Cash in reserve ....
Amounts due the trust funds ....

CURRENT LIABILITIES AND RESERVES

Immediate demands for cash ....
Accounts payable ....
Bank overdraft ....
Interest on funded debt due and payable ....
Cash reserve ....
Loans to be repaid from current revenues ....
Due to other accounts ....
Reserves against assets other than cash ....
For uncollectible taxes ....
For rebate on taxes ....
For interest on funded debt accrued not due ....
Current surplus ....

CAPITAL LIABILITIES AND RESERVES

Loans to be repaid from sale of bonds ....
Bonded debt ....
Bonds issued ....
Less bonds unsold ....
Bonds outstanding ....
Less sinking fund reserve ....
Net bonded indebtedness ....
Due to other accounts ....
Reserve ....
For depreciation of capital assets ....
Capital surplus ....

SINKING FUND LIABILITIES AND RESERVES

Due to other accounts ....
Reserve to retire bonds when due ....

SPECIAL AND TRUST FUND LIABILITIES AND RESERVES

Due to other accounts ....
Reserves for special and trust funds ....

*So long as the several funds now required by law exist, a separate balance sheet should be prepared for each fund. A general summary balance sheet, however, is the only one which would present the true condition of the city's finances.

111.—*Statement of Receipts and Disbursements.*

Fund .... Period .... 19 ....

	Current Fund	Capital Funds	Sinking Funds	Special and Trust Funds	Total
Cash on hand.........................					
Received during .... (Each class to be listed separately)					
Payments: (Each department to be listed separately)					
Cash on hand.........................					

IV—*Fund Statement.*

Condition as at.................19....

Amount.

General Fund Resources:
Net cash available for general fund purposes.
Net amount due the city for general fund purposes.
Advances to other accounts.
Balances of estimated revenues to be collected.
    Total resources

General Fund Appropriations and Reserves:
Unencumbered balance of appropriations.
Reserve for contracts and open market orders.
Unexpended balance of appropriations.
Reserves.
  Prior year's appropriations.
  Retirement of temporary loans.
  Re-appropriations.
    Total appropriations and reserves.

Excess of Resources Over Appropriations and Reserves:
Excess of Appropriations and Reserves Over Resources:

Bond Fund Resources:
  Cash held in reserve.
  Bonds issued but not sold.
  Bonds authorized but not issued.
  Additional bonds required to be sold to fund expenditures.
        Total resources.

Bond Fund Authorizations and Reserves:
  Unencumbered balance of authorizations.
  Reserves for contracts and open market orders.
  Unexpended balance of authorizations.
  Reserve against bonds issued not sold.
    (Loans made upon bonds as collateral).
  Reserve against bonds authorized not issued.
    (Loans made upon specifically authorized issues).
        Total authorization and reserves.

Excess of Resources Over Authorizations and Reserves:
Excess of Authorizations and Reserves Over Resources:

Sinking Fund Resources:
  Cash held in reserve.
  Investments.
  Cash required for sinking fund purposes.
        Total resources.

Sinking Fund Appropriations and Reserves:
  Reserve required to retire bonds when due.
        Total reserves.

Excess of Resources Over Appropriations and Reserves:
Excess of Appropriations and Reserves Over Resources:

Special and Trust Fund Resources:
  Cash held in reserve.
  Investments.

Special and Trust Fund Appropriations and Reserves:
  Reserve for special funds.
  Reserve for trust funds.

Audit and Payment of Claims, Other Than Payrolls.

Present Procedure.

Invoices are sent by the vendor direct to the city departments where the purchases originated. The administrative board requires that invoices be rendered in triplicate to those departments which are under its supervision. Only two copies of the invoice are required by other departments. After approval of an invoice in a departmental office, one of the copies is attached to a voucher form which is signed by at least one official of the department, and the voucher and invoice then forwarded to the auditor.

It is customary to accompany the vouchered invoices with a list in duplicate, showing payees and amounts of documents transmitted, one copy of which being checked and signed by the auditor is then returned as a receipt to the department from whence it came. This procedure is desirable in fixing responsibility.

The auditor's clerk then checks the invoices to the carbon copies of the purchase requisitions. which he has retained at the time the requisitions were sent him for certification, or which have been sent him subsequent to issuance. In comparing the invoices with the requisitions, the clerk inspects the extensions, additions and also looks to see that the required signatures are on the voucher. He then stamps the back of the voucher—

```
┌─────────────────────────────────────────┐
│                                          │
│          AUDITOR'S OFFICE                │
│                                          │
│   Examined by_____    │
│                    (Name of clerk)       │
│                                          │
│   Date_____ 1917         │
│                                          │
└─────────────────────────────────────────┘
```

No standard form of invoice is used. Each vendor uses his own billhead. The voucher forms are little more than a "back" for the invoices. The forms used by the different departments are practically the same size, but there is some variation in the rulings as between departments.

After the auditor's clerk has stamped the voucher as above indicated. a disbursement warrant is written for the amount and in favor of the payee named thereon. The warrant number, date and bank where payable are not filled in on the warrant at this time. The amount is inserted by protectograph method. The warrants are then placed inside of the vouchers to which they relate and attached thereto with a clip. After this the documents are placed in an alphabetical file on the counter in the auditor's office until called for by the payees or their representatives.

It is the practice to have warrants ready for the payment of claims arising in the various departments according to the definite schedule set forth below.

Department.	Day of Month.
Playground	1
Miscellaneous	1
Health	6
School	7
Water	9
Electric	10
Engineers	12
Street Cleaning	13
Gas	14
Fire	19
Police	21
Virginia Hospital	22
City Home	24
Buildings	26
Engineers	28

When Sundays or holidays fall on the above dates, the claims are made payable the day following. The schedule is posted in the auditor's office and moreover the administrative board stamps on each purchase requisition the date when payment of the claim can be obtained from the auditor's office as per the schedule.

If a warrant is not called for within thirty days after it is ready the auditor sends a postal card to the payee.

It was stated that some of the departments still continue to send postal cards to vendors, informing them of dates when their claims will be paid. They should adopt the practice of the administrative board in this respect and stamp such information on the face of their purchase requisitions. Such a plan in conjunction with the sending out of notices by the auditor is sufficient.

When a payee calls at the auditor's office for his payment warrant, it is numbered with a duplicate numbering stamp (the same number being stamped on the voucher back and on the warrant) and is recorded in a large voucher-register in which the person receiving the warrant is required to acknowledge such receipt by attaching his signature. The voucher is then dated and stamped as follows:

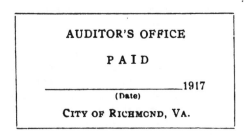

After this the voucher is put in a drawer, together with others, and later sorted by appropriations and filed.

To Simplify Audit and Payment.

Instead of invoices being submitted by the vendors direct to the several departments where the purchases originated, each invoice should be submitted direct to the auditor. The latter maintains a file of "advices" relative to contract specifications, and also a contract ledger in card form, which jointly form an adequate basis for determining whether contract purchases conform with the original agreement. Moreover, at the time the purchase requisition is issued to the vendor the auditor is furnished with a copy thereof which he files away for subsequent use when auditing the invoice.

This procedure is excellent, so far as it goes, but when deliveries are received at the various delivery points in the departments, the auditor should be sent what may be called a "blind tally" receipt from the person who receives the delivery. The auditor should file this receipt with the copy of the purchase order for use in making a better audit of the invoice when it arrives. The "blind tally" system suggested consists of a pad of blank forms distributed in advance to each receiving point in the city and on which the person who actually receives a delivery is required to write the name of the firm making the delivery and to describe in detail the character, quantity and condition of every- thing received. Thus the person receiving is compelled to ac- tually examine, count, and certify to commodities delivered in- stead of simply signing an initial or name perfunctorily on a de- livery slip or bill prepared by the vendor submitted by his repre- sentative. The slips should be written in triplicate by carbon pro- cess, the original going immediately to the auditor's office, the duplicate to the central office of the department for which the supplies were purchased, and the third (a flimsy) retained at the receiving point.

It is to be noted that the auditor endeavors to expedite the payment of all claims on which a cash discount can be obtained. This excellent practice will be facilitated by adopting the plan of having invoices sent direct to the auditor and furnishing him with a complete basis of audit so that the claim can be audited, not only thoroughly, but without waiting for the invoices to clear through the outside departments.

If the auditor desires to secure the signatures of the heads of departments relative to their approval of claims, in addition to the certification of the employee receiving the deliveries, the fore- going recommendations should be supplemented by a slight change in the present procedure. Instead of two copies of invoices (three copies in the case of the administrative board) being submitted by vendors directly to the departments, one copy should be sub- mitted directly to the auditor and the other either accompany the delivery or be sent to the departmental office. The procedure would be greatly facilitated if a standard form of voucher-invoice were adopted. At the time purchase orders are transmitted to vendors, two copies of such forms, an original and duplicate, should be enclosed. Those dealers who have contracts with the city and dealers doing a large amount of open market order busi- ness with the city, should be supplied in advance with pads of such voucher-invoice forms. The original and duplicate copies should be of different colors so as readily to differentiate them. There should be clearly set forth on the original copy either in bold skeleton type across the face, or in colored type, prominently at the top, the fact that the original copy must be sent directly to the city auditor when goods are delivered. Similarly, the duplicate copy should set forth the fact that it must accompany the delivery to whatever point the latter may be made. Dealers should, of course, be required to insert the order numbers on both copies of the voucher-invoices. The present practice of permitting vendors to use their own billheads can, if desired, be continued even with the adoption of the above procedure, but by adopting a standard form of voucher-invoice all necessary certifications can be printed thereon and no additional documents such as the present voucher "back" will be required. The use of one document instead of two will greatly facilitate handling and auditing. Moreover, it will be possible to print the directions for forwarding on the face of voucher-invoices as above suggested and thus insure conformance of all vendors in the plan of sending one copy of the invoice to the auditor and the other to the departments.

After certification in a department on the duplicate copy of the voucher-invoice, it should be forwarded promptly to the city auditor who would take the related order, "blind tally," etc., from his files and proceed to audit the claim, first, however, returning to the department the original copy of the voucher-invoice transmitted to him by the vendor. The reason for this exchange of voucher-invoices is to enable the auditor immediately to obtain an advice of the amount of the claim and fact of delivery, and enable him to follow up the claim if there is delinquency by any of the department officials in transmitting the approved documents to the central auditing office (the auditor). Upon receipt of the certified copy the auditor will no longer have use for the original and hence should return it to the department for filing and reference.

With the adoption of such a voucher-invoice procedure, the "blind tally" might be eliminated if adequate certificates to be signed at the delivery points were printed on the voucher-invoice form. However, the "blind tally" possesses inherent merit which cannot be secured by merely using a voucher-invoice, in that the person receiving the delivery is required personally to examine the commodities delivered before he can certify as to the kind, quantity delivered, condition, etc.

The routine work of auditing and bookkeeping in the auditor's office is constantly being interrupted by persons calling at the counter for their warrants in payment of claims. The procedure should be changed so that they would call at the treasurer's office and not at the auditor's office. They are now compelled to go to both offices. After the auditor has signed the warrants, he should send them to the treasurer for counter-signature and disbursement. There seems to be nothing in the charter requiring the auditor to distribute the warrants. The transfer of this entire function to the treasurer's office would not only relieve the auditor of a great deal of bother and enable the clerks of his office to devote more time to other necessary work, but would also be more convenient for the public.

Adjustment of the details incident to having payees call at the treasurer's office for their warrants instead of at the auditor's office can easily be arranged. The proposition is practicable and desirable and the working out of details should not be permitted to prevent its adoption. The auditor might take a receipt from the treasurer daily on an adding machine list of the numbers and amounts of vouchers and warrants turned over to the treasurer, or a typewritten list showing names of payees, numbers and amounts. To enable the auditor to obtain a receipt from each payee the back of the voucher form might well contain a blank receipt, acknowledgment to be signed in the presence of the treasurer's clerk by the person to whom the warrant is delivered. The receipted vouchers and invoices (or voucher invoices) should be returned to the auditor at the close of each day's business.

The vouchers might be registered by the auditor either after their return from the treasurer or immediately after being audited and prior to their transmittal. In the latter case the auditor could take the treasurer's receipt on the bottom of each register sheet. This would be similar to the present practice of the auditor in taking a single receipt signature for payrolls turned over to department heads for disbursement. If the vouchers were registered prior to transmittal, the auditor's books would be on the basis of "audited vouchers" and could be reconciled with the treasurer's books at any time by a list of the warrants not yet given out by the treasurer. Registration of the vouchers after their payment by the treasurer will keep the auditor's books on the present basis. His daily adding machine or typewritten receipts showing voucher numbers, payees and amounts would safeguard him pending the return and registration of the vouchers. The acknowledgment from each payee which would be obtained on the back of the voucher forms would protect the auditor and the city just as well as the present practice of obtaining the receipt in a column of the voucher register. In fact, the receipt would be better evidence when attached to the original document than when set forth in a separate book.

The suggested plan could be still further improved to the joint advantage of the auditor's and treasurer's offices and the vendors doing business with the city by having the treasurer mail the warrants to the payees as soon as he has signed them and inserted the name of the bank where payable. No uncalled-for vouchers for vendors would then remain in the treasurer's office, and thus the auditor at the time of transmitting the vouchers to the treasurer could register them, obtain the treasurer's receipt on the register sheet and consider the vouchers paid, the same as if they had all been called for at the counter. The practice is now general with large corporations throughout the country—public utility companies, department stores, financial institutions, etc.—to print on the face of their invoices the statement that if the claim is paid by check the endorsement of the check will constitute a receipt and no other receipt is necessary nor will be given unless specially requested. If desired, the form of warrant could easily be changed so as more closely to identify it with the claim (voucher and invoice) to which it related and the blank space provided for endorsement arranged so as clearly to show that it constitutes a receipt.

Transferring to the treasurer's office the function of distributing payment warrants, would make practically no additional work in that office, because even under the present procedure the vendor, after obtaining his warrant in the auditor's office, must come to the treasurer's office to have his warrant validated and the name of the bank inserted. The treasurer already maintains a register of vouchers paid, as required by the charter. On the other hand, the elimination from the auditor's office of the work incident to the disbursing of warrants will enable the staff of that office to devote more attention to auditing and bookkeeping, which are the real reasons for the existence of the office. The distribution of warrants is only incidental thereto, but has a disturbing and deterring effect which seriously hampers the efficiency of the office.

Irrespective of the above recommendations, the clerk to the auditor should no longer be required to countersign warrants. The signatures of the auditor and treasurer are sufficient. The auditor is elected by the council, and therefore entirely independent of the administrative departments. It is quite unnecessary for council to appoint a clerk to watch the auditor and even go so far as require him to countersign all of the auditor's warrants.

When revising the procedure so as to simplify and expedite

the auditing process, it should be noted that the auditing offices of the administrative board largely duplicate the work done by the auditor. Such duplication should be eliminated.

Better Certification Needed.

In the process of auditing claims, it is essential that full responsibility should be definitely fixed for the various factors on which the claim is based. The only certificate which is printed on the voucher forms reads as follows: "I certify that the above account is correct." To determine whether this certificate were signed either on the voucher form or on the invoice, a test was made of the vouchers and invoices which had been paid. Such documents were taken at random from the files and showed the following results.

City Home:

The invoices had been rubber stamped with the single word "approved," after which appeared the signature of the steward, superintendent or other employee of the City Home.

The printed certificate on the voucher (above cited) had been rubber stamped with a name. (No title was shown, but it was known to be that of one of the bookkeepers of the administrative board.)

Health Department:

The invoices bore in writing the word "approved" followed by written initials of some one—no title to show whom.

The printed certificate on the voucher had simply been rubber stamped with a name, the same as for the City Home cited above.

Gas Works:

Most of the invoices had simply been rubber stamped with the words "expense" and "thanks." One bore in writing "O K"—"C. F. Pryde."

The vouchers contained the same rubber stamp signature as in the case of the City Home and health department vouchers noted above.

Virginia Hospital:

The invoices had been rubber stamped "material received" and "approved," each followed by the initials of some employee; no title being shown.

Some of the vouchers bore the rubber stamped name and some another. (They were known to be bookkeepers of the administrative board, although no titles were shown on any of the vouchers.)

Electric Plant:

The invoices were rubber stamped "material received" and "amount correct." Some of them also bore "No. 45" with initials of some person; no title being shown.

The vouchers had been rubber stamped "approved" followed by the written signature and title of the superintendent of the plant. The administrative board bookkeeper had also stamped his name thereon.

Police Department:

The invoices contained neither rubber stamp name or initials except that one was marked "O. K." and followed by the signature and title of a captain.

The vouchers bore the signature of either the secretary and purchasing agent of the department or of the mayor.

Fire Department:

The invoices had been rubber stamped "approved" followed by the signature and title of chief engineer.

The vouchers had been rubber stamped "extensions checked, L. H. Jones, Secretary" and also bore the signature and title of chief engineer.

In General:

Each voucher contained a printed statement that the auditor would issue his warrant on the treasurer for the amount shown, etc. and stated that it had been "approved" by the head of the department. This statement was signed by the chairman of the administrative board, or in the case of outside departments, by the head thereof. Such statements, however, have a limited value as certifications of the correctness of the claim.

It is particularly to be noted that even the auditor makes no certification whatever as to the integrity of claims. The only auditor's marks found on either the invoices or vouchers were the rubber stamps, as already noted herein, i. e.,

```
┌──────────────────────────────┐
│      AUDITOR'S OFFICE        │
│  Examined by ..................  │
│              (Name of Clerk)  │
│  (Date) ...................., 1917 │
└──────────────────────────────┘
```

```
┌──────────────────────────────┐
│      AUDITOR'S OFFICE        │
│           PAID               │
│  ...................., 1917   │
│           (Date)             │
│   CITY OF RICHMOND, VA.      │
└──────────────────────────────┘
```

Audit and Payment of Payrolls.

Present procedure.

Only a brief description of the present payroll procedure is here included, because in general it is satisfactory and adequately serves the purpose. Payrolls are all made out in the departments and the original copy is sent to the auditor who checks the extensions, rates, and looks to see that the rolls are signed by the department heads; he also sees to it that they do not exceed the respective unencumbered appropriation balances.

The auditor draws a blanket warrant for the aggregate amount of the roll of each of the departments under the administrative board. The warrant is drawn in favor of "City of Richmond, Payroll Account." The paymaster of the board draws and himself signs a check on the above named account for each employee named on such rolls. He distributes the checks to the places where the employees are at work. Similar blanket warrants are drawn in favor of the heads of the police and fire departments in their official capacities and distributed through their captains and other officers. Individual warrants are drawn for names appearing on the roll for the central offices of the city.

The adoption of the paymaster system for the departments under the administrative board was an excellent move. It tends to minimize the danger of payroll padding and also facilitates payment without a loss of time. It might well be extended to include all departments of the government. If the administrative board is abolished an employee of the treasurer's office should be designated as paymaster.

Certifications.

Aside from the statement on the back of the payroll form to the effect that the auditor of the city of Richmond will issue his warrant on the city treasurer, etc., which is signed by the chairman of the administrative board under the statement "approved by the administrative board," the only certification on the standard payroll form is as follows:

> "I certify the above to be a correct list of men employed during the above specified time.
> (Signed) ....
> (Approved) ....
> Head of Department."

The auditor stated that he relies on the signatures of the heads of the departments as to the correctness of the rolls. An examination of the files showed that some of the street cleaning department rolls were signed only by the clerk in the department. The gas works rolls were made out in lead pencil. Some of the rolls of the general offices of the city and of the administrative board, through oversight, had not been signed at all. As a whole, the certifications are so inadequate that they fail to locate definitely any real responsibility. Considering the fact that by far the largest item of expenditure is for personal services, it is very important that every precaution be taken to establish responsibility for the entire procedure incident to the payment of employees. Every payroll should bear certificates that the time of each employee as set forth on the payroll is supported by certified time reports. There should also be certificates signed by responsible officials relative to other facts of which they have personal information, such as legality of appointment, correctness of rates of compensation, availability of unencumbered funds, etc.

As in the case of the vouchers and invoices already cited herein, neither the auditor nor any of his clerks sign the payrolls of the various departments to show that they have been audited and approved. The auditor states that he personally looks over the rolls after payment before they are filed away, but one of the clerks moves them along to payment. The only marks placed on the rolls by the auditor's office are— ·

```
┌─────────────────────────────────────┐
│          AUDITOR'S OFFICE            │
│  Examined by ...................     │
│                  (Name of Clerk)     │
│  (Date) ...................., 1917   │
│                                      │
└─────────────────────────────────────┘
```

```
┌─────────────────────────────────────┐
│          AUDITOR'S OFFICE            │
│               PAID                   │
│       ...................., 1917     │
│               (Date)                 │
│       CITY OF RICHMOND, VA.          │
└─────────────────────────────────────┘
```

Self-Identifying Check.

Payment of city employees by check is to be commended. To facilitate cashing of the checks by the employees, it is suggested that a form of self-identifying check be adopted similar to that in use in such cities as New York and San Francisco. The travelers' checks issued by the express companies and tourist agencies have the same self-identifying feature. The employee attaches his signature on the face of the check in the presence of the foreman or paymaster at the time the check is issued and as part of the condition thereof. Identification is then merely a matter of endorsing the check in the presence of the payor. Experience has shown that such a check soon becomes generally recognized with the result that they are cashed without any hesitancy and with great convenience to the payees by the banker, grocer, landlord and by the trade in general.

Uncalled-for Checks.

Payroll checks which are uncalled for usually remain in the departments until gathered up by the auditor when he finds that a balance remains in one special payroll account. A rule might well be adopted that if a department is unable to deliver a check to the payee named thereon, it should be returned immediately to the auditor's office. After a certain length of time, it should be cancelled and the amount thereof credited to a "payroll tailings" account. If the payee shows up subsequently, such account would be debited with the payment. Such a plan would enable all payrolls to be cleaned up, all payroll accounts to be closed promptly and keep the entire payroll procedure up to date.

Payment from "Expense" Appropriations.

Some of the departments have been in the habit of using the appropriations for expense purposes to pay salaries of temporary employees. To that extent budget estimates and the annual reports of the auditor have been misleading. Efforts were made when preparing the 1917 budget to stop this practice, but a "joker" inserted in the appropriation ordinance permitted the administrative board to continue such payments as before, although the board had been the worst offender in this respect.

At the time of the survey it was stated that a nurse in the health department and also a clerk in the employment bureau were being paid out of expense appropriations. Such practice should be completely discontinued.

Audit of Revenues.

Too Much "Red Tape" in Payments to Treasurer.

Owing to requirements of section 42 of the charter, it is as difficult to get money into the treasury as it is to get it out. In some respects it seems more difficult. In order that a clear understanding of the situation may be had, it is necessary to quote the entire section.

"All money to be paid into the treasury of the city, except the bills for gas and water, and such other assessments as the city council may so ordain, shall be paid by the person liable to pay the same, or his agent, to the treasurer, in the following manner: A warrant shall first be obtained from the auditor, directing the treasurer to receive the sum to be paid, specifying on what account the payment is to be made. Upon payment of the money to the treasurer he shall give a receipt for the same, which shall be carried to the auditor, and his receipt therefor shall be the acquittance of the party making the payment. Bills for gas and water, and such other assessments as the city council may so ordain, shall be paid directly to the treasurer, who shall keep an account thereof, and make daily reports of such receipts to the auditor."

In the first place it is to be noted that gas and water bills are specifically excepted. That it is unnecessary to continue the complicated procedure in the gas and other revenue collections, is clearly evidenced by the wording of the charter that council may also except such other assessments as in its judgment seems proper. To require a person to go to the auditor before being permitted to make a deposit of money in the city treasury and obtain a receipt is unnecessary and unreasonable. Payments by department heads should be made direct to the treasurer, who should issue a receipt with carbon duplicate, and the depositor should deliver the latter to the auditor as the basis for the latter to use in charging the treasurer and crediting the depositor. As an alternative the charter may be more nearly complied with by first obtaining a warrant from the auditor which shall carry a coupon receipt. Such receipt should be signed by the auditor, but there should be a stipulation on its face that it is not a release until countersigned by the treasurer. Thus the depositor would come to the auditor's office and then to the treasurer. In such case the auditor's charge against the treasurer would be made similarly as are charges for water and gas revenues, etc.

Auditing Control of Accruals and Collections.

Taxes:

The auditor charges the tax collector with the aggregate amount of the tax rolls and credits him with his daily collections as per the report of deposits with the treasurer. The auditor depends on the city accountant to audit the uncollected items at the end of the year and prepare an abstract thereof. It was stated that tests were made to determine whether the collector is holding back money pending final settlement, but this could of course not be verified as to frequency or extent thereof. The penalty for delinquency in payment only attaches once, and hence it is easy to maintain an auditing control. The tax book furnished the auditor by the commissioner of the revenue is separate and distinct from the books furnished the tax collector. It is in fact prepared after the tax collector has received his books. Tests as to the correctness of the extensions and additions should be made in the original books turned over to the tax collector.

Water and Gas:

Auditing control over water and gas bills is satisfactory except as noted in the accounting section of the public utilities chapter of this report.

Licenses and Permits:

Control over the accruals and collection of licenses issued by the city collector is derived from information furnished by the commissioner of revenue. Control over city licenses issued by the treasurer should be obtained by having the auditor charge the treasurer with the blank documents and require him to account for each one. The inspection of licenses is discussed in the chapter on "Commissioner of Revenue."

Permits:

Special attention is called to the procedure incident to the issuing of permits for the sale of milk and food. The applicant must come first to the health department, then to the auditor, then to the treasurer, then the auditor and back to the health department. Similarly for plumbers' licenses, electricians and electrical contractors' licenses. For the latter two the applicant must first go to the electrical department, then to the auditor, then the treasurer, back to the auditor and finally back to the electrical department. This procedure could be simplified without losing any degree of auditing control. It should be done without delay.

Market Rentals:

This class of revenue is controlled through tickets furnished the market superintendent by the auditor similarly as is suggested above for all licenses.

Sales and Miscellaneous Receipts.

Moneys due the city from sales and other miscellaneous sources are billed in triplicate by the departments—one copy going to the debtor, one to the auditor and one retained in the department. The auditor makes his charges against the treasurer from the copy sent him.

Pipe Connections:

To prevent damage to sewer pipes, the city makes the connections and bills the cost to the persons for whom the work is done. Copies of such bills furnish the auditing control.

Fines:

Fines collected in the courts are supposed to be audited by the city accountant by examining the court records. The extent and thoroughness of this audit could not be determined without a separate audit.

Franchises.

These are billed from the auditor's office and supposed to be checked up by the city accountant. The latter states that he does so in so far as time is available.

Interest on Bank Balances:

The auditor checks up the bank statements of interest to insure its accuracy.

Special Assessments:

Bills for special assessments of sidewalks and alleys are prepared by the special assessment clerk and sent to the auditor who lists and checks them and charges them to the city collector.

Auditor as Clerk of Finance Committee.

The existing plan of having the auditor *ex-officio* clerk of the finance committee of council is mutually advantageous. It would be better still if the auditor were made *ex-officio* clerk of council.

Examination of the minutes of the committee's meetings showed that they were neat, orderly and apparently complete.

Auditor as Custodian of Records.

Under the charter the auditor is made custodian of all deeds, mortgages, contracts, judgments, notes, bonds, etc., belonging to the city, except such as are placed in the custody of the city clerk. An examination of the records of the auditor's vault indicated that he exercised much care in filing, and all records are quickly available. Cancelled bonds and coupons are pasted in large scrap books.

Among the records and archives in the office are many large volumes containing copies of the tax valuations and assessments.

These books occupy considerable space and more space is necessary for the use of the lawyers and others who consult them from time to time. The commissioner of revenue has duplicate copies back as far as the Civil War. Records prior to that time in the auditor's office should be transferred to the commissioner of revenue, so that the latter will have a complete file. It would then no longer be necessary for the auditor to keep any of such books. Those who desire to examine them could as conveniently go to the office of the commissioner of revenue as to the auditor. As pointed out elsewhere herein, there is no good reason, except by an unfortunate requirement of the law, why a separate copy of the rolls should be made for the auditor. He should establish the integrity thereof and make his charge against the treasurer from the copy of the rolls delivered to the tax collector.

Management of Sinking Funds.

Sinking Fund Accounts.

An examination of the sinking fund accounts maintained by the auditor showed that much care and attention is given to keeping them up to date. In some respects the method of registration could be simplified, but they are very complete except that the summary accounts of the sinking fund should include a reserve to show the amount which, on an actuarial basis, should be in the sinking funds, and thus make it possible to produce from such summary accounts a complete sinking fund balance sheet.

Classes of Bonds.

The bonded indebtedness of the city of Richmond consists of two classes of bonds:

1—Those bonds which were issued by the city for city purposes.

2—Those bonds which were issued by various adjacent towns and other civil divisions, and which are now a part of the city debt through the annexation of such adjacent tertories.

The total of such bonded indebtedness outstanding January 31, 1917, as shown by the city auditor's report, is $17,048,055.

Sinking Fund Policy.

The major portion of the sinking funds of the city of Richmond are invested in the bonds of the city. The interest obtained on the sinking fund holdings is slightly in excess of 4 per cent. annually. Since the funds receive interest on the holdings semi-annually the basis for all calculations used by the city auditor and also the basis used in calculating the accompanying tables is 2 per cent. semi-annually.

Three sinking funds have been established for the redemption of the following classes of bonds:

1—$500,000 special street improvement bonds issued July, 1914.

2—$2,000,000 series (M) issued January, 1916.

3—All other city and annexed territory bonds.

In general it has been the policy of the sinking fund commission to set aside semi-annually 75 cents per each $100 of outstanding bonds. There are some exceptions to this rule, however. The annexed territory bonds assumed by the city had practically no sinking funds at the time of the assumption of the debt. These bonds matured at various dates. and in order to provide adequate sinking funds on an annuity basis, the sinking fund commission set aside arbitrary amounts, which in most instances have produced surpluses over the amount which should be in the sinking fund at the present time on an annuity basis. In the case of the special street improvement issue of $500,000 in July, 1914, the ordinance authorizing the issuing of such bonds provided that $22,832 should be set aside each January and July until the $250.000 maturing in July, 1920, had been paid off. after which time $50,000 should be set aside. This method will produce a considerable surplus in that particlar fund after the last $50,000 has been paid off in July, 1925.

The sinking fund commission has decided upon a policy of setting aside each January and July 75 cents per each $100 on bonds outstanding on such dates, except that no definite policy with respect to the annexed territory bonds has been determined upon.

The result of setting aside the above mentioned 75 cents per each $100. assuming that such policy will be uniformly followed · in respect to all outstanding bonds of both the city and the annex-ed territories except the special street improvement issue, which is covered by ordinance, is shown in the tables which have been prepared as a part of this survey and are included herewith.

Result of Existing Policy.

The result of the above mentioned policy with respect to outstanding bonds will be that the existing sinking fund holdings of

$4,018,276 on **January 31, 1917**, together with the setting aside of 75 cents per each $100 of bonds outstanding each subsequent January and July (with the exception of the special street improvement issue) will produce an amount sufficient to redeem all outstanding bonds at their respective dates of maturity, with the exception of the $2,000,000 maturing January, 1950, which, if redeemed from the sinking fund will produce a deficit of $266,549. All other bonds maturing prior to 1950 can be redeemed, and in January, 1950, there will be $1,733,451 available for the redemption of the $2,000,000 issue.

In order to produce an amount sufficient to amortize the deficiency of $266,549 which will otherwise exist in 1950, it will be necessary to set aside semi-annually, beginning July, 1917, the sum of $1,978.12.

Inasmuch as the July, 1917, period has already passed it will be necessary to base the calculation on sixty-five periods instead of sixty-six, which will necessitate the setting aside of $2,032.77.

Inasmuch as the annexed territory bonds were assumed by the city without any sinking funds, and because the sinking fund policy was only inaugurated at a comparatively recent date, the officials responsible for the administration of the sinking funds are deserving of commendation.

SINKING FUND TABLE

MATURITY DATES	Amount of Bonds Maturing	Amount of Bonds outstanding as of the dates opposite thereto and maturing the same date have been paid. (†)	Amount of Remi-annual Installments, based on 46c. per $100 Outstanding, (Installments to special improvement bond sinking funds are shown separately with a *)	Amount of Sinking Fund Holdings as at dates above, after redemption of bonds maturing as of same date. (x)	Amount Produced by the Investment of Sinking Fund Holding up to and including the period at the end of which the bonds mature.	Total Amount Available for Redemption of Bonds at the dates of maturity.
1917—January		500 000 00		$ 4,018 276 00	$	$
July		16,548 055 00	$ 22,832 00* / $1 10 00	4,245,594 00	4,098 642 00	4,245 594 00
1918—January			22,882 00* / 124,110 00	4,477,438 00	4,330,496 00	4,477,438 00
July		500,000 00	$ 2 00* / 12, 110 00	4,713,928 00	4,566 986 00	4,713,928 00
December	960,000 00	16,498,055 00		4,663,928 00	4,713,928 00	4,713,925 00
1919—January			22,832 00* / 123,680 00	4,853 498 00	4,747,006 00	4,898 498 00
July			22,832 00* / 123,680 00	5,137,860 00	4,991 868 00	5,137,86J 00
1920—January	106,500 00	500,000 00	123,680 00* / 123,680 00	5,280,610 00	5,240,618 00	5,387,110 00
July	435,000 00	14,381,555 00	123,680 00* / 123,680 00	5,106,9,6 00	5,888,222 00	5,531,916 00
1921—January	200,000 00	250 000 00	122,832 00* / 122,882 00	5,128,728 00	5,209,054 00	5,328,728 00
July	908,250 00	15,250,055 00 / 15,706,555 00	119,674 00	5,096,227 00	5 231,303 00	5,399,477 00
1922—January	946,000 00	15,920,900 00 / 15,463,905 00	50 000 00* / 118 174 00	5,168,062 00	5,198,152 00	5,314 052 00
July	490,625 00	15,307,805 00	115 900 00	4,955,868 00	5,271,413 00	5,446 218 00
1923—January	247,000 00	15,140,700 00 / 14,818,780 00	50,000 00* / 114,905 00	4,918,933 00	5,054,807 00	5,165 938 00
July	122,500 00	14,569,780 00 / 100 000 00	111,125 00	5,074,085 00	5,017 312 00	5,176 585 00
October	1,000 00	14,468,280 00	50,000 00* / 109 273 00	5,073,085 00	5,074,085 00	5,074,085 00

Date						
1924—January	150,000,000 00	100,000,000 00	108,497 00	5,188,044 0	5,174,547 00	5,325,044 00
July	852,500,000 00	14,316,280 00 / 50,000,000 00 / 13,735,780 00	50,000,000 00 / 107,577 00 / 103,613 00	4,810,577 00	5,238,705 00	5,308,077 00
1925—January	94,650,000 00	13,639,130 00	50,000 00 / 107,577 00	4,915,142 00	4,906,789 00	5,009,799 00
July	225,650,000 00	18,913,680 00	103,613 00	4,940,168 00	5,013,446 00	5,165,788 00
1926—January	489,450,000 00	18,474,130 00	50,000 00 / 102,598 00	4,703,894 00	5,088,992 00	5,143,844 00
July	140,000,000 00	18,834,130 00	104,362 00 / 101,063 00	4,769,028 00	4,707,972 00	4,999,028 00
1927—January	18,000,000 00	18,821,130 00	100,006 00	4,941,215 00	4,854,209 00	4,954,215 00
July	200,000,000 00	13,121,130 00	99,906 00	4,989,947 00	5,040,039 00	5,139,947 00
1928—January	280,000,000 00	12,861,180 00	98,408 00	4,877,154 00	5,088,746 00	5,157,154 00
July			96,456 00	5,071,155 00	4,974,697 00	5,071,155 00
1929—January	496,500,000 00	62,364,680 00	96,656 00	4,778,636 00	5,172,578 00	5,289,098 00
July	150,000,000 00	12,214,680 00	92,735 00	4,810,722 00	4,867,957 00	4,960,722 00
1930—January	81,000,000 00	12,168,680 00	91,610 00	4,987,546 00	4,900,986 00	4,998,546 00
July	120,000,000 00	12,063,680 00	91,377 00	5,088,274 00	5,068,997 00	5,168,274 00
1931—January			90,477 00	5,229,516 00	5,139,089 00	5,229,516 00
July			90,477 00	5,424,583 00	5,334,106 00	5,424,583 00
1932—January			90,477 00	5,623,552 00	5,533,075 00	5,623,552 00
July			90,477 00	5,826,500 00	5,736,023 00	5,826,500 00
1933—January	5,000,000 00	12,048,680 00	90,477 00	6,083,508 00	5,943,031 00	6,083,508 00
February	10,000,000 00			6,018,508 00	6,029,506 00	6,029,508 00
July			90,365 00	6,229,243 00	6,138,878 00	6,229,243 00
1934—January			90,365 00	6,144,198 00	6,353,898 00	6,444,198 00
July	35,000,000 00	12,013,680 00	90,365 00	6,683,442 00	6,573,077 00	6,688,442 00
September				6,029,442 00	6,663,442 00	6,663,442 00
1935—January	15,000,000 00	11,988,680 00	90,102 00	6,861,113 00	6,761,011 00	6,761,011 00
April	60,000,000 00			6,886,113 00	6,861,113 00	6,861,113 00
May				6,776,113 00	6,836,113 00	6,886,113 00
July			89,540 00	7,001,175 00	6,911,636 00	7,001,175 00
1936—January	30,530,000 00	11,968,100 00	89,540 00	7,200,209 00	7,141,199 00	7,230,789 00
May	15,000,000 00			7,185,209 00	7,200,209 00	7,200,209 00
July	15,000,000 00	11,868,100 00	89,196 00	7,408,111 00	7,328,913 00	7,418,111 00
September	10,000,000 00			7,368,111 00	7,408,111 00	7,408,111 00
1937—January			84,011 00	7,629,984 00	7,540,973 00	7,629,984 00
July			89,011 00	7,871,695 00	7,782,684 00	7,871,695 00

SINKING FUND TABLE—Continued.

174

MATURITY DATES	Amount of Bonds Maturing	Amount of Bonds Outstanding as of the Dates Opposite After the Amounts Maturing the Same Date Have Been Paid (†)	Amount of Semi-Annual installment, Based on 75c per $100 Outstanding, (Installment to special improvement street bond sinking funds are shown separately with a *)	Amount of Sinking Fund Holdings as of Dates Shown, After Redemption of Bonds Maturing as of Same Date (x)	Amount Produced by the Investment of Sinking Fund Holdings Up to and including the Period at the end of Which the Bonds Mature	Total Amount Available for Redemption of Bonds at the Dates of Maturity
1938—January	$ 699,000 00	$ 11 269,100 00	$ 80,011 00	$ 7,519,088 00	$ 8,029 027 00	$ 8,118 088 00
	334,600 00	10 934,500 00	84,518 00	7,419,387 00	7,689 419 00	7,753,987 00
1939—January	82,400 00		88,009 00	7,567 383 00	7,567,724 00	7 649 723 00
March	15,000 00	10,887 100 00		7,552 383 00	7,567,833 00	7,567 833 00
July	166,000 00	10,671,100 00	81,278 00	7,618,658 00	7,618,658 00	7,794,658 00
1940—January	304,000 00	10 887,100 00	80 038 00	7 647,064 00	7,771 081 00	7,851 084 00
July	632,500 00	9 734,600 00	77 783 00	7 143,258 00	7,696 005 00	7,775,758 00
1941—January	957,500 00	8 772,100 00	73,00 00	6,401 683 00	7,296,123 00	7,369,138 00
May	15,000 00			6,386,683 00	6,401,683 00	6,401,683 00
June	66,000 00			6,386,683 00	6,386,683 00	6,386,683 00
July	639,500 00	8,162,500 00	65 341 00	5 989,407 00	6 483,766 00	6,029 707 00
December	10,000 00			5,973,407 00	5,989,407 00	5,989,407 00
1942—January	380,000 00	7,802,800 00	61,221 00	5 800,216 00	6 060,996 00	6,160,216 00
July	289,500 00	7 513,300 00	64,521 00	5,685 241 00	5,916 220 00	5,974,741 00
1943—January	267,300 00	7,198,000 00	56 550 00	5 567,996 00	5 708 946 00	5,565 296 00
June	50,000 00			5,537,996 00	5,537,996 00	5,5 7 996 00
July	1 500 00	6,696 000 00	53,970 00	4 209,728 00	5,048,756 00	5 702,728 00
1944—January	85,000 00	5,611 000 00	42,720 00	4 329,501 00	4,266,781 00	4,329,501 00
July	66,000 00	5,566,000 00	42 088 00	4,244,501 00	4,359 601 00	4,359 601 00
				4 316 474 00	4,329,391 00	4,371,474 00
1945—January			41 670 00	4,444 473 00	4 402,808 00	4,444,4 3 00
July	1 400,000 00	4,166,000 00	41,670 00	3,115 082 00	4,583,368 00	4,575,082 00
1946—January			31,170 00	3 269,708 00	3,289,638 00	3,289 708 00
July			31,170 00	3,386 097 00	3,386 097 00	3,386,097 00

187 —January	....	....	$1,170 00	3,464 782 00	3,439 592 00	3,464 782 00
July	....	....	$1,170 00	3,085 227 00	3,434,067 00	3,085 227 00
1948—January	....	2,866 000 00	$1,170 00	2,167,702 00	8,696 532 00	3,667,702 00
July	....	....	19 920 00	2 230,976 00	2 211 056 00	2 230 976 00
December	125,000 00	....	....	2,100,976 00	2,230,976 00	2 230,976 00
1949—January	631,000 00	2 000,000 00	19,920 00	1 687,016 00	2 148 096 00	2 168,016 00
July	....	....	15,000 00	1,96	1,669,756 00	1 664,756 00
1950—January	2,000 000 00	....	15,000 00	266,549 00‡	1,718,541 00	1 738 461 00
Total	$190					

† Where bonds mature in any other month than January or July, they are considered as maturing the previous January or July.

x Where bonds mature in any other month than January or July, it is assumed that the sinking fund will not earn any interest for the fractional part of a period.

‡ Deficit arising after the payment of the $2,000,000 due January, 1950.

City Accountant

CITY ACCOUNTANT.

Present Duties.

The city accountant is under the direct control of the finance committee of the city council, and has a separate office in the city hall. His duties are more in the nature of auditing than accounting, i. e., he is really a special auditor or outside auditor supplementing the audits of the city auditor's office. For example, it was stated that he checks up the franchise payments of the local utility companies. Also the books of the tax collector, the delinquent tax collector and the treasurer with respect to the correctness of the amounts collected and deposited in the treasury. Similarly, it was stated that he checks up the financial transactions of the markets, cemeteries, dog pound, etc. His methods as described seem satisfactory, but there was little in the office to show the work actually done. The city accountant should maintain a register or day book in the form of a diary showing the work he is engaged upon from day to day. Moreover, his working papers and reports should be filed in a more systematic manner so as to facilitate reference.

It was stated that the city accountant also does extra work for the finance committee, prepares answers for inquiries which come to the mayor, etc.

Inquiry as to whether he makes any inspection or audit to determine whether deliveries of supplies, materials, etc., conform to the quantities and amounts shown on the invoices of the various departments reveal that no such independent inspection is made by the auditor's office or administrative board. The city accountant stated that he had attempted it a few times but had no basis for checking nor time to do the work systematically.

Realignment of Duties.

In the revised charter a position carrying duties similar to those of the city accountant should be continued, but it should either be called city auditor or merged in the office of the city auditor. The title and duties of the present city auditor's office should be divided so as to place the accounting and bookkeeping functions under an appointee of the mayor, and all auditing functions under an appointee of the city council (see plans 1, 2 and 3 in chapter "organization of the government.")

Special Assessment Clerk.

The employee known as the special assessment clerk is also appointed by the finance committee, but works under the joint supervision of the administrative board, city engineer and city accountant. His principal duty is preparing bills for special assessments and for sewer connections on data furnished him by the city engineer's office. He is also stenographer and typist for the city accountant. The present economical arrangement for the services of this employee is commendable, but in re-arranging the government he should not be an appointee of the finance committee because his duties are essentially administrative in character. He should be attached either to the department of engineering or to the central accounting office.

City Clerk, Clerk of Committees and Sergeant-at-Arms

CITY CLERK, CLERK OF COMMITTEES AND SER-GEANT-AT-ARMS.

These three officials are each appointed by the city council for a term of two years; their salaries are $3,000, $2,400 and $2,000, respectively. Each has a separate office—the city clerk's office comprising two rooms.

A careful examination was made of all the duties and work of the city clerk. His records are neatly prepared, in order, and seem to be complete. The entire office gives the impression of being well-administered, but it is obvious that the requirements are very light. There is not enough work to keep one energetic person busy, although the clerk employs an assistant at $600 a year, who writes up certain records for him. She is not a stenographer and hence the mayor's secretary is called upon once a month to typewrite copies of certain ordinances and resolutions which must be sent to the various departments. The present incumbent has been in office many years. He is in poor health and should be retired with a pension. His duties could easily be taken over by the clerk of committees with a resulting saving of about $2,600.

```
City clerk ..................................$ 3,000
Assistant ..................................    600
                                             --------
                                             $ 3,600
Less pension of, say, ......................$ 1,000
                                             --------
                                             $ 2,600
```

The clerk of committees typewrites the minutes of his committees in loose-leaf form and then binds them. He could do the same with the ordinances, resolutions and the minutes of the aldermen and council which the city clerk now writes laboriously in longhand. The typewriter method is quicker and produces a neater and more legible record. The clerk of committees also has been in office many years. He is clerk of all standing committees except the finance committee and is thoroughly conversant with the duties of both his own and the city clerk's office. He is required to be on hand when meetings are held at night as well as during the day but has plenty of time available to do the work of the city clerk's office.

The duties of the sergeant-at-arms are similar to those usually accompanying that office in any city. He is sergeant and messenger to both branches of council and all committees; also messenger to the city clerk. There is no need for assigning him a separate office. His desk should be located in the city clerk's office. Thus, in addition to the saving in salaries above mentioned, a consolidation of these three offices would make available for other uses the two rooms now occupied by the clerk of committees and the sergesant-at-arms. Such an arrangement would not necessarily reduce the number of rooms available for committees. If the regular committee room does not suffice at any time for committee meetings, any of the rooms adjoining the council chamber could be used for the hour or two in the evening that committees are in session.

As has been pointed out elsewhere herein, the auditor could, with advantage, take over the entire office of the city clerk, including the clerk of committees and sergeant (see "the mayor and small council plan" in chapter on "Organization of the Government"). It would mean no saving in salaries because the clerk and sergeant would simply be transferred to the auditor's staff but the consolidation would tend to facilitate and expedite the transaction of much of the business of these various offices and the city council. It would also be more convenient for the public.

In this connection it is recommended that the office should also function as a bureau of information. Citizens may be observed daily wandering about the corridors of the city hall or going hesitatingly into various offices seeking information. There should be a central office or desk on the first floor of the city hall known as the information office or information desk. It should be prominently marked by a sign at the door and in the general directory. There is no better location for such a desk than in the consolidated office of the city auditor and clerk of council because a large proportion of the business concerning which information is sought clears through these offices.

Commissioner of the Revenue and Real Estate Assessors

COMMISSIONER OF THE REVENUE AND REAL ESTATE ASSESSORS.

Office On a Fee Basis.

The commissioner of revenue is allowed by law 1-2 of 1 per cent. on the amount of the city's taxes and 1 per cent. on the state taxes, including income tax. He gets 75 cents for each state merchant's license. Also $1 for each piece of realty transferred as evidenced by the deeds, etc., recorded, although of this latter amount he gives the clerk of the Hustings Court 10 per cent. commission for collecting it for him. From the receipts of his office he pays his employees and incidental expenses. Recent state legislation (1914, amended 1916) requires the head of this office, beginning at the expiration of the term of the present incumbent, to keep a record of all earnings of the office from every source, and after deducting his own salary of not to exceed $6,500, and after paying the other salaries and expenses of the office, to pay the balance of the earnings into the state treasury. The city pays about $16,000 a year to this office on the basis of the 1-2 of 1 per cent. above cited. Whether the new law should be amended so as to return a percentage of the excess earnings to the city instead of covering them all into the state treasury is doubtful. There are good arguments both for and against such a plan.

Real Estate Assessors.

Section 171 of the constitution states that the general assembly "shall provide for a re-assesment of real estate every fifth year."

Section 437 of the Virginia state code (as amended by act approved February 28, 1910) provides that "the corporation or Hustings Courts of the cities * * * every fifth year to appoint proper persons to assess the value of all lands and lots, together with improvements thereon within their respective jurisdiction." It provides that in the city of Richmond there shall be three such assessors.

The last re-assessment under the above laws was in 1915 and became effective in 1916. Of the three men appointed to make the assessment, two were in the real estate business and one was a contractor. Instead of each assessor covering a certain district of the city, it was stated that in assessing all three traveled about the city together; also that they used no scientific basis of assessment such as has been adopted in many cities. Being of mushroom growth every fifth year, there can be no assurance under the present plan that the assessors will possess the right qualifications. The plan of appointing real estate dealers and a contractor has but limited merit and affords little assurance that the men will be qualified as assessors. Hence it is all the more important that definite factors of land value be agreed upon and scientific rules and tables used.

Very few men know how to assess land and improvements. In a city the size of Richmond such assessments should be continuous throughout the year and from year to year. Values are constantly shifting and should be immediately reflected on the assessment rolls. The experience which an assessor gains should be capitalized by the community instead of being discarded each fifth year.

It is to be noted that the constitution does not require the appointment of special assessors. It is believed that it would be entirely within the constitutional requirements for the general assembly to authorize the commissioner of revenue to make the reassessment each fifth year. That official is much better informed as to local values than is possible for any new appointees. Moreover, each fifth year finds the commissioner of revenue already supplied with men, maps and other equipment required for the work. Not only is he in position to do the work better, but there would no doubt be a financial saving. The salary cost alone of the three special assessors is $2,250. Such change of course necessitates revision of the state law herein cited, but the change would be beneficial for all Virginia municipalities alike. Those cities throughout the country which have made the most progress in property assessment have accomplished their result only after realizing the necessity of carefully selecting their assessors and retaining them in office so long as they render satisfactory service. The experience of the assessors has become a constantly increasing asset in such communities. The sooner this is done in Virginia the sooner true and equitable valuations will be obtained in the state.

Assessment of Buildings.

Supplementing the quinquennial assessment of all real estate, the commissioner of revenue each year, about November or De-

cember, revises the assessment of buildings. He takes with him
the notices which he has obtained from the building department
showing new buildings and alterations and additions in old buildings. These slips show the building department's estimate of the
value of new building or improvement and serve him as a guide
in determining the value to be assessed. He notes his appraise-
ment on the slips.

Just as in the quinquennial assessment of all real estate so in
this annual assessment of buildings, no scientific classifications or
tables are used. The commissioner stated that he aimed to deduct
from the cost of buildings the amount of the contractor's profit.
He estimated that property was assessed on about an 80 per
cent. basis, both in the quinquennial assessment and the ad interim
assessments. Just as the adoption of the Hoffman-Neill or other
similar tables would greatly assist in properly assessing land, so
also would the classification of buildings, according to the character of their construction (brick, stone, frame, etc.) and their
size. Such a classification should of course be supplemented by
definite factor values on a square foot area basis and a scale of
depreciation.

Basis of Assessing Real Estate.

The constitution (section 169) requires that all real estate
shall be assessed at its "fair market value." As cited above, it is
estimated that the average basis in Richmond is about 80 per
cent. The recent state legislation which almost provided for segregation of revenue sources as between the state and local committees,
has removed, to some extent, the arguments against assessing property at its market value. It is unfortunate that the state retained the 10 cents general property tax for school purposes, because to that extent it departed from the principle of segregation
and destroyed the full advantage otherwise obtainable therefrom.
The nearer the assessment of all property in Richmond approaches
full value. the less inequity there will be as between the valuations
of individual properties.

Assessment of Personal Property.

The commissioner of revenue stated that in assessing personal
property he sends two or three of his employees into each ward
with the blank "return" forms as soon as they are received from

the state printer. He should obtain these forms in February, but he did not receive them until May in 1917. A copy of the form is left at each house, the occupant thereof being required to fill it out and send or bring it to the commissioner's office where it is copied in the personal property tax roll.

Assessment of Poll Taxes.

The law requires that each male over twenty-one years shall pay a 50 cent poll tax to the city and a $1.50 poll tax to the state each year. Of the latter tax 50 cents is to be returned to the city for school purposes. Only the state poll tax is a prerequisite to voting and a lien on real estate. The 50 cent city tax should be abolished because it does not yield enough revenue over and above the cost of collecting to justify its continuance.

Assessment of Licenses.

Merchants' Licenses:

Each May the representatives of the commissioner of revenue canvass the city for licensable places. They leave at each place one of the state blanks which must be returned to the commissioner who uses them as a basis for making out both the state license and the city license lists. The former are delivered to the city treasurer for collection and the latter to the city tax collector. Both are payable in May. The requiring of the merchants of Richmond to pay two licenses borders on an abuse of the license authority. The adoption by the commissioner of a single return helps somewhat in that it reduces the amount of work involved and hence the cost. (This is also true of the practice of having a single return on personal property).

The revenue law which was responsible for the dual licensing system should be revised. The commissioner stated that from time to time throughout the year he sends his men out to discover additional licensable places. Such license inspection should be made by the police department in the course of the patrolmen's regular duties. Proper co-operation between these two branches of the government should eliminate all need for license inspection in the office of the commissioner of revenue. The only inspection other than that of the police department should come from the auditor's office. The present plan provides that the mayor will assign two police officers as inspectors of licenses. There would be less liability of collusion between the inspector and the licensee if on certain designated days during the year every patrolman on duty were required to report all licensable places on his post.

General Licenses:

At the time of the survey the commissioner had not yet been able to prepare his list of general licenses for the city tax collector. He stated that next year he proposes to list both kinds of licenses at the same time in the spring when his men canvass the city. Both kinds of licenses expire April 30th.

Preparation of Tax Books.

Credit is due to the commissioner of revenue for steps already taken in simplifying the elaborate and wasteful method of preparing tax records. This work is not yet completed. It should be carried to its logical conclusion and hence a description of certain methods and recommendations for improvement are here set forth. Taking the 1918 books for purposes of illustration, the commissioner described the proposed procedure as follows:

Real Estate:

With the 1917 real estate book as a guide he will begin early in the fall of 1917 to prepare his 1918 "office book." It will all be copied in longhand after which, by reference to the slips received from the building department and containing his own notations of new building valuations, etc., and by reference to cards showing transfers of ownership, he will draw lines through the items affected and interline the revised figures. He will not extend the amount of the tax in this book. With the office book as a guide the commissioner will copy a book for the tax collector to use in making collections. In this latter book the commissioner will extend the taxes and total the amount thereof before turning it over to the collector. He plans to begin delivering these books to the collector in March so that the latter will have sufficient time in which to prepare his tax bills before they become due.

With the same office book as a guide, the commissioner will then proceed to write four copies of the state book. This is now done by carbon process on a long carrier typewriter. One copy is made for the city treasurer (as state tax collector), one copy for the clerk of the Hustings Court, one for the State auditor, and one for the commissioner to retain in his own office.

Having completed the above work, the commissioner will borrow the books which he has previously furnished to the tax collector and from them make a copy for the city auditor although the auditor should already have made his charge against the city collector for the aggregate amount of the taxes because meanwhile the collector has been collecting.

The following comments on these methods of writing the real estate books should be of interest. In the first place it is noted that altogether too many copies of the books are prepared. It is doubtful if the persons who are responsible for the law were aware of the amount of work involved. Therefore, the first change which should be made in the law is a reduction in the number of copies. Pending such action it should be possible to so design the state and city rolls that six copies of the assessed valuations could be made at a single writing by carbon process. In any event the city tax bill and the city rolls should be so designed that at the time the four copies of the roll are made on the typewriter. the tax bill would be prepared at the same writing. Several cities prepare duplicate tax rolls and tax bills in this manner by the use of specially designed machines which two or three typewriter manufacturers have placed on the market. Such a method of preparing the tax bills would not only save money but would insure accuracy. Similarly, it should be possible so to design the state tax bill and tax roll that they could be prepared at a single writing when the latter is made from the commissioner's office book.

The city auditor has suggested that in preparing the city rolls each five year period, five extra columns should be allowed in which to fill in from year to year the revised value of buildings and improvements. Inasmuch as land is only assessed every five years. its valuation would need to be written in the books only at that time and the use of extra columns for buildings would obviate the necessity of rewriting the entire roll each year.

Whatever method is finally decided upon, it is obvious that the present system can be greatly simplified, the work thereby expedited and the cost reduced.

Personal Property:

When distributing the personal property "return" forms, each representative of the commissioner of revenue carriers a bound book about 10x16 inches in size. Each book is tabbed alphabetically and is complete in itself, but there are two or more books for each ward, i. e., each man on the canvass has a separate book. As the blanks are distributed, the names, addresses, etc., of the persons with whom they are left are inserted in the books. Subsequently in the office, when the returns come in, the data thereon is also copied into the books. There are 45 lines on a page and the names are not vowelized, because they are entered in sequence as the canvasser goes from house to house along the street. With these field books as a guide other bound books are then prepared for use of the city collector in preparing his tax bills and in these latter books the amount of the tax is extended and added. As in the case of the field books, there are two or more for each ward and the entries are not vowelized. Each book contains names from A to Z and hence when a persons comes to the collector's office to pay his taxes, the collector does not know in which book the property is listed even though he knows the ward. Moreover, these books contain no column for use of the collector in posting the amounts collected. It, therefore, becomes necessary for the latter official just as soon as he receives the books from the commissioner of revenue to copy the entire contents thereof into another set of books which will facilitite reference in posting and provide the necessary columns therefor.

This wasteful practice should not be continued. The commissioner of revenue when preparing the collector's books should have the latter so designed that it will meet the needs of the collector without copying the entire contents. In this connection it is to be noted that formerly the collector also was compelled to copy the entire contents of the real estate books turned over to him by the commissioner of revenue, because they did not conform to his needs. But with respect to 1917 real estate books the commissioner has adopted a revised form which obviates the necessity of copying. The same spirit of co-operation should be continued in preparing the personal property books.

If the commissioner's office book of personal property were better arranged by wards, vowelized, etc., it would be a simple matter to prepare the kind of a record needed by the collector. It is suggested that this might easily be accomplished if the field men, instead of carrying the present form of bound books, were to use cards in loose-leaf aluminum or leather binders. Then after the field men had distributed their return forms and entered the names and addresses on the cards, the latter could be assembled in the office for each ward, properly vowelized, etc., before being copied into the office book. Such a set of cards might, in fact, be used in lieu of the office book, or if desired, the office book and the collector's book might be prepared from the cards by type-writer carbon process at a single writing. In any event there is need for correcting the present defects in the system and the remedy is comparatively easy.

Having prepared the collector's book of personal property, the commissioner with his office book again as a guide, proceeds to write up his state book of personal property. The form used for this latter purpose is very cumbersome and could be much simplified. The personal property book of the city has been greatly cut down, as compared with the office book and with the form used by. the state. The commissioner hopes to be able to secure support in also simplifying the state book.

Property and Polls of Colored.

Elsewhere in this report reference is made to the obligation of the city to provide better sanitary and living conditions for its colored population. In this connection it is naturally of interest to know what percentage of property is owned by the colored people and what percentage of taxes they pay. The following figures were therefore obtained:

Real Estate:

	Valuation.	Per Cent.
White	$ 117,030.740	.977
Colored	2,817,741	.023
	$ 119,848,481	1.000

Personal Property:

	Valuation.	Per Cent.
White	$ 7,429.011	.938
Colored	490,860*	.062
	$ 7,919,871**	1.000

Polls Assessed:

	Valuation.	Per Cent.
White	$ 26,354	.71
Colored	10,877	.29
	$ 37,231	1.00

It is impossible without a great deal of analysis work to show the amount of colored polls collected or even the total polls collected because the amounts thereof are included in the personal tax collection.

---

*Exclusive of $10,760 for intangibles.
**Exclusive of polls.

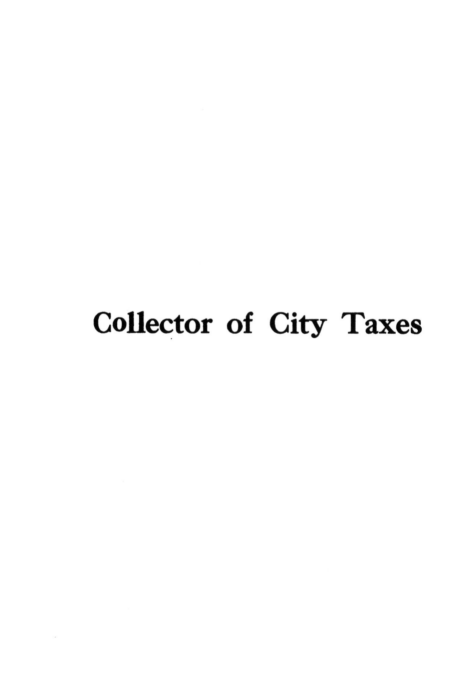

Collector of City Taxes

COLLECTOR OF CITY TAXES.

Duties.

The collector of city taxes is charged with the collection of the city taxes, merchants' licenses and "regular" licenses (such as restaurants, real estate offices, lawyers, etc.) which accrue to the city and also with the collection of bills for sewer pipe connections and pavement cuts.

Organization.

The office is organized with the following staff:

City collector	$ 3,600
Deputy city collector	1,800
1 Assistant city collector	1,500
1 Assistant city collector, Southside.........	1,020
2 Clerks at $1,020 each.....................	2,040
	$ 9,960

Office Should Be Abolished.

The charter section which provides for establishing and maintaining the collector's office includes the following clause:

> "Provided, however, that the council of the city of Richmond may, if they deem proper so to do, abolish said office of collector of city taxes and confer the power and duties imposed upon said collector upon the treasurer of the city of Richmond * * *."

Effective organization in a city government should not include both a city treasurer's office and a city collector's office. Either one or the other is sufficient. If there is to be a treasurer's office then it should be charged with the collection of all city revenues. If one of the local banking institutions is to be made the official custodian of the city's funds in lieu of a separate treasury office in the city hall, then naturally a collector's office must be provided.

In the city of Richmond, part of the city's revenues are collected by the treasurer, part by the city tax collector and practically every other department of the government participates in collecting the rest.

Taxpayers are accustomed to going to the treasurer's office to pay their state taxes, their water and gas bills and also certain license fees. Therefore, it would be equally convenient for them to pay all of their taxes, licenses, etc., directly to the treasurer. Moreover, the plant, equipment and staff already provided by the treasurer would not need much enlargement to include also the collection of those revenues now delegated to the city collector. Even assuming that the treasurer's staff were increased by three clerks, there would still be a saving of approximately half the payroll of the collector's office or approximately $5,000 per year. Such a consolidation would be in direct line with the desired simplification of the government and would make one less elective office.

In making this recommendation for the abolition of the collector's office not the slightest reflection is intended on the present collector or his staff. On the other hand there was evidence of a conscientious desire to administer the office efficiently.

Quite aside from the abolishment of the entire office, attention is called to the wasteful policy of the city in maintaining a branch collection office on the south side of the river. An employee at a salary of $1,020 is stationed there throughout the year. The rental of this branch office for the employees of the collector and treasurer is $600 per year.

Prebilling and Advertising.

The collector wisely follows the plan of making out the tax bills in advance of the date when taxes become due. This is of much assistance to the office, but its principal advantage is the convenience afforded to the taxpayers in that they are not compelled to wait in line in the collection office while tax bills are being prepared. Several cities prepare the tax bills in duplicate or triplicate on typewriters by carbon process. In Richmond the bills are written in longhand with fountain pens. Although no definite cost records have been maintained relative to the preparation of these bills, the statement of staff members relative to the average number they write per day indicates that the cost is not much above what would be required by the typewriter process. However, as the city grows and the number of tax bills increases, it will no doubt be found cheaper and more convenient to use the mechanical process. It is probable that the bills could be so designed that they could be written automatically in the assessing office at the time the collector's tax books are prepared without any extra cost. (See chapter on Commissioner of Revenue).

Real estate taxes are payable in two installments. Bills for both installments are made out at the same writing. Those for the first installment are not mailed but simply filed by wards, alphabetically and vowelly and placed in wall cabinets for convenient access when called for by the taxpayers. For all properties on which taxes are not paid by July 1st, postal card notices are mailed. The tax bills are never sent out as they are in other cities, the reason given being that the Richmond tax rate has been practically stationary and hence the information shown on the tax bills does not vary greatly from year to year.

The collector uses the local newspapers to inform the people as to the dates when taxes are due, and also to urge them to request their tax bills in advance of the final dates and to make their payments by check through the mails. This is an excellent plan because it simplifies the clerical work by preventing a congestion thereof during the last few days prior to the date when the penalty becomes effective, and obviates the necessity of taxpayers coming to the city hall.

Copying Personal Property Books.

As explained in the chapter of this report on the "commissioner of revenue," the collector is still under the necessity of transcribing all of the entries contained in the personal property books turned over to him by the revenue office. The collector realizes that this work could be eliminated if a properly designed book were used originally by the revenue office. Extra effort should be made to that end and thereby reduce the amount of clerical work in the collector's office.

Method of Posting Tax Collections.

When the first installment of the real estate tax is paid, the collector makes his credit posting from the carbon copy of the bill which remains in the office, the original copy being given the taxpayer as a receipt. Although this carbon copy is in fact the bill for the second installment, the amounts are the same as shown on the bill for the first half and hence can safely be used as a

posting medium. The entries are first made in the cash book
and show bill number, name, ward and amount. From the cash
book postings are made to the proper lines in the tax roll so
as to show opposite each assessment the amount actually paid.
There would be less liability to error if postings were made direct
to the tax roll, and the cash proved and summary postings made
in the cash book from lists of bills paid. However, the present
form of bill provides no coupon or extra carbon which can be
retained in the office in support of such a list. After the first
installment is paid all that remains is the bill for the second installment and after the latter is paid, nothing remains as a posting medium. In revising the form of tax bill, this situation should
receive due consideration. It applies not only to real estate tax
bills, but also to the bills for personal property. The latter are
payable in a single installment and neither carbon nor coupon is
prepared.

Accounting Control Over Taxes.

Neither the city auditor nor the collector maintains an accounting control over real estate taxes, and personal taxes separately.
It is, therefore, impossible to ascertain the amount of each collected until settlement time when the open items remaining on each
roll are deducted from the total amounts thereof respectively. Although it is unquestionably an advantage to ascertain monthly or
at any time the amount of each of the classes of taxes remaining
uncollected, no serious criticism is justified of the failure thus far
to maintain a separate accounting control. However, as the number of entries and the amount of the taxes become larger because
of increase in the city's population, it will be desirable to maintain such a control for the purpose of allocating the errors quickly
and accurately. In fact, large cities find it helpful to maintain
a separate accounting control over each volume of the tax rolls.

Collector of Delinquent Taxes

COLLECTOR OF DELINQUENT TAXES.

The office of collector of delinquent taxes is separately provided for in the city charter. The incumbent is elected by the city council whereas the city collector is elected by the people. For convenience these two officials occupy joint offices. If the collector's office is consolidated with that of the city treasury, the office of collector of delinquent taxes should likewise be consolidated, i. e., should be abolished and the duties thereof delegated to the treasurer. Even though the city collector be continued as a separate office, it should be appointive instead of elective, and should include the collection of delinquent taxes. There is no need for having a separate official for such purposes. The duties thereof could be performed by the city collector with perhaps the help of the clerk now employed by the delinquent collector. This would mean a saving of $3,600 a year.

The delinquent collector was formerly paid on the basis of 5 per cent. of his collections, and out of such commission he was required to pay the expenses of his office. He retained the balance. in lieu of a fixed salary. Recently this plan was abolished and his salary fixed at $3,600, which, together with the expenses of the office, are provided for in the annual budget appropriation, and the collections are turned in to the city treasury.

The 1917 appropriation for this office was as follows:

Delinquent collector	$ 3,600
Deputy collector	1,500
Deputy collector for Southside..............	300
Expenses	500
Total	$ 5,900

After the delinquent tax office has tried for seventeen months to collect delinquent taxes. they are turned over to an employee who works outside, on a fifteen per cent. basis. It was estimated that the latter earns about $800 a year. The work of this office would be greatly reduced if the fifty cent city poll tax were abolished, as elsewhere recommended herein. It was stated that the 28.000 bills for personal taxes turned over to the delinquent tax collector last year averaged less than two dollars each. The amount of such bills which it is possible to collect scarcely justified the work involved.

The Treasurer

THE TREASURER.

As Collector.

Although the larger portion of the city's revenues are received in the office of the city tax collector, the treasurer nevertheless collects directly all water and gas bills, such licenses as wagons, cabs, automobiles, peddlers, etc., and certain miscellaneous revenues.

The licenses issued by this office are not under any documentary accounting control. The treasurer purchases his own license forms, application is made to the treasurer direct and the licenses are issued by him, irrespective of any other office, except in the case of the health and milk and food licenses and also for electricians and electrical contractors. The cumbersome procedure incident to the issuance of these licenses has already been mentioned in the chapter on the city auditor's office, and recommendation made for simplification.

The office appears to be well organized, the floor plan is good and the work well distributed. It would, however, be possible for the present force, without extra assistance, to distribute payment warrants, as recommended in the chapter on the city auditor. The present force could also, with very little assistance, collect the city taxes.

Just as soon as it is possible, under the law, the southside branch of the treasurer's office should be abolished. The treasurer maintains two men throughout the year—the salary of one is $1,500 and the other $720. They collect gas and water bills and issue dog and wagon licenses. All other southside revenues are payable to the treasurer at the city hall. It was estimated that only about 9 per cent. of the water bills originate on the southside, and the auditor estimates that about 8 per cent. of them are paid through the city hall office. It is also estimated that only about 7 per cent. of the gas bills originate on the southside and of these a considerable proportion are likewise paid at the city hall. It is to be noted that if this branch collection office were abolished, the people of Manchester (southside) would not travel as far in coming to the city hall office as do the people of Ginter Park, Forest Hill, and some of the other sections.

There is a commendable plan in operation whereby the treasurer has seven sub-stations on certain days in various sections of the city. These sub-stations are mostly in drug stores. The representatives from the treasurer's office spend one or two days a month at each station. The collection in Manchester (southside) could just as well be made through a similar sub-station, as to maintain a permanent office there. The rental for the space occupied by the treasurer and tax collector in this branch is $600 a year.

As Custodian.

The city council specifies by ordinance the banking institutions in which the city treasurer shall keep the city moneys. ' At the time of the survey the general funds of the city were deposited in sixteen different banks (there are about twenty-five banks in the city). Active checking accounts were maintained in three banks—the American National and the State and City on the north side, and the Mechanics and Merchants on the southside. Checks are drawn on the two north side banks in alternate months. The accounts in the other thirteen banks are not very active. Several of them had small balances running from $4,000 to $8,000 at the time of the survey.

The number of city depositories has been increased from time to time as new members are elected to the city council and make request for additional banks to be designated as city depositories. It is suggested that better interest rates might be secured if the city did not scatter its accounts in so many small parcels throughout the city.

A reduction in the number of depositories would not lessen the city's security because adequate safeguards could be adopted to insure the safety of the funds. An excellent plan is to apportion the latter on the basis of a certain percentage of the capital, surplus and deposits of the respective institutions. The banks should be required to submit competitive bids. A specified number of the high bidders should then be selected and the funds apportioned between them according to a predetermined plan. At the present time the city obtains three per cent. on all city deposits, irrespective of whether the account is active or inactive, and on the sinking fund cash the same as on general fund cash.

Under the ordinance the auditor requires each bank to furnish a security company bond in an amount which approximates the average deposit of city money therein. The banks select the security companies, but the city pays the premium on the bonds. It amounts to about $1,300 a year.

The treasurer furnishes a bond of $50,000 and himself pays the premium thereon.

As Disbursing Officer.

Persons to whom the city owes money obtain their payment warrants from the city auditor, but must present them to the treasurer for countersignature and to have the name of the bank where they are payable inserted theron. This holds true with respect to all claims other than payrolls. The only payrolls he disburses are those of the general offices.

As soon as the claims have been audited, warrants drawn therefor and signed by the auditor, he should transmit them to the treasurer for disbursement. Payees should not be required to call at the auditor's office. Detailed procedure for the revised plan is suggested in the chapter of this report relating to the city auditor. Instead of having payees call at the treasurer's office it would be still better if he mailed their warrants to them the same as do many of the large private corporations throughout the country.

Bookkeeping and Preparation of Tax Bills.

Various registers are maintained in connection with the collection of licenses and other miscellaneous revenues. If the form of license documents were revised so as to provide a chasier's coupon (for proving the cash and posting) it would simplify the work incident to such transactions. The principal books of accounts in the treasurer's office are:

1—Settlement book. There is one of these books for each receiving teller, and although they could be somewhat simplified, they should not be dispensed with.

2—Cash book. This is practically a consolidation of number 1 above.

3—Disbursement book. This is a large record kept on the counter and is posted currently as warrants are countersigned. It is practically the same form as a similar record kept on the counter in the auditor's office. It is required by section 44 of the charter.

4—Receipt and disbursement book. The debit side of this book is the exact copy of number 2 above and the credit side is a recapitulation of number 3 by appropriations chargeable. Although a summary of number 2 would suffice for the debit side of this book, the treasurer's point that it does not require much time is for the present excuse enough for its continuance. With respect to the recapitulations of expenditures by appropriations, it should be sufficient for the treasurer's office to show only the disbursements according to funds. In fact, the charter uses the word "fund." If only a classification by funds were required. it would be readily secured by distribution columns in number 3 above and obviate the necessity of recapitulating by appropriations in number 4.

5—Daily balance book. The continuance of this book is essential.

6—Individual bank ledger. The accounts contained in these various books might with equal facility be contained in a single volume, but there can be no objection to maintaining a separate book for each bank.

7—Susidiary distribution ledger. The columnar titles on the debit side of this book are the same as the line titles of number 2. They are written in all sorts of positions on the various pages and serve the purpose of recapitulating the entries of number 2. The titles on the credit side are about the same as the columnar titles of number 4. So long as the treasurer continues to show details by appropriations, the continuance of this book is necessary.

8—General ledger. This book is posted from the totals of number 7. What has been said above with respect to maintaining accounts with each appropriation applies to this book also. It is used in balancing with the auditor.

With respect to the preparation of State tax bills there has been considerable criticism of the treasurer for not preparing the bills in advance similarly as the city tax collector prepares his tax bills. The treasurer holds that he ought to be furnished with both the real and personal State tax books prior to September, so that he can have ample time to prebill before November 1, the date the State taxes become due. The fact is that if the treasurer did not receive the tax books early in September, he would have to employ additional assistants and up to the end of 1917 he would have to pay them from his own commission. Hence the treasurer's complaint is based on his getting the books sufficiently early so that he can use his regular employees in preparing tax bills.

The Treasurer's Salary.

In addition to his duties as the city treasurer, he is ex-officio collector of State taxes, State licenses, collateral inheritance taxes, etc.

The treasurer's office is divided into two distinct parts, one side being given over to the collection of city revenues and the other to the collection of State revenues. The present survey did not extend to that part used for State purposes nor to the methods incident thereto. The treasurer stated that being State business it could not be comprehended within the scope of the survey.

The collector has been paid a commission on a percentage basis for the State revenues collected. From such commission he has paid his employees who are engaged on State work, the other expense of such work and has retained the balance. A recent State law (1914, amended 1916) provides that beginning at the expiration of the term of the present incumbent the treasurer shall report each year all fees earned by the office from every source to a fee commission composed of the governor and other State officers. He will be permitted to deduct the salaries of his State employees, certain expenses and a personal salary of not to exceed $7,500. The balance must be turned into the State treasury. The city now pays him $2,000 a year as city treasurer. Thus he will be allowed to retain $5,500 additional from the earnings of the office and still be within the $7,500 limit prescribed by law. The present incumbent contends that the city should pay him a salary more commensurate with the amount paid him by the State, inasmuch as such a large amount of work is required to collect the city revenues. It is submitted that $7,500 salary provided by the new law is adequate to cover any and all duties which may be delegated to him by either the State or the city. In fact, it is excessive. Frequent observation of the treasurer's office during the survey indicated that the treasurer himself does comparatively little work. The business of the office would get along just as well if he were not there.

Police Department

POLICE DEPARTMENT.

The police service for many years was under the immediate supervision of a large and unwieldly board of commissioners, its members selected and promoted in the past upon the basis of political patronage, its policies dictated by the partisan political leaders, its development along progressive lines impeded by the failure to provide for the adequate training of the men, and its efficiency impaired by exposes involving the integrity of some of the past administrative heads. But it is now at a stage where, by the application of modern methods of control and management, it can be made a highly efficient agency for the suppression of crime and the apprehension of criminals.

In considering the efficiency of the police department, it is to be remembered that improvement can only be accomplished gradually and not by any hastily applied remedies.

It is no simple task to raise to the standard of high efficiency a department which has been practically since its very beginning under the control and domination of many masters, who were not seeking to produce efficiency in police work, but whose every desire was to use the police department for political purposes.

That the department in the past few years has shown marked improvement and a spirit of progressiveness is obvious, and that those in charge of the department have made an effort at modernizing its procedure is equally apparent; but the most that can be said in appraising the department is that a step in the direction of efficient management has been taken and its officials show a marked willingness to perfect its organization and procedure.

Mayor Does Not Receive Adequate Information Concerning Police Department.

The administrative head of the department is the mayor who, by charter, is given general control and management of the police force. Vesting the mayor with these powers likewise places upon him responsibility for its efficiency. He is expected to direct and advise the chief in the management of the force. To do this intelligently, he must be able to speedily test the efficiency of the service and to have a thorough understanding at all times of the crime conditions. In other words, he must be able to tell from records so compiled as to facilitate reference whether crime is on the increase or decrease, whether the number of complaints received by the department is greater or less than for previous periods, whether juvenile delinquency is increasing or decreasing, whether the detectives are efficienly investigating the complaints assigned to them and obtaining results, and such information as will serve as a guide in determining whether or not the policemen are performing their duty.

Under the present plan of procedure, it is not possible for the mayor to answer, even after careful review of all of the records. all of these questions; therefore, he is unable to give the proper direction and advice and to exercise complete control over the management of the service.

It is true that the mayor has a daily conference with the chief, at which are discussed events of the previous day. He is also furnished a tabulation of the arrests made, but of course information as to the number of arrests does not of itself serve as a guide to the crime conditions or the efficiency of the force. Even the information furnished him as to arrests is not complete because, while he is informed as to the number of persons arrested and the offenses for which they are apprehended, he is not informed as to the disposition made of these cases in the courts.

It is of little value for the administrative head to know, for example, that there were twenty arrests for burglary in a month, unless he knows the number of burglaries actually reported during the month because, if there were twenty burglaries reported and there were twenty arrests for burglary, it might mean that the police were efficient in apprehending the burglars; but if on the other hand there but twenty arrests for burglary and two hundred burglaries committed. there would surely be cause for inquiry, if not investigation. Moreover. there might well be twenty arrests for burglary without a single conviction. which would at least suggest to the administrative head the need for questioning the officers who made these arrests.

At present, the mayor lacking information of this kind. is furnished no leads for inquiry. and at best can only pass judgment upon the efficiency of the force on a fictitious basis, namely, that of arrests made.

It is, therefore. recommended that the mayor require the chief of police to furnish him with a daily report. on a special printed form. designed to give an accurate picture of the service rendered by the police during the preceding twenty-four hours, the strength of the force, and the crime condition of the city as indicated by the complaints received. The mayor should also require the chief to furnish him with a monthly report of arrests made, the disposi-tions of the cases and the complaints received, classified as to sub-jects complained of. This report should be prepared on a compara-tive basis, comparing one period with another, as for example, the present month with the same month of the preceding year, the present year to date, as compared with the same period of the pre-ceding year.

In connection with suspected vice, the mayor should require a weekly report, signed by the captain of each of the three districts and approved by the chief, containing a list of the premises sus-pected of being operated for immoral purposes and the action taken by the police in their effort to suppress such traffic.

Under the present conditions, no information is furnished the mayor on this subject, except as the chief may informally discuss such conditions with the mayor at the morning conference.

Chief is the Executive Head.

The executive head of the force is the chief, who is appointed by the mayor to serve "during good behavior and efficiency." His salary is $2,500.00 a year. He is made responsible, by the charter, "to the mayor for the discipline and efficiency of the force." He is empowered "to appoint from the force, subject to the approval of the mayor, as many captains and sergeants as he may deem neces-sary for the efficient discipline of the force and the enforcement of the criminal laws of the commonwealth and the enforcement of the charter and ordinances of the city of Richmond." (Chapter 6, Sec-tion 86, Charter.)

Chief Should Be Selected as Result of Promotional Civil Service Examination.

While the chief is appointed to serve during good behavior, thus implying that he would be entitled to a trial before removal by the mayor, he is nevertheless not protected against arbitrary removal for political reasons, nor does the charter require that he shall be selected upon the basis of merit, the position not being placed in the classified civil service. Although it may be said that the present statute fixing the term of the chief during good be-havior is a step in the right direction and makes it a little more diffi-cult to remove the chief for political reasons, nevertheless he is not surrounded with the protection necessary to permit him to perform his duties in a courageous and fearless manner without fear of removal as punishment. Moreover, the method of selecting his successor, who must be selected from among the members of the force, would not necessarily be upon a merit basis and might easily result in the immediate advancement from the rank of patrolman to chief of police of some member for purely political purposes.

That the police service of America has not progressed as rapidly as have other branches of government, and that in many respects its efficiency is not equal to that of the European police service is because it is invariably the last branch of city government to be released from political control and domination.

The efficient chief of police, in the performance of his duty, must necessarily make many enemies. Unfortunately, it is only too true that in the make-up of cities those who by reason of their pernicious activities come under the constant surveillance of the police, are powerfully influential with certain dominant factions, who are able to control appointments and removals of public servants. These persons are frequently able to exercise this power against efficient police officers as a penalty for their having interfered with their illegal practices through arrest and prosecution.

If a chief of police is to be wholly efficient, he must be surrounded by every possible protection against removal for a faithful performance of his duties. He must be able at all times to perform his duties without regard for the enemies he may make. Moreover, with a system whereby the mayor may arbitrarily select the chief of police without regard for competitive civil service, the chief is necessarily forced, in order to protect his position, to remain in competition with his own subordinates for the favor and good will of his immediate superior.

Therefore, it is recommended that the charter be amended so as to provide that the chief of police shall be selected as a result of a competitive civil service examination, which examination shall not be confined to the members of the department, but open to any person who may desire to enter the competition. In such an examination, however, generous allowance should be made in the form of credit to the members of the department so as to give them some preference over persons competing from without the department.

The charter amendment should also provide that the chief cannot be removed from office except after a hearing upon charges before the mayor, at which hearing he should have the right to subpoena witnesses in his behalf, and upon dismissal by the mayor, he should have the further right of appeal to a court of record.

Information Furnished Chief Not Properly Compiled.

An examination of the records shows that, unlike many other police departments, there is every desire upon the part of the chief to cause to be recorded all of the complaints and all of the activities of his force. The procedure at present in force provides for recording this information at the district stations and at headquarters, but it is never compiled in such a manner as to keep the chief currently advised of the crime conditions as represented by complaints and the success of his force in coping with them.

The rules of the department at present require that the captains of the districts make daily reports to the chief, listing thereon the important complaints received at the districts, the strength of the force during the preceding twenty-four hours, the arrests made, the ordinance violations reported and the miscellaneous services rendered by the police.

Thus there are delivered to headquarters each morning four regular form reports from each of the three districts and special reports on complaints requiring detective attention. The reports of arrests, ordinance violations and complaints requiring detective attention are not reviewed by the chief, except the reports affecting the commission of serious crimes, in which cases the captains file special reports with the chief. But even if the chief did undertake to review all of these reports each morning, he would then merely secure information as to the current events, but would not have any picture before him of the general crime conditions. Moreover, what is equally important, he would not be in possession of information as to the success of his officers in the investigation of the complaints and in the prosecution of their cases in the courts. Therefore, it may be said that the chief does not receive information compiled in such a manner as to enable him to determine either the crime conditions or the efficiency of the force. Without such information, it is not possible for a chief of police capably to direct the activities of his subordinates.

Therefore, it is recommended that the chief install a reporting system which will bring to his desk in concise, tabulated form each morning a detailed report of the crime, complaints, the arrests made and the service rendered by the members of the force during the preceding twenty-four hours. This report should be known as a "consolidated daily return," and should be made upon a special printed form, such as will be found fully described in the section of this report headed "Records and Reports." A copy of this report should be delivered to the mayor each morning. Each Monday morning the captains should be required to file a detailed report as to the vice conditions in their districts, showing thereon a list of all places suspected of being conducted in violation of the law and the action taken by the commanding officers to suppress these conditions. Every care should be taken to preserve secrecy in the filing of this list, since the captains should be permitted to place thereon a house which, in their opinion from a police standpoint, is being illegally operated. As a protection to the reputation and character of the owners and occupants of such property, in the event of the opinion of the captain and his officers being based on erroneous information, this record should not be open to public inspection. It is evident that the captains are misinformed as to their legal right to maintain such a list, believing that should they maintain such a record of suspected places and report the same to the chief, they would be liable to prosecution if they were unable to prove their suspicions. This opinion is not based upon law, since the police are entitled to maintain such records so long as they do not maliciously injure the character or reputation of any one by wilfully publishing misinformation. Again it is evident that the captains hesitate to maintain such records, for the reason that they believe reporting a suspected place to the chief to constitute an admission of their inefficiency upon the theory that if a house is suspected by them, they should be able to suppress it. This again is a fallacious theory because, in the first place, it may well be that it would not be possible for the captain of a district to suppress a place which he may have under observation, through the use of his own force, and in the second place, since the chief is responsible for the preservation of peace and order and the suppression of vice, he is entitled to know at all times which places his captains have under observation or surveillance.

The mayor should secure from the city attorney an opinion making clear the rights of the captains to maintain a suspected list and a copy of this opinion should be delivered to each captain.

Monthly Report of Crime Complaints Should Be Compiled.

The chief should require each captain to submit on a special printed form a tabulation of the complaints received, classified as to subjects complained of, at each of the three districts and at headquarters. These reports when received should be tabulated and placed upon a consolidated crime report, showing a complete tabulation of this information for the entire city. The consolidated crime report should show the total number of complaints received for the current month and the disposition of them, the total received for the same month of the preceding year and the dispositions, the total number received for the current year up to date and the dispositions, as well as the total number received for the preceding year and the dispositions.

Captains' Daily Meeting Unnecessary.

Each morning the captains are required to leave their districts and attend a conference with the chief at headquarters. When the chief installs a proper reporting system, this daily conference of the captains should be discontinued and the captains permitted to remain in their districts. If the chief desires to confer with any captain upon any special subject, he can send for him without the necessity of having all the captains present.

Chief Does Not Devote Sufficient Time to Field Observations.

The chief remains at his desk at headquarters during the entire day and frequently during the early part of the evening. This procedure does not afford him ample opportunity for observations in the field.

It is, therefore, recommended that the chief devote more time to patrol, keeping in touch with headquarters by telephone. This procedure will unquestonably result in better discipline being maintained on the patrol posts than is at present.

No One in Command of Force During Night Hours.

While the captains for the most part remain on duty until before midnight and, one night a week, one captain remains on patrol all night, there is no one person in command of the force during all of the night. When the chief and the captains retire, the desk sergeants in each district are practically in control.

It is recommended that a captain be assigned each night in charge of the force, making his office at police headquarters, or when in the field, keeping in touch with headquarters by frequent telephone calls. The force should not at any hour be without a commanding officer in complete control. The sergeants should not have to depend upon the telephone operator on night duty in headquarters for instructions, as at present.

Captains Should Maintain Better Discipline on Patrol Posts.

There are five captains of police, each of whom receives $1,440.00 a year. Three of these captains are assigned in command of districts, one is in charge of the detective bureau and the fifth serves as secretary and purchasing agent. The captains are appointed by the chief, subject to the approval of the mayor. These appointments are made without competitive civil service examination. The captain is the next ranking officer to the chief. His promotion to that rank should be by virtue of competitive civil service examination, to which only the sergeants should be admitted. The captains are in theory held responsible for the police conditions in their districts, but because of the absence of a proper reporting system, it is not possible for the chief to check the work of the captains cr to keep informed as to the conditions within the districts. The captains are supposed to be held responsible for the discipline maintained among the members of the force. but judging from the lack of discipline displayed by the patrolmen on post. it is apparent that the captains do not exercise the control over the members of their command which it is both expected and desired they should.

It is, therefore, recommended that the captains use every effort possible at their disposal to see to it that the patrolmen are more alert and better disciplined while on patrol.

Elsewhere in this report it is recommended that steps be taken as promptly as possible to abolish the police station on the south side of the city known as "The Third District" and to consolidate that district with the first, thus making available an extra captain. If this is done, it would then be possible for the chief to have one captain on night duty at all times at headquarters without inconveniencing the other captains.

Plain Clothes Patrolmen Assigned to Captains Should Be Under Supervision of Detective Bureau.

There are assigned to each of the captains in the first and second districts two patrolmen detailed to duty in plain clothes. For reasons that will be fully explained in the section of this report entitled "Detective Bureau," these plain clothes patrolmen should be junior detectives serving under the direct supervision and control of the captain of detectives.

Sergeants Supervise Patrol and Perform Desk Duty.

There are nine patrol sergeants and seven desk sergeants, who receive $1,212.00 a year salary. The desk sergeants maintain the records and, in the absence of the captain, are in command of the district. The patrol sergeants supervise the patrol force.

Need for the Appointment of Additional Sergeants.

The efficiency of a police department may be said to be dependent upon the intelligence of its detective service and the faithfulness of its patrol force. To maintain a faithful and diligent patrol, the patrolmen must be closely supervised by sergeants. By supervision of patrol is not meant merely determining that the patrolmen are on their posts. Supervision of patrol is observing the method of patrol employed by the patrolmen, studying the conditions of their patrol posts, seeing to it that the patrolmen diligently report conditions observed by them and are alert and active in covering their respective posts. To do this, there must be enough sergeants to cover all of the posts and to observe the work of their subordinates. Thus, in order to determine whether a patrolman is efficiently performing his duty, it is necessary that the patrol sergeants spend sufficient time on the posts to ascertain the conditions and make proper observations and not merely to travel about the streets meeting the patrolmen for the purpose of making sure that he is on duty. With the present number of sergeants on patrol it is not possible to afford the kind of supervision necessary to produce good patrolling. Under the present conditions, a sergeant is just about able to cover his district once on a tour and meet each man of his platoon. Indeed, in the daytime the sergeants are scarcely able to accomplish this. It is no economy to attempt to supervise a patrol force with an insufficient number of sergeants, for the reason that under such conditions considerable of the money paid in salaries to patrolmen is almost entirely wasted because of the poor character of patrol secured. The distribution of sergeants at present provides no sergeant on patrol in the third district at all, and but one sergeant on patrol between the hours of midnight and 8:00 A. M. in the first and second districts.

From midnight to 8:00 A. M. is what is termed the "crime period," and is also the time during which patrolmen are most likely to neglect their duty. Thus it is the time during which the patrolmen are most in need of supervision. During the second tour, which is from 4:00 in the afternoon to 12:00 midnight, there are two sergeants on patrol in each of the first and second districts. It should be noted that during the hours between 4:00 and 12:00 midnight the captains are on patrol, the chief is usually observing and practically the entire population of the city is active, while from 12:00 midnight to 8:00 A. M. these conditions do not prevail, thereby making it much easier for the patrolmen to shirk their duty and avoid detection.

It is, therefore, recommended that there be appointed as promptly as possible three patrol sergeants, so as to provide two sergeants on patrol in each of the first and second districts on the third tour and one on each tour in the third district.

The patrol sergeant now detailed to plain clothes duty in the third district should be remanded to active patrol duty.

If sufficient funds are not available to provide for these appointments, it would be far more efficient and economical to reduce the patrol service by three men and increase the force of sergeants by three. Too much emphasis cannot be placed on the need for the additional sergeants.

That the sergeants do not enforce proper discipline on the patrol posts is apparent. The lax manner in which the patrolmen cover their posts, engaging in conversation with citizens and other patrolmen for long periods and loitering when they should be performing active patrol, and the general untidy appearance of a number of the patrolmen, indicate that the sergeants are not efficiently enforcing the rules. That this condition prevails is not due entirely to the insufficient number of sergeants because these conditions were found to exist during the tour from four to midnight when the number of sergeants on patrol is adequate.

Whenever patrolmen are observed standing in idle conversation for long periods, loitering on their posts and spending time in moving picture shows and theatres, there is but one reason for it and that is that they are not afraid of their sergeants reporting them for violation of the rules.

It is, therefore, recommended that the chief and the captains hold the sergeants strictly responsible for enforcing the rules and maintaining discipline on the patrol posts.

Sergeants Should Report Time and Place of Meeting Patrolmen.

Formerly, it was the rule of the department for sergeants to report, in writing, the time and place of meeting their patrolmen. This practice was abandoned, according to the chief, because, in his opinion, the sergeants were not diligently patrolling their posts, but instead were concentrating their efforts on meeting all of the patrolmen. Moreover, it was intimated that the sergeants, in order to accomplish this, would make appointments to meet the patrolmen at definite hours. ·

That this condition prevailed may be true, yet this was not a defect in the reporting system but was due to the failure of the captains adequately to supervise their sergeants and because there were insufficient sergeants to meet the needs of the city.

It must be remembered that a sergeant is but one step above the rank of patrolman, and he, as a non-commissioned officer, is in as much need of supervision by his captain as is the patrolman; consequently, some method of checking the work of the sergeants is necessary.

The particular advantage of requiring the sergeant to note the time he meets the patrolman is that it enables the chief or the captain, when reviewing these reports, to see which of the patrolmen require the most supervision from the sergeants. For example, if a sergeant's book shows the name of some patrolman whom the sergeant "sees" two or three times a night, it will indicate either that the patrolman is so derelict that he needs the constant attention of the sergeant or that the sergeant is "pounding" the patrolman. In either case, through the use of this record, the captains and the chief will have an opportunity to investigate and to admonish the policeman or discover from him that he is a victim of a sergeant who entertains a grievance against him.

Not only should the sergeant be required to keep this record but likewise the patrolman. Thus the superior officers would, from time to time, be able to check the patrolmen's memorandum books with the sergeants' in order to discover the accuracy of the reports. These records have from time to time proved of great value upon trial of delinquent policemen or sergeants, as well as in the investigation of crime conditions on posts. A careful review of these records will serve to prevent a repetition of the condition which prevailed when the system was in practice in this city.

Sergeants on Day Tour Should Patrol on Bicycles.

Because of the large area to be covered by the sergeants on the day tours, they should patrol on bicycles.

Only Sergeants Should Be Eligible for Promotion to Rank of Captain.

As the law now exists, the chief has the right to promote to the rank of captain any member of the force, subject of course to the approval of the mayor.

A police department is essentially a quasi military organization, and so far as possible the army plan of organization should follow. Promotions should be from rank to rank.

Therefore, it is recommended that the law be amended so as to provide that captains be selected from among the sergeants as a result of a competitive civil service examination. The civil service rules should require two years' service in the rank of sergeant before a candidate becomes eligible for promotion to the rank of captain.

Appointments.

All of the appointments in the police department are made by the chief of police, subject to the approval of the mayor, while all of the appointments to the fire force are made by the board of fire commissioners. Neither policemen nor firemen are appointed as the result of competitive civil service examination in accordance wth the merit plan, although applicants for appointment in the police department are required to subject themselves to what is termed a civil service examination. This examination is conducted by the chief and consists of a series of questions as to the location of public buildings, streets, routes of street car lines, railroad terminals, hospitals, churches and hotels. The examination includes a test in spelling and simple arithemetic. No such examination, however, is given applicants for appointment to the fire department. While the examination to which applicants for the police department are subjected might be termed a fairly good test, yet the examination is not wholly competitive in that a man's position on the eligible list may not necessarily guarantee appointment either in the order in which his name appears, or at all.

Each applicant is required to file a written application on a regular printed form which corresponds in a large measure to the standard form of civil service application; in fact, the form has printed upon it at the top "Civil Service Examination." Each applicant is required to swear to the accuracy of his answers and to have four citizens of the city vouch for his character and habits. This part of the appointment procedure is in force in both the police and fire departments, except that in the fire department each applicant must receive the endorsement of the chief of the department and the first and second assistant chiefs, each of whom are required to observe the applicant and to conduct such investigations as to his character and habits as to either approve or disapprove of the application.

But for the fact that no regular competitive civil service examination is conducted by persons not connected with the department, the procedure is good and at least shows an effort to prevent undesirable persons being appointed to either department.

After the applicant for appointment to the fire department has been approved his name is placed upon either one of two eligible lists in accordance with whether he lives in the eastern or western half of the city. As vacancies occur the appointments are made from these lists alternately, the first from one side of the city and the second from the other side, and so on.

The character investigations made of applicants for the police and fire departments are in accordance with good practice, in that officers of both departments are required to conduct a careful examination and to report the results of their investigations in writing.

Appointment Should Be Made as Result of Civil Service Test.

In order to prevent favoritism, the use of political influence in appointments, and in order to encourage young men of good character and physique to enter these two services, it is recommended that the law be amended so as to require all appointments to be made as the result of competitive civil service examination, and in the order in which their names appear upon the eligible list.

Maximum Age Too High.

The minimum age for appointments in both departments is twenty-one and the maximum thirty-five. It is the experience of most progressive communities that better results can be obtained in the training of policemen and firemen by fixing the maximum age for appointments at thirty years on the date of appointment. This provision further serves as a protection to the pension fund. However, in view of the fact that the maximum age for draft in the national army has been fixed at thirty-one years, it is suggested that no change be made in this regulation at this time, but that at the conclusion of the war the maximum age be reduced to thirty years.

Fee Charged for Physical Examination.

Applicants for appointment to the police and fire departments are given a thorough physical examination by doctors representing the respective departments at the time of taking the mental test. If their names are placed upon the eligible list they are subjected to a physical examination just prior to appointment, except that applicants for appointment in the fire department whose appointments might be made within three months after the first physical examination, are appointed without a second examination. This is not in accordance with good practice, since it must be obvious that it might be entirely possible for an applicant who passed the first examination to contract a disease or injury within the three months prior to his appointment and secure appointment without his condition being detected. No appointments should be made without subjecting the applicant to a physical examination at the time of appointment.

While the applicants are given a thorough physical examination, they are not subjected to an athletic test. Good practice requires that applicants for police and fire departments be given a thorough athletic test. It is recommended that the athletic test be made a part of the physical examination and that the standard used by the New York civil service commission be applied.

No Physical Examination at the End of Probation Period.

In order that the police and fire departments shall be fully protected against physically unfit men entering the service, it is necessary that at the end of six months' probation they be subjected to another physical examination. This is urged for the reason that the surgeons can better determine the fitness of candidates after six months of service than at the time of appointment, because during this period of service the physical condition of the policeman and fireman will indicate whether or not he is physically equipped to meet the requirements of this kind of service. Therefore, it is recommended that the regulations of both departments be amended so as to require a physical examination at the end of a probation period.

Proof of Age should be Required.

Applicants for appointment to the police and fire departments should be required to furnish proof of age. Since it is important that a minimum and maximum age for appointment be established, it necessarily follows that care must be taken to see to it that statements made as to age are truthful.

Therefore, it is recommended that each applicant be required at the time of filing his application to furnish proof of his age in the form of a birth or baptismal certificate or an affidavit from those competent to state his age.

Probationary Period Should Be Established.

Although a probationary period for firemen has been established, at the end of which commanding officers and the chief are required to certify to the board as to the competency of the probationer, appointment to the police force is not subject to any probationary period. This practice should be discontinued and all newly appointed policemen required to serve upon probation for a period of six months before final appointment, and at the end of this time the mayor should have the right to drop from the rolls any probationer whose service is unsatisfactory. In all such cases, the mayor should require a written report, over the signature of the chief, and certify the same to the proposed civil service commission.

Captains and sergeants should be required to make monthly reports in writing upon all probationary policemen within their commands. These reports should be detailed and not merely a general statement. The kind of service rendered should be adequately described so as to enable the mayor at the end of the probationary period to judge the fitness of the probationer for police service.

Training of Policemen.

No Adequate Training Provided.

As already stated, the efficiency of a police force is largely dependent upon the efficiency of its patrol service. Policing a city is no longer a matter of merely assigning a number of night watchmen to patrol the sidewalks and to be content with arresting those whom they witness committing a breach of the peace. Police work is now a science, and those who have studied the police problems of America are convinced that police failures are, for the most part, due to lack of training and a lack of understanding of the functions of policemen. Not only do those to whom are entrusted the management of police forces fail to appreciate what constitutes police work, but unfortunately, in general, the public has a misconception of the functions of a police force. It can be said that upon the training of a police force depends success or failure. Large sums of the taxpayers' money are wasted in most communities in the payment of salaries to what are called policemen, who in reality are nothing more than street watchmen. A few well-trained police officers accomplish more in reducing crime and in serving the police needs of a community than a large number of untrained men.

Again, the mistake is only too frequently made of believing that military drill constitutes sufficient training for policemen.

Therefore, in order to obtain the best results from a police force, not only has the chief and the administrative head to provide for the proper training of the policemen, but for the education of the general public as to the functions of the policemen. One has only to analyze the few records maintained by the average police department in the United States to appreciate the vast amount of police time devoted to answering useless calls and performing trivial service in response to public demands, due entirely to a misconception on the part of the general public as to the functions of a police force. Because of this fact, valuable time which should be devoted to solving the crime problems of a community and to performing social service functions is completely lost. It did not require much study or observation of Richmond's police force to determine its principal weakness and defect, namely, lack of training which, fairness to the officials of that department, it should be said constitutes the principal weakness of a majority of the police forces in America. In other words, the test as to the efficiency of a force may be found in the answer as to how the policemen are trained.

In Richmond, upon appointment, a policeman is assigned immediately to a precinct and detailed to work with an older officer for a period of a few days or a week. The older officer, of course, received no more training than the officer appointed today; in fact, if anything, he received less. To him the new policeman is assigned.

At the expiration of this time the new policeman is sent on patrol to develop himself by what is commonly termed in police circles "experience." His captain is supposed to see to it that the officer learns the rules and regulations of the department.

Revolver instruction and rifle training, in which a small number of the force took part, were conducted in the past, but recently were discontinued.

For his understanding of the many intricate criminal statutes which he is called upon to enforce; for the development of his mind in the direction of astuteness in the ferreting out of crime and the apprehension of criminals; for his knowledge as to how to prepare the case which he is to present in court, appreciating the value of evidence and understanding the modern methods of preserving and presenting evidence; for his conception of police service with relation to observing and reporting conditions; for his appreciation of proper discipline; for the proper understanding of alert patrol and courteous deportment, and the many other factors important in the training of a policeman, the newly appointed patrolman must depend upon a twenty-minute lecture, at which he is required to be present once in three weeks. Even the twenty-minute lecture, it is to be rememberd, is delivered by one of the commanding officers who had to depend for his training in years gone by upon experience gained while on patrol. Consequently, the citizens of Richmond must not expect a full measure of efficiency, and what is more, will never get a proper return for the money invested in the police service until the policemen do receive training under competent instructors. To cite the evidences of the lack of training apparent at every hand would be a needless repetition, and to have found the policemen alert, active and efficient in their methods of patrol, would indeed have been surprising.

During the course of the survey the attention of the chief was called to the absence of discipline among patrolmen while on patrol. One of the evidences of this, pointed out to the chief, was the large number of policemen who were observed loitering on their posts in conversation with citizens and other policemen. In answer to this criticism the chief ordered every patrolman on a given day to supply him with a report showing the time of each conversation and the matter discussed. The purport of this report was to prove that the policemen observed engaged in conversation were, for the most part, serving the citizens by directing them and giving them information requested. Indeed, it would have been interesting in the extreme to have found among these reports many statements showing the subject of conversation to be other than police business. Nevertheless, the inquiry made by the chief had its value, in that it tended to show the amount of time consumed by the policemen in answering queries. But it surely could not have been expected to show the amount of time consumed in idle conversation. Notwithstanding the numerous inquiries of a legitimate character made of the policemen, many were observed standing in conversation for periods of twenty-five to twenty-eight minutes and the attitude of both the policeman and the person in conversation with him did not serve to intimate that the subject was one of inquiry or of police business. But a day or two after the test was made, one traffic officer upon a very busy thoroughfare was observed standing in conversation with a citizen for exactly twenty-eight minutes, and the conversation was evidently so interesting to both, that there were times when traffic was considerably delayed because the officer did not desire to interrupt his conversation. At the same time that this incident took place, the policeman on patrol was standing in conversation with a citizen for fifteen minutes on the street corner, and neither of these officers seemed disturbed in the slightest degree by the fact that one of the sergeants of the district passed them both by, saluted them and made no effort whatever to enforce the regulations of the department. Without in any way discrediting the reports made by the members of the department or the motive of the chief in requiring the reports, the fact remains that continuous observations made during the course of the survey showed that there is both a lack of discipline on the patrol posts and a disregard for the rules with respect to patrolling.

In but comparatively few instances were the patrolmen observed on the late tour trying doors or looking into the stores.

Many policemen, in full uniform, were observed smoking on the streets, but owing to the fact that the rules do not prohibit the officers from smoking when off duty, it was not possible to discover whether the men who were observed smoking were on or off duty, but indeed, so far as the general public was concerned, the appearance was the same.

Policemen make a practice of attending theaters and moving picture shows in uniform; consequently, it was difficult to learn whether the many policemen who were observed in attendance at moving picture shows and theaters were supposed to be on duty at the time, but in one instance a patrolman was observed seated in a moving picture show for thirty-five minutes, and it so happened that this patrolman was supposed to be patrolling his post at the time. Another policeman who should have been patrolling his post, was observed standing in the back of one of the theaters during practically the entire performance, and singularly enough, there were in the theater at the time two officers of the department, neither of whom even suggested to the patrolman that he perhaps could perform better police service by patrolling his post.

These few incidents are merely offered as evidence of lack of training. Many others could be cited, particularly the demeanor of the policemen at their station houses and when in attendance at the police court.

Training School for Police Service.

It is, therefore, recommended that the members of the force be given proper training for their work. Instructions should be given, not only to recruits. but to all members of the force. This can be done only by establishing a training school for police service. That the force is small in numbers does not make impossible or difficult the maintenance of a training school.

Such a school could easily be conducted, either after regular school hours in one of the public schools, or in headquarters, where there is ample room for at least two classes.

But if such a school is to be established. it must be remembered that a competent instructor must be retained. Little will be accomplished, and this is said without any desire to reflect upon the intelligence of the officers, if the training is to he left to the members of the department, who have little or no training themselves.

The school should be used to determine fitness for police duty, as well as for the instruction of the force.

The course should include continuous instruction for a period of from thirty to ninety days in the following:

Field work,
First aid to the injured,
English and report writing,
Ethics in conduct,
Practical civics,
Development of powers of observation,
Possibilities for social service work by policemen,
The powers and duties of a policeman,
The rules and regulations of the department,
The general laws of the State and the ordinances of the city,
The humane handling of prisoners,
Pistol practice and the care of the pistol,
Criminal identification methods,
The elemental rules of evidence.
Court procedure.

Probationary Parolmen Should Be Assigned to Work With Specially Selected Policemen.

No newly appointed patrolman should be assigned to duty until he has completed his course of training. During the course of study at the school the recruit should be given considerable field experience by assignment to duties in different sections of the city

with policemen selected because of their special fitness of training, and not merely because of their years of service. By assigning
the recruit to different sections of the city and with different policemen, he would be subjected to a variety of police experience.
The recruit should be required to report in writing upon all matters occurring during his tours of patrol with the older man, and
these reports should be reviewed by the instructor at the school
and given a rating.

In classes for other policemen, care should be taken to obtain
and review reports made by them in the regular course of their
duty and ascertain from them the errors made. Without humiliating these policemen. their errors should be corrected and they
should be instructed not to repeat such mistakes in the future.

*Instruction and Training for Detective Work Should be Given
at School.*

As will be seen by a reading of the section of this report headed, "detective bureau," the percentage of results obtained in the
investigation of cases is so low as to emphasize the need for detective training. In no branch of police work is scientific training
more essential to efficiency than in detective work. The members
of the detective bureau receive no training whatever other than
that received during their work as patrolmen. While it is important for the policeman to know how to apprehend a criminal, it is
just as important for him to understand that evidence is necessary
to secure a conviction, how to prepare his case for court, how to
obtain a confession in such a manner as to make it admissible as
evidence, how to preserve evidence and how to make memoranda
at the time of arrest which will be admissible as evidence.

It is now recognized that as criminals specialize in their work
and become more scientific in their methods to defeat the police,
the need of specialization in the scientific training of detectives becomes more imperative. Because of the skill with which criminals
today operate, a city can no longer hope to safeguard its citizens
through the use of the old type "plainclothesman" whose only claim
to assignment for detective work is political influence. The detective must be more than a patrolman without a uniform.

It is a frequent error to disregard the importance of the uniformed patrolman in connection with the apprehension of criminals
and the detection of crime. Hence the patrolman's education in
criminology and in methods of criminal identification is neglected.

Instead of regarding every policeman as a detective, most departments regard their patrolmen merely as watchmen. Through this mistake, according to the experience of police officers all over the country, the blunders of the untrained uniformed policeman who first arrived at the scene of a crime often resulted in the failure either to catch the criminal or to make possible his conviction after arrest. Therefore, it is urged that every member of the force be given adequate training, so that all will be qualified to perform detective duties.

Court Procedure Should Be Observed.

The conduct of the policemen in the court should be carefully observed by superior officers. There should be present at every session of the police court in the morning one of the captains. He should note deficiencies in the presentation of cases and the policemen especially deficient should be required to devote additional time to study in the school. The captain of detectives should likewise occasionally attend the sessions of the hustings court for purposes of observing the manner in which his detectives testify.

The recruits should be taken from time to time to listen to the trial of cases in the hustings court and in the police court.

In order that the policemen may become familiar with their part in court procedure, "moot" courts should be held at the school and the recruits required to prepare cases and to testify. From time to time the commonwealth attorney and the judge of the hustings court, or in fact any of the other courts, should be invited to assist or preside in the "moot" courts.

Members of the Force Should Have Printed Instructions as to Procedure in Homicide Cases.

The commonwealth attorney should be requested to prepare a set of instructions as to the procedure necessary in obtaining evidence in homicide cases, including.

Preserving evidence,
Examining prisoners while in custody of the police,
Obtaining statements from witnesses,
Recording of information,
Statements or confessions of prisoners apprehended in connection with the crime, etc.

These instructions should be printed and a copy furnished to each member of the force, with the understanding that he carry it with him at all times. They should be prepared in such a manner as to enable the policemen to carry the instructions in his loose-leaf memorandum book.

Lectures By City Officials.

For the purpose of minimizing the cost of conducting the training school and increasing its efficiency, city officials competent to instruct the police should be requested to lecture at the school.

The medical officer of the department should be required to prepare and deliver a complete course of lectures on hygiene, including the care of the feet and first aid to the injured.

The commonwealth attorney should be requested to lecture on court procedure and the rules of evidence.

The Bertillon operator should be sufficiently competent to lecture on methods of criminal identification and to give practical demonstrations in the taking and recording of Bertillon measurements, observing facial characteristics of criminals, taking and classifying of fingerprints, protecting against erasure of fingerprints at the scene of crime, searching for fingerprints, and all other matters in connection with criminal identification.

The health officer of the city should be requested to lecture upon the health ordinances and the manner in which the police should enforce them.

The city engineer and the head of the street cleaning department should be requested to lecture upon the reporting of matters affecting their departments observed by policemen.

The city attorney should be requested to lecture upon the ordinances and the manner of enforcing them, and the different public officials should be requested to instruct the patrolmen in all such matters as affect their respective departments.

Written Tests Should be Conducted.

At the conclusion of each course of lectures, a written test should be conducted and the ratings obtained by the patrolmen in these tests should be given consideration in determining their efficiency records.

The instructor in charge of the school should submit a written report to the chief as to the efficiency shown by the recruits during the course of their instruction. This report should be based upon the results of written tests and of observations of patrolmen in the field. Upon these reports the mayor should rely for information as to the advisability of making final appointments.

Promotions.

Promotions in the police and fire departments are made without regard to civil service requirements. Policemen are promoted by the chief, subject of course. to the approval of the mayor, and after a form of examination conducted by him and the secretary of the department.

Promotions in the, fire department are made by the board of fire commissioners without any examination, and occasionally against the recommendations of the chief of the department; thus, a policeman or fireman, upon entering the service is offered no guarantee nor even can he be given the most ordinary assurances of his being promoted to higher rank based upon continuous and faithful service and study.

While perhaps the officials in charge of these departments make promotions at present without regard to political influence, and, of course, under such a system, it is not possible to discover the motives underlying a promotion, it is nevertheless true that promotions in the past have been in a large measure the direct result of suggestion and advice from political leaders. Nothing is more important as a means of securing efficiency in police and fire service than that the men study and perform their duties conscientiously. Nothing is more conducive to stimulating enthusiasm and prompting the policemen and firemen to improve themselves and to perform their duties efficiently than the promise of reward through promotions based upon merit. No matter how conscientious the mayor and the board of fire commissioners may be in their attempt to select the men best fitted for promotion to higher rank. there always lingers in the minds of those who do not secure promotion a suspicion that their associates who are fortunate enough to be promoted were advanced because of "political pull" or favoritism, and the psychological effect produced upon a force of men because of these suspicions tends to destroy enthusiasm and reduce the efficiency of the service. If these two forces are to be developed to a high state of efficiency, it can only be done by attracting to the service men of a high type or moral and physical courage and by fully developing the men brought into the service. But it is difficult to attract ambitious young men to join the ranks of the police or fire force unless they can see before them at all times an opportunity to advance themselves to the rank of officers as a result of their own good work.

Inasmuch as no efficiency records are maintained and no tests conducted, it is difficult to understand on what basis a new chief or board of fire commissioners or mayor would select commanding officers. At best they would be required to rely upon the opinions of their subordinates, which opinion only too frequently may subconsciously be the result of spite or prejudice rather than competent judgment upon merit. Therefore, it is all-important that promotions be made in the police and fire departments only as the result of a competitive civil service examination conducted under the auspices of civil service officials independent of and apart from either of these two departments.

It is urged as one of the means of improving these departments that the promotions be made through civil service examinations.

Efficiency Records Should be Maintained.

In order that efficient service may receive due consideration and reward in promotional tests, it is recommended that the civil service commission require the police department to install a system of efficiency records which will truly describe the quality of the work performed by the policemen.

There are no efficiency records maintained at present and, except for the record of the policemen's delinquencies, the only basis of judgment as to the work performed by the policemen is the record of arrests. As already stated, this record is of little or no value in determining the efficiency of a policeman. Under such a plan the policeman who succeeds in ridding his post of vicious characters and in suppressing crime, would reduce the number of arrests which would be necessary in his territory. By his very admirable activity, his record for arrests would be so reduced as to make him appear less efficient. while as a matter of fact, he would have performed the highest kind of efficient service.

The promotional test which does not provide a method of rating the policeman upon the kind of service rendered by him does not succeed in securing the best kind of commanding officers.

In giving efficiency ratings to the members of their commands, captains should consider carefully the following:

1—General neatness and appearance,
2—Intelligence in making of reports,
3—Intelligence and success in presenting cases in court,

4—General carriage of the men while on patrol; whether they are alert and active, or careless and slovenly,

5—Condition of the policeman's memorandum book and the grade of the notations therein,

6—Efficiency of patrolmen in observing and reporting matters of importance to other city departments, such as broken pavements, encumbered fire-escapes, encumbrances on sidewalks, street lamp outages, etc.

7—Punctuality,

8—Discipline,

9—Reporting of suspected gambling and disorderly houses and other suspicious places on post,

10—Willingness to perform extra duty.

In connection with the efficiency records, a merit and demerit system should be developed which would provide merits for efficiency of service and demerits for delinquencies.

These monthly efficiency reports, after having been reviewed by the chief, should be forwarded to the administrative head.

In no branch of municipal service is it more difficult to determine through a written civil service test the qualifications for promotion than in the fire service. The fact that the fireman in the congested value district has performed continuous and efficient fire service helps him but little when competing with the fireman from the suburban district who has performed little or no active fire duty, but who has had ample opportunity to study and prepare himself for the written test, thus making competition not only unfair to the men, but likewise unfair to the department, in that it results in securing the less efficient man for commanding officer; therefore the efficiency of the service rendered by the firemen should be given every consideration in promotional tests through the use of efficiency ratings.

Practical Tests Should be Given in Fire Department Promotional Examinations.

Many a fireman whose efficiency in practical work is far below the standard is well informed in the theory of fire-fighting and well equipped to describe on paper his theories, while many thoroughly practical firemen who are capable of rendering valuable service and whose ability as fire-fighters exceeds that of well-informed, theoretical firemen, are not capable of recording their knowledge in written tests. Therefore, it is recommended that as part of the examination for the promotion of firemen there be conducted under the supervision of the chief, the first and second assistant chiefs and the civil service commissioners, practical tests, and that a proper rating be given the firemen competing in these tests, combining the practical test with the written test and giving adequate consideration to the efficiency ratings. This will enable the efficient, practical fireman to earn a rating which will aid him in the promotional examinations and thus relieve him of any handicap.

Board of Honor Should Be Established.

While in the police department a board of commissioners within the past few years, recognized continuous faithful service for a period of twenty-five years by awarding medals to a few of the members who had served for this period, distinguished acts of bravery or extraordinary police or fire service received no special departmental recognition.

Moral and physical courage may be said to be the chief qualifications of efficient firemen and policemen. Each is equally important. Moral cowardice is more dangerous than physical cowardice, yet it is of importance in developing efficiency in police and fire work that the members possess physical courage in the highest degree.

There are times in the life of every policeman and fireman when they are called upon to risk their lives in order to protect the lives of others. Therefore, no act of bravery involving the risk of life in its performance should go unrewarded,

For purposes of making annual awards, there should be established for the police and fire departments a board of honor. This board should consist of the administrative head, the chief of the police department and president of the proposed civil service commission, when considering police cases, and the chief of the fire department when considering fire department cases.

To the members of the police and fire service who perform the most distinguished act of bravery, in the opinion of the members of the board should be awarded gold medals to be officially known as the "department medals" and to become the property of those to whom they are awarded.

The presentation of these medals should be made with fitting ceremonies by the mayor.

The policemen and firemen to whom medals are awarded should be authorized to wear a gold star or other insignia on the sleeve of the uniform, while those receiving recognition in the form of "honorable mention" should be authorized to wear a silver star.

Care should be taken to investigate carefully all cases of bravery reported to the departments, and evidence or testimony submitted should be recorded in the records and be open to public inspection.

In promotional examinations special weights should be given to the holders of medals for bravery and to those to whom "honorable mention" has been awarded.

Other members of the force performing acts of bravery should be awarded "honorable mention."

Medals Should be Awarded for Best Suggestions.

To encourage policemen and firemen to study improved methods and procedure and to keep them interested in the development of their departments, it is urged that they be invited to make suggestions to the respective chiefs or administrative heads as to improved methods and procedure.

To the member of the police department and the member of the fire department making the most practical suggestion for the improvement of the service during each year, there should be awarded by the board of honor a medal and the civil service commission, when established, should grant a special weight in promotional tests to those to whom such medals are awarded.

Medical Care of Policemen and Firemen.

For the medical care of policemen there is employed a police surgeon whose functions include the examination of applicants for appointment, the general medical and surgical care of the members of the force and the instruction of policemen in rules of hygiene and first aid to the injured. The relation of the surgeon to the police department is peculiar, in that while he is appointed by the mayor and removable by him at will, he receives no compensation directly from the city but by charter provision, must be paid by each member of the force one dollar per month for his services, whether he renders any aid to them or not. In the case of chiefs and captains, however, the surgeon waives the fee. His income from the members amounts to more than $2,000 a year.

The procedure for reporting illness is in accordance with good practice as is also the procedure for caring for the medical and surgical needs of the men. Not only does the surgeon perform minor operations, but likewise major operations without extra cost to the policemen. The service rendered by this physician is efficient and the men are well cared for, but the arrangement for employing a surgeon is to be condemned for the reason that the policemen are compelled to contribute out of their already low salary for their medical care. It is distinctly the obligation of the city to provide medical and surgical treatment without any cost to the men.

Time Lost Due to Illness Excessive.

Although the men are given a thorough physical examination at the time of appointment and competent medical aid during their service, the number of days lost due to illness is in excess of normal.

During the year 1916 a total of 1,821 days was lost, due to illness, or an average of nine days for each member of the force. The time lost, due to illness, cost the city approximately $5,500.

The following table shows the causes of illness and the number of cases:

Disease or Injury.	*No. of Cases.*
Appendicitis	5
Apoplexy	2
Abscess (of tooth)	2
Bronchitis	1
Burns	1
Backache	2
Bilious attacks and liver disorder	23
Cholo cystitis	1
Cancer of tongue	1
Carbuncle	2
Colds (ordinary)	57
Conjunctivitis	3
Diarrhoea	8
Dislocation	1
Fractures	2
Gout	1
Gun shot wound	1
Hernia (inguinal)	1
Hemorrhoids	1
Heart disease	3
Indigestion (acute)	5

Indigestion (ordinary) 59
Infected foot 2
Kidney colic 1
Laryngitis 3
LaGrippe 27
Malaria 2
Neuralgia (facial) 18
Neuritis 2
Nephritis (acute) 1
Pneumonia 2
Rheumatism 5
Stricture (urethral) 1
Sprain (ankle) 3
Syphilis 2
   (Removal of glands 1)
Sinusitis 1
Sore feet 5
Sciatica 1
Tonsilitis 10
Toothache 3
Tuberculosis 1
Toxemia 2
Uriticaria 1
Vertigo 1

Total 279

There are various ways in which to account for the excessive time lost due to illness by policemen. The probable causes are, first, the failure of the city years ago adequately to protect the department against persons physically unfit for police service being appointed; second, continued illness covering a long period in the case of several of the policemen, and third, and perhaps the most logical reason, that the city pays full time to policemen when absent on sick leave, regardless of the cause of their illness.

Just how far these causes are responsible for the excessive time lost due to illness, of course, cannot be actually estimated.

Police Surgeon Not Prohibited from Having Business Relations With Members of Force.

While the rules do not prohibit the police surgeon from having busines relations with members of the force by including their families among his private patients, the present incumbent is careful to avoid such relations and except in a few instances does not include among his private patients members of the families of policemen. The few isolated cases in which he serves as a family physician to policemen are accounted for by the fact that prior to his appointment to the police department he had served in this connection. Without in any way reflecting upon the present incumbent, but merely as a matter of good procedure, inasmuch as the police surgeon is a disciplinary officer of the department, it is recommended that a rule be adopted prohibiting him from having any business relations whatever with members of the force.

No Health Records Maintained.

Except that the surgeon makes an informal report of cases attended by him and makes a monthly report to the mayor of officers reporting sick and the cause of their illness, no standard health records of the force are maintained.

Fire Department Without a Surgeon.

No regularly employed surgeon is provided for the fire department and consequently the city does not furnish medical or surgical aid to the firemen. It is true, however, that by virtue of an arrangement with the board of fire commissioners and a local physician, all examinations for appointment are made by the same physician, for which a nominal fee of $1 per examination is paid. Moreover, through the courtesy of this physician and without compensation, firemen are occasionally given free treatment in emergencies.

Time Lost By Firemen Due to Illness Excessive.

The number of days lost due to illness by firemen during the year 1916 was 1,561 days. The following table shows the causes of illness and the number of cases during last year:

Diease or Injury.	*No. of Cases.*
Hallux volgus	1
Rheumatism	3
General breakdown (died)	1
Acute bronchitis	3
Bronchitis	6
Prostatitis and cystitis	1
Asthma	2

Lumbago 3
Articular rheumatism 1
Muscular articular rheumatism 1
Laryngitis 1
Nephritis 1
Frontal sinusitis 2
Inflammation of kidneys 1
Sprained knee 2
Sprained ankle 3
Sprained back 4
Cut hand 2
Scalp wound 1
Fractured ribs 1
Fractured arm 1
Tonsilitis 5
LaGrippe 25
Lobar pneumonia 1
Pneumonia 2
Acute indigestion 4
Biliousness 5
Appendicitis 1
Operation for appendicitis 3
Toxemia 2
Eczema 1
Colitis 2
Chickenpox 1
Gall tract infected 1
Malaria 2
Tonsilar abscess 1
Infection of head and arm 1
Infected foot 1
Infected hand 1
Infected finger 1
Infected toe 1
Fractured ankle 1
Fracture of base of skull 1
Broken collar bone 1

Total 105

Thus, it will be seen that the average number of days lost by each member of the fire department was seven and one-half days, and that the cost to the city of the time lost by firemen, due to illness, was approximately $5,000. The probable causes for the excessive time lost due to illness of the firemen are the same as the causes for lost time in the police department.

Medical Services of Police and Fire Departments Should be Consolidated.

The very nature of the police and fire service makes necessary, in fairness to the men as well as in fairness to the city, that all policemen and all firemen be furnished medical and surgical services without cost to themselves. Therefore, it is recommended that there be appointed, as the result of a competitive civil service examination, a physician who will serve as the medical officer of the police and fire departments and that such doctor be paid a salary by the city of Richmond commensurate with the services rendered. All fees in connection with examinations should be abolished.

Health Records Should Be Maintained.

In connection with his conduct of the medical division, the medical officer should be required to maintain complete and detailed health records of all policemen and firemen, which records should begin with the original examination for appointment and should continue throughout the service of each policeman and fireman. In reporting to the heads of the departments and to the mayor as to the cases of illness treated by him, the surgeon should show with respect to each case not only the cause of illness and the number of days lost in the current case, but the total number of days lost during the current year by the firemen and policemen. The record should show the number of visits made to the homes of these officers, the number of visits received from policemen and firemen at his office, the number of minor operations or dressings, and the number and kind of major operations, the total number of days lost during the month, and the total number during the year to date.

Should Conduct Clinic.

In order that the policemen and firemen shall be kept in the best of health, each member of both departments should be subjected to a thorough physical examination at least once each year, and there should be maintained and conducted by the medical officer at the police and fire headquarters on certain days of each week a clinic, to which the men may come for medical advice.

Equipment to Be Supplied.

The medical officer should be provided with a complete equipment with which to conduct his examinations and treatments, this equipment to remain the property of the city of Richmond.

Policemen and Firemen Should be Paid Half Pay When Absent Due to Ordinary Illness.

An excessive amount of illness among members of the forces is not only costly to the city from an economic point of view, but the efficiency of the service is greatly reduced because of it. Not only does the city pay policemen and firemen when absent because of illness, but the departments must be operated during such times at reduced strength; therefore every effort should be made, both for the benefit of the men and the city, to reduce the amount of illness among policemen and firemen, and thereby reduce the resulting loss of time.

One means which in a number of large cities has produced good results in this direction, is to allow the policemen and firemen when absent on sick leave, due to ordinary illness, half pay and full pay only when the illness is a direct result of an injury received in the performance of duty.

It is therefore recommended that this plan be adopted in Richmond. The medical officer should be the sole judge as to whether a man should receive half or full pay.

The rules should also provide that if in the opinion of the medical officer, the illness is the result of carelessness, immorality or inebriety, no pay should be allowed.

Physical Disability Should Result in Immediate Retirement.

It is the custom in the police department to continue on the sick list for indefinite periods, at full pay, members who are suffering from a chronic condition which renders them permanently disabled.

Several cases appear upon the records where men have been carried on the sick list for more than a year, and in which it is the professional opinion of the medical officer that these men will never be restored to a condition that will permit of their returning to the service. Instead of retiring such members on a disability pension, they are continued in the service at full pay, for the reason that the trustees of the police pension fund seeking to keep their moneys invested and to operate the fund on interest and ordinary contributions, request the surgeon not to recommend the retirement of these men. Not only is this unfair to the city from the point of view that it is paying full salary to men who are rendering no service, but it is unfair to the police department because it reduces the strength of the force and prevents the chief from securing the appointment of active men in the places of those disabled.

This difficulty arises, primarily, out of the fact that the pension fund is a privately incorporated institution and not in any manner under the control of the municipal authorities.

(For a discussion and recommendations with respect to the pension fund, see the section of this report on the benefit funds.)

Regardless of whether or not the city establishes a properly organized and financed municipal pension system, the surgeon should be required in all cases where, after a reasonable period, in his opinion, the disability of the policeman is of a permanent character, to recommend the retirement of such man on a pension.

Trial of Delinquent Policemen and Firemen.

Policemen against whom charges have been preferred are tried by the chief of police, who invariably follows the custom of having the three captains sit with him during such trials. The policeman may subpoena witnesses and is given every opportunity to make a defense. The testimony taken at such trials is stenographically recorded and transcribed. During the year 1916 charges were preferred in 127 cases. The following table shows the charges made and the disposition of the cases:

NATURE OF CHARGE	Number of Cases	DISPOSITION									
		Excused	Required to Perform Extra Tour of Duty	Fined and Reprimanded	Not Sustained	Dismissed from Force	Reprimanded	Fined	Retired	Charge Withdrawn	Transferred to Day Duty
Absent without leave	1	1									
Absent from beat	1							1			
Conduct ... an officer	14	2		2	5	2	1	1		4	1
Failing to report for reserve duty	3	4						1			
Failing to report by box	7		1								
Failing to pay just debts	1		1								
Intoxication	1			3		1	1	1			
Insubordination	1							2			
Late at roll call	52	31	18					5			
Late reporting by box	16	6	5					1			
... city without permission	1							4			
Not found on beat	4	1						7			
Neglect of duty	11		2					1			
Physical disability	3		2				1	1	3	1	
Sitting ... while on duty	10							7			
... under influence of liquor	1							1			
Total	**127**	**45**	**27**	**5**	**5**	**3**	**3**	**30**	**3**	**5**	**1**

While under the general conditions of the charter the mayor would have the right to suspend a policeman and to try and dismiss him in the same manner as he has the right to suspend and try any city employee, nevertheless the special provisions of the charter pertaining to police place the matter of the trial of delinquent policemen under the chief of police. This procedure is most defective. The theory under which it was established in the charter is that the responsibility for maintaining discipline in the police department is placed in the chief, and consequently he should have the right to impose penalties for infractions of rules. The law is somewhat inconsistent, in that the policeman tried and dismissed by the chief of police has no right of appeal whatever, while on the other hand, a policeman tried and dismissed by the mayor would have the inherent right of all city employees to appeal to the judge of the hustings court.

While the theory of making the chief of police responsible for maintaining discipline is good, yet it must be remembered that the law makes him responsible to the mayor, in whom is vested responsibility for the entire control and management of the police service. The chief of police was selected from among the members of the force, having served within its ranks for many years, and might naturally in that time have accumulated many prejudices and biases which would tend to reduce his efficiency as a trial officer. Moreover, it is the experience of most cities that trial by members of a uniformed force does not always result in obtaining the best discipline. Policemen in all cities, whether chief of police or captains, are prone to lean towards members of the force in matters of complaints made against them by citizens. This frequently results in dissatisfaction. Since the mayor is responsible for the entire management of the force, it is recommended that the charter be amended so as to vest him with the right of disposing of delinquent policemen. All trials should be heard before him and all punishments imposed by him. However, the law should provide that all cases of minor infractions of the rule be disposed of by the chief, and his power of imposing punishment should be limited to that of ordering extra tours of duty and reprimanding.

Delinquent firemen are tried by the board of fire commissioners. They are given a public hearing and accorded the privilege of interposing a defense and subpoenaing witnesses. During the year 1916 there were but seven firemen placed upon charges. The delinquent report during the past five years and the disposition of cases are shown by the following table:

Charges and Punishments in the Richmond Fire Department During the Past Five Years.

YEARS	Intoxication	Absence With-out Leave	Insubordina-tion	Conduct Pre-judicial to Good Order, Etc	Neglect of Duty	Discharged from Department	Fined	Reprimanded	Deprived of "Relief Days"	Reduced in Grade	Charges Not Sustained and Dismissed
(Captain)											
1912	3	4	2	2	1	5	1	3	2		1
1913	6	1				4	1	1	1		1
1914	10	5	2	1		1	2		8	2	5
1915	6	5		2		2	3	3	5		
1916	4	3					3	2	2		

The procedure in the fire department may be said to be in accordance with good practice.

Sanitary Conditions in Station Houses.

All of the buildings occupied by the police department were inspected and observed and found to be clean and orderly. The building occupied by the second district force is in poor repair, but this station is to be transferred to the new building now in course of erection and nearing completion. But even this building, old as it is, is clean and well kept. However, the cost of cleaning these stations is unnecessarily high, in that in each of the stations there are employed a janitor and janitress. The buildings are small and only a part of them is in actual use, and the services of a janitor should be dispensed with at once. Moreover, a further economy could be produced by dispensing with the services of the janitress and using prisoners from the city jail for the cleaning of the station houses.

Uniforms and Equipment.

The uniforms worn by the members of the force are of the approved modern type, except in minor respects.

The patrolman's uniform coat has a roll collar which tends to make the uniform appear untidy. The modern standing military collar should be adopted for all uniform blouses or coats.

The policemen at present are permitted to wear varied styles of collars and ties. Because of this fact, the general appearance of many of the police officers are anything but tidy.

Under the present rules policemen are only required to keep the top button of their uniform blouse buttoned; thus, the coat appears to be entirely open and, as a matter of fact, in many instances is entirely open, which gives the men a careless appearance. There is no justification for allowing a military uniform, such as is worn by the police, to remain unbuttoned. The rules should be amended so as to require the uniform to be completely buttoned at all times.

It is customary for the policemen to have less regard for their general appearance when off duty, but in uniform. A policeman is never off duty, although he may be temporarily relieved from his post. The rules with respect to the appearance of policemen relieved from their assignments should require that policemen be neat and tidy at all times. The rules with respect to uniforms should be enforced just as rigidly when men are going to and from their district stations as when actually on patrol. A policeman should never be permitted to smoke while in uniform, regardless of the time.

Many of the policemen wear their caps either tilted to one side or on the back of the head. This practice should be prohibited, and the caps worn squarely on the head. Nothing tends to disfigure the appearance of a policeman more than the wearing of a hat tilted to one side.

New Design of Shield Suggested.

The shields worn are of a very old design.

The numbers on the patrolmen's shield are not sufficiently distinctive to enable their being readily observed. At such time as new shields are adopted, a shield of a modern design, having on it the seal of the city and the patrolman's number conspicuously displayed, should be used.

The sergeants' shield should be of a different design from that worn by the patrolmen.

The shield worn by the captains should be made of gold and of much more dignified design than the present one.

Methods of Purchasing Uniforms Defective.

Policemen are required to purchase and pay for all of their uniforms. The average cost of a policeman's uniform and equipment during his first year of service is about $50. The city makes no contribution towards this sum, nor is provision made to advance money to the recruit.

For the purpose of securing a uniform grade and color of cloth, the purchasing agent secures the cloth by the roll as needed and pays for it out of the police department cost fund.

The policemen are then required to pay for it as they receive it, and the money is turned back into the fund.

The cloth is purchased by the brand, no specifications being used, and no laboratory tests are made of deliveries to determine whether the cloth is manufactured and dyed in accordance with the company's agreement.

The policemen are at liberty to have their uniforms made by any tailor they choose, and it is apparent that many of the tailors do not quite understand how to make a uniform. The result is that all of the uniforms are not made exactly alike.

It is recommended that the city supply and pay for the uniforms and equipment used by policemen and firemen, and a provision made to purchase all these things by contract. If the city is financially unable to defray this expense, the department should at least make arrangements to furnish them by contract, having them all made by one tailor and charged to the policemen at the actual cost of production. The city should pay the original cost and then collect it from the policemen in equal monthly installments.

Revolvers Should be Carried in the Blouse Instead of the Hip Pocket.

The city supplies the patrolmen with a 38 Colt's police modern revolver.

The present practice of carrying the revolver in the hip pocket should be abandoned and the regulations amended so as to require that revolvers be carried in a holster in the blouse on the left side, so as to be available in emergency and to reduce the danger of accidental discharge.

Distribution of Force.

The police force is organized as follows:

For Administration:
1	Mayor	————*
1	Secretary and purchasing agent	$1,440.00

Uniformed force:
1	Chief	2,520.00
3	Captains	1,440.00
7	Desk sergeants	1,212.00
9	Patrol sergeants	1,212.00
114	Foot patrolmen	1,002.30
14	Bicycle patrolmen	1,002.30
18	Mounted patrolmen	1,002.30
1	Disabled officer—receiving full pay	1,002.30
1	Patrolman, night duty headquarters	1,002.30

Detective Service:
1	Captain	1,440.00
**6	Detective sergeants	1,212.00
2	Patrolmen—detailed	1,002.30

For the Maintenance of Criminal Records:
  1 Bertillon operator 1,002.30

For the Regulation of Traffic:
  1 Sergeant 1,002.30
  12 Patrolmen 1,002.30
  2 Auto speed officers 1,002.30

For the Maintenance of the Signal Service:
  2 Patrolmen—telephone operators 1,002.30
  1 Civilian operator 900.00
  2 Linemen at respectively $960.00 and....... 900.00

*Mayor's salary not charged to police.

**Two of these detective sergeants receive $150.00 each per anuum as court officers of the Hustings Court.

For the Transportation Service:
  4 Chauffeurs $1,020.00
  2 Chauffeurs 780.00
  1 Chauffeur 900.00

Assigned to Courts:
  2 Patrolmen—court attendants 1,002.30
  3 Patrolmen—probation officers juvenile court. 1,002.30

For Clerical Service:
  1 Patrolman 1,002.30

For the Care of Female Prisoners:
  1 Matron 720.00

For the Care of Buildings:
  2 Janitresses 240.00
  5 Janitors 780.00

For the Medical Care of Members of the Force:
  1 Surgeon (per month) 203.00
    (Salary paid by assessment against each member of the force of one dollar per month).

For the Care of Horses:
    1 Civilian hostler 780.00
Mayor not included.

Unit of Distribution Police Districts.

The city is divided into three districts, namely, the first, second and third.

In each district, there is a station house which is under the command of a captain, who is empowered under the rules to distribute his men within the precinct in such a manner as he deems wise, transferring them from post to post. This method of distribution is in accordance with good practice.

The distribution of the force by districts and hours of duty is as follows:

First District:
    One captain in command.
      8:00 A. M. to 4:00 P. M.—
        1 Desk sergeant.
        1 Patrol sergeant.
        2 Mounted patrolmen.
        1 House duty.
      10 Foot patrolmen.
        ——
      15

      4:00 P. M. to 12:00 M.—
        1 Desk sergeant.
        2 Patrol sergeants.
        3 Mounted patrolmen.
        3 Bicycle patrolmen.
        1 House duty.
      18 Foot patrolmen.
        ——
      28

      12:00 M. to 8:00 A. M.—
        1 Desk sergeant.
        2 Patrol sergeants.
        2 Mounted patrolmen.
        3 Bicycle patrolmen.
        1 House duty.
      17 Foot patrolmen.
        ——
      26

In addition to the above force there are attached to this district six patrolmen assigned to traffic duty, two patrolmen performing duty in plain clothes, one patrolman detailed to the detective bureau and one patrolman detailed to headquarters for night service.

There are also employed and assigned to this district the following civilian employees:

  1 Matron.
  1 Hostler.
  1 Janitor.
  I Janitress.
  2 Patrol chauffeurs.
  —
  6

The total for this district is 86.

Second District:

One captain in command.

8:00 A. M. to 4:00 P. M.—

  1 Desk sergeant.
  1 Patrol sergeant.
  10 Foot patrolmen.
  3 Assigned to traffic duty.
  1 Bicycle and house man.
  1 Auto traffic patrolman.
  2 Mounted patrolmen.
  2 Patrolmen detailed in plain clothes.
  —
  21

  1 Janitor.
  1 Janitress.
  1 Mechanic.
  —
  3

4:00 P. M. to 12:00 M.—

  1 Desk sergeant.
  2 Patrol sergeants.
  18 Foot patrolmen.
  3 Assigned to traffic duty.
  1 Bicycle and house man.

1 Auto traffic patrolman.
3 Bicycle patrolmen.
3 Mounted patrolmen.
———
32

12:00 M. to 8:00 A. M.—
1 Desk sergeant.
1 Patrol sergeant.
18 Foot patrolmen.
1 Bicycle and house man.
1 Auto traffic patrolman.
2 Bicycle patrolmen.
4 Mounted patrolmen.
———
28

2 Chauffeurs of patrol working on twelve-hour shifts.
Total roster for district, 87.

Third District:
One captain in command.
8:00 A. M. to 4:00 P. M.—
1 Desk sergeant.
1 Sergeant detailed to duty in plain clothes.
3 Foot patrolmen.
1 Mounted patrolman.
———
6

4:00 P. M. to 12:00 M.—
1 Acting desk sergeant.
5 Foot patrolmen.
1 Mounted patrolmen.
———
7

12:00 M. to 8:00 A. M.—
1 Acting desk sergeant.
6 Foot patrolmen.
1 Mounted patrolmen.
———
8

2 Chauffeurs of patrol working on twelve hour shifts.
Total on roster of district, 24.

The total number of employees is 222, of whom 203 are members of the force and 19 are civilian employees.

Policemen Detailed to Duties Other Than Patrol and the Supervision of Patrol.

Of the 203 members of the force there are detailed to duties other than patrol and the supervision of patrol, the following:

To traffic duty	15
To detective bureau	9
To courts	5
To clerical work	1
As Bertillon operator	1
As telephone operators	2
To plain clothes duty in precincts	5
	38

Thus the actual patrol force and supervisory officers consist of but 165.

Details Which Should Be Abolished.

It will be noted, upon reading the above tabulation, that the duties performed by eight of the policemen detailed, namely, clerical work, the operation of telephone board and court attendants, are not such as require the services of a policeman. The detailing of these policemen to this work further reduces the actual strength of the force for police work.

It is, therefore, recommended that the following details be abolished and that civilians be employed to perform the work now done by these policemen:

The two details to the police court.

The three details to the juvenile court.

The two details as telephone operators.

The one detail to clerical work.

In the place of the policeman detailed as clerk, there should be employed a civilian clerk, while in the place of the two policemen assigned to the telephone board, there should be employed two telephone operators.

The employees, such as court attendants and probation officers retained to replace the policemen, should be charged respectively to the police court and the juvenile court budgets and should not be, as at present, included in the cost of operation of the police service.

The use of policemen for duties other than actual police work has long since been condemned as unnecessarily expensive and destructive to discipline within the police service, for the reason that such details are usually regarded by the members of the force who do not succeed in obtaining them, as "easy berths" obtained through the use of political influence.

Third District Station Should Be Abolished.

For the policing of the newly annexed section known as the "south side" which was formerly the city of Manchester, and the several small communities included within that annexed territory, there is maintained a station and a separate set of officers. This section is known as the "third district" and to it there are detailed a total of twenty-four members of the police department.

To answer the calls for transportation of prisoners, there is operated in the third district an automobile patrol wagon.

That this territory has been established as a police district with a separate station house is the result of a provision of law enacted in connection with the annexation agreement. Whether or not this statute can be interpreted as having required the maintenance of a separate police station for a period longer than five years after annexation is questioned by most of the police officials and many of the lawyers in the city.

But whether or not the law as at present in force, compels the authorities to maintain this station house and to continue the section as a separate police district, the fact remains that such a procedure is wholly unnecessary and results in a waste of public funds.

It is, therefore, recommended that even to the extent of amending the law, if necessary, the third district be abolished and the territory now included within it be made a part of the first police district and placed under the command of the captain of that district.

All calls for the patrol wagon in that section should be answered by the motor patrol now serving the first district, and all prisoners arrested therein should be detained in the first district station and arraigned in the police court of the city of Richmond.

During the year 1916, according to the annual report of the police department, there were 1,723 arrests made, and 482 ordinance violations reported in this district. Thus it will be seen that the average number of arrests per day in this district during that year was slightly less than 5. This, however, is further reduced by the fact that the 1,723 arrests do not necessarily mean that 1,723 persons were taken into custody because of the practice of crediting as an arrest each charge made against a defendant. In other words, if a person were arrested and charged with 8 different offenses. 8 arrests would be credited. Since the enactment of prohibition legislation, this number of arrests has been greatly reduced. until now the average number of arrests made in that section is about 3 a day. It must be obvious that in a section of the city wherein there are so few arrests made that there is no occasion for maintaining a police station with the consequent overhead expenses involved.

Number of Police Used to Patrol South Side Excessive.

To patrol and supervise patrol in this sparsely populated section of the city, the major portion of which is undeveloped and highly suburban. there are employed twenty-four members of the police department.

Prior to annexation the police force of the south side consisted of five men.

Wholly aside from the question of whether or not the use of the police station is discontinued, the number of men assigned to this section is excessive and should be greatly reduced.

The use of foot patrolmen in this section is not only a waste of funds. but likewise. a waste of the time of the men assigned.

Pending the adjustment of the law with respect to the abo¹' tion of the station house. it is possible even with the law as at present in force, to reduce the number of men assigned to this district.

Therefore, it is recommended that the mayor immediately cause to be discontinued the patrol wagon assigned to this district. transfer the captain for night service at headquarters and place the district under the command of a sergeant.

It is further recommended that the assignments to this district be as follows:

One sergeant in charge.

Three patrolmen detailed as desk sergeants.

Nine patrolmen.

The nine patrolmen, instead of being assigned to patrol posts, should be located in police patrol booths and all operate as motorcycle or bicycle policemen.

This would result in a saving in so far as the policing of this section of the city is concerned of $11,000 per year without reducing the police protection.

If the use of the station house were abandoned a further saving of the salaries of the three policemen detailed as acting sergeants on desk duty would result, thus increasing the total saving to $14,000 a year.

It is the practice at present to assign a policeman to duty within Forest Hill Park. This park is owned and operated by a private corporation as an amusement park. It is the business of the corporation owning this park to provide therein, though the use of its own employees, whatever police protection is required, and the city should not be called upon to bear the expense of policing such an enterprise any more than it should be called upon to place a policeman within a department store or a hotel.

It is, therefore, recommended that this detail be discontinued at once.

Detailed Policemen Should Not Be Assigned to Districts.

The traffic policemen, the policemen serving at headquarters during the night, and those detailed to the detective bureau, are assigned to districts and carried on the rolls of such stations. This practice should be discontinued and all such detailed officers carried on separate rolls, such as a payroll for the traffic division, a headquarters payroll and the detective bureau roll.

No Need for Additional Patrolmen.

According to the plan of distribution in the city of Richmond at present, there are 165 members of the force available for patrol and the supervision of patrol, which is an ample number of men, in view of the crime conditions of the city, and the character of the population to meet the needs of the community.

However, better results could be obtained by an improved distribution of the force which will be referred to later.

By abolishing the right details and restoring these men to active service, the force will be further increased by eight, making the total available force 173, approximately one policeman for every 1,000 population, exclusive of the detective service and the supervision of traffic.

Increases in Strength of Force and Appropriations Have Been Liberal.

That the city has been liberal in the matter of increasing the strength of police force and in its appropriations for the management thereof is disclosed by the following table, which shows that the strength of the force has been increased since 1907, when the population was but 106,227, from 126 to 203 in 1917, with a population of 172,178; while the annual appropriation has been increased from $160,618.35 in 1907, to $303,849.61 in 1917:

Table Showing Increase in Strength of Force and Appropriations Since 1907.

Year	Area Sq. Miles	Popula-tion	Chief	Cap-tains	Ser-geants	Patrol-men	Detec-tives	Appro-priation	Arrests
1907....	9 959	106,227	1	4	14	102	5	$160,618 35	9,602
1908....	9.959	107,844	1	4	14	102	5	153 659 83	8 989
1909....	9.959	109,461	1	5	14	101	5	146,458 00	9,290
1910....	11.079	127,628	1	5	15	107	5	152,818 13	9,608
1911....	11.079	129,291	1	5	15	137	5	193,026 25	10,497
1912....	11.079	130,668	1	5	15	136	6	205,755 80	11,072
1913....		132 045	1	5	15	136	6	218,000 00	12,428
1914....	24.383	154,675	1	5	15	151	6	248 587 50	12,170
1915....	24.383	156,687	1	5	15	151	6	259,272 06	12,728
1916....	24.383	158,700	1	5	16	175	6	313,484 71	13,220
1917....	24.383	172 178	1	5	16	173	8	303 849 61	*4,821

*Arrests to June 30th, inclusive.

Need for Re-apportionment of Patrol Posts.

The city is divided into 60 patrol posts, the shortest of which is 3 blocks, while the longest in the outlying districts is approximately 3 miles and the average about 10 blocks. These are divided into 30 day posts and 60 night posts. In other words, the day posts are in most instances a combination of 2 night posts.

Because crime records are not kept in a proper form, it was not possible to make a comprehensive study of the posts in the time allowed, but practically all of the posts located in the center of the city and a number of those in the suburbs were observed. Those studied indicated the need for re-apportionment since some were found to be unnecessarily short, especially those on Broad Street, and others too long, while still others, such as those on the south side and the ultra-suburban sections, should be abolished as street and mounted posts and patrol booths established instead.

The patrol posts are established by the chief upon the recommendations of the captains of the districts. Their location and length are determined first, geographically, second by the general character of the neighborhood, and third, with reference to the number of policemen available. The department is without proper information to form the basis of an efficient apportionment of posts.

To divide the city into patrol posts on an equitable basis, it is necessary that the person establishing the posts have before him accurate information concerning the conditions as to crime, character of buildings, population, kind of business transacted and nationality of the population of every block in the city. Upon no other basis can posts be equitably established. This information must be brought up to date from time to time since the uninhabited block of today may be the congested tenement or business block of tomorrow. The conditions as to population, buildings and occupants, etc., are changing continually, and with these changes come new and different police problems which make it necessary to change the methods of giving protection.

Therefore. it is recommended that the chief of police cause a census to be taken of every block in the city, not only as to the number of people, but also as to block conditions, which in any way affect the police problem. The information thus secured should be recorded upon cards having printed headings similar to those contained in the following illustrations:

POLICE DEPARTMENT

	PRECINCT	POST	BLOCK	LENGTH OF BLOCK	KIND OF PAVEMENT	TRAFFIC	CHARACTER OF BLOCK	NO. OF BUILDINGS

BLOCK DESCRIPTION

DATE

STREET OR AVENUE ____ BETWEEN ____ AND ____

BUILDINGS ON BLOCK

STREET LIGHTING	RESIDENCE	MAJORITY NATIONALITY	BUSINESS	MIXED	OTHER	HOUSES IN REAR	TENEMENTS	FURNISHED ROOM HOUSES	NO. OF FAMILIES IN BLOCK

ESTIMATED POPULATION	NIGHT OR DAY POST	OTHER PATROL SERVICE	ALLEYS	TRANSPORTATION LINES

IMPORTANT RISKS

BANKS ____

LARGE BANKS ____

PRIVATE BANKS ____

BANKS WITH SAFE DEPOSIT VAULTS ____

JEWELRY STORES ____

RETAIL ____

WHOLESALE ____

STORAGE WAREHOUSES ____

MERCANTILE LOFT BUILDINGS ____

OTHER STORES WITH VALUABLE STOCK ____

FURTHER DESCRIPTION ____

EXCISE AND VICE CONDITIONS

SALOONS ____

WITH BACK ROOMS ____

SELL TO WOMEN ____

DISORDERLY ____

REPUTABLE ____

RENT ROOMS ____

HOTELS ____

RAINES LAW ____

DISORDERLY ____

REPUTABLE ____

SUSPECTED GAMBLING

HANDBOOKS ____

POOL ROOMS ____

NIGHT GAMES ____

POKER CLUBS ____

POLICY SHOPS ____

GENERAL ____

DANCE HALLS ____

REPUTABLE ____

DISORDERLY ____

SELL LIQUOR ____

POOL AND BILLIARD ROOMS

REPUTABLE ____

QUESTIONABLE ____

TROUBLESOME ____

SUSP'D DISORDERLY HOUSES ____

HOUSES OF PROSTITUTION ____

DISORDERLY FLATS ____

DISORDERLY FURNISHED ROOMS ____

RED HOUSES ____

MASSAGE PARLORS ____

INSPECTIONAL GROUP

PAWNSHOPS	STANDS (STOOP LINE)	THEATRES
REPUTABLE	CIGAR	RESTAURANTS AND LUNCH R'MS
CHARACTER	SODA WATER	OPEN ALL NIGHT
SECOND-HAND DEALERS	FRUIT AND VEGETABLE	SELL LIQUOR
JUNK	NEWS AND MAGAZINE	DISORDERLY
CLOTHES	GENERAL MERCHANDISE	PUBLICLY OWNED BUILDINGS
GENERAL	PUSH-CART	MUNICIPAL BATHS
REPUTABLE	BOOTBLACK	LIBRARIES
SUSPECTED FENCE	CLUBS, (SOCIAL, ETC.)	AUDITORIUMS
MOVING PICTURE SHOWS	REPUTABLE	FIRE HOUSES
REPUTATION	QUESTIONABLE	STABLES
GARAGES	TROUBLESOME	MISCELLANEOUS
STABLES	NO. OF GROUND FLOOR STORES	
	NO. OF BASEMENT STORES	

EXTRA SERVICE GROUP

SCHOOLS	CHURCHES	PLACES OF PUBLIC ASSEMBLY
PUBLIC	CATHOLIC	"CLOSED FOR PLAY" AREAS
PRIVATE	PROTESTANT	OTHER
HOSPITALS AND SANITARIUMS	HEBREW	
PUBLIC	OTHER	
PRIVATE		

CRIME RECORD

COMPLAINTS—NO. OF MISDEMEANORS _____ NO. OF FELONIES _____

ARRESTS—NO. OF MISDEMEANORS _____ NO. OF FELONIES _____ NO. OF SUMMONSES ISSUED _____

MISCELLANEOUS _____

After the chief has collected the essential information concerning the above conditions he should then have a tabulation prepared of the crime complaints affecting each block in the city, and based upon this information should make a re-apportionment of the posts which should be laid out for the most part on a straight way patrol plan; that is, a definite number of blocks on an avenue or main street with a half block of each intersecting side street to compose a post. Thus, if the policeman is on his post the citizen can readily find him, the sergeant can easily overtake him, and the policeman can have a continuous view of the greater part of the post for which he is responsible.

The mistake is made in Richmond of having practically all circular posts. The circular posts should be abandoned as promptly as possible.

Maps of Patrol Posts Should Be Provided.

Each district station house should be equipped with maps showing the location of. patrol posts in the districts with the relief points indicated thereon. A set of these maps should be kept at the offices of the chief and the mayor.

Broad Street Over-policed.

Because of the failure to provide a proper apportionment of patrol posts, Broad street, which is the busiest thoroughfare in the city, and which, by reason of the number of people walking to and fro, receives a large percentage of self-protection up to midnight, is very much over-policed.

The posts on Broad street are entirely too short, so that walking along Broad street between four in the afternoon and midnight, one will find policemen standing about at most every corner.

In addition to the regular patrol posts on Broad street there are three traffic posts. A majority of the relieving points are located on Broad street; thus, at least twice a day, namely, four in the afternoon and midnight, a large per cent. of the force is assembled on Broad street. There are twenty-two relieving points located on Broad street. Of course the natural custom of the policemen is to spend the most of the last hour of the tour in the vicinity of their relieving points, and it is also the custom for the policemen upon coming on duty to spend considerable time at the relieving point.

All this tends to reduce the amount of police protection furnished the other parts of the city. It is wholly illogical and against good police practice to centralize relieving points in any one section of the city. At such time as the posts are re-apportioned, the relieving points should be distributed so as to provide for an equitable allotment throughout the city.

A re-apportionment of the patrol posts on Broad street as promptly as possible is urged, and when this is done the posts should be arranged on the straight way plan. There is no need of having any day posts in the section of Broad street where there are located traffic posts, and there is no reason for having short posts on the tour from 4:00 to 12:00 midnight, on this thoroughfare. A straight way post of ten blocks should be established on each side of Broad street in the center of the city.

That Broad street is over-policed is primarily due to the fact that before the enactment of the prohibition law a large number of saloons were located on Broad street and near Broad on the intersecting streets. It was then deemed wise to have short patrol posts in this section. These saloons no longer exist, and consequently there is now no necessity for short posts.

No Adequate Means of Reaching Patrolmen.

To reach the patrolmen on their posts the department depends upon communicating with the men who call in on their hourly call over the signal boxes, and upon two flashlights in one section of the city.

It is important that the police department be able to meet all emergencies by dispatching the required number of policemen promptly. This cannot be done at present because of the absence of a proper signal system and a reserve force. It is therefore recommended that arrangements be made as soon as the financial condition of the city will permit, to install throughout the city a system of signal lights by which the patrolmen may be notified when wanted. It is not necessary that any high-priced and extremely costly patented system be adopted. The mechanics involved in the installation of such a system do not call for the expenditure of any large sum of money. The city electrical department should be instructed to submit an estimate as to the cost of such a system.

A Reserve Force Should Be Established.

The force is now operated on the straight three-platoon plan, but does not provide for any reserve force, thus leaving the department without any available means of meeting a riot call or any other emergency. As at present organized, but one man is available in each district in case of urgent calls. It is recommended that there be established at once a reserve in the first and second districts. This reserve should consist of not less than four men on all tours. Each member of the force should be required to serve on reserve duty in his turn. Provision should be made for permitting these men on reserve to sleep at the station, and the rule should prohibit their being disturbed or called from their sleep for anything except a real emergency.

Method of Appointing Special Policemen Defective.

Special officers are appointed by the mayor pursuant to section 87 of the ordinance. There are at present but six of such officers exclusive of city employees who are vested with police powers. The procedure in making appointments involves merely the filing of a request with the mayor by the employer.

The appointment is made without referring the application to the police chief and without even notifying the department after the appointment has been made; there are no regulations as to uniforms or badges. The special officer is permitted to have any kind of a badge made he desires. Most of the badges used resemble closely the regulation department shield. They are not required to furnish the city with any bond.

Special policemen should be appointed only after they have been thoroughly investigated and with the approval of the chief of police. They should be required to furnish the city a bond in the amount of not less than one thousand dollars and should be furnished a shield vastly different in design from that worn by regular policemen. Their uniform should be designed by the chief of police, and while it should be distinctive, neat and of good design, it should not in any way resemble the police uniform.

Co-operation With Other City Departments Said to Be Good.

Although no definite formal procedure through the use of standard report forms has been adopted as an aid to the policemen in reporting matters observed by them on patrol, the co-operation between the police department and the other departments has been said to be good except with relation to violation of sanitary laws. The procedure is for the patrolmen to report such matters to his sergeant and to make an entry of them in his memorandum book. These are entered by the sergeants in what is called the "miscellaneous report sheet" and forwarded each morning to headquarters.

At headquarters a clerk copies from these reports such matters as are to be called to the attention of other departments and forwards to the department a written report.

This is a cumbersome procedure and does not serve to stimulate the policemen in the matter of reporting such conditions. No reward whatever is given through any efficiency rating for special diligence in the matter of reporting, nor are policemen punished in any way when it is discovered that they have neglected to report matters observed. Moreover, there is no special review of reports made by the policemen, thus furnishing no encouragement whatever.

In the matter of reporting violations of ordinances, however, the records indicate that the policemen are fairly efficient, but the failure of the judge of the police court to co-operate by adequately punishing offenders reported has served to discourage the policemen, and thus reduce their interest in this most important work. It is further apparent that because of a proper lack of understanding as to what matters to report pertaining to street cleaning and highway defects, and how often such conditions should be called to the attention of the street department, the co-operation of the police with this department is not effective.

The reporting of matters observed by policemen is a matter of prime importance. Nothing existing in violation of an ordinance and no condition in need of repair should go unobserved and unreported, and on the other hand, no such matters reported should fail to receive the prompt attention of the departments to which they are reported.

The present memorandum book in use is the old-style grocery credit book, and does not lend itself to a good procedure for reporting. It is therefore recommended that the present style of memorandum book be abandoned and in its place a standard loose-leaf memorandum be adopted, in which the policemen should be required to carry special printed forms upon which to report conditions observed. These reports should include among others the following forms:

Report of highway accidents,
Report of unusual occurrences,
Report of gas and electric outages,
Report of street pavements and highway conditions,
Report of arrests,
Report of violations of corporation ordinances.

These forms should be printed so as to permit the use of check marks Instead of having to write lengthy reports. They should be designed somewhat in accordance with the following illustrations:

POLICE DEPARTMENT —Form For Reporting Accidents.

Pct. | No. | TIME AND DATE OF OCCURRENCE: | PLACE OF OCCURRENCE:

A. M. | P. M.

TOTAL NUMBER OF PERSONS KILLED OR INJURED.............. (If more than three, use extra cards for their names, etc.)

NAME OF PERSON KILLED OR INJURED	ADDRESS	AGE	SEX	SERIOUSNESS OF INJURIES
(1)				
(2)				
(3)				

FAULT OR INCAPACITY OF INJURED PERSONS: ☐ Intoxicated; ☐ Ill; ☐ Crippled; ☐ Blind; ☐ Deaf;

☐ Crossed street, not at crossing; ☐ Stealing ride; Careless.

IF UNDER 16, WAS CHILD GOING TO OR FROM SCHOOL? YES NO — IN FRONT OF SCHOOL? YES NO

NAME OF WITNESS — ADDRESS

NATURE OF ACCIDENT

GENERAL LOCATION
☐ Intersection of streets
☐ Crossing
☐ Protected by stanchions
☐ Isles of safety
☐ Car stops, unprotected
☐ On one way street
☐ Street, other than above
☐ Bridge
☐ Sidewalk
☐ Traffic post
OTHER THAN ABOVE

CAUSE OF ACCIDENT

FRONT

ANSWER EVERY QUESTION. STRIKE OUT IRRELEVANT MATTER.

(VEHICLE No. 1)	(VEHICLE No. 2)
Driver's Name and Address — License Number	Driver's Name and Address — License Number
Owner's Name and Address — License Number	Owner's Name and Address — License Number

DRIVEN BY—Owner, Family, Employee, Other:
Sex...... Age...... No Driver
Violation of Traffic Regulations

DRIVEN BY—Owner, Family, Employer. Other:
Sex...... Age...... No Driver
Violation of Traffic Regulations

VEHICLE—Street Car No...............

Heavy Truck   Taxicab   Train
Light Truck   Carriage   Bus
Private Auto   Buggy   Cab
Motorcycle   Bicycle   Hack
Ambulance
Saddle Horse

POWER — Electricity, Gasoline, Steam. Horse, Foot or Hand
Other

DEFECTS OF VEHICLE — Steering Gear, Brakes, Lights Out
Other:

SKIDDING?   Yes   No
Was Vehicle Equipped with Tire Chains?
Yes   No

FAULT OR INCAPACITY OF DRIVER—
Intoxicated, Ill; Crippled, Deaf
Other:

VEHICLE—Street Car No................

Heavy Truck   Taxicab   Train
Light Truck   Carriage   Bus
Private Auto   Buggy   Cab
Motorcycle   Bicycle   Hack
Ambulance
Saddle Horse

POWER — Electricity, Gasoline, Steam. Horse, Foot or Hand
Other:

DEFECTS OF VEHICLE — Steering Gear, Brakes, Lights Out
Other:

SKIDDING?   Yes   No
Was Vehicle Equipped with Tire Chains
Yes   No

FAULT OR INCAPACITY OF DRIVER—
Intoxicated, Ill, Crippled, Deaf
Other:

Damage to Vehicles or to Other Property

WEATHER—Clear, Foggy, Raining, Snowing, High wind

STREET CONDITIONS—Slippery, Wet, Snow, Ice, Street Lights Out, Poorly Lighted, Excavation, Obstruction, Encroachment

PAVEMENT—Kind   Condition   Broken?   Yes   No

Was the Officer who makes this report a witness of the Accident?   Yes   No
Was a Traffic man on post at the time of accident?   Yes   No

Broken pavement was reported?   Yes   No
By whom?
Date

(Signature)
Rank................ Shield No........

REVERSE

PRECINCT	POLICE DEPARTMENT	POST No

DATE_____191

REPORT OF....................................... ....
(Indicate subject here.)

TIME OF OBSERVATION.................. ....

LOCATION ....

DETAILS ....

....

....

....

....

....

ACTION TAKEN ....

....

....

....

....

(Rank)	(Signature)	(Shield No.)

NOTE

On this general form the Patrolman shall report Fires, Unlocked Premises, Suspicious Places, etc.

Each report of an occurrence or observation shall bear a subject title in the blank space provided.

POLICE DEPARTMENT

PRECINCT | POST No.

LAMP OUTAGES

DATE_____191

LOCATION OF LAMP	Post No.	Time Lamp Went out	Time Lamp Was Re-lighted	Broken Globe	Broken Mantle	Kind of Lamp

Use check mark for broken globe or mantle.

ACTION TAKEN _____

(Rank)   (Signature)   (Shield No.)

Precinct

Post No

POLICE DEPARTMENT

PATROLMAN'S REPORT

Date..191

To the Commanding Officer of the Precinct:

At.....................M., I observed the following condition and took the action noted:

Location _____

Matters Affecting Department of Public Works

BROKEN CURB STONE	BROKEN SIDEWALK	
DANGEROUS TREE	DEFECTIVE SEWER CATCH BASIN	
HOLE IN STREET	BROKEN MANHOLE COVER	

NAME DEPARTMENT OR CORPORATION
CONTROLLING BROKEN MANHOLE COVER

Matters Affecting Department of Water Supply, Gas and Electricity

DANGEROUS GAS BOX	BROKEN ELECTRIC WIRE	
LEAKING GAS	SAGGING ELECTRIC WIRE	
BROKEN STREET LAMP	LEAKING HYDRANT	

BROKEN ELECTRIC LIGHT STREET FIXTURE

Matters Affecting Bureau of Buildings

UNPROTECTED EXCAVATION	DANGEROUS FENCE	
DANGEROUS CONDITION OF BUILDING	DANGEROUS SHED	
DANGEROUS CONDITION OF SIGN, ELECTRIC OR OTHER		

Matters Affecting Bureau of Encumbrances

SIDEWALK ENCUMBRANCE, PERMANENT	
SIDEWALK ENCUMBRANCE, TEMPORARY	
HIGHWAY ENCUMBRANCE	

Matters Affecting Department of Licenses—Unlicensed Places

STORES, 2D HAND		STANDS		POOL ROOMS	
PAWNBROKERS		AUCTIONS		JUNK SHOPS	
DANCE HALLS		BOWLING ALLEYS		SHOOTING GALLERIES	

Matters Affecting Department of Street Cleaning

SIDEWALK OR STREET ENCUMBRANCE (RUBBISH)	

Matters Affecting Department of Health

DEAD CAT		DEAD DOG		DEAD HORSE	

(over)

FRONT

REPORT HERE ANY MATTER NOT LISTED ON CARD

ACTION TAKEN

(Rank)   (Signature)   (Shield .)

REVERSE

PRECINCT

POST No.

REPORT OF ARREST

POLICE DEPARTMENT

DATE OF ARREST | TIME

NAME OF PRISONER (SURNAME) (FIRST NAME)

AGE	NATIONALITY	SEX M F	COLOR BLACK WHITE	MARRIED OR SINGLE	OCCUPATION

CHARGED WITH

PLACE OF ARREST

PLACE OF DETENTION

DETAILS COVERING ARREST AND CHARGE

PROPERTY TAKEN FROM PRISONER

NAME AND ADDRESS OF COMPLAINANT

NAMES AND ADDRESSES OF WITNESSES

FRONT.

COURT TIME RECORD

| Date | Court and Judge Grand Jury, Coroner or District Attorney | Disposition | Time | | | Total | On or off Duty |
			Of Arrival	Of Arraignment	Of Disposition or Adjournment		

(Signature of Arresting Officer)   (Rank)   (Shield No.)

REVERSE

| PRECINCT | POLICE DEPARTMENT
VIOLATION OF CORPORATION ORDINANCE
CIVIL ACTION | POST No. |

I HEREBY REPORT HAVING OBSERVED THE FOLLOWING VIOLATION OF CORPORATION ORDINANCE:

| DATE OF REPORT | DATE OF VIOLATION | TIME
A.
M.
P. |

LOCATION

NAME AND ADDRESS OF VIOLATOR

NAME AND ADDRESS OF OWNER

NATURE OF VIOLATION

(OVER)

FRONT

WITNESSES

_____

_____

_____

_____

REMARKS

_____

_____

_____

_____

_____

_____

_____

_____

_____

_____

_____

_____
(Signature)

REVERSE

When these reports are delivered to the desk officers a report should be made at the station house and the original forwarded to headquarters and from there to the respective departments having jurisdiction. At the end of the month the copies of reports maintained at the station should be examined by the captains and used as a guide in giving efficiency ratings. In order that the patrolmen may be kept informed as to conditions reported on their respective posts and to avoid unnecessary duplication of reports, the matters reported should be entered by posts and placed on the bulletin boards now maintained in the stations. Each patrolman on reporting for duty should make a copy of these matters so as to avoid duplicating the reports upon these subjects.

An arrangement should be made with the heads of the various departments affected whereby they will inform the police department as to how frequently such matters should be called to their attention. The reason for this is obvious, since it would be wholly unnecessary for the police department to keep reporting a hole in the street pavement day in and day out until repaired, since weeks may necessarily elapse before such repair is made.

Method of Issuing General Alarms.

General alarms on missing and on wanted persons are read at each outgoing roll call, and the police are supposed to remember the descriptions. In certain important cases the descriptions of persons wanted are mimeographed and each member of the force is furnished with a copy.

It has been found by experience that the reading of general alarms to policemen is not an effective means of causing the arrest of persons wanted; first, because the men are unable to remember the descriptions, and indeed only too frequently do not even understand the sergeants when they are reading them. The practic of furnishing printed and written descriptions has likewise been condemned because the police invariably put them in their pockets and do not even read them.

The modern procedure and the most effective method yet designed is now in operation in the police department in the City of New York, and that is to post a printed or written copy of descriptions of missing and wanted persons on the bulletin board in the station house and to require each member in the command to make a written copy of this description in his memorandum book. The theory involved in this is that when the policeman is required to write down the description he will be more likely to remember it.

When the men are assembled on the floor for roll call and orders, the sergeant should inspect the memorandum books and see to it that the policemen are faithful in making these copies. It is recommended that this procedure be adopted in Richmond.

Number of Mounted Men Should Be Reduced.

There are detailed to mounted duty for the patrol of suburban districts 21 members of the force.

As a means of policing a city mounted patrol service is the most expensive and the least effective. While mounted policemen are most valuable in suppressing riots or handling large crowds of people, they can accomplish little in the matter of regular patrol. The theory of having mounted men in suburban districts is that being mounted they can cover large areas, thus making unnecessary the assignment of a number of patrolmen to foot post. While a man mounted on a horse can of course travel a long distance, it is to be remembered the mere fact of having a policeman seated high in the air upon a well-groomed mount by no means gives police protection. Because of the necessarily very long post assigned to mounted men in keeping with the theory of their use, it is not only difficult to supervise them, but it is, to say the least, not easy for a citizen when in need of police service to locate them.

The patroling of posts in a suburban district, through the use of either foot or mounted policemen is for the most part a waste of funds as well as of the time of the policemen assigned to duty therein.

The theory of requiring a policeman to wear uniform is that the uniforms produce a psychological effect which results in preventing the commission of minor offenses. However, in a suburban section there is no native crime. Such crimes as are committed are what are termed crimes of invasion, such as burglary and hold-ups. In other words, people living in the suburban sections do not require a policeman to keep them in order, but they do require protection against burglary, and the uniformed man is of little use as a protection against burglary. The prevention of burglary can only be accomplised through detective service.

Whatever little value there may be in foot patrol service in such sections, certainly nothing can be said in favor of mounted service. While the mounted man riding to and fro can observe practically nothing, he can be readily observed, and indeed, where the streets are paved with asphalt or hard pavement of any kind, the patter of his horse's hoofs can be heard long before he is seen.

Therefore, it is recommended that the mounted force be reduced so as to provide for a small force of about four, to be used as an escort for a parade or in the event of riots.

Patrol Booths Should Be Established.

Police booths should be established in the suburban sections, at which should be stationed patrolmen equipped with motorcycles or inexpensive motor cars. In order to provide watch service for night fires, one patrolman on the late tour should be always kept patroling in a motor car. He should patrol between the booths. The procedure should be arranged so as to provide that each policeman assigned to booths will take his turn on patrol on being relieved by another officer. By adopting this procedure the suburban sections can be given bastly better police protection with about one-third the number of policemen now used and without the expense of maintaining horses.

Each of the booths should be equipped with a telephone connected with the public exchanges as well as with the police signal service box. The number of public exchange telephones should be conspicuously displayed on a sign placed on the outside of the booth, and the residents of the neighborhood should be informed of the number and advised to call when in need of a policeman.

Traffic Division.

For regulation of traffic and the enforcement of the rules of the road, there are assigned to traffic duty one acting sergeant, twelve policemen and three automobile speed patrolmen, making a total force on traffic work of sixteen.

While the traffic men are supervised by a patrolman, who is given the rank but not the salary of sergeant, there is no regularly organized traffic squad, and the patrolmen assigned to traffic are carried on the rolls and report at the stations in the districts in which their posts are located.

This plan is defective in that it does not provide proper control over the traffic men. They should be organized into a regular squad and report at headquarters to the traffic sergeant, receiving from him their orders and instructions each day. The organization of such a squad is recommended. The fact that their commandng officer is a sergeant in name only has tended materially to reduce his control for disciplinary purposes over the traffic policemen. It is a mistake to attempt to supervise a force through a man of equal rank, even though he may have a title distinctive from those whom he supervises. It is therefore recommended that the patrolman in charge of the traffic squad be regularly promoted to the rank of sergeant and be given a sergeant's pay.

Traffic Men Untrained for the Work.

No special training is afforded for the traffic men, nor are they selected because of special fitness for this work. The very fact that there is an utter lack of discipline among the traffic men and that they remain in conversation with citizens on the crossings for extended periods demonstrates fully their lack not only of training, but of appreciation of the responsibilities entrusted to them. The traffic officer who is not alert and constantly watching the vehicles and pedestrians and who engages in idle conversation, thus preventing his concentrating o/his work, is not only an inefficient policeman, but he creates a condition more dangerous to the drivers of vehicles and their passengers than if there was no traffic man on the crossing. The drivers of vehicles and pedestrians seeing that a traffic officer is on the post feel relieved of exercising extreme caution, because they are depending on the traffic officer to direct their travel and to protect them against accidents. The officer who is not alert and who does not concentrate on his work thus creates an extra hazardous conditon at the crossng.

No matter what may be given as an excuse for conversation by policemen on patrol posts, no excuse can be considered valid with respect to idle conversation of traffic officers. Because of the character of the duties imposed upon a traffic officer, it is vastly important that he not only be given regular training for police work, but that he be given special training for traffic duty. Moreover, it is again important that the utmost care be used in the selection of men for traffic duty, because the very nature of the work requires a high order of intelligence, a good disposition and freedom from nervous disorders.

An excitable policeman on a traffic crossing cannot only cause congestion, but indeed loss of life. Therefore, it is recommended that every effort be made to afford special training for the traffic officers, and that the greatest care be exercised in selecting men for these posts. Observations made of the methods employed and the men assigned indicate the need for making changes in the present assignments. The regulation of traffic and the planning for the control of traffic is no easy task. It implies not only a knowledge of local conditions, but a thorough study of procedures in effect in other communities. For this reason it is recommended that the sergeants in charge of traffic be permitted to visit the city of New York and there attend the traffic lectures and observe under the supervisor in charge of traffic the methods employed in various sections of the city. The methods to be employed in directing traffic cannot be entirely standardized for all points in the city, but must be revised and controlled in accordance with the traffic and street conditions at the points to be regulated.

Traffic Booths of Unattractive Design.

At all except one of the traffic crossings there are used traffic semaphores of a modern design, and each traffic post has upon it, with the exception of one, small shelter booths in which the policemen remain while directing traffic. The theory in using shelter booths is to protect the officer against inclement weather. While it is not conceded that there is an absolute need for such booths in connection with the direction of traffic in this city, no serious objection can be made to the use of these houses, but if they are to be retained in use they should be of an ornamental design and add to the beauty of the highway rather than detract from it. The type of booth used at present is of homely construction and poor design.

Patrolmen Should Not Be Permitted to Sit Down in Booths.

The traffic men are permitted to remain seated in these shelter houses while directing traffic. Observations made show that at all times they take advantage of this permission. Indeed, they not only remain seated, but at several times they were observed with their feet propped up so as to make their positions so extremely comfortable as to prevent their being alert and ready for any emergency. Patrolmen who remain seated cannot completely observe the traffic conditions. It is therefore recommended that seats or chairs in these shelter houses be removed and that the rules require the traffic men to remain standing while on duty. In no other way can they be kept on the alert for emergencies.

If these booths are to be retained in use they should be equipped with telephones connected with the central switchboard at headquarters. Plans are now under way for the installation of telephone service.

Arrests.

The records of the police department show that during the year 1916 there were 13,202 arrests made and 6,565 ordinance violations reported, thus, in effect, making the total number of arrests 19,767. The number of arrests made, independent of the ordinance violations reported, has increased year by year from 11,073 in 1912 to 13,202 in 1916. However, these figures do not represent an accurate tabulation of persons arrested, for the reason that for many years it has been the custom to count as arrests each charge made against a prisoner. Therefore, without an exhaustive analysis of the records it would not be possible to ascertain the actual number of arrests. As an indication of the effect this practice has had upon the statistics as to arrests it is only necessary to cite a tabulation of the record of arrests made by detectives during the first six months of the present year, which tabulation shows that while the records alleged 251 arrests there were but 172 arrests made, or 79 less than the total reported.

Because of this custom it is not possible to determine whether or not the arrests made in this city are excessive.

In order that the department shall have accurate statistics as to arrests it is recommended that this practice be discontinued at once, and that in tabulating arrests only the actual number of persons arrested be included. For purposes of showing the number of charges filed against persons arrested a separate tabulation of such information should be made. In other words, the records should show that during the year 1916 there were arrested a certain number of persons against whom a total of a certain number of charges were filed. It would then be possible for the chief and administrative head to determine whether or not the number of arrests made was excessive.

Arrests Made on Magistrate Warrants Should Be Tabulated Separately.

Because of a system of issuing warrants upon a fee basis, many hundreds of useless and unnecessary arrests are made. The police department is in no wies responsible for this condition, inasmuch as the law compels the police to serve these warrants when issued. Since the records as tabulated do not disclose the number of arrests made by the policemen of their own volition and upon warrants secured by policemen upon their own initiative as against those made upon magistrates' warrants, it is not possible to determine whether or not the police are making too many arrests or whether their arrests are greater or less than during previous periods.

It is therefore recommended that in all cases of arrests the records clearly show upon whose initiative the warrant was issued and when the arrests are tabulated they be classified so as to sh w those made as results of police investigation or observation and those made through the service of a warrant obtained by a complainant from a magistrate.

Arrest Procedure in Accordance With Good Practice.

The procedure for making arrests, delivering prisoners to the station and reportisg information as to arrests is for the most part in accordance with good practice. The record of prisoners, or what is termed their pedigree, however, is not sufficient to provide complete information for statistical purposes. In addition to the information now reported in connection with the history of a prisoner there should be reported the following: the nativity of his father and mother; the length of time prisoner is in this country; whether employed or unemployed at the time of arrest; whether married or single, and whether the offense charged was committed in a licensed premises or in connection with a licensed premises, and whether or not the defendant was sober or drunk when arrested. For statistical purposes there should also be entered the number of post on which the alleged offense was committed, and if possible the name of the patrolman on post at the time of the occurrence.

No record is maintained, either at the station or at headquarters of the disposition of the case, thus leaving the police officials without any information as to what happens to their cases in the courts. They are unable to determine what percentage of cases result in conviction or dismissal, without which information it is not possible to judge of the efficiency and indeed frequently of the integrity of the policeman.

All policemen should be required to report to their sergeant on desk duty the disposition of their cases in court and provision should be made for recording this information in the record of arrests alongside of the entry of the pedigree.

The record of arrests at present maintained, while of much better design than many such records maintained in other cities, could be greatly improved. It is therefore recommended that as soon as the stock of arrest record books now on hand is depleted a new record be designed in accordance with the suggestions contained in the section of this report headed "records and reports."

As a protection to the officers of the department the rule should require that apparent bruises and wounds on prisoners at time of arrest be noted in the record of arrest when the pedigree is entered. By doing this the officers would be protected against malicious persons alleging falsely that they were wounded while in the custody of the police.

Erasures and Pasting of Documents in This Book Should Be Prohibited.

An examination of the records at the station showed that when errrs were made in making entries it is customary to erase such entries, and that at least in one station it is the practice in warrant cases to paste in a typewritten sheet containing information as to the warrant. This practice should be prohibited by the rules, which should provide that all errors be corrected by drawing a red ink line through the erroneous entry and writing in the correction immediately above or below with the initials of the person making the correction entered alongside. All entries should be written and no papers pasted is this record.

Arrests By Magistrates Should Not Be Carried in This Record.

In cases where persons for whom warrants are issued by magistrates surrender themselves to the magistrates and are bailed, it is the present practice for the magistrate to notify the district sergeant, furnishing him with a statement concerning the arrest. The sergeant enters such a case in his record of arrests, thus carrying it as a district arrest. This practice is defective and should be discontinued at once. No arrest should be reported in this record except such as are actually made by the officers of the department.

Detective Arrests Should Not Be Carried as District Arrests.

Persons arrested by members of the detective bureau are brought to the police station of the district in which the arrest is made, and the record of the arrest is made in the same manner of all other arrests. This practice should be discontinued and the the record of prisoners arrested by members of the detective bureau and brought to the station should be entered as "detained for detective bureau" and should not be included in the tabulation of arrests for the district. The complete record of such arrest is and should be maintained at the detective bureau.

Method of Handling Women Prisoners Should Be Revised.

All white female prisoners are brought to the first district station, where a matron is on duty at all times. Colored women arrested are detained at the station located in the district where the arrest is made. Although white women are placed under the care of the matron and detained in cells set aside for their use and located within the matron's quarters and under her observation, colored women prisoners are detained in the male cell blocks, although not in the same cell with men. While the practice of segregating black and white women is justified, the custom of placing colored women prisoners under the charge of men and in the same cell block with men is not only totally unfair to the colored women and against good practice, but is indecent and not conducive to morality. All women prisoners, whether black or white, should be sent to the first district station and placed under the care of the matron, who should make ample provision for segregation.

Matron Should Personally Receive Women Prisoners at Desk.

It is the present custom for the policeman to deliver white women prisoners to the matron's quarters. This practice results in giving the policeman access to a section of the station set aside for the exclusive use of women. It is therefore recommended that women prisoners be delivered to the matron at the station desk regardless of the time of day or night they are received. In so far as is decent they should be searched by the matron in the presence of the desk sergeant and their property delivered to the sergeant. The procedure now in effect offers no protection to the matron against allegations which may be made by malicious prisoners of having their property stolen while in her custody, since they are searched by her in her own quarters and without a witness. No member of the department should be permitted in the female detention cells or the matron's quarters except for purposes of making inspection and rendering aid to the matron in restraining disorderly prisoners.

All Property Should Be Removed From Prisoners.

When prisoners are searched only such articles as might be required as evidence or with which prisoners may inflict bodily harm or effect an escape are removed from them. They are permitted to retain in their possession money, jewelry and other valuables. This is not in accordance with good procedure. It is necessary as a protection to the prisoners' property and as a protection to the officer of the station against fraudulent claims that all property be removed from prisoners when searched. The property should be placed in an envelope, as at present, but if the prisoner is sober, he should be required to sign his name on the face of the envelope, which should show a complete list of the property. The searching officer should also be required to sign as well as the desk sergeant, and the envelope should be sealed. If the prisoner desires to pay counsel or make any other legitimate expenditure out of his funds retained by the police, he should be required to furnish a written order, on a special form, and a receipt should be taken from the person to whom the funds are delivered, and both the order and receipt should be placed in the envelope and kept by the department as its record of the transaction.

Inasmuch as prisoners are in the habit of defacing the walls of the cells through the use of lead pencils, it is important that when searched lead pencils and fountain pens be removed as well as all other property.

Marked Decrease in Arrests Since Enactment of Prohibition Law.

The decrease in crime and is the number of arrests since the enactment of the prohibition legislation has been very marked and is worthy of noting in this report. The prohibition law went into effect on November 1, 1916. During the six months from January to June, 1916, there were 6,601 arrests made, while during the same six months of this year, with prohibition in effect, there were but 4,821 arrests, showing a decrease of 1,780, or about 26 per cent.

The falling off in arrests for crimes which may be directly attributed to the excessive use of liquor is even more marked than the total decrease, as shown by the following table:

Crime.	Jan.-June 1916.	Jan.-June 1917.
Assault and battery	641	398
Felonious assault	183	86
Disorderly conduct	1,249	834
Drunk and disorderly	503	189
Drunkenness	531	762

Fights on streets	215	64
Neglecting children	27	20
Non-support	141	98
Vagrancy	462	294
	3,952	2,745

Comparative Statement of Arrests, January to June, Inclusive, 1916—January to June, Inclusive, 1917.

Crime.	1916.	1917.
Incorrigible children	17	40
Interfering with police	36	21
Involuntary manslaughter	6	7
Keeping disorderly house	22	9
Keeping gambling house	22	30
Keeping house of ill-fame	36	10
Libel	...	2
Lunacy	59	54
Laboring at trade and calling on Sabbath..	157	29
Murder	14	6
Neglected children	27	20
Non-support	141	98
On capias	2	16
Peddling without license	10	7
Perjury	1	5
Petit larceny	462	294
Receiving stolen goods	15	8
Resisting police	40	14
Robbery—felonious	16	11
Rocking railway train	...	4
Selling liquor to minors	1	...
Selling liquor without license	63	
Selling cocaine illegally	2	...
Selling cigarettes to minors	...	1
Street walkers	81	50
Suspicious characters	105	80
*Speeding motor vehicles	7	...
Seduction	17	14
Surrendered by bondsman	2	4
Trespass	120	103
Unlawful cohabitation	303	145

Using auto without permission	9	8
Vagrancy	551	161
Violating parole	7	10
Violating pure food law	7	· 5
Violating health law	13	1
Violating labor law	1	16
Recklessly running auto	62	57
Slander	...	2
Byrd liquor law	1	...
Violating game law	...	2
Violating prohibition law	...	304
Drug addicts	...	6
United States registration law	...	23
Total 6,601		4,821

*Now reported under ordinance.

Thus it will be seen that there has been, a decrease in arrests for these offenses of 1,207, or about 30 per cent.

The following table shows a comparison of all arrests made during the first six months of last year and the first six months of the present year:

Comparative Statement of Arrests, January to June, Inclusive, 1916—January to June, Inclusive, 1917.

Crime.	1916.	1917.
Arson	15	2
Adultery	...	5
Abduction	2	1
Abortion	1	1
Assault and battery	641	398
Assault—felonious	183	86
Assault—criminal	9	4
Burglary	25	4
Buggery	4	1
Bigamy	...	2
Cruelty to animals	51	35
Contempt of court	99	78
Child delinquency	41	36
Contributing to child delinquency	24	20

Carrying concealed weapons	59	23
Disorderly conduct	1,249	834
Drunk and disorderly	503	189
Drunkenness	531	762
Defrauding building housekeeper	47	65
Deserters—army and navy	1	2
Detained witnesses	1	...
Defacing city property	1	4
Doing business with no license	9	4
Exposing person	18	3
Embezzlement	3	...
Expectorating on sidewalk	1	2
Exposing children to vice and crime	3	2
Escaped prisoners	4	11
Forgery	15	42
False pretence	54	34
Fighting on street	215	64
Fugitives from justice	89	67
Fugitives from parents	15	14
Gambling	133	231
Grand larceny	32	27
Highway robbery	1	...
Housebreaking	87	88
Harboring minors for immoral purposes	...	3

Policemen Should Not Be Permitted to Request Dismissal of Their Cases.

Since no record is maintained of the disposition of the cases arraigned in the police court, and because that court does not make a report which would disclose the number of convictions and the number of dismissals, it was not possible to ascertain without exhaustive tabulation and analysis of the court records the success or failure of the police in the prosecution of their cases, nor was it possible to learn to what extent the court co-operates with the police through convictions of persons arraigned.

But observations made in the court and an examination of its records disclosed the existence of a practice which is not only irregular but indeed might well lead to corruption and malicious prosecution. This is the practice of permitting policemen to ask and secure the dismissal of persons arrested by them without even going into a hearing of the case. That this practice has well-nigh become a recognized habit is evidenced by the fact that during the first six months of the present year 66 cases appearing upon the criminal docket were dismissed at the request of the police officer in the case, and 114 cases appearing upon the ordinance docket were similarly dealt with. Of the 66 cases appearing upon the criminal docket and which were dismissed, the following list shows the offenses charged and the number of cases under each heading:

Offense.	No. of Cases.
Possession or transportation of ardent spirits	24
Cruelty to animals	1
Fugitive from justice	1
Deserter United States Navy	1
Immoral acts	6
Carrying concealed weapons	4
Larceny	6
Vagrancy	6
Assault and battery	1
Forgery	2
Disorderly house	2
Gambling house	1
Gambling—policy	2
Peddling without license	2
Burglary	1
Pandering	1
Adultery	2
Housebreaking	2
Suspicious character	1
Total	66

Of the 24 cases involving the violation of the prohibition act, 15 of the cases were dismissed at the request of one officer while the same officer had dismissed at his request 4 other cases, making a total of 19 of the 66, or more than 28 per cent. dismissed at this officer's request.

Of the 114 ordinance cases dismissed at the request of officers, 28 were for violations of the ordinance relating to automobiles and 24 were for violations of the traffic regulations.

The following table shows the number of cases of ordinance violations dismissed in the police court at the request of the arresting officers. It is interesting to note that one officer during this period had dismissed at his request twelve cases involving violation of the auto ordinance:

Number of Cases Dismissed in Court at Request of Police Officers.

Date	No. Cases	Offenses
1- 9-17	1	Failing to make sewer connections.
1-10	1	Disorderly conduct.
1-11	2	Violation speed law.
6-14		Auto ordinance.
1-11	1	Operating automobiles without lights.
1-13	3	Violation of health ordinance.
3-16		Violation of health ordinance.
4-13		Violation of health ordinance.
1-13	2	Violation of water department.
6-21		Nuisance on premises.
1-13	7	Nuisance on premises.
1-19		Nuisance on premises.
5-12		Nuisance on premises.
7- 6		Nuisance on premises.
2- 9		Nuisance on premises.
7-13		Violation of health department.
5-12		Maintenance of nuisance.
1-16	2	Obstructing street with lumber.
1-16		Obstructing street with lumber.
1-16	2	Traffic ordinance.
7-14		Obstructing alley: no lights on same.
1-23	3	Obstructing street with lumber.
3- 8		Auto ordinance.
6- 1		Auto ordinance.
1-23	1	Obstructing street, no lights on same.
1-25	3	Traffic ordinance.
4-26		Traffic ordinance.
5-22		Traffic ordinance.
1-25	1	Health department.
1-26	1	Auto ordinance.
1-29	2	Disorderly conduct.
4-30		Suspicious characters.
1-29	1	Disorderly conduct.
1-30	4	Obstructing entrance to theater.
4- 3		Auto ordinance.

5-19		Traffic ordinance.
2- 6		Traffic ordinance.
5-30	1	Auto ordinance.
2-20	2	Drunk.
6-20		Suspicious characters.
2-12	1	Drunk.
2-27	1	Disorderly and gambling.
2-27	3	Violation of street ordinance.
4-24		Violation of street ordinance.
4-26		Violation of city ordinance.
3- 3	2	Disorderly.
2-13		Drunk.
3- 6	1	Auto ordinance.
3- 6	1	Drunk.
3- 8	3	Allowing minors in pool room.
6-11		Disorderly and fighting.
7- 9		Traffic ordinance.
5-10	1	Disorderly on street.
3- 8	2	Disorderly.
5-30		Traffic ordinance.
3- 9	1	Drunk.
3-10	1	Traffic ordinance.
3-14	2	Nuisance to remain on premises.
3-16		Nuisance to remain on premises.
4- 3	1	Disorderly house.
2- 2	3	Auto ordinance.
6-21		Auto ordinance.
2-14		Auto ordinance.
2- 6	12	Auto ordinance.
3- 2		Auto ordinance.
4-17		Auto ordinance.
5-12		Auto ordinance.
5-18		Auto ordinance.
5-25		Traffic ordinance.
6- 2		Auto ordinance.
6- 5		Auto ordinance.
6- 5		Auto ordinance.
7-11		Auto ordinance.
7-17		Auto ordinance.
2-14	4	Traffic ordinance.
4-30		Drunk.

5-16		Traffic ordinance.
6- 9	.	Traffic ordinance.
4- 9	2	Disorderly and fighting.
2- 6		Auto ordinance.
4-10	1	Disorderly house.
4-20	1	Auto ordinance.
4-23	1	Fighting and disorderly.
5-22	1	Disorderly on street.
4-23	1	Drunk and disorderly.
4-27	2	Health department.
4-27		Health department.
4-28	1	Street ordinance.
5- 7	1	Disorderly on street.
5- 8	3	Health department.
5- 8		Interfering with officer.
5- 2	.	Traffic ordinance.
5-10	1	Disorderly.
5-12	1	Obstruction street with stone.
5-12	1	Obstruction street with stone.
5-23	1	Traffic ordinance.
5-25	1	Auto ordinance.
5-28	1	Drunk (wrong man).
6- 2	1	Traffic ordinance.
6- 9	1	Drunk.
2-12	1	Disorderly.
6-16	2	Auto ordinance.
6-16		Auto ordinance.
6-18	1	Disorderly.
6-21	1	Resisting officer.
7- 2	1	Suspicious character.
7- 6	1	Health department.
7-11	1	Drunk.
7-19	1	Traffic ordinance.
2- 8	1	Peddlers' ordinance.
2- 9	1	Cellar cap open on sidewalk.

While in a few cases the policeman makes a statement to the court when he makes a request to dismiss the case, in the majority of cases, however, no such statement is made, but the officer merely requests the court to dismiss the case.

During the observations made in the police court, one case of a violation of a traffic ordinance was observed in which the defendant did not even take the trouble to appear, and the policeman upon whose complaint the summons was issued succeeded in having the case dismissed.

It is difficult to understand why policemen should make arrests or cause the issuance of summonses for violations of ordinances and then ask the court to dismiss the cases. It is true in all police departments that occasionally policemen make arrests which are not based upon sufficient evidence to warrant the defendants being convicted or held for a higher court, but in such cases the court, as a matter of justice, dismisses the action after having heard the statements of the officer and frequently the statement of the defendant. In such cases, the records of the court show that the case was dismissed because of lack of evidence.

Judges who are co-operating with the police department, upon observing policemen repeatedly presenting cases not supported by evidence, communicate such information to the police chief or administrative head, and an investigation is promptly made into the causes. If it is found that the policeman is inefficient, he is dealt with by his superiors, while if it is found that there is reason to suspect corrupt practice in connection with such cases, the policeman is placed under observation.

But in Richmond the superior officers of the police department do not even take the trouble to inquire of the officers why they arrest people or summon them and then fail to prosecute. The judge of the court not only makes no effort to communicate this information to the police department, but indeed, according to his notion of the law, feels that he is adequately protected by entering upon his docket in each such case "dismissed at the request of the officer." While the time available for this study was not sufficient to make any detailed investigation of the causes of these dismissals, in the absence of which it of course is not possible to even suggest that they were the result of corruption or malicious prosecution, nevertheless, the system is most emphatically condemned as being conducive to fraud and indicative of inefficient police work.

There is a grave question as to the legality of the court's dismissal of such cases upon the request of the officer without going into the facts. It would be just as logical to dismiss the case at the request of any citizen who might be interested in the defendant or at the request of the defendant's counsel without holding a hearing.

It is therefore most urgently recommended that the mayor prohibit the policemen from requesting the dismissal of cases, and moreover, it is suggested that the greatest care be exercised by the mayor and the chief of police in reviewing the results obtained in the police court by the officers making arrests. The policemen should be warned against making unnecessary arrests or unnecessarily applying for summonses, and when a large percentage of their cases in court result in dismissals, they should be questioned, and if need be, disciplined. Frequent dismissals upon arrest spell only two things, namely, inefficiency or dishonesty, both being sufficient cause for investigation and punishment.

It is interesting to note in this connection that notwithstanding the fact that the cases are dismissed, under the present system of using a tabulation of arrests as a means of determining the efficiency of the officers, all these arrests are scored in their favor.

Detective Bureau.

For the suppression of serious crimes and the apprehension of those committing them, and the prevention of larcenies, burglaries and housebreaking, a city must reply upon its detective service. The work of a detective bureau differs vastly from that of the uniformed branch of police service. The uniformed force is essentially an observing, reporting and social service agency, the uniformed patrolman, walking back and forth over a given territory for eight hours continuously, day in and day out, is constituted as the eyes and ears of the city government, while the detective service is essentially, or should be, a secret service agency for the ferreting out of crime and criminals and for the keeping of a city free of a criminal element. Its duties are different, its methods must necessarily be different. Upon its efficiency must depend in a large measure the efficiency of the entire service. To obtain the best results, all policemen must receive detective training and must co-operate one with the other to bring about a successful administration of the service. Just as a house divided against itself will fall, so also will a police department with the uniformed force not in harmony with its detective service fail in its results.

Richmond's police department maintains what is called a detective bureau. This bureau is under the supervision of a captain of detectives, who is appointed by the chief to serve during good behavior, but who can be reduced to the ranks by the chief after a hearing at any time. The captain of detectives receives the same salary as a captain of the uniformed force, namely, $1,440.

Organization of Bureau.

There are detailed to the detective bureau 'six detective sergeants and two patrolmen operating in plain clothes, making the total force eight. The six detective sergeants are paid the same salaries as sergeants of the uniformed force, namely, $1,212 a year. For the maintenance of the records of the detective bureau and the photographing of fingerprints and measuring of criminals, two patrolmen are detailed. This constitutes the organization of the bureau.

Method of Selecting Detectives Defective.

The present method of selecting detectives is for the chief to conduct what he terms a sergeant's examination, and from among those attaining an average of seventy, he selects the detectives asd they are given the rank of sergeant. To remove these detectives, it is necessary to give them a hearing and to formally demote them. This method is against wise administration of a detective service.

Assignments to detective duty should be made by the chief upon recommendation of the captain of detectives, who should be permitted broad powers of selection. All of his selections should be made from among men tried out and tested in the detective service as junior detectives before they are finally appointed. The tenure of their office as detectives should be dependent entirely upon the efficiency of service rendered and at such time as the captain of detectives may find them no longer useful by reason of lack of results or because of their becoming too well known in the community, he should be permitted to recommend their return to the ranks, and the chief should act in all cases upon his recommendation. If he is to be held responsible, as he should be, for the efficiency of this most important branch of the work, he must be given the broadest latitude in the matter of handling, selecting and organizing his staff. In no other way can harmony between the two branches of the service be produced, and unfortunately such harmony does not exist today. The detective service as at present organized is in direct conflict with the uniformed force, and especially its commanding officers, and in fact there is not even harmony between the detectives and their captain. While such a condition prevails, little in the way of results can be expected, and it may be truthfully said that the moneys expended for this kind of detective service are largely wasted.

It is recommended at the very outset that the mayor seek to produce harmony between the commanding officers of the uniformed force and the captain of detectives, even at the expense, if need be, of making a complete change in the personnel.

Administration Defective.

To accomplish the best results the detective bureau should be organized with a staff of senior detectives, and not detective sergeants, who should receive an increased salary over that paid patrolmen and junior detectives who would be selected from among the uniformed and retained at their salaries as patrolmen. After having developed them and after they have proved their efficiency, they should be able to look forward to promotion by being designated as senior detectives with the increased salary.

District Plainclothesmen Should Be Under Command of Captain of Detectives..

There are at present four patrolmen performing duties in plain clothes, two in the first district and two in the second. These patrolmen serve under the command and jurisdiction of the captains in the districts and are in no way responsible to the captain of detectives. The result is that the rivalry existing between these plainclothesmen and the detective force is not conducive to efficient detective service.

Therefore, it is recommended that no plainclothesmen be assigned to duty under the captains, but that all policemen performing service in plain clothes, except such as may be detailed by the mayor or chief of the department and confidentially investigating vice conditions or traffic in liquor, operate as a part of the detective organization.

Two of the detective sergeants, by virtue of a statute, receive $200 a year each extra compensation from the hustings court. These two men are subject to the call of the court and perform such service as the judge may select. This law should be amended so as to relieve the police department of the necessity of assigning policemen to this court. Such service as the court may desire in connection with the business thereof should, under ordinary circumstances, be performed by the sheriff and his deputies. If the court desires or needs the services of police officers to investigate cases pending before him, he should be required to make application to the chief of police, who will then assign to him temporarily and during the course of such investigation the number of officers necessary for the work. The contention of the officers who are now detailed to this service is that the amount of work they are called upon to perform for the court is so little as to prevent its interfering with their general service as detectives. If this be true, and it undoutedly is, there is surely no justification for the state being called upon to contribute $400 per year for payment for this service.

Eight Detectives Insufficient to Meet Needs of Community.

In the proposed reorganization the detective staff should be increased from eight to twelve. To do this would impose no additional expense on the city, because there are enough patrolmen available to permit of this increase. Is fact, if the recommendation to reduce the force of the third district is complied with, the men will be available to provide for this increase, but even if this is not done, there are still sufficient patrolmen to allow for a reduction in the patrol force and an increase in the detective service. When re-organized, the force should then consist of six senior detectives and six junior detectives. Two junior detectives should be assigned to each of the two districts, these men to operate under the sole direction of the captain of detectives, reporting directly to him and receiving their orders directly from him.

One senior and one junior detective should be assigned to specialize in the observation of pawnshops, secondhand dealers, and large department stores. One senior and one junior detective should be assigned to specialize in observing pickpockets on the main streets and at and about the railroad terminals. The other four senior detectives should be required to investigate directly from headquarters all important cases, one of them as at present, specializing in the investigation of homicide cases, but all should be used to investigate complaints of a detective character.

Procedure.

The procedure should then be revised so as to require that all minor cases requiring detective investigation be referred to the district detectives, and that in cases of importance occurring within those districts the preliminary investigations should be conducted by the district detectives, but only for such a period as will permit of dispatching to the district the senior detective, who should then take charge of the case and direct the activities of the juniors.

The chief should require and see to it that the captains of the uniformed force co-operate in the highest degree with the detectives in investigation of cases. In all important cases care should be taken to avoid the mistake only too often made of allowing the members of the uniformed force to bungle the case while trying to master it, rather than turn it over to the detectives. Their instructions in each case should be specific, and the effort to gain commendation for the uniformed force for effecting arrests in important cases requiring detective attention should be discouraged. Under present conditions no such order prevails. The uniformed force is permitted to undertake investigations which properly should be conducted by the detectives, and frequently they continue in the investigation of such cases up to a point where they see failure and then only are the detectives called in.

Results of Investigation Prove Need for Training.

Assignment to the detective force is not contingent upon any special training for the work, but according to the officials it is dependent upon the opinion of the chief or mayor as to the ability of the respective officers, plus a written examination.

Upon promotion to detective sergeants they are assigned to cases and are then regarded as detectives. No effort whatever is made to train them, and indeed it can scarcely be said that under present conditions there is any officer in the department who himself has received adequate instructions to conduct such training.

A tabulation of the complaints and results obtained upon the investigation of them tells the story of lack of training and emphasizes the need for a reorganization of this division. While it may be said that the percentage of crime in the city of Richmond, as disclosed by the records of the department, is comparatively low, and the type of crimes committed not especially serious, nevertheless such crimes as are committed and reported to the police in the majority of cases go unpunished. For example, out of 305 cases of housebreaking reported during the last six months of 1916 and the first six months of 1917, in but four cases, or .013 per cent., were there arrests made, while out of 116 cases of petty larceny called to the attention of the police an arrest was effected in but one. and of the 66 cases of grand larceny reported but one arrest was effected, while of 10 burglaries reported, no arrests were made and no results obtained in 8 of them, although in two cases a recovery was effected. The same tabulation shows that of 48 cases of robbery reported involving the loss of $3,323.63, but one arrest was made and only $826 recovered. The table which follows is the best evidence that could be offered of the failure of the detective service of the city to produce results:

Summary of Police Activity in Richmond.

OFFENSES	Value Stolen	Value Recovered	Percentage of Recovery	No Results	Partial Recovery	Arrests. No Recovery	Arrest and Recovery
Housebreaking—605 cases..	$6,015 28	$1,269 70—21 %	29 cases—10 %	256 cases—83 %	1 case—.003 %	4 cases .013 %	15 cases—.05 %
Petit larceny—116 cases....	2,778 13	748 85—26 '	28 " —23 "	83 " —71 "		1 " —.006 "	4 " —.03 "
Grand larceny—66 cases....	7,401 17	2 404 93—35 "	21 " —31 "	40 " —61 "		1 " —.015 "	4 " —.061 "
Lost property—70 cases.....	4,969 08	2,283 00—46 '	23 " —33 '	47 " —67 "			
Robbery—48 cases..........	3,323 63	896 00—24 '	18 " —27 "	31 " —64 "	1 case—.02 %		3 " —.06 "
Pickpocket—30 cases........	1,159 98	154 00—18 "	5 " —17 "	24 " —80 :"			1 " —.03 "
Burglary—10 cases.........	624 00	16 35 03"	2 " —20 "	8 " —80 "			

Stolen Autos.

*59 cases. Value stolen, $1,150. Value recovered, $1,150—100 %. No results, 6 cases—10 %. Recovered, 53 cases—90 %.

*Only two machines valued of the 59 stolen—one at $500, the other at $650, each, recovered.

Missing Persons

CASES	Colored Males Under 18	White Males Under 18	Disposition No Results	Disposition Number Found	Colored Females Under 18	White Females Under 18	Disposition No Results	Disposition Number Found
57	9 cases 15 per cent.	20 cases 34 per cent.	26 cases 44 per cent.	6 cases .01 per cent.	5 cases .08 per cent.	6 cases 12 per cent.	6 cases .08 per cent.	5 cases .08 per cent.

Colored Males Over 18	White Males Over 18	Disposition No Results	Disposition Number Found	Colored Females Over 18	White Females Over 18	Disposition No Results	Disposition Number Found
1 case .01 per cent.	13 cases 22 per cent.	10 cases 16 per cent.	4 cases .06 per cent	1 case .01 per cent.	4 cases .06 per cent.	2 cases .025 per cent.	2 cases 0.5 per cent.

Total amount of property reported lost or stolen.............. $27,377 25
Total amount of property reported recovered 8,943 23
Total percentage of property recovered.............. .32 per cent.

Result of Investigations Not Reported Upon.

While it must be apparent to any one even without police training that in no other way than through such a tabulation as is given above currently made and reviewed can the chief or the mayor determine the efficiency of the detectives, it is nevertheless a fact that no such tabulation as this was ever before made in the department, and the chief or mayor possessed no information which would even serve as a substitute.

While the procedure required that all complaints involving the loss of property in an amount to exceed $25 or the commission of any felony, be reported upon special forms and forwarded promptly to the detective service, which, according to the statements of the officers, has always been done, nevertheless at no time were these complaints tabulated so as to indicate the crime conditions; but what is even more serious, there was no review of the results obtained in the investigation of the complaints, so that those responsible for furnishing police protection to the city did not even know and could not have known under existing conditions whether the complaints were ever investigated, and whether the investigations terminated in the arrest and prosecution of the criminals.

That the department did not understand the necessity of such reports cannot be alleged, because the officials in charge are to be commended for the modern form of reporting installed in the department, but which, unfortunately, was not administered as it was intended it should be.

Detectives' Daily Reports of No Value.

At some time past there was prepared and installed a system of daily reports for detectives, and indeed the rule as to reporting was conscientiously enforced, but the reports submitted were of no value whatever. nor were the requirements as indicated by the rules lived up to.

The printed daily report form, which each detective is required to file, called for information concerning the activities of the detective for the preceding twenty-four hours, indicated by the following columnar headings.

Nature of case assigned to.

Disposition made of the same.

Ascertain if violations of law are going on, and where, and state positively what action taken by you.

Give names of thieves and suspicious persons met and conversed with, and location where same congregate.

Name of person arrested.

Charge.

Disposition.

Supposed unlawful places entered and for what purpose.

State if any other business attended to, and whether for this department or not.

A number of these daily reports were examined, and for the most part contained about the kind of information such as is found in the daily reports of detectives in a great many cities. The reports examined contained such voluminous information as to the work performed as follows:

No special assignments.

Work on previous assignments.

Did not see complainant.

Saw complainant; tried to get information as to complaint.

Visited pawnshops.

Looked for stolen automobiles.

In no cases where the reports found to contain any comments under the headings calling for information as to violation of the laws, suspicious persons, or supposed unlawful places entered. None of the reports as prepared would tend to give the captain of detectives the most vague idea, much less information which he could check, as to the work performed.

No written reports are filed by the detectives in connection with the cases investigated by them, except that whenever a recovery was effected or in the few cases in which arrests were made, this information is informally noted on the back of the complaint form.

If any person should complain that the detectives did not investigate a case referred to them, there is not a single record in the detective bureau or the police department which could be produced that would in any wise describe the action taken by the detectives. In view of this failure to check the work of the detectives and to review their activities, it is not surprising that a tabulation of the complaints reveals the condition shown above.

Method of Assigning Cases.

As the reports of complaints are received from the districts they are reviewed by the captain of detectives, who indicates upon the back of the complaint the name of the detective he desires to assign to investigate it. At the morning assembly of the detectives these complaints are distributed to the men. Complaints received during the day and after the detectives have left headquarters must wait until one of the detectives calls up on the telephone, at which time he is given the assignment.

No record beyond the placing of the detective's name on the back of the complaint is made of these assignments, and inasmuch as the detectives are not required to make written reports on their cases, no further records in the case are compiled; thus, the detectives may carry about with them indefinitely any number of complaints without any check or review, or indeed, without the department having any knowledge of what action is being taken towards an investigation of them. In fact, at the time the captain of detectives makes his assignments he has no method of knowing whether the detective to whom he is assigning a case has ten, twenty, fifty, or for that matter, a hundred cases under investigation. Thus, he is without any guide to enable him to make an intelligent assignment.

Because the detectives are permitted to carry with them unlimited numbers of complaints, a detective who might be enjoying a social visit in most any section of the city at any time while on duty is always in position, if detected, to justify his presence there through any one of a dozen or more cases that he may be carrying about in his pocket.

In view of the fact that the detectives are not assigned to any particular districts and not required to specialize in any particular kind of work, of course they cannot be held responsible for crime conditions nor for the existence in the city of pickpockets or the operations of criminals. The responsibility of the detectives in Richmond, in theory at least, is confined to the investigation of the individual case assigned to them, and as shown above, he is not even held to account for these.

This description of the method of procedure should indeed be convincing to the taxpayers that a large portion of the moneys expended for their detective service is wasted.

It is therefore recommended that there be installed as promptly as possible the system of records described in the section of this report headed "records and reports," and that the mayor and the chief provide a procedure which will result in a careful review of the reports made by the detectives. The chief should require a detailed daily report from the captain of detectives and a comparative monthly report.

Procedure for Checking Pawnshop Lists Should Be Improved.

There should be installed in the detective bureau the standard card record system for use in checking and controlling the pawnshop lists and reports of stolen property. It is not necessary that any highly expensive patented system be employed. The secretary to the department should be required to draft the forms for the card records and filing cabinets of the ordinary type should be purchased.

Pawnbrokers Should Have Buzzer Connection With Headquarters.

The ordinance requiring a buzzer connection between the pawnbrokers and headquarters has never been enforced and the buzzers have never been installed. Action should be taken at once to bring about the installation of these buzzers.

Division of Criminal Identification.

There is maintained in connection with the detective bureau and under the supervision of a detailed patrolman a bureau of criminal identification. Bertillon measurements are recorded, fingerprints taken and photographs of persons convicted taken and filed in the gallery. The pictures in the gallery are placed in their numerical order of receipt, no attempt being made to classify them either as to the class of criminals or facial characteristics. The Bertillon operator, while given little or no chance to secure adequate training for his work, nevertheless has a fair understanding of taking and classifying fingerprints. It is recommended that he be permitted to visit New York's police department and there study the methods of taking, photographing, recording and classifying fingerprints, as well as the advanced methods of criminal identification. Upon his return he should be required to lecture in the school for police service.

Suppression of Vice.

Since the abolition of the so-called "segregated district" and the declaration of a policy of suppression, the police department, through its officers, has been especially active in enforcing the laws against prostitution.

While no moral survey of the city was made, nevertheless the utmost care was taken upon inspection tours of the city to observe all police conditions. Such observations show that the department has reduced to a minimum soliciting for purposes of prostitution on the streets, and that it has succeeded at suppressing practically all of the commercialized houses of prostitution.

It must be a source of considerable satisfaction to the administrative heads and the officers of the police department to know that their efforts in the suppression of vice have resulted in practically eliminating from the city an industry which thrived within it for years.

That a few of the prostitutes who operated in the city during the days of the so-called "segregated district" still reside in the city and are successful in evading arrest is true, but that the police encourage, tolerate or willingly permit their operations is not true: while, on the other hand, it is apparent throughout the city that the officers of the department are vigorously performing their duties with relation to this branch of the work.

However, there still remains a field of endeavor for the police in the matter of suppressing vice.

The automobile and so-called "jitney" now presents a new problem for the police in connection with prostitution. Instead of prostitutes soliciting upon the streets, automobile chauffeurs and many jitney drivers now solicit for the women and conduct negotiations for clandestine meetings with prostitutes. It is true that such clandestine meetings are not arranged for at houses within the city. The practice is for the chauffeurs as managers for the prostitutes to call for the women, introduce them to men, and drive them to points outside of the city limits. So far has the automobile become a factor in this business that all financial arrangements in connection with prostitution are practically conducted with the chauffeurs.

There should be no difficulty in ridding the city of this new vice condition. It is comparatively easy to detect the chauffeurs in these illegal operations. Indeed, it would not require any astute trained detective to apprehend chauffeurs guilty of this conduct, for the reason that their operations are conducted openly and without fear of arrest. So prevalent is the practice that one need make no advances whatever to the chauffeur, since in most cases he will invite the passenger to meet his female friends.

Particularly in view of the fact that there is located in close proximity to the city one of the government military camps, it is recommended that the mayor and the police department secure the co-operation of the state officials in the matter of revoking the automobile licenses in cases where such practice is discovered. It is true that under the existing law the license is issued to the vehicle and not to the driver; nevertheless it is recommended that, if need be, the statute be amended so as to provide that any person holding a license for a car whose car is permitted to be used in connection with the vice traffic or for immoral purposes, shall forfeit by revocation the license for his car and that no new license shall be issued to such person for a period of one year after the date of revocation.

It is essential in the interest of morality that the police conduct at once a vigorous campaign against this form of vice. To do this, it is important that the police receive the heartiest co-operation from the judge of the police court. The chief must exercise every care in seeing to it that his subordinates are faithful to the trust imposed in them, in that they pursue their prosecutions in the courts as vigorously as possible.

That this is not done at present must be admitted; in fact, in one case observed in the court where a "jitney" driver had permitted the use of his car for immoral purposes and where the immoral acts were actually observed by the policeman, the occupants of the car were all of them convicted and fined, but the person in whom the police should have been most interested in convicting, namely, the "jitney" driver, was discharged and the case against him dismissed at the request of the officer who made the arrest. Thus, the court did not even pass upon the guilt or innocence of the driver or go into the question of the evidence that might be introduced against him, but merely dismissed him at the request of the officer.

It is but fitting that in this report the police department should be wholly commended for the success obtained by it in the suppression of commercialized vice within the city, but in commending the department it is necessary to call attention to the need for continuing their efforts in this direction and to warn the officers against ceasing their activities, because it is the experience of other cities that the first indication of inactivity on the part of the police rapidly results in a return of the old conditions.

It is further necessary to point out that although the police have been reasonably successful in eliminating commercialized vice this does not mean that the moral conditions of the city are by any means perfect. Quite to the contrary, there is need, as proven by observations made, of an energetic campaign along other lines in the interest of morality on the part of the clergy and the educators in the community. In such a campaign the police can exercise no power because their activities must be necessarily limited to the suppression of commercialized vice and the preventing, so far as possible, of conditions conducive to vice.

Contributory Causes Should Be Removed.

The public parks are inadequately lighted and insufficiently patrolled. Because of these facts, they constitute a contributing cause to immorality. An effort should be made as soon as possible to properly light the parks and to provide a patrol service within them which will tend to eliminate this condition.

Prohibition Laws Rigidly Enforced.

The study of the city also showed that the policemen are to be commended for the success obtained in the enforcement of the prohibition laws. While it is true that some people in the city succeed in evading detection in the matter of bringing into the state ardent spirits and of disposing of them for a price, nevertheless the instances in which such persons are successful in evading the police are so few as not to result in any wholesale evasion of the law or free distribution of liquor.

Services of Police Woman Needed.

In connection with the constructive preventive work in the suppression of vice, the services of a woman officer are necessary. While, as stated above, the police department is successfully attacking commercialized prostitution, little is being done by outside agencies toward preventing contributory causes. The cities of Denver, Rochester, Los Angeles, San Francisco and others, through the use of women police officers, are accomplishing good results in this direction.

However, the success of this work is wholly dependent upon the type of woman selected for the position, and great care must be taken in choosing a woman police officer. The selection should be made through competitive civil service examination, in which a generous weight should be allowed for experience and personality.

Purchasing Methods.

For the maintenance of certain records and the making of purchases for the department, there is employed pursuant to charter provision a secretary and purchasing agent who is given the rank of captain, thus making him a regular member of the department. The purchasing agent is appointed by the mayor to serve during good behavior. His salary as established by the appropriation ordinance is $1,440 a year, but by virtue of a resolution of the old board of commissioners, which is no longer in existence and the acts of which are no longer binding upon the department, he is paid $300 a year out of the funds received by the police department through costs in court cases, thus making his salary $1,740 a year.

Wholly aside from the question of whether or not the total income of the secretary and purchasing agent is commensurate with the services rendered, this procedure is, to say the least, irregular. The salary of all employees of the city government should be fixed by council, and when fixed by council should constitute the only income to be derived by the employee by virtue of his position. Of course, no criticism is to be made of the incumbent of this position for accepting this extra compensation allowed him by the board of commissioners, since when originally granted it was by virtue of a resolution of the board.

It is recommended, however, that the mayor, as the head of the police department, discontinue the payment of this extra money out of this fund.

It is further recommended that the provision of the charter giving to the purchasing agent the rank of captain be amended, and the council be given the absolute right of establishing such positions as are required in the police department. There is no logical reason for a civilian employee who performs none other than clerical functions being made a member of the force and given an officer's rank. It is quite apparent that the theory and motive which prompted this legislative act was merely a desire to secure a higher rate of pay for this employee.

As purchasing agent, all purchases for the police department are made by this official. During the year 1916 there was expended for supplies and materials, including equipment and repairs, approximately $20,000. The procedure followed by the purchasing agent in the making of purchases is in accordance with good practice, care being taken to obtain the best prices and to make purchases as a result of competitive bidding. The records maintained in connection with the purchases are in accordance with modern procedure.

A full discussion with recommendations concerning purchasing methods will be found elsewhere in this report.

Duties as Property Clerk.

The purchasing agent, by virtue of a recent ordinance, also serves as property clerk, and as such is custodian of properties coming into the possession of the police as evidence, etc. The records maintained by him as property clerk are fairly good, but could be considerably improved by the establishment of a complete property register. No regular procedure is followed in the storing of the property. Some of it is kept in the safe, some in the basement, and some in a locker. No one but the property clerk has access to the property stored, and consequently in his absence the officers of the department experience difficulty in obtaining property to be used as court evidence, etc. It is therefore recommended that in connection with the care of property there be maintained a standard property register, that regulation sacks of various sizes which will permit of locking or sealing be used, and upon each sack there be placed a tag showing the contents of the sack, the name of the case, the name of the officer or person delivering the property, the date of receipt, and the approximate value. The chief of police should have access to this property at all times.

Duties as Secretary.

As the secretary of the department, the purchasing agent maintains all of the records with respect to the finances, personnel and statistics. He attends to all the correspondence of the mayor with relation to police and performs stenographic service for the chief, including the reporting and transcribing of trials of delinquent policemen. For the most part, the records maintained by the secretary are in accordance with good practice and his work is efficiently performed. However, his functions do not include the supervision of all of the records of the department, in that records maintained in the office of the captain of the detectives and those at the stations do not come under his supervision.

It is therefore recommended that the title of this officer be changed by council at such time as the charter is amended to that of chief clerk of the police department and that his duties include those now performed by him, and in addition, general supervision of all of the records of the department and the drafting and installation of new and improved records and reports.

He should be directly responsible to the chief instead of to the mayor as at present, and should at all times be subject to orders, advice and direction of the chief. Under the present arrangement, because under the old form of organization he represented the board of commissioners, he operates largely independent of the chief. Since the abolition of the board he has continued to maintain his branch of the service in the same manner, establishing similar relations with the mayor to those previously held with the board. This relationship is not conducive to efficient service and has established a feeling between the uniformed service and the office of the secretary, which does not tend to obtain the best results. It should be distinctly understood that as chief clerk of the department, he is subordinate to the chief..

Financial Operation and Appropriations.

For the operation and maintenance of the police department, the funds appropriated by council are classified as follows:

Payroll account,
New station account,
Police signal account,
Expense account.

The total appropriation for the year 1916 was $316,734.71, while the total expenditures for the same period out of appropriated funds were $276,986.53.

In addition to the moneys appropriated by council, there is also made available for use of the police department, to be expended in any manner it desires, a fund which accrues out of police court costs. This fund amounted to $6,810.19 in 1916. There was also in this fund a balance from the preceding year of $1,178.33, making a total of $7,988.52. There was expended during the same period out of this fund $6,976.63, making the total expenditures for the operation and maintenance of the police service for the year 1916, $283,963.16.

So-called "Department Fund" Uncontrolled.

By virtue of statute, all costs accumulating in cases in the police and juvenile courts in which the policemen have made arrests revert to the police department to be expended by that department for police purposes. The construction put upon this law by the department is such that the fund is used for any purpose desired. For example, the salary of the chauffeur who drives the car used by the mayor and the chief is paid out of this fund. An employee of the police court who serves as a sort of janitor and messenger is also paid out of the fund. $300 a year is paid to the secretary and purchasing agent from these moneys, and about $8 a year is expended for cigars which are distributed among the policemen while in attendance at the instruction class. Of course, this amount is trivial, but it nevertheless illustrates the liberal interpretation of the law under which expenditures are made from this fund. While it may even.be desirable to furnish the policemen with cigars, thus adding to their comfort during instruction periods, nevertheless it is quite doubtful if the council would appropriate funds for this purpose. $25 a month of this money is donated by the department to the privately maintained pension fund, and newsboys are paid a small fee for the delivery of newspapers at headquarters and the police stations.

As pointed out in the section of this report devoted to the police court, the present system of costs should be abandoned, but pending such legislative change, certainly this money should revert to the general funds of the city and should not pass directly into the hands of the police department for expenditure within the discretion of the officers of that department. This is a most irregular procedure and should be changed at once. The moneys to defray the operating and maintenance expenses of this department, as of all other departments, should be appropriated by council in accordance with regular procedure and no special funds, the result of diverting revenues, should be permitted.

It is to be noted, however, that in making this recommendation it is not intended to intimate that the expenditures made by the police department out of this fund have been any other than legitimate and regular. It is the procedure that is criticized rather than the manner in which the fund was administered.

The following is a financial statement as given in the annual report of the police department:

FINANCIAL STATEMENT.

Payroll Account.

Appropriation ....$ 238,147.86
Expended 236,901.68

Balance ....$ 1,246.18

New Police Station.

Appropriation ....$ 52,236.85
Expended 14,,343.84

Balance carried forward ....$ 38,494.01

Expense Account.

Appropriation ....$ 25,250.00
Expended 23,248.89

Balance ....$ 1.11

Signal System Account.

Appropriation .... $ 2,500.00
Expended 2,493.12

Balance ....$ 6.88

Department's Fund.

Amount brought forward January 1, 1916..$ 1,178.33
Amount derived from court costs......... 6,810.19

Total ....$ 7,988.52
Expended 1916 .... 6,976.63

Balance carried forward Jan. 1, 1917...$ 1,011.89

Records and Reports.

Many of the records maintained in the police department are
in accordance with good practice, but are not properly compiled
nor adequately reviewed. It is, therefore, recommended. that the

mayor direct the secretary and purchasing agent to revise the records and reporting system in accordance with the suggestions hereinafter contained. As a guide in the drafting of new records, it is recommended that the record system now in use in the police department of the city of Harrisburgh be selected. This system was installed by the New York Bureau of Municipal Research. Copies of the forms used in Harrisburgh have already been supplied the police department through the courtesy of the chief of police of Harrisburgh.

District Daily Return.

Each captain is required to file with the chief daily reports as follows:

a—Report in printed form as to strength of force.

b—Report of arrests.

c—Miscellaneous report.

d—Report of ordinance violations.

It is recommended that the daily reports from each district consist of one report to be known as the district daily return. This report should contain printed headings calling for complete and detailed information as to the activities and operation of the force and the precinct during the preceding twenty-four hours.

The form should be drafted in accordance with the following illustration. It should be made out in duplicate, one copy to be retained in the district in the captain's office and the original to be filed with the chief. It should be of convenient size for binding in a loose leaf binder.

It will be noted that not only does this form provide for recording the strength of the force, and the causes of absence, but likewise the service rendered and arrests made. The reverse side of the form calls for a comparative statement of arrests, complaints and miscellaneous service, thus giving a complete picture of current activities and at the same time affording a means of comparison with previous periods.

COMPARATIVE STATEMENT

ARRESTS AND DISPOSITIONS

OFFENSE	ARRESTS				CONVICTED		DISCHARGED		ACQUITTED		Held for Higher Court		Held for Other Court		PENDING
	This Day	This Year to Date	Last Year to Date	Increase	Decrease	This Day	To Date this Year	This Day	To Date this Year	This Date	To Date this Year	This Day	This Day	This Year	
Burglary															
Homicide															
Juvenile Delinquency															
Vagrancy															
Traffic Violations															
Miscellaneous Misdemeanors															
" Felonies															
Disorderly Practice															
Disorderly Conduct															

COMPLAINTS TODAY AND PREVIOUS

SUBJECT OF COMPLAINT	This Day	This Year to Date	Last Year to Date	Increase	Decrease
Burglary					
Homicide					
Highway Robbery					
Felonious Assault					
Assault and Battery					
Pocket Picking					
Robberies and Larceny					
Crimes Against Nature					
Disorderly Houses					
Street Soliciting by Prostitutes					
Gambling					
Bunco Games					
Forgery					
Mendicancy					
Malicious Mischief					
Miscellaneous					
Total					

GENERAL INFORMATION

SUBJECT	This Day	This Year to Date	Last Year to Date	Increase	Decrease
Value Property Stolen					
" Recovered					
Fires Discovered					
" Attended					
Outrages Reported					
Open Doors Reported					
Street Defects Reported					
Suspected Disorderly Houses Reported					
Suspected Gambling Houses Reported					
Number Meals Furnished					
" Wagon Calls					
" Ambulance Calls					
" Missing Persons					
" Complaints Against Policemen					

Day of Week _____

Morning Report for 24 Hours Ending at Midnight _____ 19__

PRESENT

DETAILED AND ABSENT FORCE

RANK	SQUAD			NAME	RANK	DETAILED			ABSENT					Time of Absence
	1	2	3			To	By	Extra Pay	With Leave		Sick		Suspended	
									With Pay	Without Pay	Full Pay	Half Pay		
Chief								$						
Captain								$						
Lieutenant								$						
Sergeant								$						
Patrolmen								$						
Operators								$						
Chauffeurs								$						
Totals								$						

ARRESTS

OFFENSES	Misdemeanor		Felony		Juvenile Delinquents		Summons Issued	Total
	Male	Female	Male	Female	Male	Female		

PERSONS AIDED

CHARACTER OF AID	Male	Female	HOW DISPOSED OF						Total
			To Hospitals	To Home	To Morgue	Claimed	Released	Miscellaneous	
Sick									
Injured									
Rescued Drowning									
Suicide									
Attempted Suicide									
Found Dead									
Missing Adults Found By Police									
" " By Others									
" Children " By Police									
" " By Others									
Foundlings									
Lodgers									
Safekeeping									
Intoxicated Persons									

Consolidated Morning Report.

From the daily district reports there should be prepared what would be termed a "consolidated daily report" which should contain a complete recapitulation of the information reported upon the daily return. These should be made out in duplicate, one copy to be retained by the chief and the original to be forwarded to the office of the mayor for his review.

Court Returns.

All arrests and violations of corporation ordinances are reported to headquarters where they are copied on special sheets and forwarded to the police and juvenile courts. They are then posted in index books, thus requiring considerable unnecessary clerical work at the central office.

It is, therefore, recommended that there be established a report to be known as a "court return" to consist of a printed form with headings calling for information as to arrests and violations of ordinances reported.

These reports should be prepared by the desk sergeant on the late tour and forwarded each morning directly to the police court. There should be provided a column calling for the disposition of the case. Under this heading the clerk of the court should be requested to enter the manner in which the case was disposed of and the court return. At the close of the session it should be forwarded to police headquarters, in order that the dispositions of the cases may be entered in the records of the police department.

Card Record of Arrests and Ordinance Cases.

For maintaining a complete index to arrests and ordinance violations, there should be established a card record of arrests and ordinance violations. These cards should have printed upon them headings similar to those which should be contained in the proposed record of arrests and in the proposed record of ordinance violations. They should be filled out by the desk sergeants immediately after the pedigree of· the prisoner is entered in the record of arrests, and held at the police station until the morning following the arraignment of the prisoner in court. Each policeman should be required, under the rules, to report to the desk sergeant the disposition of his case in court, and the sergeant should then post this information on the arrest card. They should then be forwarded to police headquarters and there filed alphabetically. The same procedure should be followed with reference to violations of ordinances. When this is done, the present index of arrests and ordinance violations should be discontinued.

Monthly Report of Complaints.

Each month the captains of districts and the captain of detectives should be required to file upon a specially printed form a report of all complaints received during the month and action taken upon them. The complaints should be classified in accordance with the modern standard classification of crime and the following illustration should be used as a guide in drafting this report form:

CRIME
CLASSIFICA

...rease	Complaints This Year To Date	Complaints Last Year To Date	Arrests in Cases of This Month	Arrests in Cases Previously Reported	Total Arrests		CRIME CLASSIFICATION
							Municipal rules and regu- tion of,
							Sabbath law, violation of (
							Motor vehicle laws, violatio
							Operating without a licen
							Speeding,
							Miscellaneous,
							Firearms—
							Carrying concealed,
							Discharging,
							Illegal sale of,
							Labor law, violation of,
							Tenement house law, violati
							Usury,
							Condition of boilers,
							Miscellaneous,
							COMPLAINTS CONCERN
							REGULATIVE (
							Health, violation of sanitar
							Sale of exposed foodstuff
							Expectoration in public p
							Food adulterations,
							Miscellaneous,
							Fire protection and prevent
							Sending of false alarms,
							Reckless blasting,
							Storing combustibles wit
							Sale of fireworks without
							Failure to comply with fi
							regulations,
							Miscellaneous,
							Ordinance with relation to
							violation of,
							Licenses—
							Operating without licens
							Miscellaneous,
							Traffic conditions—
							Speeding,
							Congestion,
							Miscellaneous,
							Park regulations,
							Dance halls—
							Disorderly,
							Admitting minors,
							Improperly conducted,
							Miscellaneous,
							Pool and billiard parlors—
							Disorderly,
							Admitting minors,
							Improperly conducted,
							Pawnbrokers, affecting or c
							Theatres, regulations concer
							Overcrowding,
							Ticket speculating,
							Miscellaneous,
							Mendicancy,
							Unnecessary noises on highw
							Push cart peddlers,
							Miscellaneous,

	This Month	Last Month	Increase	Decrease	Complaints This Year To Date	Complaints Last Year To Date	Arrests in Cases of This Month	Arrests in Cases Previously Reported	Total Arrests
lations governing, viola-									
t ihe—									
I'n of—									
ses,									
A									
t									
a									
t									
ons of,									
g									
l									
[									
ING VIOLATIONS OF									
ORDINANCES									
g sade—									
s,									
isaes,									
ion—									
hout permit.									
permit,									
re prevention rules and									
weights and measures,									
s,									
oncerning,									
aleg—									
ays.									
—									

Record of Arrests.

The record of arrests as already explained in this report, is not in accordance with good practice. A new record of arrests should be provided as soon as possible, and should be designed in accordance with the following illustration:

This form should be re-arranged of course to meet local conditions, as, for example, classification of crime under the heading "degree," and the word "saloon" might be omitted.

This illustration is a copy of the form now used in the police department of the City of New York, and was designed by the Bureau of Municipal Research.

Report of Ordinance Violations.

A bound book having printed headings, to be known as the "record of ordinance violations" should be designed and installed. Such a record should be similar in form to the "record of arrests." There should be maintained, as a separate record, a bound index to the record of arrests and record of ordinance violations.

Record of Accidents and Aided Cases.

Accidents and aided cases are now reported on what are termed the "miscellaneous report" which contains reports upon various subjects. Such accidents as are reported upon by the police should be recorded in a book specially provided for this purpose. In this book should be entered under proper printed headings a complete and detailed account of all persons aided through the police department. The record in each case should include the complete pedigree of the person or persons aided, similar to the pedigree required in arrest cases, and a statement of facts in connection with the case, including the name and addresses of witnesses and in brief any statements made by them. Each case should be numbered consecutively beginning the first case with the number 1. This book should be indexed to the entries and recapitulated each month.

Because of litigation arising out of street accidents, constant demands are made upon the police of most cities for certified copies of the police record as to accidents. Therefore, the record of aided cases should be compiled in such a manner as to facilitate ready reference and furnish detailed information.

Card Record of Accidents and Aided Cases.

Cards should be supplied to each precinct having headings similar to those contained in the record of accidents and aided cases. The details of each case should be entered on one of these cards and forwarded to headquarters, where the cards should be filed alphabetically. No other report need be made except in such cases as require investigation through the detectives, in these cases there should be filed at headquarters a detailed special report in addition to the card.

Citizens' Complaint Book.

A "record of complaints" is maintained at present in each precinct. The complaints are entered in a bound book having no printed number, and only such complaints as are specially reported upon should be given a serial number. Complaints involving loss of property are entered in a bound book with printed headings, a method which was established in January, 1917.

Other complaints received over the telephone are entered in what is called the "telephone complaint record." This method of recording complaints is not in accordance with good practice in that there is no one record in which all complaints are entered. It is, therefore, recommended that there be established in each district, at headquarters and at the office of the captain of detectives a register of complaints. This book should have printed headings calling for detailed information concerning the complaints and the action taken upon them. Every complaint received should be entered chronologically in this record and given a serial number. Complaints referred to the detective bureau for investigation should be recorded under the heading of "disposition" as referred to the detective bureau. The time at which they were referred, the name of the detective at headquarters receiving the message and the name of the officer who acknowledged it should also be entered in this record. Thus there would be a complete history of each complaint entered in such manner as to facilitate ready reference. This book should be indexed both according to the name of the complainant and the subject complained of.

Card Record of Complaints.

A card record of complaints requiring detectives attention and stating action taken upon them, should be established at headquarters. Upon these cards should appear complete and detailed information concerning each complaint. The following illustration should be used as a guide in drafting the form for recording complaints of this character.

BUREAU OF POLICE

COMPLAINT CARD
DETECTIVE CASES

COMPLAINT NO.

CRIME CLASSIFICATION

NAME OF COMPLAINANT

ADDRESS

OCCUPATION

PLACE OF OCCURRENCE	DISTRICT NUMBER	TIME AND DATE OF OCCURRENCE	REPORTED TO BUREAU OF POLICE
		A. M. _____ 19___	BY _____ A.M. / P.M.
		P. M.	AT

NAME OF PATROLMAN ON POST AT TIME

BY WHOM RECEIVED

DETAILS OF COMPLAINT

IMMEDIATE ACTION TAKEN

NAMES OF DETECTIVES ASSIGNED

TIME ASSIGNED

TELEGRAMS SENT

DESCRIPTION OF PERSONS WANTED

NAME	ALIAS	ADDRESS	SEX	COLOR	AGE	HEIGHT FEET	HEIGHT INCHES	WEIGHT LBS.	COLOR EYES	COLOR HAIR	COMPLEXION

DESCRIPTION AS TO DRESS AND MARKS OF IDENTIFICATION

DESCRIPTION OF PROPERTY
STOLEN AND RECOVERED

QUANTITY	ARTICLES	ESTIMATED VALUE	RECOVERED DATE	VALUE	QUANTITY	ARTICLES	ESTIMATED VALUE	RECOVERED DATE	VALUE

VALUE OF PROPERTY STOLEN $

VALUE OF PROPERTY RECOVERED $

BY WHOM RECOVERED:

BURGLAR INSURANCE CARRIED, $
BURGLAR INSURANCE REGISTERED, $
NAME OF COMPANY

ARRESTS AND DISPOSITIONS

NAME	ADDRESS	BY WHOM ARRESTED	DATE	FINAL DISPOSITION
				(KNOWN COURT — SENTENCE — DATE)

PROGRESS

FINAL RESULTS

UNFOUNDED

NO RESULTS

PARTIAL RECOVERY

RECOVERY

ARREST - NO RECOVERY

ARREST AND RECOVERY

CASE OTHERWISE CLEARED BY

DATE

Card Record of Complaints from Other Jurisdictions.

In order to keep the records affecting complaints investigated for other jurisdictions, and not involving the City of Richmond, it is recommended that a separate complaint card record be maintained. The card should be designed precisely in the same manner as the local complaint card, except that it should be printed upon a different colored card and filed separately. A separate serial should be maintained for such complaints.

Cross-Index to Complaints.

In connection with the card record of complaints there should be maintained a cross index to name of complainant, .by street location, by property clasification, and by crime classification. The index should be printed upon heavyweight paper rather than regulation cardboard, which would reduce the amount of filing space necessary and at the same time permit of the four index cards being typewritten in the same operation through a carbon process. These index cards should be printed on four different colored papers and should contain six cards on a strip so as to make their typewriting convenient. In designing the index card, the following illustration should be used as a guide:

Name of Complainant	Address		Property	Crime

Complaint No.		Date	

DESCRIPTION OF PROPERTY

Kind of Watch	No. of Case	No. Movement

Monograms—Initials—Inscription—Marks, etc.

Name of Complainant	Address		Property	Crime

Complaint No.		Date	

DESCRIPTION OF PROPERTY

Kind of Watch	No. of Case	No. Movement

Monograms—Initials—Inscription—Marks, etc.

Name of Complainant	Address		Property	Crime

Complaint No.		Date	

DESCRIPTION OF PROPERTY

Kind of Watch	No. of Case	No. Movement

Monograms—Initials—Inscription—Marks, etc.

Special Card Record of Reports of Homicide.

The information required concerning murders differs considerably from the information concerning other complaints, and, because of the seriousness of the crime, a separate card record of reports of homicide should be maintained. The following illustration should be used as a guide in drafting this form:

Similar report forms, but printed on loose leaves, should be provided each district station and should be used by the precincts in reporting homicides. When received at headquarters, this information should be transferred to a card.

SERIAL No.	**REPORT OF HOMICIDE** **Bureau of Police**	Time and Date Reported ___ A. M. ___ P. M. ___ 19	By Whom Reported Address

NAME OF PERSON KILLED	Address	Age	Sex	Color	Nationality	Nationality of Parents
Surname First Name		Married or Single	No. of Children	Occupation	Yearly Income	

PERSON KILLED, UNIDENTIFIED—Description :

Approximate Age _____ Apparent Nationality _____ Occupation (if evidenced) _____

Sex _____ Color _____ Age _____ Height ____ Ft. ____ In. Weight _____ Color Eyes _____ Color Hair _____ Complexion _____

Dress, Clothing, Personal possessions, Marks of Identification, Etc. _____

_____

Circumstances of Death:	Place of Occurrence	Nature of Injury
Time of occurrence A. M. P. M. 19		

Name in which received _____

Details of occurrence _____

Character of premises _____ If licensed, give license number _____

Name of Persons Arrested Suspected	Address	Age	Sex	Color	Nationality	Nationality of Parents	Married or Single	No. of Children	Occupation	Yearly Income

DESCRIPTION OF PERSONS ACCUSED—Unidentified

_____

_____

_____

Known motive _____

Possible and suspected motive _____

Witnesses taken into custody (Name and Address) _____

_____

Witnesses not taken into custody (Name and Address) _____

_____

_____

Person with whom accused lived (Name and Address) _____

_____

IMMEDIATE POLICE ACTION TAKEN

Persons Notified _____ Address _____

Department or Institution notified _____ Time _____

Time _____ By whom: _____

Name of Coroner attending _____ Time of Arrival _____

Name of Prosecutor attending _____ Time of Arrival _____

Body pronounced dead for _____ hours

Name of Physician so pronouncing _____ Address or Hospital _____

REMARKS AND COMMENT

Detectives Assigned on Case _____

Card Record of Licensed Places.

In order that the police may exercise proper control over licensed premises and aid in the inspection of them, a card record of all premises and persons in the district operating under licenses should be maintained at each district station. These cards should show the name, address, character of business, number and kind of licenses issued, date of issuance and expiration, and on the reverse side provision should be made for recording under proper printed headings a report on inspection of premises and arrests made or complaints received in connection with it. These cards should be filed, classified as to kind of license, such as pool and billiard parlors, moving picture shows, bowling alleys, etc.

From the information contained on these cards the captain of each district should be required to file an annual report, which should contain a complete history of the complaints received and the action taken by the police in connection with the premises and persons licensed. This information should be of great value to the licensing authorities in determining whether or not a license should be renewed.

Card Record of Members of the Force.

A card record of the members of the force assigned to the precinct should be maintained. These cards should show for each member the name, age, residence and date of appointment, the home telephone number of the policeman, whether married or single, number of children and former occupation. Upon the reverse side of the card should be kept a record of the efficiency ratings, record of complaints received concerning the policeman and also his delinquencies. Thus, a card should contain a complete history of the policeman from the day he enters the force until he ceases to be a member. At such times as he is transferred to another precinct he should take the card with him and deliver it to the commanding officer of the precinct to which he is assigned. At the date of appointment three of these cards should be prepared—one to be retained in the office of the administrative head, one in the office of the chief of police, and the third at the precinct station to which he is assigned.

Card Record of Vacant Houses.

When a citizen notifies the police precinct that his residence is about to become vacant for any reason, the "vacant house officer" is notified and he is supposed to observe the premises from time to time. In this way it is hoped to furnish protection to the vacant houses against robbery. It is recommended that this practice be abandoned and that the procedure be changed so as to provide for a card record of vacant houses, a copy of which should be retained at the precinct station, and a copy furnished the patrolman on the post upon which the house is located. This card should show among other things the location of the house, the name of the owner or occupant, the name and address of the person to be notified; in case of any unusual occurrence at the house, and the name and description of any caretaker, watchman or other person who might, from time to time return to the house. Such persons should be given an identification card signed by the captain of the precinct, in order that they may be properly identified if discovered in the house by the police during the absence of the owner.

The sergeants should be instructed from time to time to inspect these premises to see that the doors and windows are locked.

Annual Report.

The annual report issued by the department is compiled for the most part in accordance with good practice, but it does not contain sufficient statistics to serve as a guide to council or the mayor as to the efficiency of the service, in that the information contained in it has not been compiled upon a comparative basis, and it does not contain any information as to the complaints and character of complaints received and the disposition of them. In this connection the report should contain a section showing under the heading "Detective Bureau" and in tabular form—

1. Complaints received requiring detective attention, showing the number investigated, the number unfounded, the number upon which arrests were made, those upon which no action at all was taken, and the number upon which no results were obtained after action had been taken.

2. Arrests for felonies made by members of the detective bureau classified as to crime, showing the number of males and females, and the disposition of the cases under the headings "convicted," "acquitted," and "pending."

3. Arrests for misdemeanors. The same classification as for felonies should be used.

4. Separate table showing arrests upon warrants, pick-ups and those brought back from other cities.

5. Number of murders committed and reported each year for the five preceding years, with the number of arrests and dispositions stated in the same table.

6. Cases of burglary and house-breaking reported. This table should show how the burglary was effected under a form heading, such as false keys, breaking doors insecurely fastened, etc., and the hours between which the burglary was believed to have been committed, the total value of property stolen, the total value of property recovered, the number of cases in which no ultimate loss occurred, number of cases in unoccupied houses, and the number of cases in which violence was used.

7. Number of arrests and investigations made by each member of the detective bureau, classified as to crime and place under proper headings.

Under the heading "uniformed force" the fullest detailed statistics should be furnished in tabular form as to the following:

1. Complaints received and investigated by the uniformed force, showing the number investigated, the number unfounded, and the number upon which arrests were made, those upon which no action at all was taken, and the number upon which no results were obtained.

2. Arrests for felonies made by the members of the uniformed force, classified as to crime, showing the number of males and females, and the disposition of the cases under the headings "convicted," "acquitted," and "pending."

3. Arrests for misdemeanors. The same classification and headings as for felonies should be used.

The report should contain a separate table of arrests classified by crimes in which should be noted all arrests made by motorcycle men, together with the disposition of same. All of these tables should show the total number of arrests under the same heading for each of the preceding five years.

There should also be included in the report a table showing disposition of cases. This table should show—

1. The amount of fines tabulated in amounts from $5.00 to $1,000, with side columns for terms of imprisonment from five days to over ten years.

2. Terms of imprisonment tabulated to show prison sentences imposed from five years to life, classified as to crime.

3. Arrests for intoxication, disorderly conduct and prostitution on holidays.

4. Disposition of all arrests, classified as to offense, showing total number of arrests made for each crime, records of convictions and acquittals (with sub-classification as to convictions by plea of guilty or by trial and acquittal by direction, by verdict), or discharged, (sub-classified as to discharges by magistrates, or grand jury, by dismissal of indictment, or on own recognizance) and cases pending, sub-divided as follows:

> In jail;
> On bail.
> Under parole and forfeiture.

The list of fugitives from justice arrested, and the roster of the force should be omitted from the annual report, as these are matters which are duly recorded in the records of the department and are of little or no value in an annual report.

The Police Benevolent Association

THE POLICE BENEVOLENT ASSOCIATION.

A lengthy discussion of the methods employed in the operation of the Police Benevolent Association of the City of Richmond is hardly within the scope of this survey of the city government of Richmond, because any analysis of the problems of the association must necessarily be superficial, unless founded on the results of a thorough actuarial investigation of the association. However, the Bureau wishes to draw the attention of the directors of the association to certain matters pertaining to the fundamental organization and management of the association which will require special attention in the near future, not only if the association is to yield the full benefits to the police department and the community, which an association of its type is capable of yielding, but even if it is to be continued. An examination of the majority of pension and relief associations in this country which has been made by the Bureau has shown that a neglect of actuarial principles in the establishment and operation of these systems is widespread, with the result that costly re-organization or complete bankruptcy is imminent or has taken place. The Police Benevolent Association of Richmond is not unlike many of these associations, which have actually been proven unable to shoulder the financial burdens consequent upon their development. For this reason the following discussion should be of peculiar importance to the members and directors of the association, and all who are desirous of securing the maximum efficiency in the police department of the city.

Similarity of Pension Systems to Old Fraternal Orders.

The rapid growth of fraternal or benefit orders in this country and the final dissolution or radical re-organization of the majority of such societies is probably well known to the readers of this report. Many of these associations attempted to collect assessments from their members and to pay benefits to others, or to the dependents of others, without sufficient knowledge of the acturial principles which should have been respected, and without carefully taking into account the contingent liabilities which they were assuming. This can be easily understood when we remember that the majority of claims matured only after members had been in the societies a number of years, while the income from these members began immediately upon their entrance. Without use of actuarial principles it was impossible to ascertain what the claim of each contributing member and each new member upon the resources of the society would ultimately be. The neglect to obtain this information on the part of many honest and sincere organizers of such societies has caused the dissolution or painful re-organization of their associations with very considerable hardship to many of the members.

Pension systems in this country are now being established in accordance with the same unsound principles which undermined the fraternal societies, so that shortly most of these systems must be abandoned and, indeed, many have already become unable to meet their claims. Several cities in this country have only recently undertaken to reconstruct their unsound retirement plans which were founded on the old basis. The neglect of scientific principles in the operation of retirement systems has arisen easily because the importance of the operation of the laws of mortality, which is even more important than in a death benefit association, is clouded by the fact that the benefits are payable in the case of a persons's living, instead of in the converse case of dying. The disastrous results attendant upon the absence of information whereby the future mortality rate of members of their association may be measured has not been generally brought to the attention of managers of retirement systems who are usually influenced to rely on precedents set by other unsound systems.

Data Which Board of Directors Now Has at Its Disposal.

The twenty gentlemen now constituting the board of directors of the Police Benevolent Association, are charged with the operation of an insurance business covering the life of every member of the police force of Richmond. The business is unlike that of an insurance company because it is not operated for profit and it is not expected that every active member shall provide the cost of his probable benefits from the system; nevertheless, the directors must undertake to receive and invest money for subsequent disbursement for the benefit of the active members. This is in the nature of the technical work peculiar to insurance companies handling annuities. The board of directors of an insurance company would have at their disposal the services of an actuarial staff which would furnish them the information essential to the sound management of their company. Unfortunately, the present Benevolent Association does not provide this information for its board of directors.

The treasurer of the association very properly furnishes to the board at certain intervals a statement of the income, disbursements, and accumulation of the funds. For example, the reports of the five years ending November 2, 1916, show that each year the fund has received considerably more than it has disbursed for benefits and expenses, and that on that date it had accumulated approximately $130,913.51. These reports are apparently correct and give all of the information which ought to be obtained from this source, but they should be supplemented by a statement of the prospective benefits which the fund will be called upon to provide and by the prospective assets which may be anticipated. The treasurer's report shows what appears at first glance to reflect a prosperous condition of the association, but there is no one who, from these reports, and the list of members or pensioners available alone, can tell whether or not the association is now in a prosperous condition or whether it is on the road to bankruptcy. The information now available does not place the directors in a position to know whether or not their fund is sound and with the present available information they would not know if it were unsound until their disbursements had actually exceeded their income. This condition might not occur for a number of years when it would be too late to make the slight changes in the fund which, if made at this time, might be sufficient to maintain the fund in a sound condition.

Information Which Shoud Be Supplied to Directors.

The future cost of the benefits which the association will be called upon to provide under the present scale, will depend upon the number of policemen who will live to become disabled, upon the number who will remain in the active service until they are dropped by the commissioners because of old age, and the probable time each of such members awarded a benefit will live to draw his benefit. This number can be accurately estimated only after an investigation has been made showing the rates of mortality, resignation and dismissal, and disability obtaining among the active members of the police force. This information should be available to the board of directors. Predicated upon these data and other information regarding dependents which is also necessary for obtaining the future cost of a benefit plan, the board should have calculated for it the prospective cost of all benefits which it may be expected to award on account of present policemen. A calculation should then be made of the probable dues which will be received from the present force. The excess of this liability or cost of prospective benefits over and above the present assets of the fund and the future dues from present active members will show the amount which must be derived from other sources if the benefits are to be paid. If money must be derived from other sources, the directors will know just how much must be raised each year to maintain the system. If this amount cannot be secured under the present system of operation, then the directors should advise the active members of the conditions so that some further source of revenue may be provided or the benefits reduced to exactly the amount which the income will provide for all prospective beneficiaries. Otherwise certain members will obtain more than their share of the benefits while others will be forced to take less than they are entitled to. If, perchance, there is no excess of liabilities, but rather an excess of assets, then the directors will be in a position to determine how much the scale of benefits may be increased without exceeding the available assets.

Another point upon which the directors should have definite information is in regard to the cost of benefits to new entrants. The cost of the contingent liability assumed on account of the admission of a new member should be known together with the value of the prospective dues to be received from that member. If the prospective liability incurred on account of a new entrant is in excess of the prospective dues, then *every new member admitted represents more liability to the fund*, so that new members are weakening the fund and are taking away from the benefits which might otherwise be paid to the present members. If the converse is the case (this does not appear to be the case from a superficial examination) then the admission of new entrants is a benefit to present members, so that if the fund is short of assets the excess of the dues of new entrants over their prospective cost may be considered as an additional source of income which may be employed in increasing the benefits of the new entrants or otherwise as is deemed expedient.

So long as the association is operated by those who are not provided with information of this character, it is operating under conditions which may result in its either collecting from its members more dues than are necessary or else running so far into bankruptcy that when the deficiency becomes apparent it will be necessary to cut short expeditures and deprive many of the present members of benefits which they have justly anticipated. It may then be too late to avert the hardships which are always attendant upon the failure of such organizations.

Steps Which Should Be Taken by Association to Obtain Information.

No matter in what condition the directors of the association may believe it to be, as a matter of sound business procedure they should immediately arrange to have a thorough actuarial investigation of the association made and the definite financial status of the association ascertained. This work is complex in detail, and cannot be developed in a report of this type, however, some of the main steps in such an investigation may be enumerated. A set of tables should be prepared and made available to the association, which will present in a form ready for use the laws of mortality, which obtain among members in active service and on pension, and the other factors upon which the cost of the benefits depend, namely, the rates of resignation, dismissal, disability, etc. A balance sheet showing the present and prospective assets and liabilities should be prepared in a form so that the actual financial condition of the association shall be plainly exhibited to members of the association who may not be experienced in insurance work. If there be a surplus of funds in the association, the amount of this surplus should be shown and, if, on the other hand, a deficit is developing the various ways of checking the further development of a deficit should be indicated. A table should be prepared showing the actual cost as a single payment or on an annual or monthly payment basis the amount which should be provided to cover the cost of the benefits allowable on account of various policemen entering at various ages. Reference should be made to the chapter on the Firemen's Mutual Aid Association for the discussion of the steps to be taken in making an actuarial investigation of that association where the possibility of combining the investigations required for the firemen and the policemen is suggested.

To state the various uses which will be made of the investigation and the various steps which may be taken to benefit the association as the result of the investigation is difficult in this chapter, but enough has probably been said to indicate to the reader the fundamental importance of such a chart or compass to guide the directors of the association in steering the association safely in a permanently solvent condition.

Obtaining the Information Necessary.

The Bureau of Municipal Research has established a department which is organized for such work as herein discussed, and which is engaged exclusively in furnishing to the managers of retirement systems service of this character. It is suggested that when the association determines to undertake the work, it secure the services of an organization or actuary of recognized standing in matters of this kind, who has had experience in the valuation of retirement systems. The actuary will probably outline in detail what it seems advisable to do, and will give a detailed statement of the probable cost of his services. The board of directors may be assured that the financial advantage to the association and its members which will result from a thorough actuarial investigation will be many times its cost.

Fire Department

FIRE DEPARTMENT.

As at present organized, the fire department is established more or less as an independent unit of government. It is administered by a board of four commissioners who are elected by the council for a term of four years. The charter provides that the board must comprise a representative of each of the four wards of the city, and their terms are so arranged as to provide for the expiration annually of the term of one commissioner. No salary is paid the commissioners for their services. All of the present incumbents are representative business men and have served as commissioners for a number of years, one having served continuously for a period of thirty-two years.

The functions of the board include the business management of the department which in effect means the supervision of purchases and the administration and executive control, including the making of appointments, promotions, dismissals and retirements. The board meets monthly, and at these meetings receives reports from the chief concerning the routine operation of the department and from the secretary as to the business management. A careful examination of the minutes of the board shows that the commissioners are faithful in their attendance and interested in their work.

Board of Commissioners Should be Abolished.

The powers conferred by charter upon the board in its management of this service, tend to remove the department from the remainder of the government and thus prevent close co-operative relationship and reduce efficiency. While it is not to be inferred that the present commissioners have not been enthusiastic and energetic in their efforts to bring the department to a high standard of efficiency, nevertheless, wise administration and efficient service demand centralized responsibility and control such as cannot be had through administration by a board in the management of any business.

The work of the board divides itself chiefly into two parts, namely, purchasing and control of supplies, and administration, as represented by the making of appointments, promotions, transfers and dismissals.

The making of purchases is a function which belongs properly to a central purchasing agent, a position the establishment of which is recommended elsewhere in this report. All appointments and promotions should be made as the result of competitive civil service examinations, while the transferring of firemen and officers is a function which should be exercised exclusively by the chief of the department. Thus, with the purchases made and controlled through a central agency and appointments and promotions controlled by civil service regulations, and transfers made by the chief, there would be little to occupy the time of four commissioners in the management of the fire department.

The fire service is a highly technical branch of the government, and its main operations are and should be under the control of the chief, who shoud be selected because of his expert technical knowledge and experience. Consequently, the departmnt could best be administered if placed under the supervision of the central executive to whom the chief would be directly responsible.

Therefore, as a means of securing centralized responsibility and bringing all of the activities of the city under the supervision and observation of one official who would hold his immediate commissioners or heads responsible for the efficiency of their departments, and in turn directly responsible to the people, it is recommended that the charter be amended so as to abolish the board of fire commissioners and to place the fire department under the control and supervision of the central executive, regardless of what may be his title.

Administrative Head Should Be Currently Advised Through Proper Reporting System.

While the commissioners and the chief are to be commended for the record and reporting system which they have installed, nevertheless, it must be pointed out that the system does not provide for keeping the administrative heads currently advised of all of the activities of the department. It is true that the chief reports monthly in letters addressed to the board on matters of routine, but these reports do not advise the board of the work performed in connection with the most important function of the fire service, namely, fire prevention. While the department has made very few fire prevention inspections, the type of buildings inspected, the results obtained through such inspections, the conditions removed and the orders issued are matters on which the board receives practically no information. The same is true in a large measure with respect to the success or failure of the department in the matter of fire extinguishment. While the chief reports to the board as to the number of alarms and the kind of alarms received during the month, he does not inform the commissioners of details in connection with the fires, such as losses, character of buildings, results obtained through confining a fire to its place of origin, or methods employed in the extinguishment of fires. Moreover, no comparative data is furnished currently which would enable the administrative heads to determine whether the number of fires during a given period is greater or less than during a similar previous period, whether the number of fires is increasing or decreasing, and whether the fire losses are high or low. Unless the administrative heads have before them such information affecting the fire extinguishment and fire prevention service, it can scarcely be possible wisely to direct and administer this branch of the government.

Therefore, it is recommended that the administrative heads be currently advised of all activities of the department through a proper reporting system. The members of the fire board or the central executive should not be required to wait a period of a month before being informed officially about the fires occurring within the city. The chief should be required to furnish each member of the board (or the central executive) with a detailed report upon each fire within twenty-four hours after the fire. This report, commonly known as a "fire service report," should give complete information, and an estimate of the loss. It should be made upon a specially printed form of a convenient size for binding and should be delivered to the office of the members of the board or the central executive. At the monthly meetings the chief should be required to submit upon a specially provided form, instead of informally in letters, a comprehensive report of the entire month's operations in tabular form upon a comparative basis. As relating to fire prevention work, this report should show the number of inspections made by officers and firemen classified as to type of buildings inspected, the number of violations observed, classified as to kinds of violations, the number corrected immediately, the number corrected only after written order, the number remaining uncorrected and requiring legal action.

Pertaining to training of the men, the report should disclose the number of company drills held, the number of drills held at the fire school, the number of men in attendance, and the time of attendance in hours and minutes, and the efficiency of the firemen as shown at such drills.

At such time as the board is abolished and the department placed under the jurisdiction of the central executive, the chief should be required to file a complete daily report which would be in effect the consolidation upon one sheet of the information now received by him upon the daily company returns.

Purchasing Methods Defective.

The methods employed in making purchases and the recommendations concerning the function of purchasing for the city will be found fully discussed in that part of the survey report relating to the purchasing methods. It is, however, essential to point out as relating to the fire department, some of the defects of the present system and remedies which should be applied pending the establishment of a central purchasing division.

Supplies and equipment are purchased for the fire department, some by the chief, some by the superintendent of fire alarm, and others by the secretary. The chief purchases all coal, forage and minor suppies, the superintendent of fire alarm purchasing everything pertaining to the service of his division except when the amount involved exceeds $100, in which case the board passes upon the bids and directs the superintendent to make the purchases. The secretary buys the stationery and any other supplies which the board may direct. All bills are forwarded to the secretary and vouchered by him. His control consists merely of seeing to it that the additions and extensions are correct. If bids are secured by the chief or the superintendent of fire alarm, they are retained by them and not forwarded for the files of the central office. The bills are approved by the chief and the superintendent of fire alarm, but are not signed by the officer receiving the supplies.

Pending the establishment of a central purchasing division, it is recommended that the board of commissioners adopt a revised procedure for the making of purchases. All purchases should be made upon requisition through the secretary of the board and all bids secured should be filed in the office of the secretary. In no other way can there be exercised proper control over the purchase of supplies and equipment. A copy of every bill upon presentation should be forwarded to the company officer or division head who received the supplies for signature and comment. No bills should be vouchered to the financial officers until certified to by the person who actually received and inspected the goods.

Secretary of Board Should Be Civilian Employee.

For the maintenance of the records and the recording of the minutes of the board there is employed a secretary to the fire commissioners and the fire department who was appointed by the board to serve during good behavior. The salary is $1,718.88 per year. His appointment as secretary according to law gives him the rank of third assistant engineer, thus making him a commanding officer in the fire department. The duties of the secretary as third assistant engineer are defined in the rules and regulations of the board as follows:

The third assistant engineer is assigned to such special duty at fires as the chief engineer may direct, and shall respond to such stations in the mercantile or business sections or other important stations to be designated by the chief engineer, subject to the approval of the board of fire commissioners, and shall also respond to all second, third, and general (6-6-6) alarms and special calls.

He shall be the fourth ranking officer in the fire department, and shall assume such authority as may devolve upon him by the absence of the chief engineer, the first and second assistant engineers .

He shall, in case of, and during a general alarm (6-6-6), report to headquarters and assume charge of such apparatus as is not at the fire: order transfers, and place in active service any reserve apparatus or equipment that he may deem proper, and respond to any other alarm, and have charge during the said period, and until a superior officer reports for service after the said general alarm.

He shall report to the chief engineer any indifference or neglect which he may observe on the part of any officer or member in complying with the rules and regulations established by the board of fire commissioners, and he shall have power to suspend a subordilnate when, in his opinion, there has been a breach of discipline or violation of the rules, reporting the same immediately to the chief engineer.

If the secretary is to be efficient as a recorder of the records and the office manager it must be apparent he cannot perform fire duties of a character which would enable him to obtain the training required to become a commanding officer. Therefore, the charter should be amended so as to provide that the secretary of the board be a civilian employee appointed as a result of a competitive civil service examination and should be required to qualify as a stenographer and typewriter. He should not be a member of the uniformed force, nor have any duties or powers with relation to the management of the uniformed service. In amending the charter with relation to this position, however, care should be taken to protect the rights of the present incumbent with relation to his equity in the pension fund. By virtue of his having been given a rank in the fire department, he has been made a participant in the pension fund and has for many years contributed a portion of his salary, consequently, nothing in this report is in tended to recommend that he be deprived of the benefits of this fund. The present incumbent, however, by reason of his many years of service and his attendance at a majority of the fires, in addition to having made some special studies in the fire service, unquestionably has a better knowledge of fire fighting than would the average secretary. His opportunity for acquiring this knowledge, by reason of his former duties as secretary which included the supervision of the delivery of fuel at the fires, and his service with the department when it was much smaller than at the present, was such as would not be afforded a secretary who might succeed him.

Records Should Be Centralized Under Control of Secretary.

Under the present arrangement records are maintained both in the office of the chief and in the office of the board. The records maintained in the chief's office are under the supervision of a lieutenant, who acts in a clerical capacity and who also responds to alarms with his company. This procedure should be revised so as to place all of the records of the department under the control of the secretary who should be required to maintain and supervise the same. His title should be "secretary" or "chief clerk" of the fire department and he should report directly to the chief. The lieutenant detailed to clerical duties should work under the supervision of the secretary.

In order to maintain the records of the department in accordance with the approved plans of the secretary of the board, it is essential that there be employed a clerk for the fire department who should be selected as a result of a competitive civil service examination and who should be required to qualify as a stenographer and typewriter. It is not now possible for the secretary, in addition to his many other duties, to maintain the splendid cost record system which has already been installed, but which in the past few months has not been posted. All original records and reports should be filed in the central office and copies of them retained in the office of the chief and the assistant chiefs.

Secretary of Board Should Be Civilian Employee.

For the maintenance of the records and the recording of the minutes of the board, there is employed a secretary to the board and fire department who was appointed by the board to serve during good behavior. His salary is $1,718.88 per year. His appointment as secretary, according to law, gives him a rank of third assistant chief engineer, thus making him a commanding officer in the fire department. The secretary serves directly under the board of commissioners and as such is not under the command of the chief, except at such time as he may choose to exercise the powers of an assistant chief. The rules of the department provide that the secretary takes command as third assistant engineer in the absence of the chief, first and second engineers, and report for duty at fire headquarters as assistant chief when the other chiefs are in attendance at a general alarm. (6-6-6).

While the secretary is to be recommended for the manner in which he maintains such records as are under his jurisdiction, it is nevertheless necessary to point out that he has had no training for fire service, and consequently should at no time be placed in command of the fire fighting forces. He should be a civilian employee without any rank in the department.

Under the present arrangement, records are maintained both in the office of the chief and in the office of the board. The records maintained in the chief's office are under the supervision of a lieutenant who acts in a clerical capacity and who also responds to alarms with his company. This procedure should be revised so as to place all of the records of the department under the control of the secretary, who should be required to maintain and supervise them. His title should be "secretary" or "Chief clerk" of the fire department, and he should report directly to the chief. The lieutenant detailed to clerical duties should work under the supervision of the secretary.

In order to maintain the records of the department in accordance with the approved plans of the secretary of the board, it is essential that there be employed a clerk for the fire department selected as a result of a competitive civil service examination, who should be required to qualify as a stenographer and typewriter.

Chief the Executive Head.

The executive head of the department is the chief who is responsible to the board of commissioners and who is paid $2,520 a year. The chief is appointed by the board to serve during good behavior. He can only be removed after a hearing of charges by the board and has no right of appeal. The present incumbent is an experienced fireman having been a member of the department for thirty-seven years and chief of the department for the past nine years. He was promoted to the office of chief after having served in the various subordinate ranks. He is an efficient practical fireman, a good disciplinarian and of the progressive type of chief, maintaining good discipline and adequate control over his force.

The chief's control over the force, however, is somewhat weakened by reason of the present method of making promotions without competitive civil service examination. Promotions are made, as already pointed out in this report, by the board, and not always upon the recommendation of the chief. Thus even pending the introduction of the merit system for promotions, the chief's control over his force would be strengthened considerably if the board acted solely in the matter of promotions on the recommendations of the chief. It can be readily understood that the selection of officers by the board over the opposition of the chief is not conductive to good discipline or an aid in removing politics from the fire service.

Method of Selecting Chief Defective.

While the charter aims to protect the chief against what may be termed arbitrary removal without cause, the method of appointing the chief is defective and not in accordance with the best practice. Nothing in the charter prevents the appointment of a chief from without the force, nor must the promotion be made from among the commanding officers.

In the interest of efficiency and as a protection to the service, it is urged that the charter be amended so as to provide that the chief shall be appointed as a result of a competitive civil service examination and that such examination be open only to the assistant chiefs.

Sufficient weights for superiority should be given in order that the assistant chiefs shall have an advantage over captains, all other things being equal.

Additional Assistant Chief Should Be Appointed.

There are three assistant chiefs, each of whom receives $1,718. The first assistant chief is next in command to the chief and he is in charge of one of the two districts, while the second assistant chief is in charge of the second district. The third assistant chief serves as secretary of the board of fire commissioners and the fire department. The duties of the first and second chiefs are similar. It is recommended elsewhere in this report that the secretary of the department be a civilian appointee and be relieved of the title "third assistant chief," but because of the size of the city and the manner in which the risks are segregated, it is necessary that the city be divided into three districts, and that there be an assistant chief in charge of each district.

Therefore, it is recommended that there be appointed as a result of a competitive civil service examination, to which only the captains of the department shall be admitted, an additional district chief to be assigned to the newly established third district.

Under present conditions, in the absence of one of the assistant chiefs, it is necessary to detail a captain as acting assistant chief which is not in accordance with good practice. With three active assistant chiefs this woud not be necessary, as the assistants, during the absence of one of their number, could assume temporary charge of an additional district.

Assistant Chiefs Not Required to Keep Complete Records.

While it is true that one of the assistant chiefs maintains informal records of the activities of his subordinates and of the personnel of his command, the rules do not require that such records be kept. It is essential to good management that the district chiefs be required to keep standard records covering the activities of the companies within their respective districts. These records should include among others—

A card record of the personnel containing a record of the efficiency ratings.

Detailed and complete descriptions of all buildings within their districts. These to be maintained upon cards.

A complete and detailed record of fire prevention inspections made by themselves, by the officers in the companies under their command, and by firemen, showing orders issued and the results obtained.

A record of the properties of the department for the care of which they are responsible, showing the dates of inspection of fire houses and apparatus, and the results thereof.

A complete fire service record as affecting the runs made by the companies in the district, and copies of all company reports which have been forwarded to the chief.

Captains Should Be Selected from Among Lieutenants.

There are twenty captains, each of whom receives an annual salary of $1,212. These captains are in command of their companies, respond to alarms with them, maintain discipline at the stations, maintain the records at the fire stations, and make fire prevention inspections.

The captains are selected by the board of commissioners and may be selected without regard for the duties previously performed by them. Under the present procedure it is possible for a fireman who has been in the service only a short time to be promoted to the rank of captain. This procedure is defective. Captains should be selected only as a result of a competitive civil service promotional examination to which only the lieutenants should be admitted. At least two years of service as a lieutenant should be required of a candidate before he is eligible to compete for promotion to the rank of captain. The present number of captains is deemed adequate to meet the needs of the service.

No Regular Grade of Lieutenant.

There are nine Grade A firemen who are given the title of lieutenant, and who receive $1,091.52 a year salary, and thirteen Grade B firemen who are also designated lieutenants, and who receive a salary of $1,018.80 a year. Lieutenants are the next ranking officer to captains, and in the absence of the captain are in command.

There is no regularly established grade of lieutenant. The designation is an informal one and not established as a budget title, although they are given powers of commanding officers and supervise firemen in some instances receiving more salary than themselves. This procedure is most irregular and not conducive to good discipline. It was apparent throughout the department that because of this condition, the firemen do not show the proper respect for the orders of the lieutenants either at the stations or in service. It is most important that the rank of lieutenant in the fire department be established at once by law and that the lieutenants be selected as the result of a competitive civil service promotional examination which firemen and engineers may be permitted to enter. They should receive a salary slightly less than that paid captains, but certainly more than the salary paid firemen of any grade and engineers. It is, therefore, recommended that council, through ordinance, establish the grade of lieutenant.

Engineers Should Have More Training.

There are sixteen engineers and sixteen stokers. The engineers receive $1.190.64 per year, while the stokers or assistant engineers are paid the salary of Grade A firemen, namely, $1.091.52.

While most of the engineers showed a thorough understanding of their duties, others showed decided lack of training. The engineers are selected by the board, but are not required to pass any examination proving their fitness for this most important position. The efficiency of the fire service in fire extinguishment is dependent in a large measure upon the efficiency of the engineers of steamers and gasoline pumpers. The lack of understanding of their duties tends greatly to reduce the quality of the service and can easily result in increased fire loss. It is important that engineers and stokers be thoroughly trained and they be selected for their positions only as the results of an impartial and thorough examination. Every engineer should be required to hold a stationary engineer's license. They should not be eligible for promotion to the rank of captain, but should be permitted to compete for the position of lieutenant. This is essential in order that they may have experience as commanding officers serving as lieutenants before being promoted to the position of captains. Their salaries should be slightly less than lieutenants, but more than the firemen. They should be required, in addition to their regular duties, to instruct all members of the engine companies as to the operation and care of the steamer.

Appointments.

For a discussion of the methods of making appointments and the recommendations affecting them, see section of report on survey of police department headed "Appointments."

Promotions.

For a discussion of the methods of making promotions and the recommendations affecting them, see section of report on survey of police department headed "Promotions."

Medical Care of Firemen.

For a discussion of the methods of medical care of firemen and the recommendations affecting them, see section of report on survey of police department headed "Medical Care of Policemen."

Trial of Delinquent Firemen.

For a discussion of the methods of trial of delinquent firemen and the recommendations affecting same, see section of report on survey of police department headed "Trial of Delinquent Policemen."

Method of Training Firemen.

Although there is maintained a poorly equipped training tower and one of the captains is assigned as instructor, no regular school of instruction is conducted and no adequate means for the training of the firemen is provided. When appointed, a fireman is assigned to a company in which there may exist a vacancy, regardless of the location of the company as to suburban or congested value district. Thus, upon appointment, it is not uncommon for a fireman to be assigned to an engine company in the outskirts of the city where he is permitted to remain without having any opportunity for active fire service. The captain of a company is supposed to instruct the recruit and the rules require that there be conducted a weekly drill at each station. It was apparent that these drills do not consist of the kind of instruction which firemen require for their work. and indeed, that in some of the stations the drills are not held regularly. Twice a month elaborate drills in which the engine companies participate are held, but all of this instruction is unsupervised and not conducted in accordance with any standardized procedure. Each captain determines for himself the character of instruction and the kind of control.

It was customary in the past to hold instruction classes at the drill tower under the supervision of the instructor, but for a considerable period past these classes have not been assembled.

During the course of the survey there occurred but one large fire at which the firemen labored under such difficulties because of lack of water that it was not possible to determine the efficiency of the force in fire extinguishment. but even at this fire the lack of training was apparent.

The absence of any definite procedure and the failure to afford opportunity for adequate training, however, should be sufficient evidence to prove that the men are not properly trained for their work. Success in fire extinguishment is dependent upon the intelligence of the superior officers and the training of the firemen.

It is now well understood by fire experts that something more is required of efficient firemen than a good physique and the ability to "eat smoke." Special training is required at every step in a fireman's work, but since principles of fire control and extinguishment have practically been standardized, the training of men to put out fires is no longer a difficult matter, and its need is no longer questioned. Even the ability to extinguish fires promptly and with a minimum loss is not all that is necessary to make an efficient fireman. He should also be specially trained to prevent fires by careful inspections and should be familiar with every modern requirement for adequate fire prevention.

The absence of scientific training is perhaps the chief defect of Richmond's fire department. Therefore, it is recommended that a training school for fire service be established. This school should provide a course of instruction in all phases of fire service and fire prevention work. Not only should the recruits be given this instruction, but likewise all members of the department. The school should be centrally located and have adequate equipment so that the drills and instruction may be continued throughout the year without regard for weather conditions. A special course of instruction should be given the officers of the department in order that they may be properly equipped to conduct courses of instruction in their company headquarters. This is necessary so that company drills may be standardized and the instruction put upon a scientific basis. The course of study in the school should include, in addition to practical instructions now given, lectures and instruction upon—

1—Administration:
  Discipline (respect for authority).
  Reports and records.
  Responsibility for city property.
  Rules and regulations.

2—The art of fire extinguishment:
  a—General fire fighting.
  b—Care of apparatus and equipment.

c—Auxiliary fire appliances.

d—Sprinkler system and stand pipes.

e—Conservation of property and burning buildings.

f—Water pressure systems.

g—Fire alarm system.

h—First aid to the injured.

3—Fire prevention:

a—Fire prevention laws and ordinances.

b—Method and time of reporting upon fire prevention inspections.

c—Combustibles and explosives.

4—The duties of firemen at theatres and places of public as-
semblage.

District Chiefs Should Supervise Training.

District chiefs should be required to supervise the training of
the members assigned to their districts. From time to time company drills should be held under their direction and the efficiency
of the firemen reported upon.

The district chiefs should take every care to prevent the use
of company "nicknames" for department tools and equipment.
Every tool and piece of equipment should be known throughout
the entire service by its standard name, and firemen referring to
the tools by other than the recognized department name should be
disciplined. Nothing is more confusing at a large fire where several companies are in service than to have firemen calling for
tools and minor equipment by various names.

Written Tests Should Be Held.

No day should pass without giving the firemen some formal
instruction. Text books upon these subjects should be secured and
furnished the firemen. They should be required to study them,
and frequent tests should be held by the captains or district chiefs
in order to determine the familiarity of the firemen with the subjects studied.

Need for New Pompier Tower.

The training tower now in use is wholly unsuited for the
training of firemen. It does not compare favorably in construction with the average building to which firemen are called for
duty.

It is, therefore, recommended that as soon as possible, there be erected a standard Pompier training tower.

Need for Squad Car.

In order to permit the department to maintain its school throughout the year and to assemble classes composed of firemen from different sections of the city, it is necessary that the department be equipped as promptly as possible with a high powered squad car. which should be kept at the training school when the classes are in session, and used to convey the firemen upon second alarm. In this way there will always be available, when the school is in session, a reserve force which can be quickly delivered to a large fire. A properly equipped city service truck,' which would also constitute a reserve truck, should be furnished for use of the firemen at the training school. The school should also be supplied with complete equipment, independent of the equipment owned by the company located at the training school.

Frequent Transfer of Firemen Necessary to Good Training.

If the firemen are to be properly trained. it is necessary that they perform service in all parts of the city and in truck companies. as well as engine companies. It should not be possible. as it is at present for a fireman upon entering the service to be as-. signed to a suburban company, and there to remain during his entire career. The board should adopt a procedure which would require the firemen from time to time to be transferred from one company to another. This could be done in the first instance by the district chief, with the approval of the chief. Thus the district chiefs could transfer men from the engine companies within their districts to their truck companies, and vice versa. After the firemen have been given this experience, they should then be transferred into another district. so that they will have the advantage of having worked under both of the assistant chiefs, thus becoming familiar with their methods of fire extinguishment. It is not intended that wholesale transfers should be conducted, thus disrupting the general organization. but it is suggested that these transfers be made in accordance with a definite schedule from time to time throughout the year.

Definite Period for Making Transfers at Request Should Be Established.

While it is desirable that the convenience of the firemen be considered in the matter of transfers. attention is called to the fact that the residence of the firemen should not be considered as the dominant factor in the matter of an assignment. It is now the practice to make transfers throughout the year at the request of the men or for purposes of punishment. This procedure is not conducive to efficient management, especially since the transfers are made largely for the convenience of the men and not with regard to their training.

It is, therefore, recommended that once in each year at a time established by the board, general transfers at the request of the men be considered and actual transfers in such cases be encouraged when they do not conflict with the scheme of training or with the good management of the service. If this plan is adopted, no transfers upon the request of the firemen should be made during the year, except in cases especially warranting immediate action. The transfers referred to in this recommendation are those affecting the convenience of the men and not those to be made for training purposes.

Fire Prevention Inspections by Firemen Should Be Part of Training.

Efficiency in fire extinguishment demands that the men, as well as the officers, be familiar with the interior construction of the more important risks in the city, to which the firemen may be called for service. The more familiar the firemen become with the structural condition of the buildings in their districts, the more successful they will be in effecting prompt extinguishment with a reduced loss. It is just as important in the training of a fireman that he be given knowledge of the structural conditions of the buildings in his district as that he understand the technique of delivering water and extinguishing flames. To accomplish this, it is necessary that the uniformed firemen be used to make fire prevention inspections. The procedure should be for the officers of the company to conduct an independent inspection of the important risks and large hazards, and to report upon their inspection in great detail. Their reports should be upon specially provided forms, copies of which should be available for the information and study of the members of their company. They should then select from among the risks in their district, a building which all members of the company, during a given period should be required to visit and inspect. After all the firemen in the company have been given this opportunity, the company should be assembled on the apparatus floor and examined by the captain as to their knowledge of the building. A general discussion of the methods which will be employed in the extinguishment of a fire in that building should be had, and the firemen should be permitted to discuss these matters. Hypothetical questions should be prepared and asked the firemen. In this way all members of the company in time would become thoroughly familiar with the structural conditions. They would know the location of the sprinkler shutoffs, gas connections, elevators, hatchways and all other matters which it is necessary that a fireman shall know, in advance of being called to extinguish a fire. If this plan were adopted, it would not be long until these sessions in the fire halls would furnish the basis of discussion for the men, and a subject for thought which is not now provided.

Firemen Should Be Taught to Operate Elevators.

As a part of their training, all firemen should be taught to operate elevators so that upon responding to a call in the building where the elevator operators have left the building, they will be in a position to put the elevator into service at once, and thereby perhaps effect a prompt delivery of the people in the building to the streets.

Firemen Should Be Taught to Operate Steamers.

In Richmond's fire department, like all other fire departments, members of engine companies receive no instruction as to the operation of the steamer or gasoline engines. The result is that there are usually but two men in a company capable of operating the steamer. There is no reason why several men in an engine company should not be given detailed instruction by the engineer of a steamer as to the duties of an engineer. They should be as familiar with this piece of apparatus as the engineer himself, and in the event of emergency should be able to take charge of the steamer at the fire. For this purpose the rules should require each member of an engine company to receive instruction and perform service as a stoker.

Drivers of Motor Vehicles Should Receive Special Training.

The number of accidents resulting in damage to apparatus and department property is excessively high. Without doubt the inefficiency of many of the drivers because of the lack of scientific training is directly responsible for much of the damage done to apparatus. The drivers of motor driven apparatus receive practically no training for their work other than that involved in a demonstration furnished by the concerns selling the apparatus, and advice from other drivers who received their training in a similar manner. Their knowledge for the most part is limited to the starting and stopping of the machine. Repairs of the most ordinary character, which should be made by the drivers at the fire stations must now be made by the master mechanic, and in most instances, this involves taking the apparatus out of commission. The driving of a motor fire apparatus is not an easy task. It is by no means to be compared with the ordinary touring car or roadster. Much greater skill is required to handle a large, heavy piece of motor apparatus traveling at a high speed through congested thoroughfares than is required in the driving of a pleasure vehicle.

It is essential both as a safety measure and an economy that the drivers receive thorough training not only as to driving but as to the mechanics of an automobile as well. For this reason it is urged that the officials of the Mechanics Institute be requested to organize a special class for firemen desiring to be trained as automobile enginemen. All members of the department should be invited to attend the class, the hours of which should be arranged so as to cause the least inconvenience of the fire department through the weakening of its force. As many firemen as possible should be induced to take this course, and none should be assigned to drive motor apparatus until he has completed the course.

Moreover in this connection it is recommended that before assigning firemen as drivers to motor apparatus, they be subjected to a special physical examination in order to determine not only their physical fitness, but their mental capabilities as well. It was stated by the officials of the fire department that the head of the Mechanics Institute had offered the services of his instructors upon a previous occasion to the fire department, but for some reason the offer was not taken advantage of.

Setting Up Exercises Should Be Conducted.

Because of the lack of exercise in a large number of the districts where the runs are few, it is necessary that the firemen be given proper exercise. It is, therefore, recommended that the rules provide that captains or lieutenants conduct setting up exercises each morning similar to those used in the U. S. Army. These exercises should be conducted on the apparatus floor and should occupy not less than thirty minutes.

Firemen Should Be Graded As To Salary By Years of Service and Efficiency.

Fireman are appointed to service as Grade B firemen at a salary of $1,018.80 a year. They may be advanced at the will of the board without regard for their length of service or their efficiency. This procedure is most defective, in that it does not provide for advancement as the result of meritorious service.

It is, therefore, recommended that the firemen be divided into four grades, A, B. C. and D. Each fireman should be required to remain within his grade for a period of a year. Advancement to the next higher grade should only be made after certification of the efficiency record of the fireman to the board at the end of a year's service therein and only in case the service rendered by the fireman has been in all respects satisfactory. Advancement from grade to grade should carry with it a salary increment.

Sanitary Condition of Fire Houses.

All of the fire houses were visited and inspected and were found to be generally in good repair and of a modern type of construction, built with due regard to the comfort of the men residing in them. The buildings occupied by Engine Company No. 7 and Truck Company No. 2, however, are in especially poor condition. This is particularly true of the building occupied by Engine Company No. 7. At such time as the city is financially able, these companies should be quartered in newly constructed modern fire stations.

Organization and Personnel.

The department is organized as follows:

For Administration.

Number	Title	Salary
4	Commissioners	None
1	Secretary	$1,718.00

For the Extinguishment of Fires and the Enforcement of Fire Prevention Ordinances—

1	Chief	$2,520.00
1	First assistant chief	1,718.00
1	Second assistant chief	1,718.00

20	Captains	1.212.72
16	Engineers	1.190.64
9	Lieutenants. firemen Grade A	1,091.52
13	Lieutenants, firemen Grade B	1,018.80
44	Grade A firemen	1,091.52
99	Grade B firemen	1,018.80

For the Instruction of Firemen—
1 Drillmaster $1,212.72
     (Captains detailed to perform service with
     his company).
    Included in the 20 captains.

For the Making of Repairs to Apparatus and Equipment—
1 Master mechanic $1,500.00
1 Assistant master mechanic 1.212.00
    Firemen detailed to repair shop as needed.

For the Distribution of Alarms and Maintenance of Signal Service—
1 Superintendent (fire alarm and police signal
    service) $2,684.50
1 Assistant superintendent 1,449.00
3 Alarm operators 1,209.60
1 Inspector and lineman 1,102.50
2 Linemen 945.00

As shown by the payrolls, the total number of employees in the fire department, exclusive of those employed in the fire alarm division, is 211, of whom 4 are commissioners and 1 serves as secretary, thus making the strength of the force for fire service 206.

The department is organized in accordance with the modern plan of organization, and the supervision exercised over the force by the commanding officers may be said to be good.

Single Platoon System In Operation.

The force is operated under the supervision of the single platoon system which provides for the company's service. The firemen are allowed one day off in six, and three hours a day for taking meals at home. An annual vacation of fifteen days is allowed each member. It is recommended that the schedule of furloughs be revised so as to provide for each member being allowed one day off in five.

Distribution of the Force and Apparatus.

Additional Districts Should Be Established.

For purposes of distribution and control, the city is divided into two districts and each district is placed under the supervision of an assistant chief. The force is divided into engine, truck and hose companies as follows:

16   Engine companies.
 1   Hose company.
 5   Truck companies.
——
22   Total.

As suggested elsewhere in this report, the city is sufficiently large and the risks and hazards distributed in such a manner as to make necessary the establishment of a third district, making the other two districts smaller and providing for better control of the force by the assistant chiefs.

Distribution of Fire Stations.

The manner in which the force is divided and the apparatus distributed, as well as the work performed by the various companies throughout the year 1916, is shown by the following table:

Statement of Kind of Apparatus, Alarms Responded To, and Duty Performed by Each Company During the Calendar Year 1916.

Co. No.	LOCATION	ENGINE	Officers	Firemen	Least No. on Duty	WAGON	Total Hours in Service (H. M.)	Hose Carried 2½+	Hose Carried 3"	Reserve Hose 2½"	Reserve Hose 3"	Total Alarms Responded to	Perform Duty at No. of Fires
1	306 N. 25th Street	Knox, triple comb., motor	2	8	5	Hose wagon, motor comb.	124 45	1,000	1,000	1,000		138	138
2	2016 E. Main Street	LaFrance, horse-drawn	2	9	7	"	138 45	600	800	400	700	119	119
3	310 E. Broad Street	Amoskeag, horse-drawn	2	9	7	"	97		1,000		1,000	80	80
4	Grace	Knox, triple comb., motor	2	7	5	"	135 46	1,000		1,000		169	131
5		LaFrance, 3 horse-hook	2	9	6	"	91 16	800		1,100		88	84
6	Laurel and 23d St.	Waterous motor	2	8	8	motor comb'n.	117 30	800	200	800	200	112	80
7	990 East Cary Street	LaFrance, horse-drawn	2	10	8	horse-drawn	146 16		1,000		1,000	87	86
8	Deony and Hopkins Street	Amoskeag, horse-drawn	2	8	8	motor comb'n.	41 25	850	160	1,000		41	35
9	6th and 23d	LaFrance, horse-drawn	2	9	6	"	111 21	850	150	850	150	95	68
10	Broad Street near Lombardy		2	8	6	"	128 40	1,000		860	150	108	102
11	28th and 23d Street	Clapp & Jones, 2	2	8	6	horse-drawn	60	1,000		1,000		66	45
12	Jefferson and Cary	"	2	8	6	motor comb'n.	40	1,000		1,000		33	33
13	10th and Bainbridge	LaFrance, horse drawn	2	8	3	"	68 30	800		1,000		43	43
14	901 Chamberlayne Ave.	Knox, triple comb., motor	1	3	3	"	15 80	1,060		2,000		112	47
15	104 Stuart Street	Waterous, triple comb'n.	2	3	4	"	13 25	1,000		760		2	7
16	30th and Bainbridge Streets	Waterous, motor	2	5		motor comb'n.	30 45	1,000		1,000		95	95

HOSE

Co. No.	LOCATION	ENGINE	Officers	Firemen	Least No. on Duty	WAGON	Total Hours in Service (H. M.)	Hose Carried 2½+	Hose Carried 3"	Reserve Hose 2½"	Reserve Hose 3"	Total Alarms Responded to	Perform Duty at No. of Fires
16	715 Lamb Avenue		1	3	2	Hose wagon horse-drawn.	9	900		500		14	14

TRUCK

Co. No.	LOCATION	ENGINE	Officers	Firemen	Least No. on Duty		Total Hours in Service	Ladders	No. of Ft.			Total Alarms Responded to	Perform Duty at No. of Fires
1	912 East Broad Street	LaFrance, motor	2	9	6		72 28	11	305			81	81
2	Grace bet. 18th and 19th Sts.	Hays Truck, Knox, Martin	2	10	5		71	11	298			75	66
3	Broad and Lombardy Streets	Amer. Automatic, horse	2	8	8		96 49	13	283			106	99
4	S.E. corner 28th and South Sts	Gleeson & Bailey, horse	2	4	8		71	8	190			43	20
5	10th and Bainbridge Streets	LaFrance, horse-drawn	2	7	6		90 35	9	266			19	11

The twenty-two companies are housed in eighteen fire stations, which, for the most part are efficiently distributed. There is need, however, for the establishment of another station. The board has already acquired property at the corner of Kensington Avenue and Cleveland Street upon which it is planned to erect a new station, and to establish a new company. A bond issue of $5,000 was provided some years ago for the purchase of a site upon which to erect a fire station in this neighborhood. The board of fire commissioners succeeded in acquiring the transfer of title of the property referred to above from the board of education and subsequently succeeded in enacting legislation which made the $5,000 bond issue available for expenditure in connection with the erection of a fire house. The needs of the city at this time make imperative the establishment of a company in this vicinity as promptly as possible, and it is, therefore, recommended that sufficient funds be appropriated to erect a station, establish a company, and furnish apparatus which should consist of a motor-driven combination chemical hose wagon.

Adequate Street Signals Should Be Installed.

Considerable damage to department property and injury to the members of the department have been caused by collision of apparatus with street cars. Aside from the fact that some of these accidents have perhaps, in part, been due to the lack of training of drivers, it is nevertheless true that the street car companies do not co-operate sufficiently with the fire service through the maintenance of proper signal devices. It is urged that council request the co-operation of the street car companies, and that a signal service which will provide for bells and red lights along the lines of the trolley system at points near fire stations be installed, these lights and bells to be operated in connection with the fire-alarm system. In some cities, particularly in Denver, at the more dangerous points there is constructed an electric cut-off which operates with the fire-alarm gong by shutting off the control current in the vicinity of the fire house. The cars are thus required to stop and can only be started again by the motorman throwing in a switch which is placed on one of the poles near the fire house.

The adoption of an ordinance establishing "fire streets" at which all cars will be required to stop without a signal, is recommended. It is suggested that the board of fire commissioners secure from the commissioner of safety of Denver, Colorado, a description of the street car signal system in operation in that city.

Apparatus Should Be Redistributed.

While, generally speaking, the distribution of the apparatus may be said to be good, it is nevertheless pointed out that because of certain alleged agreements in connection with the annexation of the outlying sections, an improper assignment of certain of the apparatus has resulted. This is particularly true with respect to the house located in Ginter Park.

It is recommended that the board direct the chief and his two assistants serving as a committee to make a complete examination of the distribution of apparatus and to file with the board a plan for the redistribution of the apparatus. This should be done as promptly as possible, so as to bring into active service such of the apparatus as is now assigned to the outlying territories.

Complete Motorization Recommended.

Fifty per cent. of the department apparatus has been motorized, 50 per cent. is horse drawn. It is the experience of most all of the large cities of the United States that motor apparatus results not only in an economy, but in increased efficiency. All of the tests made within recent years indicate that not only can motor apparatus be delivered with greater speed, but that because of this fact the run of districts for motor apparatus can be increased almost 100 per cent. over those served by horse-drawn apparatus. The saving which could be effected through complete motorization of Richmond's fire department would be two-fold, first, because there would be saved the maintenance cost of horses, and second, by a re-arrangement of the stations and redistribution of the apparatus, certain of the houses could easily be eliminated. It is not suggested that complete motorization at this time would necessarily reduce the force, but it would, however, make unnecessary increasing the force for a number of years to come.

Every effort should be made to effect a complete motorization as promptly as possible. The major portion of the cost of the motorization would, in a few years' time, be returned to the city through the savings effected, to say nothing of the increased efficiency of the service that would be secured.

Strength of Force Has Been Increased In Proportion to Population.

The appropriations for the maintenance and operation of the fire department have during the past ten years been liberal and commensurate with the needs of the service. The fire-fighting force has been strengthened in proportion to the increase in population and area. The following table shows population, area, expenditure and strength of the force for the past ten years, beginning 1907 and ending 1916:

Table Showing Ratio of Population and Area to Expenditures and Size of Fire Department 1907-1916.

YEARS	Population	Area in Square Miles	Expenditures* Fire and Fire Alarm Departments	Chief Engineer	Asst. Engineers**	Captains*	Lieutenants	Stationed Firemen	Call Firemen	Machine Shop	Superintendent	Asst. Superintendent	Operators and Linemen
1907	113,418	9.969	$143,346 06	1	2	19*	15	78	49		1	1	3
1908	114,790	9.969	172,700 27	1	3	15	15	76	48		1	1	3
1909	116,167	9.969	169,646 52	1	3	16	16	80	48		1	1	3
1910	127,989	10.979	173,285 04	1	3	16	16	80	48	1	1	1	4
1911	129,721	10.979	200,001 27	1	3	17	17	88	48	1	1	1	4
1912	131,453	10.979	209,141 53	1	3	17	17	105	32	1	1	1	5
1913	133,185	10.979	235,573 89	1	3	18	18	129	16	1	1	1	5
1914	134,917	24.388	252,786 69	1	3	19	21	149	0	1	1	1	6
1915	154,674	24.388	280,359 62	1	3	19	21	155	0	2	1	1	6
1916	156,687	24.388	287,279 72	1	3	20	22	160	0	2	1	1	6
			$2,134,410 60										

* Four captains in 1907 were call captains; since that year all stationed.
** The secretary is also an assistant engineer.

Fire Loss Moderate.

The gross fire loss in the past five years (1912-1916) inclusive, as shown by the records of the department, amounted to $1,358,-855.55, the annual loss varying from $90,749.79 in 1913 to $458,-414.30 in 1915. The number of fires varied from 456 in 1912 to 650 in 1916. The average number of fires was approximately 519, and the average loss per fire was approximately $524—a moderate figure.

Repair Shop.

For the repair of apparatus there is conducted a repair shop under the supervision of the master mechanic. There is also employed in this shop an assistant master mechanic and occasionally firemen are detailed to assist. This shop is efficiently managed and under the care of a competent mechanic who has a thorough understanding of his duties. The cost of repairs to apparatus is exceptionally high, but as already explained, this is due primarily to the street paving conditions in certain sections of the city and the evident lack of training of the drivers of motor apparatus. Much of the time of the master mechanic and his assistant which should be devoted to the making of important repairs is taken up in making minor repairs to motor apparatus, which should be done by the drivers themselves at the stations. The shop is fairly well equipped and located at a convenient point. The master mechanic also makes engine tests and supervises the engineers when in service at fires, responding to practically all second alarms throughout the city and to most first alarms in the congested value district. A proper reporting system is in effect which serves to develop the unit costs.

The department is, however, without adequate reserve apparatus, there being but an old and previously condemned steamer and a dilapidated city service truck on reserve. The result is that when serious accidents occur the master mechanic is not able to promptly replace the damaged apparatus from reserve. There should be provided adequate reserve apparatus as soon as possible so as to relieve this condition.

Hose.

Hose is purchased upon the National Board of Fire Underwriters' specifications and as a result of public bidding. The hose in the department is for the most part in good condition.

Pressure tests are applied to newly purchased hose, a few lengths being selected from each case. No laboratory test, in order to determine whether the report complies with the specifications is made. It is recommended that a laboratory test be made by the city chemist of each consignment of new hose. All hose is tested semi-annually and redistributed in accordance with its condition. This is in accordance with good practice.

That the department has exercised proper care of the hose is evidenced by the fact that during the past ten years it has only been necessary to purchase a total of 35,100 feet of hose, or an average of 3,500 feet a year. The price paid for the two and one-half inch hose has varied from 52 cents per foot to 60 cents, while the price paid for three-inch hose has varied from 65 cents to 70 cents per foot, which prices indicate that the department has used good judgment in the matter of specifications and purchasing of hose.

The following table shows the purchase of hose and the prices paid per foot during the past ten years:

Year	2½ In. Ft.	3 In. Ft.	Brand of Hose	Cost Ft.	Contract Price	Total Cost By Years
1907	1,000	....	Yale...................	.55	$ 550 00	
	1,000	....	Yale...................	.f0	600 00	
	1,000	....	Yale...................	.60	600 00	
	1 000	....	Yale.....	.60	600 00	
	4,000	....				$ 2,350 00
1908	4 000	....	Spec. Middlesex........	.55	2,2,0	2 200 00
1909	2,500	....	Spec. Middlesex........	.55	1 375	
	....	500	Spec. Middlesex........	.75	375 00	
	....	2,000	Spec. Middlesex........	.75	1 500 00	
	500	....	....	.55	275 00	
	3,000	2 500				3,525 00
1910	....	....	None purchased..... ..			....
1911	3,000	....	Spec. Middlesex........	.60	1,800 00	
	....	500	Spec. Middlesex........	.75	375 00	
						2,175 00
1912	500	....	Spec. Middlesex........	.60	300 00	
	....	1,000	Spec. Middlesex.......	.75	750 00	
						1,050 00
1913	....	1,000	Spec. Middlesex........	.70	700 00	700 00
1914	1 500	....	Spec. Middlesex........	.60	900 00	
	....	500	Spec. Middlesex........	.70	550 00	
	2,500	... .	Spec. Middlesex.	.60	1,500 00	
	4,000					2 750 00
1915	1 000	....	Spec. Middlesex.... . .	.60	600 00	
	....	1,000	Spec. Middlesex.......	.70	700 00	
	1,500	....	Spec. Middlesex.......	.60	900 00	
	....	500	Spec. Middlesex........	.70	350 00	
	2,500	1,500				2,550 00
1916	1 000	....	Hewitt	.55	550 00	
	....	1,000	Hewitt	.67	670 00	
	....	2 600	Hewitt	.65	1,690 00	
	2,500	....	"B.F.G."	.52	1,300 00	
	3,500	3,600				4,210 00
Total	24 500	10,600				$ 21,5 0 00

Note.—"Yale Brand" from Fabric Fire Hose Co.
" Middlesex" from Boston Woven Hose & Rubber Co.
"Hewitt" from Hewitt Rubber Co.
"B. F. G." from B. F. Goodrich Co.

Complete and detailed records of the life of the hose and its use are maintained.

Horses.

All of the horses of the department were observed, and showed evidence of good care and training. The department is fortunate in having in its membership a fireman who is competent to care for the horses and attend to their medical needs. Due to his efficiency, but a small amount is expended annually for veterinary service.

Water Service.

While there has been a normal development of the fire department as a fire-fighting and fire prevention service, the development of the water service for fire purposes, due to many reasons, has not kept pace with the needs of the city. The efficiency of the department is greatly reduced because of the difficulties experienced by the firemen in securing the water in certain sections of the city and even in the handling of large fires in the high value district. The National Board of Fire Underwriters' trained engineers upon at least three occasions carefully studied the water conditions of the city with relation to fire service, and upon each occasion reported in great detail the condition observed and pointed out remedies to be applied. Some of the recommendations of the board were complied with and others ignored. Another reference to the water service for fires will be found in the section of this report devoted to the survey of the water department, but it is necessary to point out in this report that the conditions observed by the engineers of the fire department as recently as February of the present year, during the course of a fire on Main Street near Mayo were practically repeated at a fire observed during this survey at Boulevard and Broad Streets, when, because of the inability of the fire department to secure an adequate supply of water, the chief and his men were at a disadvantage at all times while the fire was in progress. It was only after fighting the fire for practically two hours, and when he had it under control, that the chief was receiving a quantity of water at a pressure such as was needed at the beginning of the fire, notwithstanding that the fire occurred when practically all the domestic service was at a standstill, namely, three o'clock in the morning.

Unless the water service is improved, no matter how well trained its firemen become or how carefully the strength of the force may be increased, Richmond stands in danger of serious conflagration.

Fire Alarm and Telegraph.

The fire alarm and telegraph system and the police signal box system are under the supervision of a superintendent who receives an annual salary of $2,684.50 a year. The present superintendent has been in charge of the system since 1884, and is not only well qualified to perform the duties of a superintendent, but is enthusiastic and energetic in his supervision of this most important service. The equipment of the fire alarm division is of the combined automatic and manual Gamewell type, and was originally installed in 1885. Since that date it has been added to and in parts improved, but never completely replaced. Consequently much of the apparatus is now of an antiquated and obsolete type, and not suited to meet the demands now made upon it, and which necessarily will be made upon it in the future as the city grows.

System in Danger of Destruction by Fire.

While it is essential that the obsolete equipment be removed and the fire alarm system brought up to date, it is far more important that the terminal boards of all of the equipment be removed as speedily as possible from the present quarters to a fire resisting structure. Upon the efficiency of the fire alarm service must depend in a large measure the safety of the city against destruction by fire. It is the nerve center of the whole organization. Delays in this service are counted in fractions of a second; a minute's delay may easily result in serious loss both of property and of life. Not only must it be well equipped and competently manned, but it must be protected against any injury or damage which would in any way tend to cause delay. Notwithstanding this, the controlling apparatus and equipment of the fire alarm system are housed upon the third floor of the city hall, which is a building of inferior fireproof construction, although not seriously exposed. All of the trim and the floors in the room in which this apparatus is housed are of wood. A small fire occurring in the city hall and reaching the fire alarm headquarters might easily destroy in a few moments the entire controlling apparatus of the fire alarm system.

To continue to house these valuable instruments under these conditions is but to invite destruction and to cause the city to be temporarily without any means of despatching alarms. It is no economy to continue this condition since the property loss, and indeed the loss of life itself because of it, may be far greater than any sum which may be saved by refusing to remove the headquarters to a fire resisting structure.

Therefore, it is not only recommended, but urged upon council that funds be appropriated as speedily as possible for the construction of a fire resisting fire alarm headquarters, to be located in one of the public parks, where it will be protected against surrounding hazards, and in which should be housed an up-to-date fire alarm system. Such a building, while it should be ornamental, need not be of a costly type.

Of course, the principal cost involved in this would be in the replacing of the apparatus and equipment. As a guide in the construction of a fire resisting central office and as a guide as well to the manner in which it should be equipped with apparatus, it is suggested that the central fire alarm office of the city of San Francisco be used as a model. In this connection, the superintendent of fire alarm should secure from that city detailed information concerning the cost of the erection of the building and the furnishing of the apparatus, practically all of which was made and constructed in the shops of the fire alarm division.

Insufficient Fire Alarm Boxes.

There are at present 213 publicly-owned fire alarm boxes and 104 privately-owned boxes. making a total of 317 boxes in the city. These boxes are for the most part of the Gamewell type. Twenty-four of them located in the high value district are equipped with telephones connected with the central office switchboard. They are practically all of the non-interfering type. An inspection of a number of the boxes shows them to be in good operative condition, indicating a good inspection service. The number of boxes, however, is insufficient to meet the needs of the city, especially in the suburban districts. where in most instances, the boxes are from three to five blocks apart. This is true even in the high class residential section. Notwithstanding the large territories annexed to the city and the rapid development of some of the suburban sections, the installation of new boxes in the city during the past six years has averaged about sixteen boxes per year. This is true despite the fact that prior to this period the number of boxes in the city was deemed insufficient to meet the needs.

It is, therefore. recommended that as rapidly as the finances of the city will permit additional fire alarm boxes be installed so that there will be a box within five hundred feet of every building in the mercantile and manufacturing sections and within eight hundred feet of every valuable group of buildings.

Boxes Should Be Equipped With Red Lights.

None of the boxes is equipped with a red light for night service. but all are painted red. The boxes upon light poles or telegraph poles are indicated by a red band painted on the poles or in some instances by a red metal band affixed to the pole.

It is recommended that all of the alarm boxes be equipped with a red light to be used during the night so as to indicate the location of the box. The need for these lights is even much greater in the suburban districts than in the business section.

Boxes in and on Fire Houses Should Be Removed. .

Each fire station is equipped with a fire alarm box, this notwithstanding the need for additional boxes for public use. These boxes were located in the fire houses prior to the establishment of the watch system and upon the theory that a person desiring to report a fire upon arriving at the station would turn in an alarm, and again upon the theory that in case a company responded to a silent alarm it could notify headquarters of the fire over the regular alarm system. This practice should be discontinued and these boxes removed to points where most needed. There is always a fireman on watch duty in each of the houses to receive silent or telephone alarms, and companies when responding to alarms should notify headquarters by telephone. There is no need for a fire alarm box in the station or immediately adjacent to a station.

There Should Be Two Operators on Duty During the Night.

The alarm operators serve on eight-hour shifts, there being but one operator on duty at a time. During the night hours one of the linemen is required to sleep in a room immediately adjoining the alarm headquarters. This is to insure emergency calls for line service in case anything should happen to the operator on duty. While it is good practice to have a lineman available for emergencies, it is not affording proper protection to assume that he is available in the event of an accident or the death of the operator on night duty.

It is, therefore, recommended in the interest of safety and good practice that an additional operator be appointed so as to provide for having two operators on duty on the night shift.

All Alarms Should Be Treated Alike.

There is in effect a well arranged running card which, while making provision for the despatch of apparatus on first alarms, does not provide for companies automatically "filling in" in the event of two or more alarms. The filling in of the companies is left largely to the discretion of the alarm operator and alarms received verbally at stations and not over the telephone or box are termed silent alarms. In some instances but one fireman with a hand chemical extinguisher is sent in response to the silent alarms, while telephone alarms are responded to in accordance with the statement of the person telephoning as to the size of the fire. At most, one company responds to a telephone alarm. Thus, the captain of the company, upon arrival at the fire in ascertaining that he needs more apparatus must either telephone or use the Morse key in a fire alarm box to summon additional apparatus, thereby causing considerable delay and inviting a possible large loss. This practice has been condemned by fire experts throughout the country as conducive to delay and positively dangerous.

The development of a running card for service in response to box alarms, is upon the basis of the needs of a fire in the given community from which the alarm is received. Consequently, if the notification of fire is received by some other means than over the box, the basis for despatching the apparatus in such cases should be precisely the same as that upon which the running card for that district was established. All alarms should be treated exactly alike, regardless of how the information arrives at the fire headquarters. A silent alarm received by a company should be telephoned immediately to headquarters and an alarm should then be sent out over the manual system for the box number located nearest the fire. This procedure is essential to efficient fire fighting service and should be adopted at once.

The running card should be perfected so as to provide for an automatic filling in of companies in the event of second, third and subsequent alarms and no discretion should be allowed the operators in this connection. The movement of the apparatus is distinctly the function of the superior officers of the department and no apparatus should be moved by any subordinate except under direction from a superior. A commanding officer desiring additional apparatus at a fire should specify the company number desired and it should not be discretionary with the operator as to which company should be sent. The duties of the operator should be confined to the delivering of the alarms and the execution of orders of superiors and not to transferring or despatching apparatus in accordance with his own opinion.

Tower Bell Should Be Removed.

As a relic of the old volunteer fire department days and the call service there are still retained in use tower bells which announce to the community the location of fires. Nothing is gained by the ringing of these fire bells, but their use serves rather to hinder the fire department in that it encourages crowds to assemble at the scene of the fire and automobiles to speed through the streets in an effort to reach the fire. A congestion of automobiles and people at the scene of the fire interferes with the firemen and they interfere with the apparatus in transit.

It is. therefore, recommended that the superintendent of fire alarm be authorized by the board to discontinue at once the use of the fire tower bells.

Special Telephone Trunks Should Be Reserved for Fire Department.

Almost forty per cent. of the alarms are received over the telephone and no special trunks are reserved at the telephone exchanges and the switchboard at the central office for despatching fire alarms by telephone. Subscribers must wait their turn in getting a connection with fire headquarters when desiring to report a fire, although the traffic managers of the telephone companies will use every means possible to clear the wires if a subscriber is intelligent enough to request this of the operator. When a fire occurs and the fire bell rings, citizens in large numbers call up fire headquarters, requesting information as to the fire and its location, thus immediately causing a congestion of the telephone wires at the central office to say nothing of diverting the attention of the operator from his regular alarm service. The result is that should a second fire occur at the same time, considerable delay would be experienced in trying to secure a connection with fire headquarters to notify the department.

It is therefore recommended—

1. That the board instruct the operators to refuse any information over the telephone concerning fires, except to public officials and regularly accredited newspaper reporters.

2. That there should be reserved one trunk line at each of the exchanges over which fire alarms should be despatched. Thus a person desiring to inform the fire department of a fire on calling headquarters, would be immediately connected over the special trunk.

The city of Buffalo, New York, has a special light and gong service attached to its switchboard which lights and rings as soon as the central in the telephone exchange "plugs in" on the fire trunk. The co-operation of the telephone company for this service should be sought.

Maps and Charts.

The maps and charts of the circuits are incomplete and not arranged so as to provide a complete and detailed index to their location. It is, therefore, recommended that the city engineer's department be requested by the board of commissioners to prepare as speedily as possible in co-operation with the superintendent of fire alarm a complete set of modern, standard circuit maps, which should be arranged and filed so as to make possible speedy reference and current changes.

Private Telephones Should Be Removed from Fire Houses.

Some of the fire stations are equipped with private telephones paid for by the fund. Inasmuch as the fire department acts entirely upon signals, it is inadvisable to allow additional telephones in the fire houses. There is no reason why the firemen should be permitted to be in communication with their friends or others during their working hours. These private telephones create an additional bell in the fire house and have a tendency to divert the attention of the firemen from their work. It is, therefore, recommended that they be ordered removed, and that no telephones be permitted, except the department instruments.

Tappers at Firemen's Homes Should Be Removed.

Much of the time of the department and of the employees of the alarm division is unnecessarily consumed in the installation, transfer and repair of "tappers" in the homes of the firemen. Each fireman is permitted to have installed in his home a small tapper. These tappers running into small buildings are a fire menace in themselves, as they cannot be given the proper protection to prevent their causing fires from spreading. Very often it is imposing an unnecessary burden on the fire alarm division and overtaxing its battery systems. The "tapper" in the house of the fireman is but a relic of the old call service. There is nothing much to be gained by this system because the quota of the fire department is sufficent to meet its needs, making proper allowance for days off, vacations and meal leaves. The fireman who is on his day off or at his meals should not be called back unless in the event of a conflagration. The ordinary second alarm should result in an adequate number of men responding, regardless of those away on leave. As a matter of fact, there are comparatively few second alarms, and it should be entirely unnecessary for a fireman to return from his home for a one alarm fire.

It is, therefore, recommended that the board order the discontinuance of this tapper service.

Police Signal Service.

The superintendent is required to supervise the police signal service, which includes the central Gamewell board and 134 police signal boxes of the Gamewell type. Three operators are assigned to this work, two of whom are policemen detailed. One lineman and a lineman's helper are also employed.

The use of complicated and costly signal boxes for communicating between the patrol posts and the precinct stations should be discontinued, and as new boxes are installed or old ones replaced it is recommended that ordinary small boxes be used. These boxes should be placed on the walls of buildings, thus eliminating the cost of pedestals and their erection. The efficiency of the telephone as a means of communication between the patrol posts and the stations is no longer questioned. The primary object of these boxes should be to establish communication rather than to check the patrolmen since, as pointed out in the report of the police department, the only efficient method of checking the patrol service is through the use of competent patrol sergeants.

Switchboard Should Be Installed at Police Department.

While each of the three police stations is connected directly with police headquarters, as are all of the signal boxes, the telephone in the office of the chief, the purchasing agent, and the other officials at police headquarters are each independent telephones connected with the local exchanges. Thus, many calls which should be received and answered by subordinates in the department, are transmitted directly to the chief at his desk, and other calls which should be properly transmitted to the chief are received by subordinates, the result being that persons desiring to communicate over the telephone with the police department frequently have to make three or four calls over different exchanges before they communicate with the proper person.

It is, therefore, recommended, that the superintendent of the signal service cause to be installed in connection with the police switchboard at headquarters, exchanges from trunk lines so that the police department will have but one telephone number and all calls will be received at the switchboard and transmitted to the person for whom they are intended.

Fire Prevention.

The fire prevention inspections are made by the captains and occasionally, by lieutenants. All of the large mercantile establishments and what are considered important risks, are also inspected by the assistant chiefs. During the year 1916, 25,717 such inspections were made. For purposes of conducting routine fire prevention inspections the city is divided into twenty-two districts, each in charge of a captain and, in so far as possible, the inspections are made semi-monthly. The general conditions observed throughout the city and especially in the large mercantile plants indicate that the inspections are efficiently made and that the department is strict in enforcing its orders.

Chief Without Adequate Power.

The method of reporting fire prevention inspections, however, is defective in that no detailed description of the premises inspected is recorded, and no record is made of orders issued, except in such cases as it is necessary for the chief of the department or the board of commissioners to issue the orders in writing. Each month, the captains file a written report showing a list of places inspected. This report does not contain any information as to the conditions found except when the conditions require special attention from the chief or the board of commissioners. While the board of commissioners is empowered to order conditions to be corrected which tend to increase the fire hazard, such as accumulations of rubbish, overloading floors, etc., the ordinances do not provide the chief or the commissioners with adequate power to make rules and regulations affecting fire prevention conditions or to order structural changes which would tend to reduce the fire hazard.

The Establishment of a Fire Prevention Commission Recommended.

The adoption of a law creating a fire prevention commission with broad powers. is recommended. This commission should consist of the centralized executive, the superintendent of buildings or building inspector, the chief of the fire department and one citizen appointed by the mayor to serve without pay. The chief of the fire department should be the executive officer of the commission. The commission should have full power to make rules and regulations and to issue orders which should have the effect of law. - The commission's power should not be confined to certain types of buildings but should cover all buildings and conditions within city limits, regardless of what state authorities or departments might have similar jurisdiction.

The protection of life and property is a function of the municipality and this protection should not be taken from persons working in factories or buildings that are subjected to the control and inspection of State labor departments. The need for the inspection of dwellings is emphasized inasmuch as in most cities of the United States the majority of fires occur in residences. Large mercantile establishments and institutions which now receive the closest attention of the officers of the fire departments are for the most part subjected to frequent inspections by other authorities and agencies, such as State department officials, the fire underwriters and owners or managers themselves, while the residences generally are not subjected to any inspection. Owners of large industrial institutions secure the advice of experts and usually seek to make their buildings as safe as possible for commercial reasons, if for no other, while the builders of residences, especially small homes and houses of cheaper construction, have not the advantage of this advice.

Therefore, it is urged that the department conduct a house-to-house inspection as soon as possible.

Commission's Powers Should Be Especially Broad.

It has been found by experience in other cities that it is scarcely possible to adopt laws upon fire prevention which will be wholly adequate in furnishing the protection necessary, and at the same time fit all conditions found in the city. Therefore, it must be apparent that the commission should have adequate power to issue orders in specific cases which shall be in keeping with the conditions in each case, and that these orders should have the same force and effect as statutes.

The powers of this commission should include, among others, the right to—

1. Inspect any building, structure, enclosure, vessel, place or premises.

2. Remedy any condition found in violation of any law or ordinance with respect to fires or the prevention of fires.

3. Establish rules and regulations with regard to fire drills, the storage, sale, manufacture or transportation of explosives and combustibles, and to enforce the same under a penalty.

4. Require the installation of automatic fire alarm systems, fire extinguishing equipment, and adequate and safe means of exit.

5. Require to be vacated any building or structure which, in its opinion, is adequately protected against fire.

6. Require a vessel anchored near any dock to be removed to a place designated by the commission or its executive officer, providing the vessel is on fire, or in danger of fire, or from the nature of its cargo a menace to the shipping property on the water front.

7. Require regular and periodic fire drills in factories, stores, schools, hospitals and asylums.

8. Declare a building deficient in fire-extinguishing equipment or one which by reason of contents or over-crowding is perilous to life and property to be a nuisance and direct such nuisance to be abated.

9. Direct the owner of such property within a reasonable time to place his building in a condition of safety, and if he fails to do this, to take the necessary steps to remove the dangerous conditions.

Uniformed Firemen Not Used for Inspection Work.

It is the experience of fire chiefs throughout the country that assigning firemen to fire prevention inspections not only makes possible an increased number of inspections, but adds considerably to the efficiency of the service in that the firemen are given an opportunity of studying the exterior of the structures inspected. Therefore, it is recommended that uniformed firemen be used to make fire prevention inspections.

Firemen Detailed to Theaters.

A fireman is detailed to each theatre while the theater is occupied by an audience. These firemen are required to inspect the house before the performance begins and to visit different parts of the theater during the performance. They are not equipped with electric torches or lanterns so that in case of a fire or an accident causing lights to be extinguished, these firemen would not be of much service to the audience.

Firemen detailed to theaters should be equipped either with electric torches or lanterns and if lanterns are carried they should be kept lighted during the time the house is occupied. Theaters are not required to pay for the service of the firemen.

The adoption of an ordinance requiring owners of theaters to retain and to pay for the services of firemen during all times when the theater is occupied is recommended.

It is the practice to detail the same firemen continuously to at least one of the theaters. This practice has been condemned for the reason that detailing the same man continuously is not conducive to effiecient service. The firemen who is constantly in attendance at a theater soon becomes so familiar with the employees of the house that he is not as likely to enforce the regulations or to make his inspections as thoroughly as if a different fireman were detailed nightly. Moreover each fireman should be given an opportunity to visit and inspect the theaters so as to become acquainted with the structural conditions. It is, therefore, recommended that this practice be discontinued and that each fireman in the companies located in the vicinities of the theaters be assigned in turn to this duty.

The firemen detailed to theaters are required to file a written report on a specially provided printed form which form, however, is not in accordance with the standard form, in that it does not call for sufficient information concerning the inspection made by the fireman at the theater. It is, therefore, recommended that this form be revised so as to require detailed information concerning exits, auxiliary fire fighting equipment, asbestos curtain and all other matters to be reported upon when the theater is inspected. In other words, the form should be so arranged as to make it impossible for the firemen to answer the questions thereon without having actually inspected the theater.

Theaters and Moving Picture Shows in Generally Good Condition.

The majority of the moving picture houses and the two theaters which were in use were inspected during the course of the survey and found to be in generally good condition.

The section of the building code with relation to the structural condition of theatres and the auxiliary fire fighting apparatus to be maintained therein is, for the most part, in accordance with the standard recommendations of the National Board.

Fire Prevention Inspection Record Should Be Revised.

The form used at present for reporting upon fire prevention inspection is wholly inadequate and not designed to promote efficient inspection service. Inasmuch as to make proper inspection of a premises, it is necessary to visit all parts of the building and to observe all conditions, the inspector should be required to make a careful record of everything observed upon specially provided printed forms. These forms should be arranged so as to serve as a guide to the firemen in making his observations, thus preventing him from overlooking or neglecting to observe certain conditions. It should describe carefully the structural conditions so as to provide for the making of copies of the report to serve as a card record of properties for the use of the chief, the assistant chief, the captains and the men in the company headquarters. A complete report at least once a year should be made upon these forms of the inspection of every premises in the city. Subsequent inspections or re-inspections should be reported upon re-inspection forms.

It is recommended that the fire prevention inspection report form now in use in the city of New York be used as a guide, in drafting a revised form for Richmond. These reports, when received at headquarters, should be filed by street locations and cross-indexed as to character of buildings and hazardous occupancy. Each captain should carry with him upon the apparatus a copy of the reports concerning the buildings within his department, and should always have them available for the review of the assistant chiefs or the chief when in attendance at fires.

As each fire service report is filed at headquarters, the fire prevention inspection reports affecting that premises should be reviewed in order to ascertain whether there were any violations reported against the premises. This is recommended for the reason that pursuant to the decision of the higher courts in the State of New York. the owner of a premises in which a fire occurs, who has neglected to comply with the orders of the fire department, is liable for damages to the city.

Records and Reports.

The records and reports of the fire department are for the most part in accordance with good practice. They provide for the current recording and reporting of all activities and operations of the department and for a review of the same by the assistant chiefs and the chiefs.

The method of reporting service at fires, however, could be much improved as could also the fire service record book.

Individual Company Fire Service Report.

It is the present practice for the assistant chiefs to prepare and file the fire service report of fires in their districts, and no company report is filed except where a company responds to what are termed "silent alarms." It is, therefore, recommended, that the rules be amended so as to provide that each company responding to an alarm of fire should file an individual company fire service report. This report should be arranged so as to conform with the following outline:

Report of fire number ...... during the year 19....
(the number of the fire should be written in at the office of the chief and not by the company).

Engine company number .... truck company number ....

Fire number......attended by this company during 19.........

Date ....

Day of week ....

Report of fire at No. ....Street.

Alarm received by telephone .... over box.......
verbally .... at station ....

Time alarm was received ....

Time (if engine company) consumed in reaching and coupling to hydrant ....

Time delayed ....

Cause of delay ....

The hydrant was found in .... condition and was used for .... hours ....minutes with .... pounds of water pressure.

Number of gallons of water used ....
(If chemicals are used, the amount of chemicals and the time chemical stream was turned on should also be shown).

Reported to ....and were ordered by........

Number of minutes consumed in getting a stream on the fire ....

Amount of delay, if any, ... and the reason ....

The pipe was taken to ....

The supply of water was adequate, inadequate (explain here any difficulty with the supply of water).

The company was out of quarters .... hours
.... minutes.
The company worked at the fire..............hours
.... minutes.
If truck company. number of feet of ladders used
.... number of searchlights used ....

On the reverse side of this report there should appear headings calling for remarks concerning department property lost, found or destroyed, accidents, etc. There should also appear a list of the officers and men of each company who did not appear at the fire and the reason for their absence. .This report should be signed by the commanding officer of the company and forwarded to the assistant chief, who should review and sign it before forwarding it to the office of the chief.

Assistant Chief's Fire Service Report.

The report filed by the assistant chiefs should be revised so as to provide for the following information concerning each fire:

Number of alarms sent in ....
Duration of fire ....: hours .... minutes.
Location of fire ....
Date ....
Day of week ....
Time alarm was received ....
Time of signal out ....
Fire company to arrive ....
·Time of arrival ....•.......
Alarm received by box signal number..............
Alarm received by telephone ....by telegraph bureau ....
Alarm received from outside telephone (orally, or in any other manner) ....
Alarm communicated by ....-
Cause of alarm .... fire .... unnecessary .... false .... other cause ....
Description of building:
Stories high ....
Material built of ....
Fire-proof ...., semi-fire-proof .... non-fire-proof ....

Character of building .... tenement ....
  private dwelling .... factory ....
  loft building ...., etc.
Size ....
Name of owner ....
Address of owner ....
Name of occupant of part of building affected by
  fire ....
Names of other accupants and floors occupied......
  ....
  ....
  ....
Part of building where fire originated............
Fire extended to ....
With whom insured ....,....
Amount of insurance .... building ....
  contents ....
Estimated loss .... building—contents........
Probable cause of fire ....
Apparatus responding to alarm...................
  First alarm:
    Engine company .... truck company ....
      chemical number .... fuel wagon ....
    Second alarm: `
    Engine company .... truck company ....
      chemical number .... fuel wagon ....
    Third alarm:
    Engine company .... truck company ....
      chemical number .... fuel wagon ....
    Fourth alarm:
    Engine company .... truck company ....
      chemical number .... fuel wagon ....
  Number of men on fire grounds .... chief
    officers .... company officers ....
    firemen ....
Time second alarm was ordered ....
Time and by whom sent in and from what box......
  ....
Time of each subsequent alarm and by whom ordered ‘
  and by whom sent in and from what box........
  ....
Remarks ....

On the reverse side of this form space should be provided for a record of all officers present at the fire, arranged in order of rank. This record should show the time the officers left, as well as the time they arrived. The lower half of the form should be devoted to a complete and detailed description of the methods used in extinguishing the fire; whether by chemical, water line or other means. Under the heading "Remarks" should appear a detailed description of any accidents, rescues or any other incidents in connection with the fire.

This service report should be made out in triplicate by the assistant chief first to arrive at the fire, or by the assistant chief in whose district the fire accurs. One copy should be forwarded to the fire chief, one copy retained upon file at the office of the assistant chief, and the original copy forwarded to the board of commissioners.

Upon the original copy, which is filed with the administrative head, there should appear at the top printed headings to be filled in by the chief as follows:

Number of fires to date.
Number of false alarms to date.
Total number of fires during the preceding year.
Total number of false alarms during preceding year.
Total number of fires to corresponding date of preceding year.
Total number of false alarms to corresponding date of preceding year.

Fire Service Record Book.

The fire service record book does not contain sufficient information concerning the methods of extinguishment, etc. It should be revised so as to conform with the standard fire service recommended by the National Board of Fire Underwriters.

Consolidated Daily Report.

While each company is at present required to file a comprehensive daily report, which is in accordance with good practice, the information contained upon these reports is not compiled in a summarized form as affecting the whole department. It is, therefore, recommended that there be prepared each day what should be termed a "consolidated daily report," which should show upon one sheet a summary of all the information contained on the several company sheets in consolidated form. A copy of this should be retained in the office of the chief and the original filed with the board of commissioners.

Annual Report.

There is issued each year in printed form an annual report which contains considerable statistical information. This report, however, could be improved by omitting therefrom the inventory of the properties of the department and inserting a tabulation showing the probable causes of fires and the character of buildings in which the fires occured.

Care should be taken in tabulation alarms in the annual report to separate false alarms and alarms for causes other than fire, so as to enable an accurate tabulation of the average loss per fire.

It is recommended that in the next annual report there be included in tables with respect to alarms and annual fire loss per alarm, appropriations and losses, contained in the report of the board of fire commissioners to the city council, dated May 1, 1917. The reason for this recommendation is that by including these figures which constitute valuable statistics in the printed annual report, they can be preserved and used for further analysis in years to come without the necessity of making another compilation.

Firemen's Mutual Aid Association

FIREMEN'S MUTUAL AID ASSOCIATION.

The preceding chapter devoted to comments upon the Police Benevolent Association makes reference to the similarity which exists betwen that association and some of the fraternal associations which have operated in this country. As the statements there made apply forcefully to the Mutual Aid Association of the. fire department, the reader should not read this chapter without reviewing part of the chapter on the Police Benevolent Association.

Data Available Concerning Association.

The board of eleven directors of the Firemen's Mutual Aid Association has operated the association so far as is evidenced by the data at hand as successfully as any group of managers might be expected to manage an association of this character under the constitution and by-laws of the association, as they now stand, and with the information which was supplied to them. Beginning with July 1, 1912, the fund of the association has paid all benefits which it was called upon to meet, and had a balance of about $50,000 in 1917. Apparently this balance will increase each year for a number of years. Needless to state, this balance is the result of the dues of active members, of life members and of contributing members, being in excess of the pension payments maturing during the corresponding period. Whether this excess of receipts over disbursements will continue, or whether it is only like the income of the old fraternals which in many cases exceeded the disbursements for over a score of years, and then was quickly exceeded by the disbursements until the dissolution of the society ensued, is not shown in the reports available. The treasurer's report gives a statement of the assets in hand of the association, but there appears to be no statement showing the amount which should be in the association if it were solvent; consequently, it is impossible to state whether the association has developed a deficit or whether it has a surplus of funds. That the income has exceeded the disbursements must be gratifying to the members, but they should not blind themselves to the fact that if their association is not solvent this accumulation may prove more harmful to them by tempting them to continue without a knowledge of their actual condition. until it is too late to prevent a collapse, than if a slight shortage had developed which would have immediately caused them to place the association on a basis which would insure its completee permanency.

Information Which Directors and Members Should Have.

To develop a statement of the information which the board of directors should have furnished to them for their guidance is unnecessary in this chapter, because it is similar in most respects to that which it was recommended that the directors of the Police Benevolent Association should have. The two retirement systems are so very similar as regards the technical work which should be done in connection with them that it seems feasible to treat them together. Because of this fact and, further, because an actuarial investigation is the first step which should be taken by the respective boards of directors to place themselves in a position of having adequate knowledge of their funds, it has been considered advisable to make a statement indicating more specifically what is meant when an actuarial investigation is recommended. The discussion and outline of procedure which follows would apply to either fund separately, and could be followed in case both associations undertook such work at the same time, when it would be somewhat more economical to handle the very considerable amount of detail work involved.

Results to be Obtained from Investigation.

Perhaps the results which will have the greatest intrinsic value to the members of either association and to the directors and other administrative officers are the mortality tables and the active service tables which will be constructed. These tables are the basic or primary tables which must be at hand in order to value or make any scientific estimates of the costs of benefits now in the plan or of any new or substitute benefits which may be incorporated in it. As a basis for computing the amount of contingent liabilities, they are to the two retirement systems what the standard mortality tables are to the insurance companies. The construction of two sets of active service tables, pensioners' mortality tables and salary scales is recommended. These will be appropriate for the valuation of all pension benefits now in force or which may be proposed for the firemen or policemen, and will furnish the basis on which any new accidental death or other benefits may be allowed to the members at cost.

Second, will be two valuation sheets, showing for the active members of each of the two associations who are in service at the date of the valuation the present value of all pensions or other benefits which may be paid to them on retirement or disability. This sheet will be similar to the valuation reports required of the insurance companies by the various State insurance departments, and will be sufficient to show the entire financial condition of the funds both as to present and as to prospective assets and liabilities, so far as the present membership is concerned.

Third, will be a table of premium or cost rates expressed as a percentage of a members's salary, or as flat amounts irrespective of salary, which would be sufficient to provide for his pension and other benefits. The rates will be given for each age of entrance and will be sub-divided to show separately the cost of each benefit included within the pension plans.

Possible Uses of Results When Obtained.

The use of the active service and other tables need hardly be described. The term 'basic" indicates their purpose. The valuation of the present provisions may be based on them; the valuation of proposed benefits may be based on them; the future experience of any set of benefits established will be checked against them from time to time, etc. Because of the great mass of data used as a basis their construction is necessarily somewhat costly, but, when at hand, they will be of use not only to the association but may be of use in other benefit plans which may be provided covering the members.

The valuation balance sheet will give the liability on account of each benefit allowable in the fund for members in each of the associations and for pensioners. If it be desired that the liability as regards any particular group of the members be shown separately this can be done. From the superficial examination that has been made it appears that the present rate of income of the associations may not be sufficient under the present system of financing to provide the benefits included in the plan for a membership of the size of the present membership.

If the valuation sheet shows this to be the case, then some change in the plan may appear desirable. Perhaps the city of Richmond may be called upon for contributions toward those benefits of the plan in which it is interested. Perhaps additional contributions may be needed from present or new members. If so, it will be found that many members are near the retirement age and that they will be unable to make contributions, which will be sufficient to pay for more than a very small proportion of their probable benefits. The present value of the contributions which the present members may feel able to make can be computed and the result compared with the liability of the fund shown in the balance sheet. The excess of the liability over the prospective receipts from other sources will represent an accrued liability to be provided for in some other manner.

If the members provide a part of the pensions and the city the remainder, or even if the members provide the entire benefits, the amount of contribution required as a percentage of salary of a member, which is sufficient to support the system, is of importance and will be available as a result of the valuation. The provision for each member in the association and for each member added to the association by means of a contribution or appropriation on the basis of the payroll, is the method of financing a pension system which has met with universal approval in scientifically constructed pension plans. This method is highly advisable in maintaining the fund in a solvent condition and is valuable to the administrative officials. If it be definitely known for each member the amount of salary which is paid *to him*, and the premium which is paid *by him* to the association, the reduced amount of his compensation may be considered when comparisons are made of the salaries paid in Richmond with those paid by other fire and police systems which have pension benefits supported entirely by the city.

Statement of Work Involved in Investigation.

The service record of every member in the police and the fire department today and of everyone who left the service during the period of years used as the basis of experience will be required. These records will be used as a basis for constructing the service and other tables and will probably be written from the records of the police and the fire departments or of the associations themselves. The information on the records may then be subsequently transferred to punched cards for use in electrical assorters and tabulators.

After the records are punched, the cards are tabulated and on the tabulations thus obtained, showing the age, service, salary, marital conditions, etc., of each member, the actuarial work of constructing the various deduced tables is undertaken. Upon the completion of the tables, the mathematical calculations of assets and liabilities are made and the results are made ready for consideration by the directors. If any changes in the funds are found to be desirable, calculations are then made of the effect of the changes and the figures are again considered until the system has been satisfactorily constructed on a basis which is acceptable to the members and which provides the technical procedure which will insure financial solvency.

The statement made in the latter part of the preceding chapter on the Police Association relative to "obtaining the information necessary" applies also to the Firemen's Association.

Police Court

Part One

POLICE COURT.

There is maintained in the City of Richmond what is termed by law the police court. This court is presided over by a police justice who is elected by council for a term of four years and who is paid an annual salary of three thousand dollars.

The present incumbent, who is seventy-three years of age, has presided over this court for approximately thirty-five years.

The police court is an inferior court, and not a court of record. It has summary jurisdiction in all misdemeanor and violation of ordinance cases and powers of examination in felony cases.

All persons arrested in this city, except those arrested upon bench warrants issued after indictment are arraigned in this court.

Chaos and Comedy Combined Rob Court of its Dignity.

Stripped of all that tends to make a police court a tribunal of human justice. with its benches crowded with curious idlers, with the officers of the law showing their disrespect almost amounting to contempt for the proceedings. with confusion everywhere and laughter and merriment at the expense of the misguided and unfortunate persons arraigned taking the place of a judicial atmosphere. the daily session of what is called the police court is commonly regarded as one of the "side shows" of Richmond.

A police court is one of the most human of all municipal institutions. The daily line of persons arraigned within it includes men and women from most every station of life, from the poor, unfortunate, misguided vagrant begging for another chance to the wealthy autoist, hastening to pay for the privilege of having exceeded the speed law.

There are those to whom arraignment in the police court means but a gamble as to whether they will be returned to prison or set free; there are those and in large numbers, men and women, black and white, to whom arraignment in the police court brings sadness and worry such as they never experienced in their lives before; and there are those who only suffer inconvenience through the necessity of having to pay fines, which mean no hardship to them for their infractions of the law. All are entitled to justice; some to be dealt with sternly, but most to be treated sympathetically. But sternness. sympathy and justice must always be administered, if respect for law is to be maintained, with dignity, precision and equity. Such a description could hardly fit the

methods employed in Richmond's police court, where there is little
to inspire those who visit it, whether to enjoy its comedy or to
be arraigned before its bar, with either the gravity of the occasion or respect for the law. The ever present desire to accumulate
moneys through fines, the continuous laughter at the comedy of
the presiding justice which is sometimes aimed at the prisoners,
sometimes at the police officer who is attempting to do his duty,
and at other times at the old court officers who are in attendance,
but always at those whose position in life prevent their retorting
to the comedy or expressing their feelings of grief at the insults;
these features are quite noticeable. The appearance in court of
lawyers of prominence tends to exchange the atmosphere and frequently results in producing a dignified proceeding.

It is not intended, in this report, to discuss at length, the observations made which created these impressions, but merely to
point out that above all a police court must serve to impress those
who for one reason or another are arraigned within it with the
dignity and importance of the proceedings, and should offer at all
times a protecting hand to those who must depend, unattended
by counsel, upon the good judgment and sincerity and earnestness
of its presiding judge. Comedy has no place in a police court
where the difficulties of unfortunates must be adjusted. It is because the lawmakers understood fully the human side of a police
court proceedings, that they invested its judge with the vast discretionary powers that he possesses and with summary jurisdiction,
enabling him even to send to prison those whose guilt is established before him without even the judgment of twelve of his
peers as a jury. Consequently, the people should look to the judge
for wisdom and judicial calmness and not for easily excited wrath.

So attractive as one of the "shows" of the city has the police
court become that its reputation has been heralded far, and because of the large attendance attracted, it became necessary to
adopt a city ordinance allowing admission to the court only by
permit issued by the chief of police. Even under this restriction,
the learned justice has not been provided with a room large enough
in which to house his audience, because many idle curiosity seekers
may be seen every day seated upon the radiators and upon parts
of the equipment of the court not ordinarily intended for this
purpose.

No Record of Disposition of Cases.

Inasmuch as the court makes no complete annual report which
would disclose the number of cases arraigned, the number held for

higher courts, the number dismissed, the number fined—classified as to the offenses charged—it is not possible to discuss the results obtained through prosecutions brought in this court. One can easily ascertain the amount of fines and costs collected because this is one of the peculiar features of this court and every care is taken not only to tabulate but even to advertise the success of the court as a financial institution. In one instance we observed a colored woman was attempting to pay a fine of five dollars for her neighbor, who had previously been arraigned, and who was not well acquainted with the conduct of the court. Because there is nothing about the court that would indicate what procedure should be followed in the payment of fines, the woman, in her effort to locate the person to whom she should pay the money attracted the attention of the judge. He thereupon shouted in a loud and severe tone: "Let that women get out of here." He was then informed by the woman that she was endeavoring to pay the fine of five dollars. The judge then remarked in an equally loud burst for the benefit of his audience: "Let her pay the fine, I'd rather have five dollars than any nigger."

Judging from the speed with which fines are imposed in this court, it is quite evident that court is more interested in obtaining fines than in imposing sentences which might tend to have a correctional value.

Term of the Police Justice Should Be Ten Years.

As the police court is an inferior court and not a court of record, it is essentially a branch of the city government, although in the State of Virginia the statutes seem to indicate that it is considered to be a State court. The justice who presides over this court should be a city official appointed for a term of ten years by the central executive to whom he would report, and to whom he should be responsible. His removal, however, should only be through impeachment proceedings, brought before a court of higher jurisdiction. His salary should be paid by the city and the cost of operating and maintaining this court should likewise be borne by the city.

Cost System Should Be Abolished.

The system of assessing costs against defendants convicted in this court is a relic of an antiquated system which long since has been abandoned in progressive cities. This system was originated for use in small communities, such as towns and villages, upon the theory that law-abiding citizens should not be taxed for the errors of those who sought to violate the law. This theory is no longer accepted as sound, but instead it is now a well-established principle that all citizens in a community should bear their individual share in the cost of caring for delinquents and of administering equal justice through the courts. Moreover, in the end, the cost system is not an economy because a great majority of the persons arraigned in police courts are poor and unable to pay the costs or the fines, with the result that they are committed to city prisons or jails, where they must be fed and maintained at the expense of the taxpayers. Thus, a man fined five dollars and costs who is unable to pay either, must remain in jail not only for a period equivalent in days to the amount of the fine, but for an additional period in days to the amount of the costs assessed; and it is not infrequent for the costs in a case to be even greater than the amount of the fined imposed. Therefore, it is suggested that the law be amended so as to abolish the cost system.

While the moneys collected as fines in the police court or, in fact, in any court, should not be regarded as a source of revenue or income, nevertheless since the city bears the expense of maintaining the court, all moneys collected by the court in fines or forfeitures should be the property of the city and turned into its general funds.

Court Should Be In Session During Entire Day.

The law guarantees to the defendant the right of a hearing before a judge as speedily as possible. This implies that a man arrested before the close of the business day will be able to secure arraignment at once. Under the present system it is not possible, since the sessions of the police court invariably end by 11:00 or 11:30 in the morning. Thus a person arrested after eleven o'clock must either secure bail or remain in the police station until 9:30 on the following morning, thereby being unnecessarily if not unjustly and illegally detained. In the meantime the city must provide for the feeding of such persons.

Therefore, it is recommended as a means of increasing the efficiency of the court service in carrying out the intent of the law and in effecting an economy in the municipal government that the court remain in session until at least 4 P. M. Afternoon sessions of part two of the police court, and frequently evening sessions are now conducted, and the presiding judge of this part is to be commended for this practice.

Part Two of the Police Court Should Be Abolished.

There is no logical reason why there should be operated a second part to the police court. making necessary the maintenance of a separate organization and the payment of salary to an extra' judge. Part two was established pursuant to the statutes providing for the annexation of the southside, formerly known as Manchester. There is considerable doubt among the lawyers as to whether or not the statutes annexing this territory require that this court be continued. many of the lawyers arguing that the original requirement was that the court, police station and branch offices of the government .must be retained in that section for a period of five years. However. an effort should be made to adjust this matter. and if need be to amend the law.

Judge of Part Two Should Preside in Absence of Judge of Part One.

For some reason, wholly illogical, the ordinance requires that during the absence of the judge of part one. upon vacation or other causes, there shall be designated a magistrate to sit in his place, whose salary shall be paid out of the funds of the police department. thus creating an improper charge against the police service of the city.

It is. therefore, recommended that, pending the abolishment of part two, the judge of that part be required to sit in part one during the absence of the judge of this court, thus effecting a saving to the City of Richmond. without in any way inconveniencing the business of the court.

Judge Should Discontinue Practice of Dismissing Cases at Request of Police Officers.

As already discussed in a section of the report on the survey of the police department, it is the practice of the judge to dismiss cases upon the request of the police officers. This is done as a matter of practice frequently without even a hearing. A person arraigned before the bar of the police court charged with an offense should not be dismissed except for one reason and that is a lack of evidence. It is the plain duty of the court to make reasonable inquiry into all such cases in an effort to learn the cause of arrest and what evidence there is tending to show the guilt or innocence of the defendant. Therefore, he should require in every case that the police officer state the facts fully, and indeed it would be far wiser for the judge to make inquiry in cases where there is no evidence to have warranted the arrest, as to why the arrest was made. The logic of this is that for a policeman to make an arrest and thereby take away the liberty of a person without having a just and good cause indicates not only that he is an inefficient policeman, but is in all probability guilty of a crime, having abused his powers and caused what might be termed a false arrest. The judge in no case should arbitrarily dismiss an action upon the request of an officer.

Judge Should Not Delegate His Powers.

So efficient has the court become in the matter of imposing fines, that in most instances he has standardized his fines so that the cashier of the court, who is a policeman detailed to this work, has a schedule of minimum fines which the court imposes in certain violations of the ordinances. The judge has delegated his judicial powers of fining to the cashier of the court. Thus a person charged with a violation of a city ordinance, who dislikes the inconvenience of remaining in court until the regular session, has begun and thereby exposing himself to the possible consequent publicity or to the sarcasm of the judge, may send a messenger to the court and pay his fine to the clerk.

This may be convenient, but it is neither legal nor in accordance with good practice. Indeed, the efforts of the police in the enforcement of the traffic statutes are frequently thwarted because of this practice. In many cases of violations of traffic law, if the facts were presented to the court by the police officers, the court might not impose a minimum fine, but would more likely impose a more severe and more fitting punishment. It is not uncommon for an officer to waste most of his morning awaiting to hear his prisoner called to the bar only to find that the case has been settled before the opening of the court by the clerk through the payment of the minimum fine.

It is recommended that the court discontinue this practice at once.

By arrangement between the magistrates and the judge of this court, he has further delegated his judicial powers in that he has given his consent to a procedure by which the magistrates may accept fines in what he chooses to call trivial offences, imposing in such cases the judge's standard fine. As already pointed out elsewhere in this report, this practice is not only an interference with the work of the police, but even if not illegal it is conducive to fraud and corruption. It is recommended that the court abrogate this agreement and warn magistrates against a continuance of the practice.

Separate Sessions of the Court Should Be Held for Hearing Violations of City Ordinances.

It is the practice at present to issue summonses for violations of regular ordinances, such as provisions of the sanitary regulations, traffic regulations and revenue regulations. These summonses are made returnable at the regular sessions of the police court, thus requiring business men, respectable women, and others who perchance have violated the regulative ordinances with respect to cleaning alleys, traffic offences and the like to appear in police court among the regular habitues of the court and offer an explanation.

This procedure is not quite fair to the citizens of the city, nor is it fair to the departments whose representatives are required to prosecute these cases, for the reason that the psychological reaction on the judge in hearing cases of murder, felonies and major crimes at the same session that he hears these ordinance violations is likely to cause him to minimize the importance to the community of such cases.

It is, therefore, recommended that as a convenience to the citizens and the city departments all summonses for violations of the regular departmental ordinances be made returnable at a special session of the police court, which should be held at least one afternoon in each week. By doing this, the judge will be able to give the attention needed in each case and will be able to have a very much better picture of their importance. With respect to the traffic violations it has been pointed out that better results are obtained by making summonses returnable for a session of the court in each week at which no cases except traffic cases are heard, and it is, therefore, recommended, that this procedure be adopted.

Women Shoud Be Tried Separately.

No preference whatever is shown women prisoners in this court. Their cases are heard in open court and in full view and hearing of the crowd of idlers who daily patronize the court, in their regular order on the docket. This procedure has long since been condemned as not only unfair to the women but indeed indecent.

It is humiliating enough for women to be brought to the court at all without subjecting them to the scrutiny of those men, whose curiosity leads them to attend the sessions of the court. In fairness to the women of the city who are unfortunate enough to commit crime and offenses, it is recommended that their cases be heard either in private chambers or after the cases of male prisoners have been completely disposed of. At such hearings no spectators should be admitted, and only the police officers and newspaper representatives should be present. That this procedure be adopted is most strongly urged.

Need for Probation Officers.

Guided by the experience of other cities and those who have made a study of the causes of crime and of the correction of criminals, the probation system should be applied in the city of Richmond. The statutes should be amended so as to provide for the inauguration of the probation system and the granting of suspended sentences by the judge. The results obtained in the United States and Europe through the discreet and wise use of suspended sentences and the probation system are too well known to make it necessary to discuss them in this report.

It is, therefore, recommended, that there be appointed a male and female probation officer for the police court. Their appointments should be as the result of competitive civil service examination in which a generous rating for personality should be given.

Summons Procedure Should Be Revised.

Under existing laws arrests for misdemeanors not committed in the presence of police officers cannot be made without a warrant, and violations of corporation ordinances must be prosecuted through the use of a summons. The procedure for the issuance of summonses is so cumbersome and unnecessarily burdensome as to reduce the efficiency of this splendid system. Many days now elapse between the reporting of a violation case and the actual hearing before the court. Considerable bookkeeping is made necessary and only too often does the person escape punishment by refusing at the time the violation is observed to give his or her name to the officer, thus making it impossible for him to effect the serving of a summons.

It is, therefore, recommended, that the statute be amended so as to provide for the issuance of summonses by police officers at the time of observing the violation. It is suggested in drafting this statute that the New York State law, with respect to summons procedure, be used as a guide.

Bail Bond Procedure Defective.

Bonds for the appearance of defendants before the police court or the grand jury or the hustings court are accepted by the police court judge or any other magistrate; except that in felony cases the magistrates are required before accepting the bond, to secure the approval of a judge of the hustings court, which is usually done by telephone.

While the bondsman is required in most cases to make oath before the judge or magistrate as to his ownership of property to the value of the bond, he is not required to describe the property and its location, nor is any record made of any statement made during the examination of the bondsman. Moreover, his address is not even recorded, so as to make possible, in the event of a forfeiture, locating the bondsman.

When a forfeiture is ordered, the police court judge forwards a copy of the bond with a formal statement thereon, of his forfeiture to the judge of the hustings court. It then becomes the duty of the Commonwealths attorney to make motion before the judge of the hustings court for a judgment, which is then delivered to the city sergeant to be executed. The city sergeant is then expected to be able to locate the bondsman whose name appears in the judgment, without having before him any address and in fact, in many cases, having merely the name of a person of whom there may be a hundred of the same name in the city. His return is filed with the clerk of the court. If he has collected the judgments, an entry is made on the court docket, but if he has not located the person and there has been no execution, no record is made. It was not possible by examination of the records, to secure an accurate tabulation of the number of bonds forfeited, but not collected. An entirely new procedure should be installed at once.

From consultations had with attorneys and such limited investigation as was possible it is apparent that considerable "straw bond" is offered to the city and that there are operating many professional bondsmen. In order to protect the city against worthless bonds, and at the same time make possible a defendant securing his liberty promptly, it is recommended that in all bond cases the bondsman be required to make on a specially prepared form a detailed statement of his property holdings, describing their location and indicating thereon such encumbrances as exist against the property, in addition to his actual equity therein. To this statement he should be required to make oath and affix his signature. He should be further required not only to give his name and residence, but likewise his occupation and place of business so that the service of an order of judgment may be made upon him. All such bonds accepted should be recorded and filed with the Commonwealth attorney. In felony cases the approval of the Commonwealth attorney should be required before the bond is accepted. His office should be equipped with a detailed record of bondsmen and their property holdings, so that it will be possible to speedily ascertain in connection with bail offered the actual number of bonds that each bondsman is reported as having offered. Bondsmen who in the past have been suspected of practicing fraud in the matter of offering bonds should be placed upon a special list, their names certified to the magistrates and instructions issued that in no instance will their bonds be accepted in the future.

The ease with which warrants may be secured from magistrates by reason of the fee system, makes the business of bondsman thrive in the city of Richmond. Every effort possible should be devoted to eliminating this form of enterprise.

Clerk of Court.

The records of the court are maintained by a clerk, who is elected by council for a term of two years. He receives an annual salary of twelve hundred dollars.

It is recommended that the clerk of this court be appointed by the central executive as the result of competitive civil service examination and be qualified by this position by a competent knowledge of stenography and typewriting.

Stenographic Report of Examinations Should Be Taken.

While it is true that the police court is not a court of record and, therefore, not required to maintain records similar to those of the courts of higher jurisdiction, nevertheless, all examinations in felony cases should be reported stenographically and in such cases as are held for the hustings court or the grand jury minutes should be transcribed and forwarded with the original papers to the Commonwealth attorney. In this way the State will be protected against possible dishonesty of police officers, and witnesses desiring to change their testimony. It would then be possible for the prosecuting attorney to compare the testimony taken at the police court examination with the testimony offered before the grand jury. The psychological reaction on witnesses and police officers. if this were done, would be wholesome and beneficial to the judiciary system as a whole.

Cashiers and Court Attendants Should Be Civil Service Employees.

The cashier of the police court is a policeman detailed to this position, as is also the court attendant. Both of these positions should be filled by appointees of the central executive, selected as the result of competitive civil service examination. The cashier of the court should be under a bond as such and should be required to maintain all the financial records of the court. The present system, pending such a change, should be revised so as to have all fines paid in the inside office rather than in the court. The confusion caused by the payment of fines in open court is partly responsible for the chaos that exists at the daily session of the court.

Judicial Order and Dignity Should Be Observed.

No persons other than the judge and the clerk of the court should be allowed to stay on the rostrum with the judge while the court is in session. All persons should be seated in the court room and when all seats are taken no other persons should be admitted to the room. Police officers should not be permitted to wander aimlessly about the court, and certainly not to smoke, as many of them do now. They should appear in full uniform when testifying, and the detectives or officers in plain clothes should display on the lapels of their coats, their shields, when in attendance at court. No persons other than counsel, police officers and witnesses in the specific case being heard should be permitted in the enclosure immediately before the judge's desk. Counsel should not be permitted, when appearing before the judge, to have cigars even though unlighted, in the mouth. Every effort possible should be made at once to restore order and dignity to this court. Until this is done, those having occasion to come within it cannot be expected to respect the proceedings held therein.

Court Should Issue Warrants.

All warrants in criminal matters should be issued by the judge of this court. Pending the abolition of the position of city magistrates, the court should issue all warrants desired by the police department. By so doing, expense would be saved to the city and care be exercised over issuance of warrants. All warrants issued should be recorded in a register of warrants and the court should likewise require that a return be made upon all such warrants, within a reasonable time after their issuance. Such return should be shown in writing within the space provided for that purpose on the back of the warrant the results obtained in the effort to serve. In cases where the police department has been unsuccessful in attempts to serve a warrant, the complainant should be notified and requested to come to the court for the purpose of giving a better address or additional information which may tend to affect the service. In all such cases the name and address of the person making the complaint should be recorded in the register of warrants as well as upon the warrant itself.

Records.

The records of the court should be greatly simplified, and it is recommended that the procedure now in effect in the magistrates courts in the city of New York be adopted as a guide in revising the procedure for the police court of Richmond.

For the guidance of counsil and the administrative officials of the city of Richmond, as well as the Legislature, the courts should be required by statute to prepare and file officially a complete and detailed statement of the business carried on in the court. This should include among other subjects the number of cases therein with classification as to offences charged, the number of prisoners convicted, the number dismissed, the number held for higher courts or the grand jury, the number of continuances granted, the number of cases pending, the number of cases in which fines were imposed, classified as to amounts, the number of summonses issued, etc.

Juvenile and Domestic Relations Court

JUVENILE AND DOMESTIC RELATIONS COURT.

The juvenile and domestic relations court, as at present organized, was established January 1, 1916. Prior to that time, juvenile cases were heard by the police justice, sitting as judge in the juvenile branch of the police court, and assisted in his deliberations by what was then termed a "steering committee" composed of seven clergymen and one medical doctor. The establishment of the juvenile and domestic relations court in 1916 was by virtue of an ordinance adopted by council as the result of an enabling act passed by the State Legislature. The ordinance creating the court provides for the election of a special justice of the peace, who shall be the justice of the juvenile and domestic relations court for a term of four years.

The powers and jurisdiction of the court are prescribed in the legislative enabling act. The present incumbent in the office of justice is a lawyer and was, for a period of four years prior to his election, as judge, a probation officer to the juvenile branch of the police court. In addition to his experience gained while serving as probation officer and his legal training, he has observed and studied juvenile court procedure and probation work in several communities throughout the country with established juvenile procedure, thus making him especially qualified to sit as a justice of this court.

Jurisdiction of the Court in Adult Cases.

This court exercises only such powers as are delegated to it by the special statute and an ordinance of the city of Richmond, is not a court of record and consequently has no final jurisdiction in cases of adults contributing to the delinquencies of children wherein the crime involved is a felony. Therefore, the court is without a power which it should have in order to complete its jurisdiction in all cases involving juveniles. While the judge of this court is empowered to issue warrants and to go into an examination in felony cases involving crimes against children, his jurisdiction ends with the holding of adult defendants for indictment by the grand jury and trial by the hustings court.

Juvenile Court Should Be Court of Record.

Because of this fact, not only is the efficiency of this most important tribunal impaired, but what is even more serious the very intent of the juvenile protection statutes is destroyed because the infant witnesses in such cases are forced to be unnecessarily exposed upon trials in the higher courts and through this exposure to be made to bear part of the punishment meted out to the defendant.

The city of Richmond in the establishment of the juvenile and domestic relations court, indicated the desire of the citizens to surround the delinquent child with adequate protection such as can only be given in a properly organized juvenile court, but in failing to establish this court as a court of record the State has failed to offer complete protection to the child who has been wronged, even through no fault of its own, and it still leaves such a child exposed to the atmosphere of the criminal courts. If the judge of the juvenile court is to be able at all times to extend his official hand toward the child in trouble, and to offer, through his official position the kind of protection which it is desired by the people the child should have, he must be provided with the broadest powers of inquiry into the causes of a child's delinquency and into crimes committed against the child. He must be vested with power not only to punish the person guilty of contributing to the delinquency of an infant, but he must likewise be able to deal with and punish, after proper inquiry, the adults who would destroy the morals of the child.

Indeed, observations made in this court and a study of cases handled by the judge and his probation officers is sufficient to convince the investigator that the Legislature would make no mistake in vesting the justice of this court with equal pwers to those enjoyed by the judges of the courts of record. Therefore, it is recommended that the act be amended so as to establish the juvenile and domestic relations court as a court of record.

Justice Should Be Selected in Same Manner As Justices of Courts of Record.

While the present method of selecting judges of courts of record, namely, election by the Legislature, is by no means conducive to keeping the judiciary of the State out of politics, nevertheless, it is to be preferred to the present method of selecting a justice of the juvenile court by councilmanic election. The best thought of today upon the subject of courts and the judiciary argues for a long term for judges of all courts and condemns the short term. Without in any manner desiring to intimate or to be understood as inferring that the present justice of this court could be influenced by political interference or suggestion, nevertheless, his election to this most important position is made wholly dependent upon the whim of members of the local council. Moreover, and what is perhaps worse, the very existence of this court is made dependent upon the will of the local council, which body without the slightest reason or without having in any manner investigated the practices of this court and without appreciating the good that has been accomplished through its officers may repeal the ordinance establishing it and destroy at any meeting of the council the efforts made to protect the children of Richmond. This is but a further argument in favor of establishing this branch of the judiciary as a court of record.

Present Procedure Defective.

While it is true that the judge of this court uses every means at his disposal to remove all of the atmosphere of a criminal court therefrom, even to the extent of refraining from making the procedings of the court come under the usual heading of the "people vs. . . . ., defendant," etc., nevertheless, none of the proceedings of this court can be conducted in chancery: thus the child must necessarily be made a defendant. It is, therefore, recommended that in the event the Legislature establishes this court as a court of record that all cases be heard in chancery, and in no instance will the child be made a defendant, but in each case the child will become the ward of the State and the inquiry shall be to determine the punishment of the person responsible for the delinquency. Inasmuch as the children who are brought to the juvenile court are of tender years and always in need of the attention of women, it is recommended that in the amendment of the statute the judge be empowered to appoint a woman as a master in chancery to sit with him in the investigations, especially in cases involving girls. It is pointed out that the Constitution of the State prohibits a woman from holding public office. This provision of the Constitution should be changed, but even though not amended, might be liberally construed so as to hold that a master in chancery is not a public officer within the meaning of the constitutional provision.

Juvenile Probation Officers Perform Efficient Service.

For the probational care of the wards of the court, there are employed two probation officers, one male and one female. The female officer receives twelve hundred dollars, and the male officer one thousand dollars per year. The records of these officers, as to the work performed by them were carefully examined and reviewed, and they were both interrogated as to their methods of probational treatment, and it may be said to their credit that the work performed by them is especially efficient. Not only do they perform the duties imposed upon them by the statutes, but indeed go further in their desire to protect the children and perform considerable work in the nature of social service. The court is particularly fortunate in being able to retain the services of the female officer, because of her splendid previous training for the work.

Need for Appointment of Additional Probation Officers.

The efficiency of these two officers, however, in the handling of their cases is necessarily greatly reduced, because of the vast number of cases which they are required to observe and direct. During the year 1916 these two officers had placed under their probational care a total of 464 children or an average of 232 per officer. They conducted, during the year, a total of approximately 543 investigations and made more than 1,500 visits to the homes and places of employment of their probationers. Thus it can be seen at a glance that these officers, as capable and interested in their work as they are, cannot devote the amount of time and energy in the follow-up of their cases that good probation work requires. Those who have studied probation work and are by virtue of their training, qualified to discuss the question, agree that no probation officer should have at any one time more than fifty cases under his care. It is true, however, that it is difficult to make an estimate as to the maximum number of cases for the reason that some cases require little or no attention while others need constant and careful observation; nevertheless, it must be apparent that no probation officer can perform efficient service in the handling of 200 cases in a year.

The members of the council in making inquiry as to the need for the appointment of additional officers to this court need go no further in order to become convinced than to analyze the records maintained by these officers and to study the work performed by them in connection with their cases. Therefore, it is recommended that at least two additional officers for the handling of juvenile cases be appointed to this court, one male and one female.

Services of a Physician Should Be Retained.

In the examination of juvenile delinquents nothing is more important and nothing serves as a greater aid in determining the cause of delinquencies than the physical examination of children by a competent physician. The organization of no juvenile court is complete unless it includes a physician. Not only is it essential. that children coming under the observation of this court be given a physical examination but indeed, if the service is to be complete as it should be, they must be subjected to a psychological and pathological examination. In no other way can the child whose delinquency is the direct result of mental deficiency or physical defects, be protected against injustice and be provided with the medical service necessary to bring about reformation. To the credit of the officers of this court it may be said that although no provision has ever been made for securing competent medical advice, in practically every case of a female child brought to the court through the diligent efforts of the female probation officer and the charity of local practicing physicians and hospitals. it is subjected to a thorough physical examination. Again. through the courtesy of the State Board of Charities and Corrections. most of the children are subjected to a psychological test. but this service is only the result of the appeals of officials of the court to the sympathy and charity of the persons who render the medical service. Therefore, it is recommended that an effort be made to secure the services of a competent physician. qualified to handle children's cases on a part-time basis. Such services could be obtained in the city of Richmond without the expenditure of any large sum of money.

Policemen Detailed as Probation Officers.

For the probational care of adults in the domestic relations cases pursuant to the ordinance creating the court. three members of the police department having the rank of deputy sergeants are detailed to this court. This practice is most irregular. first because it is not in accordance with good practice to utilize policemen in probational work. and second, because the detailing of these three policemen results in reducing the quota of the police force and moreover establishes police details which are undesirable. These officers are principally concerned in the collection of moneys from husbands in non-support cases. It is true, of course. that in the performance of their duties in this connection they render social service by aiding so far as they can in restoring good relations between husbands and wives. But their functions are those that should be performed by trained probation officers, men or women, who, by reason of their past training and study are wholly in sympathy with the probational system. While these officers perform non-police functions, for which they were appointed, their salaries continue to be charged against the expense of maintenance of the police service, which is not an efficient accounting nor quite fair to the police department. Therefore, it is recommended that these three officers be returned to active police duties and that provision be made in the next budget for three probation officers, regularly appointed in accordance with civil service requirements referred to above, to take their places in the domestic relations court.

Records of the Court Should Be Improved.

The officers of the court are to be commended for the kind of records kept and the manner in which they are maintained. The most improved recording system is used and every care is taken by the court to review the records, nevertheless, these records can be improved by making slight changes and introducing two additional records. It is, therefore, recommended that each probation officer assigned to juvenile work be required to maintain a regular chart showing graphically the progress made by the probationer week by week. Such a chart is now used with much success in the juvenile court of Denver, Colorado.

It is further recommended that each probation officer be required to submit to the judge, in writing, a monthly report, showing the progress made by each probationer. With the aid of these two records the judge can, at his leisure, analyze and study the course of development of the children and the effect of probation upon them. These two reports added to the recording system now in effect will render the record system complete. Of course, when a regular physician is attached to the court, he should be required to render a written report of each examination made by him; this report should be made on a specially provided form.

Filing System Defective.

Under the present system of filing each probation officer retains in his charge all records and documents affecting the cases upon which they are working. This system should be changed to a general filing system in which the records of all cases will be maintained. Under this plan the probation officers would then be required to obtain the papers with reference to their specific cases from the general file.

System of Handling Moneys of Court Not Effective.

Each of the three probation officers assigned to domestic relations cases collects money in non-support cases and retains the money in his possession until called for by the persons for whom it is intended. When they receive the money they issue a receipt and when they deliver the money to the wife or person representing her, they take a receipt. This receipt is maintained in an informal receipt form book which contains a blank form of stub. No control is exercised over these books, which are left carelessly in most instances on the probation officers' desks, and which could easily be lost. thus destroying the evidence of their having paid over the money to the person for whom it was intended. Through this system of making collections more than four persons in the court handle the money coming into the possession of the court. This procedure is most defective in that it does not provide either for a proper control of the funds or afford protection to the officers making the collections.

It is. therefore, recommended that the acting clerk of the court be required by the judge to receive and pay out all moneys and to maintain all records in connection with these payments. This, of course, is adding additional duties to the numerous duties already performed by the acting clerk of this court. This clerk, who is a competent typewriter and stenographer and who maintains practically all the records of the court and the filing system, receives but $720 a year. This salary is not commensurate with the services performed, and should be increased in accordance with the recommendations contained in the section of this report relative to the standardization of salaries.

Judge Should Issue Warrants.

It is the practice of the court to refer applicants for warrants in juvenile and domestic relations cases to the city magistrates who are paid fifty cents for each warrant issued. Abolishment of the position of magistrates in the city of Richmond is recommended elsewhere in this report. Pending the adoption of such legislation, it is recommended that the judge refrain from the practice of referring applicants for warrants to the magistrates. The reason for this must be obvious, since many cases wherein application for warrants are made could easily be adjusted through the use of probation officers without the necessity of an arrest upon a warrant and the humiliation which necessarily goes with it. Moreover, it would tend to reduce the commercialism involved in issuing warrants upon the payment of fifty cents and relieve the poor people of this needless payment of money.

Recreational Opportunities Must Be Offered Children.

While it is true that the officers of the juvenile court are doing all in their power to aid in reducing juvenile delinquencies and to protect and comfort the children brought under the observation of the court, there is little being done either by the government or the social service agencies of the city in the way of constructive preventive work. A careful canvass of the situation shows that little or nothing is being done to provide legitimate amusements and entertainment for children of the city and especially is this so with relation to the colored children. If juvenile delinquency is to be reduced, every effort on the part of the city government and the social service agencies in the city must be exerted to provide means for wholesome play under supervision for the children of the city. Not only is this true, as to the infants and those of juvenile age, but it is equally true with respect to the younger girls of the city who are just beyond the age of control of the juvenile authorities.

Table of Demestic Relations Cases.

In connection with the domestic relations cases presented to the court, it is interesting to note the reduction in the number of domestic relations cases since the enactment of the prohibition statutes. The following table tells its own story:

1916 WET	Non-Support		Wife-Beating	
	White Male	Colored Male	White Male	Colored Male
May	13	8	17	14
June	22	10	26	16
July	13	14	9	24
August	16	14	6	21
September	20	10	10	18
October	17	14	8	16
Total	101	70	76	109
1916 DRY				
November	15	8	3	8
December	8	5	5	4
1917				
January	11	11	7	8
February	6	10	5	5
March	8	5	6	6
April	13	10	2	7
Total	61	51	28	38

It is further interesting to note in the same connection that prior to the enactment of prohibition legislation, the number of boys arrested and brought to the juvenile court, charged with drunkenness was becoming so large as to alarm the authorities, while since the prohibition law went into effect there have been but two or three such cases brought to the attention of the court.

Probation Officers Should Be Selected by Competitive Examination.

The probation officers should be appointed as a result of a competitive civil service examination. The qualifications for this position will be found in the section of this report devoted to the standardization of salaries. However, it is essential to point out here that the most important qualification for probation officer is personality, and liberal weight should be given for this in the original civil service examination for appointment. It is to be remembered that personality counts first in probation work, for the reason that the man or woman assigned to handle juvenile cases who does not possess a disposition and temperament congenial to the children, can accomplish little. If the probation officer is to be successful in dealing with children, he or she must be capable of gaining the confidence of the child as soon as the original contact is established. No probation officer can succeed who is not capable of establishing sympathetic relations between herself and her ward.

In making this recommendation, however, it is not intended to intimate that the present employees do not possess these qualifications.

Detention Homes

DETENTION HOMES.

Juvenile Court Should Have Complete Supervision of Detention Homes.

There are two detention homes, one for white and one for colored children. Although the juvenile court is responsible for the care of children sent to these homes, the management and operation of the homes is under the direct supervision of the mayor and appointments of employees of the homes are made by him.

It is obvious that this division of authority, as regards detention homes, does not make for highest efficiency. The officers of the juvenile court, although responsible for the children quartered in the homes, have nothing whatever to say officially as to how or by whom they shall be operated. The probation officers of the court are in almost daily touch with conditions at the homes, whereas the mayor has actually little contact with the homes. It is believed that for the best interest of the children in detention homes, the complete control of the homes should be given to the juvenile court.

Detention Home for White Children.

The main building consists of a three-story and basement structure, which is used as the living quarters of the matron and members of her family and several small bedrooms equipped with iron cots for girls under detention. A general sitting room is provided on the main floor for the use of the matron and this room is also used by inmates at the discretion of the matron. About twenty girls may be accommodated in this building.

There is also a two-story annex which is used as quarters for boys, there being on the second floor sleeping quarters for four or five boys, and on the ground floor a toilet and wash room. These quarters for boys are kept locked apart from the girls' quarters.

The home is poorly equipped throughout, sleeping rooms are mere barracks without wall decoration of any kind and very unattractive from every point of view. In one so called "strong room" the beds are merely platforms, raised about four inches from the floor, and provided with cheap mattresses. Not only is the equipment of the rooms of the most meagre and cheap variety, but there is ample evidence of lack of cleanliness. For example in the window ledges was seen accumulations of dirt and filth which was evidently of long duration.

There is every reason in the world why such a detention home should be a model of cleanliness and there should be also an effort on the part of the authorities to make living conditions more agreeable. At a very nominal cost the bedrooms could be made attractive by pictures on the wall, by curtains before the windows and by other inexpensive fittings which would give the home a real home atmosphere.

The "strong rooms" would probably not be so much needed if some effort were put forth to make the children more appreciative of their care in the home. The child who can live at this home for any length of time and not become embittered by the lack of consideration given him is a most unusual child. The children of Richmond are like children elsewhere. Kindness, tact and firmness will accomplish results where sternness and repression will not. In the administration of detention homes emphasis should be laid upon the idea of "home" rather than upon the idea of "detention."

Provision of Maintenance on Per Diem Basis Should Be Discontinued.

In charge of the white home is a matron who receives $40 a month and maintenance. In addition a maid or cook is provided at $12 a month and maintenance and the husband of the matron acts as a caretaker and general utility man at $20 a month and maintenance. Maintenance is at the rate of thirty cents a day, this sum being allowed also for the feeding of inmates.

The diet provided for inmates of the home is simple in character. There is no record of dietary kept and no sample menu was available. but the matron states that the food provided is ample and satisfactory to inmates, consisting usually of cereal. bread, butter and coffee for breakfast; meat, usually a stew with potatoes and other vegetables. and bread for dinner; bread and butter, cold meat and preserve or sauce for supper. The furnishing of maintenance on a per diem basis is, however, open to criticism. In the first place it makes possible the reduction of the food for inmates so that profit can be made by the matron. It is not charged that this is the case, but the fact that there is no evidence to show whether it is the case or not is sufficient to warrant a change in procedure. Appropriations should be made for detention homes just as for other institutions. and the matrons or keepers should be required to account for their expenditures from such appropriations. The situation, with reference to the detention homes. is similar to that which formerly existed in jails and prisons throughout the country, where the warden or keeper was paid a certain sum per diem for feeding and caring for prisoners. Due to this system many abuses existed as the direct result of the procedure, and similar abuses are possible in Richmond Detention Homes.

Colored Detention Home.

The colored detention home, which is a three-story building very similar in character to the white detention home, is a far more satisfactory institution than the white home, although it is but little better equipped, having the same cheap and meagre furnishings and "strong rooms" with their platforms and mattresses. As regards furnishings the same recommendations may be made as in the case of the white detention home. The home is, however, scrupulously clean throughout, and the matron and her assistants are to be highly commended for the very evident interest which they have in the welfare of children. At this home the matron. a colored woman, receives but $15 a month and her husband $20 a month. The husband. however, is an attendant at the juvenile court and receives $20 a month additional for this service. The diet of inmates at the colored home is furnished by the matron who receives twenty-five cents a day per inmate.

The following outline of the daily dietary at the colored detention home was secured for the investigator by the acting clerk of the juvenile court:

Breakfast:
    Oat meal or potatoes.
    Corn or wheat bread and butter.
    Coffee with milk and sugar.

Dinner:
    1 meat (usually bacon or salt pork, occasionally beef) or beef stew or soup.
    2 vegetables—pototoes. cabbage or some other wholesome vegetable.
    Corn bread.

Supper:
    Wheat or corn bread with butter or molasses.
    Occasionally salt meat.
    Fruit—prunes or dried fruit or apples or other fresh fruit in season.

While it is probable that the above dietary is of higher standard than that found in many of the homes from which the colored children came, it leaves much to be desired as a dietary for children under restraint. Any one knows who has had experience in feeding children that diet is one of the most important factors, not only in treatment of physical or mental disorders, but also in securing good discipline. The apparent object of the above dietary which may be accepted as typical of the dietary in the white detention home, is to feed these children a cheap and filling ration. It must be cheap if it is furnished at 25 cents a day, and it must be filling to avoid actual hunger. Meat should be allowed but once a day and that fresh meat in the form of a stew or thick soup rather than salt meat. Milk should be substituted as far as possible for coffee, and fresh fruit of some kind is necessary, preferably as part of the morning meal. Fresh green vegetables are a valuable article of diet for children and could be used in many instances in place of meat.

Under the present method of paying a fixed sum per day for the care of these inmates, however, no changes in dietary will probably be made. The matrons of the homes cannot be expected to go into their own pockets to improve the dietary for their charges. The same recommendations relative to the methods of financing the white detention home applies to the colored detention home.

Medical Service at Homes Inadequate.

Medical service at the homes and at the juvenile court is entirely voluntary. Several physicians have very generously given their services, are called upon when an inmate is believed to require examination, and a psychologist has also given his services without compensation. The city physicians of the health department are not disposed to offer their services at the Detention Homes as they do not consider such work their responsibility.

It is recommended that more definite provision be made for medical service at the homes, and in the juvenile court, instead of depending upon volunteer service. A physician to the Detention Homes and juvenile court on part-time duty should be provided at a small annual salary,—about $600 a year. All children coming under the supervision of the juvenile court should be carefully examined by this medical officer, prior to the decision of the court as to their disposition. Physical defects are frequently the influencing factors in the delinquency of children. Children with eye defects and consequent headaches play truant from school and lacking school discipline become delinquents. Children with other physical or mental defects may, by reason of such defects, be forced into an attitude of irritability and incorrigibility. To deal properly with children coming before the juvenile court and after disposition by the court, the court should have adequate means always available for determining all the facts as to their physical and mental status.

Civil Court

CIVIL COURT.

The civil court is maintained for the trial of civil cases, wherein the amount involved does not exceed three hundred dollars, including interest. It is presided over by a judge who is elected by the Legislature for a term of six years. The present incumbent was appointed by the governor of the State to fill the unexpired term of his predecessor who died while in office. The judge of this court is paid a salary of thirty-six hundred dollars per year, which is paid out of city funds.

For the maintenance of the records of the court there is employed a clerk who is appointed by the judge and who receives an annual salary of eighteen hundred dollars. There is also employed a court bailiff, who attends all sessions of the court, preserving order therein and assisting the clerk of the court. The bailiff is paid an annual salary of one thousand and eighty dollars.

The salaries of both the clerk and the bailiff are paid out of city funds.

Judge Provided.

This court is in session throughout the year, but the regularly elected judge is allowed four weeks vacation in each year, during which time a substitute judge presides, who receives ten dollars per day, and who is appointed by the judge of the hustings court.

Magistrates Issue Civil Warrants.

All cases in this court originate through the issuance of civil warrants by the several magistrates of the city. For the issuance of a civil warrant the magistrates receive a fee of fifty cents, which they are permitted to retain. The only fees received by the civil court are what are termed trial fees which are fixed by statute at fifty cents per hundred dollars, based on the amount involved in the suit, the minimum being fifty cents and the maximum one dollar and a half. These fees revert to the city treasury and amounted during the year 1916 to four thousand eight hundred and fifty-six dollars ($4,856.00) as against approximately six thousand dollars ($6,000.00) representing the cost of maintenance and salaries of the court.

It has been recommended earlier in this report that legislation be adopted abolishing the position of magistrate. Whether or not this is done, it is urged that at least the law be so amended as to provide that all warrants in civil cases be issued by the clerk of the civil court and that the fee in such cases revert to the city treasury. The amount collected by magistrates in the city for the issuance of the warrants during the year 1916 was estimated at approximately eight thousand dollars ($8,000.00), which if paid into the city treasury would not only make the civil court self-sustaining. but would add further revenue to the city.

The records maintained by the court are in accordance with good practice as is also the procedure. The clerk of the court, however, should be required by law to file a detailed and comprehensive annual report with the city council, showing the actual number of suits begun, the number dismissed, and number resulting in judgments, and the kind of suits classified as to amounts involved and kind of proceedings. The only report filed at present is a financial statement of the fees collected.

Justices of the Peace—
Magistrates

JUSTICES OF THE PEACE—MAGISTRATES.

There are twelve justices of the peace or magistrates, all of whom are elected by the people for a term of two years, three being elected from each of the four wards. The justices of the peace receive no salary but are paid by fees which they are permitted to retain. The functions of justices include the issuance of civil and criminal warrants and the acceptance of bail in misdemeanor cases. For the issuance of warrants both civil and criminal a fee of fifty cents per warrant is allowed the magistrate, while a fee of one dollar is charged for each bail bond accepted.

Inasmuch as Richmond has a regularly established civil court for the trial of civil suits, and a regularly constituted police court for the hearing of criminal cases, there is no longer any logical reason for retaining the office of justice of the peace or magistrates in the City of Richmond.

In the matter of civil warrants the city loses fees which should be turned in to the public treasury and thus go toward the support of the civil court.

Police Justices Should Issue All Criminal Warrants.

It is only necessary to attend a few sessions of the police court and the juvenile and domestic relations court in order to ascertain the vast number of useless arrests caused by the lack of care shown by the magistrates in the issuance of warrants. Of course, the majority of magistrates' fees accrue from the issuance of warrants. Therefore, it is only natural to assume that it does not take much persuasion on the part of the complainant who is prepared to pay fifty cents to secure a warrant from a magistrate, but it does take considerable time and energy and causes considerable expense to the police department to execute these useless warrants, to say nothing of the time lost in the police court. The ease with which warrants may be secured because of the fee system indicates but a slight regard on the part of the magistrates for the right of liberty of the people. It is, therefore, recommended, that the position of justice of the peace or magistrate be abolished and that all criminal warrants be issued by the police justice at the police court.

Magistrates Exercise Powers Not Vested in Them by Law.

In what are termed by the magistrates, minor cases, it is customary for them to impose what they believe would be the fine usually imposed for the offense by the police justice and to collect the same from the defendant and then order his discharge. Not only is this practice not in accordance with law, since it is in effect exercising trial powers not vested in the magistrate, but it is indeed not conducive to good administration or court procedure and might easily lead to corruption. Most persons arrested dislike the idea of having to appear in a police court. As a matter of fact, in a majority of those cases the humiliation caused by appearing in the police court in the morning is practically the only punishment which the offender is made to bear, because the imposition of a fine readily paid can scarcely be held to be a punishment in the majority of these cases. Moreover it is not difficult to conceive of a miscarriage of justice as a result of this practice, since cases which, by reason of past convictions might result in a jail sentence, would be disposed of by the magistrates through the payment of a fine. At least one of the magistrates defended this action by stating that the judge of the police court had authorized him to do this. Of course, it is scarcely necessary to point out that the statute does not give to the police justice the right to delegate his judicial powers. Therefore, it is recommended, pending the amendment of the statutes, so as to provide for the abolishment of the position of justice of the peace that the police justice call the attention of the magistrates to this practice and direct that they discontinue it at once. It is further recommended that the chief of police direct the sergeants at the station houses to refuse to release a prisoner on the order of a magistrate, based upon the payment of a fine.

Police Sergeants Should Be Empowered to Accept Bail.

For the purpose of admitting to bail persons charged with misdemeanors, the law should be amended so as to provide that the captains and sergeants of police be empowered to accept bail when properly offered. The theory of law involved in bail is that a defendant is entitled to his liberty as promptly as possible, providing he can give to the authorities ample security to insure his presence in the court. For this reason every convenience for the bailing of prisoners, especially those charged with minor offenses, should be provided by law, and certainly no fee should be charged. The acceptance of bail, either in practice or theory, is by no means a courtesy, but is a legal right guaranteed the defendant by law. There is no more reason to believe that the sergeants who are responsible officers sworn to perform their duties in accordance with the law, would not exercise as much judgment in the matter of accepting bail as do the magistrates, and judging from the forfeitures and uncollected bail bonds it might appear that they would exercise even better judgment than do the magistrates.

Commonwealth Attorney

COMMONWEALTH ATTORNEY.

The office of the Commonwealth attorney is still retained upon a fee basis. Thus the compensation of the Commonwealth attorney, who is the prosecuting officer of the City of Richmond, is primarily dependent upon the number of cases prosecuted by him, and as far as misdemeanor cases are concerned, upon his success in obtaining convictions.

The Commonwealth attorney is elected by the people for a term of four years. The present incumbent was appointed to the office by the judge of the hustings court in September, 1915, and was elected by the people to fill the unexpired term of his predecessor in November, 1915.

The functions of the Commonwealth attorney include the preparation of cases for the grand jury, the prosecution of cases in the hustings court, the prosecution of police court appeals, the prosecution of bail bond forfeitures, the prosecution once a year in the circuit court of what are termed convict cases, and the prosecution of delinquent State taxpayers.

For his services he is allowed fees as follows: For the trial of felony cases ten dollars per case for each conviction; in a misdemeanor case five dollars, and for the prosecution of what are termed revenue cases, which are delinquent State license tax cases, he is allowed ten dollars per case. His fees in felony and misdemeanor cases are paid by the State, while the ten dollar fee in license cases is supposed to be collected from the delinquent tax payer.

The State law pays the Commonwealth attorney all fees in felony and misdemeanor cases, which in the aggregate do not exceed twenty-two hundred and fifty dollars ($2,250.00) per year. It is the practice of the present official not to assess the fee of ten dollars on delinquent taxpayers, because the majority of the defendants in these cases are financially unable to pay the fees, thus during the year 1916 he received no revenue whatever from this source, while during the same year he had earned the maximum allowance for his other fees by August, which meant that for his services during the balance of the year he received no compensation.

For some reason, which does not appear, and which is difficult to explain, the city, by virtue of an ordinance, pays the Commonwealth attorney one thousand dollars ($1,000.00) a year, thus making his total income thirty-two hundred and fifty dollars ($3,250.00) per annum.

Fee System Should Be Abolished.

The Commonwealth attorney is a State officer, and as such occupies a most important position, one requiring not only a competent knowledge of the criminal statutes and procedure, excellent judgment and efficient training as a lawyer, but likewise integrity and courage in the highest degree. His compensation should not be dependent upon fees or upon the activities of criminals or his success in securing convictions. The fee system has long since been condemned in most progressive communities as against public policy, and as a result in those places city and county officials are now retained upon a salary basis and any fees assessed or collected are paid into the public treasury.

Therefore, it is recommended, that the statutes be amended, at least so far as cities are concerned, so as to provide for the payment of an annual salary instead of fees to the Commonwealth attorney. It is further recommended that inasmuch as the prosecuting officer is distinctly a State official, the city make no contribution in its budget or otherwise towards the compensation of this official.

Prosecuting Attorney Should Be Prohibited from Engaging in Private Practice.

Although the law does not prohibit the Commonwealth attorney from engaging in private practice, it may be said to the credit of the present incumbent that he does not engage in private practice, although as he frankly stated, in one or two instances he has performed legal services for a few clients in cases having originated prior to his taking public office. Notwithstanding that the present incumbent does not engage in private practice, it is nevertheless pointed out that the best interests of the community demand because of the very nature of the duties of the prosecuting officer that he shall, during his term of office be absolutely free from any alliance which would at any time serve to embarrass him or reduce his efficiency as a prosecuting officer, and it is, therefore, recommended that the statutes be amended so as to prohibit the Commonwealth attorney from engaging in private practice.

Prosecutor Should Have An Assistant.

Since the Commonwealth attorney maintains no records as to the number of cases tried or services rendered by him, it is not possible to readily secure any definite tabulation of the number of cases in which he was engaged. But it is acknowledged that the number is sufficiently large to warrant the appointment of an assistant Commonwealth Attorney. No office staff whatever, is provided for this office. The prosecutor is not even supplied with the necessary legal stationery to carry on the business of his office, nor is he furnished with a telephone in his office. The functions of the prosecuting attorney, when efficiently performed, demand close attention and effort, and above all, privacy, which cannot be secured under the present conditions.

Because of the absence of a proper criminal procedure, the prosecuting attorney is without any formal information concerning the cases which he is to prosecute or present to the grand jury, until practically the hour of going to trial or making his presentation to the grand jury. Of course, it is possible for him personally to seek out witnesses and make such investigations as his time will permit, but when the hustings court is in session, it is necessary that he be present at all of its sessions, which necessarily limits his time and makes impossible the kind of investigation which it is all-important that a prosecuting official shall make prior to the presentation of his case.

Cases held for the grand jury by the police justice are merely certified to him in the most formal manner and such certificates contain little or no information of value to the prosecutor. He has no knowledge of what has been testified to in the police court and no means of securing this information. Were a witness in the police court to testify differently before the grand jury, he cannot determine the differences in the testimony and thus he is without adequate means for efficiently conducting the prosecution of criminal cases. One has only to visit the police court and observe the method of procedure in that court to appreciate the need for having a representative of the Commonwealth attorney present at its sessions.

Therefore, it is recommended that there be provided an assistant Commonwealth attorney who shall be required to be present at all sessions of the police court. His presence in the police court would necessarily prevent many cases from being transferred to the hustings court, which should be disposed of in the police court, and indeed, in all probability would result in cases being held for the grand jury, which now because of improper presentation in the police court are disposed of in that tribunal.

Services of a Stenographer Should Be Provided.

In order that the prosecuting attorney shall be able to carry on the work of his office, it is not only necessary, but essential that there be appointed a stenographer, who shall perform necessary clerical services, in addition to stenographic work.

Prosecuting Official Should Be Notified Promptly in Murder Cases.

That the prosecuting officials be brought to the scene of a murder as promptly as possible after the crime has been discovered is not only desirable. but absolutely necessary. Nothing is more helpful in the investigation of murder cases than the advice and assistance of the prosecuting officers.

Therefore. it is recommended that arrangements be made for the transporting of the Commonwealth attorney or his assistant to the scene of the crime as soon as possible after its discovery. If this is done. the detectives can be advised as to the course to be followed in the examination of witnesses. the collection and preservation of evidence and the obtaining and recording of confessions in a legal manner. It must be apparent that in the interests of justice and efficiency in the prosecution of cases the prosecuting officer should have part in the investigation from the very beginning and that the police should be given intelligent aid and guided absolutely and solely by the Commonwealth attorney. In this way the prosecution of cases will be facilitated.

Commonwealth Attorney Should File Annual Report.

It is recommended that the Commonwealth attorney be required by statute to maintain a complete case record which shall include complete information concerning every case handled in his office and that he be required to file annually with the judge of the hustings court a report which will truly describe all of the services rendered by him during the year. This report should be a public document.

The City Jail

THE CITY JAIL.

City Jail Under Supervision of City Sergeant.

The city jail is under the supervision of the city sergeant, who is elected by popular vote for a term of four years. The present incumbent has already served in this position for a period of seven years. In addition to his functions as warden of the city jail, he serves as officer to the hustings court and possesses co-ordinate powers with the sheriff in the matter of serving process. Thus his functions are to retain custody of prisoners committed to his care, to maintain and operate the city jail and to attend as officer of the hustings court, serving such process of that court as he may be directed. While the city sergeant has equal powers with the sheriff in the matter of serving process, he does not exercise these powers except in matters originating outside of the City of Richmond.

The city sergeant operates as a fee officer, receiving no salary either from the State or city, but being permitted to charge fees for his service, both as attendant at the court and as custodian of the jail. The fees are paid by the State pursuant to statute. For each prisoner committed to the city jail, the State pays to the city sergeant a fee of 50 cents. For the boarding and maintenance of the prisoners, the following fees are allowed:

For Federal prisoners ....40c per day
For insane persons detained in jail hos-
   pital ....50c per day
For other prisoners—
   For the first 100 ....24¾c per day
   After the population of the jail ex-
     ceeds 100, per prisoner ....18c per day

When a prisoner detained awaiting trial is sent to court either for examination or any other reason, and his case is adjourned or continued, he must be recommitted, and for each such recommitment the city sergeant receives 50 cents, regardless of the number of times during the course of the trial of a defendant the case may be continued or adjourned.

In addition to these fees, the city sergeant is paid the usual statutory fees for the service of process for the hustings or any other court.

After the expiration of the term of the present sheriff the fee
system will be changed. The city sergeant will not be allowed to
receive any compensation above $6,500 per annum and all fees
collected in excess of that and of the expenses of operating the
jail, must revert to the public treasury.

City Sergeant's Staff.

From the funds collected as fees, the city sergeant is required
to provide food for the prisoners and to pay the salaries of his
deputies.

•To assist him in the conduct of his office the city sergeant employs the following staff:

1 Chief Deputy at the jail, who receives. .$110.00 per mo.
1 Chief Deputy at the Hustings Court,
    who receives .... 110.00 per mo.
2 Deputies, each paid .... 85.00 per mo.
2 Deputies and Guards, each paid...... 60.00 per mo.
    ($30.00 of which is paid by the State
    and $30.00 by the city sergeant).
1 Matron, who receives .... 50.00 per mo.
    (which is paid by the city of Rich'd).
1 Visiting Physician, who receives...... 500.00 a year
    (which is paid by the State).
1 Resident Physician, who receives...... 600.00 a year
    (which is paid by the city of Rich'd).

Prior to the first of January, 1917, there were employed two
additional deputies, who were relieved from duty because of the
marked decrease in the number of prisoners confined at the jail.

The two deputies and guards were each paid $30.00 per month
by the State pursuant to a statute which provides that there be
employed at the jail a night and day guard, who shall be paid at
the rate of $1.00 per day by the State. These two men have also
been designated deputies and perform the regular duties of the
deputies, for which the city sergeant contributes out of his fees
an additional dollar a day: thus making their salary $60.00 per
month.

Jail Should Be Under Supervision of a Warden.

The position of city sergeant, operated on a fee basis, was for
many years one of the most lucrative offices in the government, and

the income was out of all proportion to the value of the service rendered. But since the enactment of the statutes prohibiting the sale of ardent spirits, the number of prisoners committed to the jail has so decreased as to greatly reduce the income of the city sergeant.

The city jail is essentially a municipal institution, although as at present operated, may be said to be a State institution insofar as the financing of the feeding of the prisoners is concerned.

As a municipal institution, the jail should be conducted, supervised and financed by the City of Richmond. and should not be operated upon a fee basis. The practice of feeding prisoners in jails upon a contract or fee system has been condemned, not only because it is against public policy, in that the prisoners are never as well cared for under a fee system as they are under the direct control of the municipal authorities, but because such a practice results in inefficiency and increased cost.

It is, therefore, recommended, that an effort be made to amend the statute so as to abolish the office of city sergeant.

The functions performed by the city sergeant and his deputies in connection with the hustings court should be transferred by law to the sheriff.

For the conduct of the jail, there should be created, by council, the positions of warden, guards and matrons, appointment to which should be made as a result of a competitive civil service examination, by the central executive. The salaries of these employees should be fixed by council and paid out of the city funds.

Prisoners Remain in Idleness.

Prisoners are committed to the city jail by the police court, the hustings court, the federal courts and courts of other jurisdiction located in sections of the State not equipped with jail facilities.

The maximum period of detention at the city jail is twelve months, while the average period, based on the total number of prisoners committed, is approximately seventeen days. Thus the terms of imprisonment in this institution vary from a few days to twelve months.

Persons committed pending trial of their cases and material witnesses are also detained at this jail.

Male prisoners, committed for a period in excess of sixty days, are invariably requisitioned by the State authorities for work on the roads, but no provision whatever is made for providing occupation or industries for the many prisoners detained at this jail who are not requisitioned for road work. These prisoners remain in absolute idleness during their period of detention. Approximately twelve prisoners can be used as "trusties," serving in the kitchen and performing general cleaning chores about the jail.

The cells are all opened at 5:30 A. M. and breakfast is served at 7:30.

The prisoners are permitted the freedom of the corridor on the tier immediately outside of their cells, which corridor is approximately four feet wide and about sixty-five feet long. Here the prisoners remain during the entire day. They are permitted to return to their cells at their pleasure and to congregate in groups or to spend their time on their cell tier in any manner they choose so long as they do not become disorderly.

Lunch is served at 1:30. Both breakfast and lunch are served the prisoners in their cells or on the tier corridor. No evening meal is served. The cells are locked for the night at 8:00 P. M. in the summer, and 5:00 P. M. in the winter. Thus it will be seen that detention in the city jail does not result either in correction, reform or punishment—in fact, many of the prisoners are of a type who actually enjoy the period of complete idleness afforded by commitment to this jail. As evidenced by the dirty condition of the cells, which will be referred to hereafter, the prisoners are not even put to the "inconvenience" of maintaining their cells in a clean and orderly manner.

No Attempt at Segregating Prisoners in Accordance With Types.

Except that prisoners awaiting trial are detained on the lower cell tier and that white and colored prisoners are detained in separate divisions of the cell blocks, no attempt is made at segregating prisoners in accordance with the types of criminals. Thus prisoners, when admitted, are assigned to cells, regardless of the offense for which they are committed or the type of criminal represented, thereby bringing into close association during their period of detention prisoners of all kinds and classes. Inasmuch as conversation is permitted during the entire day and night, and further since there is no other means of occupying the time of the prisoners, it may well be said that the city jail, instead of serving as a correctional or punishment institution, is merely a place of detention and serving as a school of crime.

No exercise period is provided, nor are the prisoners required to bathe. No attempt is made to provide for observation of the

prisoners, unless they become so disorderly and noisy as to attention of the guard on duty, who merely directs them to be quiet.

Admission Procedure Defective.

Upon admission, prisoners are searched by a "trusty," and only
contraband property, such as knives, files, saws or the like, removed. The prisoner is permitted to retain in his possession jewelry, money, pencils, etc. In practically all of the cases, the prisoners have been searched and contraband property taken by the
police officials before he is sent to the jail.

The prisoner having been searched, is then assigned to a cell.
He is not required to bathe; he is not given a physical examination, notwithstanding that there is a resident physician on duty
at all times, nor his clothing removed, unless it is apparent to
the guard or "trusty" that his clothing is infested with vermin.
No finger prints are taken, nor is any pedigree recorded, except
the name of the prisoner and such information as is conveyed
through the formal committment.

This method of conducting jail admissions is most defective—

1—Because the prisoner is searched by another prisoner.

2—Because the prisoner is permitted to retain moneys, jewelry, etc.

3—For the reason that no physical examination is given, it is
possible to cause the jail to be quarantined by admitting a person
with a contagious disease.

4—Because the prisoner is not required to bathe and he is
permitted to wear his own clothing.

5—Because no proper record is maintained.

Cells Used by Male Prisoners Unclean.

There are two main cell blocks for the detention of male prisoners, only one of which is now in use. The largest cell block
consists of three tiers, each of which has twelve cells on a side,
making a total of seventy-two cells. One of these cells on each
side is occupied as a shower bath, making the number of cells
available in this block sixty-six. The second, or unused cell block,
contains a total of forty-two cells, three tiers high, having fourteen
cells on a tier.

The cells are of the old type of cage construction. All of
the cells were inspected in the presence of one of the deputies.
Each cell is equipped with two bunks of the lattice iron type and

furnished with mattresses, the majority of which were totally unfit
for use, being dirty, filthy, and in most cases, bug-infested. The
cells occupied by the males, particularly in the division assigned
to colored people, were dirty and showed evidence of lack of care,
having cobwebs in abundance and large numbers of water bugs
and roaches. The dirty condition of the cells is encounraged by
reason of the fact that the prisoners are permitted to store in
their cells any quantity of old clothing and such other materials
as they may desire. Under the mattresses in many cells there were
stored materials of a vast variety.

The utility corridors were found unclean and showed evidence
of not having been inspected or visited. Because of the absence
of proper methods of lighting the utility coridors, it will be difficult to make the necessary repairs to toilets or to provide for the
inspection and cleaning of same.

Another procedure which tends to maintain the cells in a filthy
condition is the practice of requiring prisoners to retain their tin
dishes in the cell without inspection to see that the dishes are
properly cleaned after each meal. Because only two meals a day
are served, the prisoners invariably carry food to their cells after
dinner, in order that they may have something to eat later in the
day. Other prisoners, more fortunate than their neighbors, keep
on hand in their cells a large quantity of foodstuffs brought into
them by their visitors or purchased from restaurants in the vicinity
of the jail.

On the whole, the cells were unclean and showed not only a
lack of inspection, but likewise a lack of discipline on the part
of the jail officials.

It was stated by the officials that all of the cells were thoroughly cleansed once a month, and in some instances, once in two
weeks; but the conditions found, especially those affecting the
walls and ceilings, did not indicate that the cells were cleaned at
any recent date.

When this condition was pointed out to the official detailed
for the inspection, it was stated by him that the ceilings, upper
portions of the cells, were not cleaned on the regular cleaning
tours.

Many of the toilets in the cells were found so dirty as to
render them totally unfit for service, even absolutely insanitary.

The filthy condition of one of the shower baths inspected, indicated a further lack of effort to keep the jail clean.

The cell blocks are badly in need of paint; not only are the walls chipped in such a manner as to invite vermin and bug nests, but because the prisoners are permitted to carry with them to their cells lead pencils and chalk, most of them are disfigured by writing placed there by the prisoners.

That the inmates do not bathe regularly is not surprising when it is known that no towels are supplied. No towels are supplied for the use of the prisoners even for their daily cleansing.

No Matron On Duty During Night Hours.

The female division of the prison consists of four large cell rooms, or wards. such as might be termed dormitories. This division is under the charge of a matron, who is on duty from 8:30 in the morning until 3:30 in the afternoon. After 3:30, the female prisoners are under the charge of the male guards. One of the three prison wards in the female division is reserved for white prisoners. In each of these wards, there is provided a bath tub. The female prisoners are more fortunate than the male prisoners in that their time is partly occupied by sewing, washing and scrubbing. but even these three forms of industry do not provide a means of occupying the time of all the prisoners for the entire day. They do the washing of the linen for the prison hospital and themselves.

The placing of women prisoners in the custody of male guards for a period of seventeen hours of of twenty-four, can scarcely be said to be in accordance with modern prison procedure. As a matter of good practice, and in fairness to the women prisoners, no males should be admitted at any time to the female division of the prison, except in the regular course of business during the day or to help a 'matron to restrain a disorderly prisoner.

Jail Without Any Fire-Fighting Equipment.

Although the average population of this jail is approximately one hundred and ten, and the building is of non-fire resisting construction of an inferior type. it is absolutely without auxiliary fire fighting equipment. There is not even a fire bucket in the building, much less hand chemical extinguishers and fire hose.

Inadequate Staff.

For the care of the prisoners, there are on duty two deputies from 6:00 A. M. until 5:00 P. M.. and two deputies from 5:00 P. M. until 6:00 in the morning. These deputies are required to receive the prisoners, maintain the records, supervise their feeding, prepare the prisoners for court, see to their return and exercise disciplinary control over the one hundred and ten inmates. Consequently, it is not difficult to understand why the cells are unclean and no effort made towards conducting the jail in accordance with modern prison procedure.

Not only is the staff inadequate, but requiring the deputies to remain on duty for eleven and twelve hours for seven days a week is hardly conducive to efficient service.

Hospital Maintained in Prison.

For the care of sick prisoners and the temporary detention of insane persons, an emergency hospital is maintained in the city jail. A resident physician employed by the city is in constant attendance. Notwithstanding this fact, the State retains a visiting physician, at a salary of $500.00 a year, who calls at the prison a few times each week.

It is customary during the winter season to allow the freedom of the operating room to a surgeon attached to one of the medical colleges in the city for conducting major operations for the benefit of the students of the college.

There is absolutely no need of employing two physicians to attend to the medical needs of the inmates of this jail. The resident physician could render all, the service necessary and consequently it is recommended that the services of the visiting physician be dispensed with.

It is not possible, in view of the structural conditions of the operating room, to provide for proper sterilization. It is unfit for use as an operating room for major operations; therefore, it is recommended that the practice of performing major operations in the hospital be discontinued and all prisoners requiring such operations be transferred to the city hospital.

Except that the resident physician maintains an informal record of the names, date of admission and date of discharge of all insane persons detained in the hospital, he has no records showing the service rendered by him in connection with the treatment of the prisoners in the jail. It is recommended that the resident physician be required to maintain complete and detailed records of the same character as are maintained in all properly managed hospitals.

Prisoners Delivery to Police Officers Without Order of Court.

It is customary for the city sergeant, or his deputies, to permit members of the police department to take prisoners from the jail for police purposes, such as identifying persons, visiting pawnshops in search of stolen property, etc., without any written authority and without maintaining any record of the prisoner having left the jail. This practice has long since been condemned as conducive to corruption. While it is not intimated, or even suggested, that fraud has been practiced in connection with this custom in this city, nevertheless it must be obvious that certain types of prisoners under certain conditions would be very willing to pay for the privilege of leaving the jail, even for but a short period. It is, therefore, recommended that no prisoner be delivered to any person for any reason, except upon the written order of the committing judge, which order should be filed in the office of the city sergeant and an entry made in the record of the jail which will show the time of departure of the prisoner, the name of the officer in whose custody he was delivered, the name of the judge signing the order, the period of absence and the time returned.

No Proper Inspection of Visitors.

Prisoners are permitted visitors any day during the week and as often as desired. No proper inspection of visitors, so as to prevent contraband materials entering the jail, is provided, except that in cases of prisoners awaiting trial for commission of serious offenses, visits are only permitted under observation of the guard.

Inasmuch as at best the city jail can only be constituted as a penal institution because of the short terms of the prisoners, those committed upon sentence should only be permitted visitors at definite intervals, and even then, the number of visitors should be limited and the privileges of visitors should be confined to the immediate relatives of the prisoner. The denial of the privilege of visitors should be one of the forms of punishment. All persons entering the jail should be carefully examined and observed, so as to prevent contraband materials entering the jail. A record of visitors should be maintained, in which should be entered the name of the visitor, the relation to the prisoner, the time of entering and the time of leaving.

No Record of Visits of Counsel Maintained.

No effort is made to prevent lawyers from soliciting business in the city jail. Lawyers are permitted to enter and see prisoners at their pleasure. No record of such visits of counsel is maintained. It is recommended that lawyers be permitted to visit prisoners only at the request or invitation of the prisoner, and that in all cases the lawyers should be required upon such visits to place their signature in a register showing the time of entrance, the name of their client and the time of departure. Such a record has been found most valuable in many cities in connection with the trials of defendants for serious offenses.

Feeding the Prisoners.

Although the State pays for the board of all of the prisoners, no adequate inspection of the foods served is conducted. The food in the jail is prepared by prisoners detailed as "trusties" and the menu consists of——

Breakfast:
Corn meal bread, coffee and molasses. On alternate days, herring or some other fish is served for breakfast.

Lunch or Dinner:
Corn meal bread, bean soup or pea soup, and on alternate days beef stew. No coffee is served.

The corn bread, made by the prisoners, is of fairly good grade. Coffee screenings are used in the preparation of the coffee. No meal is served in the evening.

The quantity of the corn bread and other food served is liberal, the prisoner being allowed to consume as much as he wishes and also being permitted to retain a portion of his dinner in his cell. The menu is not in accordance with modern prison fare and a greater variety of nutritious food should be served at the rate allowed by the State. Of course, inasmuch as the jail is operated entirely on a fee basis, the city sergeant, in order to make the position pay, has to make a profit out of the feeding of the prisoners, which practice, as already pointed out, is against public policy. Whether or not the jail is established as a municipal institution and the fee system abolished, a more nutritious and more varied menu should be provided, and three meals a day should be served instead of two.

Prisoners Permitted to Obtain Food from Outside of Jail.

All prisoners are permitted to order meals, at their own expense, from restaurants or shops outside of the jail. While it is permissible, and indeed good practice, to allow persons detained awaiting the trial of their cases to obtain food from outside of the jail at their own expense, it is decidedly against good practice to accord this privilege to persons detained as a result of conviction.

First of all, it is totally unfair to those prisoners who cannot afford this luxury, to permit their cell-mates to purchase food from outside, and second, it tends to reduce the amount of punishment, which is supposed to accompany commitment upon sentence. A person sentenced to serve time in the city prison should be required to eat the prison fare, which should be sufficient to sustain the prisoners and be of wholesome and nutritious quality.

Jail Procedure Should Be Completely Re-organized.

The defects in the procedure of the jail, as pointed out in the foregoing description, should be corrected as promptly as possible. To this end, the adoption of the following procedure is recommended in connection with the management of the jail—

1—That all prisoners on admission, be searched by an officer of the jail and all property in his possession be removed, including money. There is no reason why a person committed to jail upon a sentence should have money in his possession, since there should be nothing in the jail that he can purchase. His valuables and money, when taken from him, should be recorded in the record book, and he should be given a receipt and also required to sign a statement showing a list of the properties taken from him. There should always be two guards present when a prisoner is searched, the second guard to act as a witness and to affix his signature to the written list of properties taken. This rule should apply to all prisoners. A prisoner detained awaiting trial, should have the privilege of issuing an order on the warden directing the payment of moneys out of his property envelope to such persons as the prisoner may desire. In all such cases, the written order of the prisoner should be retained as a part of the records of the jail.

2—That all prisoners on admission be detained in the unused cell block and not assigned to their regular cell until the evening of the day on which they are received. Each prisoner should be given an individual cell while awaiting assignment to his permanent cell. Immediately upon admission, he should be stripped of all of his clothing and bathed. He should then be given a thorough physical examination by the resident physician. Prisoners convicted and sentenced should have all of their clothing removed and should be furnished a suit of underwear and light weight prison clothes. Such clothes need not be of a striped or humiliating pattern or design, but should be clean and serviceable. The personal clothing of the prisoner should be sterilized, and for this purpose there should be installed in the jail the necessary apparatus for sterilizing. Such an equipment is neither costly to purchase or maintain. After the clothes have been sterilized, they should be pressed and put into good condition by prisoners detailed as "trusties," and the linen should be cleaned and ironed by the women inmates. This should be done in order that when the prisoner is discharged he will leave the prison with his clothes clean and in decent condition.

3—That a complete and detailed pedigree of all prisoners be taken and sufficient inquiry conducted by the city sergeant to ascertain the number of previous commitments of the prisoners to the jail. This information should be secured from the records of the police department.

4—That insofar as the structural conditions of the jail will permit, prisoners should be segregated by assignment to cells in different parts of the building so as to prevent prisoners of the hardened criminal type associating or coming into close daily contact with the younger and less serious offenders.

5—That the rules of the jail provide for a routine daily inspection of cells. This inspection should be conducted each morning in the following manner:

At a given hour, all prisoners should be required to stand at attention, immediately outside of their cells. The guard conducting the inspection should be equipped with a electric torch, and should enter each cell and inspect every part of it.

The rule should require each prisoner to keep his cell clean and in order. Where the guards finds that the cell has not been properly cleaned by the prisoner. he should direct that it be put in good order immediately, and if this is not done to his satisfaction the prisoner should be punished by solitary confinement, by being denied visitors and in such other manner as the law will permit.

6—That once in each week the city sergeant should conduct a cell to cell inspection in order to see to it that the guards have complied with the regulations as to the daily inspections of the cells.

7—That no food be retained in the cells, and that the prisoners be prohibited from storing any materials in any part of their cells.

8—That the large pen, now used for storage in the basement, be equipped as a mess-hall and that all meals be served in this room. Prisoners should be marched from their cell blocks to the mess-hall for each meal and no dishes should be carried from the mess-hall to the cells, nor should any food be carried away.

9—That a definite hour be fixed for exercising prisoners awaiting trial. These prisoners should be required to walk to and fro for a period of half an hour in the morning, and half an hour in the afternoon in the corridor outside of the cell block.

10—That a matron be employed who will live at the jail and be available for service, and in charge of the women's prison at all hours.

11—That better bathing facilities be afforded the women prisoners and that during their bathing periods they be given the privacy to which they are entitled.

12—That discipline be maintained to the extent of preventing, so far as possible, prisoners congregating in groups about the jail.

13—That all of the mattresses at present in use be condemned and that new mattresses be provided. The new mattresses should be equipped with an outer covering, which can be removed and washed at intervals. Each prisoner, upon admission, should be given a clean mattress cover and should not be required to sleep on the same ticking used by the prisoner who occupied the cell before him.

14—That all of the cells be thoroughly cleaned at once and that for purposes of destroying the bug nests and keeping the jail as free as possible from bugs, the cells be thoroughly scoured with soap and water and the runways and crevices be frequently dusted with commercial sodium fluoride mixed with equal parts of flour. No liquid disinfectants are necessary, the cleanliness of the jail should be wholly dependent upon its frequent scouring with soap and water.

Industry Should Be Provided.

There is no reason why the prisoners should be kept in complete idleness, even though the jail is improperly constructed and poorly located for jail purposes. There could be installed in the basement of the jail, at a small cost, sufficient laundry equipment to do a considerable part of the lundry work for the city institutions. The local conditions in Richmond make possible the operation of an efficient concrete plant, at which all of the prisoners committed upon sentence could be used. Concrete work requires little or no training and most inexpensive machinery. The house of correction in the city of Minneapolis, which corresponds to the city jail of Richmond, is made self-supporting through the use of its concrete plant. The average term of commitment in the Minneapolis house of correction is approximately the same as the average period in Richmond.

Need for Indeterminate Sentence Law.

Little in the way either of reform or punishment can be accomplished through the use of the city jail or the penal system now followed in the City of Richmond. The inmates of the city jail are, for the most part habitues of that institution. They are constantly coming and going and little or no regard is paid to the number of previous convictions or to the actual correctional needs of the prisoners. As a result, nothing much is being accomplished or need be expected in the way of accomplishment by the mere commitment to the city jail of persons convicted in the police court. As a matter of fact, the commitment of the average prisoner to the city jail involves for the most part only an added expense upon the State, and a period of restful idleness for the person committed. In this age of prison reform and progressiveness in the handling of delinquents, it is little short of criminal to continue this form of so-called correction. What Richmond needs is what most progressive communities are rapidly adopting, namely, a penal system which will tend to reform the prisoner or at least make him self-supporting while he is in the custody of the State. To this end, it is recommended that an effort be made to adopt an indeterminate sentence procedure, which will provide for the commitment of a person, not for a definite period, but for such time as those duly appointed to investigate and observe the prisoners may determine necessary to effect a reform or at least a punishment in keeping with the condition of the prisoner. To do this, it will be necessary to establish, by law, a board of parole for the city, which shall have jurisdiction over all persons committed for misdemeanors. It will also be necessary to establish a farm colony and proper industries at which the prisoners may be given an opportunity to labor under wholesome and decent conditions, permitting their families to share in the profits of their production. The parole law of the city of New York is suggested for the use of the city government of Richmond as a guide in drafting such legislation. Until such a procedure is adopted, every dollar spent by the State or city upon the city jail, insofar as the handling of persons convicted of offenses is concerned, is a dollar which gives little return to the taxpayers, either in reforming the delinquent or in affording protection to society against the type committed to this institution.

The Coroner

THE CORONER.*

Duties of Coroner Fixed by. Charter.

The charter of the city states that the council shall have the power to prescribe the duties of the coroner of the city of Richmond, who shall be appointed as provided by the general statutes of the State, by the judge of the hustings court, but who shall receive instead of fees, a salary to be determined by the city council, and to be paid by the city; provided the salary of the said coroner shall not be less than $2,000. He shall be a physician of not less than five years standing and shall also be a chemist. He shall hold all inquests and make all post mortem examinations without the assistance of any medical experts for whose assistance the city may be liable, without the consent of the mayor.

It will be noted in the foregoing quotation from the city charter that the city council may prescribe the duties of the coroner and may fix his salary, but that he is appointed by the judge of the hustings court. To the extent that his salary is paid by the city and his duties prescribed by council, he is a city officer and yet his appointment by the judge of the hustings court would appear to indicate that he is responsible to the State rather than to the city.

---

*When the coroner was visited by the investigator and an attempt made to interview him regarding his work, he evidenced by his manner that he was not favorably disposed to the interview or to the examination of the work of his office. At the question put by the investigator, "How much of your daily time is required by the work of your office?", he said, "I do not recognize your right to ask that question," explaining that he considered himself to be a State officer and, therefore, not to be included in the survey of the city government. The investigator pointed out to him that his salary is paid by the city, and that this fact should warrant the inclusion of the coroner's office in the survey. As the coroner insisted, however, that his position is that of a State officer, the investigator did not press the matter further. The data here given is, therefore, only such as could be obtained from available public records, and from information regarding the procedure of coroners in other cities.

Cost of Coroner's Office and Work Performed.

The present city coroner is a physician and a chemist, as required by law. For the current year the following sum was appropriated for this office:

Salary of coroner $2,700.00
Allowance to assistants 500.00
Witness attendance 300.00

Total $3,500.00

The coroner states that his assistant is also appointed by the judge of the Hustings Court, Part I, and that the judge of the Hustings Court, Part II, also appoints an assistant who acts independently. The coroner stated that he was uncertain whether or not the assistant appointed by the Hustings Court, Part II, is under his jurisdiction. In any event the services of these assistants are paid for out of the appropriation stated above, such additional assistance as the coroner may require being supplied by himself from his salary allowance, after authorization as provided by law.

The report of the health department for 1916 shows that the coroner examined a total of 426 cases in 1916, viewed ten fetuses and twenty-nine still births. The number of autopsies made or actual inquests held is not stated in the report of the health department.

The present coroner was formerly the city chemist, this position being given up by him in order to accept the appointment as coroner. As he is a chemist he continues to do private chemical laboratory work, renting the laboratory formerly used as the city chemist's laboratory at $240 a year. He is, therefore, on full time duty only to the extent that he is on call at all times. It is obvious from the foregoing statement of the quantity of work performed by the coroner in 1916 that the duties of this office do not require all of the coroner's time.

Status of Coroner Not Clearly Established; Office Should Be Abolished.

There is at the present time considerable confusion as to the status of the coroner. The city attorney has rendered an unofficial opinion that he is a State officer, but it is clear that whatever his legal status he is a part of the city government under the partial control of the city council, and his office is supported by the citi-

zens of Richmond from the taxes levied upon them for the general
support of the government. Nothing is to be gained, however,
by quibbling as to his legal status.

The office of the coroner should be abolished and, instead,
the position of medical examiner should be created, such medical
examiner or examiners to be attached to the office of the Commonwealth attorney. The duty of this medical examiner should be to
make medical examinations only and certify the facts of such
medical examinations to the Commonwealth attorney. Such chemical analyses as might be required could be performed by the city
chemist and pathological examinations could be performed in the
pathological laboratory of the medical college, on a fee basis, if
necessary. The tendency throughout the country is to eliminate
coroners, coroners' juries and inquests, subject as they are to all
manner of irregularities. It is not suggested that there are irregularities in the procedure of the present coroner, but the very
nature of the quasi-judicial proceedings held make irregularities
possible. It is not necessary to detail the evidence found in other
States and cities relative to the defects in the coroner system.
An excellent summary of the whole situation in this country with
special reference to the office of coroner in the city of New York
will be found in a report on "A Special Examination of the Accounts and Methods of the Office of Coroner in the City of New
York (1915)" prepared by the commissioner of accounts of New
York City at the direction of the mayor.

Two Medical Examiners on Part Time Recommended.

It is apparent from the previous statement of the work of the
coroner's office, that the amount of work required is not such as to
interfere with the practice of his profession as chemist. The total
number of cases "viewed." that is four hundred and twenty-six.
means that of these four-hundred and twenty-six only part of
this number required autopsy. or any procedure beyond the mere
viewing of the body. In cases where the cause of death is quite
clear from readily established evidence, the coroner simply views
the body and certifies the cause of death upon the death certificate,
autopsies being performed only when it is necessary to establish
certain facts not evident upon inspection. It is believed that all
the work now done by the coroner and his assistants could be
performed easily by two medical examiners at salaries not to exceed $1,000 each annually, one medical examiner being designated

for each side of the river. The method of their appointment by the judge of the hustings court might perhaps be continued, but their responsibility to the Commonwealth attorney should be direct, and on that account, their appointment should be preferably by the Commonwealth attorney. In the event that a civil service commission or other body charged with civil service functions may be established and a general civil service plan adopted for the entire city. the medical examiners should be chosen through competitive civil service.

Sheriff and High Constable

SHERIFF AND HIGH CONSTABLE.

For the service of process of the several civil courts, there are maintained two separate offices, viz, the office of sheriff and the office of high constable.

The sheriff is elected by the people for a term of four years. The present incumbent is now completing his second term, while the present incumbent in the office of high constable has served continuously in that office since 1906. Both the sheriff and the high constable are fee officers. receiving no salary from the State or city but being compensated for their services by the payment of fees by litigants. All of the fees are fixed by statute.

While under the present law all of the fees, when paid, become the property of the high constable and the sheriff, by virtue of a recent statute after January 1, 1918, these officials will only be permitted to retain for themselves as their compensation fees amounting in the aggregate, over and above the operating expenses of the office, to six thousand five hundred dollars ($6,500.00) per annum. Such fees as are collected in excess of this amount will revert to the State.

Sheriff's Office.

The functions of the sheriff are to serve as attendant to the law and equity, chancery and circuit courts, and to serve the process of these courts and carry out such orders as the several judges may direct. The processes served by the sheriff and his deputies are delivered to him for service by the clerks of the several courts. They are properly recorded in the records of the sheriff's office which records are maintained in accordance with statute. Upon the service of execution of these processes. proper return is made to the court of issuance and to the counsel for the litigants involved. To assist him in his work the sheriff employs two regular deputies and two deputies who serve on a temporary basis working only at such times as the work of the office requires extra service. The compensation of these deputies is paid out of the fees received by the sheriff. In addition to attending to the service of process. the sheriff is given by statute the powers of a public administrator and is allowed to retain five per cent. of the proceeds of the moneys administered by him as such.

Office of High Constable.

The functions of the high constable include the serving of all process by the civil court. His duties and powers correspond in a large measure to those of the sheriff. The fees paid to the high constable for the service of process, however. are less than those paid to the sheriff. For example. the sheriff is allowed fifty cents for the service of a summons in a civil suit, while the high constable is allowed but thirty cents for the service of a similar warrant. All of the processes served by the high constable are properly recorded in records maintained in accordance with the statutes. The records of his office show due regard for efficient management and the procedure of the office is in accordance with good practice, with the single exception that the high constable has introduced a procedure for the "speeding" of settlements in cases coming to his office, which is unwise, if not illegal and unethical. It is the practice of the high constable to serve with each civil warrant a notice to the person being sued, which notice reads as follows:

"IMPORTANT NOTICE.

You will please call at my office. Room 18. City Hall, and settle the accompanying account, and thereby keep same out of court. If it goes to a judgment it will be published in the Daily Record and by the Mercantile Agencies and will destroy your credit in the City and State.

WM. H. WYATT, JR.,
High Constable City of Richmond."

It will be seen, by reading the above notice that the high constable, over his signature, assumes the validity of every claim and, indeed, though perhaps unconsciously and without any wrong intent, conveys. in the second sentence, a veiled threat to the person being sued. A person ignorant of the law. as most of the litigants in the civil court are. could easily construe this notice of the high constable to mean that it is required of him that he make immediate payment of the claim without further protest: while of course the law is that the defendant in the action has a right to be heard in a court of law, and if need be, to dispute the validity of the claim. The high constable is frank in declaring that this practice has resulted in the prompt settlement of claims in very many cases, and in this way has increased the financial proceeds of the office. It is to be understood that in settling such cases the high constable is entitled, by law, to the same fees to which he would be entitled, had he executed a judgment in the case. In other words, the issuance of this notice by the high constable, who is legally an officer of the court, and whose duties must be performed without favor or prejudice in precisely the same manner as by the judge of a court, makes him in effect, a plaintiff's attorney.

Without in any manner desiring to reflect upon the efficiency of this official or to indicate that he was inspired by other than good motives, it is urgently recommended that he discontinue the practice of isuing these "dunning" notices.

Upon receiving a judgment for execution it is also the custom of the high constable to issue a similar notice to the judgment debtor. which reads as follows:

"IMPORTANT NOTICE.

Please call at my office, Room 18, City Hall, and make satisfactory arrangement to settle claim of .... against you. Unless you do, I will be compelled to remove your effects and sell same according to law. It would be a very unpleasant duty for me, and at the same time very humiliating to you in the neighborhood, and, therefore, try to avoid this unpleasantness.
WM. H. WYATT, JR.,
High Constable City of Richmond."

While, perhaps, there is more justification in law for the issuance of a notice to a judgment debtor that a judgment has been filed against him, and that the same can be paid at the office of the high constable, nevertheless it can scarcely be said to be ethical for the high constable, an officer of the court, to issue a notice of this kind couched in such language. The duty of the high constable and his deputies is plainly defined by statute and consists merely in using every proper and ethical means to serve the process of court and to execute its orders. These duties must be performed in such a manner as to at no time convey to the persons having business with that office any notion of bias, or interest, except to see to it that the law is complied with.

The fact that the high constable has resorted to these extraordinary measures in the exercise of his duties is the result of the fee system, which naturally makes him eager to secure as large a number of fees as is possible. It is, therefore, recommended that the high constable, in his efforts to execute judgments, rest content with the normal standardized methods, namely, the service of notice of judgment on the judgment debtor, and the collection of the proceeds of judgment without the use of this notice, which it is recommended he discontinue.

When the attention of the high constable was called to the matter, and the recommendation discussed, he immediately issued an order to the deputies to discontinue the use of these two notices.

Offices of Sheriff and High Constable Should Be Combined.

There is no logical reason for maintaining two separate and distinct officials for the service of civil process. The amount of civil business conducted by the civil courts is not so enormous as to require two separate divisions of the judicial branch of the government to perform this service. It is, therefore, recommended that the statutes be amended so as to combine these two offices in one.

Fees Should Not Be Retained By Official.

At such time as these offices are combined, the act combining them should also provide that the official in charge of this division and his deputies and clerks be paid salaries and all fees collected revert to the public treasury.

Sealer of Weights and
Measures

SEALER OF WEIGHTS AND MEASURES.

Little or no protection is afforded the honest merchant and the purchasing public of the city of Richmond, against fraud and loss, as the result of dishonesty and carelessness in the use of weighing and measuring devices. Not alone are the laws and ordinances wholly inadequate to provide protection against fraud, but the sealer of weights and measures, upon whom is imposed the duty of detecting frauds and fraudulent practices in the use of weighing and measuring devices, is unable to enforce such statutes and ordinances as are now in effect by reason of the numerous other duties assigned to him, and the failure of the city to provide an adequate force for this work.

Sealer a State Officer.

The sealer of weights and measures is appointed by and serves at the pleasure of the judge of the hustings court. His office is created by statute, and he is essentially a State officer, responsible only to the judge who appoints him. He receives no salary from the State but is authorized by statute to charge and collect a fee of five cents for each scale, weight or measure examined.

By virtue of power vested in the city council by the charter of the city of Richmond, the sealer is allowed an annual salary of $600 for conducting his weights and measures inspection without charging the statutory fees. In addition, $400 is appropriated by the city council annually to defray the operating expenses of the sealer of weights and measures, thus making the total amount expended for protecting the public against fraud in the use of weighing and measuring devices $1,000 per year. The council provides by ordinance for the appointment of a sealer for a term of two years by the administrative board, and the present incumbent has held this appointment since 1907. Since the sealer is essentially a State officer and his appointment by the judge of the hustings court is provided for by statute, there is some question as to the powers of council to provide for the appointment of a sealer by the administrative board. As evidence of a conflict of these two provisions of law, it is only necessary to poin out that if the administrative board should decide to dismiss the sealer he would still be the sealer of weights and measures, by virtue of his appointment by the court, under a state law, and would be the only officer empowered to inspect weights and measures.

Notwithstanding his dual appointment, the sealer receives no supervision whatever, either from the court or the administrative board, and makes no report which would in any wise serve to advise either the court or the administrative board as to his work with relation to weights and measures investigations. He does, however, make an annual report to the administrative board which deals almost entirely with the duties performed by him as city gauger and public weigher.

Sealer Is Also City Gauger and City Weighmaster.

The sealer is also city gauger and city weighmaster. As city gauger, he gauges liquids for private concerns, receiving fees for his services. As city weighmaster, he conducts weighing for the large coal companies, other large corporations, and all commodities purchased in large quantities under contract by the city departments. For conducting weighings for private corporations, he receives a fee, which fee is paid by the corporations employing him under agreement between them and the sealer.

According to the statement of the sealer, the total income which includes the $600 per annum paid by the city is approximately $1,500 per year. Out of this amount the sealer pays a salary of a clerk who assists him in maintaining his records and conducting weighings.

Because of the small amount paid him by the city, it is necessary in order that he may obtain a livelihood out of his position that he stimulate, as far as possible, the business of public weighing and gauging, and consequently he must devote the greater part of his time and energy to the service for which he receives fees. Not only is it necessary for him to give the major portion of his time to this work, but it is essential that he be subject to the call of corporations needing his services. Aside from the time consumed in serving private corporations, the sealer is required to spend considerable time in conducting weighings for the city, thus, for example, if the department of education receives a large delivery of coal, the sealer is required to be present at the delivery point and to weigh the entire shipment, occuping as much as an entire day at times. Thus, it must be apparent that the amount of time available for the sealer to conduct investigations of weights and measures throughout the city must necessarily be, to say the least, less than is required in order to afford proper protection to the purchasing public. That this is true, cannot be said to be the fault of the sealer who cannot be held responsible for efficient service in weights and measures investigation while he is required by law to perform these additional services in order to secure a living wage.

Need for Vigorous Weights and Measures Campaign Apparent.

The inability of the sealer to devote sufficient time to the inspection of weights and measures has resulted in considerable loss to the purchasing public. This is fully demonstrated by the result of an inspection made in various stores throughout the city in company with the sealer and his assistant. As the time available for the survey of this branch of the city government was necessarily limited. it was only possible to observe the conditions in comparatively few of the hundreds of stores throughout the city. In all, 38 places, including the First Market. were visited and a total of 156 scales inspected and tested. All of the tests were conducted by the sealer and his assistant. Of the 156 scales tested, 70, or 45 per cent., were found to be incorrect, and in nearly every instance resulting in a loss to the purchaser, while but 86, or 55 per cent., were correct. These tests were made in but comparatively few of the many stores in the city, but they were made, however, in practically all sections of the city in places selected at random, so as to make the test as rapidly as possible in the time allowed.

It is not intended or desired to convey the impression in this report that the merchants as a whole are dishonest or that wholesale fraud is perpetrated against the purchasing public, but it is intended to show clearly and distinctly that the purchasing public is sustaining a loss as the result of the failure of the city to provide for an adequate inspection and investigation of weights and measures. These conditions. pointing as they do, to the defrauding of the people, speak with considerable emphasis of the need for a vigorous campaign against short weight. While it may be contended that these conditions do not indicate intended fraud. nevertheless they do indicate the result of gross carelessness on the part of the merchants and the loss to the consumer is the same in either case. One scale observed, which was confiscated by the sealer was more than a quarter of a pound fast. which means that when three-quarters of a pound was put on this scale, it would be recorded on the scale as a pound. In almost every case of an inaccurate scale the inaccuracy was apparent without testing the scale, or to use the technical term of the sealer, it was "fast on observation." In other words. the pointer of the scale, when not in use, did not stand at "zero" but was one-half to one ounce beyond the zero mark. Very few of those examined were slow or weighing against the merchant. The fact that out of a total of 156 scales tested, 70, or 45 per cent., were incorrect, proves above all that the merchant has no fear of the visit of the sealer of weights and measures. Indeed, in nearly every case the merchant expressed no indignation or surprise, but on the contrary in numerous instances admitted that he knew the scale was fast, but delayed having it repaired, while in other cases they alleged that the scales had just previously been repaired. An examination of the weights in use disclosed several two and three-pound weights which were from one-quarter to one ounce light. Scales of a type long since prohibited were found on the counters of several stores.

As bad as were the conditions observed in connection with weighing and measuring devices, far more serious were the shortages observed in package goods. In practically no case were merchants found who sold net weight, while in almost all cases all the wrappings were included in the weight of the commodity and charged for at the price per pound of the commodity. This, of course, is not the fault of the sealer, but is because of the absence of a net weight law in the State of Virginia. The fact that in several stores packages were found to contain less than even the gross weight, is the fault of the city in failing to provide adequate inspection. Of the packages tested it is interesting to note that in one store the following shortages were observed:

1 12-lb. package of meal was 2 lbs. 1 oz. short.
1 12-lb. package of meal was 1 oz. short.
1 10-lb. package of sugar was 1 oz. short.
1 10-lb. package of sugar was 1 1-2 oz. short.
3 10-lb. package of sugar was 1 oz. short.
1 3-lb. package of sugar was 1 oz. short.

These shortages existed in one of the most prominent stores in the city. While it may be true that a shortage in a package of more than two pounds may have been the result of an error, it could scarcely be contended that all of the other packages, all of which were weighed on accurate scales, were short because of error. To ascertain the amount the public would lose, one has only to multiply the sales of packages in this store by one ounce short and it will be seen that every sixteen packages sold results in the loss of a pound of the commodity to the consumers, to say nothing of the loss due to the practice of weighing in the paper bags, strings and butter dishes.

Detective Work Necessary.

The city ordinance requires that the sealer shall test and inspect every scale, weight and measure in the city at least twice in each year. Of course, under the present conditions, it is not possible for the sealer to conduct properly an annual inspection, much less two inspections a year. It is doubtful whether the sealer would be able to conduct two inspections, even if he were relieved of all of his other duties. Two inspections a year, however, are wholly unnecessary, and the ordinance requiring two inspections a year, but tends to decrease the efficiency of the weights and measures work, in that it prompts the sealer, in his effort to comply with the law to devote his entire time to inspections. While it is necessary that the sealer conduct an annual inspection for the purpose of ascertaining the general condition of the scales, and make a test as much for the benefit of the owner as for the public, it should be noted that such inspections are of little value as a protection against fraud. The observations made in the field and reported upon merely show the scale conditions and by no means do they show fraud, which is practiced by scale manipulation. Continued testing of the scales will never of itself reveal the fraud practiced from scale manipulation.

It is the experience of weights and measures experts that fraud practiced upon an unsuspecting purchasing public is based, in a large measure, on the manipulations of the scale when weighing and on short deliveries in the sale of package goods. Indeed, the history of the investigations of weights and measures in New York points out the fact that in many cases, dealers equipped with the best type of scales, and the most costly style of weighing apparatus are only too frequently the most dishonest and corrupt because their fraud was practiced by the wrongful handling of the instrument in the process of weighing. Nothing but continuous detective work will serve to detect fraud or frauds committed in this manner. In the city of Richmond such detective work is not performed. This is not because the sealer is unconcerned, nor because he does not desire it, but for the reason that, even though he would, it is not possible for him to do it because of the many other duties assigned to him.

Sealer Should Employ Woman Agent from Time to Time.

Since the sealer has not been able to devote sufficient time to instructing the housewives as to the proper method of purchasing and from the further fact that the number of complaints received by the sealer are comparatively few, it is quite evident that many of the housewives of the city are almost ignorant of the existence of such an office. The detective work can be best performed from the investigation of complaints made, but unfortunately in a comparatively small community the merchants soon learn the identity of the sealer and because of this fact, his efficiency as a detective is necessarily greatly reduced. This points the need of empowering the sealer to employ from time to time the services of a woman, to act as a shopper. It is not suggested that the sealer be empowered to appoint women deputies, for the reason that it would not be long before their identity would be so well established that their efficiency would be reduced, and also because of the fact that several would be needed, as the dress and habits of one kind of shopper would keep her from being useful in another quarter of the city. The sealer should select women for this work, who, by reason of their race or color and general demeanor, would be best adapted for the work in the neighborhoods to which he wishes to assign them. It is not necessary that they be trained in detective work, but merely that they go into the store as a regular shopper, make purchases, selecting commodities which would be delivered in their entirety, and immediately upon delivery of them the sealer should enter the store, test the scale and reweigh the commodity purchased. Under the existing laws it would be necessary for the woman shopper to pay for the materials bought, since in case the weight was accurate, the commodity could be returned to the dealer, and in case fraud was practiced, the merchant should be charged with having offered for sale short weight.

Therefore, it is recommended that the sealer be empowered to follow these recommendations, and that the fees necessary to pay for the employment of the women be provided for his department.

Sealer Should Be City Officer and Under Control of Central Executive.

If the people of Richmond are to be afforded protection against short weighing, it is necessary that the law be amended so as to enable the sealer to devote his entire time to weights and measures work. In amending the law, the fee system should be abolished and the statute provide that each city be required to employ and maintain an inspector of weights and measures. He should be paid a salary commensurate with the services to be required, and devote his entire time to the work. The same statute should prohibit him from engaging in any·other industry and particularly from having any interest whatever in the sale or manufacture of weighing and measuring devices.

He should be appointed by a central executive as a result of a civil service competitive test, such test to include a physical examination and athletic test. This recommendation is made because of the fact that the weights and measures work to be efficiently performed requires that a physically strong man be employed, one capable of handling the very heavy weights.

It will be noted that the recommendation suggests the appointment of an inspector of weights and measures, rather than a sealer. The reason for this is that the terms "sealer" and "sealed" used in connection with weights and measures are misleading and convey a false impression to the purchasing public. The term "sealed" is generally understood by housewives to mean that after the scale has been tested by the inspector or sealer, it has been sealed or locked in such a way as to prevent its subsequent fraudulent use, consequently the unsuspecting public, upon observing the seal upon a scale, which in fact may be inaccurate, is led to believe that it is an accurate weighing instrument. In this connection, it is recommended that the sealer conduct an educational campaign, through the newspapers, instructing the public that the seal is no guarantee of the accuracy of the scale.

Assistant Inspector Should Be Appointed.

The functions of the department of weights and measures include the enforcement of all laws and ordinances relative to the use of all measuring and weighing devices as well as a general inspection of all commodities in so far as weights and measures are concerned, the testing and inspection of all weighing and measuring devices, the investigation of complaints of purchasers and detective work. All these are to be performed in connection with the thousands of business places in the city using scales, weights and measures. The work cannot be done successfully in a routine manner. Many of these scales are of the large platform type, such as are used in coal yards, freight yards, and by ice companies, and require the services of two men in making the test because of the numerous heavy weights which must be used.

Thus, it is a physical impossibility for one man to efficiently perform all of those services. Moreover, it is essential that there be available some time during the day an inspector at the office of the sealer to receive complaints and to test scales and measures brought to the office.

Therefore, it is recommended that the council make provision for the appointment of an assistant inspector of weights and measures, whose salary should be considerably less than the salary of the sealer. The assistant should also be selected as a result of a competitive civil service test.

The ordinance requiring semi-annual inspection should be amended so as to require but one general inspection a year.

City Should Be Divided in Two Districts.

As a convenient means of conducting an annual inspection the city should be divided into two districts. One of the districts should be under the supervision of the inspector, and the other under the assistant. From time to time the sealer and his assistant should exchange districts so as to prevent their becoming too well known to merchants.

Need for New Laws and Ordinances.

The State laws and city ordinances affecting weights and measures are entirely inadequate to meet the needs. First, because the sealer is without sufficient power to perform his duties, and, second, because no provision is made in the law for the sale of commodities by net weight or for control over the manufacture and production of weighing and measuring devices. There should be adopted by the Legislature, as promptly as possible, a net weight law, which would compel the sale of all package commodities by net weight, the weight to be indicated on the outside of the package. As a guide in drafting such a statute, the "Brooks Net Weight Law of the State of New York" is recommended.

The inspector should be given broad powers, which would include the right to promulgate and enforce, under a penalty, rules and regulations governing the sale, manufacture, and use of weighing and measuring devices, and the power of confiscation and destruction, not only of inaccurate and fraudulent scales, but likewise of inferior and defective type. The ordinances now in use in the cities of New York, Los Angeles, Philadelphia, and Chicago are recommended as proper types from which a proper ordinance could be drawn for use in the city of Richmond. That the inspector be given power to promulgate rules and regulations is of importance. The need for this will be appreciated when it is known that the owners of scales cannot be compelled to place their scales in such a position as to make reading of the scale by the purchaser easy. The ordinance should provide also that the owners of small scales which have been condemned, should be required to bring them to the office of the sealer for re-inspection, after repairing. This would save considerable time to the inspector and his assistant. The law should prohibit the use of any scale, weight or measure in the city of Richmond until after it has been properly tested, stamped and approved by the sealer, and the use of such scales, weights and measuring devices in violation of this ordinance should result in a penalty of not less than $50.

Peddlers Should Be Required to Have Scales and Measures Examined and Licenses Issued.

As a further aid to the inspector and as a protection to the public, the ordinance should provide that no license should be issued to peddlers and hucksters not presenting a certificate of inspection, showing that his measures and scales had been properly approved by the inspector of weights and measures.

Equipment Inadequate.

The testing equipment now in use by the sealer is of an ancient and antiquated type, and not conducive to efficient service. It is recommended that council make provision in the next budget for furnishing the sealer with a complete new testing outfit. He is unable, at present, because of the lack of equipment, to make any tests except the most routine and ordinary, and has no equipment whatever for the proper marking of scales, weights and measures.

Office Poorly Located.

The office of the sealer is located in the cellar of the city hall. Aside from the fact that at present it is used as a storage room for ardent spirits, and is so located as to make it undesirable, if not unhealthful to work in. it is poorly located as a weights and measures office, being in the cellar. thus requiring the hauling of heavy weights up and downstairs, and adding to the inconvenience of the public having business with the inspector. It is recommended that ample provision be made in one of the public markets for an office and quarters for the sealer and his assistant. In providing a place in a market adequate equipment should be furnished for the use of the sealer, who should be in a position at all times to make reweighings and tests for shoppers. There should be located in each of the markets conspicuous signs, calling attention to the location of the sealer's office and advising the purchasing public to visit the office and have purchases reweighed from time to time.

Public Scales Should Be Under the Supervision of the Sealer.

The public scales and the public weighmaster of the city should be under the immediate supervision of the sealer of weights and measures.

Sealer Should Be Relieved of Gauging Functions.

In order that the sealer should be able to devote his entire time to weights and measures work, he should be relieved at once of his functions of city gauger and public weighmaster. The weighings for the city of all commodities purchased under contract should be conducted by representatives of the department making the purchases, while the gauging of liquids should be performed by a city gauger specially appointed for such service.

Records and Reports.

The sealer maintains practically no reports except memoranda of fees collected by him. It is recommended that provision be made immediately for recording the activities of the sealer and his assistant, and that the sealer be required to make a daily report to the central executive showing thereon the work performed by him each day. Among others, the department should establish and maintain the following records:

Citizens' Complaint Book:

In this book should be recorded the day, date, time, name and address of person making complaint; name and address of firm or corporation complained of; character of complaint; the result of the investigation and when and by whom the complaint was investigated.

Record of Violations and Prosecutions:

This should be a card record of all violations discovered, showing the name, address, location, and character of store or business, and a detailed description of the violation reported and the action taken upon it.

Record of Confiscation:

> This record should be kept in a bound book, showing the day, date, time, place, reason, and a detailed description of the scales, weights and measures confiscated.

Card Index of Merchants in City Using Weighing and Measuring Devices:

> A card record of merchants will be comparatively easy to maintain if the inspector is provided with a proper form of certificate of inspection. Certificates of inspection should be in a bound book, which should contain three duplicate copies of each certificate with carbon paper between them. The first certificate, or original, should be given to the owner of the inspected scales, etc., the second, which should be printed on much lighter paper, should remain permanently bound in the book, the third, which should be printed on stiff cardboard, should be removed and filed in the office of the sealer. These cards would then form a card record of all the merchants whose scales, weights and measures are inspected. They should be filed according to streets, sub-divided as to class of business, and cross-indexed as to the name of the firm or corporation. The procedure would be for the sealer and his assistant each morning before leaving the office to remove these cards from their books and place them in their proper position in the files. Upon the back of those cards should be proper printed headings calling for information on any violation found. Space should be provided upon which to enter the final dispositions in such cases. Thus, upon one card would appear the name, address, class of business, number, and kind of weighing and measuring devices, date inspected, condition in which they were found, a record of any inaccuracy or any violation of law, and the result of the proceedings against the owner.

Record of Inspections:

> The present form of record of inspections should be maintained, as in accordance with good practice.

Annual Report.

In order to indicate the efficiency of the work and to be of real statistical value, the annual report of the department of weights and measures should contain the following tables:

1. A table of places inspected according to character of business, including the following headings:

> Character of business.
> Total number of inspections.
> Number of violations found.
> Number of inspections where no violations were found.
> Arrests made.
> Convictions in criminal cases.
> Cases where more than one violation was discovered in a
>   year.

Under the first general heading should be included:

> Bakers.
> Butchers.
> Butter dealers.
> Caterers.
> Coal wagons.
> Produce commission merchants.
> Candy and confectionery.
> Milk and cream dairies.
> Delicatessens.
> Drug stores.
> Dry goods.
> Feed and grain.
> Fruits.
> Fish.
> Etc.

2. A table showing inspection of peddlers and hucksters as differentiated from inspections of stores and regular mercantile establishments. Inspections of push-carts and hucksters in the field are made so quickly and with such little difficulty that a proper impression of the efficiency of the bureau is not given if they are included in a general table of inspections. A combined table does not enable the reader to determine whether fraud or carelessness is greater among peddlers than it is among storekeepers.

3. A table showing tests made of institutional and city departments scales.

4. A table showing classification of apparatus, and number of each type condemned and violations put upon them.

5. A table showing apparatus confiscated and destroyed as well as condemned, a term used in the sense of disapproval.

6. A table showing number and classification of new scales, weights and measures sealed during the year. This table would show the number of new apparatus coming into use, bringing added responsibility and work to the department.

7. A comparative table by years, showing number of routine inspections made, as compared with special inspections. By routine inspection is meant the annual inspection required by ordinance as compared with the special inspections made because of installation of new apparatus or of suspicion, or on complaint of citizens.

8. A table of purchases made for the purpose of testing, not the scales, but the manipulation of the scales and the results found. This table should also show the amount of money spent by the bureau and its inspectors in purchases, as well as the disposition of the commodities purchased. For example, if the inspector purchased a ham for the purpose of testing the honesty of the butcher, this table should show the cost of the ham and the disposition made of it—whether it was turned over to a city institution or hospital, etc.

9. A table showing the number of tests made of packing companies' products and results.

10. A table of complaints received.

11. A table showing number of household weighing equipments tested upon request. The purpose of this table should be to show the number of families equipped with scales for their own protection.

12. A table showing the number of inspections made by the inspector or assistant, arranged by months; the number of violations and condemnations made; arrests, convictions, penalties or fines imposed. Such a table should include the following headings:

Inspector's name.
Total number of inspections made.
Number of articles condemned.
Number of violations.
Amount of money collected.
Number of arrests.
Dispositions.

13. A table showing by classification as to business, the number of inspections and violations in public markets.

14. Tables showing, under classification as to business and apparatus, violations where actual fraud was practiced, classified as follows:

Tampering with a scale.
Fraudulent instrument.
Operators of scales detected manipulating.

Public Welfare Functions

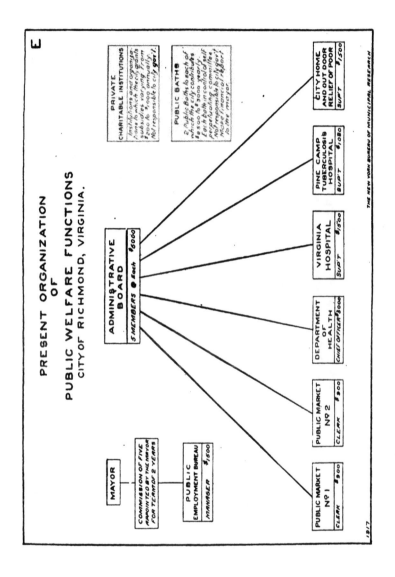

PRESENT ORGANIZATION
OF
PUBLIC WELFARE FUNCTIONS
CITY OF RICHMOND, VIRGINIA.

THE NEW YORK BUREAU OF MUNICIPAL RESEARCH

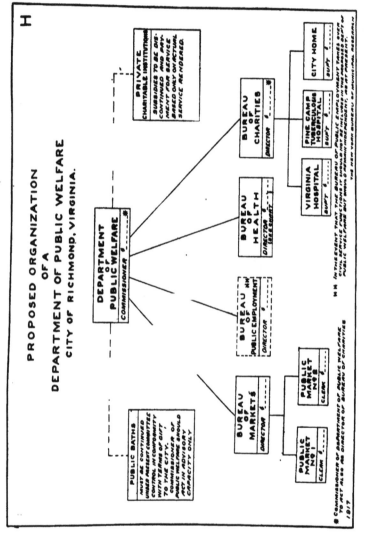

PROPOSED ORGANIZATION
OF A
DEPARTMENT OF PUBLIC WELFARE
CITY OF RICHMOND, VIRGINIA.

PUBLIC WELFARE FUNCTIONS.

Department of Public Welfare Recommended.

In view of the need for closer co-ordination of the public health and social welfare work of the city, as will be shown in subsequent pages of this report, it is recommended that a department of public welfare be created under a commissioner of public welfare appointed by the mayor. In this department there should be the following bureaus, each with a director at its head who should be appointed by the proposed commissioner of public welfare or through civil service:

1. A bureau of health.

2. A bureau of charities—including the City Home, Virginia Hospital and Pine Camp Hospital.

3. A bureau of markets.

4. A bureau of public employment.

The director of the bureau of health should be the present chief health officer, who should have under his supervision the execution of the public health program recommended subsequently in this report.

The bureau of charities should include the City Home, the Virginia Hospital and the Pine Camp Hospital, and should include as a staff agency this corps of city physicians. No director would be required for this bureau as each institution is in charge of a superintendent, who should report directly to the commissioner of public welfare. In other words the commissioner of public welfare would act as director ex officio of the bureau of charities.

The bureau of public markets should be in charge of a director who should assume responsibility for general market operation and the promotion of public market service. This is a new position which should be established.

The bureau of public employment of the proposed department of public welfare should be in charge of a director who should be the present manager of public employment bureau, and the present commission having direction over the present public employment bureau should be abolished. In the event that the scope of this bureau is broadened, as is later suggested, to take over the functions ordinarily performed by a civil service commission, it should not be included as one of the bureaus of the proposed department of public welfare, but should remain, as at present, under the control of the commission appointed by the mayor, in order that it may retain that freedom of action which is required in the exercise of civil service functions.

Outline of Proposed Organization.

On the following page will be found charts showing the present organization of the public welfare functions of the city and also the proposed organization of a department of public welfare.

It will be noted in the latter chart of the proposed organization of public welfare functions that effort has been made to bring together related activities under one control, and to fix responsibility on the fewest possible number of executives. The bureau of public employment, as shown in this chart would, of course, continue as at present, an independent unit of government, if its scope is broadened to include civil service functions, as later suggested.

Health Department

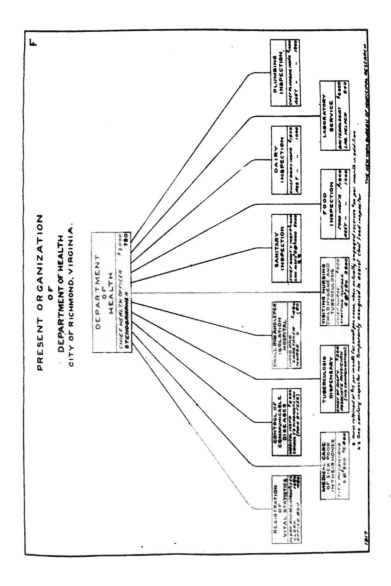

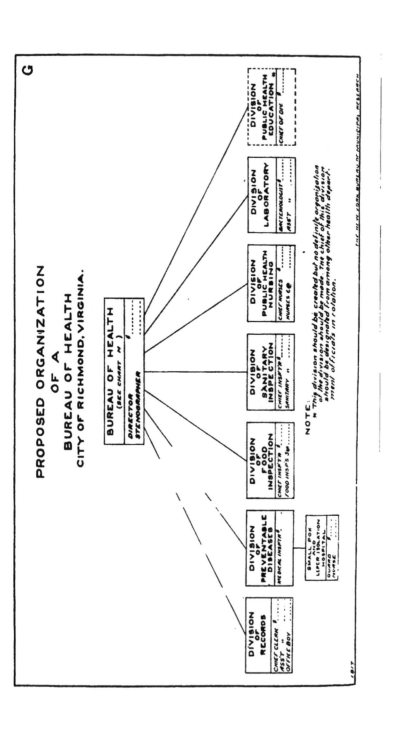

PROPOSED ORGANIZATION
OF A
BUREAU OF HEALTH
CITY OF RICHMOND, VIRGINIA.

G

THE HEALTH DEPARTMENT.

Foreword.

The public health service of the city of Richmond has many excellent features, and it is largely to the credit of the former health officer that the progress along public health lines, during the past ten years has been so marked. Ample opportunity remains, however, for the present health officer to extend existing activities and inaugurate new ones. It is believed that the health officer, provided he is not hampered by private and political interests, can accompilsh fully as much in the next ten years as has been accomplished in the preceding decade. Much remains to be done in further reduction of infant mortality, in the prevention of communicable diseases, chiefly tuberculosis, gonorrhea and syphilis, in the correction of bad housing conditions, in the improvement of the food supply, in the dissemination of public health knowledge through educational publicity and in securing better citizen co-operation.

While the purpose of this report is primarily to criticise those branches of service which are found defective and to suggest measures for improvement, many features of the city's health department work have been found worthy of high commendation and credit has been given where credit is due. Recognition has also been given to the recommendations of the former chief health officer, as found in the annual report of the health department for 1916.

On the whole the personnel of the department is excellent. There is to be found in all branches of service a spirit of co-operation and receptiveness to suggestion which augurs well for the future work of the department. With but few exceptions, it is believed that appointments to health department positions have been made upon merit and with the best interests of the service in view. It is unfortunate, however, that no adequate salary schedules have been adopted, for the lack of opportunity for employees to improve their positions financially through efficient and conscientious work has resulted in the loss of competent employees from the department. A few employees are certainly underpaid, and the remainder though perhaps adequately paid, have no assurance of promotion, even though their increased efficiency may warrant it. This matter will be more thoroughly discussed in another section of this report, relative to standardization of salaries and grades.

In the report which is to follow, it has been impossible within the limits of the space and time available to discuss in detail all features of health department work, but effort has been made to lay stress upon those features of work in which there is believed to be the greatest possibility of increased efficiency and economy. By economy is meant the adoption of methods and means which will at the lowest added initial cost, produce greatest results in improved public health. In recommending extensions of service which involve increased initial cost, it has been kept in mind that the city of Richmond can have only such health service as it is willing to pay for, and that if it contemplates increased and improved health service, it must be prepared to pay the cost. There are, however, certain economies which may be effected in the present service without decreasing the quantity or quality of service rendered.

General Administration.

Inadequacy of Administrative Control.

The health department, in common with many other departments of the city government, is under the control of the administrative board.* Prior to July, 1916, administration of the health department was in the hands of a board of health of five members. three of whom were physicians and two laymen. By charter change the board of health was abolished on the above date. That this change. in so far as the health department was concerned. was a wise one, may reasonably be doubted. It is true that administration of large city departments of health by unpaid boards of health is very often ineffective because of lack of proper selection of the members thereof, conflicts of interests, politics, and other factors. but so far as can be ascertained from the records of performances left by the board of health, the control exercised by this board was more in sympathy with the health program of the city and also more effective in its co-operation with the chief health officer and his associates than is the present administrative board. In short, the only thing that was accomplished so far as the health department is concerned, was the substitution of a lay administra-

---

*For description of the activities of this board. see section on "administrative board."

tive board with many diverse interests for a technical board of health with health interests predominant.

The administrative board has under its supervision a large number of departments and offices of the city government. Supervision of these departments and offices is exercised by the members of the board acting jointly, there being no definite partition of the departments or offices among the various members of the board. In other words, it is impossible for any one member of the board to give to the health department alone, sufficient time and attention to make his supervision effective. The health department is merely one of a number of departments and the amount of time and consideration given to it must necessarily be slight.

To be most effective, any administrative board must be a planning board; it must have such intimate contact with the department or departments under its supervision as will enable it to know what the needs of the department are and how best they may be provided for. The health officer is an executive merely and though he must make plans also they cannot be put into effective operation unless he has the co-operation of an understanding and sympathetic administrative officer.

In attempting to discover the contact which the chief health officer has had with the administrative board, and to estimate the value of the supervision given him by it, no attempt has been made to go beyond the records available for the period of incumbency of the present chief health officer, that is, from May 1, 1917, to the present time, but such records as are available for this period indicate clearly that the present administrative control of the department of health is not satisfactory. In other words, the administrative board has not exercised any function nor furnished any service which could not as well have been provided if the board had not existed. The correspondence shows that contact with the health department has been chiefly by correspondence and this correspondence relates almost wholly to complaints which have been received by the administrative board, and referred to the health officer for his advice, together with other routine communications relative to the financial side of the health department's work, and the appointment of employees.

The chief health officer states that since his appointment on May 1st he has not had a single visit from the administrative board as a whole, nor has he been asked to submit any reports of work performed, and his course of conduct in his new and unfamiliar position has been, therefore, of necessity guided by his own judgment. He states that after one month of service, he submitted a report on his activities for the first month, but was informed that this was unnecessary and need not be continued. It is obvious that if a board is to administer—and this means planning for future work—it must have either personal contact through visits to the department of health and conferences with the chief officer of that department, or it must have periodically complete written reports of work done, and to be done. Without information gained in one of these two ways, it is apparent that the recommendations of the health officer cannot be properly understood and properly dealt with by the administrative board, and this statement is borne out by the records of several instances in which, although the health officer was asked for recommendations as to the appointment and promotion of employees, his recommendations were ignored. It is recommended, therefore, that whatever the type of administrative control that is exercised over the health department, the chief health officer be required periodically to submit complete statements of work performed, work on hand and work proposed, and that the administrative officer or officers make an effort to inform themselves, by personal observation, of the needs of the department. Even if reports are merely pigeonholed, there will at least be some record what has been accomplished and what recommended, and also to what extent the action of the administrative board has been responsible for the success or failure of health work.

In preceding pages of this report a plan is offered for the co-ordination of existing health and welfare work of the city in a department of public welfare under a single commissioner. The adoption of such an organization would result in the removal of the health department from the control of the administrative board. If this is not not done, it is not easy to see how any very satisfactory relation can be established between the chief health officer and an administrative board which, however conscientious and well-intentioned it may be, has neither a proper understanding of public health work nor apparently the time or inclination to inform itself on public health matters.

Present and Proposed Organization of the Health Department.

The present organization of the health department is shown herewith on Chart F. As shown on this chart there are at present under the direction of the chief health officer, eleven major divisions of health service, each reporting directly to the chief health officer.

On chart G an outline of a proposed re-organization of the health department as a bureau of health is shown. The purpose of this re-organization is to center the supervisory authority of the eleven divisions of public health activity in a smaller number of officers and to co-ordinate existing activities now closely related as to function but separate as to supervision. The titles and functions of the proposed divisions are as follows:

1. *A division of records*—to be in charge of a chief clerk (the present registrar). The functions of this division should be the recording, tabulation and analysis of vital statistics, and the co-ordination and supervision of all other record keeping and statistical work of the proposed bureau of health. This division should include, in addition to the present registrar, the present assistant clerk and an office boy.

2. *A division of preventable diseases*—to be in charge of the present medical inspector. The functions of this division should be the control of preventable diseases, except for those functions in the control of preventable diseases that are delegated to visiting nurses. The officer in charge of this division should be made responsible also for the work of the tuberculosis dispensary which now acts independently. Supervision of the work of the Smallpox Hospital and Leper Isolation Hospital should be in charge of the head of this division.

3. *A division of food inspection*—to be in charge of a chief food inspector who should be the present chief dairy inspector. This division should include all functions of supervision of the food supply now exercised by two divisions, namely, the division of dairy inspection and the division of food inspection.

4. *A division of sanitary inspection*—to be in charge of the present chief sanitary inspector. This division should include all functions now performed by the division of sanitary inspection in the investigation of nuisance complaints as well as general supervision of sanitary matters throughout the city.

5. *A division of public health nursing*—to be in charge of the present chief nurse and to have supervision of all functions now performed by visiting nurses in the prevention of infant mortality and the control of tuberculosis.

6. *A division of laboratory*—to be in charge of a bacteriologist. This division should be responsible for all laboratory work of the department as at present.

7. *A division of public health education.* This division is new and is not represented by any existing division or branch of service in the health department. It is proposed to create such a division in charge of a chief, designated from among the present officers of the department if possible, for the purpose of collecting and making available for the information of the public the facts regarding health work in Richmond. No additional appropriation is requested for this purpose at this time, but it is believed that the importance of public health education as a recognized branch of public health work should be recognized by the creation of such a division.

The existing divisions of the city physicians and the division of plumbing inspection are omitted in this proposed organization, these two divisions to be transferred to other city departments as recommended elsewhere.

It is believed that this proposed organization represents a much more effective instrument for public service than the present organization. It centralizes responsibility, co-ordinates related activity and eliminates functions which are not properly public health functions.

The Health Officer; His Duties and Salary.

The present chief health officer is a physician of experience and training in public work and prior to appointment as chief health officer was an officer of the State health department. It is believed that his experience thoroughly qualifies him for his present position and his willingness to co-operate in any movement which makes for better health of the community should assure his success. He receives $3.000 a year, an amount less by $300 than that paid to the former health officer. While it is not the purpose of this section of the report to recommend salary increases, that matter being discussed more fully in another section, it should be pointed out that this salary of $3,000 is entirely inadequate as compensation for all the time of an experienced health officer. That an able health officer held this position for years at $3,000 a year (later $3,300), and that another able physician has been secured at the same rate, is not an argument in favor of such a low salary. The city of Richmond can afford to pay what such service is worth, and it will unquestionably get more as it pays more. Mere figureheads can, of course, be secured for even less money than $3,000, but Richmond needs an able, aggressive, trained man, and it has apparently secured one. The city should, therefore, see to it that he is adequately paid.

Stenographic Service Underpaid.

THe stenographer of the department who acts as secretary to the chief health officer is an unusually competent woman. All of the stenographic work of the department, including the preparation of reports of the various divisions, routine correspondence of all division heads, and the preparation of material for the annual reports is done by this one stenographer and done exceptionally well. She receives a salary of $720 a year which is woefully inadequate and considerably less than that paid secretary-stenographers of other departments. (Salary schedules for stenographers will be found in that section of this report which deals with salary standardization.)

Advisory Public Health Council Recommended.

Whether or not there is a general re-organization of public welfare activities of the city of Richmond along the lines previously suggested, it is believed that the chief health officer should take steps to organize at once an advisory health council. This council should be made up of representatives of all unofficial agencies in the city doing public health and social work, including the visiting nurses' association, the anti-tuberculosis association, mother's clubs, settlement house organizations, associated charitie, etc., together with representatives of the medical societies of the city. This council should meet with the health officer to consult with him regarding local health problems, but it should act in an advisory capacity only. Through consultation with such a council, a thoroughgoing plan of co-operative public health service could be worked out and all private agencies fitted into this program.

The Finances of the Health Department.

For the current year (1917) the following appropriation for the health department was authorized by the appropriation ordinance:

Payroll ....$ 38,850.00
Expenses, prevention of disease, improve-
    ment of milk supply, etc.............. 14,860.00
Special vaccination, expenses, and hospital
    quarantine 1,000.00

Total ....$ 54,710.00

In 1916, the appropriation and expenditures authorized thereby were as follows:

	Appropriation.	Expenditures.	Balance.
Payroll	$ 31,585.00	$ 31,240.84	$ 344.16
Expenses ....)		(12,881.87)	
Sanitary improvement of)		( )	
milk supply ....}	·22,472.45	5,026.79}	1,201.37
Tuberculosis campaign ..)		(3,069.08)	
Educational campaign ...)		(293.34)	
Special vaccination	1,000.00·	456.76	543.24
Smallpox quarantine and			
hospital	1,500.00	1,457.71	42.29
Total	$ 56,557.45	$ 54,426.39	$ 2,131.06

The following reimbursements were made from the health department appropriation:

Unexpended balance ....$ 2,131.06
Food permits 504.00
Sale of 320 pounds of potassium permanga-
    nate 473.45
Sale of remnants of old buggy......... 4.25

Total ....$ 3,112.76

The net cost of health service in 1916 was, therefore, $3,112.76
less than the appropriation of $56,557.45 or $53,444.69. On this
basis the per capita cost for health service in Richmond is only
about 34 cents. If the cost of plumbing inspection service which
is not primarily a health function, is deducted from the net cost,
the per capita for health service is brought down to about 30 cents.
The department should receive a great deal of credit for its ac-
complishments with its present funds.

Arrangement of Offices.

Re-adjustment of Office Space Recommended.

The office of the health department is located in the city hall. There are five principal rooms, one large room being occupied by the health officer and his secretary; one by the clerk of the department, plumbing inspectors, sanitary inspectors, food inspectors and nurses; one by the registrar of vital statistics and the dairy inspectors; one by the bacteriologist and the medical inspector, and one used by the bacteriologist as a laboratory. The large room in which the assistant clerk, the plumbing inspectors, food inspectors, sanitary inspectors and nurses have their desks is reached by a doorway from the main hall. A railed passageway leads to the desk of the assistant clerk, who acts as information clerk. There are other doorways leading from the main hall of the building to the health department offices so that it is very difficult to keep the general public out of the offices.

It is believed that a re-arrangement of these offices is desirable to relieve the crowding of the room for the inspectors and nurses, and to prevent the general public from invading the offices. There is a doorway to the inspectors' room opening directly from the main hall, but this doorway has been permanently closed. It is suggested that the doorway be opened and made the regular entrance to the department. A small space should be fenced off here as a waiting room and the desk of the assistant clerk or information clerk should be at this enclosure. All other entrances to department offices should be permanently closed to the public. This would permit the clerk to see everyone who enters the health department office, find out his business and make the necesary appointments for him, and register the time of arrival of all employees of the department.

The room now used by the registrar of vital statistics and the chief dairy inspector should be turned over to the use of the registrar of vital statistics alone, as this work requires not only concentration but also plenty of room for working. If, as previously suggested, the dairy inspection and food inspection services are combined under the chief dairy inspector, one room for this division should be provided. The room now used by the bacteriologist and the chief medical inspector could well be used for this division, the medical inspector being given desk room in the inspectors' room and the bacteriologist being moved back to the laboratory room. The chief medical inspector is not in his office much of the time and he needs desk room only. The transfer of the plumbing inspection division to the building department would leave ample space in the inspectors' room, so that the visiting nurses and the sanitary inspectors would then have ample space for their desks.

Prevention of Communicable Diseases.

The Medical Inspector and His Duties.

A medical inspector is employed on full time at a salary of $2,000 a year. The present incumbent was appointed at the beginning of the current year to fill the vacancy resulting from the resignation of the former medical inspector to join the medical service of the army. The present medical inspector was appointed by the administrative board, although the chief health officer recommended another applicant.

It would have been a better policy to have permitted the new health officer to select his chief medical officer, as it is largely upon the efficiency of this officer. in preventing communicable diseases that the health officer depends. If a health officer is to be charged with full responsibility for the carrying out of a public health program, his recommendations for the selection of subordinates should be given full weight. If there were an adequate civil service provision, the question would not arise, for employees would be selected upon merit and proof of ability—but lacking civil service, the health officer's recommendations should be accepted unless there is a clear evidence that they are not in accordance with the best interests of the department.

The present medical inspector is a physician who was formerly engaged in general practice in the city. He has had experience both as a former city physician and as a local health officer in the south. In view of his experience, his service should prove satisfactory to the department and to the physicians of the community, and there is every evidence that it is. Without criticism of this officer, however. it is believed that the administrative board would have done well to select a younger man with a reputation to make and who would have been glad to take the work at the salary offered, for the experience to be gained.

The duties of the medical inspector are to receive and record reports of communicable diseases. and to visit such cases for the purpose of confirming the diagnosis of attending physicians, and to see that the rules of the department relative to placarding, isolation and disinfection are properly observed. He is furnished with an automobile for use in visiting cases of disease reported to him.

Division of Preventable Diseases Recommended.

The medical inspector of the department, the medical officers of the tuberculosis dispensary and the custodian of the Smallpox Hospital report to the health officer independently. As all of these agencies are directly concerned with the prevention and control of preventable diseases, it is recommended (see Chart G) that all of these agencies be included in a division of preventable diseases with the medical inspector as chief. It should be his duty to exercise such supervision of the tuberculosis dispensary and Smallpox Hospital as the health officer may direct, and be responsible to the health officer for information and reports relative to their work.

Reporting of Diseases.

All physicians of the city are furnished with boxes containing complete outfits of all forms and blanks for reporting births, deaths and contagious diseases. On the cover of this box is a statement of the regulations of the department relative to such reports. They are required to report within twenty-four hours *after making their diagnosis*, all cases of the following contagious diseases:

> Small pox and varioloid.
> Diphtheria and membranous croup.
> Measles.
> Mumps.
> Chickenpox.
> Whooping cough.
> Infantile diarrhoea (under two years).
> Pulmonary tuberculosis.
> Laryngeal tuberculosis.
> Scarlet fever.
> Typhoid fever.
> Infantile paralysis.
> Pellagra.
> Cholera.
> Yellow fever.
> Malarial fever.

The regulations of the department as to reporting are defective on two main grounds. In the first place the physicians are required to report within twenty-four hours "after making diagnosis." The physician may not make a diagnosis for several days after his first visit, and yet the case may be one of which the health department should be informed of immediately. The present regulation permits physicians to put off reporting indefinitely. The physician may not make a diagnosis at his first visit but he should at least inform the department of the existence of the case if it is one of suspected contagious disease. In all well-devised regulations regarding the reporting of disease, it is the rule to require reporting "within twenty-four hours after first observation of the patient." The present regulation should be corrected to conform with the usual and better practice.

Then too, several preventable diseases have been omitted from the list, namely, opthalmia neonatorum (infective conjunctivitis of the new born), epidemic cerebro-spinal meningitis, epidemic or streptococcus, sore throat, rabies, glanders, tetanus or lockjaw. trachema (infectious disease of eyes), mumps, and several other diseases of varying degrees of importance in Richmond. Venereal diseases also are not included in this list, although within the past few years progressive health authorities have been making efforts to secure registration of these diseases. It is recommended that this list be revised to include at least all diseases which are not too infrequently found in Richmond—and also venereal diseases. The matter of control of venereal disease will be discussed later.

Methods of Investigation and Record Keeping Satisfactory.

The methods of investigating communicable diseases and the manner in which they are recorded and followed up is in accord with the best procedure elsewhere. Efforts are made to secure laboratory specimens in all cases where laboratory tests are helpful in diagnosis, and to encourage physicians to report promptly. Telephone reports are encouraged, but the telephone report is not accepted as a complete report unless the proper card is also sent in. Special report cards are furnished physicians for use in cases of tuberculosis and infantile diarrhoea cases, which are followed up by the visiting nurses in co-operation with the medical inspector. A special record of the investigation of all typhoid fever cases is kept.

Quarantine and Release.

Quarantine is established only for diphtheria, scarlet fever. measles, infantile paralysis and smallpox, and the cases are terminated as follows:

Diphtheria, only after two successive negative cultures.

Scarlet fever, after all discharges and desquamation have ceased.

Measles, twelve days after the beginning of the eruption.

Infantile paralysis, indefinite—upon approval of medical inspector.

Smallpox, after all discharges and desquamation have ceased.

The regulations regarding quarantine are sensible and thoroughly in accord with good pubic health policy. The practice of routine terminal fumigation following contagious diseases has been discontinued, but the department will provide fumigation when it is especially desired by the family. This also is the proper procedure—and follows the recommendation of the former health officer as made in his annual report for 1916.

New Procedure Recommended.

It is suggested that a new procedure be adopted following the termination of cases of these contagious diseases of which one attack usually confers immunity. When such cases have been terminated and the patient is discharged a certificate should be given the patient stating that he has had the particular disease and has been discharged from the surveillance of the department. The patient should be urged to keep this certificate so that it may be available for future reference. Then, if another case of disease occurs later in the same household, the medical inspector will be informed quickly as to the persons whom it is necessary to keep in strict quarantine. A child having once had scarlet fever, for example, would not be required to be kept at home from school.

Exclusion from School.

Children suspected of having contagious diseases are examined by the city physicians who visit the schools daily and are sent home if found to have a contagious disease for which exclusion is necessary. When a case of contagious disease appears in a family in which there are school children, the patient, if a school child, and other children in the family, are excluded from school according to certain specific regulations covering each of the following diseases; Varicella, (chicken pox), diphtheria, German measles, measles, mumps, scarlet fever, smallpox. The rules governing each particular case are well formulated, and physicians and school authorities are kept informed of their responsibility in the matter.

Importance of Reporting Ophthalmia Neonatorum.

As previously noted, this disease of the eyes of the new born is not required to be reported although the medical inspector states that midwives and physicians are advised to report this condition when found. This, however, is not sufficient and it is certain that there are in Richmond many cases of this disease which are not known to the department. It is the experience of every city where the reporting of this disease has been required that there are far more cases than were believed to exist. With the facts of the prevalence of venereal disease known, and with the knowledge that some 1,200 babies are delivered every year in Richmond by ignorant midwives, it would be the most surprising thing in the world if there were not dozens of cases of this disease. Blindness frequently results from the disease if it is not properly treated, and yet, without knowledge of the existence of cases, the health department has no way of insuring that the eyes of babies will be properly treated unless the disease is discovered by a visiting nurse. and even if it is discovered in many cases it cannot be properly treated unless the infant is taken to a hospital.

It is suggested that effort be made to secure the co-operation of the State health authorities in requiring that the physician or midwife attending at birth, state upon the birth certificate whether or not the proper preventive means have been used. Prevention of opthalmia neonatorum can be accomplished only if physicians and midwives make it the rule to instill in the eyes of the new-born infant a few drops of a weak solution of silver nitrate. No baby is too high born to be exempted from this procedure. The requirement of a statement on the birth certificate from physicians and midwives as to whether or not this procedure has been followed, will call their attention to the matter and will probably mean the carrying out of the procedure more generally. That the department of health should require physicians to report the disease, goes without saying.

Reporting and Control of Venereal Diseases Urged.

The reporting of venereal diseases has not yet been attempted although the need for a beginning of preventive work along this line was suggested in the annual report of the health officer for 1916. As pointed out in the report, the prevention and control of these diseases is a very difficult matter. for there is and always will be a tendency on the part of the patient and his physician to conceal the facts. Other cities throughout the country have had success, however, not only in securing reports of the disease from physicians, but also in placing patients under observation and a limited control. It is certain that until health officials regard venereal disease as they regard other communicable diseases no great progress can be made.

There are four fundamental steps in any program for the prevention of venereal disease. These are:

1. The reporting of venereal disease by physicians, aided by laboratory facilities offered by the health department for making Wasserman tests for syphilis. New York City is having considerable success in securing reports by this means.

2. The provision of evening clinics of the pay-clinic type in operation in Brooklyn. N. Y., and Boston, Mass. Under this plan, patients pay a small fee for dispensary consultation and treatment. This eliminates the charity idea from the dispensary and makes the patients feel responsibility in the matter. The clinics are in the evening so that patients are not obliged to leave their work, and so that they may have a certain amount of privacy.

3. An educational program. including lectures, bulletins, exhibits. etc. A good example of educational publicity is that provided in the bureau of health of the city of Rochester, N. Y. Dr. G. W. Goler. the health officer of Rochester, even competes with the quacks by putting his publicity material in public toilets and bar-rooms.

4. The elimination of the quack venereal disease cures and the fake venereal disease specialists.

Any thorough-going program for the prevention of venereal disease should include all of these features, and none of them requires the expenditure of any considerable amount of money.

Typhoid Fever in Richmond.

In 1916 the death rate per 100,000 from typhoid fever was 23.6. the highest death rate from this disease since 1909. There were 37 deaths out of a total of 224 cases. 17 being among whites and 20 among colored people. The death rate per 100,000 among whites was, therefore. 17.1 and among colored 34.8.

Of the total number of cases 48 were known or, from the best evidence, believed to be contracted outside of the city and 176 (known and estimated) cases were contracted in the city. No evidence was available from careful investigation of all of these cases that the milk supply was responsible for the disease, and daily analyses of the city water showed no evidence that it was responsible. The former health officer states in his annual report that neither the studies of the health department nor the investigation of the State department of health revealed the cause of the general increase of typhoid fever in 1916. The probability that the city water was responsible for part, at least, of this increase warranted the health officer in recommending the boiling of drinking water and the further chlorination of the water supply during the period of the outbreak. The State sanitary engineer, according to the health officer's statement, was inclined to believe that a considerable number of cases were contracted in the business sections of the city through special cans of milk which may have become infected from the drivers, but he was unable to bring the responsibility home definitely to any given driver.

It is probable, although there is no direct evidence to support the theory, that much of the typhoid fever existing in Richmond is due to the infection of one individual from the bowel discharge of another. Proper disposal of excreta is a very important factor in the prevention of typhoid fever, and as there are in the city some 3,500 dry closets used by about 17,500 persons, this condition might well be responsible for the extension of the disease. These dry closets are found chiefly in the newly-added portions of the city, which have not as yet been sewered, and although they are well-supervised by the sanitary inspectors, the necessity of adequate sewers for these sections of the city is apparent.

To what extent contamination of food by flies is responsible for the existence of typhoid fever, it is impossible to say, but if conditions at the local markets where flies are swarming and have direct access to food in stalls and in restaurants nearby, is any criterion of conditions elsewhere in the city, the fly is probably responsible for much of the infection.

Then, too, there are approximately 2,500 wells in the city, many of which are unquestionably contaminated, although no systematic effort has been made to eliminate these wells. To mention one example of the use of water that was possibly contaminated: The investigator witnessed a colored woman dipping up water from a small "spring" or pool beside the Brook Road. This "spring" was simply a shallow excavation in the roadside which received surface water from the adjacent hill slope. This condition was reported immediately to the sanitary officer who took the necessary steps to close this source of water supply.

The former health officer called attention, in his annual report of 1916, to the necessity of having a "most thorough survey of the entire water distributing and purification system." This should, of course, be done, so he suggested, by a trained specialist in water collection, purification and distribution. Such a survey should be undertaken without delay, but in the meantime the health authorities should make a thorough survey of all wells, springs and other sources of water supply apart from the city system, and should take prompt and effective steps to remove all possible dangers from the open contamination of food by flies. The necessity of providing sewers for the unsewered portions of the city is apparent.

Mortality In Measles and Whooping Cough High.

With the exception of measles and whooping cough, of which there were very considerable outbreaks in 1916, the records of acute contagious diseases for the past year showed a very satisfactory condition. The death rates from diphtheria (3.2 per 100,000) and scarlet fever (1.3 per 100,000) were low.

The death rate for measles, however, of which there were 6,784 cases reported was 25.5 per 100,000 in 1916. Although, as far as can be determined from the records, everything possible was done to check the spread of the disease through all the forces of the department and the co-operation of private individuals, the disease ran through a six months' epidemic period, from January to July. Measles apparently reveals itself in Richmond in epidemic form at three-year intervals. This cyclic tendency on the part of this disease has been noted in many other cities. The former health officer predicted a measles epidemic in 1916, because of his experience in previous epidemics. The fact that these outbreaks do appear at regular intervals and can be predicted with considerable accuracy, should put physicians on guard, and if they are required to report "within twenty-four hours after first observation" instead "after making diagnosis" improved control should result. The danger period in measles is before the rash appears, that is during the stage of increased secretions of the eyes, nose and throat. If the physician waits until the appearance of the rash before making his diagnosis, he has wasted valuable time and the greater part of the damage has probably been done. It is desirable also that some publicity of the known facts regarding measles should be furnished the general public in preparation for the next probable epidemic in 1919 or 1920.

Whooping cough was a particularly fatal disease in Richmond. Out of 328 cases of whooping cough in 1916, there were 45 deaths, giving a mortality of 29.4 per 100,000 for this disease. The total deaths almost equalled the combined deaths from scarlet fever. measles and diphtheria. Whooping cough is, in Richmond, the most fatal of all diseases of infancy and childhood, and the difficulties of control are obvious because of the very nature of the disease. Here again, however, educational publicity is perhaps one of the most important factors of control, and the efforts of the department should be directed along this line during the coming year.

Within the past year the use of pertussis (whooping cough) vaccine as a preventive of the disease, has been found an exceedingly valuable procedure by Dr. George W. Goler, health officer of Rochester, N. Y.

He found that of children in the infectious disease wards of the Rochester General Hospital, no children came down with whooping cough who had been exposed to it, if they had previously been given three protective inoculations of pertussis vaccine four days apart. As a result of his experience, supported by that of other health workers, Dr. Goler conducted an energetic campaign for whooping cough vaccination by advertisement in the street cars, newspapers, etc., and distributed the vaccine to physicians without cost. All told, about 10,000 children were vaccinated. and it is certain that this work will have a very salutary effect in reducing the incidence of the disease in Rochester.

Infantile Paralysis Well Controlled in 1916.

The prompt and energetic efforts of the health officer and his staff resulted in the suppression of what might have been a serious epidemic of infantile paralysis in 1916. There were twenty cases during the year, and of these but three died. Sixteen of the cases were apparently contracted in Richmond and of these but one died—a white child, no deaths occurring among the six colored patients. Two of the four cases contracted outside of Richmond died. There was, according to the records, no apparent connection between the local cases, and nothing to indicate direct contagion from one individual to another. The department received excellent co-operation from private physicians, from the Richmond Academy of Medicine, and from the State department of health. but, as in other cities, no very definite facts were developed as to the method of infection in the twenty cases. The usual methods of strict quarantine were put into effect, and circular letters addressed to all physicians of the community resulted in the prompt reporting of suspected cases. An emergency appropriation of $2,000 was granted by the city council, and this sum was used by the health officer as he saw fit without interference by the administrative board. The success of the department in combating the disease is sufficient evidence that the money was well spent.

The fact that prompt publicity was given to the known facts, and that physicians were encouraged to report promptly all *suspected* cases, even before actual diagnosis was made, should be a lesson to the department in dealing with other communicable diseases.

Deaths from Malaria Greatly Decreased.

The effectice work of the health department during the past ten years in eliminating mosquito breeding places has borne fruit in the almost complete elimination of malaria and this has meant a reduction of the average death rate from malaria from 23.1 in the period 1904-1907, to 0.8 in the period 1911-1916. As the former health officer points out, this reduction of the apparent death rate is in part at least due to improved methods of diagnosis of malarial fever, many cases of disease having been recorded as malaria or malarial fever in the earlier period without accurate diagnosis. It is a fact, however, that at the present time Richmond is comparatively free from mosquitoes of any kind, both the harmless mosquito and the malaria mosquito, and it is equally certain that this result is due to the daily vigilance of the department in eliminating mosquito breeding places.

Improvement In Housing Conditions Necessary for Control of Disease.

To say that housing conditions are bad in certain sections of Richmond signifies nothing. Every citizen who knows anything at all about Richmond, knows it and it has been told him many times. It avails little to describe the filthy and indecent housing conditions found in certain negro districts of the city. There are rooms occupied by negroes in which the sunlight never enters, and in these same rooms scores of others negroes have probably lived and died; there are houses which are about ready to drop apart and are infested with all manner of vermin; there are houses without ordinarily decent facilities for washing or bathing, and there are houses in which promiscuity of sexual relations among inmates is encouraged by the very manner in which they must live. Hardly a stone's throw down the hill from the Jefferson Hotel is a row of negro houses of the two-story and basement type. The basement is far below the street level so that it is as dark as the tomb and is always damp because of the drainage from the street level. They are dilapidated and broken down and apparently no repairs have been made on them in years. The rooms in these houses rent from 50 cents a week up to $3 a week, so that the total rental received varies from $12 to $16 for each house—a very satisfactory rental for wrecks of this kind.

On Baker Street and on Calhoun Street small shacks or cottages are found in no better condition than those described except that they are all above ground and get some of the sunlight. Along the Shockoe Creek are found other negro "cottages" in indescribably disreputable condition; on William Street, on Duval Street and on St. Peter Street, similar conditions may be seen by anyone interested.

The question is not how bad they are, because they cannot be worse, but what can be done about it? It is useless to talk vaguely about philanthropic plans for building beautiful rows of cottages for negroes—although even that is found to be good business rather than philanthropy by large industrial corporations. The only effective way to put an end to existing conditions is to secure such laws as will enable the health authorities to condemn and destroy buildings unfit for human habitation. This has been done by other cities and can be done by Richmond if only the public has the will to do it. Any talk about putting these hovels in repair is nonsense for the necessary repairs would cost far more than the houses are worth.

It is claimed that many of these houses which are unfit for habitation are owned by residents of Richmond, who are themselves poor, and must have the small rental from the houses. If this is true, special arrangements can be made to meet special conditions. But even if it is true, it is an explanation rather than an excuse. Richmond need not have bad housing conditions if it does not want them, and if Richmond wishes to encourage its colored citizens to remain in Richmond it should at least guarantee them proper living conditions.

The matter of housing conditions thus briefly discussed in the foregoing paragraphs, requires more careful investigation than was possible in the course of this study. It has been given place in this report, however, because of the bearing which it has upon the problem of prevention of disease, and the further reduction of mortality, particularly the mortality among negroes.

Negro Mortality a Serious Problem.

The problem of negro mortality is one that very seriously concerns the city of Richmond. As the former health officer has shown in his report for 1916, the mortality of the colored race is higher than that of whites, both as a whole and from almost every special cause of death. The general death rate of the colored population was 56 per cent. higher than that of the white population, nonresidents included, and 8 per cent. higher, non-residents excluded. The higher mortality among colored people is particularly marked in the case of tuberculosis, lobar pneumonia, broncho pneumonia, syphilis and diarrhoeal diseases.

In the same report recommendation is made that an intensive study should be made of the problem of negro mortality, and that a preventive program based on such a study developed. An intensive study of negro mortality is of course advisable but many of the causes of high negro mortality are not far to seek, nor the reason why negro mortality in Richmond is so much higher than the mortality of whites.. In the first place, Richmond does not guarantee its colored citizens even ordinarily decent housing conditions. This has already been discussed in greater detail. Further, the city of Richmond does not protect its people and particularly its colored people from the exploitation by quack doctors and patent medicine fakers. The negro, because of his ignorance and childlikeness, is an easy prey of such quacks and fakers.

Richmond does not provide proper facilities either for the entrance of colored babies into the world, or for the care of sick colored babies after they get in, nor does it provide as good facilities for the care of the colored adult sick as for the white adult sick. Richmond does not provide adequate means for the diagnosis and treatment of venereal diseases with which all classes and both colors suffer. Richmond provides no public bath for its colored people, although the negroes need baths just as the white folks do. In short, Richmond is doing very little indeed to prevent a high negro mortality. The causes of negro mortality are to a considerable extent the same as for white mortality, but when living conditions are worse for colored than white, when hospital and dispensary facilities are fewer and less satisfactory, when the ignorance of the negro can be prayed upon by quacks and fakers as in Richmond, it is not reasonable to expect that the mortality record of negroes will be satisfactory as that of the whites, even if the negroes were otherwise as well adjusted to modern civilized life as the whites.

Industrial Hygiene Program Recommended.

The importance of industrial hygiene in the public health program cannot be overestimated and this work should be begun by the department of health at the earliest opportunity. Physicians should be asked to co-operate with the department in reporting cases of industrial disease and such cases should be followed up by the physicians, nurses and inspectors of the department with the view of eliminating the causes of such disease among workers. The reporting of such diseases is, of course, the first and most important step, and the following up of cases the next step. Supplementing these two procedures. there should be educational publicity directed especially to employees and employers. Health department placards containing "do's" and "don'ts" for workers should be placed in the establishments where they work and employers should be urged to consult the city dispensaries or the deparement at the first symptoms of disease.

The provision of such preliminary measures would cost very little. The next step, perhaps, would be the development of a clinic for industrial diseases, to be conducted in connection with the dispensary of the medical college. It is not recommended that any special division or staff be created to carry on this work. For the present the medical inspector should be made responsible for working out the program.

Need for Physical Examination of Children Applying for Working Papers.

Children under 14 are not permitted to work without a permit from the court, and children over 14 and under 16 must present to the employer a certificate of age issued by a notary public. In the report on the public employment bureau this matter is further discussed, but it is desired to emphasize here that there is no provision made for the certification by competent authority that the child is physically able to work. To require that such a certificate of health be obtained would require amendment of the law, but the health department should be able to secure the co-operation of the courts to the end that no child under 14 be given a permit until the court has received the approval of the health department

Smallpox Hospital.

Smallpox Hospital Should Be Under Supervision of the Chief of Division of Preventable Diseases.

The Smallpox Hospital and the isolation house for the leper are under the supervision of a superintendent who receives $40 a month and maintenance. The superintendent is allowed also to derive such profit as he may from the twenty acres of land which he has under cultivation. In addition to the superintendent, a nurse is kept on a retainer at $15 a month, and when actually employed at the hospital is paid $50 a month with maintenance. This arrangement would appear to be satisfactory to all concerned.

In the outline of the proposed organization of the health department (Chart G) it is suggested that the chief of the proposed division of preventable diseases be made responsible for the work of the Smallpox Hospital and Leper Isolation Hospital. The object of this is to fix upon the person logically competent for such work the responsibility of seeing that the affairs of this institution are satisfactorily conducted.

Repairs Needed at Smallpox Hospital.

The Smallpox Hospital is a one-story and attic frame building situated on a plot of about 17 acres, belonging to the city, about three miles from the center of the city. It affords accommodations for about twenty persons, in addition to the quarters of the superintendent and his family of which there are four members. At the time visited, there were three bedrooms and a bath-room available for patients, one room containing 3 beds, and 2 rooms containing 6 beds each. Nine patients were in quarantine at the time visited, all of whom were colored. Of the nine, however, only two male adults were actually ill with the disease, the remaining seven, women and children, being regarded merely as suspected cases.

The building is old, having been erected more than ten years ago and is of very flimsy construction. Originally, there were separate buildings for white and colored, the present building being used for white patients only. A still older building on the premises was used for colored patients but this building has disappeared. All cases, therefore, both white and colored, are now cared for in the one building. Fortunately, white patients are rare, but in the event of any considerable increase of cases, both white and colored, it would be necessary for both white and colored to occupy the same rooms.

The bedrooms are large, amply lighted and capable of proper ventilation. The equipment is meagre, consisting merely of small iron cots, badly worn and rusted. Bedding is of the cheaper kind, but so worn and dingy that though fairly clean it presents a very uninviting picture. The bathroom for patients is also a very uninviting place because of its worn and battered equipment. The poor construction and worn condition of the floors of the building make satisfactory cleanliness difficult. The health officer, in his report for 1916 (page 30) called attention to the unsatisfactory conditions at the Smallpox Hospital, and it is desired to emphasize his statements. Much could be done at very slight expense to make the place not only more attractive, but more easily kept clean. The old cots should be painted and repaired where necessary, the bathroom and its equipment improved by the liberal application of soap, water and paint.

Flies in Abundance.

At the time visited flies were in abundance throughout the building. This condition was apparent to the medical inspector who was present and he stated that new screens had been ordered and would be shortly installed. It is recommended also that several large fly traps be installed in and about the building.

Although the superintendent states that he removes all manure daily from the stable, which is located about one hundred yards from the house, it is apparent that the very dilapidated condition of the stable makes real cleanliness impossible. The superintendent houses in this old stable a horse and two mules. The manure from these animals, no matter how promptly removed, leaves behind sufficient material due to the rotting and leaky condition of the stable floor to promote the breeding of flies. This stable, under the rules of the health department, would be prohibited if it were in the city of Richmond and privately owned. There is certainly no warrant for its existence as the property of the health department. It is recommended that the health department apply its own regulations to its own stable at the Smallpox Hospital.

Common Drinking Cups Should Be Abolished.

At the time the hospital was visited, a drinking glass, much soiled, was noticed on top of the refrigerator in the main corridor of the hospital. It is assumed that this is used only by the superintendent and his family. As patients have free access to this corridor, however, there is no assurance that it may not be used by patients also. It is recommended that this possible source of infection be eliminated.

Removal of Smallpox Hospital to the City.

The former health officer in his annual report for 1916, expressed himself as being in favor of removing the Smallpox Hospital to the city. On the side of convenience and in view of the fact that the patients could be given better care, with no more danger to the general public than from other existing conditions, this matter should be given proper consideration. There is a certain advantage, however, in the present location. The majority of patients are ambulatory and because of the wide limits of the farm they are able to roam about and have considerable freedom. This makes their detention in quarantine less irksome and also gives them the benefit of plenty of sunshine and fresh air, both of which are important factors in treatment. It is, therefore, recommended that the hospital be continued in its present location for the present at least; but that it be put into better repair and better provision be made for the separation of the sexes and those of different color.

Extra Nurse Employed As Needed.

Under ordinary circumstances such as existed at the time of visit by the investigator, the patients require little attention and are able to wait upon themselves. In case of emergency the medical inspector is called upon and a nurse provided from the special fund for Smallpox Hospital quarantine.

Care of the Leper.

Little need be said regarding this patient. A small house has been provided him within an enclosure and within these limits he is very comfortably situated. He works his own garden, prepares his own meals and attends to his own wants without difficulty. The health department is to be highly commended for the satisfactory manner in which the patient has been dealt with and for its broad-mindedness in accepting this responsibility. The bill for a national leprosarium has passed both branches of Congress, and no doubt it will be soon possible to have this patient removed to such an institution.

Further Utilization of Farm Possible; Suggestion for Extension of City Farm Program.

At the present time only about 20 acres of the city farm of 167 acres are under cultivation. The soil is poor, but in the opinion of the superintendent much more of it could be utilized for garden truck. The area now under cultivation produces only enough for the superintendent and his family. It is recommended that the State agricultural school be asked to make a soil survey of this property with the view of offering some definite recommendations as to its further utilization. If the land can be put into productive condition without too great expense, and labor supplied by means of prisoners or inmates of the City Home, the city would have a valuable source of income. If the land is suitable, sufficient garden truck could no doubt be raised to supply the majority of its institutions.

The success of the dairy inspection division in guaranteeing proper supervision of commercial dairies suggests the advisability of the city operating its own dairy upon the land available at the farm. The annual cost of milk, buttermilk and cream at the three city institutions, namely, the Virginia Hospital, the Pine Camp and the City Home, aggregates between $7,000 and $8,000. This cost could be very materially reduced and an excellent supply of milk furnished for all institutions by the operation of such a dairy. It is urged that the chief dairy inspector of the department be required to investigate this matter and make a complete report with recommendations relative to the probable cost of herd, dairy barn equipment and labor in connection therewith. Under his supervision the dairy could also be used as a demonstration station, at which experiments in reduction of the cost of production, as well as in the improvement in the quantity and quality of the product, could be made for the benefit of the city and its milk producers.

Considerable thought has already been given by the administrative board to a much broader conception of a city farm program, but as yet no satisfactory solution of the problem has been reached. The present farm is so located that it is of more value for use as building lots than as farm property because of its easy accessibility and because it is in the line of the suburban growth of the city. Furthermore, the present farm is not adequate for a complete development of the city farm idea, either in size or in soil resource. It is believed that the city of Richmond would do well to consider the sale of the present property, and the purchase of a larger tract of unimproved land, even at greater distance from the city. If a tract of 600 or 700 acres of unimproved land could be secured at a distance of from 5 to 10 miles from the center of the city, which when cleared, could be utilized as a farm for male and female prisoners and able-bodied indigents, and also for tuberculosis patients, there can be no doubt that such a farm would be of great advantage in the care of these persons. The work of clearing and cultivating the land could be performed practically without cost to the city, for prisoners and able-bodied indigents could do all the work at less cost for their maintenance than is now required in caring for them in the prisons and other institutions. Furthermore, such work would have a very beneficial effect upon the health and rehabilitation of workers themselves. Enough produce could be raised to provide for all city institutions, and a municipal dairy could be conducted with economy and efficiency. The success of the city of Lynchburg in developing the city farm idea should be an example to other Virginia municipalities.

City Bacteriologist.

Personnel and Duties.

The city bacteriologist is a physician with special training in bacteriological work. He devotes his entire time to the work of the department and receives a salary of $2,000 a year. He had at the time of this survey, a girl assistant or laboratory helper, who has received technical training in the preparation of media, routine preparation and examination of specimens and care of laboratory equipment. She receives a salary of $20 a month, which is by no means adequate compensation for the service which she renders. One of the janitors of the city hall is supposed to assist in keeping the laboratory cleaned and in order, and the office boy, who receives $35 a month renders such assistance as the bacteriologist may require.

At the time of this survey the bacteriologist had accepted an appointment to the medical corps of the army, and no definite arrangement had been made to fill his position. In view of the fact that the present laboratory helper has had adequate training in routine work, it is recommended that the position of bacteriologist be left open temporarily. The present technician is well able to do the greater part of the routine work required, and it is suggested that such supervision as she may require and special examination needed be provided either by one of the assistants of the State bacteriological laboratory, or by one of the staff of the medical college. The salary of the technician should be increased to about $75 a month, and the supervising bacteriologist who may be appointed should receive in the neighborhood of $60 a month.

Such an arrangement, though not as satisfactory as the present plan, is believed by the present bacteriologist to be sufficient. There would be considerable difficulty at this time in securing and retaining a competent bacteriologist owing to the demand for trained men in the military and naval forces of the government, and it would be extremely difficult to secure any bacteriologist not of military age at $2,000 a year for full time service.

Laboratory Arrangement and Equipment.

The bacteriologist now has his desk in the same room with the medical inspector and does much of his technical work there. As previously recommended in the discussion of the general arrangement of departmental offices, the office of the bacteriologist should be moved into the laboratory room so that he may not be disturbed by the medical inspector and the persons who wish to consult him. The medical inspector should be moved to the general room used by inspectors.

The laboratory is quite well equipped except that the lack of a hood to carry off vapor from the sterilizing apparatus makes the laboratory very uncomfortable at times. There is also a home-made apparatus for distilling water which requires too much attention during its operation and is otherwise unsatisfactory for the purpose. This should be replaced by a modern distilling equipment.

A janitor of the city hall is supposed to keep the laboratory clean and in order, but his service is by no means satisfactory. There is constantly an accumulation of laboratory refuse to be seen on and under tables which is, to say the least, unsightly. It is hardly proper to require the bacteriologist or technician to do this janitorial work.

The bacteriologist keeps in his laboratory a stock of drugs used for supplying the tuberculosis dispensary. This is a constant source of annoyance to him and to his assistant, because the laboratory is being invaded several times a day by clerks and others who wish access to this material. It is recommended that this cabinet be placed in the outer office under the supervision of the clerk, and that it be kept locked and under his control.

Routine Laboratory Work.

The bacteriologist performs all routine examinations of specimens sent in by private physicians and furnishes them with the necessary equipment for taking such specimens as may be required. These tests include examination of diphtheria cultures, blood cultures and Widal tests for typhoid, sputum tests, examinations for malarial parasite, etc. The diphtheria culture tests constitute the bulk of his work. In addition he makes tests of water samples which are secured by sanitary inspectors from wells, springs, etc., examinations of city water being made by the water department. Milk samples collected by food and dairy inspectors are examined for bacterial content. The bacteriologist is also required to vaccinate persons applying at the department for vaccination against smallpox and typhoid fever.

In 1916 the bacteriologist examined 4,559 diagnostic specimens as follows:

Diphtheria	2,146
Typhoid fever—	
a—Widal tests	571
b—Diazo tests	12
c—Other tests	316
Tuberculosis (sputum)	863
Malaria	407
Other diagnostic tests	244
Total	4,559

In addition, 132 persons were vaccinated against smallpox and approximately 600 injections of typhoid vaccine were administered. Bacteriological examinations of 2,176 samples of milk and cream were made.

The record of work performed by the bacteriologist is very satisfactory and represents a most excellent service on the part of this division of health service. The methods of record keeping adopted by the bacteriologist are well designed and the records well kept.

Wasserman Tests Should Be Made.

The bacteriologist states that he is prepared to perform Wasserman tests for syphilis, but as yet no effort has been made to secure the co-operation of physicians to this end, or to furnish the service. Unless a competent full time bacteriologist is appointed to take the place of the present one on his retirement (and this is not recommended as immediately necessary) it would not be advisable to begin this work at the health department. It has been suggested later in this report, that a resident physician be appointed at the City Home, and that such a resident physician be one properly qualified for laboratory work. The City Home laboratory could then be fitted up properly for the purpose and Wasserman tests made there, as the making of Wasserman tests on City Home inmates should be routine procedure.

Outfits Furnished Physicians.

Outfits are furnished to physicians for the taking of specimens for diagnostic examination by the bacteriologists, including outfits for taking blood specimens for typhoid and malaria tests and outfits for taking specimens of sputum, and diphtheria antitoxin and culture outfits. All such material is kept in a refrigerator in the laboratory to which the clerk has access. The furnishing of this material to physicians is a very proper procedure and should be continued in order to secure their co-operation in reporting cases.

There are in the city seven stations where physicians may leave specimens for examination by the bacteriologist. These specimens are collected daily by the sanitary inspectors and brought to the department at the close of their day's inspection work in the field. No change in this procedure is suggested.

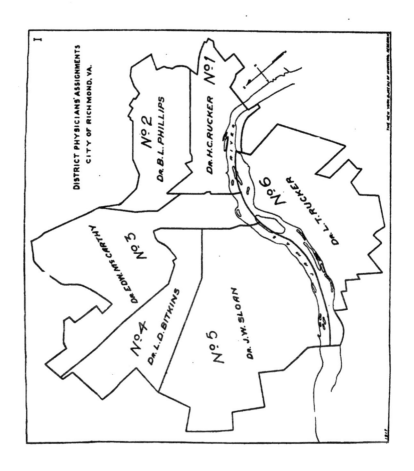

DISTRICT PHYSICIANS' ASSIGNMENTS
CITY OF RICHMOND, VA.

City Physicians.

Duties of City Physicians.

There are at present six city physicians, who receive $75 a month for their services. Each reports directly to the health officer and there is no supervision of their work, except that which the health officer may give through their weekly and monthly reports. The city is divided into six districts, as shown on the accompanying map, and in his district each physician visits and treats such of the sick poor as may summon him and also makes daily visits to the public schools for the purpose of examining children referred to him by the teachers or school nurses as suspected of contagious disease. Each physician his six or seven schools under his supervision and they are required to 'visit these schools "as early as possible" each morning. In addition, the city physician must vaccinate newly registered school children, who do not show evidence of previous satisfactory immunization against smallpox.

One of the city physicians who was interviewed, stated that the school work of the physicians averaged from one and one-half to two hours daily, including the time required in going from school to school. Physicians furnish their own means of transportation.

Summary of Work of City Physicians in 1916.

The following summary shows the work performed by city physicians in 1916, as shown in the annual report of the health department. Under the head of "visits" are included all visits made, both visits to sick patients and visits to public schools.

Summary of Reports of City Physicians (1916)

District Number	Total Visits	Total Patients	Total Deaths	Number Sent to City Home	Number Sent to Virginia Hospital	Number on Hand Dec. 31	Remarks
District 1....	1,564	736	2	35	0	12	
District 2.....	1,181	641	3	10	0	8	
District 3.....	579	173	0	10	15	2	On duty Sept. 10, 1916 to Dec. 31, 1916, only.
District 4.....	700	438	8	28	38	1	
District 5.....	4,416	3,498	15	47	Includes Virginia Hospital also	12	
District 6.....	1,686	900	7	41	0	7	

It is apparent from the foregoing summary that in so far as the number of visits made by city physicians is concerned, the work is very unevenly divided. This may be accounted for in part by the fact that some of those making the fewest visits have a more extensive territory to cover. It may also be due in part to the fact that some of the physicians are more generous with their services than others.

Of the total 10,128 visits made by city physicians the physician in charge of District No. 5 made over forty-three per cent. while the physician of District No. 4 made only 6.9 per cent. The other physicians, except the physician of District No. 3, who was on duty slightly less than four months, made the remainder of visits as follows: District No. 1, fifteen per cent., District No. 2, eleven per cent. and District No. 6, sixteen per cent.

Abuse of City Physician Service.

There is but little doubt that this free service is abused. Any person is privileged to call the city physician who is supposed to determine on his visit whether or not such person is a proper charge on the city. As a matter of fact there is no evidence that any are refused service because they are not proper charges, and even if they are not, it is doubted that the city physician could determine the facts in the matter with a merely casual inspection of home conditions and interview with the patient or members of the family. One of the city physicians who has been longest in service states that it is the practice of many people to call the city physician in emergency when the city ambulances are out, although such patients may have private physicians to whom they have been paying fees. It may be argued that this is justifiable so long as the city has city physicians who are available, but the doing of such work means that the city is undertaking to meet obligations for private citizens which they should themselves meet and pay for.

The almost complete lack of supervision of the work of city physicians and the lack of reports, except the weekly and monthly summaries warrants the belief that the city is giving far too much service along this line. In the city of Springfield, Mass., which is practically the same size as Richmond, only one city physician is employed, and in the City of San Francisco also, which is about three times as large as Richmond, there is but one city physician. Without any more restriction upon the service of city physicians than is now made by the health authorities, it is certain that there is much more work being done free than there is reason for. It is realized that Richmond has a large colored population which demands free medical service, but from the records of the City Home, it would appear that the indigence among colored people is relatively less than that among the white. The large colored population cannot be made the basis of argument for so many city physicians.

City Physicians Should be Transferred from the Health Department.

In the outline of a proposed department of public welfare it is recommended that the city physicians be transferred from the department of health and made a staff agency of the bureau of charities of the proposed department of public welfare. The work of city physicians in the care and treatment of the indigent sick in their homes. is not primarily public health work, although in some respects closely related to it. Public health service should be preventive rather than curative, and for that reason a bureau of charities is proposed which will assume responsibility for those functions of government which have to do with the actual care and treatment of the sick.

If the proposed department of public welfare is established, the city physicians should be responsible to the director of the bureau of charities. As the office of the director of the bureau of charities under the proposed organization plan is not essential to the proposed plan, in view of the fact that each of the three institutions of this bureau has its own superintendent, the city physicians would be under the direct supervision of the commissioner of the department who would act ex officio as the director of the bureau of charities. ·

The school work now done by the city physicians should be transferred wholly to the school medical inspection service of the education department. We can see no reason why the school health inspection work should be divided, and since the department of education already has physicians and nurses who must visit the schools regularly, for the examination and correction of the physical defects of children the transfer of this work to these physicians and nurses will not cause any great additional burden.

In the annual report of the former health officer for 1916 he recommends that the district physicians be relieved of the daily visiting of schools for the recognition and exclusion of cases of contagious diseases, and that in lieu of this twelve physicians be appointed in the health department at $200 a year each. He recommends also that the district physicians be transferred to that department having charge of hospitals. This latter recommendation is exactly what is proposed in transferring city physicians to the bureau of charities of the proposed department of public welfare, but it is believed that the appointment of twelve physicians at $200 each for the school work now done by city physicians would not be as effective as to have all school health work done by the medical department of the board of education. It may well be doubted that twelve physicians of the type desired for this work can be secured for $200 a year each—and further it is an unnecessary expense. If the present medical staff of the department of education cannot assume this responsibility with the present force, its force could be increased adequately for less than the $2.400 which would be required for twelve additional physicians in the health department.

Division of Public Health Nursing.

Organization and Scope of Work.

The division of public health nursing employs six nurses. In addition two nurses are supplied by private organizations, namely, the Federation of Mothers' Clubs and the Zionist Institute. Each of the two nurses supplied by the private organizations is assigned to an infants' milk station under the supervision of the health department. but operated by the organization employing her. Each of the six nurses employed by the department, except the chief nurse, is assigned to a district and performs all public health nursing work required in that district. Such public health nursing includes the visiting of expectant mothers for the purpose of instructing them in prenatal and postnatal care, and the follow-up of all cases of tuberculosis reported to the department for the purpose of instructing the patient and others in the family in the home care of such cases. The nurses are also required to be observant of the general health of all persons in the homes visited, and to report to the department sanitary conditions requiring the intervention of the department.

Personnel and Salary Compensation.

All nurses in the employ of the department are graduate nurses of experience and ability. The chief nurse and four of her assistants are upon the regular payroll of the department, their positions being authorized in the appropriation ordinance, the chief nurse at $900 a year and the four assistants at $780 a year each. The remaining nurse, who serves in the same capacity as other nurses, also receives $780 a year, but is paid from the expense appropriation of the department, no special authorization for this position being stated in the appropriation ordinance. This nurse is a temporary employe for the summer months only. Although there can be no question but that the services of this nurse are needed, the utilization of the expense appropriation of the department for salaries should not be continued. Provision should be made in the appropriation for salaries for such positions as may be required during the summer months; otherwise the appropriation for the health department will not give the information to which citizens are entitled. It can readily be understood that an expense item of appropriation which is not detailed could be used for the employment of a large number of temporary employees, and yet the citizen who pays the bills would have no way of determining the facts without special inquiry.

The compensation of nurses by the health department is inadequate and should be increased in accordance with the schedules set up in that section of this report, which deals with the standardization of salaries and grades.

Colored Nurse Should Be Employed.

The prevention of infant mortality among the colored people requires more intensive work along this line. At the present time each nurse has upon her list about 250 infants who must be visited. It is frequently a month before the nurse can complete her round of visits and even though she makes a special effort to visit the most seriously ill. it is impossible for her to cover the territory as it should be covered. It is believed that an additional nurse would very considerably relieve the situation by permitting a decrease in the size of districts, and therefore the quantity of work required. If an additional nurse is employed it is suggested that she be a colored nurse. It is apparent that the need is greatest among these people and yet the nurse in charge of the district harboring the largest number of colored people, namely, the Jackson Ward, states that it is extremely difficult to secure the necessary co-operation of the colored people. A colored nurse would no doubt secure such co-operation more readily, because of a better understanding of the negro's nature.

Centralization of Nursing Service Suggested.

It is suggested that some consideration be given by the health authorities to the possibility of centralizing the nursing service of the city under one control. At present all private organizations doing nursing work operate independently, each with its own quarters, its own supervisory officers and individual program. There is, of course, great waste in this method of work. If all nursing services of the city could be centralized under the supervision of the health officer, it would be possible to district the city and assign each nurse to a small district in which she could perform all nursing work required. This plan does not contemplate the elimination of private agencies but merely their co-ordination for more effective service. As a first step in the devlopment of such a program, the creation of an advisory public health council as already recommended is necessary.

The plan thus briefly outlined is not by any means a theoretical one, for the Dayton, Ohio, department of health has already been operating on this basis for several years. Private agencies, recognizing the fact that there was duplication and overlapping of nursing service and by reason thereof a greatly increased cost to the city, voluntarily placed their nurses at the disposal of the health department. Quarters were furnished them at the health department, which bears all overhead expense. The salaries of nurses are still paid by their respective organizations. Formerly, there were in Dayton three public health nursing centers, each maintaining its own organization, offices and equipment. Now there is but one center at the health department. With reference to the success of the plan the commissioner of welfare states:

"Instead of three public health nursing centers in the city, there is now one, the city providing rent, heat and janitor service, each organization paying the salaries of its staff, the nurses all supervised by the one superintendent of nurses and all the staff under the direction of the commissioner of health. The city is divided into districts, one nurse serving in each district and doing all types of field nursing. The benefits of the plan are:

"a. Economy of money by cutting out overhead expenses of two officers and reducing control of all public health nursing to one salaried official.

"b. Economy of time. Overlapping of nurse service is wholly eliminated by centering one nurse to cover the entire service in a limited given district, and securing a prompt reporting of calls from one branch of health service to another.

"c. Increased efficiency by centralizing responsibility, co-ordinating three services under a central plan of action, thus securing a single policy and a balanced scheme of development.

"d. Reduction of the size of districts, thus bringing nurses into closer relation with the families.

"e. Deals with the family as a unit with better results in promoting the health of the family.

"f. Meets the demands of business efficiency."

This plan may seem a very radical one, but when it is realized that the citizens of Richmond publicly or privately are supporting all of these various agencies it is in the interest to every citizen to eliminate unnecessary cost and unnecessary overlapping of work. There are sufficient visiting nurses going about through the city of Richmond to do all the work that is required, if their work is co-ordinated. The chief nurse of the health department believes that the health department alone should have three more nurses, and no doubt other agencies think that their forces should be increased. There will, therefore, be an ever-increasing cost of nursing service to the community until some effort is made to bring all nursing work together to one common program.

At the present time several private agencies of the city are co-operating splendidly with the department by furnishing nurses to assist the department, but no concerted effort has yet been made to definitize the problem and program.

Co-operation of Health Department In Community Center Idea.

In his annual report for 1916 the former health officer strongly recommended that the health department co-operate with the community center work now being done by the nurses' settlement of Richmond. This recommendation should be strongly supported by the present health administration, and the recommendation of this report for the creation of an advisory public health council will no doubt be effective if followed as an aid in bringing about such co-operation.

The health officer is now co-operating with the Federation of Mothers' Clubs, and with the Zionist Institute in the operation of two infants' milk stations. A nurse is assigned to each of these stations by the private organization which supports it, and the visiting nurses of the health department are encouraging mothers to take their babies to these stations where they may receive modified milk prepared by the nurses in charge upon physicians' prescriptions. Infant clinics are also being held three days each week and at these clinics volunteer physicians are in attendance to instruct mothers. This is a step in the right direction, and although it is yet too early to estimate the benefit derived from the work already done, it is believed that much good will result.

The present tendency in infant clinic work is not to dispense milk but to utilize the clinics only to give advice and instruction of mothers in the proper care of their babies. The present plan is, however, believed to be advisable under existing conditions. Mothers, particularly colored mothers, whom it is especially desired to reach, will be much more likely to attend the clinics if they are given something besides advice. When once the habit of attending clinics has been established and a feeling of confidence is then engendered, the dispensing of milk may, perhaps, be discontinued.

Eventually it is believed the city should establish, at least during the summer months, clinics in school buildings for the benefit of mothers and prospective mothers. Several centers where the need is greatest should be selected and volunteer service by the physicians of the city should be solicited. The nurses of the health department should receive definite assignments to their clinics in rotation so that all may have an opportunity to assist. The use of school buildings during the summer months is advised for several reasons, chief of which is that the public school should be the starting point for all community center works. The school buildings are empty in summer and there would be no interference with regular school work. Furthermore, it would be much easier to induce parents to go to the public schools than to other places.

Emphasis should be laid at these community centers upon prenatal work, and instruction of mothers in the care of themselves and babies before confinement should be provided. The services of several of the obstetricians of the city might be enlisted for this work.

Training of Pupil Nurses in Public Health Work.

The importance of the public health nursing in the general health program is so evident and the need for efficient, tactful nurses so great that it is believed that all nurses should receive training in public health work. The additional nurses who are needed by the health department, particularly in the summer months, should be pupil nurses from the various training schools of the city. No nurse should be graduated until she has had such experience and it would be a comparatively simple matter for nurses' training schools so to arrange their curricula that pupil nurses could be assigned in rotation to the chief nurse of the health department. It is, therefore, urged that effort be made to put this plan into effect as soon as possible, through co-operation with the hospital training schools.

Control of Tuberculosis.

The fact, as pointed out by the chief health officer in his annual report for 1916, that the colored death rate from tuberculosis was, in 1916, 2.63 times as high as the death rate from this disease among whites indicates the necessity of more intensive work in the prevention and control of the disease, particularly among the colored people.*

The tuberculosis work of the department is carried on by the visiting nurses co-operating with the Tuberculosis Dispensary. The dispensary is located at the Medical College and here, on separate days, both white and colored patients are given advice and treatment by the clinic physicians. The chief physician is paid $300 a year and his assistant serves without compensation. Each visiting nurse spends about two hours a week in attendance at the dispensary.

As reports of cases of tuberculosis are received by the chief nurse, the district nurses are assigned to make an investigation, and if the patient is not under a physician's care they refer the case to the dispensary. If the patients require home nursing and are unable to provide it themselves, the nurses of the Virginia Instructive Nurses' Association visit the patients as indicated by the health department.

---

*There were 277 deaths from pulmonary tuberculosis in 1916, giving a death rate of 176.8 per 1,000. Of these 110 were white (a rate of 110.8 per 100,000), and 167 were colored (a rate of 290.9 per 100,000).

The combination of health department investigation, free dispensary, free treatment by city physicians, free home nursing care and the hospital service at the City Home (for colored patients) and the Pine Camp Hospital (for white patients), is an excellent arrangement. The dispensary is doing effective work at very small cost to the city and the public health nurses are also doing excellent work. Conditions for the care of white patients at Pine Camp Hospital are very satisfactory, and the colored pavilion for tuberculosis patients at the City Home is the most well-conducted branch of the City Home's service.

It is quite evident from the available records that many cases of tuberculosis are not reported to the department. Prompt and complete reporting is of course an essential, but here again as in the case of venereal diseases, both the patient and likewise the attending physician are reluctant about reporting, because of the attitude of the public toward sufferers from tuberculosis. The health department provides examinations of sputum and the services of competent physicians and nurses to assist the physicians of the city in combating the disease. It should, therefore, have their complete co-operation and also that of every citizen.

To sum up the tuberculosis situation, it may be said that the city health department and private agencies are doing excellent work, but in the words of the chief physician of the dispensary "anyone who has observed the home conditions of the average tuberculosis dispensary case wonders what improvement is possible where there is lack of sufficient quantity of suitable food, with poor ventilation, crowded conditions and almost everything else present that militates against a lung condition."

Transfer of Patients from One Nurse to Another Causes Difficulty.

The chief nurse states that one of the present difficulties in the supervision of cases of tuberculosis is due to the transfer of patients from one nurse to another. For example, the patient is first visited by a health department nurse and then, in the event that the patient requires home nursing care he is turned over to a nurse of the Visiting Nurses' Association. Naturally, the patient does not like this, and it is, therefore, sometimes very difficult for the second nurse to secure the necessary co-operation of the patient.

As has already been suggested, this difficulty would be met by the consolidation of nursing service and the districting of the city so that one nurse would do all the work required in that district.

Tuberculosis Dispensary Should Be Open on Saturday.

The work of the Tuberculosis Dispensary is well summarized in the annual report for 1916. Although this service costs the city very little, quarters being furnished by the medical college and only a salary of $300 being allowed the chief physician, the dispensary is rendering very efficient service. The dispensary is open every day except Saturday between 12 and 1. The chief physician attends the dispensary four days a week and his assistant one day each week. The dispensary is not open on Saturday. The character of the work performed is excellent, and the method of record keeping and reporting very satisfactory.

It is believed, however, that the Tuberculosis Dispensary should be kept open on Saturday, as working people are better able to attend the clinic on this day. If it is necessary to increase the salary of the chief physician or to make an allowance to his assistant for this purpose. it is urged that this be done.

Need for Additional Law for Control of Tuberculosis.

Another serious difficulty in controlling tuberculosis in Richmond is the lack of an adequate law which will permit the compulsory removal and isolation of cases of tuberculosis which have become a distinct menace to others. In the State of New York a very effective law, relative to the control of tuberculosis, has been passed. Under this law the health officer may, if he deems it necessary, require a hearing before a magistrate relative to any tubercular case which he believes to be a distinct menace to the health of others in the household. If the magistrate approves the health officer's findings he may commit such person to a hospital for tuberculosis and such person is deemed to be committed until discharged upon the approval of the chief medical officer of the hospital after a period of sixty days during which time the patient shall have obeyed all rules and regulations.

It is recommended that effort be made by the Richmond health department to secure the enactment of such a law.

As a further aid in controlling tuberculosis, it is recommended that following a death from tuberculosis, the health officer shall order the premises properly cleaned and disinfected and be given the power by law of prohibiting further occupancy until all regulations have been complied with. In the event of failure to comply with these regulations within forty-eight house the house should be placarded, and the placard kept in place until the proper procedure has been carried out. To what extent house infection plays a part in the spread of tuberculosis in Richmond it is impossible to say, but it is quite certain that in many of the rooms into which the sunlight never enters house infection is a positive fact.

Further Reduction of Infant Mortality Possible.

It is quite evident from thé records available and from the reports of the department (see report of health department 1916) that there has been a consistent reduction of infant mortality, particularly in the mortality of infants under two years from diarrhoeal diseases, during the last ten years. As pointed out by the health officer, reduction of the infant mortality rate in Richmond is largely a problem of more effectively dealing with infant mortality among the colored people, since the infant death rate among colored people is about twice as high as that among white people.

In view of the fact that infantile diarrhoea, which results in high mortality of infants, is largely due to the infection of one child from the diarrhoeal discharges of another, the visiting nurses have made special effort to impress upon mothers the necessity of proper disinfection of stools and the exclusion of flies from contact with the person or food of their babies. Stress is laid by the nurses in their instructions to mothers upon the importance of breast feeding, and in 1916, of 1,225 babies under supervision, 998 or 81.5 were entirely breast fed. Since 1907, about at the beginning of re-organized health department service, when the death rate from diarrhoeal diseases under two years was 142 per 100,000, there has been, with the exception of 1911, an almost steady decrease of the death rate per 100,000 from infantile diarrhoea, and since 1912 the decrease has been particularly marked, dropping from 100 per 100,000 in 1912 to 65 per 100,000 in 1916. This effective work supplemented as it is during the present year with infant clinics should prove even more effective as time goes on.

Much remains to be done, however, for the further prevention of infant mortality. Suggestions have already been offered relative to the improved control of communicable diseases, the improvement of housing conditions, and the better co-ordination of nursing service. In subsequent pages of this report additional measures, all bearing upon this problem will be suggested, chiefly among which are the improved control of midwives, day nurseries and infants' homes, the further elimination of the fly nuisance, and better hospital facilities for infants.

Control of Midwives Inadequate.

Under the present State law any ignorant white or colored woman may practice midwifery without restraint or supervision. Midwives are required to register with the health department, but neither State law nor local regulation provides that they shall be trained or competent to do the work required. There are 100 such midwives practicing in the city and of these about 90 per cent. are colored, without technical training or any other qualifications except experience. Such experience as they have had may as well be a disqualification as a qualification.

What is needed, of course, in Virginia is an adequate State law, but even lacking the State law the city of Richmond has the right to protect itself against these ignorant and unqualified midwives. The records of the health department show that out of 3,902 infants born in 1916, 1,213 were attended at birth by midwives and 2,689 by physicians, although there are but 100 midwives registered with the health department, as compared with 275 physicians registered. How many unregistered or unlicensed midwives may be practicing is impossible to state, but it is safe to say that there are many. Since the attendant at birth is required to sign the birth certificate, the unregistered midwife obviously would not send in a birth certificate unless she could get some registered midwife to sign it for her. The result would be and probably is that because of this fact there are many unrecorded births, particularly among the colored people.

The health officer should demand that all midwives practicing in Richmond show evidence of their competence to do so, and further than this, he should require that all midwives and their equipment be given frequent and thorough inspection by the visiting nurses of the department. If gone about in the right way, the co-operation of the intelligent and competent midwives could be secured, and it should be possible to arrange courses of instruction for midwives, either at the public schools in the evening or at the health department. It would be too much to hope that even a majority of midwives would attend such courses, but a beginning could be made and a few instructed, and co-operating midwives would accomplish much in securing the co-operation of others.

The midwife is a useful person, but unless she is subject to some regulative control by the health officials she is likely to become a distinct menace to community health. What per cent. of colored infant morbidity may be due to the improper actions of midwives it is hard to say, but undoubtedly much of it may be traced to this souce. If the city of Richmond sincerely wants to decrease the mortality of its colored people, there is no better place to begin than with the entrance of the colored baby upon life.

Need for Infants' Summer Camp.

In the report on the Pine Camp Hospital, it is suggested that a summer baby camp for both white and colored babies be established. This should be emphasized here. Any citizen who is interested in finding out for himself what the conditions are under which small infants are reared, particularly in the colored hovels of the community, need but take a trip through these hovels with the visiting nurse of the health department. He will see, as the investigator said, infants wasting away with diarrhoeal diseases. mere wisps of humanity, starved into semi-consciousness in some cases, tormented by flies and vermin, and dying in spite of the earnest efforts of the health department nurses.

In one colored baby home and day nursery fourteen babies were seen, many of them mere skeletons and all of them badly cared for. Flies were in abundance and the babies that were not suffering with actual disease were exposed to the infection from the bowel discharges of others. The health officer had this particular home under surveillance at the time of this study, and he was putting forth every effort to make it decent. These day nurseries are a necessity because colored mothers must work and their babies must be cared for somewhere while they are at work, but so many of the babies need nursing care by competent nurses that, they should be in special hospitals where such care may be given them.

There are many such day nurseries, and although the health authorities are endeavoring to inspect and supervise them, it is well nigh impossible to give them the supervision they need with the force available. Fortunately, conditions are not as bad as those described in all of the homes, but there is obvious need for more supervision and for the transfer of such infants as are seriously ill to a babies' hospital.

Dairy Inspection.

Personnel, Salaries and Duties.

This division is in charge of a chief dairy inspector, at a salary of $1,800 a year. He has one assistant at $1,000 a year. The duties of the chief inspector are to supervise and be responsible for the production, handling and sale of milk in the city of Richmond. This requires that all dairies shall be regularly scored, that pasteurizing plants shall be inspected, that milk samples shall be taken and analyzed for bacterial content and chemical constituents, and that the retail sale of milk throughout the city shall in all respects conform to the very excellent standards of the health department.

To the work of the chief inspector and his assistant the highest praise is due. The chief inspector is an especially competent man who has developed a splendid degree of co-operation with producers. As a result of this effective work on his part, and on the part of his assistant, it is believed that the system of dairy inspection now in effect and, what is more important, the quality of the milk secured thereby for the citizens of Richmond is second to none in the country.

Chief Dairy Inspector Shoud Be Placed in Charge of All Food Work.

In earlier pages of this report, it is recommended that a division of food inspection be established in the bureau of health of the proposed department of public welfare. In the event that such a re-organization takes place and even if it does not, the present division of dairy inspection and the present division of food inspection shoud be combined under the supervision of the present chief dairy inspector. There is need, as will be shown later, for better organization of the routine food inspection work of the city and the success of the chief dairy inspector in making dairy inspection efficient justifies the belief that he will be able to do as much for the general food inspection work. The lesson which may be learned from this branch of the service, namely that effective supervision of food establishments can be maintained provided there is adequate authority and competent supervision, should be the basis for similar work along other public health lines.

Dairy Permits Should Be Issued Annually.

Dairies are required to secure a permit from the health department. This permit is issued by the health department only after personal investigation of the application by the chief dairy inspector. A fee of two dollars is charged for this permit as in the case of other food permits issued by the health department— the permit being good until revoked. While no criticism is made of the method of issuing permits, it is recommended that these permits be issued for the period of one year only, to be renewed at the end of that period and that the amount of the permit fee be decreased to one dollar. This would not impose a heavy burden upon dealers and yet at the same time it would increase the revenue of the city.

Dairy Inspection Problem and Inspection Methods.

There were at the time of this survey, about 160 dairies supplying milk to Richmond. About 89 per cent. of these are located within a radius of twelve miles from the center of the city, the others being at distances varying from twelve miles to one hundred and ten miles. The problem of transportation is, therefore, not a serious one—as the greater part of the milk is received at the distributing plants in Richmond within about eighteen hours from the time of milking. There are but five small producers selling directly from wagons to consumers, and these dealers handle only about 200 of the 8,500 gallons used by Richmond daily. The greater part of the milk consumed is distributed by two large pasteurizing plants.

Dairies are scored once a month by means of a numerical score card based upon that adopted by the Federal government. The card is well designed and meets Richmond needs satisfactorily. The majority of dairies are scored at least once a month, and more frequently if the bacteria counts of milk samples show unusual contamination. At the present time all dairies under the supervision of the department, have adopted the standard type of dairy barn construction, equipment and methods advocated by the department of health and the results are evidenced by the low bacteria counts. Richmond may justly boast of its dairies and of its dairy inspection service, and it is a pleasure to record that in more than twenty cities visited by the writer, he has not before found such excellent dairy equipment nor higher standards of dairy product.

Rules and Regulations for the Production and Handling of Milk.

The rules and regulations of the health department, as revised by the board of health in 1910, provided in general for supervision of the physical condition and feeding of dairy cattle, sanitary conditions of dairy barns, health and hygiene of milkers and methods of handling milk at the dairies, the cooling and transportation of milk to the market, cleaning of milk receptacles, etc. These regulations declared that milk containing as many as 250,000 bacteria per cubic centimeter on its arrival at the Richmond market, evidenced improper handling of milk and producers of such milk were to be warned of the fact. Milk containing more than 500,000 bacteria per cubic centimeter was declared to be unfit for human consumption and the health officer was directed to exclude such milk from the Richmond market.

In 1913 the milk regulations were revised to require the tuberculin testing of cattle. All producers were required to submit evidence by record of tuberculin tests that his cows were free from tuberculosis. The regulations provided also that after first of May, 1913, no cow or cows should be added to any herd from which milk was being shipped to Richmond, without evidence that such cows were free from tuberculosis.

For the further improvement of the milk supply in 1916, the board of healt adopted rules and regulations for the grading of milk which are still in force. These regulations provided for three grades of milk as follows:

1. *Grade A, Raw Milk*—to be obtained from cows free from disease as determined by the tuberculin test and physical examination of cows by a qualified veterinarian approved by the chief health officer; to be produced and handled by employees free from disease, as determined by medical examination by a qualified physician; to be produced under sanitary conditions such that the bacteria count at time of delivery to the consumer should not exceed 25,000 per cubic centimeter in the cooler months (November 1st to March 31st, inclusive) or 50,000 during the rest of the year. Dairy farms producing this milk were required to score 80 points on the score card of the U. S. Bureau of Animal Industry, and 45 such points must be for "methods."

2. *Grade A. Pasteurized Milk*—to conform in all respects to the requirements of Grade A, Raw Milk: the bacteria count at no time prior to pasteurization to exceed the limits allowed for Grade

A. Raw Milk, and when delivered to the customer not to exceed 5,000 bacteria per cubic centimeter.

3. *Grade B Milk*—to be obtained from cows free from disease as determined by physical examination, of which at least one each year should be, by a qualified veterinarian, approved by the health officer; the milk to be produced and handled under sanitary conditions such that the bacteria count at no time should exceed 250,000 per cubic centimeter; all milk of this class to be pasteurized under the official supervision of the Richmond health department and the bacteria count at time of delivery to the consumer not to exceed 25,000 per cubic centimeter; dairy farms to score at least 70 on the score card of the U. S. Bureau of Animal Industry.

Under these regulations, cream was classified under the same grades as milk, except as to bacteria standards; in 20 per cent. cream the bacteria count in excess of five times the count of the corresponding grade of milk not being allowed. These regulations also provided that all other rules and regulations of the department should be observed and permits issued to producers only on the basis of the grades of milk produced, the permit of any dealer whose product should fall below the requirements of Grade B being revoked. Labeling of the grade of milk on the bottle cap was also ordered, such labeling to be of a specified kind approved by the chief health officer.

Results of Grading Regulations.

The adoption of grading regulations and their enforcement is never an easy task, and it was not easy in Richmond. Considerable criticism was directed against the health officer and a certain amount of opposition still exists among those ignorant of the benefits derived from such regulation—but the producers themselves have come to see the benefit of the regulations and are now co-operating very well indeed with the department through a Producers' Association.

Unquestionably the quality of milk has been improved by this grading regulation, and this is evidenced by the bacteria count which is a fairly accurate index to the methods of producing and handling milk. The establishment of definite scoring standards for the various grades has made it necessary for producers to put their dairies in sanitary condition and to keep them so if they desire to sell milk in Richmond. The consumer knows now from the label just what he is getting and if he wants the very best he can get it. The producer is given an opportunity to get more for his product when he fulfills the highest requirements of the milk regulations.

The improvement of the milk supply is in part at least responsible for the reduction of infant mortality in Richmond, although the improved milk supply is not perhaps the most important factor in such reduction during the last four years. To what extent the general reductions of morbidity and mortality in the past four years may be due to the improvement of the milk supply it is impossible to say but it is certain that it has played an important part.

Records of Dairy Inspection.

The chief dairy inspector made 1,660 visits to dairies in 1916 and scored 165 dairies, making in all 1,430 different scorings of these dairies. The report of the dairy inspector for 1916 shows in detail what was accomplished by his visits to dairies.

All scores are kept on file in the department and are bound in indexed volumes, 250 scores to the volume, the scores being numbered consecutively. Special files are kept for all producers of the various grades, a card for each producer showing the chemical analysis, results of medical examination and tuberculin tests and the bacteria counts of milk. All records are very well kept and it is possible for any citizen to know from these records exactly what the conditions are in the dairy which supplies him with milk.

Purchase of Additional Automobiles for Dairy Inspectors Recommended.

The chief dairy inspector is furnished with an auto for the use of himself and his assistant. A horse and buggy is also provided by the city and the cost of this equipment in 1916 was as follows:

Board of horse ....$ 248.76
Hire of horse 8.25
Repairs to buggy and shoeing horse........   66.80

Total ....$ 323.81

The chief dairy inspector states that another automobile would be more serviceable than the horse and buggy for his work in view of the fact that the roads are passable for automobiles all the year round except possibly for about twenty days during the year. The loss of time in making visits to dairies by horse and buggy is considerable—for an auto can go in fifteen minutes a distance which would require an hour with a horse and buggy. It is recommended, therefore, that an additional automobile be purchased, the yearly cost of the horse and buggy being about equivalent to the cost of purchase of a new automobile.

Food Inspection.

Personnel, Salaries and Duties.

This division is in charge of a food inspector at $1,200 a year. Ordinarily this inspector has one assistant at $1,000, he being the only assistant authorized by the appropriation ordinance. This assistant is an old man whose physical condition makes it impossible for him to perform active duty and the health officer has, therefore, made a temporary transfer of one assistant sanitary inspector at the same salary to the division of food inspection. There are, therefore, at the present time, two inspectors on active duty and one inspector on occasional duty, only because of physical disability. It is urged that some more satisfactory arrangement be made as soon as possible. The infirm inspector should be retired from active duty or if retained should be given minor clerical work at reduced salary.

Originally all food inspection work, including dairy inspection, was under the direction of the chief food inspector, and he states that he is still nominally the head of all work in connection with the supervision of the food supply. As a matter of fact, the dairy inspector and his division work independently and perform all work in connection with the supervision of the milk supply except the taking of milk samples, this being done by the food inspector proper and his assistant.

While there is clearly a division of service between the dairy inspectors and the food inspectors proper, it is recommended that the dairy inspector who has evidenced such a high degree of ability in planning and execution of work in connection with dairy supervision be given the title of chief of the division of food inspection and made responsible for all food inspection work both as to dairies and other food establishments. It is believed that this officer is capable of applying the same efficient management to other lines of food work that has been applied to dairy inspection work.

Scope of the Work of Food Inspection.

Leaving out of consideration the matter of dairy inspection which is elsewhere discussed, the food inspection requires that *outside of the public markets* of the city all persons engaged in the business of selling meat, butter, fish, fruit or vegetables shall secure a permit for such privilege from the health department and that by virtue of the granting of this permit the recipient thereof shall conform to the rules and regulations of the department relative thereto. To enforce this ordinance and to see that such storekeepers obey the regulations of the department, inspection is, of course, required.

It should be noted that the ordinance mentioned specifically states that permits are to be required only from such places *outside of the public markets* of the city as sell or expose for sale *meat, butter, fish, fruit or vegetables*, the places over which the department has complete jurisdiction being thus limited to places handling the five classes of food named. Later in the ordinance, however, we find the statement that before a permit is granted places selling or exposing for sale the above named foods "and other food supplies" shall be inspected and subject to the rules and regulations of the department. The ordinance is, therefore, somewhat confusing, and it is quite evident that if the permit authority is limited to those places selling, meat, butter, fish, fruit and vegetables, a large number of food establishments do not require permit from the department, and yet later inclusion in the ordinance of places selling "other food supplies" would appear to indicate that the intention of the ordinance was to give the health department supervision of all food supplies.

The city attorney ruled in a communication to the department, dated July 28, 1908, that the health department does not have jurisdiction in the matter of supervision of the management of restaurants, eating houses and soda fountains. To anyone familiar with conditions in these establishments, when they are not supervised, it is clear that one of the most important branches of food inspection service must be left unsupervised according to this rule. It is recommended, therefore, that a new ordinance be devised, which will meet actual conditions of need. Such an ordinance should require a permit from all establishments manufacturing, handling, storing, selling or exposing for sale food or drink intended for human consumption. There should be no ambiguity as regards the letter, as well as the spirit of the law.

Issuance of Food Permits.

Permits are issued by the clerk of the department with the approval of the food inspector. A fee of $2 is required for each new permit issued and this permit, though not transferable, is good until revoked. The fee is paid to the city treasurer and the money derived therefrom goes into the general funds of the city. In theory no money is handled by the clerk of the department, but he states that under a ruling of the auditor he is allowed, in order to save annoyance to the payee, to collect the $2, issue the permit and then turn the money over to the auditor, who issues him a receipt therefor. No serious objection can be raised to this practice as the clerk sends with each $2 received a slip on which is stated the number of the permit issued and the name and address of the person to whom issued and receives from the auditor an acknowledgment of the transaction.

Increase of Revenue Possible.

Effort is now being made by the department to round up all dealers who have not secured the necessary permits from the department. In 1916, according to the statement of the annual report for that year, $504 was collected from the issuance of food permits for 252 places. The food inspector states that this amount will be considerably increased during the coming year, there being sixty-one permits issued in the month of June alone—since the beginning of efforts to round up the delinquents.

It is believed that food permits should be issued for a limited period only, and that a fee of at least $1 should be required from each such establishment yearly for the purpose of covering the cost of inspection. Because of the fact that many establishments go out of business without notifying the department, it is impossible to determine exactly how many places there are which require permits or how many permits are still in force. The food inspector states, in his report for the month of June, that he and his assistant visited 1,288 places, and that there are, in addition, about four hundred places which were not inspected during that month. This means approximately 1,600 places which require permits. An annual permit fee of at least $1 would mean a very much increased revenue from this source, without any considerable burden on the dealer.

Records of Inspection: Improved Methods Suggested.

Prior to July, 1917, the records of inspection of food establishments were very unsatisfactory. Inspectors made their records upon small memorandum pads. These records could not be properly filed and used as a control. Since July 1, a new inspection record form has been in use. This new form calls attention to the various points to be observed by the inspector and is made into pads in duplicate. At each inspection the inspector fills out the card with the required data, the copy being given to the proprietor of the place inspected and the original retained by the inspector as the department's record. This card record required that the inspector sum up at the bottom of the card, his opinion of the condition found as "excellent," "good," "fair," or "bad." This is a decided improvement over the previous form of memorandum. At the time this file of records was examined, however, only sixty-four places had been inspected. an insufficient number on which to base conclusions as to conditions throughout the city.

This method of record keeping will eventually permit the adoption of an improved system of supervision of food establishments. As rapidly as is possible. all places operating under a permit from the department should be inspected. At the rate of inspection possible with the existing forces. all places should be scored within a period of two months. The inspection or score cards should then be filed, first according to character of business and then acording to the score as "excellent" or "good," "fair," or "bad." Those in which conditions are "excellent" or "good" should be ignored for the present and emphasis laid first upon those which are "bad." It should be the aim of the inspectors to raise the standard of all such places, so that they may eventually get into the excellent or good groups. In short, the attention of the department should be concentrated where attention is needed. This will mean the gradual reduction of the inspection field.

It should be said here, however, that the classification of food establishments as "excellent." "good," "fair" and "bad" is not the most satisfactory plan. These designations mean only what the individual inspector means. That is to say, what one inspector might deem excellent, another might think only good: what one might index as good, another would classify as fair, etc. A better plan would be the adoption of a numerical score card, based absolutely upon the requirements of the sanitary code, and the rules and regulations of the department.

Certificates of Merit Recommended.

As a further aid in improving the condition of food establishments, it is recommended that a special certificate of merit be granted to each establishment having a standing of "excellent" by the department's rating. This certificate the department should require the merchant to post conspicuously in his establishment. Provided sufficient publicity is given to the matter in the daily papers, consumers would look for these certificates in the establishments where they trade. The result would be that proprietors not receiving the "A" certificate would make an effort to bring their places up to "A" standards, so that they might secure it, the advertising value of such a certificate being very considerable.

Need for Improved Meat Inspection Service.

At present it is certain that fully 75 per cent. of the meat used in Richmond is entirely uninspected at time of slaughter. In the city markets approximately 75 per cent. of all meat sold is domestic meat, which is not inspected in any way. How much of this meat is from diseased cattle, can only be conjectured, but the investigator saw, on visits to slaughter houses throughout the surrounding country, cattle destined for slaughter which bore every physical appearance of disease.

No matter what dealers may say in regard to this matter, tuberculous cattle are unquestionably slaughtered for food purposes in Richmond, and the present force of food inspectors of the health department is powerless to prevent it, since they do not see the animals at slaughter. It is easy enough for the butcher to rid the slaughtered animal of evidence of tuberculosis, and when the meat comes to the dealer's stall all that can be said about it is that it is poor in quality. Without actual evidence of contamination, the food inspectors cannot condemn it as unwholesome.

It is an established fact that human tuberculosis may develop from bovine tubercle bacilli. This is particularly true of tuberculosis of bones and joints and abdominal tuberculosis among children. To what extent tuberculosis in Richmond may be traced to infected meat no one can say, but if we are to be consistent in our program for the control of tuberculosis, we may not ignore this factor in its causation. The first step which should be taken by the Richmond health department is to insist that all meat sold in Richmond shall bear either the stamp of the federal meat inspection service, or the stamp of its own meat inspection service. This means that all meat for sale in Richmond must be inspected at the time of slaughter, and to do this there must be at each slaughter house a veterinarian meat inspector during the slaughtering. There are at present eight slaughter houses supplying meat to the city of Richmond, apart from those which are under federal inspection. To require that a veterinarian food inspector be present in each of these establishments would result in a very considerably increased salary cost to the health department. Some alternative plan should, therefore, be put into effect.

A Municipal Abbatoir Recommended.

As previously stated there are now eight slaughter houses in operation, five in the West End and three in the East End. All of these are under nominal supervision by the health department and in the past year strenuous and fairly effective efforts have been put forth to make these slaughter houses conform to the rules of the department relative to the construction and arrangement of plants and the disposal of waste. Except for two large slaughter houses in the West End, and one in the East End, which are run upon a co-operative plan, none of these five remaining slaughter houses are satisfactory places, although at the time of this study one was undergoing extensive alterations which should make adequate sanitation possible.

There are two alternatives open to the city—either the health authorities must bring about co-operation between slaughter house men, so that all killing may be done in the two good plants and under the eyes of a veterinarian inspector of the health department, or the city must construct a municipal abbatoir, as has been recommended many times by the dairy inspector and the chief food inspector. The latter plan is believed to be the one best adapted for Richmond. A municipal abbatoir can be conducted without any cost to the city, except the initial cost of construction, provided all dealers are required to slaughter in this abbatoir. As a matter of fact, municipal abbatoirs are now being conducted at a profit in several cities in this country—and, prior to the war, in practically all the larger cities of continental Europe.

Another plan which may be suggested is in operation in one large American city. There a meat inspection station is maintained at a convenient point, to which all dealers must bring their slaughtered animals with the organs intact. At this station a veterinarian is on duty throughout the entire day to inspect carcasses on the dealers' wagons, and to stamp such carcasses with the health department's seal of approval. Carcasses which show evidence of diseases are retained or condemned immediately. If retained, they are more carefully examined later and such parts as may properly be used are stamped and turned over to the dealer for sale. A heavy penalty is exacted of dealers having in their possession in markets meat not bearing the stamp of the federal inspection service or of the city health department's veterinarian. This latter plan, though worth considering as a temporary makeshift, should not take precedence over the municipal abbatoir plan.

Sanitary Inspection.

Personnel and Duties.

This division was, at the beginning of this survey, under the supervision of a very competent and experienced chief sanitary inspector at $1,200. Unfortunately for the department of health, since the salary was not satisfactory, and there was apparently no opportunity for increase of salary, this officer terminated his service during the survey, to go into private business. The position of chief sanitary inspector was filled by the promotion of one of the field inspection force, and an additional field inspector was appointed to fill the occupancy caused by his promotion.

The policy of the administrative board in permitting the resignation of this officer, who had devoted many years to effective public service, may be questioned. A slight increase of salary would have insured his continuance in this position, and it is believed such an increase was entirely warranted. It is urged that effort be made to induce the return of this officer to the department at a salary commensurate with the value of the service rendered, the fixing of such salary to be governed by the schedules recommended in that section of this report which deals with salary standardization.

In filling the vacancy made by the promotion of a field inspector to the position of chief inspector, the administrative board again refused to accept the recommendation of the health officer, just as in the case of the appointment of the medical inspector. What the reasons were for the action of the board it is impossible to say, but certainly the health officer should have received more consideration in the matter.

Personnel, Salaries and Duties of Inspectors.

There are, under the direction of the chief sanitary inspector, seven assistant sanitary inspectors at $1,000 a year each, who are assigned as follows: Three to the investigation of complaints only, two to the inspection and supervision of stables and elimination of unsanitary conditions therein, one to the inspection and supervision of dry closets, and one to general utility work, such as special complaint investigation, stable and dry closet inspection.

In addition to this force, the officer formerly assigned to fumigation, has been detailed to this division for such special work as may be required. As all fumigation work now done, (and this is comparatively little, routine fumigation having been discontinued) is performed by all sanitary inspectors, there seems to be no reason for the continuance of this officer at $1,000 a year. In the annual report for 1916, the former health officer in recommending the discontinuance of routine fumigation suggests that the officer formerly detailed to fumigation alone be retained in some other capacity because of his long and devoted service to the department. This suggestion has been followed, but there is no warrant in actual fact for the continuance of this officer in the department. If an additional inspector is needed a younger man should be appointed, but it is not believed that additional inspectors are needed.

Use of Automobiles Recommended.

All sanitary inspectors travel on foot except the chief inspector, who is furnished with an automobile. The inspectors, however, may ride free on the street cars. In the opinion of the chief sanitary inspector, the use of two additional automobiles by the department would permit the elimination of two and probably three inspectors. The cost of purchase and operation of two automobiles would of course be considerably less than the salary cost of two inspectors. All of the routine complaint work of the sanitary inspectors could readily be handled by one man in an auto, instead of three men on foot, at a saving of time and money, and one man in an automobile could do all the work of stable inspection which now requires two men on foot. It is certain that at least one-third of the time of inspectors is spent in going from place to place, and this lost time could be cut to the minimum.

Health Department Should Purchase Uniforms.

The sanitary inspectors are required to furnish their own uniforms—namely, a suit of clothes at about $20, and cap at $2.50. As they wear the same suits summer and winter, this is of course not a considerable item, but for men receiving only $1,000 a year, many of whom have families to support, this requirement is a hardship. It is recommended that the uniforms of these men be purchased by the department—one suit and one cap being provided each year, at a cost not to exceed $20 for the suit and $2.50 for the cap. This would amount to less that $200 a year and would mean a very considerable relief to the men.

Present Method of Assigning Sanitary Officers Should Be Continued.

It has been suggested at various times that the sanitary inspectors be districted and the sanitary inspector of each district required to do all that is necessary in each district. This idea is favored by the chief health officer.

It is not believed, however, that this method of work should be followed in Richmond. There are three chief branches of work at the present time, namely, the inspection and supervision of stables, the inspection and supervision of dry closets and the routine investigation of complaints. Other work of less important ance from a public health point of view includes the inspection of premises, streets, alleys, etc., for minor nuisances. Under the district plan the inspector would be inclined to shirk his duty, as regards the dry closets and stables, because this is work of an unpleasant nature. He would be likely, therefore, to spend the greater part of his time in making routine inspections which, however desirable in improving the appearance of the city, would have little bearing on the health of citizens. It is recommended, therefore, that the present method of assignment be continued.

Too Much Time Spent by Inspectors in Office.

All inspectors, except the three on dry closets and stable work are required to report at 8 A. M. at the department. From that time until 8:30, they are supposed to be in the office writing up their reports, and preparing their schedules of the day's work. Then they go out into the field and at 5 o'clock (Saturdays 1 o'clock) return to the department, bringing in the material from the culture stations which has been left there by physicians for bacteriological examinations. The men on stable and dry closet work, however, go directly to their work in the field, in order that they may save time and report at the department at 11 o'clock, for the notices which they are required to serve. When the men are in the field, they call the department on the phone in the afternoon for special orders regarding complaints which have just come in or other special work assigned by the chief inspector.

Observation of the work of inspection leads to the belief that altogether too much time is spent in the office. It is by no means uncommon to see inspectors at their desks in the office after 9 o'clock. It is, of course, difficult to make and enforce a hard and fast rule that inspectors should be out of the office at 8:30 because more than the usual amount of clerical work may be required on certain days, but it is certain that accurate records of the time of arrival and departure of inspectors would show what needs to be done.

It has been recommended elsewhere in this report, that a rearrangement of offices be made so that the clerk may have his desk near the general entrance to the department. He should be at his desk at 8 o'clock, and should record the arrival and departure of inspectors. As an alternative a time clock might be installed so that it would be possible to determine how much of inspectors' and nurses' time is required in the office and how much in actual field work. These facts being known, one would be better able to determine the exact need as regards office work. It would be far better and more economical to employ one or two extra clerks at small salaries, than to utilize field inspectors for so much routine office work.

Discontinuance of Weed Elimination Work.

Many complaints regarding weeds are received by the department, and recently a considerable amount of valuable time has been spent by inspectors in investigation of these complaints. It is recommended that this work be discontinued because weed elimination is not essential to the public health program. If citizens are annoyed by weeds in neighboring lots they should see that they are cut in any way that suits them. The health department of Richmond, with its limited funds, cannot afford to waste the services of its inspectors in doing anything from which direct health benefit is not derived.

Co-operation of Police and Other City Departments.

Although it is stated that the co-operation of the police and inspectors of other city departments with the health inspectors, is excellent. no definite plan of co-operation has been devised. The sanitary inspectors are required to spend much of their time in making inspections which should be made by the policemen and inspectors of other departments on their regular tours. The former health officer called attention to the need for some plan of formal co-operation in his report for 1916, but no steps have been taken to put his suggestion into effect.

First of all, policemen particularly, and other inspectional forces of the city, should be required to familiarize themselves with the sanitary code and with the rules and regulations of the department. This should be done in the case of the police as part of their regular training—and a complete copy of the sanitary code and the rules and regulations of the department should be furnished each such policeman or inspector. This means, of course, complete revision of the sanitary code and its publication in compact, pocket-size form. The policemen should know his sanitary code as well as he knows his police manual, for it should be his duty to arrest violators of the sanitary code just as it is to arrest violators of the penal code.

To bring about the co-operation of all agencies of the city engaged in inspectional or investigational work, it is suggested that a uniform report form be prepared which may be used by policemen, gas inspectors, firemen, visiting nurses and social workers, etc. The following form is suggested, to be modified as may be required:

Report to Health Department of Conditions Requiring Correction.

Conditions to be noted—Please check mark (⸱) after condition observed.

N	Condition		No.	Condition	
1	Insanitary Stables	......	7	Insanitary handling food	......
2	Alleys	......	8	handling milk	......
3	Premises	......	9	plumbing	. ....
4	Dry Closets	......	10	Mosquito breeding	......
5	Wells	......	11	Etc	......
6	Garbage	.....	12	Etc	......

No.	Location	Owner or Agent	Address Owner or Agent
1	515 Jones Street	J. T. Smith	128 Gray Avenue......................
......	217 Main Street.......	W. B. Brown	217 Main Street.....................
4	17 Williams Street...	F. L. Taylor	423 Avenue B ....
10	84 Grand Street	J. T. Phillips	84 Grand Street ....

Signed...

Date...

In using the foregoing form on which all of the conditions needing correction should be listed and numbered, the policeman or other inspector should check the condition noted below under the heading "No." he should place the number corresponding to the condition found. If, for example, two or more insanitary stables were noted, he should list each. Under "Location" he should give the address of the premises; under "Owner or Agent" the name of such person and under "Address," "Owner" or "Agent" the name of the person responsible. In the event that the condition is corrected by personal action of the police officer or other officer, note should be made on the back of the form to that effect. These forms should be signed by the officer and turned in to the department of health daily, where special assignments of health inspectors or nurses can be made as required.

By special ordinance the police could be given authority to serve notices upon owners or agents. If this is done, there should be space provided on the card for data regarding the serving of such notices.

Summary of Sanitary Inspectors' Work.

The following summary of sanitary inspectors' work is taken from the annual report of 1916. It is reproduced here because of the desire to point out the great amount of work done by sanitary inspectors, which could well be done by the police, as for example inspection of yards, premises, dry closets, stables, etc.

Summons served	284
Cases in court	423
Old plumbing repaired	2,846
Dry closets inspected	6,161
Dry closets cleaned and destroyed	361
Closet boxes ordered in and houses repaired...	1,865
New dry closets ordered	283
Sewer connections ordered	672
Rain conductors, gutters and roofs ordered repaired	217
Visits for plumbing inspector	145
Yards ordered cleaned	3,909
Vacant lots inspected and ordered cleaned....	584
Cellars ordered cleaned and drained	138
Alleys ordered cleaned	380
Old wells inspected—ordered cleaned and repaired	· 69

Old wells condemned and ordered filled 196
Contagious disease cards put up 1,734
Premises inspected 13,266
Premises revisited 28,060
Agents, owners and plumbers visited.......... 6,970
Miscellaneous visits and orders 3,848
City water ordered on premises 1,068
Nuisances abated 1,961
Stables inspected 6,870
Stables ordered repaired and cleaned......... 1,118

Total number of visits.................. 52,144

Stable Control Should Be Improved.

At present the chief difficulty in controlling the maintenance of insanitary stables is due to the lack of adequate regulations of the health department. As suggested by the former health officer in his annual report, the regulations relative to stables, should be completely revised. No stable should be erected hereafter without application made by the individual and approved after inspection of plans and location by the health officer. This should also apply to any alterations and to the use of existing buildings as horse stables. Upon approval of the application and plans therewith attached, a license to operate a stable should be issued and a fee for such license required. The regulations should provide for a uniform type of construction of stables and for uniform methods of handling and storing manure.

The successful experiments of the former chief health officer and the chief sanitary inspector in the construction of manure boxes, which effectively eliminite the fly nuisance incident to improper handling of manure, are a matter of public health history. As yet, however, little use has been made of the experience of these officers. It is suggested that in devising rules and regulations for handling of manure, the knowledge already gained by these officers be availed of, and that it be required that manure boxes be constructed so as to conform to the principles already established as effective in fly elimination.

Public Comfort Stations.

Attention has already been called in this report to the very insanitary toilets of the public market and the former health officer has noted in his annual report for 1916, the need for public comfort stations conveniently located throughout the city. Prior to the passage of prohibition laws the saloon was practically the only place available to men, and this of course was bad from every point of view.

The National Committee of Confederated Supply Associations, which represents a large number of commercial corporations, has created a Public Comfort Station Bureau the purpose of which is to promote the establishment of public comfort stations throughout the country. This bureau has devised plans and specifications for public comfort stations, and in several cities public comfort stations have been built, according to these plans. Such public comfort stations can be operated at no expense to the city, and if properly managed can be made a source of income, by the installation of pay toilets, pay towel service and other concessions. The initial cost of a station of standard construction is about $10,000 and if properly located and built is just as attractive and free from nuisance as the public baths in which Richmond justly takes pride.

Provision of Street Trash Cans.

Even the most casual observer of the conditions of Richmond's streets cannot fail to be impressed with the necessity of providing proper receptacles for paper, fruit skins, and other litter usually thrown upon the street. There should be an ordinance prohibiting the throwing of such material on the street, of course, but unless some place is provided for it, such an ordinance would be difficult of enforcement.

It is suggested that the health department secure the co-operation of private organizations in providing these cans if the city fails to appropriate a sufficient sum for the purpose. In several cities the women's clubs, housewives' leagues, chambers of commerce, etc., have furnished trash cans for street use and have been permitted to advertise the fact by labels on the cans. This, however, is a makeshift, for the city should do it for no other reason than to aid the street cleaning department in its efforts to keep the streets clean.

This is not to be considered as a health measure for there is probably no menace to health involved in the throwing of refuse into the street, but it should be the duty of the health department to preach civic cleanliness as well as personal cleanliness. The need for this work is mentioned in the former health officer's annual report for 1916.

Methods of Record Keeping Satisfactory.

The methods of the sanitary division in recording the complaints and the result of inspectors' investigations are entirely satisfactory and no change in procedure is recommended. Inspectors are required to keep complete records of all work performed and the result of such work and to make periodic reports to the chief sanitary inspector. From the records available it is believed that the present corps of sanitary inspectors is doing as satisfactory work as may be expected. That this is due to the excellent supervision given by the former chief sanitary inspector is certain and it is hoped that the procedure which he followed will be followed also by his successor.

Prevention of Smoke Nuisance.

The former health officer called attention to the need for the passage of a smoke prevention ordinance in his annual report for 1916. Richmond is certainly a smoky city and the prevalence of unnecessary smoke unquestionably has ill effects upon the health of citizens through irritation of the air passages of the body and through the loss of sunlight which the smoke clouds cause. The researches of the Mellon Institute of Pittsburgh have shown that smoke means loss of money and loss of health. It causes more rapid deterioration of buildings, harms vegetation, wastes money for the manufacturer and works against the interests of the business men of the city through making the city unattractive to prospective residents. It has a bad effect upon the physical and mental processes of the individual and is even believed to be a factor in the causation of crimes and misdemeanors. In short it is entirely uneconomic and Richmond should begin a campaign for its elimination.

Removal of Night Soil.

At the present time night soil from closets is removed by the private controllers once a month only, and at night in accordance with the city ordinance and the rules and regulations of the department. In the opinion of the chief sanitary inspector the present procedure is open to several objections. He states that monthly removal is insufficient and that more frequent removal is necessary if privies are to be kept in proper condition. He further states that the removal of this material at night is unsatisfactory because it is not done as carefully as it would be during the day when the scavengers are more likely to be under observation. Both of these objections are believed to be well founded and it is recommended that proper consideration be given to this matter by the health authorities in revising health ordinances and regulations. There is no objection to the removal of night soil in the day time provided the scavengers are required to have tight and properly covered receptacles or wagons,.

Vital Statistics.

Personnel and Duties.

The chief clerk and registrar is in charge of the keeping of all vital statistics. He receives a salary of $1,350 a year, and is assisted in this work by a clerk at $1,080 a year. Both of these clerks have other routine duties to perform in the keeping of the general financial and business records of the department. Their duties in regard to these latter records will be elsewhere detailed.

The statistical work required in connection with the duties of the registrar and the clerk include the receiving, examining, copying and indexing of all reports of births and deaths, the issuance of burial permits, the receiving, checking and filing of reports from cemeteries as to interments, the issuance of certified copies of birth and death certificates, and the compilation and tabulation of all records of births and deaths for monthly and annual reports.

The methods of keeping the vital statistics as adopted by the registrar and his assistant are worthy of high commendation. All reports of births and deaths are carefully examined to see that they are properly filled out. Physicians are required to use the standard international list of the causes of death in making out death certificates, and no certificate is accepted until this requirement is met. Copies of all records are made and sent to the State department of health prior to the tenth of each month.

The deaths of infants under one year are systematically checked against the birth records to ensure that births are being properly reported by physicians, and every effort is made to impress upon physicians the necessity of prompt reporting. Sanitary officers are required to obtain the names of children under one year in the homes which they visit, and nurses also are required to report new births promptly in order that it may be made certain that a birth certificate is made out by the physician or midwife attendant at birth.

Description of Special Records.

Complete card indices are kept of all births and deaths so that reference may be promptly had to the original certificates, the duplicate copies of which are indexed by consecutive number, bound and filed. In addition the clerk has derived a very interesting and valuable index of deaths by numbers and diseases or conditions corresponding to the numbers and diseases or conditions of the international list.

This index is such a valuable one that it is well worth more detailed description. A card 9x4 inches is provided for each disease or condition (a white card being used for white deaths and a buff card for negro deaths). At the top of this card is a number corresponding to the number of the international list. For example. the number 1 refers to typhoid fever of the international list, and so on through the entire list, there being one card for each number for both white and negro deaths. As a death certificate is received, the registrar enters upon the proper card the number of the certificate, and since all certificates are filed by consecutive number. it is very easy by reference to these cards to secure copies of all of the certificates relative to any given condition. For example. if it should be desired to make a special study of the deaths of infants under two years from diarrhoea and enteritis index card No. 104 (104 being the number of this condition on the international list) would give the numbers of the certificates of death in these cases and they could be quickly secured. This record has been described in detail because it is original with the Richmond health department and because it evidences that the value of these death certificates as sources of information for public health benefit is properly appreciated.

It is not necessary in this report to go into further detail as to the method of tabulating reports of births and deaths. The annual report of the health department for 1916 shows the basis for the various tabulations and the kind of information furnished. It should be said. however, that the Richmond health department takes high rank among the cities of the country as regards its vital statistics, and this is due to the fact that there has been inculcated in the present registrar and his assistant by the former health officer a statistical sense and accuracy of method worthy of high praise.

A Division of Records Recommended.

The position of "clerk of the health department" was established June 18, 1906, by ordinance, and the salary of this position was fixed at $900. In May, 1907, the position of "registrar of vital statistics" was established at a salary of $1,200. There has been for some time some confusion in the minds of these two people as to who is the "chief clerk"; as the former health officer delegated the chief clerical functions of the department to the registrar of vital statistics, and the clerk of the department of health, whose position was established by earlier ordinance, became by custom rather an assistant to the registrar. Up to the time of this survey the exact functions of these two officers were not sharply differentiated and indeed could not be. The "clerk of the department of health" acted as an assistant to the registrar of vital statistics, and the "registrar of vital statistics" assumed many of the responsibilities ordinarily devolving upon the "clerk of the department of health." This naturally caused some misunderstanding between the two employees,—the registrar having never actually been given official recognition as the chief of the clerical division of the department. The present health officer has, however, given the registrar of vital statistics such recognition and he is in fact at this time the chief clerk.

It is obvious that the work of keeping vital statistics alone is not sufficient to engage all the time of one employee, and it is equally obvious that there should be some one upon whom full responsibility for the clerical work of the department is definitely fixed in order that there shall be complete and harmonious co-operation. It is recommended, therefore, that a division of records be created in the proposed bureau of health. The present registrar of vital statistics should be designated as chief of this division and made fully responsible for all clerical work, including vital statistics, financial records and records of field work.

Fees Should Be Required for Issuance of Certified Copies of Certificate.

Certified copies of birth and death certificates are issued by the State authorities, but as the certificates are forwarded to the State department only once a month, the registrar states that he is frequently required to issue certified copies of such certificates. In this event no fee is charged, although the State charges a fee of 50 cents for such service. The registrar states that approximately one thousand certified copies of birth and death certificates

are issued by him each year. It is recommended that hereafter a
fee of 50 cents be charged for such service. This would increase
the city's revenue by about $500 annually, and would be no depar-
ture from the practice usually followed in other cities.

Methods of Increasing the Reporting of Births.

The registrar of vital statistics states that he believes from
the records available that approximately 90 per cent. of births are
being reported. This is a commendable record in view of the difficulties of securing proper registration of births, particularly among
the colored people. It is believed, however, that further improvement of this record should be aimed at because the beginning of
all effective health work, particularly among infants, depends upon
the registration of birth with the health department.

The checking of death records of children under one year
against birth records as now done, is an effective means of increasing birth registration, as are also the reports of nurses and
sanitary inspectors regarding the names of children in the houses
which they visit. There are, however, certain additional measures
which have proven effective in other cities. Among these measures may be suggested the examination of the baptismal records of
churches, the publication of birth notices in the daily papers, and
the carrying out of an educational program relative to birth reporting. The more thorough and adequate supervision of midwives as earlier recommended is also an important factor in securing better reporting of births.

As regards the printing of birth notices in the daily papers,
the registrar of vital statistics states that in his opinion this would
not have the desired result, because of the large number of illegitimate births. There would, he thinks, be a tendency on the part
of the parents of illegitimate children to conceal the birth if they
knew that the report of birth would be printed in the paper. There
is, of course, reason in this contention, but it is believed that there
would not be as great objection to the printing of such notices as
might appear. There are many persons whose co-operation is valuable and who would be glad to assist the department in securing
complete registration. The parents of legitimate children who are
in the majority, would certainly assist in furnishing the desired
information to the public, in fact they would probably insist upon
it if the publication of birth notices were made a regular procedure.

Public Health Education.

Division of Public Health Education Recommended.

At present little educational publicity work is being done by the health department, except through the newspapers. The health officer has endeavored to utilize the newspapers as far as possible and he states that they have given him excellent co-operation. The chief difficulty, however, with newspaper publicity, is that the newspapers want "news" and it is very difficult at times to put public health facts in news form, so that the educational rather than the "news" idea will be the more prominent. The newspapers are, of course, excellent mediums of publicity, in that they reach the people whom it is desired to reach, but it is necessary to supplement newspaper publicity with more direct educational publicity methods.

To carry out a proper educational publicity campaign a special division of the health department called a division of public health education should be created. In the plan of the proposed organization of a bureau of health such a division is shown. It is not intended that a chief of this division should be immediately appointed, but rather that through the establishment of such a division even without a chief the need for the work will be officially recognized.

For the present, temporary assignments of the various heads of recognized divisions should be made to this division of public health education and each should be required to outline a program of publicity with reference to his own particular work. There are in the department of health a number of men whose experience and training should enable them to contribute a great deal of material for educational use. For example, the registrar of vital statistics has a great deal of information at hand which could be utilized for educational publicity, either as special articles for newspapers, or for exhibit purposes. In the same way, the chief of the division of dairy inspection has a great deal of material which is of interest and value if properly presented, such as pictures of dairies and maps and charts of dairy field work. The chief nurse has or could readily secure sufficient material for a series of interesting articles on infant welfare work. The division of public health education should, therefore, for the present be merely the clearing house for such material. The acting chief of division so assigned should collect currently the available data and put it in form for the use of the health officer in the daily papers or for exhibit purposes.

Exhibits Should Be Provided from Available Material.

There is, as has been said, a large amount of material which could be utilized as a public health exhibit. The basement corridor of the city hall would be an excellent place for such an exhibit which could be kept there permanently and changed somewhat from time to time to suit the seasons. For example, in summer months an exhibit on infant welfare could be easily prepared. Photographs of infant clinics, pictures of babies "before and after" care at the infant clinics, placards warning of fly dangers and diseases of infants, importance of clean milk and what the department does to keep it clean, samples of approved and disapproved nursing bottes, etc., could readily be secured and arranged in an interesting exhibit. In the fall a typhoid exhibit might be staged with illustrative material showing how typhoid is contracted. how prevented by typhoid inoculation, and the service the department offers in this regard. In the contagious disease period, exhibits on diphtheria, scarlet fever, measles, whooping cough, etc., could be provided. The exhibit is one of the best methods of educational publicity and it has the advantage of being prepared at very small cost. There is hardly a day goes by that a nurse or inspector does not see something that could be made the basis for exhibit material. The collection of such material and its arrangement should be made the duty of the "acting chief" of the division of public health education.

Bulletins, Special Leaflets, Etc.

The cost of getting out a regular health department bulletin and other special leaflets, as need arises, is small, and once the department has demonstrated that it is prepared to handle a public health educational program, demands for an appropriation for this purpose might be more readily allowed. It is believed that the department would do well, however, for the present to carry on only such educational work as is possible without greatly increased appropriation.

A plan which has been found practicable in some cities, is to place in appropriate sections of the city bulletin boards where they may be readily seen by many people and to post on this board notices of special interest or importance. In one large city bulletin boards on iron standards have been set up in certain sections of the city and bulletins are changed daily. For example, during the typhoid months special bulletins on this disease will be posted.

The people have already learned to look for these bulletins and it is believed that good results are obtained from their use.

In another city the health officer has made effective use of card advertisements placed in street cars, the co-operation of the advertising companies having been secured. Cards advising people to find out whether or not their births are recorded, cards suggesting how to secure immunization from typhoid fever or how the individual may find out about his milk supply, are well worth the small cost involved.

The whole trouble with most health departments is that they have never really tried to organize publicity work. So much can be done at very small cost that no health department has done its duty when it has failed to utilize the material already at hand.

Lectures Before Private Organizations.

During the winter months a schedule of lectures or talks on special topics could be arranged by the health officer to be delivered by himself or members of his staff to mothers' clubs, visiting nurse groups, teachers' associations, nurses' associations, civic associations, etc. This would require very little additional work and would be productive of increased co-operation from these agencies.

This idea could be carried still further by co-operation with labor organizations and by arranging a schedule of talks on the health of workers and the prevention of industrial diseases. Labor organizations have always been found willing to further any program of this kind.

Revision of Sanitary Code Necessary.

Chapter 25 of the Richmond City Code, 1910, is supposed to constitute the sanitary code, but many of its provisions are now an absurdity in the light of modern public health knowledge. The most important features of the health laws, namely, the rules and regulations adopted by the former board of health, have not been compiled in proper form so that it is extremely difficult to obtain a complete understanding of what the law requires. It is, therefore, recommended that a complete revision of the sanitary code be made and the rules and regulations of the department incorporated in such a code. It should then be printed in compact pocket size form so that it may be made readily available to all health department employees and to others doing related health work. This would be an excellent work for the officer designated as chief of the proposed bureau of public health education to undertake.

Elimination of Harmful Medical Advertising.

One feature of a public health program which has apparently been ignored or neglected in Richmond is the elimination of medical quacks and fakers, and the co-operation of the newspapers with the health authorities for the exclusion of patent medicine advertising and fake medical advertisements from the daily papers. Quacks, patent medicine fakers and the like exist only because they can advertise. Once the faker's opportunity for displaying his wares is lost, his business is lost. It is particularly upon the negro and the poor white that the bane of these parasites rests most heavily. One big step in the reduction of negro mortality will have been taken when the reputable physicians of the community, the newspapers and the health authorities awake to their responsibility in this matter. One cannot pick up a Richmond paper without being confronted with advertisements of cures for "blood diseases," a veiled term for venereal diseases. Remedies for skin diseases, for kidney disease, for obesity, for tuberculosis and all other maladies to which flesh is heir, find advertising space in the papers. Richmond is no worse than many other cities of the south or north, but it is no better than most. Newspapers can purge themselves of such advertising if they wish, and the city health authorities can, if they wish, carry on an effective campaign against quacks and fakers.

Program Before Appropriation.

To sum up the whole matter of public health education, a program is needed before an appropriation. The results of educational work cannot be ignored and once the department has outlined a program and has carried that program as far forward as is possible without additional appropriation, it will be much easier to convince citizens of the need for spending more money for more educational work.

Plumbing Inspection.

Plumbing Inspectors and Their Duties.

The inspection and supervision of plumbing installations is delegated to a chief plumbing inspector at $1,600 a year who has one assistant at a salary of $1,200 a year. The duties of the chief plumbing inspector and his assistant are to receive, pass upon and approve all applications of plumbers for permits to install plumbing in accordance with the provisions of the plumbing code, and to issue such permits after approval of plans and specifications. They are required to visit and inspect all plumbing installation and upon the completion of such installations to make the necessary tests (usually water test only) of the efficiency of the plumbing installation.

The chief plumbing inspector keeps a card index which gives a complete record of all work in progress and the result of inspections of such work. In addition he keeps a file of all plumbing installation plans for a period of one year after the installation is completed. He has also a register of licensed plumbers which he keeps on a card index so that reference may be had to it to establish the standing of a plumber making application for a permit to do work.* Monthly reports of work performed are made out by the chief plumbing inspector and submitted to the health officer.

The chief plumbing inspector is provided with an automobile which is essential if he is to cover his territory satisfactorily and promptly. His assistant goes on foot or by trolley car when in the field, but spends much of his time in the office answering communications from plumbers and receiving plumbing complaints.

Plumbing Inspection Should Be Transferred to Building Inspection Department.

The chief plumbing inspector and his assistant are doing effective and satisfactory work. All records are properly kept and the reports to the health officer are promptly and satisfactorily made. As pointed out. however. by the former health officer in his annual report for 1916, plumbing inspection is not properly a health function since modern sanitary science has established the fact that the health of the community is in but a very slight degree dependent on the efficiency of plumbing installa-

---

*Plumbers are examined by a plumbers' examining board of which the chief plumbing inspector is chairman. The members of this board receive $50 a year each and meetings are held twice each month. The examination given applicants consists in the making out of a chart showing the floor plans of a building with toilets, baths, sinks, etc., the applicant being required to show on this how the various pipes, attachments. vents, trap, etc., are installed. No fee for examination is required. If there is doubt in the minds of the board as to the applicant's fitness, he is given a special test of shop work in a plumbing establishment.

tions. So far as the public health is concerned, sewer gas may be ignored, however unpleasant it may be to those who have to smell it. The health authorities are concerned of course with the proper removal of human excreta, but the entire machinery of plumbing inspection, licensing of plumbers and the installation of plumbing has been based upon the theory that the health of the community demands the prevention of leaking sewer gas. As a matter of fact sewer gas is not nearly so dangerous *as leaking* illuminating gas and yet we put the responsibility of preventing the leaking illuminating gas largely upon the householder.

In view of the fact, therefore, that plumbing inspection is not a health function it is recommended that this branch of service be transferred entirely to the building inspection department. The only argument which may be raised for keeping plumbing inspection under health department supervision is that as inspectors of the health department it is somewhat easier to enforce plumbing regulations, the courts being generally inclined to be more strict with violators of health regulations. However, this argument is not sufficient to effect the general proposition that the health department should not be called upon to bear the burden of financing work which has no direct relation to preventive health work.

Fees for Plumbing Inspection Recommended.

In view of the fact that the chief benefit of plumbing inspection is derived by the individual householder it is recommended that plumbers be required to pay fees for this service—these fees of course eventually coming out of the pockets of the householders, being included in the plumbers' bills for services. Fees should be based upon the kind of plumbing installation, the number of fixtures and the extent of the job. For example, the plumbing installation of a large building will require perhaps twenty or more inspections by the plumbing inspector before the work is completed, while that of a small house may require but two inspections. In all fairness, the owner of the large building should be required to pay in proportion to the service which he receives. Plumbing inspection should at least be self-supporting and the establishment of small fees for service would easily put this branch of service on a self-supporting basis.

City Chemist

CITY CHEMIST.

Service of City Chemist in 1916.

Prior to the present year (since 1912) a city chemist was appointed by the administrative board at a salary of $2,000 a year. The city chemist was furnished an office in a building owned by the city, for which a rental of $240 a year is now obtained. The report of the city chemist for the year 1916, shows the cost of this department to have been as follows:

Salary of city chemist ....$	2,000.00
Man to collect samples and clean building.	704.25
Fuel	16.60
Gas	31.76
Water	8.00
Electric light	.71
Miscellaneous supplies	74.48
	$ 2,835.80
Including rental value of offices of city chemist ....$	240.00
Total ....$	3,075.80

The city chemist was required to make such tests of materials as might be required by city departments engaged in constructive work; to make chemical tests of milk and cream for the health department and such other tests of foods, drugs, water, etc., as the health department might require and also to make such tests as might be required by the police and fire departments. A summary of the work performed for various city departments during 1916 follows:

Tests of asphalt and asphaltic materials......	38
Tests of cement	5,141*
Tests of coal, gas and steam.................	120
Tests of milk and cream	2,533
Miscellaneous tests including ammoniacal liquor, illuminating gas, well water, whiskey, solder, drugs and other materials	76
Total tests	7,908

*Represents 51,410 barrels.

Proposals for Chemical Laboratory Service in 1917.

At the beginning of the present fiscal year the city chemist having given up that position to accept the office of coroner, the administrative board secured bids from three parties, one a commercial chemical laboratory, one an instructor in chemistry at the Mechanics' Institute, and one the former city chemist now the coroner. Copies of the proposals of these parties which were on file in the office of the administrative board were examined and are briefly summarized as follows:

1—Commercial chemical laboratory—

This concern made two proposals as follows:

    a. To do all work previously done by the city chemist for $975 a year.

    b. Or for $2,000 a year to make all analyses required by city departments and consult with the heads of departments on any subject; to prepare specifications for the purchase of various articles which are or may be subject to chemical analyses or tests, submitting them to the board (administrative board) for approval; to test all milk samples for determining butter-fat total and non-fatty solids which are collected by the inspectors of the health department; to test all cement used by city as well as sand, gravel or broken stone sent by city engineer or administrative board; to make a weekly instead of monthly analysis of gas and steam coal received at gas works, and a sufficient number of samples of coal furnished to the electric plant. This contract to expire March 1, 1918, and not to include testing of steel or iron reinforcing bars used on Shockoe Creek or any steel for structural work or cast iron pipes.

2—Instructor of chemistry in Mechanics' Institute—

This party proposed, for $225 a month, to make the following tests

Cement—25 cars, 200 barrels each, or fraction of cars, a total of 25 series of the usual physical tests per month.

Milks and creams—210 samples per month, butter-fat and solids determinations, and when necessary, examinations for preservatives.

Coals—10 samples per month, proximate analyses for sulphur and B. T. U. determinations.

Miscellaneous samples—10 per month of asphaltic materials, sanitary water examinations, food samples, etc., making the usual required tests.

All samples to be drawn by city authorities and delivered to Mechanics' Institute laboratory and $1.25 per hour to be paid for all sampling work outside of duties described; excess samples of materials named to be paid for as follows:

Cement—$5 per report—car lots or less.

Milks and creams—25 cents per sample, butter-fats and total solids; $1 for preservative examinations.

Coal—$5 per sample.

Miscellaneous—$1 to $2.50 per determination depending on character of samples.

All expenses for apparatus, chemicals and assistance to be paid for by the author of the proposal, except when work is of special character requiring special equipment. In this event apparatus or equipment to be supplied by Mechanics' Institute. Termination of agreement to be on twelve months' notice except by mutual consent.

3—Former city chemist (present coroner)—

This person made two proposals as follows:

a. Administrative board to furnish apparatus and appliances, materials, rooms, water, gas, heat, current and janitor service, the author of the proposal to examine such samples as the board sends to laboratory at the following schedule of prices:

Cement—$25 per 1,000 barrels, including tagging of bags.

Milk and cream—10 cents per sample.

Gas and steam coal—$2.50 per sample.

Asphalt and asphaltic materials—$5 per sample.

Solder—$2.50 per sample.

Whiskey—$1 per sample.

Illuminating gas—$1 per sample.

Ammonical liquor—$1 per sample.

Drugs and poisons—$2.50 per sample.

b. The administrative board to sell to the author of the proposal the outfit of the chemical laboratory as per inventory at $1,200 and the author to pay rental of $240 a year for the building. All samples sent by the board to be examined at the following schedule of prices:

Cement—$27.50 per 1,000 barrels.
Milk and cream—12 1-2 cents per sample.
Gas and steam coal—$3 per sample.
Asphalt and asphaltic materials—$6 per sample.
Solder—$3 per sample.
Whiskey—$1.50 per sample.
Illuminating gas—$1.50 per sample.
Ammoniacal liquor—$2 per sample.
Drugs and poisons—$5 per sample.

Present Contract Most Advantageous.

After scrutiny of these proposals the administrative board very properly accepted the proposal of the commercial laboratory (1) as being the most satisfactory. It will be readily seen that the proposal of the instructor in chemistry at Mechanics's Institute (2) would have meant at the lowest figure $2,700 a year with additional cost for examinations not specifically stated or more examinations than were specified. The proposal of the former city chemist (3) would have meant in the case of proposal 3-a on the basis of work performed by him in 1916, about $1,800 for tests alone. In addition, the city would have had to pay all the expenses of the laboratory which amounted approximately to $800 a year. The total cost including the rental value of the offices, $240 a year, would have been practically what it paid for the service under the salaried city chemist. Proposal 3-b of the former city chemist would have been no more satisfactory.

Under the present arrangement the city secures excellent service at low cost. The commercial laboratory is well equipped and is able and willing to render even more service than has been given in the past by city chemists. The agreement was entered into by the city with the commercial laboratory on May 15, 1912, and the agreement expires March 1, 1918. The city secures, therefore, only nine and one-half months of service on this agreement, but the additional service offered by the commercial laboratory more than compensates. In addition, the offices formerly occupied by the city chemist are rented at $240 a year. It is believed that the present arrangement should be continued as long as possible.

Public Markets and City Weighmaster

PUBLIC MARKETS AND CITY WEIGHMASTER.

Public Markets Not Properly Administered.

As will be shown in succeeding pages, the public markets are not efficiently administered, supervised or inspected. Even the most casual investigation of market conditions would demonstrate this fact to the satisfaction of any citizen. Conversation with a member of the administrative board regarding the condition of markets indicated to the investigator that this member of the board at least was aware of the unsatisfactory conditions existing. If this is the case, one wonders why nothing has been done about it by the board which is responsible for the operation of markets. Furthermore, conditions in the market indicate neglect of duty and incompetence on the part of the health department inspector and of the clerks of the markets.

Bureau of Markets Should Be Established as Bureau of Proposed Department of Public Welfare.

The inclusion of the public markets as a separate bureau of markets in the proposed department of public welfare has already been suggested. It is recommended that in the event that such re-organization takes place a director of markets be appointed at a salary of approximately $1,800 a year, who may be made completely responsible for the operation of these markets. The development of an adequate marketing system, the encouragement of producers to deal directly with consumers and the prompt and proper remedying of insanitary conditions of markets are all very important factors in the promotion of public welfare and particularly important at this time. That such problems can be satisfactorily handled under the present irresponsible and haphazard system is doubtful.

Duties of Market Clerk and Assistants.

There are two public markets each under the general supervision of a clerk, responsible directly to the administrative board. These clerks receive $900 each. In addition to the clerks, a force of sweepers is attached to each market, three sweepers in the case of the first market and two in the case of the second market. These sweepers are paid $2.15 per day, seven days of the week, because of the late market hours on Saturday night.

The market hours of the first market are from daybreak until twelve noon, five days of the week and on Saturday until ten or eleven P. M.; the hours of the second market are from daybreak until two P. M., five days of the week, and until ten or eleven P. M. on Saturdays.

At each market the clerk is charged with the leasing of stalls subject to the approval of the lease by the administrative board. He also is required to render all bills for rental on the first of each month and to follow up collections from delinquent stall holders. In addition, he issues tickets and collects sanitary fees or taxes from dealers occupying street market space. It is also the duty of the clerk to see that the market is kept in a cleanly and sanitary condition and each clerk is given police authority with badge in order that he may enforce order in the market.

Clerk of First Market Should Have Office in the Market.

The clerk of the first market has his office in the scale house with the city weighmaster. This small frame building is situated at the north end of the market about two hundred feet from the market building. It is believed that it would be more conducive to proper supervision of the market by the clerk if office room could be provided for him in the market building. One reason perhaps why the market is not properly supervised, is because there is every inducement for him to retire to the scale house to while away the hours. The farther removed the clerk is from his job, the less likelihood of proper conditions in the market.

Method of Leasing Stalls.

Persons desiring to rent market space are requested to make written application on a special form, specifying the number of the stall and the market, together with the amount of annual rental payable in monthly installments. If this application is approved by the administrative board, a lease is given by the board and signed by the chairman of the board and the dealer, one copy of the lease being given the dealer, and one copy retained by the board. This lease or "articles of agreement," as it is called, binds the lessee to the rental of a specified stall in the market at an annual rental payable in monthly installments, the amount of annual rental and the amount of installments being stated. It specifies also that rentals shall be due and payable without demand on or before the tenth day of each current month in default of which a penalty of 10 per cent. of the monthly rental will be demanded.

The lease further requires that the lessee shall leave the stall "in good repair, ordinary wear and tear excepted." Recently there has been added to the "articles of agreement" a typewritten slip which is pasted upon the lease, setting forth the following additional terms:

"Further that the party of the first part leases unto the party of the second part Stall No. ...... in the First Market from the first day of ...., 1917, for a term of ...., on the following conditions. the acceptance of this lease by the party of the second part being an acceptance by him of all the conditions:

(1) That the party of the second part shall keep clean, by washing and sweeping, the stall, the windows on the interior of the stall, also the floors on the interior of the stall.

(2) That the party of the second part and all his employees shall wear at all times during market hours a coat of some white material, the said coat to be kept clean and sanitary.

Failure as to any of the foregoing conditions shall act as an immediate revocation of the lease of said stall by the Administrative Board."

As will be shown later, little attempt has been made to enforce the term of the lease, as regards anything except the monthly rental.

Stalls Should Be Auctioned to Highest Bidders.

Certain stalls, by reason of their location, command higher rentals than others, but in the majority of cases the amount of rental has apparently been determined largely by precedent. It is believed that a more satisfactory plan would be to auction stalls to the highest bidders in order that all dealers may have equal opportunity of securing the most advantageous locations. This policy should be adopted as soon as present leases are terminated.

Collection of Rentals.

On the first of each month the clerk makes out a bill for each stall rented. this bill being presented to the proprietor thereof. On or before the tenth of the same month the stall holder is required to go to the city treasurer's office to pay this sum. If he fails to do this on or before the tenth of the month. the treasurer adds to the bill an amount equal to one-tenth of the monthly rental. It is the duty of the clerk of the market to encourage prompt payment and he is furnished with a statement of those who are in arrears in order that he may warn them of their delinqueicy. The clerk does not collect any of the rents.

The Sanitary Tax.

A tax, called the "sanitary tax," of ten cents a day, is made upon those who have stands or wagons in the market area, but outside of the market buildings. Tickets serially numbered and bearing numbered spaces corresponding to the days of the weeks are furnished the clerk by the auditor. These tickets are sold for ten cents to the persons desiring to occupy market space on the date which is punched on the card. Each month the clerk must turn over to the city treasurer an amount sufficient to account for the number of tickets used.

Capacity of First Market.

The first market comprises two modern brick and concrete market buildings well built and well designed for market purposes. One of these buildings is used as a meat market almost exclusively and contains fifty-four stalls, varying in price from $10 to $14 per month, and two stores at $50 and $52.50 a month, respectively. The distribution of stalls and stores according to rental is as follows:

```
26 stalls at $10.00 a month.
13 stalls at  11.00 a month.
10 stalls at  12.00 a month.
 5 stalls at  14.00 a month.
 1 store  at  50.00 a month.
 1 store  at  52.50 a month.
```

On this basis the total possible revenue from the rental of stalls and stores is $8,346. At the time visited all of the stalls and stores above listed were occupied and the report of the clerk of the market for 1916 shows that these stalls were occupied practically all of the time during the year.

The other market building is used as a vegetable, live poultry and fish market. This market contains twenty* vegetable stalls, and five fish stalls distributed as to rental as follows:

```
4 vegetable stalls at $ 9.00 a month.
8 vegetable stalls at  10.00 a month.
8 vegetable stalls at  12.00 a month.
1    fish    stall  at  10.00 a month.
2    fish    stalls at  12.00 a month.
2    fish    stalls at  14.00 a month.
```

On this basis the total possible annual income from stalls in this market building is $3,288. All stalls in this market were occupied at the time of inspection and were so occupied in 1916 according to the clerk's report.

Inspection of First Market.

The first market was visited in the afternoon after market hours (July 19th) when, as the clerk said, it had been "cleaned up" for the day. On this visit the investigator was accompanied by the chief sanitary inspector of the health department in order that there might be no difference of statement or opinion as to the conditions found. The market was generally in filthy condition. In the meat market in which there are fifty-four stalls, every stall was inspected and not a single one found which would pass inspection. All were indescribably dirty. The porcelain-topped counters were dirty and decaying filth was found in crevices of the top; utensils such as meat grinders, knives, saws, etc., were also unclean and in some instances had not been washed at all. Meat blocks were not scraped clean and scrubbed, and in crevices of the wood fly pupae were found. Clothing used by the stall holders was found hanging on hooks or merely thrown in a heap on the floor and in a disgustingly dirty condition. On the floors behind the counters were found scraps of meat, bones, boxes, bags, barrels and refuse of every description, unprotected in many instances from the flies with which the market swarmed. In several instances evidences of rats were noted, and in one stall two large rats were seen.

The responsibility for this wretched use of an excellent market building lies partly upon the administrative board, partly upon the clerk of the market, and partly upon the food inspector of the health department, who visits the market several times each week. No matter whose the responsibility, conditions should be corrected immediately and the terms of the lease enforced. As previously stated the lessee binds himself

1—To keep clean, by washing and sweeping, the stall windows and floors of the interior of the stall.

2— To wear a coat of some white material, the said coat to be kept clean and sanitary.

---

*These twenty stalls are double stalls and the capacity of the market building is ordinarily said to be forty stalls. Each stall holder, however, occupies a double stall.

The lease further states that failure as to any of these conditions shall act as an immediate revocation of the license and yet there was not a single stall holder of the meat market who would not have had his license revoked had these rules been enforced.

In the vegetable and fish market conditions were somewhat better because of the fact that the majority of articles sold in this market can be handled in a more cleanly manner, but even here the insanitary methods of handling food products and the refuse therefrom needs immediate attention.

Unprotected Refuse Pile Should Be Eliminated.

The refuse from the market is simply dumped into the middle of the street at one end of the market. It is not protected from flies in any way and naturally flies swarm upon the refuse pile and about the market. Within thirty feet of this refuse pile are two quick lunch restaurants, and across the street about fifty feet away is a bakery. The contact of flies with food is thus readily established and since the role of the fly as a carrier of disease is already established, it is not too much to conclude that this refuse pile is a distinct menace to health, since the refuse is removed by the street cleaning department but once or twice a day.

A refuse storage room was built at the end of the market where the refuse pile is now located, but the clerk of the market stated that owing to the difficulty of loading the refuse from this room, the room was not used. A refuse box was also devised but this also proved unsatisfactory. The most satisfactory way of handling this refuse would be to place it directly into a wagon which could be properly covered and drawn away when necessary, another wagon being left in its place. This would require an extra wagon of course. Another alternative would be to have a sufficient number of garbage cans which could be kept covered. The disposal of refuse at this market is by no means a difficult problem and some such plan as has been suggested should be immediately adopted.

Toilets Should Be Improved.

The connection between filth, flies, food and disease has already been suggested in the description of the method of handling refuse. There is, however, a still more serious menace in the toilets of the market. At one end of the market is a toilet for colored persons used by the public and the stall occupants. This the clerk of the market keeps locked because, as he said, it is abused when left unlocked. This toilet contains two bowls, one urinal, and two wash bowls. The bowls must be flushed by the user and because of neglect of the users to do so, the bowls are frequently left filled with excreta. As there is nothing but a wide mesh screen through which flies find ready ingress and egress,—thus again the contact of flies with filth and food is established. No toilet paper was supplied in this toilet room, except old pieces of newspaper, the use of which made it well nigh impossible to flush the bowls properly. Although there are two washbasins in the room supplied with running cold water, no hot water being supplied, the handles of the faucets were broken off, so that it was practically impossible to use them. Nor was there soap, nor anything upon which the user might dry his hands- provided he did manage to wash them. There is naturally then no inducement for users of the toilet to wash their hands, and as many of those who use it go back to the market to handle foods, a distinct danger to citizens results. The proper disposal of excreta and proper cleanliness of food handlers is impossible under conditions existing in this market.

The toilet for whites at the other end of the building was found in somewhat better condition. The toilet has practically the same equipment as the one for colored people, but like the other, it is not supplied with toilet paper or soap and towels for cleansing the hands. This toilet had, however, the advantage of having automatic flush closets so that the flushing of the closet is not dependent upon the carefulness of the individual.

These toilets should, of course, be put into proper condition for use immediately, they should be properly screened, toilet paper, soap and paper towels should be supplied; water faucets should be put in condition for use, and automatic flush closets should be installed in the colored toilet. It should then be made the duty of the clerk of the market to see that these toilets are kept clean and in proper condition. If they were visited frequently by this officer he could prevent any serious abuse of equipment. Signs posted in the toilets warning users about the dangers to themselves and others from improper use of toilets or improper cleansing of their hands would perhaps help. People can be educated in a few principles of common decency, if an effort is made to do so.

Capacity of Second Market.

The second market comprises two buildings, one of which is used exclusively for market purposes. The other building being an armory, is used as a market only on the ground floor. This latter building, because not built for market purposes, is not well adapted for this service. As a matter of fact, only a small part of this armory building is now in use as a market. The first building is used exclusively for market purposes and so long as the city has this propery it must be used as a market building.

In the market building proper, which is used exclusively as a meat market, there are twenty stalls which rent for $15 each per month. The total possible income to be derived from this building in the way of rental of stalls is $3,600 a year. At the time visited, all of these stalls were occupied, and the report of the clerk shows that practically all of these stalls were occupied in 1916.

In the armory building there are sixty-five vegetable and fruit stalls, which are rented at various prices as follows:

```
 1 at $ 4.00 per month.
 1 at $ 4.50 per month.
12 at $ 5.00 per month.
 1 at $ 5.50 per month.
10 at $ 6.00 per month.
 1 at $ 6.50 per month.
 6 at $ 7.50 per month.
 5 at $ 8.00 per month.
 1 at $ 8.50 per month.
 6 at $ 9.00 per month.
 8 at $10.00 per month.
 3 at $11.00 per month.
 2 at $12.00 per month.
 3 at $12.50 per month.
 4 at $13.00 per month.
 1 at $14.00 per month.
──
65......Total.
```

The total possible annual revenue to be derived from these stalls is, therefore, $6.342. At the time visited, however, only twenty-three stalls in this market were being used as follows:

1 at $ 4.00 per month.
1 at $ 5.00 per month.
1 at $ 6.00 per month.
1 at $,7.50 per month.
2 at $ 8.00 per month.
5 at $ 9.00 per month.
2 at $10.00 per month.
2 at $11.00 per month.
1 at $12.00 per month.
2 at $12.50 per month.
4 at $13.00 per month
1 at $14.00 per month.
—

23......Total.

On this basis the total possible annual income is $2,742. The city is, therefore, receiving only a little more than one-third of what it should from these stalls. The report of the clerk for 1916 indicates that this same condition existed last year.

As the armory building is not well adapted for its present use, it is believed that the use of this building for market purposes should be discontinued as soon as present leases expire. This would make it possible to dispense with the services of one sweeper and to reduce the cost of maintenance of the market very considerably. Such stalls as may be vacant in the market building proper, should be made available for the use of as many as possible of those persons who are now occupying market stalls in the armory building. To put this armory building in proper condition for market use would require a greater outlay of money than the city is justified in spending in view of the small return from it.

Inspection of Second Market.

In company with the chief food inspector the second market was inspected by the investigator while the market was in operation. This market, though less well constructed for market purposes than the first market, was found in slightly better condition but practically the same condition of uncleanliness described as found at the first market exists at the second market. The floors of stalls are not kept clean, refuse is allowed to collect on the floors under the counters, no protection of food against flies is provided, and the market swarms with flies. The general appearance of the entire market is not wholesome, and there is quite evidently lack of proper inspectional supervision.

Toilets in Bad Condition at the Second Market.

In the armory building a toilet has been constructed above the floor level, which is reached by a stairway leading up from the market floor. One toilet is provided for white males and one for white and colored females, the latter toilet being divided for the separation of the races. The toilet for white males was found in bad condition, because of the carelessness of users and lack of proper attention by the clerk of the market. The toilet for females was, however, found in fairly good condition, but in neither of these two toilets was there soap or paper towels for the proper cleansing of the hands, although there were wash basins and running cold water.

The most filthy condition imaginable was found in a toilet used by colored males only. This toilet is a small brick outhouse at the northern end of the armory. The door of this was locked when visited, the key being in possession of the clerk, who had apparently not seen the inside of the toilet for some time, as he expressed surprise at the condition found. The walls, floors and ceiling of this place beggar description. Urinals had overflowed all over the floor, so that the floor was soggy and reeking with urine. The closets, which consisted merely of a trough with several seats, were filled with fecal matter, although there is an automatic flushing device connected. The floor beneath the trough, as well as the seats themselves, were covered with excreta of human beings and rats. There were no facilities whatever for washing the hands. Ventilation was negative and it was impossible to stay in the place without nausea. When it is realized that the users of this toilet are the negro occupants of market space, the menace of food contamination is at once apparent.

The recommendation made for the improvement of conditions of toilets at the first market hold good as regards the second market also. Toilets should be kept clean and properly ventilated. They should be properly screened from flies; closets should be provided with automatic flushing devices; toilet paper, soap and paper towels should be provided, and signs posted warning against abuse of toilets and the necessity of personal cleanliness. The toilet now used by male negroes at the second market should either be put in first class condition or destroyed. It would probably be better to destroy it completely and construct a better one at some point where it could be more carefully supervised.

Disposal of Refuse at Second Market.

The same condition as regards the disposal of refuse exists at the second market as at the first market. Refuse is simply collected by the sweepers in carts and dumped on the ground in a vacant lot at the north end of the armory building, whence it is removed two or three times a day by the garbage collectors. At the time of inspection one of the fish dealers in a store adjacent to the market building had dumped a pile of decaying fish on the ground in this vacant lot and naturally the flies were in swarms. It is useless to talk about the elimination of the fly nuisance while such shipshod and slovenly methods are continued. The same procedure as recommended at the first market should be followed here. A wagon which could be properly covered should be left standing in this vacant lot and refuse placed directly in this wagon. When filled it should be drawn away and another wagon left in its place.

Hot Water and Refrigerating Plants Should Be Installed in Both Markets.

One of the difficulties in securing proper cleanliness in market buildings is lack of hot water and it is almost impossible to keep counters and implements clean without it.* There should be also better facilities for refrigeration. At present the stall holders who need to keep their products on ice have small ice boxes behind their counters. These are, in the majority of instances, mere ice chests with a lid on top and without compartments for the separation of meats and butter, etc. Many of these ice chests were leaky and in a very insanitary condition, because difficult to clean. It is urged that a refrigerating system be installed in place of the refrigerating ice boxes. In any event until this can be done, a standard type of ice box should be required, which will permit the separation of perishable and easily contaminated commodities, such as butter from meats, fish, etc., and which may be easily cleaned and inspected.

Correction of Insanitary Conditions of Markets Should Be Health Department's First Step.

Correction of the conditions mentioned means, first of all, enforcement of the terms of lease. Furthermore, health department inspection should be more rigid. In discussing the food inspection

---

*It is understood that the administrative board has already determined upon the installation of hot water service.

service of the health department in this report, it was stated that health inspection should be ecentered in those establishments most needing inspection. It would be far better for the food inspectors to give their time to inspection of markets only until the present unsatisfactory conditions are improved than to spend their time in making casual inspections of the hundreds of other places throughout the city where their control is less easily enforced.

General Suggestions for Improving Conditions of Stalls.

Under food regulations of the department, stalls in public markets are exempted from the requirement of a permit to conduct a food establishment. This permit costs $2 and the granting of it implies an inspection by the health officer prior to the issuance of a permit. It is urged that food establishments in the public market be required also to secure a permit from the health department and that the issuance and continuation in force of this permit be conditional upon the maintenance of proper sanitary conditions. Aside from the fact that the granting of such permit would increase the city's revenue very considerably, it would give the health department much better control of the market food stalls.

The display of food stuffs, particularly meat, upon the counters of the stalls, without protective coverings of any kind should be prohibited by regulation. A uniform style of glass case, open only at the rear, should be provided so that food which may otherwise be contaminated by the fingers of customers and by flies, may be protected.

Stall holders should not be permitted to keep food products on the floor. This makes it difficult to clean the stalls properly and besides promotes waste of food products. The stall holders should be required to keep all articles on benches eight inches to one foot above the floor so that proper inspection may be made and the floors thoroughly cleaned.

The floors of the markets, being of concrete, are covered by some of the stall holders with sawdust, and others have put down wooden platforms. It would be preferable to have simple wooden platforms or gratings put down and so arranged that they could be removed readily at night or at the conclusion of the market period. The gratings should be raised and the hose turned underneath the counters and about the floor of the stalls.

When once the floors of the stalls have been cleaned of accumulated debris and filth, any rat holes will be evident and these should be tightly closed with concrete.

General cleanliness of counters, utensils and clothing should, of course, be rigidly enforced. Once the habit of cleanliness has been formed, it will not be difficult to require its continuance.

Some of the above recommendations require additional expenditure, but all are needed. If it costs more to put these stalls in proper condition and to maintain them in proper condition, the increased cost should be borne by the dealers themselves. If the dealers are willing to put in the necessary fixtures according to the specifications established by the city authorities, they should be allowed to do so. If not, the city should install the fixtures and should increase the rentals because of the improved service offered.

Finances of Public Markets.

The appropriation for the maintenance of the public markets for 1917 is as follows:

Salaries—

First Market.

Weighmaster ....$	900.00*
One clerk	900.00
Three sweepers at $2.15 per day..........	2,347.50

Second Market.

One clerk	900.00
Two sweepers at $2.15 per day..........	1,565.00
	6,612.50
Expenses and repairs	3,000.00
Total appropriation ....$	9,612.50

The markets are not only self-sustaining, but produce an annual net revenue of about $11,000. The reports of the market clerks for 1916 as to receipts and disbursements follow:

---

*See paragraph on weighmaster, who is paid out of appropriations for first market.

First Market.

Receipts.

Rental of stalls	$11,613.50
Sanitary tax	1,622.80
Scale house receipts	195.59*
Cash from premium on stall.	5.00
Total receipts	$13,436.89

Disbursements.

Payroll:

Weighmaster	$ 900.00	
Clerk	900.00	
Sweepers and cleaners	2,172.00	
		$ 3,972.00

Expenses:

Water	$ 354.85	
Electricity	280.90	
Disinfectant	6.25	
Fly-killer	215.42**	
Repairs to doors, screens, etc.	173.10	
Brooms, toilet supplies, etc..	56.85	
Printing and binding	38.04	
Incidentals	21.79	
Emergencies	15.00	
		1,874.70
Total disbursements		$ 5,346.70
Net income		$ 8,090.12

The following report of the clerk of the second market for 1916 shows that the second market is also a profit-making institution. It will be noted that the financial statement of the clerk

---

*Fees for weighing loads of material collected by weighmaster. See paragraphs on weighmaster.

**It is interesting to note that there was spent in the first market $215.42 for "fly-killer." This is evidence that the fly elimination problem was attacked from the wrong end, i. e., by fly killing instead of the elimination of fly breeding and fly feeding places.

of the second market is not uniform with or in as great detail as
that of the clerk of the first market.

Second Market.

Rents.

Butcher market ....$	3,348.00	
Vegetables	2,758.90	
Sanitary day tax	1,659.10	
		$ -7,766.00

Disbursements.

Light and water ....$	735.66	
Repairs	336.75	
Expenses	149.50	
Supplies	99.55	
Payroll	2,071.30	
		$ 3,392.76

Net income .... $ 4,373.24

It is evident from the foregoing that the city is receiving a
net income of approximately $11,000 annually from the two mar-
kets. It can, therefore, well afford, if the present public markets
are continued, to put them in proper condition, and to eliminate
the certain menaces to public health which exist by the installation
of more adequate equipment and the appointment of a superintendent of markets or director of a bureau of markets as has already been suggested.

Methods of Record Keeping Unsatisfactory.

The condition of the records of the clerk of the first market
makes it impossible for one to determine what he is doing or how.
He keeps one large record book in which he notes the number of
stalls, the amount of rental and the status of the stall holder as
regards payment. This record book is also used as a diary of
weather conditions day by day, the date of appearance of certain
products on the market, and any other facts which the clerk may
think important. The book is also used as a repository for papers of all kinds—bills, newspaper clippings, copies of leases, miscellaneous memoranda, etc. It was impossible for the clerk to find
statements requested by the investigator until after a search of
about fifteen minutes. The desk of the clerk is littered with papers

and trash of all kinds. Slovenly methods of record keeping usually indicate, as in this case, slovenly methods of work.

The keeping of a diary of daily events at the market is a good thing if properly done, but the information now kept is worthless, except, as the clerk says, "to settle arguments" about past weather conditions, and similar matters. If the diary gave complete information about the daily business of the market, the complaints of citizens, disturbances which may have occurred, orders issued by the clerk, etc., it would be of considerable value.

Under any circumstances the clerk should be required to keep all records, books and papers in proper order so that the administrative officer or officers charged with the responsibility of market operation would, if they desired, be able to get some definite information as to what happens besides a mere annual statement of receipts and disbursements.

At the second market the condition of records is somewhat better. Here the clerk keeps only a record book showing the number of stalls rented, to whom rented, and the monthly condition as to payment of rental. It is suggested that a diary of transactions be kept by this officer also along the line suggested for the clerk of the first market. A uniform system of record keeping should be installed in both markets and sufficient supervision given to see that they are kept properly and uniformly.

Bad Condition of Market Streets.

The streets about the public markets are in very bad condition. Where they are asphalted. the asphalt is full of holes in which water and debris collect, and where paved with stone block they are full of irregularities so that proper cleaning of the market area is extremely difficult, if not well nigh impossible. If there is any place in the city which should be kept clean, not only as to the plant, but also its environs, it is the public market, and to keep environs clean there should be a better cleaning of the surface of streets.

As an aid in keeping the market area cleaner, it is recommended that proper receptacles for refuse be installed in the markets and at the curbs, and that dealers be requested to use these instead of being allowed to throw the refuse on the ground whence it must be swept up and carried away in carts.

The City Weighmaster.

The city weighmaster has his office at the first market in a small building used jointly by the weighmaster and the clerk of the market. The weighmaster receives a salary of $900 a year, his salary and the expenses of maintenance of his office being provided in the appropriation for the first market and included in the financial report of the clerk of the first market.

The city weighmaster receives fees for weighing as follows:

Ten cents per ton for iron, coal, stone and materials of like nature.

Fifteen cents per ton for hay, grain and produce.

These fees are paid directly to the weighmaster at time of weighing. The weighmaster has a large book containing weighing receipts serially numbered. These receipts are made out in duplicate, one copy going to the person weighing the goods, the other being retained in the book as the permanent record. The weighmaster states that he places all fees received in the bank to his personal credit and at the end of the month makes out a statement of the number of tons weighed and the receipts therefrom which is forwarded with his personal check for the proper amount to the auditor.

The above procedure of recording and issuing receipts for weighing and for accounting for such receipts is open to criticism. The amount of cash handled is, of course, small and there is not the slightest indication that any irregularity exists, but the possibility of irregularity certainly does exist and should be eliminated. It is recommended that all receipts be made out in triplicate—one copy to be retained by the weighmaster, one copy to go to the person weighing, and one copy of each receipt to be sent to the proper authority each month together with the amount of the monthly receipts. These receipts should be made in triplicate by the use of a carbon paper, so that there will be certainty of their agreement, instead of each being written by the weighmaster as at present.

The propriety of the weighmaster placing receipts in the bank to his own credit may well be questioned, but the receipts of the weighmaster are so small ($195.59 in 1916), averaging only about $15 or $16 monthly, that the present procedure is probably as economical as any that might be devised.

In 1916, according to the records of the weighmaster, the following service was rendered by this office:

Quantity Weighed.	*Receipts.*

For private persons 2,677,960 pounds of produce and merchandise $195.59
For city $12,787,480 pounds of coal, feed, etc. None
For city 139,740 pounds of old iron........ None

Although the city pays no fees for the service of the weighmaster in weighing commodities for city departments, the weighmaster keeps a record of the amount earned by his office as though the city paid the same fees as private individuals. That is, he records the earnings of his office as $195.59 from private individuals and $696.94 from the city. This latter amount is, of course, not represented by cash receipts.

As a matter of fact, there is no advantage in having a city weighmaster certify to the weight of commodities handled by private companies, since the certification of the weighmaster means only that the weight stated on the receipt is the weight of the scales and weight at the scales is not necessarily the weight received by the purchaser. That is to say, there is nothing to prevent the lightening of the load after it leaves the city scales. The city weighmaster has been long in city service and his elimination would probably mean that practically what the city now pays for the services of the weighmaster it would have to pay to others in fees, or it would have to require that all commodities purchased by the city be weighed at the point of delivery. This latter method is, of course, the right way to determine whether or not the weights of commodities purchased by the city are just, but unless large scales are established at these delivery points or a large portable scale purchased this could not be done. It is believed that this position of city weighmaster may well be left undisturbed, except that it should be put under the supervision of the sealer of weights and measures.

Public Baths

PUBLIC BATHS.

Control of Baths.

The two Branch public baths were bequeathed to the city under the following arrangement: that there shall be a self-perpetuating board in control of each bath and that for the maintenance of each bath the city shall pay a sum not to exceed $3,000 annually. The city's appropriation for each bath for the current year is $2,500, a like amount having been appropriated for each in 1916.

The board in control of each bath is made up of citizens of responsibility not connected with the city government, and is charged with all duties in connection with the maintenance of the baths, including the employment of such attendants as may be required. In charge of such bath there is a superintendent at $75 a month, and in addition there is employed at each bath an engineer at $80 a month, a janitor or male attendant at $60 a month, and a janitress or female attendant at $40 a month.

Baths in Excellent Condition.

Each bath was visited and found to be in excellent condition throughout. The baths are unquestionably a credit to the city and to the boards which have them in charge. Each is amply fitted with bath tubs, shower baths, toilets and all accessories for the comfort and convenience of patrons, and there is everywhere indication that the baths are not only well used, but well cared for. It is believed that no better arrangement for the proper administration of the baths can be devised and many of the institutions under the control of city authorities suffer by comparison with the public baths, as, for example, the public markets.

All laundering of towels is done on the premises. Towels are thoroughly washed in scalding hot water and soap suds and then rinsed several times before drying. This procedure amply protects patrons of the baths from any possible dangers from unclean towels. All small particles of soap left by bathers are collecte by attendants and used for laundry and general cleaning purposes.

Appropriation for Baths Should Be Based Upon Actual Needs.

Each board in control of a public bath makes an annual report to the mayor. The secretary of each board keeps his own records, but the reports to the mayor show in full detail how the funds of the boards were spent. In addition to the appropriation from the city, each bath receives about the same amount from other sources, including receipts from bathers. Bathers purchase tickets at a ticket window at the front of the building and these tickets are given over to the attendants who assign them to baths. Five cents is charged all persons over twelve and three cents all under twelve. With each ticket goes a small cake of soap and a clean bath towel. Prior to the present year women were allowed to do their family washing at public bath No. 1, ten cents being charged for this privilege. This has, however, been discontinued by the board in charge of that bath.

Approximately 43,000 persons use each of these baths annually, the great majority being adult men. The receipts from this source, plus the sum received from the city, is sufficient to pay the salaries of employees and all expenses and leave a balance annually, which is placed in the bank at interest. As both baths are in excellent physical condition, the cost of repairs has not, up to this time, been a very large item. Under present conditions it is believed that an annual appropriation of $2,500 to each bath is somewhat more than sufficient for their needs, particularly in the case of bath No. 2. The following summary of reports made to the mayor for the year 1916, shows the service given by the baths and the cost of such service for the period February 1, 1916, to January 31, 1917:

Summary of Financial Reports of Public Baths for Period February 1, 1916 to January 31, 1917—Financial Statement.

	RECEIPTS					EXPENDITURES								
	Balance in Bank Feb. 1	From City	From Baths*	Interest from Bank	Total	Salaries	Fuel	Water and Light	Repairs	Supplies	Insurance	General	Total	Balance on Hand Jan. 31
Bath No. 1...	$ 729 54	$2,500	$2,178 37	$21 14	$ 5,424 05	$ 3,040 67	$ 510 26	$ 357 19	$ 130 59	$ 500 19	$ 5 00	$194 22	$4,738 02	$ 696 03
Bath No. 2...	1,949 12	2,600	2,318 59	62 47	6,930 18	3,076 00	380 41	243 76	386 23	557 41			4,601 81	2,328 37
Total.....	$2,678 66	$5,000	$4,491 96	$83 61	$12,254 23	$6,116 67	$870 67	$600 95	$485 82	$1,057 60	$5 00	$194 22	$9,339 80	$2,924 40

Summary of Services Rendered

	Pay Bathers*			Free School Children	Number Using Laundry	REMARKS
	Men and Women	Boys and Girls	Total			
Bath No. 1.........	40,035	3,147	43,182	1,970	411	Permission to use this bath for laundry not allowed in current year.
Bath No. 2.........	43,143	3,047	46,190			
Total.........	83,178	6,194	89,372	1,970	411	

*Five cents charged for each adult and three cents for each child under twelve.

It will be seen from the foregoing summary that the baths are in a flourishing financial condition and also that they are rendering a very excellent service, there being a daily average of over one hundred bathers visiting the baths. While it is desirable, of course, that each bath have funds in bank for emergency use, the fact that public bath No. 2 had over $2.000 in the bank at the beginning of the current year would seem to indicate that the city's appropriation to this bath could have been reduced by at least $1,000, without hampering service. Appropriations should be based upon the financial needs of the baths, as evidenced by their financial statements and not upon mere precedent.

Baths for Colored Citizens Recommended.

It is apparent from the foregoing statement of receipts and expenditures that, granting a lower salary cost for the operation of these institutions, public baths can be made self-supporting without excessive charges to patrons. In view of this fact, it is suggested that the city government give consideration to the matter of establishing a public bath for the benefit of its 50,000 or more colored citizens. Public baths are excellent public health educational enterprises and it is believed that a public bath in the colored section of the city would be well patronized. The baths need not be built on such an expensive plan as existing baths, nor need the cost of attendant service be so high.

Public Employment Bureau

PUBLIC EMPLOYMENT BUREAU.

Organization and Duties of Board and Employers.

The public employment bureau was created by ordinance on December 19, 1914, and began actual operation on February 8, 1915. By the terms of the ordinance the bureau is under the supervision and control of a commission of five citizens appointed by the mayor and directly responsible to him. No member of the commission is permitted to hold any other public office in the city, State or national government. The members of the commission serve for a term of two years each or until their successors are appointed and qualified, but no change has been made in the original commission since the bureau was established.

The commission is empowered to elect its own officers and to make its own rules and regulations and is required to keep complete records of service rendered as to (a) applicants for positions; (b) positions to be filled as reported to the bureau; (c) persons sent to those seeking employees; (d) persons securing employment, and (e) such other records as the commission may deem necessary.

Meetings of the commission must, under the ordinance, be held at least once a month, but at present two meetings are held each month on the first and third Fridays of the month. Special meetings are held, as required, at the call of the chairman of the commission.

The ordinance further fixes the number of employees and salaries of the employees of the board, as a manager at $1,500 a year and a clerk at $900 a year, their terms of office being for two years or until removed by the board. The duties of these employees are fixed by the commission.

Complete and detailed records of the actions of the board are kept by the manager of the bureau, who acts as clerk of the board and acts also in an advisory capacity to the commission when called upon to do so for the determination of the policy and operation of the bureau. For the routine conduct of the affairs of the bureau, the manager is given full authority subject to the rules and regulations established by the commission.

Salary of Assistant Clerk Included in Expense Item.

The rapid growth of the service of the employment bureau has made it necessary to increase the clerical assistance. As the number and salaries of employees are fixed by the ordinance, additional clerical assistance has been secured at the rate of $2.25 per day, this service being paid for out of the appropriation for expenses.

It may be well to point out here that the fixing of the exact number and salaries of employees of this employment bureau by ordinance is a very unsatisfactory procedure, in that it is impossible to anticipate the growth of such a bureau or the demands of service in the future, dependent as such growth and demands are upon circumstances not anticipated at the passage of the ordinance. Further, it results in faulty reporting of costs. For example, the bureau reports that it spent in 1916 $2,400 for salaries and $1,699.58, for expenses, although as a matter of fact the item of expenses included the salary of an assistant clerk at $2.25 per day. This procedure of including salaries in expense statements is a common one throughout the city, and is discussed at greater length elsewhere in this survey report.

Qualifications of Manager and Assistants.

The manager of the bureau was selected by the commission from a list of several applicants because of his experience and general fitness for the position and it is believed that the appointment was well made. His experience with industrial employment in a large business, as well as a thorough understanding of community needs regarding employment and allied social problems make him particularly well qualified for this work.

The woman clerk, who is his immediate assistant, was originally employed as an additional clerk at $2.25 per day for the registering and interviewing of applicants at the bureau, acting as an assistant to the regular clerk at $900, who had been originally appointed at the beginning of the bureau's work. This clerk, however, terminated his service for military duty in May, 1916, but his salary was continued until February 1, 1917, when the present clerk, formerly the assistant clerk at $2.50 per day, was appointed to fill the vacancy at $900 a year. This woman clerk is also very well qualified by reason of her business experience and general training. She is a competent stenographer and keeps all records of applicants in a very satisfactory manner.

The present assistant clerk who is employed at $2.25 per day, payable from the allowance for expenses of the bureau, is also rendering very satisfactory service. His work consists in the receiving of applications, interviewing applicants and assisting the clerk in the handling of files and general office work.

So far as can be determined from the records of service performed and observation of the daily office routine, the city is receiving satisfactory service from the employees of this bureau at small cost. The matter of salaries of these, as well as other city employees, is further discussed in that section of this report which deals with the standardization of salaries of municipal employees.

Proposed Re-organization of Municipal Employment Bureau.

By reference to chart H of the proposed department of public welfare, it will be noted that the municipal employment bureau has been made a bureau under the direct supervision of the proposed commissioner of public welfare. This bureau is included among public welfare functions because of the nature of the service it renders.

In the event that such a general re-organization is effected, there will be no need for the continuance of the present commission as the controlling agency, and it should, therefore, be abolished. In recommending the abolition of the present commission, there is no thought of criticism of the commission which has from the beginning performed its work thoroughly and successfully.

Policy of Bureau and Summary of Service Rendered.

The policy of the municipal employment bureau since its inception is well expressed by its motto "a clearing house for the unemployed." It is not intended and has not been used as an agency merely for the furnishing of employment to the "down and out." but to secure employment for all persons suited to their ability and needs regardless of their social or financial conditions, and to meet as far as possible the demands of employers, both private and municipal, for skilled and unskilled labor of all kinds. That it has performed this service well is indicated by its records of service and by the contact which it has built up with private employers and the various departments of the city government. Not only has it been of vast service to the citizens of Richmond, but also to citizens of other cities throughout the State.

It is unfortunate that so little effort has been made by its critics, and even by its supporters to inform themselves intelligently as to its work, and it is hoped that this report will at least have the result of encouraging private citizens and city officials not only to inform themselves of the service rendered, but also to make wider use of the bureau's help in adjusting local industrial conditions satisfactorily for both employee and employer.

The following extracts from a report on public employment exchanges by the City Club of New York (1914) indicate that thinking people throughout the country are in hearty accord with the public employment bureau program and its policy of acting as a "clearing house" for the unemployed. The report says:

> "The labor market, the most universal, the most vital, the most important of all exchanges, is still unorganized. The buyers and sellers of leather, grain, coffee—of any important saleable article—have well defined meeting places where information is accumulated and exchanges made. * * *
>
> "What is done with reference to labor? Do the buyers and sellers in this case go to a center for their mutual exchanges? By what business-like methods do the "manless jobs" and the "jobless men" come together? Workmen go from door to door offering their services and employers hang out their "help wanted" signs. This sign "help wanted" is a symbol of inefficiency in the present disorganized state of the labor market. The haphazard practice of tramping the streets in search of this sign "help wanted" is no method at all. It does not assure the idle worker of success in his search for employment, or the employer in his search for labor. * * *
>
> "It is impossible to reckon the cost to a community of such waste of production through failure of prompt and fitting sale of labor. But beyond that there is the waste incurred by this accidental way of fitting or rather not fitting a man to a job. The law of chance decrees that misfits must be the rule, and society now permits this daily process of attempting to fit a round peg into a square hole."

The report calls attention also to the waste and possibility of fraud in newspaper advertising for labor and says:

> "Indiscriminate advertising is the present expensive makeshift for the intelligent economic treatment of this large problem."

The report also points out the menace and inefficiency of the private licensed agency—facts well known to anyone who has had experience with them either as an applicant for work or as an investigator of their method. The inefficiency of employment agencies operated in connection with charitable agencies has frequently been commented upon. The worker who is not "down and out" but merely temporarily out of employment, does not care to be considered as a problem of charity, and that is precisely the difficulty which the Richmond municipal employment bureau has been trying to overcome. It is not charity but simply good business for a community to keep its citizens engaged in work suited to their needs and to the needs of industry.

The following summary of work performed since the establishment of the bureau speaks for itself:

Summary of Service Rendered by Municipal Employment Bureau	1915	1916	1917 to July 1st
Applications from employers	1 909	2,954	1 637
Persons called for by employers	4,277	5,344	2,464
Persons referred to positions	3,642	6 39.	3,096
Positions reported filled	2.179	2,846	1,302
Registrations for work	7,222	6,725	2 945

Classification of Positions Reported Filled	1915			1916			1917		
	Male	Female	Total	Male	Female	Total	Male	Female	Total
White									
Professions	2	2	4	2		2	1		1
Clerks	115	101	216	243	121	364	152	48	200
Skilled labor	761	81	842	610	154	764	262	27	289
Laborers (ordinary)	135		135	265		265	307	32	339
Domestics	12	25	37	16	37	53	4	9	13
Horse attendants	326		326						
Colored									
Skilled labor	44	2	46	64	2	66	17		17
Laborers (ordinary)	290		290	825		825	243		243
Domestics	73	206	279	231	276	507	44	156	200
Horse attendants	4		4						
Total	1,762	417	2,179	2,256	590	2,846	1,080	272	1,302

It will be noted from this summary that there was a very considerable increase in the work of the bureau in 1916 over that of 1915. but that in the present year there has in general been a slight decrease, particularly in the number of registrations for work. This is accounted for by the fact that war conditions have demanded large increases among industrial workers and these workers have not found it necessary to resort to the employment bureau. This does not, however, point to a steady decreasing demand upon the bureau. It is true that the drafting of men for war will open large possibilities of employment for those not drafted, but the bureau can render a very efficient service in adjusting labor demands to the supply. .

The municipal employment bureau should continue to act as a clearing house for the unemployed and for employers, for the work of re-adjustment made necessary by war conditions demands that there be some organized effort to fit changed conditions. Municipal departments will also feel the need for having just such an agency to fill the gaps in their forces left by the military draft, and the registration of applicants for these positions, their examinations, etc., can well be left to the municipal employment bureau. It is believed that any decrease in the force or funds of this bureau is unjustified by the facts as to work done and to be done.

Procedure of the Bureau.

Each applicant is given a careful interview: his references are examined and his exact qualifications noted. A registry of the demands for service of all kinds is also kept and the applicant for employment is often put in immediate touch with the employer, frequently within an hour. If there is no position immediately available of the special kind desired by the applicant, he is given the opportunity of accepting some other position which is offered and which he may be qualified to fill. The manager endeavors to keep in daily contact with employers by personal visits and by correspondence. All newspaper advertisements offering employment are investigated and effort made to fill the positions offered from the lists available.

When an applicant for employment is sent to an employer. he is given a card of introduction which is a post card to be taken up by the employer and returned to the employment bureau with a statement as to whether or not the applicant was employed. A follow-up post card is sent to the employer in the event that the card of introduction is not returned stating that the applicant has been sent to him for employment, and requesting the employer to notify the bureau at once if such applicant was employed. Follow-up cards are also sent to applicants failing to report for employment, requesting them to call at the employment bureau for re-assignment or inform the bureau by return post card or telephone if still unemployed. in order that they may be re-registered.

The entire procedure is designed to keep in constant touch with employer and employee, to find jobs for men and men for jobs, and to make all of the necessary adjustments between employer and employee. That the procedure is effective is proven by the records and correspondence of the office.

Employment of Minors.

The manager of the public employment bureau states that he has complied strictly with the State law regarding the employment of minors in that no applicant under fourteen years of age has been directed to employment without a court permit. and if over fourteen and under sixteen without a certificate of age issued by a notary public. This is. of course, all that the manager of the public employment bureau can do under the circumstances. and yet he recognizes fully that the present method of issuing working permits is very defective in that there is no guarantee that the child is physically able to work. This matter is discussed at greater length in that section of this report. which relates to the department of health. but it is mentioned here because the manager of the employment bureau having ample opportunity to judge of the working of this law considers it very defective as regards the prevention of employment of physically unqualified children.

The manager is himself a notary public and issues permits without fee to children applying for working papers. It is urged that some effort be made through this office to secure data relative to the physical condition of children. The co-operation of the health department could no doubt be secured for making physical examinations of children with their consent. and that of their parents, of course. The co-operation of the school authorities should also be secured in obtaining the health record of the child during the school period. At the end of the year considerable evidence would be available as to the necessity of making the child pass some more rigid physical tests before being permitted to work.

Records and Reports.

Complete and detailed records of all applications, assignments to work and positions filled are kept by the clerk. The present system of records is an admirable one. designed by the manager and the commission. after a study of records of public employment bureaus throughout the country. A special file of applications is kept for professional and skilled labor and each application when filled out gives a complete history of the general and special experience qualifications of the individual. Space is provided on the back for the endorsement of the name of the employer, and the date of sending the applicant to him. These applications are filed consecutively by number and also cross-indexed by name of the applicant. Other applications for non-professional or unskilled labor are entered in brief upon special forms which give all the information needed for the purpose of proper reference. These are also filed by number and cross-indexed by name of the applicant. On the back of this form space is also provided for the applicant's references, and the names and dates of employers to whom the applicant may be sent. A special file is also kept which gives reference to the various applications, classified according to the trade or occupation of the applicant. For example, if four clerks or three domestics are desired, this file will furnish data as to the applicants available.

'Detailed description of all records is not practicable in this report, but it may be said without fear of contradiction that all of the information needed as to employer or employee is readily and completely available, and that is the test of the efficiency of the record keeping system.

A report is made to the commission by the manager semimonthly and is presented to the board at the meetings on the first and third Fridays of each month. This report gives for both white and colored, male and female, the number of employers' applications received, the number of persons called for, the positions offered, positions reported filled and the total registration for work from the first of the year up to the date of the report. The report also gives the total amount of expenditure against the appropriation and the balance at the time of the report.

In addition to the semi-monthly report, the board makes an annual report to the mayor of work accomplished and the cost. This annual report would be very considerably improved if a more detailed statement were made of the finances of the bureau. The financial statement, as found in the annual reports for 1915 and 1916, are altogether too meagre, being a mere statement of the appropriation for "salaries" and "expenses" and the amount of expenditure under each of these two headings. To secure public support the public should be fully informed not only as to what is being done in the way of securing employment for the unemployed, but exactly what it costs. For example, it has already been shown that the item "expense" covers the salary or wages of a clerk at $2.25 a day. Other items should also be shown under such general classification of expenditures as has been recommended for all city departments. It is believed that the municipal employment bureau is economically operated, but unless the citizen knows definitely where the money goes, he is likely to criticize and his criticism is quite often warranted.

Co-operation With Other City Departments.

Unfortunately, city departments have not made as good use of the public employment bureau as they might. The manager of the bureau has placed the services of the bureau at the disposal of city departments, and certain departments have secured competent employees thereby. In several instances, however, the department heads have failed to co-operate with the employment bureau, even to the extent of notifying the manager when positions have been filled by applicants sent from the bureau. The following summary shows the number of persons called for by various city departments, the number of persons to whom positions were offered, the number of persons who accepted positions, and the number of persons who refused to accept the positions offered:

Summary of Requests of City Departments for Labor 1915, 1916, 1917.

DEPARTMENT	Number of Persons Called for	Number of Persons Offered Positions	Number of Persons Accepting Positions	Number of Persons Refusing Positions
City Home......................	11	19	2	17
Administrative Board..........	13	13	6	7
City Attorney	1	2	1	1
Commissioner of Revenue......	5	4	3	1
Police Department	10	6	6	
Water Department.............	10	13	8	5
Playground Commissioner	2	2	2	0
Building Inspector..............	8	8	7	1
Board of Health	6	6	4	2
School Board (Shop).	83	92	37	55
Total	148	165	76	89

It is evident from the above summary that the greatest success of the employment bureau has been in securing positions for persons above the labor class at the City Home, as is shown in the report on that institution. Neither the salaries nor conditions of living are sufficient to attract persons to the service. The school board, which asked for the greatest number of employees, wanted laborers, carpenters, painters, plasterers, etc. These positions were in many instances refused by the persons sent, because of the unsatisfactory wage, or because they were not able to do the work required. On the whole, however, this is a very good record, for aside from these two city departments mentioned, the public employment bureau was generally successful in filling positions satisfactorily.

It is urged that a detailed statement of the requests made by city departments, the number of persons sent in response to these requests, the number of persons refusing appointment, and the number accepting be incorporated in the annual report in order that it may be brought to the attention of the city authorities that, lacking a civil service program for the selection of employees, the public employment bureau is the best resource.

Possible Extension of Service of Public Employment Bureau.

The success of the public employment bureau in securing municipal employees suggests the possibility of a much wider extension of its service. It is believed that with a slight addition. perhaps of only one clerk, to the present staff of the public employment bureau, this bureau could well serve in lieu of a civil service commission for securing city employees of all grades below supervisory or executive positions. That is to say, all inspectors, clerks, stenographers. nurses, mechanics. skilled laborers, ordinary laborers, etc.. could be selected by the public employment bureau on the basis of an analysis of their qualifications and experience, with such additional examination as might be deemed advisable.

In the event that the public employment bureau should act in this capacity. it should not be placed under the direction of the proposed commissioner of welfare, but should remain independent as at present.

The present commission should act as a civil service commission, and it is believed that the commission would function very satisfactorily in that capacity. Since by the terms of ordinance they cannot be public office holders themselves, there would be in such commission as great freedom from political influence as in any civil service commission. The present commissioners are all responsible business men of the community and could, it is believed. be relied upon to give efficient service in the matter.

Payments to Private Charitable Institutions

PAYMENTS TO PRIVATE CHARITABLE INSTITUTIONS.

Appropriation for Private Institutions and Organizations, 1917.

The following appropriations to private institutions and organizations of the city were allowed by appropriation ordinance for 1917:

1—St. Monica's Mission ....$	200.00
2—St. Paul's Church Home	300.00
3—Retreat for the Sick	500.00
4—Eye and Ear Infirmary	500.00
5—Belle Bryan Nursery and Kindergarten	500.00
6—Female Humane Association	300.00
7—Foundling Home	400.00
8—St. Joheph's Orphan Asylum........	300.00
9—Sheltering Arms	2,500.00
10—Home for Incurables	1,000.00
11—Home for Needy Confederate Women.	250.00
12—Richmond Colored Hospital	200.00
13—Spring Street Home	800.00
14—Little Sisters of the Poor...........	500.00
15—Friends' Orphan Asylum	150.00
16—St. Joseph's Mission House	500.00
17—Instructive Nurses' Association.......	1,000.00
18—Nurses' Settlement	800.00
19—Society Prevention of Cruelty to Animals	500.00
20—Children's Home Society	300.00
21—Richmond Male Orphan Asylum.....	500.00
22—Colored Orphan Asylum	250.00
23—Old Folk's Home	200.00
24—Travelers' Aid Society	750.00
Total ....$	13,200.00

Summary of Reports on Private Institutions.

In the time allotted to the survey of the city government it was not possible to make a study of the above named institutions. As all except the Society for the Prevention of Cruelty to

Animals are required to make annual reports to the State board of charities and corrections, effort was made to obtain certain definite information regarding these institutions from that office. It was found, however, that the reports submitted to the State board of charities and corrections are very meager, being confined to very brief statements as to the location, names of officers, purpose of institution and finances. A summary of their reports as found in the Eighth Annual Report (1916) of the State Board of charities and corrections follows:

Name of Institution	Purpose of Institution	Capacity of Institution, Number of Persons Cared For
1. St. Monicas Mission ...	Provides weekly baskets of provisions, etc., for needy colored persons	Not stated ....
2. St. Paul's Ch. Home...	Orphanage and home for white girls	24 inmates at end of fiscal year
3. Retreat for the Sick ..	General hospital service with training school for nurses	Capacity 50 beds; days of free treatment 2,662; total patients 968; average daily attendance
4. Richmond Eye, Ear and Throat Infirmary	Hospital and dispensary treatment of diseases of eye, ear, nose and throat	Capacity 20; private patients 34; entirely free 14; total patients, including these treated in dispensary, 1,073.
5 Belle Bryan Nursery and Free Kindergarten	Day nursery and kindergarten for white children.	40 inmates at end of fiscal year
6. Female Humane Association	Home for white girls	46 inmates at end of fiscal year
7. Foundling Hospital ..	Foundling home and hospital for white infants.	7 children present at end of fiscal year
8. St Joseph's Academy and Orphan Asylum ..	Orphanage for white children....	75 inmates at end of fiscal year..
9 Sheltering Arms Free Hospital	Free treatment of indigent sick. Has training school for 15 nurses	Capacity 51 beds; total patients treated 833; average daily attendance 41.
10 Virginia Home for Incurables.........	Care and treatment of incurable diseases. $200 admission charged	Capacity 35; 35 present at end of fiscal year.
11. Home for Needy Confederate Women	Care of women relatives of Confederate soldiers	
12. Richmond Hospital..	General hospital for colored persons. Has training school for nurses	Capacity 30; private patients 181 paying patients 16; entirely free 11; total patients 208; average daily attendance 25
13. Spring-Street Home ..	Hospital and maternity for white girls	Capacity 50 adults and 30 infants infants born in institution 22; received from outside 4; 12 adults and 6 infant inmates at end of fiscal year
14 St. Sophia's Home for the Old People ("Little Sisters of the Poor")...	Home for old men and women. No admission fee charged....	Capacity 200; 150 present at end of fiscal year ....
15. Friends Asylum for Colored Orphans	Orphanage for colored children ..	18 inmates at end of fiscal year..
16. St Joseph's Mission Home	Trade school for children..........	No report of work performed or
17. Instructive Visiting Nurses' Association...	Visiting and nursing sick in their homes .... (Employs 12 nurses)	31,780 visits made, 3,579 new cases Special diet supplied to 314 Patients referred to other organizations. Employment secured and children sent to country ....
18. "The Social Workers" Department of the Nurses Settlement....	Social service work of all kinds for improving condition of the poor.....................	9 girls in boarding department; 30 clubs conducted with enrollment of 366; two classes in home nursing for 40 colored women. kindergarten of 35 pupils; bible vacation school of 35 ....
19. Society for Prevention of Cruelty to Animals,	Does not report to State Board of	Charities and Correction. ...

| Endowment | Total Valuation of Property | Indebtedness | Receipts, 1916 | | | Expenditures, 1916 | | | Remarks 8th Annual Report |
			From City	From Other Sources	Total	For Salaries and Maintenance	Other Purposes	Total	
....	....	....	$ 200 00	$ 125 00	$ 325 00	$ 325 00	$ 5 90	$ 330 00	p. 113-114
$50,000	$60,000 00	....	300 00	3,682 00	3,982 00	3,982 00	....	3,982 00	70-71
....	25,000 00	$15,000	500 00	28,872 47	29,372 47	26,020 17	1,200 00	27,220 17	132-133
50 00	11,000 00	*2,800	500 00	14,708 00	5,208 00			5,093 39	130
	5,000 00	....	600 00	6,356 26	6,856 26	3,642 79	102 34	3,745 13	75
114,200	....	....	300 00	6,608 13	6,908 13	....		6,908 13	63
....	....	....	400 00	1,500 00	1,900 00	1,826 70	211 78	2 088 48	74
....	....	....	300 00	6,800 00	7,100 00	7,100 00	....	7,100 00	70-71
....	45,000 00	....	2,500 00 not stated	11 649 66	14,149 66	13,176 83	887 87	14,064 70	133
....	6,352 11 (bal. in bank)	....	"	†8 500 00 / †11,025 87	8,500 00 / 11,025 87	8,000 00 / 11,752 58	500 00	8,500 00 / 11,752 58	115 / 112
....	8,000 00	4,500	200 00	10,705 00	10,905 00	6,347 13	4 357 87	10,705 00	131
....	No financial statement submitted.								140
....	....	....	500 00	No other financial report—except "supported by voluntary contribution					114
....	3,000 00	....	150 00	900 00	1,050 00	1,019 31	353 78	1,373 09	64
finance submitted									
....	4,108 00 (bal. in bank)	....	1,000 00	10,947 02	11,947 02	9,159 19	3,574 41	12 734 60	120
....	....	....	800 00	1,677 52	2,447 52	850 00	1,168 00	2,018 00	109

*Floating debt, $150.
†$1,500 from State.
‡2,500 from City and State
§4,000 from State.

Name of Institution	Purpose of Institution	Capacity of Institution, Number of Persons Cared For
20. Children's Home Society of Virginia........	Acts as home and placing-out agency for white children.......	29 inmates at end of fiscal year; 320 placed and replaced during year; 350 children visited in foster homes....................
21. Richmond Male Orphan Society	Orphanage for white boys.........	35 inmates at end of fiscal year ..
22. Working Woman's Industrial Home and Nursery.............	Colored orphanage and day nursery................................	32 inmates at end of fiscal year .
23 Old Folks Home for Colored People	Home for colored people—no admission fee charged.............	Capacity 30; 18 present at end of fiscal year ....
24. Richmond Travelers' Aid Society	Assist travelers, particularly young women and girls, by means of money, employment reference to other agencies, etc.; protects them from exploitation	Assistance given to 7,280 in various ways through own organization and other agencies ......

Endowment	Total Valuation of Property	Indebtedness	Receipts, 1916			Expenditures, 1916			Remarks 8th Annual Report
			From City	From Other Sources	Total	For Salaries and Maintenance	Other Purposes	Total	
....	$15,000 00	$ 3,900	$ 300 00	$ 15,770 08	$16,070 08	$ 10,082 32	$ 5,987 71	$ 16 070 08	p. 77-78
....	°95,000 00	....	500 00	5 550 00	6,000 00	6,000 00	....	6,000 00	69
....	3,500 00	950	(a)	1,150 00	1,150 00	1,400 00	48 00	1,448 00	74
....	....	....	200 00	1.840 00	2,040 00	2.340 00	140 00	2,480 00	112
....	....	....	750 00	2.301 55 ($1,000 from State; 540 from R. R.)	3,051 55	1,544 50	....	1,544 50	79-80

°Includes endowment.
(a)From all sources amount of city appropriation not stated.

Many Institutions in Flourishing Financial Condition.

It should be noted in this summary that of the twenty-four institutions, several are in a very flourishing financial condition and apparently have no need for the small dole given by the city. For example, St. Paul's Church Home has an endowment of $50,000. The Female Humane Association has an endowment of $114,200 and the Richmond Male Orphan Society has assets, including endowment, to the amount of $95,000. The Home for Needy Confederate Women has a bank balance of $6,251.11, the Instructive Visiting Nurses' Association has a bank balance of $4,108.90. In the year past, the receipts of the Belle Bryan Nursery and Kindergarten, exclusive of the $500 given by the city, exceeded its expenditures by $2,611.13. The receipts of the Travelers' Aid Society, exclusive of the $750 given by the city, also exceeded its expenditures by $757.05. It is proper, of course, that such institutions be kept free from money worries, but it is not clear why the city should appropriate money for self-sustaining institutions, particularly in view of the fact that it has no control over their methods of spending money. All of these institutions may be economically and efficiently conducted, but they do not furnish evidence in their reports sufficient to satisfy an appropriating body of the fact. Furthermore, no reports are available regarding the Spring Street Home, to which the city appropriated $800 in 1917, of the St. Joseph's Mission House, which received $500, nor of the Society for the Prevention of Cruelty to Animals, which also received $500.

Amounts of Allowance to Private Institutions Based on Precedent.

Although, as has been shown, the city of Richmond spends annually, for its private institutions, $13,200, it has little or no information from the institutions as to the character of work done, results obtained, costs of service, etc. The meager reports which are submitted to the State board of charities and corrections are quite inadequate as a basis for determining the need for the existence of these institutions or their need of funds. It was stated by the city auditor that the amounts given to homes and hospitals are intended chiefly to cover the cost of light, water, etc., which under the law, the city is not allowed to furnish free. As to other organizations and institutions, the theory is that they relieve the city of the burden of caring for certain of its poor. There is no doubt but that many, perhaps all, of these institutions are doing commendable work, but the city government has no way of knowing what they are doing other than by hearsay, or the review of the reports made to the State board of charities and corrections.

Requests for funds are commonly made by the authorities of these institutions by letter or by personal appearance before the finance committee of council. It appears from the records that the amounts to be allowed are largely established by precedent rather than on the basis of careful investigation into their needs.

Subsidizing of Private Institutions Should Be Discontinued.

The city now maintains at considerable expense a city home for the care of the sick and infirm poor, including tuberculosis pavilions for colored persons: the Virginia Hospital for the acutely ill, both white and colored, and the Pine Camp Hospital for white tuberculosis patients. That this service does not meet all the demands for the care of needy persons is quite true, and the city's service must of course be supplemented by private endeavor. As a matter of policy, however, the subsidizing of private institutions should not be encouraged. It is right and proper that the city should pay for actual service rendered, and this should be its policy under the organization of a department of health and charities, as previously recommended. All applications for relief of the poor of whatever nature should be referred to the head of that department. From such sources as are available—as the Associated Charities and other charitable organizations—the city's responsibility for the care of individuals should be determined and the city should pay for such service as may be found advisable.

In many States and cities the subsidizing of private agencies is forbidden by law—and this, it is believed, is not only good business but sound public policy. It is recommended, therefore, that donations to private institutions be discontinued, and payments made only on the basis of actual service rendered. In the care of institutions to which public charges are referred the city should pay an amount per day or per week, based on the actual cost of maintenance in such institutions: in the case of service rendered by the Visiting Nurses' Association, the Social Settlement and The Traveler's Aid Society, payment should be made for actual service, approved by the proposed commissioner of charities, and on the basis of bills rendered by these organizations. Attendance by visiting nurses upon city charges should be paid for at a fixed fee per visit.

If the discontinuance of the $200 or $300 subsidies granted by the city results in the elimination of certain small impoverished institutions, it will probably be a distinct gain in that it will place squarely before the city authorities the necessity of providing adequate and proper care of all of its charges in such a manner that the appropriation granting authority will also have administrative as well as financial control.

City Home

CITY HOME.

General Condition of Physical Plant.

The City Home is an institution for both white and colored persons, male and female, who, by reason of indigence and physical incompetence, require custodial and some degree of medical and nursing care. The plant consists of five principal buildings, the main building being the home for white males and females and an infirmary for the same, a colored home for male and feale persons with infirmary wards, a contagious disease pavilion for white persons, a tuberculosis pavilion for colored males and females, and an ambulance station for the ambulances of the Virginia Hospital.

Except for the main building, i. e., the home for whites, these buildings are all in fairly good condition. The main building, however, being the oldest and built prior to the war between the states, is in a rather dilapidated condition as to its interior. This necessitates almost constant repair work. Its interior arrangement is also unsatisfactory for efficient and economical care of the inmates. Plans have been suggested at various times for the establishment of a city farm for charitable and penal institutions and ultimately no doubt some such plan will be put into effect. For the present all that can be done with the present City Home is to make conditions as satisfactory as possible at the most reasonable outlay. Much can be done to improve conditions without great cost, and in succeeding paragraphs of this report certain recommendations will be made toward improving living conditions, increasing efficiency of service and economizing labor and cost. That any considerable economies may be effected without compensating increase of cost for improved service is doubtful, but the city of Richmond cannot afford to maintain this institution without making some effort at least to make it efficient.

Special mention should be made of the physical conditions at the colored home. In this home the general cleanliness and orderliness of all rooms and service quarters could not have been improved upon.

Organization and Personnel; Payroll.

The following summary shows the distribution of the payroll force at the time of this study:

Superintendent ....$ 1,500.00
Steward 1,200.00
Matron—white department 720.00
Matron—colored department 720.00
Day clerk 600.00
Night clerk—colored department 480.00
Superintendent of nurses (trained nurse). 780.00
Nurse (orderlies for old men, white de-
    partment) 2 at $240 .... 480.00
Nurse (orderlies for old men, colored de-
    partment) 2 at $240.................. 480.00
Nurse (practical nurse for old women,
    white department) 240.00
Nurse (practical nurse for old women, col-
    ored department) 120.00
Nurse—trained nurse, colored, tuberculosis
    pavilion 360.00
Pupil nurses—3 colored pupil nurses for
    colored department—at $20 per month.. 720.00
Pupil nurses—2 colored pupil nurses for
    colored tuberculosis pavilion 480.00
Orderly—colored infirmary 240.00
Internes—3 at $5 per month............. 180.00
Engineer 1,080.00
Baker 720.00
Cook—white department 240.00
Cook—colored department 180.00
Cook—officers' mess 120.00
Wagon driver 240.00
Laundress 240.00
Night watchman—white department 300.00
General utility man 300.00
Chauffeurs—ambulance Virginia Hospital,
    2 at $1.080 .... 2,160.00
Clerk for outside poor 600.00
                            ——————

    Total ....$ 16,200.00

It will be noted that the payroll, as here summarized, does not agree with the payroll as set forth in the appropriation bill. The total payroll, as scheduled in the appropriation bill is $17,040, of which $180 is for "emergency nurses" not represented by nurses on the payroll at the time of this survey. Since the passage of the appropriation bill, other minor changes in personnel and salaries have been made which account for the discrepancy between the appropriation bill schedule and the actual payroll.

It should be noted in the above schedule that the two chauffeurs of the Virginia Hospital ambulance service are paid from the payroll of the City Home. This is, of course, not fair to the City Home, as it increases the payroll cost of the institution without any service being given directly to the institution by the chauffeurs. The charge for this personal service should be against the Virginia Hospital, as well as all other charges in connection with the ambulance service.

In general, it may be said that the payroll of this institution is smaller than would be expected, but economies in personal service do not in this instance represent efficiency. Exceptionally low salaries are paid in certain instances. For example, the trained nurse in the tuberculosis pavilion is paid only $360 a year. By all rules and precedents this nurse in charge of colored tuberculosis patients and exposed as she is to the hazards of such work, should receive at least $50 a month or $600 a year. The internes who are third year men, receive only $5 a month in lieu of laundry. The character of service is such that there is no particular inducement for internes to accept this service. The cook for the colored department who receives only $180 a year does all the cooking for the entire colored department of about 150 persons without assistance, except such as can be secured from inmates.

Superintendent Should Be Business Executive.

The superintendent is a physician who is directly responsible to the administrative board. His duties are nominally to exercise general supervision over the business affairs of the institution and the professional and custodial care of patients. While no personal criticism is directed against this officer, it is apparent that his supervision of institutional affairs is only nominal. In other words, a study of this institution does not convey the impression of a strong personality at its head. The superintendent of nurses is, in general, responsible for the nursing care of the sick and the steward is responsible for the business affairs of the institution. Medical service is under the direction of a group of attending physicians who supervise the work of internes. The superintendent is, therefore, merely the figurehead through whom orders are promulgated and upon whom the administrative board has placed responsibility.

If this institution is to be raised and maintained at a higher level of efficiency it must have a trained superintendent at its head—preferably not a physician but an executive man or woman with business ability. Such a superintendent probably cannot be secured at a salary of $1,500 a year, but the additional salary paid to an institutional executive of the type described would be more than offset by the improved service which he would give.

Capacity of Plant; Admissions 1916 *and* 1917.

The entire plant accommodates between 350 and 400 inmates without crowding, approximately as follows:

White department 200
Colored department 150
Tuberculosis wards 24
Contagious disease wards ..../.............. 8
                                            ——
                                            382

In 1916 the average daily occupancy was 302. The number of inmates has very materially decreased since the beginning of the present year, this condition being due, according to the superintendent and steward, to the passage of prohibition laws. The following table compares the admissions, white and colored, of the first six months of 1916 with the first six months of 1917 (M—men; W—women, C—children):

	1916 (First Six Months)								1917 (First Six Months)							
	White				Colored				White				Colored			
	M.	W.	C.	Total	M.	W.	C.	Total	M.	W.	C.	Total	M.	W.	C.	Total
January	27	7	1	35	45	30	4	79	15	11	2	28	26	18	4	48
February	29	8	4	41	35	20	11	74	12	7	3	22	23	21	6	50
March	38	19	2	59	34	23	9	66	15	5	4	24	24	22	4	30
April	29	14	6	49	20	30	14	63	15	9	11	35	14	23	9	46
May	40	20	5	65	31	27	15	73	11	6	3	20	8	21	9	38
June	33	11	1	45	18	22	11	54	2	7	1	10	14	30	2	46
Total	196	79	19	292	183	160	64	409	70	45	24	139	109	135	34	278

Grand total white and colored—601   Grand total white and colored—417

1916 (Second Six Months)								
	M.	W.	C.	Total	M.	W.	C.	Total
July	21	15	11	47	23	25	7	55
August	22	22	16	60	11	20	16	47
September	18	11	6	35	12	20	9	41
October	26	13	2	41	10	23	8	41
November	11	4	1	16	15	12	5	32
December	10	7	3	20	8	13	5	26
Total	108	72	39	219	79	113	48	240

A decrease in the second six months of 1917 comparable to that in the first sixth months of that year would give for this period approximately 320 admissions

Grand total white and colored—459

It will be noted in the foregoing table that there has been a reduction on the total admission of the first six months of 1917 as compared with the first six months of 1916 of approximately thirty per cent. It would be improper to draw definite conclusions from these figures as to the results of prohibition laws in the community in general, but the superintendent and the steward state emphatically that this reduction is due to fewer admissions arising from indigence incident to inebriety and drug addiction. It is believed that comparison of the last half of 1916 with the next six months of the present year will show somewhat similar results. In so far as indigence is concerned and the infirmities usually found associated with it, the conditions during the first half of the year give the best test because of the severity upon the poor and infirm of the winter and early spring.

It will be noted also in this table that the greatest reduction of admissions has been of whites rather than colored, the percentage reduction of white admissions being fifty-three per cent. and that of colored admissions only thirty-two per cent. The reduction was much the greater in the case of white females than in the case of colored males and greater also in the case of white males than colored females. If the reduction of admissions is due, as stated by the superintendent to the fact that there is an effective prohibition law, the above figures would need to indicate that indigence and destitution due to liquor and drug addiction are greater among the whites than among the colored people. It is dangerous, however, to draw inferences from the figures of a six months' period only. The above facts are stated merely as an interesting side light on the possible result of prohibition laws.

Costs of Operation, 1916 *Compared With* 1917.

In view of the very considerable reduction of the number of inmates of the City Home in the first six months of the present year, it would be reasonable to expect a corresponding reduction in the cost of operation of the institution. The appropriation for 1916 for salaries and wages was $17,040, the same amount as was appropriated for this purpose for the current year. The appropriation for expenses in 1916 was, however, $35,000, as compared with $30,000 for 1917, a reduction of $5,000 being made in this item.

There has been practically no change in the payroll of 1917 as compared with that of 1916. The following table shows comparatively the cost of maintenance, exclusive of salaries and wages, of the first six months of 1916 and 1917, as taken from the annual report for 1916 and the records of the steward for the first six months of the current year.

Comparison of Costs (Exclusive of Salaries and Wages) 1916 and 1917.

Item of Expenditure	1916 (First Six Months)							1917 (First Six Months)						
	January	February	March	April	May	June	Total	January	February	March	April	May	June	Total
Drugs includ. medicines (in key)	$1,867 45	$2,092 96	$2,013 89	1,817 90	1,886 36	1,878 22	$11,496 78	$1,770 88	$1,644 28	$2,158 19	1,875 09	2,296 30	4,072 21	$13,816 96
capital sup-	104 78	113 71	117 30	130 04	88 40	172 46	726 33	80 98	75 52	113 31	106 36	104 51	106 02	586 70
provements	37 75	16 80	37 16	16 80	42 91	31 27	182 69	35 58	37 00	43 80	73 80	43 00	45 27	278 45
implements	459 45	345 32	475 85	19 16	61 88	58 83	1,430 47	304 28	262 85	266 40	22 06	836 36	61 61	1,091 96
Repairs and cloth-	153 77	178 80	282 28	96 06	65 69	65 57	841 97	118 96	90 20	245 16	104 88	91 34	2 50	712 16
Hardwa	29 96	12 50	289 79	28 21	5 80	32 41	378 07	81 46	66 13	32 35	11 63	20 63	2 90	214 60
	2 12	3	4 50	5 68	8 40		24 69	4 55	4 24	9 56	2 62	3 25		27 11
icies	67 58	175 07	126 32	153 75	24 60	209 12	736 42	14 03	5 30	130 98	27 84	6 80		184 43
equipment	21 80	80 90	60 65	145 84	113 77	99 71	520 67	29 12	129 90	139 30	35 90	97 90	28 63	460 75
e and postage	56 50	40 50	38 25	336 80	56 63		528 68	1 25	8 00	110 39	43 95		58 75	222 54
and stationery	2 82		21 96	3 78		23 40	51 96			20 50	2 00		12 45	34 95
ation	3 75		10 10	29 33	4 76	71 23	119 17		4 95	34 00	10 88	16 92		65 75
boilers	25 00	25 00	25 00	25 00	25 00	25 00	150 00	25 00	25 00	25 00	25 00	25 00	25 00	150 00
													67 41	67 41
Total	$2,842 06	$3,025 56	$3,482 95	2 788 35	2,394 18	2,665 01	$17,158 10	$2,466 11	$2 353 87	$3,329 53	2 341 96	3,541 01	4,482 75	$18,513 73

* This total given by steward as $2,506 11 which is incorrect total of amounts in this column.

** " " " " " " " $4,502.93

*** " " " " " " " 4,502.93

From the preceding tabulations it is seen that although the number of admissions in the first six months of 1917 was decreased by thirty per cent. as compared with the same period in 1917, the cost of operation and maintenance, exclusive of salary cost, which is a more or less fixed quantity was greater for the first six months of 1917 than in 1916 for the same period by $1,325.63. It will be noted that the cost of "subsistence" in the six months of 1917 exceeded that for the six months of 1916 by $2,320.17. It is true that the cost of food products has risen considerably during the past six months, but this increase should have been more than offset by the reduction of the number of inmates. The average number of inmates per day for the first six months of 1916 was 331, while for the first six months of 1917 the average number of inmates per day was 272 the monthly average number of inmates varying between 256 and 284. This is a reduction of the daily average by fifty-four patients per day. In the course of a year on the basis of a cost of forty-three cents per day per inmate this should mean a reduction of total cost of over $7,000 in 1917.

At the present rate of expenditures the City Home will exceed its appropriation for expenses in 1917, by several thousand dollars. While there is no evidence of extravagance in the provision of food for inmates and lower grade employees, observation of meals served at the officers mess certainly indicates extravagance there. For example, at two meals eaten by the investigator at the City Home the table was laden with the greatest variety of vegetables it has even been his good fortune to see on one table. At one dinner there were fresh cucumbers, fresh tomatoes, lettuce, black-eyed peas, corn, buttered beets, pickled beets, string beans and potatoes, and at another dinner an almost similar profusion of fresh vegetables in addition to the usual staples of meat, bread and butter, coffee, tea and dessert. These vegetables are purchased fresh at the market daily, and at the present price of fresh vegetables, cannot be said to be cheap food. Under present conditions two or possibly three vegetables is all that the ordinary citizen can afford,—and the city of Richmond cannot afford to be any more extravagant. The officers of the institution naturally expect to have somewhat better food than the inmates, but there is altogether too much discrepancy in the two diets. If economy is being practiced at the City Home it is certainly not being practiced at the expense of the officers' table. The experience of institutions all over the country has proven that unless there is some curb put upon the food supply, particularly of officers, extravagance results.

It is, therefore, recommended, that separate records be kept of the cost of feeding inmates and employees. This can be readily done by the steward with the present records kept. At the end of a year it would then be possible to determine whether or not the food costs of the officers' table are justifiable.

The cost per inmate per day is stated in the annual report of the superintendent for 1916 as forty-three cents. Accepting this figure as accurate, it is evident that the inmates of the City Home are being cared for at low cost—but as will be shown there is lack of adequate service in caring for inmates, and there is need for certain very definite improvements of service along other lines. Efforts to reduce the cost of institutional inmates are commendable only when the kind of service given them conforms to accepted standards.

There are, however, certain economies which may be practiced, which will eventually reduce cost, although in certain instances requiring increased initial cost. This will be discussed in subsequent paragraphs.

Records of Inmates.

Persons are admitted to the City Home, upon the approval of the superintendent. Any city physician may send patients to the City Home, and these are usually admitted without question. Other physicians and citizens may request that persons be admitted and such persons when they appear are interviewed by the superintendent to determine whether or not the application is a proper one. The superintendent says that if the individual is not known to him he seeks information regarding such person from the Associated Charities. When admitted, an admission slip is made out for each person on which is stated the name, color, address, disease, if any, physician recommending, age, sex, civil condition and other data necessary for identification. There is no routine physical examination of the inmate at the time of admission, although if he is ill he is later examined by a member of the medical staff or an interne. Adequate records are not kept of such physical examinations, however.

From this admission slip the clerk enters the data in a daily admission register, (one for white and one for colored admissions) calling for number (serial number) date of admission, name, address, age, sex, civil condition, occupation, nativity, length of time in the city, admitted to hospital or home, officer by whom admitted, date of discharge, date of death. This record calls also for information as to diagnosis, treatment and results of treatment but data on these matter are not entered in the record. For each of the above registers, i. e., white and colored, there is an index book in which the names of the persons admitted are arranged alphabetically and by serial number corresponding to the serial number in the admission register.

Each morning the clerk prepares a consolidated morning report of the house count which shows for the preceding day, classified as white or colored, and as men, women and children, the number remaining at previous report, the admission discharges, deaths of the preceding day and the number remaining at the close of the preceding day.

These reports are summarized monthly and yearly, and the summary for 1916 will be found on page eleven of the annual report of the superintendent for 1916.

The records above described show several defects. In the first place they are unnecessarily cumbersome and in 'the second place there is no proper record of the physical condition of inmates on admission. The first defect can be easily remedied by the substitution of a card index for the registers now in use. A card or sheet of ordinary letter size should be devised, which will give space for all necessary entries of identification data, as well as the health record desired. Such cards could be indexed in several ways—as for example, alphabetically, by serial number, by physical condition, by occupation, etc. With this card index should go a simple register showing for each patient the number of days actually in the home.

There should be an examination by an interne of every inmate on admission—and the data secured at this examination should be entered on the inmate's history card. If the inmate is able to work, he should be so certified by the physician with a statement of the kind of labor he is best fitted for. On no other basis is it possible to determine the working ability of inmates nor the kind of labor which they must perform without injury to health. Illnesses should also be reported to the central office on special slips so that entry can be made on the record card.

Instead of the card record containing all data, it might be advisable to have an envelope for each inmate into which could be placed all records and memoranda relative to that individual

659

while an inmate. Either the card or the envelope system may be used satisfactorily, the idea being merely to have available in one place a complete record of each individual. At the present time there is no such record. Persons may live, die and be buried at the City Home with little more information left behind regarding them than the notes made on admission and the date of death.

The medical records are very unsatisfactory and should be completely revised. Unless the individual is ill enough to require routine nursing care, no adequate record of his condition is kept. There should be for every patient, as has been said, a record of physical examination on admission. If that patient is ill a clinical record should be kept. which will show what is done for him and the result of pathological tests, surgical treatment, medication, etc. Not only does the City Home need such records for its own protection but the patient also needs them for his protection.

Dietary of Inmates.

The steward makes out the daily diet list for inmates and requisitions are made upon him by the head of the various departments. There are three general types of diet called "general," "low," and "full" diets. The "general" diet is that furnished those in good health, i. e., those not requiring special articles of diet; the "low" diet is that given generally to the sick as recommended by the physicians, and the "full" diet which is a combination of the "general" and "low" diets is that given to those who are in physical condition requiring extra food such as convalescents or debilitated persons not classed as sick.

The "general" diet which is the one commonly served to inmates, is as follows, this schedule being given by the steward as typical:

Breakfast—
Coffee, bread, herring.

Dinner—
Regularly, thick soup and bread: twice each week fresh vegetables with bacon: once a week. hash.

Supper—
Bread. coffee, sliced meat.

The "low" diet is what is prescribed by the physicians and consists of bread, butter, milk, tea, eggs, etc., as required. Fresh meats are furnished as ordered and dried fruits—apples, peaches and prunes three times a week.

The "full" diet combines the general diet and the low diet, and includes in addition such special articles of diet as may be ordered by the physicians.

Effort is made to vary all diets sufficiently to prevent monotony. The "general" diet, as outlined above is, however, not varied greatly from day to day. Corn bread is added frequently, however, and is apparently much relished. The white bread which is baked on the premises is excellent in quality, and other foods, though coarse, are wholesome. It is, however, recommended that some additions be made to the general diet so that it may be made somewhat more nourishing and palatable. If cost is increased thereby, it should be considered money well spent. Cereal should be added for breakfast, and dried fruits for supper. Dried fruit can be purchased in large quantities and stored and when served with the evening meal adds considerably to it without adding greatly to the cost. Many of the bodily discomforts of the aged are caused by constipation and such a diet as is now offered favors this condition. Dried fruits would have a salutory effect in such conditions.

Dietitian Should Be Employed.

It is believed that the services of a trained dietitian should be provided at the City Home. Dietetics is a science and scientific feeding of hospital patients and institutional inmates means not only better results in the care and treatment of such patients but also in the saving of waste, and curtailing of extravagance. The duties of a dietetian should be to

1—Plan daily menus for staff, other employees and patients.
2—Take entire charge of kitchens and dining rooms.
3—Direct the purchasing of food supplies.
4—Inspect deliveries of food and kitchen wastes.
5—Check food bills of the institution.
6—Instruct nurses.

The salary which should be paid in an institution of this kind should not exceed $900 a year with maintenance.

Medical Service.

The attending medical staff is composed of ten practicing physicians of the community, seven of whom are connected with the medical college. Each of the physicians, except the chief of staff, is assigned to a special branch of service. The chief of staff visits the hospital weekly and the other members of the staff visit it when called.

The internes, three in number, are third year students of the medical college, who live in the institution and perform such routine medical work as is required by the members of the visiting staff. As these men are non-graduates, their work must at all times be under the direction of one of the qualified physicians of the staff. This, however, is well nigh impossible owing to the infrequency of visits of the members of the visiting staff.

The report of the superintendent for 1916 shows that the hospital work at the home is very considerable, including as it does, the care of general hospital patients, tuberculosis patients and contagious disease patients. In 1916, 656 patients were admitted to the hospital, 135 died in the hospital and 532 were discharged. From the detailed statement of the annual report regarding patients admitted to the various departments it is found that patients were distributed as follows:

1—Department of surgery—52 patients with surgical conditions of all degrees of severity.

2—Department of isolation (contagious diseases)— 70 patients including cases of scarlet fever, diphtheria, erysipelas, measles, infantile paralysis, meningitis, etc.

3—Department of nervous diseases—40 patients with mental and nervous diseases, many of which were of serious nature.

4—Department of eye, ear and throat—9 patients including cases of tonsilitis, otitis and corneal ulcer.

5—Department of tuberculosis—104 patients of whom 46 died (these patients are all in a late stage of the disease).

6—Department of drug habitues—63 patients of whom 50 were white and 13 colored.

7—Department of obstetrics—69 patients of whom 15 were delivered at the City Home, and 53 sent to the Virginia Hospital, 1 case being an abortion.

8—Department of venereal diseases—140 patients, including 120 cases of syphilis, 16 cases of gonorrhea, and four of chancroid.

9—Department of orthopedic surgery—seven patients of whom five were suffering from tuberculous disease of the bones and two with rickets.

10—Department of general medicine—245 patients, including 60 cases cf cardiac disease. 36 cases of chronic kidney disease. 5 cases of pneumonia, two of typhoid fever. and others with conditions varying in severity.

From the above summary it is quite evident that there is ample medical and surgical work to be performed and from observation of conditions at the home it is believed that there is need of a resident physician who can, in the absence of the members of the visiting staff. assume full responsibility for medical work. Such a resident physician could be secured for about $900 and maintenance.

Internes Should Be Graduate Physicians.

Although there is little inducement to graduate internes to accept positions at the City Home. because of the character of service, and admitting the difficulty at the present time of securing graduate internes in institutional work in Richmond. it is believed that effort should be made to raise the standard of interne service by requiring that internes be graduates. Two graduate internes on full time should be sufficient and if the opportunities for improved medical service at the City Home are taken advantage of. there would be sufficient inducement to graduates to accept service there. Furthermore. small salaries should be offered to internes as suggested in the section of this report which deals with the standardization of salaries and grades.

Pathological Service Should Be Improved.

A small laboratory has been fitted up in the hospital but it is little used by the internes. There is, however, an abundance of pathological material which should be utilized not only for the benefit of patients. but also for the benefit of the medical staff. There is decided need, as pointed out by the former chief health officer, for a laboratory which may perform the Wasserman test for syphilis. As previously noted. there were 120 cases of syphilis cared for at the Home in 1916. and it is more than probable. in fact. certain. that many other inmates of the Home are suffering with this disease. Provided a resident physician can be secured for the City Home. it would be possible for this officer after proper training to perform with the assistance of internes such tests, as well as other routine tests of blood and urine, and to perform also such autopsies as might be desirable.

It is recommended also that a visiting pathologist, preferably one associated with the medical college, be attached to the medical staff to supervise the pathological work of the Home, and develop a more extensive and satisfactory service.

Colored Tuberculosis Pavilion Should Be Transferred to Pine Camp.

In view of the fact that the same classes of patients are cared for at the Pine Camp Hospital as at the City Home it is recommended that the colored tuberculosis pavilion at the City Home be removed to the Pine Camp property. There is no reason why the colored patients should not have the same advantages as white patients in the treatment of tuberculosis. There is ample room for the colored quarters at the Pine Camp, and the cost of providing for these patients there will be no greater than that in their present surroundings. One of the present difficulties in providing for colored patients with tuberculosis is that the hospital is at the City Home and the environment, though pleasing, perhaps, to the eye, is not such as to induce contentment. One of the greatest services rendered by Pine Camp is that of keeping its patients, the majority of whom are hopelessly ill, from losing their enjoyment and desire of life. The surroundings are pleasant, more freedom can be allowed them, and better results secured because of these conditions.

The removal of the tuberculosis wards for colored persons to the Pine Camp would not necessitate the construction of new buildings there. The entire pavilion could easily be removed in sections from the City Home and set up at Pine Camp.

Nursing Service.

The superintendent of nurses is a trained nurse of ability and experience, but except for one assistant nurse who is assigned to the tuberculosis pavilion there are no other graduate nurses. Except for the five colored pupil nurses who are assigned to hospital wards in the colored department, such other assistants as she has are without technical training. Two of these untrained "nurses" are male orderlies in the hospital for colored males, one female practical nurse is assigned to the hospital ward for white females and one to the hospital ward for colored females.

It is not believed that the present nursing service is adequate in view of the extensive medical and surgical service of this institution. It is a physical impossibility for the superintendent of nurses to exercise adequate supervision of all hospital wards in both the white and colored departments, and at the same time be responsible for the dispensing of drugs. The fact that cases of acute venereal diseases must be kept in the home without proper facilities for isolation; that there are large numbers of cases of syphilis; that children must be cared for at the home among old people; that many of the inmates are mentally deficient and require careful observation and almost constant care to prevent their becoming a menace to others,—all these conditions point to the need for improvement of nursing service. It is recommended that two additional trained nurses be employed at salaries conforming to the standards suggested in the report on the standardization of salaries and grades, one to be assigned to the hospital for whites and the other to the hospital for colored patients.

In this connection it should be noted that the salary of the superintendent of nurses is inadequate. This nurse should receive at least $840 a year. The salary of the nurse of the tuberculosis wards is also insufficient. She should be paid the usual rate of trained nurses in charge of wards, namely about $600 a year. The other so-called "nurses," not including pupil nurses, receive salaries which range from $120 to $140 a year.

The salaries offered make it well nigh impossible to fill vacancies properly. For example, from March 22, 1915, to August 29, 1916, the City Home made application to the public employment bureau at various times for nine orderlies, but of about twenty persons sent to the hospital all but two refused appointment at the salaries offered. To expect satisfactory nursing service at the City Home, the city must be prepared to pay for it. The man or woman who accepts a position in an institution of this character at such a low wage is not likely to be efficient in this kind of work or to be able to inspire inmates with respect. To pay these assistants a fair salary would mean a very considerable increase in institutional cost, but if the institution is to be made efficient necessary costs must be met, and this may well be considered a necessary cost.

Care of Children at the City Home.

Unfortunately the city of Richmond has no facilities for the proper institutional care of children. At the City Home there were at the time of this survey seven young children, one of whom was suffering with a serious infection involving the entire face, and two of whom were obviously mentally defective. These children were found mingling with the aged sick, and in several instances being cared for by inmates. This is a condition which should be remedied at once. A city home or almshouse is not a good place for children under any circumstances, but as there is no other place, apparently, where they can be cared for the best that can be done is to provide them with a special ward where they can be given the attention which children need. This is a matter to which the city government should give its immediate attention.

Cells for Patients Suffering With Venereal Disease Should Be Abolished.

In the home for whites, special wards are provided for both male and female patients with open lesions of syphilis and gonorrhea. These patients have their own lavatory and eat apart from other inmates, all dishes used by these patients being washed separately. In addition there are in use for special cases of acute gonorrhea, two cells for males and two cells for females. These cells were originally used for cases of alcoholism and acute mania. Such cases now being rare, the cells are used for gonorrheal cases requiring strict isolation.

In the colored home, isolation wards are provided for both males and females with venereal disease, as in the white home, and there are also two cells similar to those described above which are used in special cases for colored patients.

The propriety of using such cells in a hospital may well be questioned. Certainly there is no warrant in actually putting behind the bars any sick person white or colored. Even alcoholics and cases of acute mania can be restrained without iron bars and this is done in all large hospitals. The effect upon the patient who finds himself placed in a cell is distinctly bad because it arouses in him a feeling of resentment and makes him more inclined to resist discipline and isolation. It is recommended that these cells be eliminated and that ordinary ward rooms be provided in their places.

Isolation for Contagious Diseases.

There is a small building within the enclosure of the City Home and at the rear of the Home for the isolation of patients with contagious diseases. This small pavilion has five rooms, four of which are utilized for patients. Each of the four rooms contains two beds. Eight patients may thus be cared for easily and in an emergency ten.

This building not by any means a satisfactory isolation hospital but under present circumstances is the only place available. Nothing would, however, be gained by making any extensive alterations in the construction or arrangement of this building, for Richmond needs a contagious disease hospital badly—in a different location and built according to modern idea of isolation and sanitation. It should be in the city and not in the country, and it should not be connected in any way with the City Home. The question of need for an isolation hospital is further discussed in the report on the health department.

Reports of Medical Work of Little Value.

Little information is to be gained from the reports of the medical staff of the hospital as found in the annual report of the City Home for 1915. The report on the department of surgery shows merely the number of surgical cases cared for but tells nothing of what was done or the results of treatment. The same is true of the report of the department of isolation, the department of mental and nervous diseases, department of eye, ear and throat, department of venereal diseases, department of orthopedic surgery, department of obstetrics and department of general medicine. The report of the department of tuberclosis gives the number of cases admitted, the number that left without treatment, or were treated and recovered, improved or died and the department of drug habitues gives the number of patients admitted, discharged and died.

Such reports are of little value in determining what medical service is doing for inmates. It would be interesting to know for example, how many major operations were performed, for what conditions performed, and the results of operation; how many of the patients cared for in the isolation hospital recovered; how many obstetrical patients were delivered normally and how many otherwise, and what happened to the infants; how the drug habitues were divided as regards the drug used and what was accomplished by their treatment beyond their discharge; what happened to the patients with tuberculosis disease of the bones, to patients with heart and kidney diseases, etc. The material for medical research at the City Home is excellent and no doubt physicians are doing good work, but if they are to make reports at all, the reports should at least tell what they accomplish.

Fly Menace Should Be Abolished.

The fly nuisance at the City Home is one which should receive immediate attention. Many of the windows were unscreened and the rooms were consequently filled with flies. In an institution of this kind where all manner of communicable diseases are treated the menace of flies is not a matter to be lightly considered. There are patients with open sores, patients with contagious disease, patients with open lesions of venereal disease and the flies have ready access from one patient to another, and to the patients' food and drink.

The superintendent states that it is difficult to keep screens in the windows because the patients take them out. This can be easily prevented. Full length screens should be nailed to the window casings outside of the windows so that screens need not be removed to close or open windows. The use of fly traps and other ordinary methods of fly elimination should be adopted as a matter of course.

Common Drinking Cups and Roller Towels Should Be Abolished.

Water tanks are located conveniently about the buildings, but these are provided with common drinking glasses. Here again is another possibility of spreading infection which should be eliminated. It is recommended that bubble fountains be installed, and the use of water tanks discontinued. One bubble fountain of cheap type at each end of each corridor of the main building would be sufficient under any circumstances the use of common drinking cups should be discontinued at once.

Roller towels, another serious menace to health and prohibited by many cities and States, are found in use in the toilets throughout the institution. Many of these were in filthy condition, and this is not to be wondered at for even if they were changed a half dozen times a day they would probably always be found dirty. It is recommended that sanitary paper towels be installed in place of roller towels for common use in toilets and wash rooms, or one of the many cotton towel dispensing devices which are now on the market. Each inmate should be allowed, in addition, one full size towel each week for his own use, and he should be required to turn in that towel before getting a new one. Additional towels should be allowed in special cases, of course.

Method of Dispensing Drugs Extravagant.

The drug room is under the supervision of the superintendent of nurses. Internes are allowed access to the drug room and they go to the drug room and take such drugs or medicines as they may require. Sometimes if the prescription is a large one, a record is left by the interne upon the file in the drug room, but ordinarily no record is left. If the interne needs pills, tablets, stock solutions, etc., he takes them without restriction.

The closet containing narcotics is kept locked by the superintendent of nurses, but in order that the internes may secure morphine, codeine, etc., when required, small quantities of these drugs are kept in another closet to which internes have access. The whiskey store room where surgical supplies are also stored is kept locked by the superintendent of nurses at all times.

Although the Federal law, relative to the dispensing of narcotics, is very strict in its provisions and penalties, it is not enforced at the City Home. No records are kept of the dispensing of such drugs as required by law. This is a very serious situation and should be corrected at once.

It is apparent that under the present procedure it is impossible to check waste, extravagant use or even misappropriation of drugs. It is not charged that drugs are misappropriated, but it is a fact that loose methods of control make it possible. First of all there should be some responsible person in charge of this drug room at all times, and a complete record should be kept of each prescription issued. Prescriptions should be put up by a pharmacist, and not by an interne who is not yet a graduate in medicine or by a nurse. The employment of a pharmacist would mean too great an expense for the small amount of dispensing done at this institution, and this is not recommended at this time.

It is recommended, however, that the attending medical staff prepare a formulary of the prescriptions best suited for City Home needs. Such a formulary would meet all needs except in acute cases where special medication might be demanded. The prescriptions listed in this formulary should be the simplest possible and the most economical, instead of allowing each physician to prescribe what he sees fit. The formulary system is not a new thing, being in use in many of the large hospitals of the country, where considerably more work is done than at the City Home. If such a formulary were used, it would be possible for the majority of prescriptions to be made up in stock, and these could be issued by the superintendent of nurses each morning. Such tablets, narcotics and other items as physicians and nurses might require should be issued on requisition to the various wards where they should be kept under lock and key by the person in charge of the ward. Physicians should secure emergency drugs from these sources and sign for them. When there is need of replenishing drugs in a ward the person in charge should make a complete report to the superintendent of nurses who may then issue additional quantities. There is no necessity for any one excepting the superintendent of nurses having access to the drug room.

The total cost of drugs, medicines and whiskey used at the City Home in 1916 was according to the superintendent's report for 1916, $1,472.84: at the Virginia Hospital, where each patient is a bed patient requiring almost daily medication, the total cost of drugs was $2,119.18 and for wines, liquors and waters, $391.83, a total of $2,511.01, as compared with the $1,472.84 at the City Home. The total drug cost at the City Home was, therefore, fifty-eight per cent. of that at the Virginia Hospital. This, it is believed, indicates extravagance in the use of drugs. It is difficult to understand how there could fail to be extravagance without a better check on the dispensing of drugs.

Handling of Stores.

The steward is in full charge of the receipts and disbursement of stores for both the institution proper and for out-door relief, subject to the approval of the superintendent. Staple articles, such as meats, milk and cream, potatoes, meal, coffee, sugar, clothing, fuel, etc., are purchased on contract by the administrative board for all institutions. Before letting contracts, the administrative board submits the proposals to the steward of the City Home, and his recommendations are generally accepted. Articles not included in city contracts such as fresh meat, fresh vegetables, household supplies, etc., are purchased by the steward at market rates. For all such purchases on open market, an order signed by the superintendent is issued to the dealer, who returns the orders with his bill on or before the tenth of the succeeding month.

All goods received are checked upon special memorandum books kept by the matrons, and when the dealer returns his bill with the original orders at the end of the month's period the items of the bill are checked by the steward against the entries of these memorandum books. For articles in the commissary an order similar to the one which goes to the dealer is sent by the head of the department needing the articles to the steward who issues what is requested, unless he has reason to believe the demands are not justified, in which case he uses his discretion to to the amount or number of articles requested.

The major books of record kept by the steward are the following:

1—A journal in which is kept a chronological statement of all bills approved and sent forward for payment.

2—A ledger in which all purchases chargeable against the expense item of the appropriation bill are entered under the following headings—date, name of firm, and amount of warrant, the amounts being classified according to the nature of purchases as

    · Subsistence.
    Drugs, medicine and whiskey.
    Surgical and hospital supplies.
    Fuel.
    Light and water.
    Improvements and repairs.
    Hardware and implements.
    Shoes, clothing and dry goods.
    Household articles.
    Furniture and equipment.
    Postage and telephone.
    Printing and stationery.
    Extras for officers and nurses (articles not included
        in regular commissary).

These items are totaled for each month and form the basis of the annual report of expenditures from the expense item of appropriation.

3—Special stock record books, for (a) food and drug supplies and (b) household supplies, shoes, clothing, etc., for each of these two classes of supplies there are two books, one showing quantities of the various supplies on hand, and receipts throughout the year, and the other the disbursement of such articles.

It is believed that the present record keeping system, though furnishing very complete and detailed information regarding all of the steward's transactions, can be greatly simplified by the substitution of stock record cards in place of the present cumbersome book system. There should be for each commodity carried in the commissary a stock record card, which will show for such commodity the quantity on hand at the beginning of the year, subsequent daily receipts and disbursements, and a daily balance of goods on hand. Such a card record might also show the value of receipts and disbursements of stock and the value of the balance on hand. The unit price of commodities being known, the values of receipts and disbursements could be readily entered on these cards. The card should also be arranged to show the various units of the institution to which disbursements were made. Stock cards of this kind are in use in the majority of institutional store houses as they are more convenient than the books of record, and are very easily kept.

In recommending the above change in the record keeping system, it must be acknowledged that the present system is completely and accurately handled by the steward and practically all of the information desired is now available although kept in many books.

Uniformity of Stores Procedure Recommended.

At present each city institution,—Virginia Hospital, City Home and Pine Camp Hospital,—does its own purchasing and handles its stores, according to its own individual system. At the Virginia Hospital and the Pine Camp Hospital because of lack of room, goods can be handled only in small quantities. Furthermore, the method of accounting for stores varies in each institution, and there is no common basis for comparing institutional costs. The City Home schedules its expenditures, other than salaries, according to an outline previously shown, while the Virginia Hospital has an entirely different scheme of classification.

A uniform classification of items of expense would be easily adapted to the use of all institutions since all use food, fuel, clothing, household supplies, drugs and medicines, etc. Its use would make it possible to compare the expenditures of the various institutions for special items and would make annual reports much more readily understood.

It would be quite practicable also to establish the City Home as the central store house for all commodities which are not delivered as per contract by the merchants direct to the institutions, and also such articles of food as need not be purchased fresh daily, for example, household supplies, such as brooms, mops, dust pans, soap, clearing powder, etc.; linen and bedding, towels, gauze, bandages. etc.: stock drug preparations, whiskey, etc. There is ample room at the City Home for the storage of such articles which might then be bought in larger quantities at reduced prices. Deliveries could be made to the various institutions on requisition upon the steward of the City Home. a bill being rendered by the steward at the City Home to the institution receiving supplies.

Worn Out Articles Should Be Returned to Stores.

It is the practice of the steward to issue requisitions from stores without requiring that the articles to be replaced be returned to stores. For example. worn out bed linen is not returned to the store room when new linen is issued. The same applies to other articles of like nature. The steward states that it is the practice to scrutinize all requisitions to satisfy himself that the quantity or number of articles is actually needed but a better plan would be to require the return of used or worn articles to stores before new issues are made. Worn linen. towels, brooms, kitchen utensils. etc., have a salvage value, and unless proper care is taken much useful material may be wasted.

Employment of Inmates.

There is not at present a satisfactory plan for the employment of inmates at the City Home. although there is much to be done which inmates may do. It is true that some inmates are employed regularly in kitchens and dining rooms and others at odd jobs. but the employment is casual and haphazard rather than based upon any definite program.

It is obvious that any attempt to assign inmates to work without first having knowledge of their physical and mental condition would be unsatisfactory, and as elsewhere recommended physical and mental examination of inmates should be the first step in this progress. There is plenty of work to be done. and no inmate who is able to work even for only short periods of the day should be idle. It may tax the ingenuity of the superintendent or matrons to find work for inmates, but it can be done somewhere in the house or on the grounds. Physical or mental inaction means more rapid physical or mental deterioration for old people. There is much useful work in the making of baskets and chair bottoms, repairing old furniture and equipment. cleaning windows. mowing lawns. cutting wood. attending to horses. etc., that inmates may do without overtaxing their strength. Old women who cannot move about would no doubt be glad to sew or knit if materials were furnished them. The man or woman who has a job, no matter how insignificant that job may be, gains in self-respect over the sitter who idles the whole day away on his cot or in a chair on the veranda.

Laundry Service Should Be Extended.

At the present time laundry for inmates only at the City Home is done in the laundry there. The uniforms of nurses and such other minor articles as are done outside is paid for by the lot, and in 1916 this amounted to $208.55, which is paid out of the funds for relief of outdoor poor. At the Virginia Hospital likewise laundry work is done outside the institution and this cost $2,947.03 in 1916. At the Pine Camp also laundry work is sent out (but the figures of cost for 1916 are not available).

It would seem entirely practicable to equip and maintain at the City Home a laundry for all institutions; labor could be largely furnished by inmates under competent supervision, and the cost of laundry service for all three institutions materially reduced. The initial cost would be for equipment and for the enlargement of laundry quarters at the City Home, where there are but two laundry rooms, one for washing and one for drying. This could be done by putting an extension on the laundry wash room, there being sufficient ground space for such extension.

Ice Plant at City Home.

At the present time ice is purchased from local dealers as required by each of the three institutions, City Home, Virginia Hospital, and Pine Camp. At none of these institutions are there proper facilities for ice storage. The cost of ice at the City Home was $455.73 in 1916, and at the Virginia Hospital $1,281.72. Figures of ice cost at the Pine Camp for 1916 were not available at the time of this study. The total cost of ice for all three institutions is in the neighborhood of $2,000 a year.

It is suggested that consideration be given to the establishment of an ice plant at the City Home. The labor cost of the operation of such a plant would be low, as inmate labor could be used and city power could be utilized for the operation of machinery. A plant with a capacity of about 1,000 to 1,500 pounds daily would probably be sufficient for the needs of these three institutions, and this could be provided at relatively small cost. Small ice plants which operate automatically by a time clock are on the market, and the investigator has seen several of these giving good service. At the San Francisco Isolation Hospital, for example, such a plant is in operation at a cost which is practically negligible.

Fire Prevention at City Home Inadequate.

Although the City Home is of fire resisting construction, it is not by any means fire-proof, due to the wooden floors and stairways, wooden windows, furniture, etc. In view of the fact that so many of these inmates are old and infirm there should be adequate protection against fire. A sufficient number of large chemical extinguishers is provided on each floor, but this is not all that is needed.

There should be first of all a regular assignment of all employees and working inmates to stations in the event of fire, and fire drills should be held occasionally. In several places on each floor fire buckets should be kept filled with water, and in addition sufficient length of fire hose with attachments should be installed so that any part of the building may be reached.

The rear outside stairways of the white home would have to be used in the event of fire—but as these are of wood they would be probably the first to burn. There should be on each of the City Home buildings over one story in height proper iron fire escapes with large entrances properly lighted and with doors opening outward. The platforms of these fire escapes should be wide enough to permit the handling of a stretcher and the stairways should be wide and not so steep as to endanger the footing of old patients. All fire exits should be plainly marked with red signs and with red lights at night.

The fact that there has never been a serious fire does not mean that there may not be one. The best fire insurance is proper prevention against fire and the best life insurance for inmates is adequate means and methods of emptying the buildings quickly.

Outdoor Poor Relief.

The city appropriated in 1916, $15,000 for the outdoor relief of the poor, and in 1917 a similar amount. The expenditure of this sum is under the direction of the superintendent of the city.

Outdoor relief of the poor consists of the distribution of shoes, coal and wood to the needy poor. When an application for relief is received by the superintendent he refers the matter to one of the eighteen visitors of the City Mission for investigation. The city is divided into districts and one visitor is assigned to visiting the poor within her district. The visitors are women of the city who volunteer their services for this work, and the organization called the City Mission is affiliated with the Associated Charities. There is also a City Mission of twelve colored visitors which co-operates with the superintendent in the same way.

If the application for relief comes through some person well known to the superintendent, emergency relief is given and the visitor of that district in which the applicant lives is asked to make an investigation. The applications received from the city physicians are also honored by the superintendent, and in cases of the illness of a poor person, a "sick" ration so-called, consisting of flour, bacon and other food supplies may be issued on the order of the city physician.

Coal is furnished and delivered in one-half ton lots by the dealer having the coal contract. Wood is delivered in one-hundred block lots, and shoes, clothing, etc., as needed. No goods may be delivered by the dealer without an order signed by the superintendent of public charities, and these orders must be returned monthly with his bill to the steward. These orders are made out in duplicate, one copy going to the merchant and the other being kept in the order book. The orders are serially numbered and an index book for each kind of commodity furnished is used as reference to these orders by name and serial number of the order.

Prior to the present year, corn meal was also furnished, but this practice was discontinued during the current year. In addition to the furnishing of fuel, food, shoes and clothing, as previously described, the city has made arrangement with local druggists whereby prescriptions are furnished to the poor at ten cents each. In addition the city pays certain fixed sums quarterly to these druggists as follows:

```
1—$39.07 quarterly
2— 37.50     "
3— 40.62     "
4— 39.06     "
5— 37.50     "
6— 37.50     "
7— 37.50     "
           ———
Total   $268.75      "      or $1,075 yearly.
```

The following summary compares the expenditures for outdoor poor relief of the first six months of 1916 with the expenditures for the first six months of 1917:

676

mparative Summary of Costs of Out-Door Relief of Poor—1916-1917.

Item of Expenditure	1916 (First Six Months)							1917 (First Six Months)						
	January	February	March	April	May	June	Total	January	February	March	April	May	June	Total
Dispensaries	$127 09	$124 96	$268 75	68 85	$127 38	$268 75	$ 587 50	$ 15 05	$127 80	$268 75	$ 73 44	$178 43	$268 75	$ 587 90
Maintenance of ambulance	247 50	262 50	199 32	246 00	158 00	183 68	831 68	287 60	277 55	182 07	56 86	4	4 85	529 64
Meals	218 05	248 85	235 00	31 65	49 55	99 00	1,268 80	287 40	1,961 63	456 60		23 10	10 15	456 00
Beds	1,639 26	3,226 55	143 15			33 75	729 80	1,907 90	5 76	117 76	4 50	88 82		773 22
Fuel	4 50	3 00	25 68	6 00	4 50	3 00	4,891 46	2 25	55 62	1 87	4 50	4 50		8,954 22
Horse shoeing, veterinary		40 54		20 76	89 22	26 00	21 00	33 20		4 50	7 08	68 06		21 50
Forage			42 82				169 34	30 00		21 78				175 64
Burial					7 25	20 50	7 25						20 25	30 00
Repairs to harness, vehicles	30 00	7 10	6 85	42 15	7 40		114 40				31 60	18 40	29 98	51 85
Uniform and sundry	purchased for med. call	inspect	or of	health d	epartme	nt	4 55	nil				360 00		43 88
Automobile	4 55											75		390 60
Miscellaneous								1 25						$ 00
Total	$2,270 95	$3,913 50	$995 77	$415 41	$598 10	$685 29	$8,570 02	$2,276 75	$2,428 25	$1,003 82	$173 47	$719 56	$533 96	$6,936 32

It will be noted in the foregoing table that there has been considerable saving in 1917 as compared with 1916 in the cost of ambulances, maintenance and the issuance of meal and fuel. It is quite probable that this reduction in cost, representing as it does a reduction in the number of applicants for relief, will continue if prohibition continues, and it should be upon complete and detail reports of actual service rendered that the budget for the coming year is prepared, provided the city still continues this form of relief. But as will be noted from the foregoing summary, the city should not use from the fund money which should be used for City Home purposes or for equipment for other city departments.

Outdoor Poor Relief by City Should be Discontinued.

The whole matter of outdoor relief of the poor is one that deserves serious consideration by the city government. It is not believed that the present plan of furnishing relief upon the recommendation of volunteer investigators should be continued. The Associated Charities is performing a similar work and spends annually about $10,000 for outdoor poor relief. Leaving out of consideration the cost of relief furnished by the numerous other agencies of the city, which are acting entirely independently, the city of Richmond pays annually for outdoor poor relief about $25,000. It is safe to say that the total cost of outdoor poor relief in Richmond is in the neighborhood of $30,000 a year.

The tendency at the present time in cities throughout the country is to turn over to Associated Charities all outdoor poor relief work, and this has been found to be the most satisfactory plan, unless the city is prepared to assume the responsibility of organizing its own poor relief on a proper basis with paid social investigators. This latter plan is not believed to be a good one for Richmond, and it is believed that Richmond should discontinue as a municipal enterprise the furnishing of outdoor relief. All this work should be turned over to the Associated Charities, which is better able to render this service satisfactorily than is the city. This would centralize in the Associated Charities the greater part of the relief work of the city and would permit a more satisfactory scrutiny of cases requiring relief.

The transfer of this function to the Associated Charities would of course increase the financial burden of this organization, but it is believed that the citizens of the community could better afford to furnish the additional support needed by the Associated

Charities than to continue the present loose system of giving relief. The visitors of the City Mission, both white and colored, are no doubt performing their voluntary duties with the best of intentions, but unless there is some one with knowledge of existing conditions and thorough understanding of social problems to pass upon their recommendations, there is almost certain to be waste of public funds. The superintendent of the City Home has not the knowledge of social conditions and problems necessary to make his supervision effective, but the general secretary of the Associated Charities has, it is believed, such knowledge because of long experience in social service in the city.

Provided the Associated Charities takes over this work for the city, the city should accept definite responsibility for bills for articles furnished by the Associated Charities for the relief of such persons as might be proper charges of the city, such bills being approved, of course, by the head of the proposed department of public welfare. It is impossible to offer definite recommendations on this point, but it is believed that a thorough study of the work of the Associated Charities will convince the city authorities that this organization is much better prepared to handle outdoor relief work economically and efficiently than is the city. Once this fact is settled, a working arrangement can be made with the Associated Charities.

Virginia Hospital

VIRGINIA HOSPITAL.

General Character of Service Excellent.

The Virginia Hospital accommodates approximately 125 patients, the number varying in 1916 from 86 to 141, with a daily average of 102 patients. The main building of three stories is used for white patients and the annex for colored patients, the number of white patients cared for being about the same as the number of colored patients.

Although this building, with the exception of the annex, was not originally designed for hospital purposes, and is, therefore, not so arranged as to make for most efficient service, the work which is being done is to be highly commended, and with the facilities at hand the nurses, physicians and other employees are rendering an excellent community service. There is no evidence of uncleanliness or lack of proper attention to patients, but on the contrary many evidences of efficiency. In this report no recommendations will be made for any radical changes in construction, but rather for certain improvements in methods which it is believed will make for improved service.

Within the limits of this study it was not possible to go carefully into all details of hospital management and operation. It is believed, however, from such study as has been made that the Virginia Hospital compares very favorably with other hospitals of its character and size throughout the country. The criticism of this report has, therefore, been limited to those defects of service which are easily remedied under existing conditions, i. e., without radical change of hospital plan or organization.

Organization and Personnel.

The Virginia Hospital is under the direction of a superintendent* responsible directly to the administrative board. Owing to the illness of the superintendent at the time of this survey, the assistant superintendent was acting as superintendent until the vacancy could be filled.

---

*Since this report was written the superintendent's resignation was accepted and the position left vacant. A medical director at $50 a month was appointed by the administrative board to exercise medical supervision over both the Virginia Hospital and the Pine Camp Hospital.

The following summary gives the number and title of employees together with their annual salaries at the time of the survey:

Superintendent	$ 1,500.00
Assistant superintendent	780.00
Superintendent of nurses	1,000.00
Superintendent of operating room	780.00
Night superintendent	780.00
Head nurse	660.00
Pupil nurses—27 at $108	2,916.00
Anaesthetist	600.00
Chief resident physician	720.00
Ambulance surgeon—2 at $300	600.00
Internes—5 at $60	300.00
Clerk	900.00
Telephone operator (day)	600.00
Telephone operator (night)	600.00
Housekeeper	600.00
Cook	420.00
1st Assistant cook	240.00
2nd Assistant cook	180.00
Dishwasher—2 at $180	360.00
Kitchen helper	300.00
Kitchen helper	240.00
Head waiter	240.00
Maids—6 at $180	1,080.00
Seamstress	180.00
Floorman	300.00
Engineer	900.00
Furnaceman	240.00
Elevatorman	240.00
Orderly	360.00
Orderly	300.00
Orderly	240.00
Night orderly	300.00
Night orderly	240.00
Operating room orderly	300.00
Total salaries	$ 20,076.00
Total force	71

Ratio of Patients to Employees.

In modern well equipped and adequately manned hospitals it is generally considered that the ratio of patients to employees should be about one to one. That is for a one-hundred-bed hospital. which furnishes service along all lines, including out-patient and social service work, there would be needed about 100 employees. It is of course not possible to establish this as a definite ratio for much depends upon the convenience of arrangement of the hospital and the individual ability of employees. Accepting this, however, as an approximate standard, it is evident that the Virginia Hospital is being run with a very small force, the patient employee ratio being considerably greater than one to one. Furthermore, the salaries paid employees are unusually low. In succeeding pages of this report, recommendations for increasing the hospital force will be made.

Records of Patients.

The clerk of the hospital is to be highly commended for the manner in which the records of patients are kept. All records are examined by her as they come down from the wards and no record is accepted for filing until it is complete. The records as well as filing methods now in use are well designed and satisfactory for the present service. Special card index history records are kept for all patients on which are summarized the salient facts of the history, and in addition a card record is kept of diseases and injuries classified according to the approved hospital nomenclature in international use, reference being made to the history record number so that any physician desiring to study a special group of cases has ready access to the proper records.

The matter of keeping records of patients is such a vital one, and yet the manner of history record keeping in the majority of hospitals of the country is so open to criticism that it is indeed gratifying to find a hospital in which the attention is given to this matter which it deserves.

Visiting Medical Staff of the Hospital Should Be Increased.

The visiting staff, which is made up largely of physicians and surgeons affiliated with the medical college, comprises a chairman, a chief surgeon and two assistants, a chief physician and five assistants, and in addition, specialists in eye, ear, nose and throat diseases, in orthopedics, nervous and mental diseases, skin diseases, and in oral and dental surgery.

Although the present medical staff is rendering excellent service, as judged from available reports, it is believed that the medical staff of the Virginia Hospital should be increased by the addition of a number of the young physicians of the city as an assistant or adjunct attending staff. The function of a city hospital is not only to care for the indigent sick, but also to give opportunity to the young physicians of the community to receive the experience and training in hospital, medical and surgical work which they need. It would be simple to provide such a rotation in service if this adjunct or assistant medical staff were established and organized so that each of its members could have three or four months at least of active hospital service each year. The members of the attending staff should be recruited from this assistant medical staff.

The physician in chief of the medical staff recommends in his annual report for 1916 the appointment of a resident surgeon. a resident pediatrician, a resident obstetrician and a resident pathologist, in addition to the present resident physician. It is not believed that these appointments are advisable at the present time with the possible exception of the resident pathologist. The need for such additions to service would, however, be largely met by additions to the visiting staff, as recommended above. (Note).

Visiting Pathologist Recommended.

In view of the fact that internes doing pathological work are undergraduates. it is recommended that a visiting pathologist be appointed who may supervise the work of internes and instruct them not only in the routine work of the laboratory. but also in the technique of the more highly specialized bacteriological and pathological work. The need for a department of pathology has been pointed out in the annual report of the superintendent. It

---

Note.—Since this report was written the administrative board has appointed a "medical director" to assume responsibility for the efficiency of medical service in the Virginia Hospital and the Pine Camp Hospital. The need for such medical director is not apparent. nor is it reasonable to assume that a medical director at $600 a year will be able to give sufficient time and attention to the work to make his influence of value. It is believed that with a responsible superintendent in charge of each institution. all the supervision needed can be readily given.

is not believed desirable at this time for the hospital to employ
a paid pathologist, but if the necessary service cannot be secured
on a voluntary basis, a pathologist should be employed on part
time at small salary—preferably one connected with the medical
college who may act also as visiting pathologist to the City Home.

Autopsy Work Should Be Increased.

Little autopsy work is now done although such work is most
important from the standpoint of the physicians and surgeons
connected with the hospital, and also the faculty and students of
the medical college. Autopsy records show that even in some of
the best hospitals of this country with all modern facilities for
diagnosis, only about 50 per cent. of diagnoses are verified at autopsy. It is, therefore, suggested, that following the appointment
of a visiting pathologist, a systematic effort be made to secure the
consent to autopsy of friends and relatives of the deceased. This
is by no means always easy to secure, but in a free public hospital
of this type many cases may be brought to autopsy by the effort
of the physicians, surgeons and others connected with the hospital.

Resident Medical Staff.

Ordinarily there are, in addition to the resident physician, who
is a graduate physician and receives $720 a year, two graduate
physicians who act as ambulance surgeons at $300 a year each,
and six undergraduate house physicians, who receive only $5 a
month in lieu of laundry. These latter house physicians are students of the medical college. At present there are a graduate resident physician, two graduate physicians as ambulance surgeons,
and five undergraduate house physicians.

The service of house physicians is for one year, and prior to
the present year the service of these men was so arranged that
they were rotated through all departments of the service, but
owing to the present lack of a full complement of house physicians, it has been necessary to change this schedule somewhat. A
paid anaesthetist is now employed and no anaesthetics are administered by internes. Laboratory work, which with the administration of anaesthetics formerly was a rotating assignment, is now
done by all, each interne doing all laboratory work of the floor
or department to which he is assigned.

The present arrangement and schedule of interne service is
perhaps as satisfactory as could be devised to meet the present

situation, as regards medical service. It is believed, however, that the present service presents several defects, which may be pointed out here as worthy of consideration, as soon as normal conditions are established.

1—Internes should be graduate instead of undergraduate physicians, and should be paid small salaries of $120 to $240 a year.

2—Interne service should be for eighteen months rather than one year, in order that men may have ample time to become thoroughly familiar with hospital methods and procedure.

3—Not all internes should come on service at one time, but the service should be so arranged that there will always be a complement of experienced internes to help the newcomers in adjusting themselves to the service.

4—The assignment to laboratory work should be a definite assignment to each interne in rotation—otherwise laboratory work, which is an important part of the internes' training and essential to efficient hospital service, will be neglected for work more interesting to him.

5—Ambulance service should be assigned to internes in rotation, provided all are graduate physicians. This service is educationally valuable to internes.

Internes Should Receive Instruction in Administration of Anaesthetics.

Although the present plan of having a paid anaesthetist is to be preferred to the assignment of undergraduates to this work, it is essential that undergraduate internes be given all possible training in the administration of anesthetics. The hospital is the only place where these men are able to secure such experience, and it should therefore be the duty of the paid anesthetist to see that the internes are given as much instruction as possible. The resident physician should make definite assignments of internes for such instruction as far as this is possible without disturbing the routine schedule of their work.

Reading and Recreation Room for Internes Recommended.

Although it is recognized that the present available space for internes is quite limited, it is recommended that effort be made by rearrangement of internes' quarters or readjustment of other space on this floor to provide a reading and recreation room for internes. The opportunities of internes for recreation under present circumstances are very few, and yet efficiency of interne service demands that more consideration be given to furnishing them the comforts and conveniences of a hospital home. There are eight rooms now available for internes, and it believed that by a readjustment of this space the necessary additional room recommended could be provided.

Internes' Quarters Should Be Provided With Shower Baths.

The bathroom for internes is provided with a tub bath only, which is by no means as convenient for use as would be a shower bath. Experience in hospital service, where the demands of the service cannot be anticipated, teaches that the interne suffers frequent annoyance and inconvenience because of lack of proper toilet facilities. In view of the fact that the city is securing satisfactory interne service at very low cost, it owes it to the internes of the hospital to provide all conveniences within reason.

X-Ray Laboratory Should Be Provided.

The need for an X-Ray laboratory at the Virginia Hospital has been commented on by the superintendent, the chief surgeon and the chief physician in the annual report for 1916. This is a very evident need and one which should be met. X-Ray work for the Virginia Hospital is now done by the Roentgenologist of the Memorial Hospital at the cost of the plates, but the Roentgenologist keeps the plates. X-Ray service in a hospital of this kind is of the greatest value not only to the patient, but also to physicians and internes, and the plates taken should become in all cases part of the official hospital record of patients.

Additional Trained Nurses Recommended.

Routine nursing service is provided by pupil nurses almost exclusively, there being but six trained nurses attached to the hospital, namely, the superintendent, assistant superintendent, night superintendent, operating room superintendent, superintendent of nurses, and head nurse. There are twenty-seven pupil nurses engaged in regular ward work under the general supervision of the superintendent of nurses.

It is not believed that the supervision given to pupil nurses is by any means adequate. It is obvious that the superintendent of nurses cannot give the individual attention to these pupil nurses which they require, and there is apparent a lack of the strict discipline of pupil nurses which efficient service demands. It is believed that there should be in immediate charge of each main nursing department of the hospital a trained nurse of experience and ability who may give immediate supervision to pupil nurses. This would mean the employment of at least three additional trained nurses, one for each patient floor of the main building and one for each patient floor of the annex.

Furthermore, it is not believed that the number of pupil nurses is sufficient, and effort should be made to increase the number in so far as this can be done with the present facilities. It is far better to have too many than too few pupil nurses.

Admitting Room Should Be Equipped As Out-Patient Surgical Department.

The admitting room which is in charge of the resident physician is on the ground floor of the main building. There are, however, no adequate facilities for emergency dressings and treatment, and minor surgical cases which could be well taken care of in such admitting room must be taken to the operating room, which is on the second floor. It is recommended that this admitting room be properly equipped for emergency work and utilized as a surgical out-patient department as far as possible. Properly equipped, such an emergency surgical room or accident ward would be of considerable service, not only as a first aid station for cases to be admitted, but also as an accident room in which internes could receive training in first aid and accident work. Although the space now available for such service is rather limited, it is believed that it could be utilized effectively by equipping the present lavatory connected with the admitting room as a private surgical dressing room, the large admitting room being utilized as a waiting room and for the keeping of such records of the service as are desirable.

Ambulance Service Decreasing.

There are two ambulances regularly in active service, and these are housed at the City Home. The chauffeurs of these ambulances live at the City Home and their salaries and maintenance are charged, very unjustly, against the City Home. Two ambulance surgeons of the Virginia Hospital are detailed to ambulance duty only.

The records show that the number of daily calls varies from ten to fifteen, the great majority of these calls being for patients who are treated by the ambulance surgeon and left at the place of call. Only about twelve to fifteen per cent. of the patients seen on ambulance calls are removed to the hospital. The following comparison for the first six months of 1916, in which year there was a total of 4,538 calls shows that since the beginning of the present year there has been a very considerable decrease in the number of calls.

Ambulance Calls—1916 and 1917.
(First Six Months.)

	Jan.	Feb.	Mar.	Apr.	May.	June	Total
1916	362	315	330	385	405	496	2,293
1917	284	259	238	318	291	384	1,774
Decrease	78	56	92	67	114	112	519

From the above figures it will be seen that there was a total decrease for the six months' period of 1917 of 519 calls, or an average decrease of about three calls a day. This decrease of ambulance service is significant in view of the statement of the secretary to the visiting staff who states in the annual report of 1916 that there was a marked decrease of injuries due to drunken brawls since prohibition became effective in November, 1916.

Condition of Ambulances and Equipment.

The ambulances of the Virginia Hospital, which are kept at the City Home garage, are cared for by the chauffeurs, who do all minor repair work. The city has three large ambulances, one of which was purchased during 1916. Two of these ambulances only were in regular use at the time of this survey.

Although no records are kept of mileage costs, the records of the cost of maintenance of ambulances, together with the salary cost for chauffeurs, are shown in the report of the City Home, the ambulance costs being included in the costs of outdoor poor relief and the salary cost for chauffeurs in the payroll costs of the City Home. According to these reports, ambulance maintenance, exclusive of the salaries of chauffeurs, amounted to $1.760.28 in 1916. It is suggested that individual records be kept of the cost of operation and maintenance of each ambulance, showing the cost per mile operated. Comparison of ambulance costs from these records would give an indication of the relative efficiency of these machines and would be of considerable value not only in determining how machines are being operated by chauffeurs, but also in indicating the most satisfactory machines for future purchase.

Both ambulances are fitted with the old style ambulance bed which lies flat upon the ambulance floor, and takes up the whole width of the floor. These beds are very unsatisfactory from the standpoint of the patient and also from the standpoint of the physician, who must climb over the patient in order to minister to him if any treatment is necessary while en route to the hospital. The more modern type of ambulance bed is only about one-half the width of the ambulance floor, and is supported in spring brackets which make for the comfort of the patient and convenience of the surgeon. In the event that the physician must attend the patient during the journey to the hospital, there is ample space between the bed and the opposite side of the ambulance. It is suggested that estimates be secured from the manufacturers of these ambulances as to the cost of equipping them with more satisfactory beds. If the cost is excessive, this may be left to a later day, when complete overhauling of the ambulances becomes necessary.

The ambulance bags carried by the surgeons were found to be in improper condition, one bag in particular being in the greatest disorder and carrying an equipment of surgical instruments which were so rusty as to warrant immediate discarding. There is no standard equipment for ambulance bags, and the ambulance surgeons therefore stock up their bags with whatever they think they need. One of the bags which was found at the ambulance station had evidently not been put in order since the last call, and the gauze originally wrapped in sterile packages was exposed to contamination by other articles in the bag. It is of course difficult to keep articles sterile in an ambulance bag which is in frequent use, but certainly ordinary care should be taken to prevent the infection of wounds through dirty instruments and dressings.

First of all, there should be a specified list of articles which are to be carried in ambulance bags, and only this equipment should be permitted. Before the bag goes out this list should be checked by a nurse to see that it is complete. When the bag is returned, if there is opportunity before the next call, the nurse should clean the instruments and put the bag again in order with full equipment. A list of this equipment should be posted in the admitting room and a copy of the list pasted on the lid of the bag.

In addition to the bag and equipment, the lockers in the ambulances for larger articles, such as rolls of cotton, splints, large bandages, oil for burns, etc., should be properly equipped and kept in order. There should also be a list of the articles to be carried, and the ambulance surgeon should be charged with seeing that this locker is kept in order.

Care of Children.

As pointed out by the superintendent of the hospital in the annual report, the facilities for the care of sick children, particularly during the summer months, are entirely inadequate, and the superintendent recommends that the children's ward be enlarged. Since the need for more accommodations for children is greatest in the summer months, it is believed that if the present accommodation for children were supplemented by the provision of a summer baby camp at the Pine Camp Hospital, as recommended in the report on the Pine Camp Hospital, immediate needs would be met, although it is admitted that they are not satisfactory. The need for better provision for children is most evident in the case of colored children, who must now be kept in the corridor on the second floor of the annex.

Improvement in Obstetrical Operating Room Recommended.

The reports of the obstetrical department show clearly that good results are being obtained in this branch of service. A special delivery room with a sterilizing room and toilet facilities for the use of physicians is provided and is in general satisfactory as regards equipment except that the basins used by physicians in cleansing and sterilizing the hands are not properly equipped with foot levers so that water may be turned on or off without the necessity of using the hands. This requires that surgeons turn off the water themselves at the faucet, thus contaminating their hands just sterilized, or that a nurse or other assistant assist them. It is suggested that these basins be equipped with foot levers similar to those used in the main operating room.

General Operating Room Service.

The general operating room of the hospital is on the third floor and well lighted, heated and otherwise equipped for satisfactory service. An operating room superintendent is in charge of this room and also in charge of instruments and other surgical equipment. This nurse is required to keep the records of operation in a register which calls for the following information: Date of operation, number of operation, name of patient, color, name of operator, diagnosis, nature of operation, anaesthetic used. name of anaesthetizer, and result. This record is well kept and satisfactory in detail, as it is designed merely as a summary of operative procedure from which the annual report of the operating room superintendent is made up. The annual report of operative procedure as given in the annual report is, however, not satisfactory, in that it states merely the nature of operations performed, and the number and color of patients. Further comment will be made on this point in a discussion of the annual report.

Need for Social Service Department.

The need for a social service department has also been pointed out by the superintendent in her annual report for 1916. Such social service department should, if it is established, be run in connection with the dispensary of the medical college. The value of social service work cannot be overestimated, and the addition of such a department to the Virginia Hospital service would greatly increase the community service which that hospital is rendering. The initial expense should not be great. All that is needed in the beginning is a secretary who can work out a plan of co-operation with all the visiting nurse agencies of the city so that the follow-up work necessary for patients discharged from the hospital can be carried on by these visiting nurses.

Care of Patients' Clothing.

The clothing of patients after being listed is placed in bags which are hung upon hooks in a clothing room, the clothing of each patient thus being kept separate from that of other patients. As a result, when the patient is discharged. he obtains his clothing in the same condition as it was when he was admitted plus the wrinkling and disorder incident to their being packed in the bags. The patient therefore goes out of the hospital with his clothing in disorder and looking "seedy." This is entirely unnecessary, and the present procedure should be radically changed as follows:

When a patient is admitted his clothing should first be thoroughly brushed and cleaned. If much wrinkled and disordered, it should be pressed and then hung upon holders which will keep the clothing unwrinkled. If the clothing requires mending, it should be mended, buttons should be sewed on and missing articles supplied as far as possible. If it is necessary to secure an additional employee for this work, the hospital should provide it, as the gain in self-respect and respect for the institution which the outgoing patient will have will more than offset the small salary necessary for such an employee.

At the San Francisco Hospital, for example, a tailor is employed who cleans, repairs and presses garments, and from his stock of uncalled-for clothing adds missing articles, such as socks, hats, neckties, etc. The patient who leaves the San Francisco Hospital does not go out looking like a tramp and feeling like one, but goes out with head erect and with consciousness of being fit for his return to work.

Use of Formulary in Dispensing Drugs Suggested.

The drug room of the hospital is under the supervision of the operating room nurse, because of the location of the drug room near the operating room. Prescriptions from the stock preparations are filled by this nurse, other prescriptions which require compounding being filled by the medical college, which is affiliated with the hospital. It is believed that a very considerable economy would result in the handling of drugs if a hospital formulary were adopted by the medical staff for use by them and the resident medical officers. It would then be possible to make up stock prescriptions of practically all preparations needed, and these could be dispensed as at present. This plan has also been recommended for use at the City Home. If such a standard formulary could be adopted for use in these two institutions, a pharmacist might be employed on part time to compound for both institutions the preparations called for by this formulary.

The records of the dispensing of drugs from the drug room are also kept by the operating nurse. These records include a record of drugs dispensed from the drug room, prescriptions compounded at the medical college and a special record of narcotics as required by the federal law relative to the recording of data on the dispensing of narcotics. These records are very satisfactorily kept.

Fire Prevention Inadequate.

Chemical fire extinguishers are provided in sufficient number on each floor, and on the first floor there is ample length of fire hose. Fire escapes are provided leading from all floors at the east and west sides of the building and exits to fire escapes are properly indicated. There is, however, no fire hose on the second floor. The iron fire escapes are altogether too narrow at landings and stairways are too steep to permit any one except a person in complete control of his faculties to get down without danger of injury. The landings of fire escapes are too narrow to permit the rapid and safe handling of stretchers. No fire drills are held and proper assignments of employees to fire stations are not made.

The fire risk of this old building is considerable, and once a fire gained headway in the hospital it would be doomed. It is therefore incumbent upon the city to see that all facilities for fire prevention, fire fighting and rapid emptying of the building are available. First of all, there should be sufficient hose with connection on all floors, and in addition to the present equipment of fire extinguishers, there should be racks of water buckets kept constantly filled with water. The fire escapes should be improved by making the landings and stairways wider so that stretchers could be properly handled, and the exits to the fire escapes should be widened with larger doorways opening outward on a level with the fire escapes. Fire drills should be held and all employees should be assigned to stations and instructed in the most prompt and effective way of removing patients by stairways and fire escapes. Instructions to employees should be posted throughout the building so that they may have an opportunity to familiarize themselves with the procedure in the event of fire. Without at least the organization of employees for fire fighting and the handling of patients, it is certain that great loss of life would occur in the event of fire at this hospital.

Common Drinking Cups Should Be Abolished.

It was noted that at the Virginia Hospital, just as at the City Home, the ice cooler with a common drinking cup is in evidence and daily use. It hardly seems necessary to point out the menace of this common drinking cup, particularly in a hospital. It is recommended that the ice water tanks and drinking cups be abolished, and that either individual paper cups or bubble fountains be provided.

Handling of Stores.

The storekeeping of the hospital is in charge of the housekeeper who orders, receives, inspects and issues all food and household supplies, linen, drugs and medical and surgical supplies being under the control of the superintendent of nurses.

The present housekeeper is a competent and efficient woman, and is performing her work in a very satisfactory manner. Supplies are issued only upon written requisition of the proper officer.

these requisitions being filed and entered in a book which shows the distribution of supplies to the various units of the hospital. A record book is also kept in which are listed goods received and the prices thereof.

Purchases are made upon contract for all goods for which contracts have been let by the administrative board. Other articles are purchased as required on open market order and at market prices. In the report on the City Home it is suggested that the storeroom at the City Home be made the storeroom for all institutions for such supplies as are not purchased on contract or which must not be purchased fresh daily.

Lack of adequate refrigerating systems and the use throughout the hospital of small ice chests means a very considerable ice consumption. It is not recommended that the city go to the immediate expense of installing a modern refrigerating system, although this would no doubt be an ultimate economy. In the report on the City Home, however, the possibility of reducing ice costs for all institutions by the establishment of an ice-making plant is pointed out. In 1916 the ice bill of the Virginia Hospital was $1,281.72, indicating the need for economy along this line.

Under the present plan of handling stores it is believed that there is an adequate check against the misuse of stores, and no change in the present procedure is therefore recommended. The stores kept on hand are in such small quantities as to make any more detailed stores record keeping plan inadvisable.

Trained Dietitian Should Be Employed.

It is believed that the Virginia Hospital would do well to engage a trained dietitian to take full charge of the purchase, distribution, preparation and serving of all foods. This would relieve the housekeeper of the greater part of her responsibility in these matters. She should then be given full charge of all housekeeping work proper—that is, the cleaning of the hospital, the handling of household linen, supervision of the sewing room and other functions properly falling in the sphere of housekeeping. This recommendation does not imply criticism of the work of the present housekeeper, but the proper and economical control of the food problems requires scientific training and experience which the housekeeper lacks.

Costs of Hospital Service.

The cost per patient per day, as given in the annual report for 1916, was $1.50. The clerk states that this figure should be

$1.58, which of course in a year's period means several thousand dollars' difference in cost from that stated. This cost is not a high one, in view of the generally increased cost of food and drugs, and compares favorably with the patient day costs of other institutions of like character throughout the country. It is largely due, however, to the relatively low salary cost of this hospital that the patient day cost is low. As a matter of fact, it would be considerably higher if the service of the hospital were adequately manned.

Reductions in cost, therefore, if there are to be any, will have to come through reduction in maintenance costs through better coordination of purchasing and service operations of the Virginia Hospital with that of other institutions under city control. In the report on the City Home the possibility of utilizing the storeroom at the City Home as a general storeroom for certain supplies to be purchased in larger quantities and distributed from that point has been suggested. The possibility of a reduction of costs for laundry service and for ice by having a general laundry plant and an ice-making plant at the City Home has also been suggested. This closer co-ordination of services can be worked out more satisfactorily if there were one individual responsible for the administration of these institutions, as is proposed in the recommendation for a department of public welfare under a single commissioner.

As has already been noted, there are certain costs, namely the salaries of chauffeurs and the cost of ambulance maintenance which are properly charges against the Virginia Hospital, but are now included in the costs of the City Home. The stated patient day cost of $1.58 does not therefore represent the true cost, and if there is to be any proper comparison of costs, these costs should be included in the Virginia Hospital reports.

For the first six months of 1917 the total number of patient days was 18,172. The salary cost for this period was $9,155.48, and the expense cost $19,914.70, a total of $29,070.18. On this basis the patient day cost for the first six months of 1917 was $1.59. As the annual appropriation for salaries was only $17,100 and the appropriation for expenses $35,000, it is apparent that on the present basis of expenditures there will be need for a further appropriation to make up a deficit at the end of the present year. It is therefore important that effort be made to reduce cost wherever possible.

This report has recommended increased cost as regards salaries and wages. It is, however, recommended that no immediate additions be made to the force, but that future appropriations provide for as many of the additional employees recommended as may be practicable. By savings resulting from more economical operation of the City Home, by the discontinuance of subsidies to private institutions, and the discontinuance of outdoor poor relief at the City Home, as recommended, it is believed that sufficient can be saved to put the Virginia Hospital on a basis of efficiency to which it is entitled. in view of the excellent work which it is now doing.

It should be pointed out in this connection that if cost figures are to be worth while, they should be properly determined. For example, permanent repairs and improvements, the life of which extends over a period of years, should not be charged against the operating costs of any one year, but should be distributed over the life of the improvement. Similarly, all costs, including that of ambulance maintenance, which properly belongs to Virginia Hospital, should be considered in calculating Virginia Hospital costs.

Annual Reports Should Be Improved.

As a document intended to inform the administrative board and the general public of the work and results of work in the Virginia Hospital, the annual report leaves much to be desired, particularly as regards the medical and surgical work of the hospital. There is also much material which could well be omitted.

For example, the report on the surgical operations of the hospital is of very little value because it does not give any information as to the results of operations. A general statement of all medical and surgical conditions properly classified is given in the report, but it is impossible to determine how many of the surgical cases therein noted were operated upon. On the other hand, two and one-half pages of the report are devoted to listing the occupation of patients—facts which are of little service in determining the value of hospital work.

A brief outline of what a small hospital's report should contain may be helpful in this connection:

1—The superintendent's story of what the hospital does, its aims and aspirations, and the difficulties it encounters. Here should be all recommendations for improvements in the interest of increased efficiency, in other words, a report of an annual survey of the hospital.

2—The organization of the hospital, showing how salary costs are distributed and how the supervision of employees is exercised.

3—The report of the medical staff, showing the number and kind of cases treated, the results of treatment, with special data on cases of more than ordinary interest: this report should also offer recommendations and criticism as regards medical work.

4—A financial statement, showing what the hospital owns and owes, a statement of past operations showing in comparative form unit costs for salaries, food, household supplies, equipment, etc., wherever possible for a period of about three years past, together with a statement showing the sources of revenue and an estimate of funds needed for the ensuing year on the basis of the progress outlined in the superintendent's report.

These represent the minimum features of every good hospital report. Other statistical matter relative to age, sex, social condition, religion, occupation, etc., is interesting for statistical purposes, but not of great value, and should occupy as little space as possible. In so far as the administrative board or other administrative head is concerned, the chief information desired is as to costs and the need for additions or reductions of appropriations, but the public wants to know what the hospital does for its patients, what it hopes to do, and how the service which it offers helps them and merits their support.

Pine Camp Hospital

PINE CAMP HOSPITAL.

Location of Plant and Character of Service.

The Pine Camp Tuberculosis Hospital is situated on the city farm of 167 acres about three miles from the center of the city. The Pine Camp plot comprises about thirty acres of this farm, and except for small areas devoted to lawn and gardens is woodland, chiefly pine. A more satisfactory place for such a hospital would be hard to find in a location convenient to the city.

The camp consists of the following buildings:

1—Administration building and nurses' home.
2—Infirmary pavilion for bed patients, including dining room for ambulatory patients.
3—Pavilion used as sleeping and rest quarters for ambulatory or up patients.
4—Two shacks used as living quarters for two special male patients, one of whom is an employee.
5—Ice house.
6—Fumigating house.
7—Storage house.
8—Stables.
9—Chicken houses and yards.
10—Pump house.

The hospital buildings at Pine Camp are all in fairly good condition and in general well adapted to their purpose. The administration building is somewhat in need of painting within and without, but otherwise little is to be recommended in the way of repairs. One of the patients, who is an employee of the hospital, acts as general utility man and the superintendent is quick to see and remedy conditions requiring minor repairs. There are, however, a few matters relative to the physical plant, which should receive attention. These will be discussed in detail subsequently in this report.

Only white patients, male and female, are cared for at the Pine Camp. Accommodations exist for approximately forty patients and this number is almost constantly maintained. The camp is designed only for the care of tuberculosis patients who have reached the more serious stage in the development of the disease, patients with incipient tuberculosis not ordinarily being admitted. The purpose of the camp is to furnish quarters to which can be removed those patients who by reason of their illness, cannot be properly cared for at home or who are a menace to the health of others.

Organization and Personnel.

The following statement shows the force on the payroll at the time of this survey:

	Per Year.
Superintendent	$ 1,080.00
Interne	60.00*
Ward nurse (trained in tuberculosis work)	780.00
Nurse (practical)	360.00
Nurse (practical)	300.00
Night nurse (practical)	360.00
Ward maid	360.00
Day orderly	360.00
Night orderly	450.00
Orderly (General utility man)	336.00
Laborer (gardener)	420.00
Cook	360.00
Waiter	336.00
Dishwasher and utility man	216.00**
House maid	168.00
Laundress	432.00***
Laundress	144.00****
Total	$ 6,522.00

The above schedule varies considerably from that set up in the appropriation ordinance for the current year, owing to changes in salary rates, which have been made since the passage of the appropriation ordinance. The total payroll, as given in the appropriation ordinance, includes an item of $770 for extra help, and this sum has been drawn upon for increasing salaries and for the employment of an interne and the two laundresses. The total payroll at the present time is, therefore, $6,522, as against $6,500 in the appropriation bill.

*Interne receives $5.00 a month in lieu of laundry.
**This employee formerly a patient and acts as general utility man.
***Laundress paid salary for home laundry work for patients.
****Laundress paid salary for home laundry work for nurses.

The changes in payroll are the result of a general re-organization effected by the present superintendent when she took office in April. Prior to this time the general supervision and care of patients is said to have been very unsatisfactory and complaints of inefficiency were not infrequent. With the coming of the new superintendent many of the employees under the former regime left the hospital, and it was necessary to re-organize the nursing force almost completely owing to the difficulty of securing new and efficient employees at the former rates of pay. Small increases were allowed—and very justifiably so. From careful observation at the Pine Camp Hospital at several visits, it is believed that the present organization is none too large, and the payroll is as low as may reasonably be expected. The character of the superintendent and nurses is such as to inspire confidence in the adequacy of the organization.

Pine Camp Under Excellent Management.

The city is to be congratulated upon this institution and upon the character of service which it renders. The present superintendent is a very competent nurse and executive, trained in the Bellevue and Allied Hospitals of the City of New York, and with experience in executive positions in both the City Home and the Virginia Hospital. It is certain that this superintendent is largely responsible for the present general excellence of the service and the discipline now maintained at this hospital.

At the time of this study the superintendent of the Virginia Hospital was ill and it was the intention of the administrative board to transfer the superintendent of the Pine Camp Hospital to the superintendency of the Virginia Hospital. It is believed that such a move would make for increased efficiency at the Virginia Hospital but if this transfer is brought about it is recommended that no new appointment to the superintendency of the Pine Camp Hospital be made at this time, but that the superintendent of the Pine Camp Hospital act also as superintendent of the Virginia Hospital. The executive authority relative to the Pine Camp Hospital should be delegated so far as may be necessary to the chief nurse at Pine Camp, who should act as acting superintendent at slightly increased salary.*

Care of Patients.

The care of patients at the Pine Camp Hospital is in every way satisfactory. The patients are given adequate nursing care and everything compatible with good discipline is done for their comfort and well being. The food is wholesome and nourishing though not extravagant. Owing to the craving of these patients for meats, meat in one form or another is served generally twice a day. The following sample of daily menu illustrates the dietary of patients and this with only an occasional exception is the dietary of the superintendent and her staff.

---

*Since this paragraph was written the administrative board has appointed a medical director for the Pine Camp and Virginia Hospital at a salary of $600 a year. The duties of this officer are said to be to co-ordinate and exercise supervision over the medical work of these two institutions in the interest of economy and efficiency. It is not clear why such an officer should be considered necessary. So far as the Pine Camp Hospital is concerned, the present superintendent is absolutely able, with the advice and assistance of the visiting staff to work out in co-operation with the Virginia Hospital authorities, any or all of the co-ordinating measures deemed advisable. Furthermore, it is not probable that a medical officer without considerable previous hospital experience will be able to give enough time and attention to this work to make his influence of great value.

The Pine Camp Hospital needs nothing more than its present competent superintendent, and the position of superintendent of Virginia Hospital should, of course, be filled as soon as possible. Until this can be done, the plan above proposed for placing both hospitals temporarily under the supervision of the superintendent of the Pine Camp Hospital, who should transfer her location to the Virginia Hospital, should give satisfactory results. If this cannot be brought about satisfactorily then a trained superintendent at the Virginia Hospital should be immediately appointed and the newly created position of medical director abolished. Such co-ordination of services as is deemed advisable could be satisfactorily worked out by the head of the proposed department of public welfare recommended earlier in this report.

Breakfast:

Cereal, friend hominy, bacon, corn muffins, bread, coffee and milk.

Dinner:

Roast beef, boiled cabbage and potatoes, milk and bread.

Supper:

Cold roast beef, black eyed peas, bread and milk, oranges with cocoanut.

For patients too ill to eat the regular meals provided, special diets suited to their needs are prepared and served by the nurses—eggs, milk and fruit constitute the major part of such diets, with occasional chicken and squab, which are raised at the camp.

Change in Procedure of Admission to Pine Camp Recommended.

At the present time patients on being admitted are supposed to have a card of admission from the health department, but this does not mean that they must necessarily receive an examination by a health department physician. That is to say there is no certainty that the patients sent to the Pine Camp Hospital are such as require the kind of care that Pine Camp gives, or even that they have tuberculosis. It is, therefore, recommended that hereafter all patients requiring hospital treatment for tuberculosis be sent first to the Virginia Hospital, where they may be fully examined and kept under observation a sufficient length of time to establish a diagnosis at least. If their condition is such as to require their care at Pine Camp they may then be transferred there. In other words, the Virginia Hospital should be the clearing house for the Pine Camp Hospital.

Medical Service.

The hospital has a medical staff of four members who are practicing physicians of the community. One of them is the chief of the tuberculosis clinic of the health department. These men serve without compensation and at least one of them visits the hospital and makes rounds of patients at least twice each week.

Prior to the coming of the present superintendent, no medical interne was employed, and the superintendent states that as a result some very bad practices in connection with the dispensing of narcotics existed. Upon her insistence that an interne be employed, a third year student of the local medical college was secured and since his coming the medical care of patients has been materially improved. This interne receives only $5 a month and maintenance, and at the beginning of the college year will be required to attend his regular classes. It is believed, however, that the service rendered and the risk run by the interne is sufficient to warrant the increase of his salary. There is extra hazard in a tuberculosis camp, and this fact should be recognized in salary allowance for employees.

It is believed further that it would be preferable to have a graduate interne at the Pine Camp eventually if the service of this institution is increased, as recommended in this report. Under such circumstances the interne should receive a salary within the limits established for the grade of medical interne, as suggested in that section of this report dealing with the standardization of salaries and grades. No criticism of the efficiency of the present interne is intended, for this interne is rendering as satisfactory service as may be expected under the present plan.

Extensions of Service at Pine Camp.

The need of more adequate care of infants during the summer months is recognized by the health department which is doing intensive work for the prevention of infant mortality. It is evident. however, that many of these infants, particularly colored infants. need to be removed from their home surroundings if they are to be made well. The educational work of the visiting nurses is producing excellent results but there are many cases where their efforts are of little avail. For such cases there is need of a summer camp where these babies can be cared for under more favorable conditions than prevail in their homes, even under the supervision of the visiting nurses; a place where they can have plenty of air and sunshine. good food and good care. It is believed that the Pine Camp offers a splendid opportunity for such a babies' summer camp—there should be pavilions for both white and colored infants, such pavilions to be of the shack type of cheap construction and simply equipped. Additional nurses for infants would of course be needed, but two nurses would be able to care for twenty or thirty babies easily. The superintendent of the Pine Camp could readily assume the additional responsibility for this baby camp.

It is believed that a year's experience with such a baby camp would demonstrate its usefulness. The beginning should be small and as an experiment. If the experiment succeeds, extension of the plan may be provided according to needs.

It is believed also that more satisfactory results in handling colored tuberculosis patients would be secured if the colored tuberculosis wards were removed from the City Home to the Pine Camp Hospital. This has been discussed at greater length in the report on the City Home.

Improvement of Nurses' Home.

The administration building contains the superintendent's office, the sitting room for the staff, dining room and kitchen on the main floor, and has three bedrooms with a bath for nurses at the front of the house on the second floor. In the rear, reached by an outside stairway, there is a bedroom and bath for the interne, and a large room now partly used for storage purposes. There are, as previously noted, but three rooms for nurses and this necessitates that their quarters be shared with the superintendent. In order that the rear room, now partly used as a store room may be utilized as a bedroom for nurses, thus making it possible for the superintendent to have her own private room, it is recommended that a doorway be cut through from this store room to the nurses' bath room, thus giving access to the room frm the front of the building. The back veranda from which the doorway to the internes' room, the internes' bath room and the vacant store room now open, should be divided by a partition between the storeroom and the bathroom. Access to each part of the veranda should be provided by dividing the rear stairway so that there will be a separate stairway leading to each side of the partition of the veranda. This would permit the nurses occupying this room to have access to the nurses' bath and thence to the front of nurses' hallway and when the bath was occupied the room could be reached by the back outside stairway. This room would thus be completely separated from the internes' quarters.

Recreation for Nurses.

It is particularly important in an institution of this kind that sufficient opportunity be given nurses and doctors for healthful recreation. At the present the only means of recreation is indoor amusement with piano and phonograph. It is suggested that a tennis court be constructed on the grounds so that nurses may find adequate recreation out of doors. This would serve the additional purpose of making nurses more contented with their lot at

Pine Camp. Good nurses are not easily secured and they should be encouraged in every possible way to remain.

Bath Rooms in Infirmary Should be Enlarged.

The baths and toilets in the infirmary building are very unsatisfactory. In this building there is a bath room containing one bath and two closets for each group of ten patients, male and female. The bath room is very small and is heated with a stove so that when this stove is in use. it is difficult for the patient to avoid the stove while drying himself. In view of the fact that these patients are seriously ill and likely to be seized suddenly with dizziness or fainting. the bath rooms should be considerably enlarged so that there will be no danger from these stoves. It is preferable. of course. that a heating plant be installed so that the stove menace to the entire plant may be eliminated If stoves are continued proper metal sheathing of the walls adjacent to the stoves should be provided.

Need for Morgue Building.

At present there are no facilities for the care of the dead other than the small so-called recovery rooms in the infirmary. It is suggested that a small frame building be constructed for the care of the dead until they can be removed for burial. Their presence in the infirmary is depressing to patients who cannot help but be constantly aware of the situation.

Records.

The superintendent keeps all records of patients upon a well-designed card index. Charts of daily pulse, respiration, temperature, feces, sputum, blood pressure. and weight are also kept of such patients as required special nursing care. Records of medication and treatment are kept by nurses in charge of patients, but no special charts are kept of physical examination. It has been recommended elsewhere in this report that all tuberculous patients be first admitted to the Virginia Hospital, where they may have thorough physical examination. with such tests of blood. sputum, etc., as may be necessary before being sent to Pine Camp. If this is done. copies of these records should be forwarded to the Pine Camp Hospital with the patients and subsequent observations as to the physical condition of these patients made by the attending physician and the interne.

Annual Report Should Be Prepared.

In order that the administrative board or other responsible authority may have more definite information regarding costs at the Pine Camp, it is recommended that an annual report be prepared at the termination of the present fiscal year and thereafter, showing in detail the cost of maintenance per patient day, with special reference to food costs. While it is believed from the evidence available that this institution is being conducted as economically as is consistent with the proper care of patients, statistics showing all costs should be available at all times.

Laundry Service.

Laundry for patients is sent out to a laundress in the city who receives a salary of $432 a year for the work. Laundry for nurses is done by a laundress in the city at $144 a year. The interne recently appointed is allowed $5 a month in lieu of laundry, which he has done wherever he chooses. It is recommended in that section of this report which deals with the City Home that all laundry work for Pine Camp and Virginia Hospitals be done at the City Home.

Poultry Farm Should Be Enlarged.

Although the hospital has four poultry houses with yards and about forty fowl, it is obliged to purchase eggs from local dealers. In view of the fact that there is ample space for greatly increasing the extent of egg production and as the labor cost is not a considerable item in connection with the care of poultry, it is recommended that this feature of the Pine Camp service be extended at least to meet the needs of the Pine Camp Hospital. It is believed that it would be a considerable economy to establish at Pine Camp a poultry farm sufficient in size to provide for the major needs of the camp, the City Home and the Virginia Hospital. To do this, however, it would be necessary to employ at least one additional laborer.

No figures of cost of the Pine Camp Hospital in 1916 were available at the time of this study, but at the City Home in 1916 $2,477.85 was spent for eggs and $555.15 for chickens, a total of $3,033. At the Virginia Hospital in 1916, $1,896 was spent for eggs and $743.28 for chickens, a total of $2,639.28. For the three city institutions, therefore, the annual cost for eggs and chickens is in the neighborhood of $6,000 or $7,000, a very considerable item. Raising fowl is not a difficult matter under conditions existing at Pine Camp, and if there is profit in this business for private enterprise there should be profit in it for the city.

Stables Should Be Improved for Fly Elimination.

Considerable difficulty has been found in properly screening the nurses' home from flies. On the recommendation of the superintendent, arrangement has been made for the installation of full length screens to be nailed to the window casing so that windows may be closed without removing the screens. This does very well so far as exclusion of flies from the house is concerned, but something more is needed in the stables. The stable is merely a shack, without adequate provision for 'drainage and thorough cleaning of the stable floor and without proper provision for the handling of manure. It is recommended that for the elimination of the fly nuisance, a well drained floor with gutters be constructed in this stable and that a manure bin having the approval of the chief health officer be built and used.

Improved Ice House Should Be Constructed.

The small tin roofed shack now used as an ice house from which ice is taken to smaller refrigerators and ice boxes is poorly adapted for this purpose. · It is of flimsy wooden construction and has a tin roof, so that when the sun is out it is actually hotter inside the icehouse than outside. Ice is received twice each week. and there is considerable difficulty in keeping it, although only small quantities of ice are purchased at a time.

Plans for a model ice house have been worked out by Dr. Geo. W. Goler, of Rochester, New York, and ice houses built after this plan are being used by dairies supplying the city of Rochester. Such an ice house could be constructed at small cost and would. it is believed. within a year effect a saving equivalent to its own cost. A brief description of this ice house follows:

The ice house should be built on drained ground not too much sheltered from the wind nor in a situation too shady. It should be built of hemlock boards and two by four joists with a half-pitched roof that opens all around between the uprights and the gable and with a large opening at either end of the gable for ventilation. The joists should be laid up with hemlock boards on either the inside or outside of joists. At one side of the ice house should be a small can into which sawdust may be thrown to dry. When ready to fill the ice house with ice, the bottom should be covered with litter or shavings and the ice put in one layer above another, so that the joists do not come opposite. At least twelve inches of space should be left between the ice and the walls of the ice house, and as each layer of ice is put down this space should be filled with clean dry sawdust tightly tramped down. Where the ice is put in the opening in the front part of the house should be laid up with hemlock boards. When the house is full to the topmost layer, the ice should be covered with about a foot of sawdust.

Such an ice house could be readily built at small cost to take care of a season's supply of ice, or the present ice house, with slight modification according to the above plan, could be used. The weekly buying of ice on the scale of an ordinary housekeeping establishment is an extravagance. In the report on the City Home it has been suggested that an ice-making plant be operated at the City Home for supplying all institutions with ice at lower cost.

Fire Protection.

The Pine Camp Hospital buildings are equipped with small Pyrene fire extinguishers. Water is secured from a large tank located on a water tower about fifty feet high at the rear of the house and about one hundred feet of fire hose is provided for connection with this tank. There is also available about two hundred feet of garden hose for connection with water faucets. The superintendent has instructed her nurses and helpers what to do in the event of fire, and a general utility man has been designated in charge of fire equipment. The superintendent states that the equipment has been examined and approved by the fire department.

In view of the fact that the area covered by buildings is wide and the danger of forest fire considerable, it is recommended that additional equipment be provided. Pyrene extinguishers do not meet the needs at this camp—three-gallon hand chemical extinguishers should be provided, one for each floor of the nurses' home; two in each of the buildings for patients, and one in each of the other small buildings. In addition to the fire extinguisher, there should be on each floor of the nurses' home and in each of the buildings used for patients a rack containing three fire buckets, which should be kept constantly filled with water. Many people become confused in trying to use fire extinguishers, but all know how to use water in a fire bucket. The fire hose should be increased in length sufficient to reach the farthermost building of the camp and somewhat beyond. This hose should be kept on a hand reel mounted on a small cart so that it will not deteriorate rapidly, and so that it can be quickly extended to the fire. A small shack should be built to house the hose cart. Fire drills should be held occasionally, all employees and ambulatory patients being assigned to stations.

Produce Garden at Pine Camp.

A small garden at the rear of the plot is utilized for raising beans, potatoes, onions, squash, cucumbers, lettuce, tomatoes, and cantaloupe. The extent of this garden could not well be increased without clearing additional land. The labor required and the cost of putting the land in condition for production would no doubt be in excess of the value of the products. It has been suggested in that section of this report which deals with the Smallpox Hospital that a survey of the farm in connection with this hospital be made by the experts of the agricultural school. If the land is suitable, the products of a small garden of the Pine Camp could be supplemented by products of the more extensive garden at the Smallpox Hospital.

Garbage and Sewage Disposal.

Garbage is removed from the hospital daily and burned at some distance from the hospital building at the edge of the woods. This is a satisfactory method of disposal of garbage, provided the fire is properly safeguarded.

A new sewage disposal system is being installed which, when completed, will be a very considerable improvement. The old sewage system was very defective, and a very great nuisance because of poor construction and lack of covering over the cesspool, and its location near the nurses' home. The new system which includes new drains throughout and a septic tank located in the woods at considerable distance from the house has none of the objections of the former method. It is recommended that as soon as the new system is in operation the old cesspool be filled up and obliterated. At present the superintendent finds it necessary to keep the cesspool covered with lime, but its presence is a menace to health and comfort under any circumstances.

Improved Drainage About Nurses' Home Should Be Provided.

Due to the fact that adequate drains are not provided beneath the leaders in the nurses' home, the road about the house is continually wet in the vicinity of these leaders. While this is not a serious matter, it is of considerable annoyance to the inmates of the nurses' home and should be remedied by the installation of proper basins and drains. Such work as is required could be done at small expense by employees of the hospital.

Path Should Be Built to Main Road.

The camp is somewhat difficult to reach from the city, except by carriage or auto. A trolley line passes about a half mile from the house, but in order to reach the road leading to the trolley station at Westbrook without making a long detour, it is necessary to cross a cultivated field which, in wet weather and at most other times, is difficult footing. It is suggested that a gravel or cinder path be constructed from the dirt road in front of the camp to the macadam road on the other side of the field. Permission could no doubt be secured for the construction of this path from the owners of the field.

The Administrative Board

THE ADMINISTRATIVE BOARD.

The organization and salary cost of the administrative board is as follows:

5 Commissioners at $5,000 each.........	$ 25,000.00
1 Chief clerk	2,400.00
2 Clerks at $1,500 each	3,000.00
1 Clerk	1,200.00
1 Chauffeur	1,080.00
	$ 32,680.00

also

1 Bookkeeper (paymaster)	$ 2,100.00
1 Bookkeeper (paymaster)	1,500.00
	$ 36,280.00

In that chapter of this report on "organization of the government" it has been shown that executive leadership is an attribute which can be exercised by but a single individual, and that therefore it is fundamentally impossible for the city to secure executive leadership through its administrative board irrespective of whether the members thereof be appointed or elected.

In discussing the administrative board, it is specifically not the intention to cast any reflection on the personnel of the board. The organization and its methods have been studied without reference to the personal qualifications of persons. It is understood that the original administrative board began its work by dividing the departments among its membership—each member assuming to administer some particular department or group of departments. That plan did not work satisfactorily and was changed so that for some time past the members have been acting jointly on all business over which the board has jurisdiction.

The men engaged on this survey attended various sessions of the board, which are held daily at ten o'clock, in a room which has a setting similar to that of a high court of justice—the desks of the five commissioners being arranged in a semi-circle facing the clerk of the court, a witness chair and audience benches. Here the commisioners sit each day for from one to three hours, and sometimes longer, transacting what is mostly mere routine business such as could be performed as effectively and more expeditiously by a single executive. These five commissioners sit in formal state and listen to their secretary (chief clerk) read over the details of purchase requisitions, vendors' bills, and similar routine matters which no efficient commercial organization in the country would think of bringing before a board for consideration. Complaints such as should be handled through a central complaint office are given a hearing before the full board. Detailed minutes are kept by the secretary, written up in much detail each day in various large volumes and formally submitted at the board meeting the following day.

Not only is the time of these five officials thus occupied on matters which should be handled by a single executive, but the board has provided itself with a large automobile and chauffeur, and the entire board, as a body, motors about the city inspecting pavements, curbs, and various physical conditions incident to the work of the departments under the board's supervision. An additional automobile runabout has been acquired for the use of the chairman just prior to the survey.

Careful examination was made of the character of work performed by the four clerical employees in the board offices, and even as described by themselves in writing, it consists almost entirely of writing up minutes, correspondence, filing, etc.. the need for which would entirely disappear if the board were abolished. The work of this clerical staff was being well performed, and there was plenty of it, but the existence of the force is not justified.

With respect to the two bookkeepers who serve as paymasters, most of the auditing work duplicates that of the auditor's office. The accounting work, although well done, could either be transferred to the central accounting office of the city or to the various departments. The paymaster functions should be transfered to the city treasurer. A purchasing agent should be appointed to buy not only the supplies, materials and equipment of the departments now under the administrative board, but his duties should extend to the entire city government.

As shown above, the salary cost alone of the board and its staff is over $36,000. Assuming a year of 300 working days—although there are not that many after eliminating Saturday half-days and holidays, it is to be noted that the cost to the city is approximately $120 per day throughout the year.

Whatever advantage there may be in having the administrative judgment of joint minds as members of the board, can be obtained just as readily and at no extra cost by having the department heads (see plan No. 1 on "organization of the government") sit from time to time as a board or cabinet to discuss matters concerning the city's welfare and the administration of its current business.

It should of course go without saying that in abolishing the administrative board, the city council should not return to its former practice of performing administrative work. The latter should be restricted by charter exclusively to the administrative departments and the city council should be restricted to matters of legislation.

Department of Engineering

722

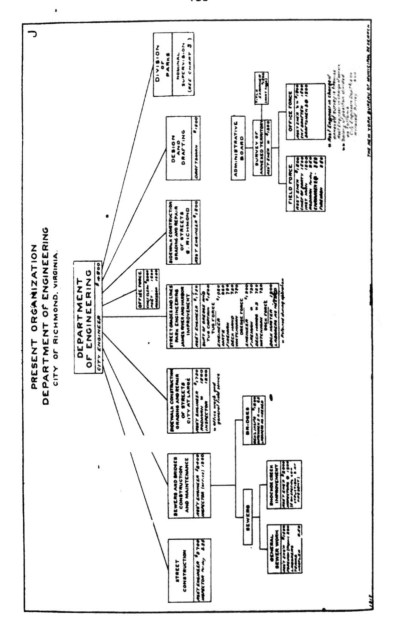

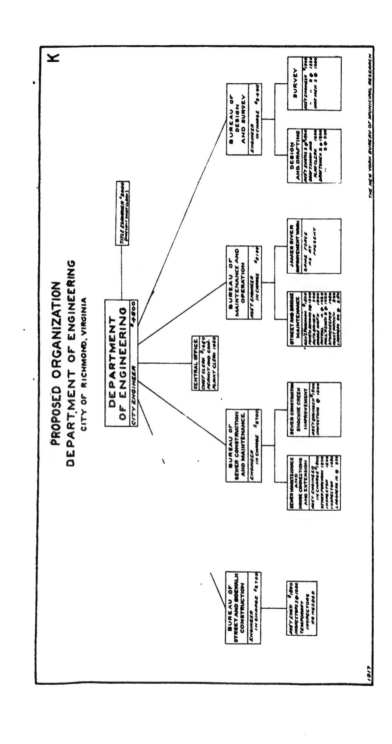

PROPOSED ORGANIZATION
DEPARTMENT OF ENGINEERING
CITY OF RICHMOND, VIRGINIA

K

THE NEW YORK BUREAU OF MUNICIPAL RESEARCH

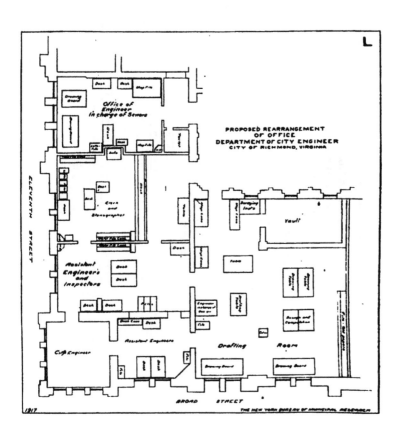

PROPOSED REARRANGEMENT
OF OFFICE
DEPARTMENT OF CITY ENGINEER
CITY OF RICHMOND, VIRGINIA

DEPARTMENT OF ENGINEERING.

The department of engineering is established under section 62 of the city charter, which provides for the appointment of the city engineer. The city engineer is the administrative head of the department, and is appointed by the administrative board for a period of two years. He receives a salary of $4,800, and is required to furnish a bond of $10,000. It is interesting to note that during the last fifty years there have been but two incumbents in this position.

Appointment of Subordinates.

The city engineer, under section 63 of the city charter, is vested with power to appoint or remove such assistants or clerks in his department as may be authorized by ordinance. -This power of removal and appointment, however, is subject to the approval of the administrative board.

Duties of City Engineer.

The duties of the city engineer, as fixed by section 64 of the city charter, include general supervision over streets, culverts, public buildings, and all public improvements, and also include the carrying out of surveys, preparation of plans, specifications, estimates and reports, and performing such professional service as may be required in connection with public improvement work throughout the city. The position also carries with it the title of superintendent of parks, but at the present time supervision over the work of that department is largely nominal. In the case of public buildings, responsibility for their care and maintenance has been transferred to the building inspection.

Organization of Department.

The nature and distribution of the forces under the supervision of the city engineer are shown in the accompanying organization chart. It will be noted that the organization, exclusive of park work, includes the following divisions:

Street construction.
Sewer construction and maintenance, including care of bridges and viaducts.
Street lines and grades, care of parks and grounds.
Supervision of James River improvement.

Sidewalk construction, grading and repair of streets, and paving of sidewalks, city at large.

Sidewalk construction, grading and repair of streets, South Richmond.

Design and drafting.

Annexed Territory Survey.

In addition to the above organizations, there is an engineering force reporting directly to the administrative board, but working under the supervision of the assistant engineer in charge of sewers and bridges, in the city engineer's office. This latter force, the nature and distribution of which is shown in the accompanying chart, is engaged in making a survey and developing drainage studies and plan of the territory recently acquired by the city by annexation.

Defects of Present Organization.

Aside from the illogical division of organization between the city engineer's office and the force engaged in conducting the survey of the annexed territory, the organization of the department is defective in the following respects:

Distribution of force along geographical rather than functional lines.

Inadequate provision for design and drafting work.

Poorly defined lines of responsibility and badly articulated organization.

The requirements of the engineering department of a city such as Richmond, excluding special needs necessitating the temporary employment of specialists, may be roughly divided according to the following functional lines:

Construction of streets and sidewalks.

Construction and maintenance of sewers.

Maintenance and repair of streets, bridges, etc.

Design and survey work.

Office force.

With these divisions in mind the accompanying organization chart is submitted as indicating the nature and distribution of an engineering force adequate to serve the city of Richmond. The relation of the organization recommended for the city engineer's office to the present one is discussed later in the report, together with a consideration of the character and scope of the work carried on by that office and the methods employed.

Policy of Administrative Board as Affecting the Administration of City Engineer's Office.

Before considering in detail the scope of the work carried on by the above force and the methods employed, it is desired to call attention to the procedure followed in the matter of public improvements and also the policy followed by the administrative board and the city council as affecting the administration of the city engineer's office.

Public Improvement Procedure.

All public improvements are initiated by the city council and recommendations concerning them are transmitted by that body to the administrative board. The improvements initiated and consummated are not based on any definite comprehensive work program developed by the city engineer nor has the latter official any voice regarding the general desirability of the proposed improvement. in so far as he is consulted by the administrative board or the council.

After approval by the council the administrative board directs the city engineer to furnish estimates, plans and specifications for the improvement. If approved by the board the extent and character of the improvement is stipulated by that body and the city engineer is authorized to advertise for bids.

Advertisements are inserted in not less than five issues of two local papers and where the work is of sufficient magnitude to attract reputable outside contractors. advertisements are likewise published in the technical journals and the manufacturers' record. Blank proposals for submitting bids are furnished by the city engineer's office and such information as is desired is also given out by that office. There is no preferred list of bidders.

Revision of Estimates and Award of Estimates.

Bids received are opened in public by the administrative board and tabulated in the office of the city engineer. On the basis of this information estimates are revised to include such extras as can be anticipated. also the cost of cement and other construction supplies which are furnished by the city and these estimates are then returned to the administrative board. If the administrative board then decides to authorize the work the city engineer is directed to prepare the contract and the award is made to the lowest responsible bidder. A bond is required from the contractor for 50 per cent. of the amount of his bid, a guarantee company's bond being required for work over $500, while personal bonds are permitted for work involving an expenditure of less than $500.

Defects in Policy of Administrative Board.

The policy followed by the administrative board in the general matter of public improvements and its resultant effect in the administration of the city engineering department is open to serious criticism in the following respects:

Appropriation of funds for improvement work.
Restriction of the power of the city engineer.
Employment of outside engineering service.

Appropriation of Funds.

The greater part of the public improvement work is financed out of tax levy funds provided in the annual appropriation ordinance. In some few cases involving extraordinary expenditures, as for example, in the case of the Shockoe Creek sewer, funds for the work are provided out of bond issues. The amounts of these funds from both of the above sources made available for public improvement work from 1913 to date are shown in the accompanying tabulation:

Appropriations From Tax Levies For City Engineer Department.

Year	STREETS			SEWERS	JAMES RIVER	
	Engineer Department Payroll	General	Repair	General, Including House Connections	James River Improvements	TOTAL
1913....	$25 910	$488,619	*	$20,000	$29,820	$564,349
1914....	31,510	447,836	*	20,000	18,020	517 366
1915....	32,010	284,940	$10 000	20,000	23,020	369,970
1916....	30,510	306,352	35,400	20,000	19,020	411,282
1917....	30,510	110,000	32,200†	21 370	18,020	261,800
		39,700‡				
		10 000‖				

*No special allotment
†Force not under jurisdiction of city engineer
‡Sidewalk improvement charged against abutting property.
‖Survey for annexed territory

Bond Issues.

Since 1913, the only bond issues authorized by the city which were specifically designated for public improvements, are as follows:

Issue	Amount	Purpose	Remarks
1914	$ 500 00	Street improvement	All expended
1914	170,000	Sewer construction	" "
1915	10,000	Annexed sewers	" "
1914- 1918	653,500	Shockoe Creek Improvement	Expended to date, $610 285

Defects in Present Financial Policy.

An analysis of these figures discloses that no bond issues for public improvement of streets have been made since 1914, while funds provided out of bond issue for sewers outside of those authorized for the Shockoe Creek storm sewer were in very moderate amounts. Moreover, the annual appropriations for these purposes out of tax levy funds have decreased from approximately $508,619 during 1913 to $213,270 during the present year 1917. The unwisdom of such a policy is evidenced by the deplorable condition of most of the streets in Richmond and the crying need in many sections of the city for additional sewer facilities.

In the case of funds appropriated for public improvement work, if these funds are not expended within the fiscal year up to January, the general policy followed is to cancel such appropriation, the balance reverting to the general fund. The annual appropriation for public improvements cannot be made until after the approval of the budget for the ensuing year, which means that funds for public improvement are not available until about the middle of March of any year.

The policy followed of cancelling at the end of the fiscal year unexpended funds appropriated for public improvements, together with the delay in making available funds for the ensuing year, restricts the intelligent planning of work on the part of the city engineer and tends to demoralize the administration of his department. Furthermore, the delay in appropriating funds causes the advertisements of proposed work and the award of contracts to be deferred beyond the ordinary season for such work, and in this way tends to eliminate from competition the more desirable and progressive type of contractor, and also results in the submission of higher bids than woud prevail if work were advertised during the season when competition is keen. The restriction in the construction season due to the above policy is probably not serious, as climatic conditions in the city of Richmond are such as to permit practically all the year round construction.

In considering the restricted funds available for public improvements in Richmond, it should be borne in mind that under a state law no public improvements except paving of alleys and sidewalk contracts are paid for by special assessment. Property owners are subject to a spcial annual tax for sewer construction, but this cannot be interpreted as a special assessment. Obviously, this is a matter vitally affecting the financial and economic welfare of the entire city, and prompt action should be taken by the citizens of the city as well as the city government to secure the enactment of legislation adequate to relieve the city of its present limitations in respect to assessing for public improvements.

Restricted Powers of City Engineer.

The city engineer at the present time has practically no voice in the determination of the character of any public improvement, for example, the type of pavement most suitable for any given locality or the extent of the work. It is true that he is occasionally consulted in such matters, but the administrative board is in no way bound by his advice or recommendations. This is a distinctly pernicious system, and that it has proven an expensive one for the city is reflected in the character and distribution of smooth pavements throughout the city and the street conditions in the outlying districts. Many miles of streets have been paved with asphaltic block and asphaltic concrete where the traffic requirements could have been met by a properly constructed macadam surface with oil treatment at a fraction of the cost involved in constructing the existing improvements. Furthermore, the improvement of certain sections of streets with smooth pavements where abutting sections are of gravel, macadam or granite spalls would indicate that in some cases, at least, personal convenience rather than community advantage had actuated the carrying out of the improvement. The scope of this report does not permit going into detail in the matter, but there are sufficient examples of this character throughout the city to indicate not alone an unintelligent policy on the part of the city government, but a decided misuse of public funds.

The city of Richmond must be brought to a realization of the necessity of a comprehensive program of public improvements and the further necessity of providing adequate funds to carry out such a program. Furthermore, all decisions in respect to design, construction and exigency of public improvements should be made by the city engineer, and he should be held responsible for the satisfactory execution of the work. A change in the present policy of the administrative board is of particular importance at this time, as in connection with the development of the territory recently 'acquired by annexation the city is confronted with a problem requiring the most careful study in order to develop a property co-ordinated system of public improvements.

Two other examples of policy on the part of the administrative board which have militated against securing an effective administration of the city engineer's department are:

> The establishment of a separate engineering organization to carry on a street and drainage survey of those sections of the city recently acquired by annexation: this organization reporting directly to the administrative board while working under the supervision of an engineer reporting to the city engineer on other phases of engineering work in the city.

> Placing the forces engaged in street repair and maintenance under the supervision of the superintendent of street cleaning.

Annexed Territory Forces.

The appointment of a separate engineering force with independent offices to carry on the survey of those sections of the city recently acquired by annexation, creates an anomalous situation in the engineering department that is without justification. The value of the work carried on by this force depends to a considerable degree upon its co-ordination with the work of the city engineer's office elsewhere in the city, and it should be carried on under his direct supervision. It is recommended that the necessary action be taken by the administrative board to effect this change.

Street Repair Forces.

There appears to be no justification for the action of the administrative board in transferring the forces engaged in the repairs of unpaved streets from the jurisdiction of the city engineer to the superintendent of street cleaning. The repair and maintenance of streets is essentially an engineering function and responsibility for carrying it on should be vested in the city engineer's office.

Employment of Outside Engineering Service.

It has been the practice of the administrative board in cases where engineering information relating to proposed improvements has been desired, to employ local engineering firms or surveyors to do this work in place of securing the necessary service from the office of the city engineer. In this connection it should be noted that the nature of the work involved was not of a highly technical character, requiring special training and qualifications, but of a purely routine nature involving making of surveys and supervision of minor construction work.

In a city the size of Richmond the principal justification of maintaining a relatively permanent organization such as has existed in the office of the city engineer, in spite of the fluctuations in the work of the office from year to year, is to make available to the city government engineering service when required. Facts disclosed in connection with the study on which this report is based, indicate that outside engineering service has been retained when the required service was readily available in the city engineer's office. Furthermore, it appears that this practice has resulted in a serious waste of the city's funds both by reason of the inadequacy of information received and submitted by outside engineers, necessitating re-surveys by the city engineer's forces, as in the case of the survey of the drainage project for Shockoe Creek and Bacon's Quarter Branch, and also in imperfect construction as in the case of the Gambles' Hill Park retaining wall.

While it is not within the scope of this report to pass professional judgment on individual projects for public improvements, it is desired to call attention to the conditions attending the contemplated viaduct and boulevard construction along Chamberlayne Avenue, designed to provide a direct route from Ginter Park to Broad Street. In considering this project, which is a public improvement that should, without question, have been handled by the city engineer's department, the city government retained outside engineering service to make the necessary surveys and prepare plans for the proposed construction. In connection with this work separate routes were surveyed and location plans submitted to the city council and administrative board. The location approved by the city council, and for which property to the extent of about $38,000 has already been acquired and the preparation of plans for the required viaduct construction has been authorized, was opposed by the city engineer. In opposing these plans and endorsing another location, which contemplates an extension of Chamberlayne Avenue through Brook Avenue to Broad Street, the city engineer's office submitted information to the city council and administrative board showing a saving of $200,000 in property damage alone over the route approved by the council.

The policy of the administrative board and city council in restricting the power of the city engineer, as indicated by the acts above cited, tends to discredit the office of the city engineer in the minds of the public and break down the effectiveness of the department as a part of the city government. To what degree that policy has been responsible for the present somewhat demoralized condition of the city engineer's department, it is impossible to determine, but that it has been a factor in this demoralization appears to be beyond dispute.

At the same time aside from the forces working directly under the supervision of the engineer in charge of sewers there is a lack of effective administration of the city engineer's department that indicates a need for a complete re-organization of that department. The claim made that present conditions are due to a lack of adequate engineering service is not borne out by the facts of the case. Aside from the absolute necessity of providing an adequate labor force and equipment for maintenance work and additional inspectional service, the present forces connected with the city engineer's department and the annexed survey should be entirely adequate to meet all ordinary needs of the city for service rendered by that department.

It should be noted that engineering, drafting and inspectional service in the city engineer's department and annexed survey forces, not including any clerical service, or forces connected with the James River improvement work, at the time the study of the department was made included a payroll of approximately $49,210. This represents approximately 23 per cent. of the funds made available for the public improvement work for the entire city. What the city engineer's department needs is not additional forces but an effective co-ordination and administration of the present forces. As a first means towards accomplishing this, it is recommended that the entire department, together with the forces concerned with the survey of annexed territory be re-organized along the lines indicated in the accompanying organization chart. Obviously, the success of such an organization will depend upon its administration, and if it is not possible to secure effective administration under the present administration, drastic measures should be taken to secure it.

Too much emphasis cannot be placed, however, in the necessity for a discontinuance of the pernicious policy followed by the administrative board in restricting the powers of the city engineer and the usefulness of his department, and in usurping prerogatives vested in him by the city charter.

Relation of Present Organization of Office of City Engineer To That Proposed.

The following discussion is designed to point out certain of the defects in administration and procedure existing in the present organization with special reference to central office conditions. Details of construction, policy, maintenance needs and scope of work will be discussed subsequently.

Central Office.

The main offices of the city engineer's department are located in the city hall. The work incidental to the survey of the annexed territory is handled from offices in the Lyric building, one square from the city hall. The general layout of the offices in the city hall is shown in the accompanying diagram. The architectural design of the building does not permit of the utilization of the available space to the best advantage, but the present arrangement is susceptible of decided improvement.

Proposed Changes in City Engineer's Office.

In the proposed re-organization of the city engineer's department it is intended to provide accommodations in the present offices of the city engineer for the forces now concerned with the survey of the annexed territory which are now located in the Lyric building. That it will be perfectly feasible to provide such accommodations is indicated in the accompanying floor plan of that department. The main features of this proposed plan include the removal of the grille partition at the entrance to the room occupied by the assistant engineer in charge of sidewalk construction, the extension of the vault in the drafting room now used as a dark room and for the storage of miscellaneous junk, in order to make provision for the storage of plans under relatively fireproof conditions, the purpose for which the vault was originally designed, and a re-arrangement of the office furniture.

As an indication of the extravagant use of space in this department, attention is called to the size of the present draughting room which has an inside area of 1,620 square feet and an area of approximately 1,470 square feet, exclusive of that occupied by the present vault. This room is at present used by two draughtsmen, and furnishes desk room for one of the assistant engineers and the general inspector.

In connection with the office arrangement, attention is also called to the inadequacy of telephone facilities, a condition which apparently prevails throughout the city hall. It is recommended that desk extensions be made to every room in the city engineer's department including the draughting room; also the substitution of flat-top desk furniture for the roll-top desks now in use at as early a date as possible.

Adequacy of Equipment.

The office is well equipped with calculating machines and other time-saving devices. But there is no central filing system and with few exceptions an antiquated, obsolete type of filing case is employed, the greater part of the equipment not being fireproof. A considerable amount of valuable space is occupied by old records that could be stored elsewhere with advantage. Steps should be taken to provide up-to-date filing equipment and provision should be made for the storage in fireproof vaults of such records as are not needed for routine work.

Office Force.

The office organization includes the following:

Chief clerk $2,000.00
Assistant chief clerk, stenographer and pho-
    tographer 1,500.00

Duties of Chief Clerk.

The present incumbent of the position of chief clerk has been identified with the department for over forty years. His title does not adequately describe his duties. He prepares all contracts in longhand, tabulates bids in co-operation with the assistant engineer in charge of the proposed work, and keeps miscellaneous minor records. At least two-thirds of his time is employed in the investigation and examination of titles and the preparation of reports for the city attorney. His work in this capacity is practically invaluable to the city. Furthermore, his entire time could be devoted with advantage to this class of work in connection with the survey of annexed territory, thereby discontinuing the present practice of employing outside professional service for this purpose.

It is recommended that this official be released of his present routine duties as chief clerk, and be transferred to the city attorney's department or retained in the city engineer's office and assigned to the specific duties of title examiner, his services in this capacity to be available as needed.

Assistant Chief Clerk and Stenographer.

The duties of this position are practically those of the chief clerk in a department of this character. They include the routine work in connection with the preparation of contracts and specifications, the drafting of reports to the administrative board and council committees, issuance of all permits emanating from the City engineer's office, furnishing stenographic services required to the city engineer 'and his assistant, filing of correspondence, etc., and acting as photographer for the department. Much of the work involved, particularly in respect to the procedure incidental to the issuance of permits, could be simplified by a suitable looseleaf system of permit forms, but aside from that feature the demands of the position are entirely too multifarious for one man. It is recommended that the position of stenographer and clerk be added to the office force of the city engineer. Suggestions in respect to modification in the present permit procedure and the distribution of work will be discussed in a subsequent section of this report under "permits and complaints."

Present Division of Streets.

The present division of streets is concerned with the preparation of plans and estimates for and the supervision of the construction of all paved streets and curb and gutter construction. The construction of gravel macadam streets, sidewalks and the paving of alleys are not included within the work of this division. The engineer in charge of this work is frequently called upon for miscellaneous engineering service.

Organization in Charge of Street Construction.

. At the time the study of the department was made, the organization in charge of street construction included the following:

One assistant engineer, $2,700.
One rodman and inspector $3.25 per day, extra pay for overtime.

The actual construction work under way was limited, owing to the small appropriation allowed for street improvement during the year 1917.

It is desired to call particular attention to the fact that all details of the work, such as making surveys, giving line and grade, inspection of construction and preparation of estimates, are handled directly by the engineer in charge of the work. Obviously, the utilization of a highly-paid engineer to render service that could be done equally well under supervision by young engineers or inspectors, is open to serious criticism.

In a city the size of Richmond, it is desirable to centralize the responsibility for all construction work relating to streets, alleys and sidewalks, and the proposed organization is drawn up with that in mind. It should be noted that no definite assignment of engineering assistants is made to the proposed bureau.

It is recommended that service of this character should be centralized in the bureau of design and survey and should be made available as needed to the heads of the other functional divisions of the city engineer's department. The force indicated in the organization chart is deemed adequate to meet the ordinary needs of supervision and inspection. Obviously, additional inspectors, preferably per diem men, should be provided when the extent of construction work justifies their employment.

Division of Sidewalks, Grading, Graveling of Streets and Paving of Alleys.

The work of this division at present includes the construction of sidewalks, the paving of alleys and the so-called graveling of unpaved streets. Responsibility for this work is divided between two men, one of whom has jurisdiction over that done in South Richmond, and the other over the rest of the city. Conditions do not justify any such division of responsibility. Formerly, the work of this division included supervision over the repair of streets both when done with city forces, and when handled under contract, but on April 1, 1915, the administrative board transferred the responsibility for the repair of streets other than by contract from the city engineer's department to the department of street cleaning. The needs of the city of Richmond in the matter of street maintenance and repairs are discussed later in the report under "street maintenance and repair."

Organization of Division.

The organization of this division at the time the study of the department was made included:

City at large:
One assistant engineer $1,750.00
One rodman and inspector, part time...... 1,200.00
One inspector 1,200.00

South Richmond:
One assistant engineer $1,800.00
One laborer acting as driver, per day...... 2.50

The engineer in charge of the work of sidewalk construction and graveling of streets in the city at large is supplied with a Ford runabout, while the engineer in charge of work of that character in South Richmond has to depend on the part-time use of a horse and buggy assigned to the city engineer's department. Additional equipment and force assigned to the work in South Richmond included one mule and cart.

Under the proposed organization the present work of this division would be divided between the bureau of street construction and the bureau of street maintenance.

Division of Street Lines and Grades—Care of Grounds and the James River Improvements.

The work of this division includes furnishing the public on request with information as to line and grade of streets and alleys, furnishing engineering service to the assistant superintendent of parks, and general supervision over the James River improvement work.

Organization of Division.

The organization of this division. aside from the force employed in connection with the James River improvement work, comprises:

One assistant engineer $1,750.00

Under the proposed organization all engineering work in parks relating to design would be handled in the bureau of design, and that involving construction should be under the direct supervision of the construction bureau of the department. The force employed in connection with the James River improvements would be placed under the supervision of the engineer in charge of maintenance. The work of furnishing information in respect to line and grade, being essentially a routine service, would be handled in the bureau of design and survey. The present force assigned to this latter work is inadequate.

Division of Sewers, Bridges and Viaducts.

The work of this division is concerned with the design, construction and maintenance of sewers and the maintenance of bridges and viaducts. The only contemplated change in the organization of this division in connection with the proposed reorganization of the department, relates to the force engaged in the maintenance of bridges and viaducts. It is proposed to include this work in the bureau of maintenance.

Proposed Bureau of Design and Survey.

The purpose of this bureau is to centralize the design and survey forces of the department in such a way that they may be used to the greatest advantage, and at the same time make such service available to the construction divisions as needed. The need for some such separate organization unit in the department is serious. At present the only drafting force in the organization includes one draftsman, recently assigned to this work and a so-called assessor of damages, whose work includes the preparation of damage and assessment plans and the issuance of house numbers to property owners. This work should obviously be handled as part of the routine work of the bureau and not as at present as an independent activity.

There is no co-ordination in the preparation or filing of plans and while the workmanship is in general excellent, and the policy followed in the preparation of plans is commendable, there is a laxity in the control exercised over this part of the work that is open to serious criticism. The preparation of all designs and other plans and maps, together with the filing and use of plans should be under a central control. The bureau of design and survey should also have under its jurisdiction all work incidental to the survey and mapping of the territory recently annexed by the city.

It should be borne in mind that this proposed bureau is essentially for service, and while the development of designs, etc., should be under the direct supervision of the head of the bureau, there should always be a co-operative relation between the heads of this bureau and the heads of the other functional bureaus of the department. The organization of the bureau, as shown in the chart, is designed to include a force adequate to serve the normal needs of the department, including the survey of the annexed territory.

Construction Policy.

On all construction work the city furnishes the cement required and also in connection with sewer construction, all terra cotta pipe, castings for manholes and catch basins. These supplies are contracted for annually, the price bid being based on delivery on the line of work. This practice has resulted in securing low prices and is commendable.

A further extension of this policy to include furnishing such materials as asphalt, gravel and broken stone should be considered. In the matter of asphalt, particularly it should be borne in mind that the city has at present a considerable mileage of asphalt paved streets, and that material will undoubtedly be used extensively in future construction. As a means towards securing the effective maintenance of asphalt streets, the city government should give serious consideration to the establishment of a city-owned asphalt plant, of sufficient capacity to furnish asphalt for new construction as well as repair work. The experience of other cities in the operation of such plants in securing suitable asphaltic materials and in the more advantageous handling of repair work than results from having that work done under contract, fully justifies the installation of a city-owned asphalt plant for Richmond.

Also consideration should be given by the city government to the acquisition of gravel pits and possibly stone quarries in the vicinity of Richmond, and their development, as a means toward securing suitable materials for the improvement of the many miles of unimproved roads within the city limits.

Grading Contract.

The city also makes an annual contract for grading involving excavation and back-fill required in connection with pipe-laying, repair work, etc. This work in the streets is handled directly by the department concerned, as for example, the water department or the gas department, and it is not in any way supervised by the city engineer's office. This applies not alone to the matter of grading, but also to the replacement of pavements.

This practice is extremely undesirable and should be abandoned. It is obviously essential that the various city departments, such as water and gas, should have the right to make necessary cuts in pavements and excavation in streets to carry on their work. However, when this is done the city engineer's office should be informed of this work and the back-filling of trenches and all replacement of pavements should be subject to the inspection and supervision of that department and it should be held responsible for the standards employed in carrying on this work.

Testing of Construction Materials.

All testing of construction materials is done by a reputable local concern under a yearly contract with the city. The procedure followed in respect to sampling of material and method of testing and reporting is in accordance with the best practice.

Specification.

The specification for cement, concrete paving blocks, etc., and the standards employed in connection with the construction of granolithic sidewalks and curb and gutter construction conform to accepted standards.

Asphalt Specifications.

The specifications for asphalt are being revised to conform with the requirements of the American Society for testing materials. The present specifications are somewhat loosely drawn, but present no serious defect.

Mileage of Streets in Richmond.

There are approximately 400 miles of streets within the city limits and 250 miles of alleys. The amount and character of paving on these streets and the mileage of unpaved thoroughfares are shown in the accompanying tabulation:

Amount and Character of Paved and Surfaced Streets and Un-improved Roadways in Richmond.

Type of Paving.	Mileage.	
Asphaltic concrete	9.08	
Asphalt block	15.61	
Bitulithic	2.25	
Vitrified block	0.12	
Sheet asphalt	0.28	
Bituminous macadam penetration	2.58	
Total smooth paving		29.92
First class granite block	1.52	
Granite spall paving	51.27	
Total block paving		52.79
Total mileage paved streets		82.71
Graveled road beds		88.05
Total improved roads		170.76
Total unimproved roads approximately		229.24

Data on mileage of improved alleys were not available.

It will be seen from the above figures that the mileage of streets in Richmond improved with some sort of a permanent pavement is approximately 20.5 per cent. of the entire mileage of streets within the city, and that the total mileage of streets improved in any way, constitutes less than 43 per cent. of the total mileage. These figures are a sufficient commentary on the needs of Richmond in the matter of street improvement.

Asphalt Concrete Paving.

In 1914, the city initiated the policy of laying asphaltic concrete paving. The extent of this work arranged according to years up to the present time is shown in the following tabulation:

Asphaltic Concrete Paving.

Year.	Square Yards Laid.
1914	55,397
1915	100,303
1916	2,827
1917 (Up to June 30th)	23,620

The bulk of the work has comprised a 2-inch wearing surface on a 5-inch broken stone concrete base, the proportion of concrete being 1-3-5.

Natural asphalt has been generally used in the construction of the top course, although the specification permits the use of residual asphalts and the latter have been employed to a limited extent.

The construction methods employed and the general condition of pavements under service are commendable, particularly in view of the fact that there is no systematic maintenance of streets.

Asphalt Block Pavements.

There are at present within the city of Richmond 15.61 miles of asphalt block paving, some of it dating back to 1895. The greater portion of the asphalt block pavement is laid on a 5-inch gravel or broken stone base with a 2-inch sand cushion, although the more recent construction of this character is laid on a 6-inch concrete base.

The general condition of the asphalt block paving throughout the city is good, particularly the construction laid a few years ago. Of late the quality of the blocks received, although manufactured under precisely the same specification requirements as formerly, has proven distinctly inferior to those used in earlier construction.

Restriction of Asphalt Block Construction.

There has been a somewhat extravagant policy followed in the past in the matter of laying asphalt block pavements. In many cases this material has been used to pave side streets and streets where traffic conditions are very light and where the streets could have been improved at a fraction of the cost incurred, with a pavement entirely adequate to meet the traffic demands of the districts. The present cost of this type of construction, including the cost of cement, which is furnished by the city, and the cost of all other than extra grading is approximately $3.10 per square yard.

There are few streets in Richmond where traffic and other conditions would justify the construction of this type of pavement and it is recommended that its use be discontinued.

Granite Spall Paving.

There are few streets in Richmond where traffic and other Richmond. The specifications for this type of pavement permit the use of blocks with the following range in dimensions:

Depth—6 to 7 inches.
Width—top and bottom—3-6 inches.
Length—3 to 10 inches.

The blocks are laid on a sand cushion not less than four inches in depth and the joints are filled with fine gravel. Under traffic, pavements of this character rapidly become uneven, producing most undesirable conditions for hauling or other purposes. Furthermore, it is practically impossible to keep such pavements clean.

The use of this type of construction is probably justified on certain streets with excessive grades, of which there are a considerable number in Richmond with grades as high as 12 per cent. Elsewhere in the city, however, there appears to be little justification for the use of granite spall pavements. Experience has shown that in districts subjected to heavy hauling ultimate economy requires the construction of permanent pavements presenting as smooth a wearing surface as possible, such, for example, as is secured with first-class stone block paving laid on a concrete base.

The present cost of granite spall paving ($1.60 per square yard) is excessive in view of the objectionable features inherent in this type of construction. It is recommended that its use be restricted to streets with exceptionally heavy grades.

It is desired, however, to call attention to the possibility of utilizing granite spalls to greater advantage than at present by turning them to more uniform dimensions and laying them on a concrete base in a manner similar to that employed in laying "Durax" block pavements. This would cost materially less than first-class granite block construction and would give a serviceable pavement for heavy hauling.

Gravel Macadam Streets.

The greater portion of the street mileage of Richmond is made up of graveled or unimproved dirt streets. Of these about 88 miles are surfaced with gravel. There is a considerable supply of "cementitious" gravel suitable for road construction, both within the city limits and in the immediate vicinity. This material, when placed on a suitably drained sub-grade and surfaced, gives a satisfactory wearing surface for streets in the outlying residential sections of the city, provided:

First—That it is given a surface treatment with asphaltic oil.
Second—That it is adequately maintained.

There is no provision made for systematic maintenance of the gravel macadam streets in the city, and few of them have received any surface treatment. As a result, these streets are practically all in a state of disrepair.

It is essential that provision be made for an adequate force to maintain this class of construction. Also it is urged that these roads be treated with a heavy asphaltic oil as a means of preserving the surface against disintegration from traffic, and action of the weather.

Curb and Gutter Construction.

There are two types of curb and gutter construction in Richmond. The first of these, granite curb with granite spall gutters, five feet wide, predominates in the older sections of the city. In the outlying residential districts combined concrete curb and gutter construction is largely used.

Authorization of Curb and Gutter Construction.

A policy is followed to a considerable extent of authorizing the construction of curb and gutter construction without regard to the general improvement of the street. When this is done, if the construction of an improved surface of the street is soon to follow, the policy is to grade the street to the proposed sub-grade. If, however, as is frequently the case, the improvement of the street is not immediately contemplated the policy is to bring the grade of the street surface to the established grade.

In many cases, however, notably in those streets in that section west of the Boulevard between Cary Street and Monument Avenue, the practice is followed of leaving the street at approximately sub-grade subsequent to the construction of the curb and gutter. As a result, quite frequently the gutter is undermined resulting in many cases in local failure. This practice is a distinctly pernicious one and in fact the entire policy of authorizing curb and gutter improvement in Richmond is open to serious criticism. There are many miles of such construction in the city of Richmond, involving a very considerable expenditure of public funds, which serves no purpose other than possibly to stimulate the sale of real estate.

Conditions such as the above furnish an example of the evil results attending the inability of the city to assess for the improvement of the public streets.

It is strongly recommended that no improvement work of this character be authorized except in connection with the improvement of the street as a whole.

Sidewalk Construction.

There are two types of sidewalk construction permitted in the city of Richmond, brick and granolithic. The specifications governing the work are in conformity with accepted standards. The space reserved for sidewalks is fixed by ordinance as one-fifth the width of the street. although some latitude is allowed in the matter of actual paved area required. Obviously this arbitrary method of fixing the width of the sidewalk by ordinance is both unscientific and illogical. The width of a sidewalk should be determined on the basis of traffic needs with due regard to local conditions. It is recommended that the policy of the city in this matter be modified in the above respect.

In residential streets the general policy is followed of providing space at regular intervals for the planting of shade trees. This practice is commendable and has aided materially in beautifying the streets of the city.

Authorization of Work.

The construction of sidewalks is in general initiated by property owners although in some cases it is specifically authorized by the administrative board. Application for permits to construct sidewalks is made to the city engineer on a blanket form used in connection with all permits affecting the use of streets. Before a permit is issued by the city engineer the applicant is required to have the application approved by the gas and water departments, in so far as the proposed construction may affect the work of these departments, and also by the commissioner of revenue, who certifies as to the ownership of the property. This procedure while commendable, in so far as it is designed to prevent the tearing up of new construction in order to make necessary house connections, is unnecessarily cumbersome and should be simplified.

Issuance of Permits and Control of Work.

After approval by the city engineer. permits are issued in duplicate on a blanket form, used for all street work. one copy being given to the applicant and the other retained in the city engineer's office. Control over the construction work when carried on by private parties is exercised by casual inspection on the part of the engineer in charge of sidewalk construction and one inspector. There is no fee exacted for the issuance of the permit and subsequent inspection.

The same force is also responsible for the supervision and inspection of all sidewalk construction by contract with the city, vault construction and the control over encumbrance. This force is entirely inadequate to meet the demands of the work.

Sidewalk Construction By Contract.

When the construction of sidewalks is carried on by contract, the engineer in charge prepares an assessment list on a prescribed form giving significant data in respect to the location and magnitude of the work, the owners of the property affected and the amount of assessment on each piece of property affected. This information is submitted to the special assessment clerk and by him transmitted to the city collector, who includes the amount due in the taxes levied on this property for the ensuing year.

The expense involved in connection with the supervision and inspection of the work is not included in the assessment charge made, although it constitutes a legitimate element of expense. It is recommended that this item be included in all charges for assessment work and in order to determine the amount of this charge there should be a daily time record kept by each man connected with the work, showing a distribution of his time over the various classes of work in which he is engaged.

Basis of Assessment for Sidewalks.

Where the property fronts on sidewalks laid by the city, the entire cost of the construction, minus the cost intersection, is levied against the property benefited. Where the new construction is adjacent to but not in front of the property benefited, as in the case of a corner lot, the city pays one-half the expense involved plus the cost of intersection and the property owner the remainder.

In general, the practice has been to provide funds for the city's share in the cost of sidewalk construction out of current revenues, but in 1916 the sum of $50,000 out of a $1,000,000 bond issue was set apart as a rotary fund for this purpose.

Records of Sidewalk Construction.

The records kept by the engineer in charge of sidewalk construction are to be commended. They include weekly detailed reports of the inspector, a complete record of each job, including materials used and payments made, together with a detailed history of the contract. This is filed with the inspector's notes on the work is a concise, readily available form. It is suggested that the inspector on the work be also required to submit a daily report in the form of a postal card, thereby enabling the engineer to exercise a somewhat closer control over the work than is possible under present conditions.

Paving of Alleys.

The grading and paving of alleys is carried out on petition of 75 per cent. of the property owners affected, the entire expense of the improvement being assessed on the property abutting on the alley.

This policy is modified at times by the administrative board in so far as securing the consent of 75 per cent. of the property owners is concerned before authorizing the work. Also there is no personal notification of the property owners in respect to the proposed improvement, the only notice being the publication of allegations. This practice has frequently resulted in undue hardship to individual property owners who are assessed for the cost of alley improvements from which they derive no benefit.

The entire policy of the administrative board in this matter is open to criticism and should be revised.

There is a decided need for improving the alleys in certain sections of the city. In many cases these alleys, although connecting paved streets. have not been graded and in times of severe rainfalls which frequently occur, mud and clay are washed out from these alleys onto the paved streets, clogging the catch-basins and producing undesirable conditions generally. The city should have the power to remedy such conditions and to levy the expense against the abutting property, and if legislative action is necessary to accomplish this, steps should be taken at once to enact such legislation.

Alleys in general are paved with granite spalls. This practice was doubtless justified when such pavements could be laid for from 75 to 85 cents per square yard, but under present conditions the use of this form of construction is not justified and it is recommended that concrete be used for this purpose.

Condition of Railroad Areas.

The condition of the railroad area throughout the city is almost universally open to criticism. The traction companies are required by ordinance to maintain the street area between their tracks and for two feet outside in repair, but there is no delegated responsibility in the city engineer's department for enforcing these requirements and as a result these areas are in a general state of disrepair. One of the main factors in producing the present unsatisfactory condition is permitting the traction companies to use other than concrete foundation for their track system within the city limits.

Track Foundation.

The practice of using ballast for track foundation which has been permitted by council against the protest of the city engineer's office, cannot be too severely condemned. It results in the rapid deterioration under traffic of the pavement area adjacent to the tracks causing local failure in the street section. The lack of systematic maintenance accentuates these conditions which in some places constitute a distinct hazard to the public.

An additional reason for requiring concrete foundation under street railway tracks is the protection this affords from electrolysis due to stray currents from the track. It is recommended that the city government take appropriate action to prohibit the use of other than concrete foundation for street railway tracks within the city limits.

Street Maintenance and Repair.

At the present time there is no provision made for the maintenance of streets in Richmond. It is true that there is a certain amount of repair work carried on both by contract and also by a force connected with the department of street cleaning, but this work is limited in scope and is not carried out in accordance with any well-defined policy.

Street Repair by Contract.

At the beginning of each year the city advertises for bids to do general repair work on streets, and the contract for the ensuing year is awarded to the lowest bidder. The items included in the contract cover practically all phases of street construction although the work actually done is largely confined to the replacement of pavements. During the present year this work is divided between two contractors, each of whom bid low on certain kinds of work.

Authorization and Control of Work.

The powers of the city engineer are restricted in authorizing and controlling this work. In the first place, there is no patrol inspection of streets and hence the need for repair work is generally brought to the attention of the engineer in charge of this work by some outside agency such as the police department, or some other member of the city engineer's organization. Frequently no report is made until the condition of the street is distinctly hazardous to the public.

When the report of conditions requiring repairs is brought to the attention of the city engineer or his representatives, he has not the power to authoriez immediate repairs, except when conditions are such as to constitute a hazard to the community. Otherwise he must first cause an inspection to be made and then request the administrative board for authority to have the required repairs made. This applies to work done by contract. In cases where the work is not included in the repair contract, the city engineer may notify the superintendent of street cleaning in respect to the conditions noted, but he has no authority over the method of carrying on the work.

When authority is received from the administrative board to undertake the required repairs, the engineer in charge notifies the contractor to go ahead and also indicates the extent of the repairs. The work of repair is inspected in so far as the limited force available permits and careful records are kept of the extent and character of the repairs made. At the end of each month the engineer in charge sends to the auditor a statement of the amount due the contractor. The character of the records kept and the general control over this work are commendable.

It is illuminating to note the extent of the expenditures made for repairs to streets during the past five years under contract. These expenditures are as follows:

Year.	Street Repair By Contract.
1913	$16,000
1914	38,000
1915	15,000
1916	11,000
1917 (Up to July 1st)	3,500

(It is assumed that amount for year will be $7,000).

Data are not available. in respect to the distribution according to type of repair of the expenditures shown in the above tabulation, but it will be seen that whereas a considerable mileage of improved pavements has gone out of guarantee during that period, thereby increasing the necessity for street repair and maintenance, yet the actual expenditures by the city for that purpose has decreased to a considerable extent. This is a very short-sighted policy.

Criticism of Street Repair Work By Contract.

The present policy of contracting for the repair of paved streets is open to criticism because it fails to give the city engineer the necessary power to make repairs as needed, and it ignores the fundamental requirement for the economical upkeep of city streets, that of providing for continuous maintenance in place of periodic repair.

The city of Richmond has at present a considerable mileage of paved streets which are being added to every year. It is probable that the bulk of the street improvements in the future will involve the construction of asphaltic concrete or bituminous macadam pavements. The economic life of these types of pavement depends to a considerable degree on the care with which they are maintained. Local failure in such pavements can be readily detected and, if promptly repaired, the rapid deterioration under traffic that results in the formation of pot holes can be avoided. To carry on this work effectively, it is necessary to provide for a system of patrol inspection and also a repair force adequately equipped to make the necessary repairs promptly.

The only true economy in street work lies in providing for constant and continuous vigilance in the maintenance of the streets.

Street Repairs By City Forces.

At present the repair of streets other than by contract is conducted by a force working under the direction of the superintendent of street cleaning. This force, which was formerly connected with the city engineer's department, was transferred early in 1915 to the street cleaning department by order of the administrative board.

Organization of Repair Force.

The present organization of the repair force includes:

1	Foreman	$1,200.00
1	Foreman, per day	3.00
2	Steam roller engineers, per day........	2.75
25	Laborers, per day	2.50

Ordinarily the force is divided into two gangs working independently.

Equipment.

The equipment includes:

    2   10-Ton road rollers.
    2   Road machines.
    12 Watson bottom dump-wagons.
    22 Mules and 4 horses.

Each foreman is supplied with a horse and wagon. The mules and horses are stabled at the department of street cleaning stables. The equipment, with the exception of the road rollers, is stored in the street cleaning yard. The practice is followed of allowing the road rollers when not in use to remain by the roadside without protection of any kind.

Scope of Repair Work.

The work of the repair force is primarily concerned with the surfacing and repair of gravel macadam streets although the men are also called upon to do miscellaneous repairs involving pavement work. In carrying on this work a considerable amount of intelligence and energy have been displayed, and certain of the results obtained are distinctly creditable. At the same time, there has been no intelligent work program followed, and in many cases streets have been graded without respect to established grades.

Maintenance and Repair of Unpaved Streets.

The gravel macadam streets, that are classified as unpaved, serve rapidly-growing residential sections on the outskirts of the city, or as connecting thoroughfares between such territory and the business section of the city. The condition of most of these streets at the time of the survey beggars description. The lack of any maintenance or repair work, wash-outs, the ravelling of road surfaces, etc., not only make many of them almost impassable but constitutes a distinct hazard to the traveling public.

Such conditions as these represent a distinct economic loss to the community to say nothing of the discomfort to the public. It is essential that funds be provided to maintain and equip a force adequate to keep these roads in a state of repair.

Defects In Present Policy of Street Repair.'

It is desired to emphasize the fact that street maintenance in all of its phases is distinctly an engineering function and should be directly under the supervision of the city engineer's department. The present policy followed in handling this work in Richmond is esentially unsound, and the alleged economics that have resulted from that policy are misleading and fallacious. The condition of the streets in Richmond is sufficient proof of its ineffectiveness.

Maintenance Organization Recommended.

It is obvious that the nature of the organization required to maintain paved streets differs to a considerable degree from that required for unpaved streets, and in the tentative organization shown in the accompanying chart the attempt is made to indicate the character of the force required rather than the exact number of employees. It is safe to say, however, that a conservative estimate of the amount of money required to maintain the streets of Richmond in a suitable condition would be not less than $100,000 a year.

Maintenance Yard and Storehouse.

In connection with the maintenance work of the city engineer's office, it is important to emphasize the desirability of a general storehouse and yard to serve as a headquarters for the field maintenance forces and provide adequate housing for the equipment of the city engineer's department. The latter is of particular importance as the life of equipment depends to a considerable degree upon the protection it receives from the weather during periods of disuse. The practice, for example, of leaving the steam rollers on the public street, when not in use, should not be tolerated.

In connection with this yard there should also be a storehouse for small supplies and tools used on the work. It is desirable but not essential to keep in the yard a small stock of construction material such as paving blocks, terra cotta pipe, man-hole covers, etc., for which there is a more or less emergency demand from time to time. Such a yard should be fenced in, with a yardmaster on duty during the day time. The yardmaster should have control of all supplies of all kinds going out of the yard and procedure should be developed and records installed for this purpose.

Sewer Construction and Maintenance.

The organization concerned with sewer construction and maintenance, aside from the special force employed in connection with the construction of the Shockoe Creek sewer, included at the time the study of this department was made:

1	Assistant engineer	$1,500.00
1	Sewer foreman	900.00
10	Laborers and pipe layers, per day.....	2.50

The work of this force includes supervision over the construction of sewer extensions, the installation of house connections and general repair work, such as the removal of obstructions in sewers, cleaning out of catch-basins, etc.

Sewer Construction Policy.

All sewer construction is carried on by contract, the usual procedure being followed in the award of such contracts as in the case of other public improvements.

Terra cotta pipe is used for sewers ranging in size from 6 to 29 inches in diameter. Above those sizes the general policy is to construct sewers of brick masonry, although concrete has been used to a limited extent, and there are some stone sewers in the older sections of the city. The mileage of sewers constructed up to the present time is shown in the accompanying tabulation:

Type of Construction.	*Mileage.*
Terra cotta pipe	105.58
Brick sewers	77.21
Stone sewers	7.14
Concrete sewers	2.81
House connections, terra cotta pipe.........	122.71
Total	315.45

In connection with all sewer construction, except trunk sewers, the policy is followed of placing all Y's for house connections and laying the necessary pipe to the property line at the time the sewer is constructed. The distribution of these Y's is based on the lot division of the property abutting the sewer, connection generally being placed at about the center of the lot.

Control of Construction Work.

The control exercised over sewer construction both in the matter of inspection and supervision is worthy of special note. Standards of construction covering practically every phase of sewer work have been developed, and this information with a variety of dimensional data showing their application to different sizes of sewers together with definite instructions are given to each inspector of the work. The inspectors are also required to keep accurate records of the work as it progresses. This information is recorded in a compact form suitable for ready filing and reference. The inspectors are also required to plot the location of all completed work. This information is promptly transferred to record plans and the result is that the sewer department has fairly complete, up-to-date records of the work done.

Desirability of Permanent Inspection Force.

The inspectors of sewer construction are not included as a part of the permanent organization of the department but are employed on a temporary basis. The needs of the city in the matter of sewer maintenance and construction fully justify the employment of a limited number of qualified inspectors on an annual basis, and it is recommended that provision be made for the permanent assignment of two inspectors to the division of sewer maintenance, house connections and extension.

Type and Adequacy of Sewer System.

In the older sections of the city, the combined system of sewer construction is in use. This system is fairly adequate. In new work in the outlying districts the separate system is being installed to some extent. The existing drainage and sewer systems in the territory recently annexed by the city are generally inadequate and one of the most serious problems facing the city at the present time is the design and construction of a comprehensive sewer and drainage system to serve the outlying districts of the city. Considerable progress has been made in this work, largely in connection with the survey of the annexed territory, and the methods employed and policy followed in developing this design are particularly commendable.

Sewer Outfalls.

All sewers of the city within the watershed of the James River and its tributaries, are discharged into the James River through suitable outfalls. There is no treatment of this sewage. In the western section of the city, a portion of which is located on the watershed of the Chickahominy River, it will, however, be necessary to provide for the treatment of city sewage before it is discharged into the stream. This is a problem that should receive the consideration of the city government.

Flush Tanks.

There are no flush tanks used in the older sections of the city. Owing to the prevailing grades there is little need for them. Provision is made, however, in the designs for sewer system in outlying districts where the grades are light for the installation of flush tanks.

Sewer Assessments.

No assessment for sewer construction, based on the actual cost of construction is levied on the property benefited, but an annual tax of ten cents per front foot is levied providing the property benefited is also served with city water. This annual tax can be commuted for all time by the single payment of $1.50 per front foot.

Obviously, such a practice is unscientific and illogical. The cost of sewer construction other than trunk sewers should constitute a legitimate charge against the property benefited and this cost should be apportioned in the form of an assessment on that property.

In the case of trunk sewers, where there is more than a local benefit involved, the cost should either be apportioned over the city at large or preferably on the drainage area directly tributary to the sewer in question.

When the construction of a service or lateral sewer is completed, the engineer in charge makes out an assessment list, giving all significant data in respect to cost, amount of pipe laid, etc., and also prepares a sketch on the back of the assessment list showing location of all property affected, and its relation to the completed construction, which is sent to the special assessment clerk.

The above procedure, although commendable as to completeness of information presented, is unnecessarily cumbersome and entails useless labor on the sewer division. It is recommended that the form used in transmitting the information to the special assessment clerk be simplified so as to include only the essential data as to location and ownership of property affected and the cost. Other data are readily available in the office of the sewer division if at any time required.

House Connections.

Work involved in connection with the installation of house connections is of two classes: First, that involving making the necessary connection with an existing sewer tap; second, where the connection involves making a tap in the sewer.

House Connection Permit Procedure.

The procedure for the issuance of permits to make connections with sewers requires the owner of the property to make application to the city engineer's office for a permit, on a prescribed form, the applicant agreeing to pay all costs incurred by the city in carrying on the work. The application must first be personally approved by the city engineer before the permit is issued. When approved by the city engineer, it is then referred to the division of sewers to ascertain if a connection with the sewer exists. The application is then referred back to the assistant chief clerk and the permit is issued in duplicate by him, the original being retained in the office and the duplicate, not a carbon copy, being given to the plumber engaged by the property owner. The application is filed and indexed according to location. If the work does not involve tapping the sewer, the work of the plumber is merely inspected by the plumbing inspector to insure that the workmanship meets the requirements of the department.

Work Done By City Force.

When the sewer connection involves making a tap to a sewer the tap is made and the pipe laid to the property line by city forces under the direction of the sewer foreman. The latter keeps an accurate record of the cost of the work in respect to labor and materials, on a well-designed form. When the work is completed the cost information is transmitted to the assistant chief clerk who makes a report to the special assessment clerk as to the property affected and the amount chargeable to the property owner. This amount does not include such elements of expense as supervision and clerical work.

A similar procedure is followed in connection with the unstopping of sewers, the property owner being charged with the cost of the work when the obstruction is due to any fault of his.

Defects in Procedure.

While the control exercised over the work is satisfactory in so far as field inspection and reporting is concerned, the procedure followed in the handling of the application and permit is open to criticism. The type of permit form could be improved and unnecessary steps in procedure eliminated.

These defects could be easily corrected by the use of carbon copies for permit forms and developing a procedure for handling application and permits that would not involve the circumlocution that exists at present.

Adequacy of Force and Equipment.

The present force in charge of sewer construction and maintenance is entirely inadequate to give the service required in a city the size of Richmond.

The assistant engineer in immediate charge of this work has a horse and buggy at his disposal. while the foreman and his gang have one mule and wagon. The work is of a character that frequently requires prompt action and the use of a motor truck would greatly expedite it. Further consideration is given later in this report to the general question of transportation for the city engineer's department.

The force should also be equipped with modern apparatus for the cleaning of sewers and catch-basins. At present there is no systematic cleaning of the latter. and the failure to keep them clean frequently results in stoppage and overflow of sewers, resulting in property damage that could otherwise be avoided. The city is subject to frequent heavy rain falls when a considerable amount of clay and silt is washed onto the street, and thence into sewers and catch-basins. and systematic cleaning is essential.

In this connection consideration should be given to the discontinuance of the use of catch-basins and the installation of direct connections to the sewers. It is conceded that this is the best practice in sewer construction. and it has been adopted to a considerable extent in many cities throughout the country.

Miscellaneous Projects and Methods.

In addition to the construction and maintenance work previously noted, the assistant engineer in charge of sewers, has supervision over the construction of the Shockoe Creek and Bacon's Quarter Branch storm sewer and some improvement work along the dock bordering the canal.

Shockoe Creek Storm Sewer.

The Shockoe Creek storm sewer improvement includes the construction of a storm sewer designed to carry the drainage from the watershed of Shockoe Creek and Bacon's Quarter Branch and thus relieve an area that has been in the past subject to frequent inundation, causing loss and damage to property. The sewer is of approximately rectangular section, built of re-inforced concrete with a carrying capacity of 8,000 cubic feet per second. This work was commenced in 1912 and approximately two-thirds of it has already been constructed at an expenditure of $610,285. Bonds to the amount of $653,500 were issued to defray the expense of the construction.

The lower section extending from Washington Street to the James River is yet to be constructed, and while suitable location plans and estimates have been prepared under the direction of the engineer in charge of sewers and presented to the council for their approval, council has failed to act in the matter although the resulting delay has materially increased the ultimate cost of the work. The importance of this improvement cannot be over-estimated as it will result in the reclamation of an extensive area of the city peculiarly available for manufacturing and industrial development. That the benefits to be derived are real, is evidenced by the recent acquisition and prospective development by the American Locomotive Works of a considerable section of the area served by the construction already completed. It is urged that this city government take suitable action to avoid delay in the completion of the project.

Annexation Survey.

Mention has already been made of the drainage and topographical survey of the territory recently annexed to the city and attention has been called to the illogical placing of the responsibility for this work on the administrative board rather than on the city engineer's office. The methods employed in connection with this work are distinctly creditable, but the force provided as shown on the organization chart of the department is too large both in the field and in the office. The employment of an assistant engineer at $1,800, a chief of party at $1,500, and an instrument-man at $1,200 with four assistants, serving as rodmen and chainmen is not justified in this class of field work. There is no justification for the employment of a chief draughteman at $1,500 to supervise the work of three draughtsmen each receiving $1,200 per year, all working under an assistant engineer receiving $1,800, when the work required is of but a purely routine character.

Furthermore, the employment of a title examiner who receives for part-time services a salary of $1,800, is not justified when service of this character is at present available in the office of the city engineer and city attorney. It is recommended that this position be abolished.

No specific recommendations are made in respect to other organization changes as provision is made in the proposed re-organization in the bureau of design and survey, as submitted in the proposed re-organization of the department, for a force adequate to render service of this character for the entire city.

Bridge Repair.

In addition to the above activities the engineer in charge of sewers and annexed section survey is also responsible for the up-keep of bridges within the city limits. This work is directly under the supervision of a general inspector, who makes periodic investigations of the condition of bridges and supervises such repairs as are required. No special repair force is assigned to this work, but men are hired as needed or when the work is of sufficient magnitude special contracts are awarded.

There are also three bridge watchmen each receiving a salary of $65 per month, included in the organization, having the care of bridges. One of these watchmen is assigned to Mayo's bridge, which is a re-inforced concrete viaduct, and two are assigned to the Ninth Street bridge, which is a steel structure with a timber deck. These men are vested with police authority, and are supposed to regulate traffic over the bridge.

There is no justification for their employment and it is recommended that these positions be abolished.

In connection with the care of bridges it is desired to call attention to the laxity displayed by the administrative board in failing to carry out the painting of the steel work on the Ninth Street bridge, after the urgent necessity for such painting was brought to the attention of that body by the city engineer's department. The importance of adequate care of bridge steel work in the matter of painting cannot be overrated, both from the point of view of ultimate economy and also as a means of safeguarding the public against possible failure of the structure due to progressive deterioration in the steel work.

It is further recommended that the care of bridges being purely a maintenance function, be included under the bureau of maintenance and operation of the city engineer's department rather than in the bureau of sewers.

James River Improvement.

The so-called James River improvement work, which is under the jurisdiction of the city engineer, includes the general care and dredging of the harbor of Richmond, which is at the head of the navigable section of the James River and also the maintenance and operation of the lock, located at the foot of Twenty-eighth Street which gives access to the James River and Kanawha Canal.

Dock and Harbor Master.

The operation of the dock is under the direction of the dock and harbor master, who also is responsible for the collection of freight tolls from ships passing through the dock and the movement and berthing of ships within the harbor. He receives an annual salary of $1,200.

The harbor master is not provided with any permanent force but hires laborers as needed to operate the lock gates. The records kept and the control exercised over the work which is of a purely routine character are fairly adequate.

Dredging Improvement Work.

The dredging work is carried on under the direction of the superintendent of the dredge, and captain of the tug who receives an annual salary of $1,500. The dredging equipment includes a combination bucket dredge and sand sucker. The material dredged is largely good quality sand and is used principally in reclaiming land along the waterfront, although recently the city has sold a limited amount to contractors. A 250 H. P. tug is provided for general use along the harbor.

The United States Government maintains a turning basin in the harbor of Richmond, and the dredging work done and men employed on the tug are subject to government regulation. The supervision exercised over the work by the city engineer's office is of a routine character involving occasional measurement of material deposited, etc., and it is suggested in the proposed re-organization of that department that it be placed under the supervision of the engineer in charge of maintenance.

Transportation.

At present the city engineer's office is equipped with the following transportation equipment:

1 Ford runabout, used by the engineer in charge of sidewalk construction.

1 Ford runabout, used by the engineer in charge of line and grade work and James River improvement.

1 Horse and buggy. used by the chief engineer.

1 Horse and buggy, used by engineer in charge of street construction.

1 Horse and buggy, used by' engineer in charge of sewer construction and annexed territory survey.

1 Horse and buggy. used by engineer in charge of sewer construction and maintenance.

1 Horse and buggy. for general use by engineering force.

1 Mule and cart, used by sewer foreman.

1 Mule and cart. used on the Southside.

The Ford machines are kept in private garages. while the horses and buggies are kept in the stables of the department of street cleaning.

While it is appreciated that for some time to come the city will have to depend on some horse-drawn equipment. particularly in connection with the grading and repair of gravel streets, yet the horse-drawn equipment used for other than this class of hauling should be replaced in so far as possible by motor-driven equipment. The latter equipment should include Ford runabouts or their equivalent for use by the engineers in charge of the three divisions of street construction, sewer construction and street maintenance.

In addition. a Ford truck or its equivalent should be at the disposal of the forces engaged in emergency repair work. and a second Ford truck should be available for general service of the department. It would also be desirable to provide a larger truck of about two-tons capacity for special hauling purposes where a considerable amount of material is to be handled. It is estimated that such equipment would make it possible to dispense with all of the present horse-drawn equipment in the department with the exception. possibly. of the horse and buggy used by the chief engineer, and would materially increase the efficiency of the department through the saving in time alone that would result.

Miscellaneous Complaints.

In addition to the permits for making sewer connections and sidewalk construction, there are other miscellaneous permits issued by the city engineer's office. Among these are permits to occupy portions of the street for construction purposes, permits to construct areaways, courts, balconies, bay windows, cornices, marquises, to install gasoline pumps, etc. The application for all such permits requires the personal approval of the city engineer before the permit is issued. No fee is charged in connection with the issuance of these permits and the procedure followed does not insure adequate control ovr the permit after it is issued.

This policy is open to particular criticism, in so far as it relates to the issuance of permits for the use of the streets for any purpose. At the time of inspection, extensive areas in certain of the main thoroughfares, for example Marshall Street, were occupied by construction materials without any protection for the street surface. In one place a contractor was observed dumping a load of brick directly on the surface of a street paved with asphaltic macadam. Such practices are indefensable and should not be tolerated. It is appreciated that a city ordinance permits the use of streets in this way, but steps should be taken at once to revise this ordinance in such a way as to protect the interests of the city.

Furthermore, no permit to use the streets for any purpose should be issued without the payment of a fee adequate to cover the overhead expense involved in issuing it and the subsequent inspection and control of the work. In addition the applicant should be required to make a deposit sufficient to protect the city against possible damage to the pavement used, and where the work involves the replacement of any section of this pavement this should be done by city forces under the supervision of the maintenance bureau of the city engineer's office, and the cost of this work should be deducted from the deposit required of the applicant.

A uniform size of permit forms should be employed, preferably utilizing a loose-leaf system. Also the procedure followed in issuing permits should be such as to avoid unnecessary duplication of the work involved, and should afford automatic control over the inspection of the work involved when desired.

To exercise adequate control over various classes of permits will involve a certain amount of routine inspection. This inspection should be handled in part by the police and in part by the inspectors attached to the maintenance bureau of the city engineer's office.

Furnishing Line and Grade.

In addition to service rendered in the matter of permits, the city engineer's office is frequently called upon to furnish information in respect to the line and grade in order to enable property owners to construct garages and other structures on ungraded streets and alleys. This work frequently entails the making of surveys and the actual establishment of the lines and grades on the ground. At the present time such service is given without charge upon application by the property owner. The procedure followed in recording the information thus secured in order to make it subsequently available to the office is entirely satisfactory. This service, however, is one that the city engineer's office should not be called upon to give free of charge. While the expense involved is not large, it being estimated to amount to approximately $425 for 1916 and $340 for 1915, yet it is those gratuitous services rendered by the city which unnecessarily increase the cost of city government.

It is recommended that the expense involved in this work shall be paid by the property owner desiring the service. In order to arrive at the cost of this and similar work, each member of the staff of the city engineer should be required to keep a daily time record, which will show the distribution of his time according to the work on which he has been engaged.

Encumbrances.

There are comparatively few encumbrances or encroachments on the streets of Richmond. Those that are left include principally stone blocks formerly used for carriage steps, and some few show-cases along the main business streets.

The control exercised over this work, both in the matter of records kept and the procedure followed, insuring the removal of encroachments, is commendable.

Sidewalk Vaults.

The right to construct and maintain vaults extending beyond the property line under the sidewalk is subject to a permit issued by the city engineer's department. There are also standard plans covering vault construction, the minimum requirements of which must be met before the construction of any vault is permitted.

The city derives a revenue from the maintenance of vaults. This revenue is based on the number of square feet of vault lights on the sidewalk section, at the rate of six cents per square foot. During 1916, revenues from that source amounted to approximately $6,100.

This policy is commendable, but it is suggested that a more equitable basis of charging for space would be according to the cubic feet of space occupied by the vault rather than the area of vault lights. Also the location of the vault, that is in respect to the taxable value of the property to which it is connected, should be considered in fixing the charge rather than the establishment of a flat rate for space occupied irrespective of location. It is suggested that consideration be given to this matter by the city government.

Department of Street Cleaning

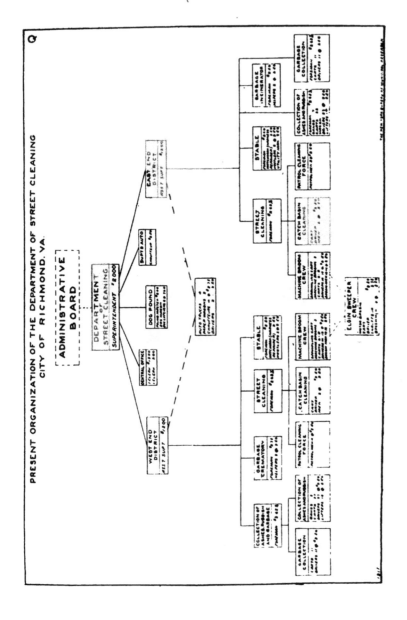

PRESENT ORGANIZATION OF THE DEPARTMENT OF STREET CLEANING
CITY OF RICHMOND. VA.

DEPARTMENT OF STREET CLEANING.

Introductory Statement.

Functions Performed.

As in many cities the title "department of street cleaning" is not sufficiently inclusive to indicate the scope of this department's activity in the city of Richmond. The functions of refuse collection, refuse disposal, repair of streets and the operation of the dog pound are delegated to this department in addition to the cleaning of streets.

The chapter of this report, which deals with the city engineer's department contains certain recommendations with respect to the location of responsibility for highway maintenance and repairs. It is mentioned in passing, that the inclusion of this particular function among the street cleaning department's activities is both illogical and uneconomical.

In order to create a title for the department of street cleaning which will be descriptive of the functions performed. and sufficiently inclusive, it is recommended that the title "department of sanitation" be employed.

Street Cleaning.

The general conclusions reached on the basis of the information contained in subsequent sections of the report on the street cleaning department. are that the effectiveness and economy of the cleaning of smooth pavements can be improved through a change in the methods employed and the manner in which the work is routed. and further that the physical condition of a large part of the granite spall pavements preclude an effective cleaning by other than intensive hand patrol work.

The following sections recommend definite changes in methods. the abandonment of machine broom cleaning on smooth paved streets. and the abandonment of this latter method on many of the granite pavements where this type of cleaning equipment is decidedly ineffective.

Garbage Collection.

The principal criticisms in connection with garbage collections are directed. not at the department. but at the public at large. for the lack of co-operation and the absence of effort to maintain a standard of cleanliness and sanitation proportionate to the size and importance of the city.

To improve the service rendered it has been recommended that the responsibility of garbage collectors be somewhat further definitized through the establishment of definite collection routes which shall constitute one day's work.

The condition of garbage receptacles and their lack of uniformity in size is commented upon in detail. The conclusion reached and recommended is to the effect that standardized receptacles are essential, and that the sanitary condition as existing can only be improved through the co-operation of the public at large, or by a broadening of the police powers to enforce regulations, and through the co-operation of the judicial authorities in connection therewith.

Collection of Ashes and Rubbish.

Only a very small portion of ashes and rubbish is collected separately. In most cases householders do not separate ashes from rubbish which consequently necessitates the use of the same wagon or cart for the transportation of both. Inasmuch as the same equipment is used in summer and winter, the weight per load of the material collected in summer is very much less than for a load of winter material. The use of small capacity carts in summer is far from economical.

As a remedy for this condition it is recommended in the section of this report covering the subject that ordinances and laws be enacted requiring the separation of ashes from rubbish in order to permit of the use of greater capacity carts for the collection of the latter material. This will result in a considerable saving.

Refuse Disposal.

The question of the disposal of ashes and rubbish by dumping is discussed and commented upon with the general conclusion that this method should be continued and that more careful supervision be exercised over the dumps now in use.

The use of incineration as a means of disposing of garbage is undoubtedly the most satisfactory for a city of the size and geographical location of Richmond.

A comparative cost analysis of the operation of the two plants has been made and conclusions drawn therefrom. In general it may be said that the plants are operated in a satisfactory and economical manner.

Organization.

The department of street cleaning is one of the several units of the city government which are under the jurisdiction of the administrative board. All employees are appointed by the board, including the superintendent of street cleaning who acts as the chief administrative officer of the department.

The general organization is built up on the district basis, the city being divided into an east and west district, the dividing line being Fifth Street and the James River. The west district includes all territory west of Fifth Street and north of the James River. The east district includes all territory east of Fifth Street and south of the James River.

For convenience, the entire organization of the street cleaning department is shown in graphical form on a chart included in this report. The comments and references on organization may be easily understood through reference to this organization chart.

District Organization.

Each district is supervised by an assistant superintendent who is responsible for all the activities carried on in his district, with the exception of the dog pound, which is not considered as a part of either of the district organizations.

Generally speaking, each function is supervised by a foreman who reports to and is supervised by the assistant superintendent of the district. It may be observed from the chart that each district is sub-divided into: (1) street cleaning; (2) collection of refuse; (3) disposal of refuse; (4) stable operation. These four functions are still further sub-divided as may also be seen by reference to the chart.

In the east district, the two functions of garbage collection and collection of ashes and rubbish are each supervised by a separate foreman, whereas in the west only one supervising foreman is employed. These two functions are so operated that the employees carrying on the work are separated by a considerable distance during the day's work. Ash and rubbish collection is carried on under a gang system and is confined to a relatively small area each day, whereas garbage collection is performed by individual collectors covering the entire area included in each of the two districts.

It is impossible for a foreman to supervise the collection of garbage from the area included in one district when he is provided with no means of transportation. It is also impossible for one foreman to supervise both ash and rubbish collection and the collection of garbage.

The work performed in the two districts did not differ in the quality of service rendered, chiefly for the reason that the supervision over garbage collectors is in reality performed by the assistant superintendent of the district rather than by the foreman directly in charge.

It is recommended in this particular respect, that the position of foreman of garbage collection in the east district be abolished, and that the supervision continue to be exercised by the assistant superintendent of the district.

It is recommended that the position of foreman of ash and rubbish collection be retained in each of the two districts in order to provide constant supervision over the gang organization utilized in connection with this function.

Assistant Superintendents Should Be Provided With Motor Transportation.

The assistant superintendents should be provided with automobiles in order to cover the large area over which they must exercise supervision. The assistant superintendent in charge of the west district is already provided with such transportation, the other superintendent however utilizes a horse-drawn vehicle.

It is recommended that the east end assistant superintendent be provided with motor transportation similar to that used in the west district.

Unassigned Employees.

There are certain employees of the department who are not definitely assigned to either the east or the west district. They are the chauffeurs of motor equipment and the drivers of the paper wagons. These men may be assigned to work with their equipment in any part of the city.

Inasmuch as the number of these employees varies in proportion to the demand for their services, no attempt has been made to indicate their number. The organization chart provides a unit wherein these employees appear by title only and rate of wages without regard to the number employed. This group is shown to be subject to assignment by indicating the line of authority by means of a dotted line connecting this group with each of the two districts.

Repair Force.

It may be noted from an examination of the chart of the street cleaning department that no detail of the organization of the repair force is indicated. Although the assistant superintendents exercise a certain degree of supervision over this work, it may be said that it is directly under the jurisdiction of the superintendent of the department.

Detailed comments and recommendations covering the work of street repair are treated in the section of this report devoted to the activities of the city engineer's department. In order to avoid repetition it is deemed advisable to omit all comments concerning highway repairs from the report on the department of street cleaning. The detail of the organization of this branch of the work may be obtained from the organization chart accompanying the report on the city engineer's department.

Central Office.

The clerical force employed in the central office comprises two clerks who divide the work carried on therein. A considerable portion of the time of one clerk is consumed in answering telephone calls and recording the subject of the messages received. It is the practice for all garbage collectors and for foremen of the ash and rubbish collection gang to telephone to the central office three or four times a day for special instructions regarding the collection of dead animals and other complaints.

The subsequent sections of this report contain a number of recommendations with respect to the installation and maintenance of new records. The question of clerical service in connection with the keeping of these records has been carefully considered, and it is clear that no additional clerical help will be required for this purpose.

It is, therefore, recommended, that not more than two clerks be employed in the central office, with the qualifications, however, that one of the two clerks should be competent to take shorthand dictation and to act as stenographer and typist for the department.

Recommendations.

There is no inherent weakness in the form of organization of the street cleaning department, and no general changes are recommended.

The various recommendations made in the following sections, with respect to working method, equipment, etc., refer to particular phases of the activities of the street cleaning department, and are commented upon under the section titles descriptive of the functinos comprehended therein.

General Administration.

Centralized Responsibility.

The department is theoretically administered by the administrative board, through the superintendent acting as the agent of the board. Each district is supervised by an assistant superintendent, who in turn supervises the work of all foremen in charge of gangs operating in the respective assistant superintendent's district.

Although the administrative records and reports are meagre in detail, and in many cases essential records are entirely lacking, it is nevertheless possible to fix responsibility definitely for all of the functions performed by the department.

Due to the fact that the administrative board is responsible for the operation of many other city departments, it frequently happens that the routine work of the street cleaning department is disturbed to a considerable extent through compliance with orders issued by the administrative board.

During the last year the street cleaning department has been delivering all coal purchased by the administrative board to its ultimate destination. The occurrence of this class of work at unforeseen intervals has a tendency to seriously interfere with the effective and economical operation of the department. It has also a tendency to demoralize the personnel.

In addition to the hauling of coal, the department is required from time to time to deliver material for the city engineer's department, to aid in the planting of trees and perform other miscellaneous functions,

It is recommended that this method be abandoned and that coal be delivered by the contractor from whom it is purchased. It is further recommended that a program be adopted for tree planting, etc., so that it will not interfere with the routine work of the street cleaning department.

Street Cleaning.

Street cleaning functions as performed in the city of Richmond may be divided into two groups as follows:

1—Machine broom cleaning.
    a—Horse-drawn rotary brooms.
    b—Motor-driven pick-up broom.
2—Hand patrol.

The organization of this work is under a "gang system" as may be observed from the organization chart accompanying the report.

Machine Broom Cleaning.

There are two machine broom crews, each of which operates in its respective district, one being assigned to the east end district, and the other to the west end district. As may be seen from the organization chart the east end crew is supervised directly by a foreman, whereas the west end crew is supervised by the foreman in charge of both the machine broom crew and the hand patrol force.

Eliminating the supervising officer the organization of each crew is as follows:

1   Sprinkling wagon.
3   Rotary brooms.
6-8 Pick-up carts.
9-13 Broom men.

Methods Employed in Gang Cleaning.

Under ordinary circumstances, the machine brooms operate in batteries of three, preceded by the sprinkling cart. Each follow-up broom takes a position which will permit it to pick up the "strike" or "windrow," which is the material removed from the surface and thrown to one side by virtue of the angular position of the broom with respect to the axle of the running gear.

The sprinkling cart and brooms follow a definite route, which is practically standard for each particular day's work, unless interrupted by street construction or similar work.

The pick-up carts and broom men of the crew are divided according to the requirements of each particular street. The methods employed in directing the work of the broom men and the pick-up carts lead to a considerable loss of time on the part of both the men and the carts.

It is the practice for the foreman to divide the follow-up crew and assign and direct certain broom men and carts to side streets and avenues from time to time during the progress of the work.

This almost invariably leads to retracing over streets already cleaned by another cart of the follow-up organization, and requires that both men and carts proceed two or three blocks to the next point, at which active work is to begin.

This loss of time cannot be evaluated in either hours or money without an intensive time study of each particular crew, and a comparison with the most effective routing for the broom men and pick-up carts.

Detailed Study of Each Route Recommended.

It is apparent that too little stress has been laid upon the careful planning of the disposition of the follow-up men and carts.

Such a study can only be effectively carried out by the use of maps and the setting forth on such maps of the precise route to be traveled by each member and cart of the follow-up force. This can be accomplished by joint conference of the superintendent of the department, the assistant superintendents, and the foreman of the machine broom crews. Experience will indicate the approximate quantitative work demands of each particular street. The approximate time to be consumed by the follow-up men on each section of the daily route can be determined therefrom.

It is, therefore, recommended, that the maps elsewhere spoken of in this report, be utilized for planning of each machine broom route, and that tentative disposition of the follow-up force be made with the principal end in view, of precluding the necessity for retracing and for idle time between stopping and starting points.

The present machine routes are continuous for the streets traversed by the sprinkling cart and the rotary brooms, and the same degree of consecutive work is possible of attainment by the broom men and pick-up carts.

The above recommendation should result in either a considerable saving in men and carts or an increase in area patrolled by the force now employed during an equal number of working hours.

Methods Employed by Broom Men in Gutter Piling.

The usual practice is to utilize two follow-up men in each gutter, to pile the windrow or strike convenient for pick-up by the pick-up cart drivers. These follow-up men start at points 20 to 30 feet apart, and work toward each other, meeting at the half-way point, where a pile of approximately 1 cubic foot has been produced. It may be seen that this method produces lost motion on the part of each broom man, who, during the day's shift, walks approximately half again as far is is necessary. The proper method to be employed by the broom man in piling the windrow in the gutter is to assign only one man to each gutter, unless the work is of such heavy nature that it is impossible for one man to keep ahead of the pick-up cart. In such cases, two men should be assigned to each gutter.

In no event, however, should the retracing method be employed. Each man should always work along the gutter in the direction in which the work is progressing. Where two men are necessary, the second man should pass around the first to a point some fifteen or twenty feet ahead, at which point he should begin the operation of piling. When the first man has completed the fifteen or twenty feet, he should, in turn, pass around the second. This procedure will then be a continuous one, and neither of the two men will ever have occasion to face, or progress, in the direction opposite to that of the general direction of progress.

Selection of Streets to be Cleaned, by Machine Broom Method.

There are four general types of pavement in the City of Richmond:

1—Asphalt block, a smooth pavement.
2—Granite, in most cases very irregular.
3—Asphaltic, concrete, and bitulithic, rough or smooth, depending upon age and use.
4—Gravel and dirt roads.

Only three of the above four types are at all susceptible to rotary broom sweeping, as a method of cleaning, gravel or dirt streets being eliminated.

The use of machine brooms, as a method of cleaning, is ineffective, except as an adjunct or supplement to other methods. In no case will the machine remove the fine dust, or the material which closely adheres to the pavement surface. It has been found universally that only the coarsest material is removed from a surface by the machine broom, and the degree of cleanliness, resulting from such method, is principally dependent upon the absence of irregularities in the pavement.

Smooth pavements, such as sheet asphalt, asphalt-block, brick and wood-block, if subjected to considerable horse-drawn traffic, accumulate refuse material, which is principally composed of horse-droppings. This clas of material become packed down by traffic, and can only be removed by hand-operated methods, or the use of flushing equipment or the "squee-gee" machine.

On all rough pavements, which class is confined to granite, in the city of Richmond, it is found that the machine broom performs very ineffective cleaning. The broom passes over the many depressions in the pavement without removing any material therefrom. It is also found that the general action of the broom upon packed down horse-droppings is also ineffective as a means of removal. In Richmond the majority of the granite streets are constructed with a sand filler, between the pavement joints. The effect of the machine broom method is to loosen the sand filler from the intersticies between the stones, thus producing a greater quantity of dust to be blown about than if it had not been disturbed.

There are many granite paved streets, which carry only a very light traffic, and whereon there is a negligible accumulation of material. Similarly, many of the asphalt-block streets and other smooth pavements accumulate very little refuse material other than that caused by horse-drawn traffic.

The use of machine broom cleaning on the smooth pavements and the light traffic granite streets is decidedly uneconomical.

Change in Machine Broom Schedules Recommended.

For the reasons set forth in the preceding section, it is recommended that all smooth streets, viz., asphalt-block and smooth bitulithic and asphaltic concrete be entirely dropped from the machine-broom cleaning routes, and that other methods be employed as described in detail under the sections entitled "hand patrol cleaning" and "squee-gee" cleaning.

It is further recommended that a careful study be made of all granite paved streets, and that a new classification for machine broom cleaning be established, and that streets carrying light traffic, such as Eighth, Ninth and Fourteenth in South Richmond be dropped from the machine broom routes, for that reason: and further, that streets such as Seventh in South Richmond, be dropped from the machine broom route, on account of the excessive irregularities in the pavement, which precludes other than the most ineffective results.

The streets mentioned are cited only as examples of similar conditions encountered on an inspection tour of the city in general. It is further recommended that greater emphasis be laid on the hand patrol method of cleaning as a substitute for the machine broom work, on the streets of the classes mentioned above. This recommendation is treated in greater detail in the section of the report devoted to "hand patrol cleaning."

Hand Patrol Cleaning.

The hand patrol force is divided between the east and the west district, and in each instance is supervised by the foreman in charge of the function of street cleaning. Each foreman in turn is responsible to the assistant superintendent in charge of the district. The personnel of the hand patrol force consists of thirteen patrolmen, sometimes locally designated as "push-cart" men. Nine patrolmen are assigned to the east district, and four to the west. The dividing line is Fifth street, as in all other street cleaning work, all of South Richmond being included in the east district.

Hand Patrol Methods Employed.

In general, it may be said that the hand patrol work is efficiently performed, and that this is an effective method of street cleaning. It is observed, however, that the patrolmen utilize methods indicative of a lack of instruction.

The same general criticism concerning unproductive retracing and lost motion, which applies to the other divisions of street cleaning, may be made with respect to the operations of individual patrolmen.

It is observed that the progress along a street is not constant and in a uniform direction. The patrolmen frequently broom the material toward the can carrier, without regard to whether the carrier is ahead or behind them.

Wherever this method is followed, it results in traversing some twenty or thirty feet forward, returning to the can carrier with the accumulated sweepings being pushed along the broom, and the passing over of the cleaned area by the patrolmen in pushing the can carrier to the next stopping point. It may, therefore, be seen that a net advance of thirty feet in the direction of travel has been accomplished, only through traversing ninety feet in all. In other words, wherever such a method is employed from time to time during the patrolman's tour, the total distance is three times as great as necessary..

The prevalence of this condition indicates a real necessity for instruction in the most efficient and economical methods to be employed by hand patrolmen.

Hand Patrol Equipment.

The carriers used by the hand patrol force were originally designed as "bag" carriers, but have since been remodeled to accommodate the metallic cans now in use. These carriers are provided with a pan, into which the refuse material is swept. The pan is dumped into the can by raising the handle or shaft of the carrier.

The use of the pan attached to the can carrier necessitates the moving of the carrier, or the moving of the material to a fixed location, in order that the material may be swept into the pan. Not only must the material be brought to the can, but considerable manoeuvering is also necessary.

It is recommended that the cans be removed, and that a short handle shovel, and a short handle broom (a heavy whisk broom) be substituted therefor. It is further recommended that the patrolmen be instructed to utilize the push broom only where it is absolutely necessary.

Supply of Cans Inadequate.

The supply of metal cans, for the can carriers, is inadequate. At the time of writing this report, it had been found necessary to use some wooden barrels, due to the scarcity of the metal receptacles. The chief undesirable feature of the wooden barrel is its short life in comparison to the cost.

It is, therefore, recommended that one hundred metal receptacles be purchased to supply the present demand, and to care for the additional patrol force recommended in this report.

Patrol Cleaning to Take the Place of Machine Broom Cleaning.

As mentioned in the section of the report which deals with machine broom cleaning, and the elimination of certain classes of streets from the existing schedule. it is recommended that the hand patrol force be increased to take over the cleaning of the smooth pavements. now included in the machine broom routes, and further that new patrol routes be laid out for the rough granite streets which may be dropped from the machine broom schedule. In this latter case it is recommended that the patrol work in the outlying sections of the city should be performed with a single horse-drawn cart, because of the difficulty of utilizing the hand manipulated can carrier.

The principal duty of the patrolman., who should also be the driver, should be to pick up papers and similar trash together with the accumulated horse-droppings.

It is urged that careful study of each locality be made before determining upon the route to be followed by the patrolmen with the carts, and that the quantitative requirements be given careful consideration.

On all smooth streets now included in machine broom routes the necessity for periodic scrubbing by the "squee-gee" method should be considered. No street which at the present time is not cleaned by the machine broom crews should be included in the re-organized hand patrol cleaning, nor should such a street be included in the "squee-gee" route.

The question of the substitution of the "squee-gee" for the machine broom on smooth streets is discussed in detail in the section of the report entitled "squee-gee" cleaning.

"Squee-Gee" Cleaning.

It has long been recognized that the most effective method of removing the accumulations of fine material on city streets is by the use of water either in flushing by hand or machine, or by the employment of the so-called "squee-gee" machine, which both sprinkles and scrubs the street pavement. It is also recognized that flushing can only be utilized to advantage on smooth pavements, or first grade granite-block, with a cement grout, or tar filler.

The use of any kind of flushing equipment on granite streets, such as are found in Richmond, which are from third to fifth grade, is precluded, on account of the material used to fill the joints in the pavement.

Due to the wide spacing of fire hydrants, and to the low water pressure, it is unnecessary to give further consideration to the feasibility of hand flushing, with hose and nozzle.

The steep grades and low water pressure practically preclude the use of horse-drawn pressure, or power flushers, for the following reasons:

The location of and the pressure at the fire hydrants in the business section of the city which are paved with smooth pavements, would require great loss of time in filling either pressure or power flushers. This would necessitate seeking lower level hydrants for filling purposes, accompanied by corresponding loss of time, and injury in wear and tear to the horses or mules drawing the filled flushing wagons.

In considering the use of automobile flushers, the first cost and the expense of maintenance and operation must be weighed against any other method considered. The number of square yards of smooth pavement in the city which would require flushing is not sufficient to require the entire time of a battery of two flushers, operating sixteen hours a day. The entire territory of this class could probably be flushed by one machine operating sixteen hours a day, but the traffic condition would seriously interfere on the most important smooth pavement business streets. The same obstacles with respect to the steep grades and the fire hydrants, would be encountered in the operation of a motor flusher. as in the case of similar horse-drawn equipment.

As mentioned elsewhere in this report, the city is operating two machine broom gangs, with a total equipment of two sprinkling carts and six rotary brooms.

Brooms Should Be Remodeled as "Squee-Gees."

By eliminating all smooth streets, together with certain of the granite paved streets, from existing machine broom cleaning schedules, it will be possible to entirely dispense with one machine broom crew, including the sprinkling cart. three rotary brooms. eight carts and ten broom men.

The remaining machine broom crew can devote its entire activity to the heaviest traffic streets, such as Main, Cary, and other shorter streets. requiring the same attention. As a substitute for the machine broom crew. to be dispensed with, it is recommended that the three brooms in question be remodeled to provide for a "squee-gee" roller. in place of the rotary broom now used, and to utilize the existing running gear.

Development of "Squee-Gee's" Cleaning Schedule.

The development of a squee-gee schedule should be paralleled by a new machine broom schedule. the two being so arranged as to permit of the use of the minimum number of mules or horses for these two methods of cleaning.

An increase in patrol cleaning on smooth streets and the use of additional can equipment will permit of much greater speed in the collection than under the present system, and will require fewer carts than at the present time.

The use of the "squee-gee" should be considered in the light of a periodic cleaning or scrubbing to supplement the hand patrol work on smooth streets. Such scrubbing need not be performed nearly as often as the machine broom cleaning in use on smooth streets. for the reason that the machine broom only performs the same function on a smooth street 'as hand patrol work, except that the entire area is passed over, but without removing the finer particles of refuse material.

The motor-driven Elgin broom, already referred to, may effectively be used on certain of the smooth streets, where the so-called scrubbing is unnecessary, and where the hand patrol is less frequent than in the central portion of the city.

Elgin Motor Broom Sweeping Machine.

The Elgin sweeping machine owned by the city has not been in regular use for some time for the reason that competent operators have not been available.

This broom is not assigned to either the east or the west district, but works under the supervision of both assistant superintendents, depending upon the locality in which it is operating. The routes ordinarliy followed by the Elgin broom include streets which are also swept by the machine broom crews. This motor broom is accompanied by two broom men and a pick-up cart, and when not in use, the men and cart are assigned to patrol work.

The absence of cost and performance records prevents a comparison between the motor broom and the other classes of cleaning employed.

Like all other rotary brooms, the power driven pick-up broom is unable to remove the finer material from the pavement surface, and also fails to remove the packed-down horse droppings. It has one advantage, however, over the horse-drawn broom, in that the material is collected and deposited in considerable volume, which permits of cheaper cost of removal by pick-up wagons.

Inasmuch as the city is possessed of this equipment, it is recommended that its use be continued, but only on such streets as are not included in the recommended "squee-gee" routes. It is suggested in this connection that the use of the motor sweeper be confined to the rougher of the smooth pavement streets, where the "squee-gee" would not work with its greatest effectiveness.

Collection of Refuse.

Garbage Collection.

Organization.

The city utilizes 22 garbage collection carts the drivers of which load their own vehicles. This force is divided between the east and the west district, eleven carts being assigned to each. In the east district there is 'a foreman in charge of garbage collection, while in the west district this work is supervised by the foreman who also supervises the collection of ashes and rubbish.

Each collection cart driver is responsible for his route, which is covered daily in certain localities, including certain institutions and apartments. In other localities and in the outlying sections of the city, the garbage is collected twice or three times a week.

Wherever individual routes are laid out and assigned to one man, there can be no question concerning the responsibility. The responsibility should be enforced by the assistant superintendent. A foreman stands between the assistant superintendent and the collectors in the east district. He has no way of covering the territory except by walking, and it is manifestly impossible for him to cover the district, which is very large. This division of responsibility between the collectors, the foreman ind the assistant superintendent should not be permitted. The west district has no foreman, and in the east district the position is useless. It should be abolished and the assistant superintendent of the east district should assume the responsibility and do the necessary inspection work in connection with his other duties.

Collection Equipment.

The carts used in garbage collection are two-wheeled wooden body, single dump carts of approximately 1½ cubic yards capacity without allowing for any "heap." These carts are not provided with side or end boards.

The use of wooden body non-water tight carts is not considered good practice, for the reason that the carts are both leaky and insanitary, giving rise to an ever-present disagreeable odor of decaying vegetable and other matter.

In spite of this criticism, there is much justification for the present type of equipment. The alleys from which garbage must be collected are in many instances so narrow that no four-wheel vehicle could be used. The difference in weight between a steel-body and wooden-bodied cart is given as a reason against the use of the former on the steep grades and under the heavy hauling conditions which prevail in Richmond.

Condition of Receptables.

The condition in which the many varieties and sizes of garbage receptacles were found is a disgrace to the city; and to the legislative and judicial bodies responsible for the enactment and enforcement of laws and ordinances governing this question.

If the members of the city legislative bodies and the board of health would take the time to inspect the average conditions obtaining in the back yards, and particularly in and around the garbage receptacles, such city officers would see the necessity for new and strict ordinances governing the size and type of garbage container, and would further provide through the co-operation of the judicial authorities for the enforcement of such new ordinances.

To say that the so-called garbage cans are unclean, dirty and filthy is to express the condition in very mild language. Cans without number were inspected, and in a majority of cases the contents of the already emptied can were in a state of putrefaction and decomposition, and alive with vermin and maggots.

The existence of these conditions is explainable by the following facts and deductions:

1—That the cans are never washed or cleaned is self-evident.
2—That there is no desire on the part of the public to cooperate in remedying the conditions.
3—That the types and kinds of receptacles vary from tins and wooden boxes and baskets to excessively large metal containers and oil barrels.
4—That the receptacles remain near the back fence from the time of their purchase until their complete destruction is deduced from their general appearance and condition.

In only one back yard visited were conditions satisfactory. In this instance the receptacles were all covered and were placed on a cement platform properly drained. A liberal quantity of lime had been placed both inside and around the garbage and other receptacles, and no flies or odors were apparent.

It cannot be too strongly urged that the city authorities take steps to remedy the existing conditions, and to penalize citizens who fail to comply with existing and future ordinances.

The above recommendation applies with equal force to persons who, through carelessness, permit the use of non-water tight receptacles. It is further recommended that the controlling ordinance provide for the use of standard size, metal water-tight receptacles, which should be provided with metal covers, and further that the responsibility for the condition should rest with the householder entirely.

Delays in Collection.

Only a very small percentage of the city's garbage is collected from the street front. This quantity is so small as to be negligible, and it may therefore be said that all garbage is collected from the alleys.

The garbage containers are usually found somewhere within the back yard, which is usually provided with a fence and a gate. In many instances the gates were found to be locked, and garbage collectors were observed attempting to gain admittance to the locked yards.

Many complaints concerning uncollected garbage are traceable to the inability of the collector to gain admission without waiting an unreasonable length of time.

It is recommended that this situation be remedied by the enactment of a necessary ordinance.

One case was observed where it was necessary to attract the attention of the occupant of a second floor flat, in order that the garbage can might be lowered to the street level. An attitude of this kind on the part of the citizen should not be tolerated by the community at large.

Collection of Ashes and Rubbish.

Ashes and rubbish are collected once each week throughout the greater part of the city. In some cases, however, more frequent collections are made. Very little effort is made to separate the light rubbish, locally called trash, from the heavier ashes. The department operates only one paper wagon for the sole purpose of collecting light material.

For the collection of ashes and rubbish the city is divided into the east and west districts, with the same dividing line as exists for the supervision of other departmental functions.

The collection force in the west district consists of 7 gangs, composed of 3 carts and 2 helpers, the latter known as "litters." The section of the city known as North Richmond is provided with 2 gangs, each composed of 3 carts and one lifter. This force is supervised by a foreman, who also supervises the garbage collection in the west district.

The organization of the collection force in the east district comprises six gangs, of 3 carts and 2 lifters each, and one gang, of 2 carts, 1 wagon and 2 lifters. This force is supervised by a foreman responsible for only the collection of ashes and rubbish in the east district.

Inasmuch as the gang method of collection is used the foreman is able to exercise intimate supervision over the forces under his jurisdiction.

Collection Methods and Equipment Employed.

Except in the case of one wagon the equipment used in ash and rubbish collection is precisely similar to that used by the garbage collectors, viz., the two-wheeled wooden body single dump cart of 1½ yard capacity.

Practically all of the ashes and rubbish is collected from back alleys, and this would make it difficult to use four-wheeled vehicles. But aside from this point, the use of the yard and one-half cart for the combined collection of ashes and rubbish is decidedly uneconomical in the cost per ton hauled.

If filled to capacity with ashes, the yard and one-half carts would be able to carry approximately 1,800 pounds. During the summer months when the combined collections are almost entirely rubbish, except in the central portions of the city, it is probable that the load carried by one cart approximates not more than 600 to 800 pounds.

Even with the severe grades of the city streets and the condition of the unimproved alleys, it would be impossible to utilize wagons of much greater capacity than the year and one-half carts without in any way overloading or injuring the mules or horses.

It is therefore recommended that larger bodied carts be provided for back alley collections, and that large sized paper wagons be used on routes where the alleys are of sufficient width to accommodate a four-wheeled vehicle.

As a substitute for new bodies on the 1½ yard carts, it is recommended that sideboards be provided, to approximately double the capacity in the summer months in the districts where little or no coal is consumed. The use of sideboards would approximately cut the cost of collection in half, and would result in a large saving to the city.

Collection Force Can Be Materally Reduced.

There are 16 gangs engaged in the collection of ashes and rubbish. These gangs include 30 helpers or lifters. It is the practice for drivers of collection wagons working in a gang to so carry out their work that the trips to and from the dumps will overlap in such a manner that in general one cart is being loaded while two carts are en route to or from the dump.

Collection begins at the point where last left off, and the driver remains in the cart, while the lifting is performed by the two lifters. The size and weight of very nearly all the receptacles observed were such as to permit of handling by one man. It is unnecessary for the driver to remain in the cart for the purpose of dumping the receptacles passed up to him by the lifters. It is therefore recommended that the services of the lfters be dispensed with during the light season except on the routes where a considerable quantity of ashes is produced even in the summer.

It is further recommended that all drivers act as lifters, and that only one lifter be assigned to each gang except in the central part of the city where ashes are removed from hotels and office buildings.

On an inspection trip through the outlying sections. it was noticed that both lifters remained without any work to do while the carts were en route to or from the dump. This waste of time and wages would be ended if the lifters were discharged, as they are not needed.

The abolition of unnecessary positions will result in a saving of 5,500 man days at $2.50 per day, or a total of $13,750.00, obtained as follows:

25 men 4 months, 100 days...... 2,500 days
15 men 8 months, 200 days...... 3,000 days
                                 ————————
                                 5,500 days

Separation of Ashes and Rubbish Should Be Required.

There are certain sections of the city in which the alleys are sufficiently wide to accommodate a vehicle larger than the two-wheeled cart. There are certain other sections, particularly in the outlying districts, where the collection is carried on from the street instead of the back alley. In these latter cases it is also possible to use a larger collection wagon.

Assuming a figure of 1,200 pounds per cubic yard for household ashes, it follows that one cart load will weigh approximately 1,800 pound. Under the existing handling conditions this provides a sufficient load for one horse or mule. The mixed load of ashes and rubbish will of course weigh less, and as has already been pointed out, is not a sufficiently heavy load in the summer for economical hauling.

If complete separation of ashes and rubbish were made, it would be possible to utilize the same type of equipment as at present for the collection of ashes, and to provide sideboards for all carts engaged in rubbish collection. Having once established a colliection route, it would be possible for each cart driver to first collect the ashes, then put on the sideboards and collect the rubbish from the same route. By using the recommended detachable sideboards, one load of either ashes or rubbish would be a full load, as far as the weight was concerned.

Inasmuch as more than half the time of collection is spent en route to and from the dumps, it may be seen that any given quantity of mixed ashes and rubbish will require more trips to the dump than if the same quantity is separated and collected by carts with and without sideboards.

It is therefore recommended that the necessary ordinances be enacted to require all householders and others from whose premises the city collects ashes and rubbish to separate these two classes of waste. It is further recommended that the ordinance include clauses requiring that ash receptacles be constructed of metal, not to exceed a certain size, which size will permit of handling by one ·man under ordinary circumstances when filled with ashes. It is also recommended that all rubbish shall be placed in receptacles of a size that will permit of easy handling by one man, and that unless placed in such receptacle, waste material shall be wrapped up in a bundle convenient for handling.

Night Cleaning.

No night cleaning is carried on in the city except on Saturday night when the east end machine broom crew works from 7 P. M. to midnight instead of following its usual time schedule which begins at 7 A. M.

The district covered by the Saturday night broom crew comprises the smooth pavement on Broad street, Grace and Franklin, parts of Marshall and cross and intersecting streets. This section constitutes the main thoroughfares of the city and the object of the night cleaning on Saturday is to remove the litter, etc., which accumulates from the rather large crowds upon the streets on Saturday afternoon and evening. No cleaning is performed on Sunday.

The principal method of cleaning is by machine brooms which method requires practically uninterrupted passage for the brooms.

This cannot be obtained on other than the lightest traffic streets during the daytime. In any business section the parking of automobiles along the curb seriously interferes with any mechanical method which may be employed.

The preceding sections of this report contain certain recommendations with respect to changes in methods of the mechanical cleaning. In conjunction with these suggestions, it is further recommended that all mechanical cleaning be conducted at night except in those portions of the city where the traffic during the daylight hours is negligible.

The advantages derived from conducting mechanical cleaning at night are considerable. Less interference is encountered from both traffic and parked automobiles and vehicles. This results in lower cost per unit area cleaned. In addition, it is possible to clean all of the area, whereas during the daytime a considerable portion must be omitted, due to vehicles parked at the curb.

Hand patrol cleaning is for the purpose of removing foreign material from the street surface as soon as possible after such material accumulates. Consequently, hond patrol cleaning should be conducted during the daytime, and in this connection no change in the time schedule is suggested.

Disposal of Refuse.

Ashes and Rubbish.

The combined collections of ashes and rubbish are disposed of on the city dumps. These dumps are located on private property except in a few instances. The rubbish collected by the rubbish wagon, which is not mixed with ashes, is taken to the incinerator for disposal. Formerly some of this material was baled, but no purchasers have as yet been found for the quantity on hand, and the method has been at least temporarily abandoned.

Location of Dumps.

The dumps located on private property are distributed pretty generally all over the city except in the central portion. The dumping privilege is obtained from owners desiring to have the low-lying sections of their property brought to grade.

In most cases the length of haul from any collection route is not excessive. There are some localities, however, which require as much as two miles' travel to and from the dump.

An effort should be made by the city authorities, and those responsible for collection, to plan as far in the future as possible,
and to obtain dumping privileges before the actual need arises.

Condition of Dumps.

In general, the dumps visited were found to be in good condition, considering the lack of attention which they received. The
grade is generally well maintained, and in several instances, considerable areas and streets have been constructed, thus resulting in
an economic saving to the public and the city as well.

The only attention which the dumps receive is performed by
former departmental employees now on the superannuated list.
No particular attempt is made to supervise these employees, who
only work intermittently. The need for this labor does not exist.
The superannuated employees are expensive labor at $1.50 a day,
and should be dispensed with, as is recommended in the section of
this report which deals with the subject.

Several instances were noted where private collectors had
dumped garbage upon the ash dumps. This practice should not
be permitted, and drastic means should be utilized for its prevention.

Dump-Picking.

The quality of the material on the ash and rubbish dumps is
so low in salvagable material, that dump-picking would not be
particularly profitable. Only one instance of this practice was observed. It is recommended, however, that no one be permitted to
pick over the city dumps, unless it can be established that the city
will derive a slight return for this privilege.

The only dump fire observed was at the particular location
where the picking was being carried on. Dump fires usually originate from carelessness on the part of those engaged in dump-picking. The result of dump fires is a public nuisance, and in some
instances, the creation of a fire hazard, which may assume considerable proportions.

It so happened that the dump on fire was under the supervision of one of the superannuated employees of the department.
This is an added indictment against the employment of this class
of labor.

Garbage.

The disposal of garbage, decayed meats, fruit, etc., is carried on at the two city disposal plants, the disposal method used being the destruction of the material by fire.

During the heavy garbage season in the summer, it has been found necessary to utilize other than the disposal plants, on account of their inability to consume the entire quantity of material produced in the city. This excess is hauled to the farthest limits of the city.

Disposal Equipment.

The disposal equipment consists of two disposal plants, one a Decarie incinerator. rated at fifty tons capacity, which was constructed during 1909 and 1910, and was accepted by the city February 3, 1910, and old crematory. The cost of construction of the Decarie plant, including the building and stack, was $39,950. The Morse-Boulger crematory was constructed twenty-seven years ago. The exact date, however, could not be ascertained. It is believed that the cost of this plant was approximately $8,000.

The Decarie plant is located at Marshall and Fifteenth streets. adjacent to the east end stable, and serves the east end district of the city. The Morse-Boulger plant is located in the vicinity of St. John's street, near the S. A. L. tracks, and serves the west end district. Both of these types of garbage destructors are in use in many cities of the United States.

Approximate Comparative Cost Analysis.

In order to compare the operation of the two plants from a cost per ton standpoint, it is necessary to consider the interest and depreciation charges.

The Morse-Boulger plant was constructed twenty-seven years ago. If constructed from bond funds. the bonds already should have been retired, even though the period is thirty-four years in Richmond. If the plant was constructed from appropriation funds, it would no longer be reasonable to charge interest against its operation. In either event, the cost of operation as of 1916 would carry no interest charge. Regardless of the source of the funds from which the plant was constructed, the depreciation would already have been written off. Consequently, the cost of this plant contains only the items of repairs and operation.

The Decarie plant was constructed in 1910, and whether from

bond or appropriation fund, should be charged with interest on the investment when comparing this plant with the Morse-Boulger.

Inasmuch as the Decarie has only been in operation for a little over seven years, it is necessary to charge depreciation whether or not such an account has been set up.

The cost, therefore, for operating the Decarie plant, must include interest on the investment and depreciation.

The following tabulation shows a comparison between the two plants, on a cost per ton basis, the tonnage being estimated by the street cleaning department, on the basis of the actual loads destroyed:

Decarie Plant.

Total cost	$ 39,950.00	
The cost of building	4,447.00	
Estimated cost of stack	2,000.00	
Estimated cost of approach	1,000.00	
Estimated cost of furnace and appurtenances	32,503.00	
Interest on total cost at 5%		$ 1,998.00
Depreciation on furnace at 5%..	1,622.00	
Depreciation on stack at 3½%....	70.00	
Depreciation on building at 2½%.	111.00	
Depreciation on approach at 2%..	20.00	
Total depreciation		1,823.00
Cost of labor	3,103.68	
Cost of fuel	2,006.83	
Cost of water, light and repairs..	285.00	
Miscellaneous	115.76	
		5,511.27
		$ 9,332.27

Total tons destroyed, 7,053.00 tons
Cost per ton $1.32
Operating cost per ton .78

The refuse material produced by the machine broom sweeping which necessarily contains a large proportion of dust and dirt. is usually dumped at the city dumps, or other vacant property.

Care of Equipments and Horses.

West End Stable.

The west end stable, housing 67 head of stock, is located at the fair grounds. In addition to its use as a stable, the buildings and sheds are utilized for the housing of the departmental equipment assigned to the west end district.

The premises now occupied are very undesirable from every standpoint. The stable is constructed entirely of wood, and is in need of considerable repair. The department has been forced to use certain sheds and stalls for the accommodation of the stock which cannot be housed in the main stables. The buildings are likewise in a rather dilapidated condition.

The facilities for the storage of equipment are very inadequate. The sheds formerly used for the covering of carts, brooms. etc.. were at best poor shelter. At the time of the inspection of the stables, it was found that these sheds had been practically demolished by a recent severe storm.

The stables are still further made undesirable, because the department is required to vacate for a period of approximately one month each year during the "fair week." During this period all stock and equipment must be transferred to the east end stable which cannot in itself care for the entire number. This uncared for stock is stabled in the city engineer's department old stable. which is located behind the city jail. some 300 feet from the east end stable. Aside from the cost of taking up and putting down the stalls at the fair ground stables. the department is put to considerable added expense on account of the lost time consumed by the west end equipment. caused by its temporary location in the east end stables.

It is recommended that the question of locating and constructing a new stable for the west end district be given immediate attention. for the reasons mentioned above, and further, because the west end stable in its present condition constitutes a serious fire hazard to both stock and equipment.

East End Stable.

The east end stable was found to be in excellent condition. The building itself is of brick. three stories high. The portions occupied by the stalls extend two stories high, thus providing excellent ventilation and light. The facilities for handling grain and hay are of approved type, and the general appearance of the entire equipment was pleasing.

The facilities provided for housing the brooms, carts, etc., are not as satisfactory as the stable proper, but are in much better condition than those found at the west end yard.

Repair of. Equipment.

The department repairs practically no equipment with the exception of harness, which is kept in condition by the night watchman of each of the two stables. This latter method is an eminently satisfactory one, tending to produce the greatest economy in this respect.

All repair of other equipment is performed on open market orders. The apparently small amount of repair work would indicate that this method is preferable to the employment of a permanent repair force.

The push brooms and rotary brooms are purchased by contract. The quantity is such that this is probably the most economical method of obtaining this class of equipment.

Veterinary Service.

All sick or injured horses and mules are cared for by the hostlers. who are under instruction not to employ a veterinary except in the case of extreme emergency.

There are 67 head stabled at the west end barn. Of this number 10 mules were found to be unable to work on the day of inspection, viz. July 6th. Eight of these were suffering from collar sores. This is entirely too high a percentage, and indicates a lack of good care upon the part of the drivers and hostlers responsible for the welfare of the stock entrusted to their care.

It should be noted at this point that the cleaning of all stock is performed by the driver in charge.

It is recommended that more efficient supervision be exercised over cleaning the horses and mules.

Conditions at the east end stables were found to be much better in the above respect. Out of a total of 86 head in the barn. only 4 were laid up on account of sickness. It is quite possible that the difference is traceable to the relative condition in the two stables.

Motor Vehicles.

Aside from the Elgin broom sweeper, the department owns the following motor-driven equipment:

  2 5-yard dumping body Sternberg trucks.
  2 2-yard Willis body dumping trucks.
  2 Ford automobiles.

At the time of the examination of the street cleaning department, the two five-yard trucks were being repaired by the manufacturer, and neither of the two-yard trucks was in operation. The Ford automobiles are assigned to the superintendent and to the assistant superintendent in charge of the west district.

The motor trucks do not play a regular part in the operation of the department, but are used from time to time in connection with both street cleaning, refuse collection, and street repair work. The two larger trucks especially are used in the heavy garbage season as relay trucks to haul garbage to the city limits for dumping.

It is suggested that the ownership of some $12,000 worth of motor truck equipment is an expensive investment, unless the machines are in constant use. It is recommended that an effort be made to utilize these trucks to greater advantage. or to negotiate for their sale.

Financial Records.

Daily Time Reports.

Each assistant superintendent makes a semi-monthly time report of the men working in his district each day. The record shows a day or fraction of a day, but does not show the number of hours. This semi-monthly report is divided to show the personnel engaged in the several functions performed by the department. The basis for this report is a roll call each morning at each of the two stables, supplemented by the field inspection of the assistant superintendents and information furnished by the gang foremen.

The employees at the garbage plants, at the dog pound, the hand patrol force, and the driver of the Elgin broom do not answer the roll calls at the stables. These employees, however. appear on the time record of the assistant superintendent in whose district they may be working.

Superannuated Employees' Time Book.

There are 17 superannuated and incapacitated city employees carried on the payrolls of the street cleaning department. A "time record" which must necessarily be an absurdity is kept of these employees. In reality, it is merely a list of those receiving the equivalent of a pension.

Of the 17 individuals only 10 were ever employed by the street cleaning department. City employees are placed upon this superannuated list by order of the administrative board. The usual daily compensation is $1.50, although this is sometimes somewhat decreased. These men are not required to work if not so inclined, and the majority are so physically incapacitated as to make work an impossibility. The money paid to these men is nothing more or less than charity and should be discontinued as a charge against the street cleaning department.

If city employees are deserving of a pension, and it is the desire of the people and the city administration to pay such pensions, it is entirely unreasonable to load the street cleaning department appropriation with this item. This ridiculous practice is made more absurd by the inclusion of seven individuals who never were employed by the street cleaning department.

It is recommended that this practice be discontinued, and that a proper pension system be established if such is desired.

Work for Other Departments Charged Against the Street Cleaning Department.

The appropriation accounts of the street cleaning department are now being charged with the full time of six men engaged in the trimming of trees and with the full time of one man spraying ponds. These accounts are also carrying all of the miscellaneous carting of coal, etc., performed for other departments.

Aside from the interference with the work of the department this practice creates financial records which are utterly useless for unit cost determination, and do not reflect the proper distribution of the city's expenditures for its various departments and activities.

If the street cleaning department must continue to cary on the miscellaneous activities mentioned above, it is recommended that at least a proper allocation of the expenditure be made. This can be effected by an inter-departmental transfer of funds, and the removal of all employees who may be permanently assigned to other departments from the street cleaning payroll.

Administrative Records.

Department Not Supplied With Maps.

The street cleaning department is not provided with street maps, other than several duplicates of the map appearing in the city directory. It is almost essential for the proper administration of the department that the superintendent be supplied with maps showing all city streets and alleys. The purpose of these maps is to set forth in graphical form all collection and cleaning routes.

Hand patrol routes—should be shown on a separate map by means of a number of colored pencils or inks. These routes can be changed from time to time by the superintendent, after a conference with his assistants and foremen. These maps should further provide a means whereby the sequence of streets patroled by any one patrolman could be shown. Direction arrows would be convenient for this purpose. With such a picture before the superintendent, re-arrangements in schedules which are now impossible could easily be accomplished in a very short time.

Machine broom routes—could be shown on a separate map using different colors for each day's work, or by using a separate map for each day. The latter method is preferable for the reason that the crew will probably pass over certain streets several times a week.

Elgin broom routes—can be shown in a manner similar to that used for the machine boom crews.

Collection routes—for garbage and ashes and rubbish should be separately shown with arrows to indicate the direction of the collection route.

Similarly, catch-basin locations, types of pavement, and other information can be shown in graphical form by the use of maps.

It is recommended that this subject be given immediate attention, and that a map be prepared to show only the streets and alleys. It is suggested that the width of all streets and alleys be somewhat exaggerated in order to provide more space for setting forth the desired information.

It is further suggested that such a map be prepared by the city engineer's department, and that the time consumed be charged against the street cleaning appropriation.

Stable Record.

Although the stable foremen submit a daily report, this record is not utilized as a current record of the horses that are working, idle, sick etc.

It is recommended that the daily reports from the stables be transferred to a monthly horse record, which would show for each day the following information:

Number of head of stock in the stable.
Number of head of stock sick.
Number of head of stock idle.
Number of head of stock hired.
Number of head of stock loaned.
Number of head of stock stabled for other departments.

This information should be transferred to a recapitulation sheet after having been totalled each month.

Existence of such a record, in conjunction with a record of a distribution of all stock, will permit of the accurate allocation of stable expense to the various divisions supplied with horses or mules.

Horse History Record.

No record of the deed of purchase, price, age or indentification is maintained concerning the horses and mules owned by the street cleaning department. The absence of such a record prevents a scientific decision concerning the relative advisability of using horses or mules in this department. Another feature which cannot be made use of is the knowledge of the stamina and endurance of the various animals working under similar conditions.

It is recommended that a horse history record be established. This record should provide for the setting forth of all information concerning each head of stock which may be required for purposes of identification and comparison. The date of purchase, the purchase price, and the date of the death and cause thereof, should be provided for together with a certification by a veterinary concerning the cause of death. If sold, the sale price, name and address of purchaser, etc., should be shown. The dates and number and the cost of shoeings should be set forth on the record, as well as of veterinary service for each horse or mule.

Record of Distribution of Equipment.

Each gang foreman makes a daily report of the number of men working a number of carts, wagons, etc., and the streets cleaned, the quantity of material removed, and the streets from which collections are made.

Practically all of the information necessary for a set of complete operating records is available in the various daily reports submitted by foremen and assistant superintendents.

In connection with the distribution of equipment, it is recommended that the following information for the east and west districts be transferred each day from the daily report to a monthly report of the distribution of equipment. This report sheet should provide for showing the following information:

Garbage collection—
   Number of men ....
   Number of carts ....
   Number of wagons ....
   Head of stock ....

Ash and rubbish collection—
   Number of drivers ....
   Number of lifters ....
   Number of carts ....
   Number of wagons ....
   Head of stock ....

Hand patrol—
   Number of patrolmen ....
   Number of drivers ....
   Number of pick-up carts ....
   Head of stock ....

Machine broom cleaning—
   Number of sprinkling carts ....
   Number of rotary brooms ....
   Number of carts ....
   Number of wagons ....
   Number of drivers ....
   Number of broom men ....
   Head of stock ....

The monthy totals should be transferred to a monthly recapitulation sheet. In addition, all daily totals should be compared with the stable reports.

Catch-Basin Cleaning Record.

As mentioned elsewhere in this report, there is no program for catch-basin cleaning. Basins are cleaned after special complaints from individuals or other city departments, or from one of the several foremen or superintendents in the street cleaning department. All such complaints are recorded on a card, designed for the purpose, each card constituting an order to the catch-basin cleaning gang. These orders are transmitted by the assistant superintendents or the foremen in charge of the street cleaning in the sewer districts. The return of the card with the necessary notation concerning number of loads removed and the date of cleaning constitutes a report to the effect that the basin in question has been cleaned. These cards are returned to the central office by the foremen of street cleaning, who receives such reports from the basin cleaning crews.

As soon as the complaint is received, either in person, through a letter, or by telephone, the information obtained is entered in a record known as "the basin cleaning docket" which provides the following information under the columnar headings:

> District.
> Date.
> Location.
> Complaint or request.
> Made by.
> Returned by.
> Number of loads.
> Date.

This method of ordering and recording catch-basin cleanings is both expensive and ineffective. The system does not provide for the recording or tabulating of the returns on individual basins which constitutes the only basis for an intelligent basin cleaning program. Under the present scheme, the loss of time between basins is much greater than if definite routing were provided.

Card Index of Basins Recommended.

In order to make available a permanent record of each existing catch-basin and the quantity removed therefrom, which may be utilized for the purpose of laying out routes to the best advantage, it is recommended that a card index of all basins be established. This record should be arranged alphabetically by street location.

After the record has been in use for a sufficient length of time, the cards should be arranged by routes without regard to the alphabetical order of the names of streets. A map should be prepared on which all basins should be shown together with the routes in colors. This will provide an easy means for locating any particular card in the route index.

Each card should provide for the location of the basin and columnar headings under which the dates of cleaning, the quantities removed, and the name of the foreman may be shown.

With the employment of this the necessity for the docket as kept today would cease. All basins would be cleaned in the consecutive order of the particular route except in emergency cases. The docket should be retained for the purpose of recording the disposition of emergency cases.

In routing the particularly troublesome basins, it may be found necessary to place one or more duplicate dummy cards in the index to take care of such basins as may require cleaning more often than the others.

For purposes of convenience in locating cards in the index, it is recommended that each route be given a letter of the alphabet, and that the basins of each route be numbered beginning at one. The map above recommended should be lettered and numbered correspondingly.

Order Cards Should Be Discontinued.

It is recommended that the order cards now in use be discontinued on the ground of excessive cost and because the adoption of the system outlined will make their further use unnecessary.

Daily Report of Basins Cleaned.

It is recommended that a new form of daily report be drawn up, which shall provide for the recording of the location and quantity of material removed from each basin. This report should be made out by the basin crew and transmitted to or collected by the foremen in charge of street cleaning. This basin report should be attached to the daily report of the street cleaning foremen and forwarded to the central office for recording the information upon the basin cards in the index.

Garbage Collector's Daily Report.

Each garbage cart driver makes a daily written report of the streets from which this class of material has been collected by him. The report in itself is satisfactory. The sections of this report which point out the desirability of utilizing maps for indicating collection routes contain definite recommendations oencerning the setting forth of the activities of this division of the department in graphical form.

It is recommended that each collection route be given a letter or number, and that the results of the daily collections of garbage be recorded by the number of loads collected from each route. A loose-leaf binder should be provided to contain a separate sheet for each garbage collection route, and to provide columns for the thirty-one days of the month upon which collections may be made. Each sheet may constitute a running report which, when totalled for the twelve months of the year, will provide immediately an annual report for each route showing the number of collections made and total amount of material removed therefrom.

Daily Report of Ash and Rubbish Collection.

The foremen in charge of the two ash and rubbish districts submit a daily report of the activities of their respective collection crews. These reports give the quantity of material collected in loads, the streets from which collections have been made, and the number of carts engaged in the work.

It is recommended that each collection route be given a number or letter, and the daily recapitulation of collections be recorded in the same manner as that described in the preceding section for the recording of garbage collection data.

Daily Reports of Incinerator and Crematory.

Although a daily report sheet is provided for the incinerator and crematory, the department has not required the foremen of the latter to make other than a monthly report. The report in itself provides all the necessary information for recording the performance of each of these two units of disposal. The information contained, however, is not transferred immediately to a current report. It is highly desirable for the administrator of the department to follow the current activities of these two plants. It is, therefore, recommended that a loose-leaf binder be provided, each sheet thereof to show the activities for the thirty-one days of each month. The columnar headings should provide for the dates and the side headings for the quantitative information contained on the daily report. In order to economize space, it is recommended that the items be abbreviated something as follows: "Wet garbage" instead of "loads of wet garbage from city carts"; "mixed refuse" instead of "loads of mixed refuse from city carts": etc. Inasmuch as the use of the words "boxes of meat or fruit and of canned goods" indicate a uniform size which does not exist in reality, it is recommended that a unit of weight be used in all such cases.

By drawing off the total of each month's activities of the two plants, it will be possible to obtain the total consumption of each of these two plants immediately at the close of the fiscal year without having laboriously to calculate directly from the daily and monthly reports now in use.

The daily report now used should be continued as a basis for the new record recommended. The foremen of both plants should be required to render such a daily report.

Street Cleaning Foremen's Daily Reports.

Each of the foremen in charge of the two street cleaning gangs submits a daily report of the streets cleaned, the cart loads of material removed therefrom, and the number of men, carts, wagons, sprinkling carts and machine brooms engaged in the work. In addition, this daily report indicates the number of catch-basins cleaned and the quantity of material in cart loads removed.

In order to obtain unit costs for the different kinds of cleaning, and for similar kinds of cleaning on different types of pavement, it will be necessary to keep a more detailed daily record of time consumed than has been the practice.

It is recommended that all street cleaning work be laid out in routes, and that the routes shall be so designed as to include only one kind of pavement if possible. Several routes may be included in one day's work. The material removed from each route together with the time consumed by the crew should be recorded in order to distribute the total cost by routes and then by types of pavement. The unit cost of cleaning by the hand patrol method is easily obtainable for the reason that each patrolman is assigned to a definite area comprising a definite number of square yards of the several types of pavement in existence in Richmond.

The necessity for obtaining the unit costs of cleaning different types of pavement by different methods is absolutely essential for the proper and economical administration of street cleaning. At the present time it is impossible to determine which of the three methods, namely, machine broom cleaning, motor pick-up broom cleaning or hand patrol, is the most economical. No data is available which will indicate the relative costs of cleaning the different types of pavement, and no classification of the degree of cleanliness for the particular types and conditions of pavement has been determined.

Before any intelligent decision can be reached with respect to changes in methods of cleaning, it is essential that the data above mentioned be available in the form of daily recapitulation of the work oden and the cost thereof. It is, therefore, urged that the routing and reporting as outlined above, be inaugurated immediately.

Building Department

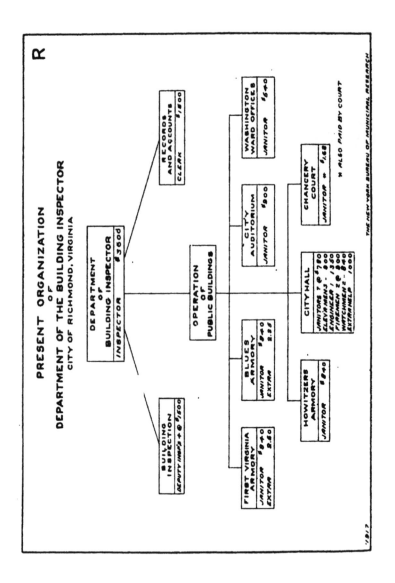

PRESENT ORGANIZATION
OF
DEPARTMENT OF THE BUILDING INSPECTOR
CITY OF RICHMOND, VIRGINIA

BUILDING DEPARTMENT.

Organization.

The organization of the building department is divided into two distinct units, as may be observed on the accompanying chart. These two units may be designated as : (1) building inspection division and (2) public building operation division. The clerk of the department keeps all records of both inspection and operation.

The administrative officer of the department is known as the building inspector, who, in addition to the supervision over inspection personally acts as an advisor to other city departments in the maintenance and repair of buildings under the jurisdiction of the several departments.

The force engaged in the operation of the buildings for which the building inspector is responsible reports directly to him and receives such orders as may be necessary. The deputy inspectors exercise no supervision over this operating organization.

Building Inspection.

For the purpose of inspecting all new·buildings and those buildings upon which repairs and alterations are to be made, the city is divided into four inspection districts. Each district is assigned to a deputy building inspector, who is responsible for all the operations carried on within his respective district.

Upon the issuance of a permit the inspector is provided with a card which sets forth the location and nature of the work comprehended on the permit. This card is used for recording.the dates of the several inspections made prior to the completion of the work. The inspector does not make any daily reports of his activities, neither are particularly designed forms used as notices of violations of the building code or for unsafe buildings.

The section of this report which deals with the office records contains detailed recommendations covering the above points.

The chief building inspector himself makes frequent inspections especially in the case of steel and re-inforced concrete buildings.

Permit Procedure and Office Records.

Applications.

Before proceeding with the erection, alteration or moving of any building, the erection of a sign, the laying of sewer pipes in an alley between houses, and the construction of areas, vaults, balconies, etc., it is necessary to make written application to the building department.

These respective application forms give all necessary information for the granting of the permit.

Submission of Plan.

All new construction work, alterations and repairs in excess of one hundred dollars must be shown by plans and sketches submitted for examination with the application. These plans are examined by the deputy inspector in whose district the work is to be performed. All plans for steel and concrete structures are personally checked by the chief building inspector.

Granting of Permit.

After the application and plans have been examined and approved and so stamped, the permit proper is issued either by one of the inspectors or by the clerk of the department.

There are only three permit forms used. The first a permit for new construction, the second the permit to repair, alter, etc., the third a permit to erect a sign.

All of these permits are issued in duplicate, the duplicate copy remaining in the stub book.

As soon as the permit has been issued and numbered, the same number is placed upon the application and upon the plans which accompanied such application. At the same time a memorandum is made out for the inspector's information and the inspection card is also prepared. The following information, namely, date, name and permit number is also entered in one of the separate memorandum books kept for new work, alteration and repairs, verbal permits and miscellaneous. These notations are entered alphabetically under the name of the owner of the property.

Filing of Applications.

All applications are filed numerically by permit number in a vertical document file under the current month. These applications are then transferred to the main application file for the current year after the lapse of which they are placed in the dead file numerically under the year in which the permits are issued.

Plan File.

All plans receive the same number as the permit and application covering the particular construction or repair work. These plans are filed according to the month and year in which the permit is issued. In order to find any particular plan it is necessary to discover the date on which the permit was issued, and to examine the plans in the particular bin corresponding to the year and month of the issuance of the permit.

Inspection Card File.

As already mentioned, it is the practice to make out a 3x5 card for each permit issued. These cars are of three colors: (1) pink is used for new work, repairs and alterations; (2) buff for frame structures, repairs and alterations thereto; (3) blue is used for verbal permits. erection of sheds and repairs thereto.

Each card shows the date of application and the date of the issuance of the permit, also the date the work commenced. Provision is made for the recording of the dates of six inspections. the final inspection and the date of completion. The reverse side shows the geographical location. the number of the permit and other information with respect to the type of structure. the names of contractors, etc.

These inspection cards are retained by the deputy inspectors until the building or work is completed. They are then placed in a file arranged numerically by permit numbers, a separate file being maintained for each of the three different types of cards.

Aside from showing the dates of inspections and other readily accessible information, this card index provides a means of locating any plan in the plan file through the date of the issuance of the permit.

It is the practice for the deputy inspectors to retain the cards for uncompleted work and to make notations from time to time showing the date of inspections.

In this particular connection it is recommended that a small cabinet with four drawers. one for each inspector, be provided and that the cards be placed therein by each inspector. rather than that these cards remain in the desk of the inspector or perhaps be taken out of the office when the inspector is at work in the field.

Building Atlas.

The department maintains an atlas which shows every building within the city limits. This atlas is posted up currently by the corporation providing this service.

A system of symbols and codes has been adopted, which transforms the atlas into the controlling index for all of the records maintained in the department. Upon the completion of any work comprehended in the permit, a symbol is used to show the type of the permit and the number and year are recorded in ink upon the map.

This method provides an excellent index to all departmental records through the fact that the system is based upon the permit number. The only record which cannot be immediately located from the atlas is the set of plans covering the work. Inasmuch as these plans are filed under the month in which the permit is issued, it is necessary to refer either to the permit stub or to the inspection card file or to the application file.

The atlas index is eminently satisfactory and the department is to be congratulated upon the effective system employed.

Violation Notices.

Whenever an inspector discovers a violation of the building code in connection with the construction, repair or alteration of any structure, he immediately notifies the builder or contractor employed. If the violation is a serious one, the inspector makes a written report to the chief inspector, who in turn may or may not notify the owner, agent or contractor to remedy the defect.

A letter book copy is made of all such letters sent out by the department. This letter book is cross indexed by the names of the persons to whom the letter may have been written. This does not provide a satisfactory method for current control over violations which have not been dismissed.

In order to provide for this important feature of the inspection work, it is recommended that the following system with respect to violations be inaugurated:

Notice to Be Served.

Each deputy inspector should be provided with printed notices to be served in the event of a violation of the building code. These notices should show the location of the building, the permit number and the name of the person served with the notice. These notices should be made out in triplicate and should be of such size as to permit of filing in an 8x5 file. The original should be delivered to the contractor or his representative on the work. The duplicate copy should be filed in the central office in a file to be known as "the pending violation file;" the triplicate copy should be retained by the deputy inspector until the violation has been abated, at which time it should be placed together with the duplicate copy in a file that will be known as "the dismissed violation file." The deputy inspector should make the proper notations on the triplicate copy to indicate that the violation notice has been complied with.

It is suggested that the notices be of three colors and made up into a pad to permit of easy handling by the deputy inspectors. The copies should be carbon copies.

The files should consist of four pending violation files and one dismissed violation file. The filing should be in numerical order by permit numbers.

Unsafe Notices.

All unsafe buildings which are brought to the attention of the department by complaint or through inspection or any other agencies are recorded on a card which is also used for complaints. All such cards are given a number and are filed numerically by such numbers.

A special examination is made of all unsafe buildings or those reported unsafe, and the findings are transmitted to the owner in the form of a letter notifying him to make certain changes to insure the safety of the building or to raze the same.

This written notice is in reality a letter and is not on a specially designed form. All such letters are copied in a copy book and indexed by page number alphabetically according to name of the owner.

It is appreciated that the number of such unsafe notices during any one year is comparatilvely small. Nevertheless, it is recommended that a similar system to that outlined for the abating of violations be employed. A special report form should be used for recording the results of all inspections on unsafe buildings. This should be prepared in triplicate. After examination of the report the chief inspector should forward a copy of the same to the owner, together with notification on a special form to the effect that the recommendations contained in the report must be complied with in a given time. A copy of this latter notice should be filed tógether with the duplicate copy of the special report. This file will constitute a tickler file for all such notices issued which have not yet been complied with. After the building has been made safe or has been demolished, the copy of the notice and the report should be filed together in a permanent file under the permit number for the particular building and the proper notations should be made upon the building atlas.

Sign Permits.

In order to receive permission to erect a sign within the city limits it is necessary to receive a permit from the building department. If such a sign extends beyond the property line and over the sidewalk, it is necessary to obtain a permit from the administrative board. If such sign happens to utilize electricity for lighting or mechanical operation, it is necessary to obtain a third permit from the city electrician.

It is recommended that a new form of sign application be drawn up which will be sumbbitted to the building department together with the sketches, etc. This permit should carry space for recording the approval of the administrative board with respect to the proposed encroachment and also for the approval of the city electrician.

The original applications should be filed with the building department, transmitted to the administrative board, be returned to the building department and transmitted to the city electrician. Upon its second return to the building department the permit may be issued, providing the application has been approved by said board and the city electrician. This will obviate the necessity for three permits and will materially simplify the procedure and control.

Inspector's Daily Report.

The deputy inspectors do not make a daily report of their activities. If any violations or unsafe conditions are discovered by the deputy inspector a written memorandum is made to the chief inspector, but if nothing is encountered during the day's inspection, the chief inspector receives no report and is not aware of the extent of the activities of the deputy inspectors except through personal interrogation.

It is recommended that all inspectors be required to make a daily report to the chief inspector, which daily report should show the address, permit number and time of each inspection made. A

notation should also be made in the event of violations or unsafe
conditions being discovered. These reports should be made in duplicate in order that inspectors may retain a copy for future reference.

The furnishing of daily reports will permit of more effective
supervision on the part of the chief inspector and will furnish
a comparative record of the work of each inspector. This system
will further permit of recording the total number of inspections
made on (1) new work; (2) repairs and alterations; (3) unsafe
buildings; (4) miscellaneous. The bottom of the back of the report can be used to show the number of inspections under the
above four classes made to date. Immediately below can be shown
the number made on the particular day covered by the report.
The sum of these two figures will be the amounts to be carried
forward to the next daily report. A code may be established for
the above purpose, such as NW new work, R&A repairs and alterations, US unsafe, and M miscellaneous. Any convenient code
may be used.

Where any lengthy special report is made by the inspector
concerning a particular violation or unsafe condition, that fact
should be noted on the daily report by means of the code symbol
applying thereto.

Principles of Regulation and Inspection.

The regulation by public officials of building construction and
inspection of the various appliances and fittings contained in a
completed structure have the following objects in view:

1—To insure compliance with the established standards of
   light and ventilation and structural safety.
2—To enforce the legal restrictions concerning the percentage
   of area which may be utilized for occupancy and to maintain the established alignment of street and property
   lines.
3—To require that appliances and installations prescribed for
   the health and safety of the people conform to established standards.
4—To control the erection of miscellaneous structures, the
   existence of which involves the safety of the community.
5—To exercise police powers to protect innocent occupants
   against criminally negligent landlords or owners.
6—To exercise control over demolition. shoring, etc.

Prevention of Encroachments.

In order to prevent the encroachment of structures upon city property and encumbrance of sidewalks and roadways, it is necessary that the location of all buildings with respect to street and property lines be carefully examined.

Conformity with the city plans is necessary in order that the aesthetic standards of the community may be maintained. It is right and proper that this function be exercised by the department or division responsible for the control over the erection of new structures and the alteration of and additions to old structures.

Light and Ventilation.

The public at large is not in a position to pass judgment upon the light and ventilation facilities afforded by a commercial or residential structure, and even though aware of the established standards, is not in a position to insist upon conformity with standards.

It should, therefore, be the duty of the inspection agency carefully to examine plans of proposed buildings and to inspect the construction in order to insure the enforcement of the minimum facilities for light and ventilation which have been determined upon.

Structural Safety.

The enforcement of the established standards of structural safety is a function of only relative importance. It may be presumed that an architect of builder is competent to erect a structure which will not constitute a source of possible injury to the subsequent occupants. The same generalization applies equally to alterations and additions to existing buildings.

In the event of carelessness or incompetence on the part of the erector, the community at large will not suffer injurious effects. The failure of any structure will involve the safety of the occupants and will not be communicated to the public at large.

The enforcement of structural safety standards and the necessary accompanying inspection is a benefit only to the owners or occupants of the particular structure. The representatives of any community are not morally obligated to pass upon the structural stability of a building, and the performance of this function should be minimized, unless the inspection agency is fully compensated for its actual expenditures and for the moral responsibility which it automatically assumes through the issuance of a favorable report.

Plumbing

Plumbing inspection in the United States has been almost universally overemphasized. The underlying principles of the regulation of plumbing and other sanitary installations are dependent upon financial rather than public health and welfare considerations. The inability of any plumbing system to withstand the pressure demands to which it may happen to be subjected results in damage to certain property. This damage is a purely economical feature of real estate ownership. No city government is morally obligated to safeguard the individual from pecuniary damage arising from the failure of equipment purchased and utilized for private gain. Plumbing, in its broadest sense, falls within the same catagory as steam heating equipment. The city is not required, nor is it expected, to pass upon the piping installation of a steam heating system. Any ramage resulting from leaking steam pipes or radiators is repaired by the owner and charged to maintenance expense. It would never occur to such owner to hold the city responsible for the failure of such a system.

It has never been proven that improperly trapped or vented plumbing fixtures result in the spreading of disease. or in other than an insult to the olfactory sensibilities of the detector. The existence of leaky gas pipes and fixtures, over which city authorities exercise no control, constitutes a far more serious source of possible danger than the presence of the slightly disagreeable odors of sewer gas.

The emphasis placed upon plumbing inspection from a sanitary standpoint is largely misdirected, and a waste of the city's funds. If the community at large insists upon a rigid inspection of plumbing installation with the resulting guarantee of immunity from the fallaciously conceivable health menace, then the individuals which benefit by this immunity should be required, not only to pay for the cost of inspection. but also for the intangible asset accompanying such inspection.

No Fees Are Charged.

All permits issued by the building department are obtained by the applicants therefor without the payment of any fee. The performance of the functions outlined in the sections immediately preceding are principally benefits to individuals through the protection afforded to them by the inspecting agency. Aside from the expense of stationery, printing, etc., the department of building expends $6,000 for the salaries of four deputy building inspectors, $3,600 for the salary of the building inspector, and $1.500 for the salary of the clerk. The deputy inspectors devote their entire time to the function of inspection, whereas the chief building inspector and the clerk most necessary devote a portion of their time to the operation of the public buildings under the jurisdiction of the department. It is reasonable to assume that of $3,600, $2,000 is chargeable against building inspection and of $1,500, $900 is chargeable against building inspection. This gives an approximate total salary expenditure for building inspecton amounting to $8.900. For this expenditure, the city of Richmond receives no return.

The theory upon which revenues are derived from permit fees of any description depends upon whether the fee is charged to compensate the city for any intangible benefit which the citizen may derive or merely for the purpose of making the agency rendering the service self-sustaining. In all cases where the permit issued is purely for purposes of regulation and does not carry with it any special privilege which may be capitalized and result in added revenue to permittee, it is the universal custom to design the amount of fees on the basis of the actual cost of performing the necessary inspection to insure compliance with the ordinances and regulations in force.

It is therefore recommended that the applicant for permit be required to pay a fee to the department before any permit is issued, and that such fees be based upon a sliding scale in proportion to the value of the work comprehended under the permit. In the case of signs a rate per square foot of superficial area should be charged, different rates being charged for electric and for non-illuminated signs. Another rate should be charged for signs commonly known as "billboards."

In connection with sign permits an annual inspection charge should be made also.

Operation of Public Buildings.

The following public buildings are under the maintenance and custody of the building department: the city hall. city jail. city auditorium, Howitzers' armory. Blues' armory, the First Virginia Regimental armory, Hustings' Court Part II and the Wash.

ington ward offices. In addition the department supervises all repairs to the two market buildings and to numbers 1108-1110-1112 Capitol street, property which is owned by the city.

Condition of Buildings.

The city-owned buildings visited, namely, city hall, city auditorium, Howitzers' armory, Blues' armory, and the First Virginia armory presented a cleanly appearance and were in a good state of repair with the possible exception of the Howitzers' armory, where extensive reconstruction work is about to be undertaken. The force engaged in the operation of the public buildings is commensurate with the needs.

Repairs to Public Buildings.

All repairs to buildings directly under the jurisdiction of the building department are made by contract under the specifications which are prepared by the department. In addition to this function the building department is extending the scope of its activities to include the drawing of specifications and the supervision of work in connection with repair of other city buildings not directly under its control. This practice is to be commended, and it is urged that repairs to all city buildings be supervised by the building department.

Rental of City Auditorium.

During the year 1916 the rentals for the use of the auditorium amounted to $910. During this period the building was occupied forty-two times at night and nine times during the day, making a total of fifty-one times, with a consequent average rental charge of $17.84.

During the same period the salary of the custodian—$900—and the other expenses—$422.80—amounted to a total of $1,322.80, which exceeds the receipts by $412.80.

It is recommended that the basis of rental be increased in order to make this building self-sustaining.

Expenditure Distribution Ledger.

All expenditures for the operation and maintenance of all buildings under the jurisdiction of the building department are entered according to a code classification in an expenditure distribution ledger. This permits of detailed analysis of the cost of operating and maintaining all such buildings, and also provides the building inspector with the current record of the distribution of all funds already expended and permits of intelligent distribution of funds for subsequent repairs.   .

It is recommended that this record be continued in force.

Department of Parks

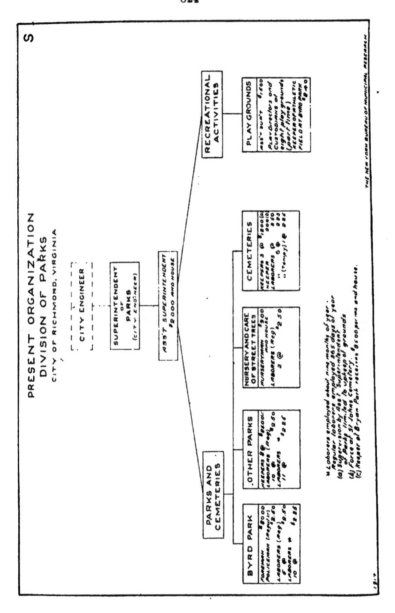

PRESENT ORGANIZATION
DIVISION OF PARKS
CITY OF RICHMOND, VIRGINIA

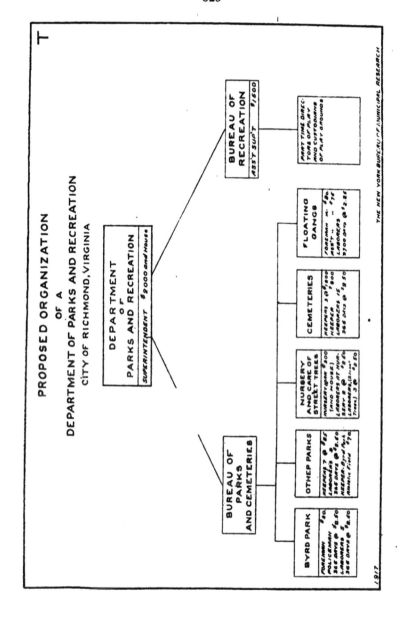

PROPOSED ORGANIZATION
OF A
DEPARTMENT OF PARKS AND RECREATION
CITY OF RICHMOND, VIRGINIA

THE NEW YORK BUREAU OF MUNICIPAL RESEARCH

DEPARTMENT OF PARKS.

The work of the park department includes responsibility for all construction and maintenance work in the parks and cemeteries, and also the operaton and upkeep of playgrounds and other recreational features throughout the city.

Under the charter, responsibility for the care of the various parks (and city owned cemeteries) throughout the city of Richmond is vested in the city engineer as superintendent of parks. In the past the city engineer exercised direct supervision over all work relating to these properties, but at the present time this supervision is largely nominal, an assistant superintendent of park appointed by the administrative board having direct charge of the work.

Construction and Improvement Work.

There is a lack of definite policy regarding the construction and improvement work in the parks and cemeteries that is open to serious critcism. In some cases this work is carried on in co-operation with the city engineer's office, a man from that office being detailed to furnish the engineering service and supervise the work. In other cases the administrative board has retained outside engineering service and has delegated responsibility for its supervision to the assistant superintendent of parks.

This policy has frequently resulted in a waste of the city's funds, due to imperfect construction or other causes, and should be discontinued. The assistant superintendent of parks should ne relieved of all responsibility for the direct supervision of construction work within the properties under his jurisdiction. In planning all improvements involving construction work he should be consulted in regard to the necessary parking features to be considered, but the preparation of the engineering design and the supervision of the construction work should be under the direct supervision of the city engineer's office. The same policy should be followed in the maintenance and repair of roads within the parks. Responsibility for this work should be centered in the proposed division of maintenance in the city engineer's office.

Proposed Department of Parks and Playgrounds.

The problem involved in the care of parks and playgrounds and the administration of the recreational activities of the city as a general rule should be handled by an independent organization.

In Richmond, particularly, the extent of the work involved in the carrying on of these activities justifies the establishment of an independent department in the city government to administer them.

It is recommended that such a department, to be known as the department of parks and recreation, be established, the scope of the work of the department to include responsibility for the maintenance and physical upkeep of the parks and city owned cemeteries, except the maintenance of roads within those properties and the operation of all recreational activities conducted by the city.

Present Organization of Park Development.

The present distribution of forces in the department of parks is shown in the accompanying organization chart. The assistant superintendent of parks receives a salary of $2.000 and a house located in William Byrd Park. The assistant superintendent of playgrounds acts as secretary to the assistant superintendent of parks and attends to the general clerical duties of the department.

Division of Parks.

The park system of Richmond includes thirteen parks, with an approximate area of 653 acres. The three largest parks total 602 acres, while the remainder are small areas distributed throughout the city. In addition there are numerous grass plots at street intersections, which are maintained by the park department. In the following discussion special consideration will be given to the following parks, which are the largest in the city:

William Byrd Park, area 300 acres.
Joseph Bryan Park, area 263 acres.

William Byrd Park.

William Byrd Park is the show park of the city. It is adjacent to a high class residential section of the city and possesses unusual beauties both natural and artificial. There is an artificial lake in the park on which the use of boats is permitted for fishing and other purposes. These boats are maintained by private parties, although the assistant superintendent of parks exercises supervision over them and the amount charged for their use. The city receives $150 a year for this privilege, which is the only park concession awarded to private parties. It is doubtful if the value of the concession justifies a higher charge.

The general conditions in the park are excellent, although the maintenance of certain of the roads should be improved.

Byrd Park Force:

The permanent force employed at Byrd Park includes the following:

Foreman, $80.00 per month.
Policeman, $2.50 per day, on duty 12 hours each day, 365 days in the year.
Five laborers, $2.50 per day, 365 days in the year.
The laborers also do police duty when conditions require it.

Extra men are employed at the rate of $2.25 per day as needed. At the time the study of the department was made there were ten extra men employed at this park.

Bryan Park:

Joseph Bryan Park is located just outside the city limits. It is an undeveloped natural park, with an area of 263 acres. This park is used to a considerable extent as a picnic ground, permits for such use being issued by the assistant superintendent of parks. No fee is charged for permits of this character.

Park Force:

The permanent force employed at Bryan Park includes—

Parkkeeper, who receives $85 per month and a house located in the park.
One laborer, $2.25 per day.

The granting of a perquisite to the keeper of this park by furnishing him with a house is open to criticism. His duties are less arduous if anything than those of the other parkkeepers who receive the same compensation. He should either be required to pay the city a fair rental for the property occupied or his compensation should be fixed with due regard to the value of the perquisite granted.

General Distribution of Park Forces.

The regular force employed at eight of the smaller parks includes:

Parkkeeper. $85.00 per month
One laborer, $2.25 per day 365 days.

The duties of the parkkeeper include responsibility for the upkeep of the parks and the preservation of law and order, even to the exercise of police functions when necessary. Parkkeepers are required to be on duty 365 days in the year, and are subject to call for night service to some extent. The regular laborers are also vested with police authority.

In two of the smaller parks located in the outlying districts no keeper is provided, but a laborer at $2.50 per day is assigned to each park for continuous service, his duties and powers being precisely the same as those of parkkeepers.

In addition to the regular force at the various parks the practice is followed of assigneing extra men to assist the regular force. These men receive $2.25 per day, working 5½ days a week and are generally employed during nine months in the year.

Defects in Present Force Distribution.

The present distribution of park forces is open to criticism in the following respects:

1—In respect to the parkkeepers. These positions are generally in the nature of political patronage, and in some cases the incumbents are not rendering other than custodial and police service. Their duties in this respect are not arduous and they should be required to assist in the actual maintenance of the area under their jurisdiction.

In the case of the Monument Avenue grass plots, a parked section extending down the middle of one of the main boulevards of the city, there is no justification for employing a parkkeeper.

It is recommended that this position be abolished. It is probable that during a portion of the year the permanent assignment of one laborer to care for the parked area would be justified.

2—With the possible exception of Chimborazo Park, which has an area of thirty-nine acres, there does not appear to be any need for the assignment of extra men for any extended period of time. Obviously this does not apply to Byrd Park, where the almost continuous employ of a considerable force is required.

It is recommended that the force now distributed among the various parks be organized into a floating gang working under a

competent foreman. It should be possible with a force of this
character to secure more efficient and economical upkeep than at
present.

Proposed Organization of Park Forces.

A proposed reorganization of the forces employed in connection with the maintenance and care of the park system of Richmond is shown in the accompanying organization chart. It will
be noted that provision is made for an additional force to work
under the direction of the nurseryman in connection with the care
of the city nursery and in the care of street trees. The need for
this force is discussed later in the report.

In respect to the employment of a floating gang rather than
assigning laborers temporarily to different parks throughout the
city, it should be noted that need for such additional service aside
from the purely routine work of the parks is essentially periodic,
and it is evident that the employment of a gang of men working
under competent supervision will result in having the work performed more expeditiously and economically than at present.

The proposed organization of the floating gang labor forces,
predicated on their employment for nine months in the year which
it is understood is a fair basis for estimating the need for such
service together with the elimination of one parkkeeper represents
a reduction in personal service of approximately $4,000 a year.

Obviously the successful handling of forces of this character
depends to a considerable degree on adequate transportation facilities for tools, etc. With this in mind it is recommended that the
park department be supplied with a Ford automobile truck or its
equivalent. The needs of the department both in the matter of
park maintenance and care of street trees fully justifies this equipment.

Park Maintenance.

The general condition of the parks in Richmond aside from
the almost universal need for road repair and maintenance is commendable. The buildings and benches, etc., are in a good state of
repair and the care of the grounds and flower beds reflects credit
on the administration of the department.

Comfort Stations.

With the exception of Byrd Park and Chimborazo Park the
provision made for comfort stations is inadequate. In certain of

the smaller parks, particularly in the outlying districts of the city, the lack of such facilities is not serious at present. However, in the case of Jefferson Park, and Monroe Park the present facilities are entirely inadequate. Provision should be made at as early a date as possible for their extension.

Tree Nursery.

The city maintains a tree nursery adjacent to Bryan Park. This nursery is under the supervision of a city nurseryman, who receives a salary of $900 a year and a house. He is also responsible for the planting and care of trees on the streets and in the parks. He is aided in this work by two laborers, each of whom receives $2.50 a day.

Condition of Nursery.

The condition of the tree nursery at the time the inspection was made was open to serious criticism. Trees were planted entirely too close together in most cases, and there was little evidence of any intelligent trimming of trees so as to produce growth suitable for street tree planting.

The stock contained in the nursery represents a potential value to the city of Richmond amounting to many thousands of dollars, but if it is allowed to continue in its present deplorable condition there is little likelihood of securing enough trees suitable for street planting to justify the expense. The present force of unskilled labor provided for the care of the nursery is entirely inadequate and incompetent to give it the needed attention.

The city government should either provide funds for the employment of a competent force to handle this nursery work or should abandon the nursery and use the ground it occupies for some other purpose.

Street Tree Planting and Care of Shade Trees.

The planting of street trees is carried on under the direction of the city nurseryman, the necessary labor service in the matter of excavating being done by men assigned from the forces of the superintendent of street cleaning. The placing of the necessary top soil and the actual planting of the trees is done by the force working directly under the supervision of the nurseryman. The same force is employed in the trimming and spraying of trees on the streets and in the parks.

As previously noted, the force assigned to the city nurseryman is entirely inadequate. If satisfactory results are to be secured in the care of the trees within the city, it is essential that additional funds be provided for competent men to carry on this work.

Division of Cemeteries.

The city maintains five public cemeteries, four of which are in use as burial grounds. These cemeteries are under the jurisdiction of the park department in so far as maintenance and improvement work is concerned. The other work of the cemeteries involving the sale of lots, supervision over burials, etc., is not under his jurisdiction. The permanent force employed at the various cemeteries is shown in the accompanying tabulation:

Cemetery Force Employed:

    Maury and Mt. Olivet—Keeper, $1,200; 4 laborers, $2.50 per day, 365 days.

    Riverview—Keeper, $1,200; 4 laborers, $2.50 per day, 365 days.

    Oakwood—Keeper, $1,200; 5 laborers, $2.50 per day, 365 days; 1 laborer, $2.25 per day—extra man.

    Shockoe—2 laborers, $2.50 per day, 365 days.

    St. John's—Keeper, $900; laborer, $2.25 per day, 303 days.

No burials are permitted in St. John's cemetery. The keeper, in addition to supervising the maintenance of the grounds, acts as guide to visitors interested in this historic church and burying ground.

Condition of Cemeteries.

The condition of the cemeteries in so far as maintenance is concerned in satisfactory and the force employed does not appear to be excessive in any case.

City Policy as Affecting Operation of Cemeteries.

It is desired to call attention to the unsound policy followed by the city in the matter of charges for burial lots and their subsequent care. The present revenue derived from the city cemeteries through the sales of burial lots and charges is not sufficient to make them self-supporting. While it is probable that any material increase in the price charged for space in the cemeteries would in many cases work a hardship, the city should adopt some definite policy in respect to an equitable charge for the maintenance of cemetery lots. At present there is practically no provision for perpetual care of graves. If this policy is continued the city will face the prospect of decreasing revenues from the sale of lots, as the space available for burial purposes is reduced while it will always have the burden of maintaining the cemeteries in a suitable condition. This is a matter that should receive the serious consideration of the city government.

Division of Playgrounds and Recreation.

The city of Richmond maintains the following playgrounds and recreational activities:

Three playgrounds for young children.
Five playgrounds with facilities for older as well as young children.
Byrd Park athletic field.
Swimming pool.

With the exception of Byrd Park athletic field, which is open and in use during the entire year, the recreational facilities are in general open from June 15th to September 15th of each year.

Scope of Activities.

All these playgrounds are equipped with play 'apparatus of various kinds and volley ball courts, while tennis courts are provided in the three largest. In the evening, folk dances and simple entertainments are conducted by the directors in charge.

Supervision of Playgrounds.

The use of the playgrounds is at all times under the direction of play directors, both men and women. The incumbents of these positions with the exception of the so-called director in charge of the playground for small colored children, are young men and women trained in recreational work. They receive compensation ranging from $80.00 per month to $21.00 per month depending upon the time they devote to the work. It is difficult to evaluate service of this character, but conditions at the playgrounds visited and the attendance appear to justify the expenditures made.

Playgrounds for Young Children.

There are two playgrounds and a vacant lot for baseball which are especially designed for the use of young children. These play-grounds are provided with sand piles and some limited play equipment. One of these playgrounds is set apart for the use of colored children. The grounds are open daily except Sunday from 9 A. M. to 12 M., and from 4 to 7 P. M. during which hours there is a woman play director and care taker in charge.

Lack of Provision for Colored Children.

The policy followed by the city in failing to provide more playground facilities for colored children under suitable directors is open to serious criticism. The children of this class in Richmond are in far greater need of being directed along the lines of legitimate amusement than the rest of the population. It is urged that in the interests of the city, steps be taken to provide additional playgrounds and other recreational facilities for the colored race.

Care of Equipment and Grounds.

The grounds and equipment at the various playgrounds throughout the city were found to be in good condition. Systematic repairs are made as needed. and at the end of the season the equipment that would deteriorate from exposure to the weather is dismantled and housed.

Swimming Pool.

The city maintains a swimming pool for men and boys in the James River. A life guard who gives instructions in swimming is on duty at the pool during the day. During the present summer, in the absence of the "Virginia Howitzers," the swimming pool in the Howitzer Armory is being used by boys and girls on alternate afternoons except Sundays. The pools are at all times under the direction of either a male or female director.

Comment on Recreational Activities.

The administration of recreational activities in the city of Richmond is in general commendable. There is no question but that these activities constitute an important factor for good. There is apparent, however, a lack of co-ordination between the work of this character carried on by the city, and by private organizations. It is urged that steps be taken to bring about such co-ordination as a means for securing more effective service to the community than exist at present.

The Municipally Owned Public Utilities

THE MUNICIPALLY OWNED PUBLIC UTILITIES.

Introductory.

The City of Richmond owns and operates three public utility properties, namely, the water, gas and electric utilities. The first two of these utilities supply all the water and gas services, both public and commercial, now furnished in Richmond, while the electric utility engages in no commercial transactions, but is operated exclusively in the service of the city. A survey has been made of the operating departments of each of the properties. Part of the survey and report has been made by the firm of Hagenah and Erickson, of Chicago, the special public utilities experts of the Bureau of Municipal Research and part by the utilities engineers of the Bureau's New York staff. The work was divided into four main divisions, which arrangement is also followed in this report, as follows:

I—Office Organization and General Administrative Methods.
II—Examination of Accounts.
III—Examination of Rates.
IV—Engineering.

Divisions I, II and III were covered by Hagenah and Erickson.

I—OFFICE ORGANIZATION AND GENERAL ADMINISTRATIVE METHODS.

Water Department.

Organization.

The administrative staff of the water department is composed of a superintendent, two assistant superintendents, a chief clerk and a general staff of twenty-three clerks, inspectors, meter readers, messengers, etc. Of the twenty-three clerks, inspectors, etc., two are directly under the supervision of the superintendent, two are under the supervision of an assistant superintendent at a separate office maintained in South Richmond, and nineteen are under the supervision of the chief clerk. The assistant superintendent on the south side is also in charge of the South Richmond portion of the plant.

The organization is not rigid. Whenever there is a pressure of business all employees of the office assist in the different activities, regardless of their regularly assigned duties. To a considerable degree of the chief clerk in the general office works independently of the superintendnt, which official, together with the first assistant superintendent, devotes most of his time to construction work and plant operations, giving less attention to the administrative work of the department.

The work of the office of the chief clerk of the water department is divided as follows:

Applications for service connection.
Applications for turning on supply.
Meter reading.
Inspection.
Billing.
Complaints.

Applications for Service Connection.

A resident or property owner desiring the extension of the water service into his premises, is required to fill out and sign an application. the form of which calls for the following data:

Number .... side of .... Street,
between ....Street and .... Street,
........inch lead to supply ....
Owner.............. Plumber..............
Date...............
Number of tap......

Immediately on receipt of the above signed application. the particulars are entered on a blotter and telephoned to the shop or headquarters of the construction force. The shop foreman enters the particulars on a numbered form, the number of which is recorded on the blotter and on the application. The plumber installing the service prepares a complete report of the installation which is returned to the office and entered in full on the application and description record. which entries are numbered consecutively. and the number of the entry is the official identifying number by which any particular tap can be located. It is interesting to note in this connection that the record of taps extends back to the installation of the first service in 1834, and the numbers of taps had been entered for the city of Richmond alone. exclusive the present time. Up to January 1, 1917, approximately 30,500 taps had been entered for the City of Richmond alone, exclusive of South Richmond.

The above method of handling the applications for service appears cumbersome. If the application signed by the property owner were printed on numbered stationery and signed in duplicate by means of a carbon copy, the duplicate copy would serve as the work order for the shop to make the necessary installation. Provision for the historical data could be made on the duplicate, which should be returned at the completion of the job, properly filled out and signed. This would eliminate the possibility of error in transmitting such order by telephone, the maintenance of the blotter record of orders and the preparation of two or more reports covering the same piece of work.

Applications for Turning on Supply.

The procedure incident to filing, granting and posting applications for turning on water is well ordered, and no suggestion is made for change therein.

Free Water Service.

The water department of the City of Richmond grants water free to widows and indigent persons on receipt of an application for such service showing name, residence, amount paid for house rent, amount of income, etc., and signed by the inspector and approved by the superintendent. A form of numbered permit is granted to the applicant on approval of the application, and these permits run for a period of one year, subject to prior cancellation at the discretion of the administrative board. Registers of the free water permits are kept for each district.

Meter Reading.

The meter readers' hand book is prepared along the lines of the consumers' register, a page being devoted to each meter and the name of the consumer and his address entered at the top of the page. Space is provided on each page for monthly readings of each meter for a period of six years, and columns are provided for the readings and the amount of the consumption. Notwithstanding the fact that bills for the water department are sent out quarterly, it is the practice of the department to require each meter to be read every month. The meter readers are expected to determine the consumption each month for each meter, and if the consumption indicated since the previous month's reading appears to exceed the proportion of the quarterly allowance under the minimum bill, notice is given, stating the number of cubic feet of water consumed since the last meter reading and advising an examination of fixtures for waste or leaks. A duplicate of the notice left with the consumer is returned to the office, where it is subsequently mailed by the superintendent to the owner or to the agent.

The meter readers, inspectors, messengers, and other employees of the water department, whose duties require them to observe the condition of the water supply, carry a book with perforated leaves for the purpose of noting sundry violations, essential repairs, etc. Such reports are submitted at the office daily, where they are given to the inspectors for attention. At the end of each month the meter readers prepare a report of their activities during the month, covering the number of days spent in reading meters, delivering bills or doing special work.

The reading of water meters monthly is unnecessary. Since bills are rendered only quarterly, no useful purpose is served by this practice except that, as stated by the chief clerk, the consumer may thereby be advised as to whether his consumption is averaging greater than allowed under the minimum bill. The existence of leaks could best be discovered by a periodical inspection of the meters, fixtures, etc., and such an inspection would be of more value than one made by the meter readers. Further, the expense of meter reading is tripled when all, instead of only one-third, of the total number of meters are read each month.

The make-up of the meter readers' hand books is also subject to criticism. The practice of furnishing meter readers with previous readings of the meters is objectionable, since it permits a meter reader to estimate readings of meter consumption without reading the meter itself. A list of the consumers could be secured as required from the addressograph machine, after which it would be necessary for the meter reader to examine each meter on the list to ascertain its registration at the date of reading. Neglect of duty on the part of the meter readers would thereby be reduced to a minimum.

Inspection.

The question of how much inspection work should be done by the water department without charge is an important one. Monthly inspection is certainly unnecessary. The only advantage gained by such frequent inspection is the possible early discovery of more or less unimportant violations, but the expense attendant thereon more than offsets the advantage gained. The inspection of water meters ordinarily is not required oftener than once a year, whereas in the City of Richmond this inspection is practically continuous and therefore constitutes an unduly large expense.

Billing.

Since January 1, 1917, the city auditor has been using as a basis of the gross revenue earned by the water department the total of bills sent out as shown by the "listing book" and the adjustment of the bills as shown by the change sheets prepared by the chief clerk's office. This is a step in the proper direction and should be continued.

Builders desiring permission to use water for building purposes must apply for permission to the office of the water department and are furnished with a permit. They are required to pay for the water consumed at meter rates, the consumption to be determined by a meter attached to the hydrant. It appears to be the practice of the department to require all bills for water incurred by the builder to be paid before the tenant of the house can secure service, in spite of the fact that the applicant for water service might not be the owner of the property. This practice of subordinating the right of the tenant to the obligation of the property should be corrected by making bills of this character a lien on the property, to be collected in the same manner as taxes or other liens are collected.

The chief criticism to be leveled against the method employed in the office of the chief clerk of the water department with respect to the function of making out and recording consumers' bills is that unnecessary records of transactions are made. The preparation of the listing book is unnecessary, but is provided for in the ordinance, and is kept in conformity thereto. Modern accounting practice, however, would seem to indicate that since the consumer's indebtedness is plainly shown on the register, which is in fact a consumers' ledger, there should be no need for a further detailed list of such indebtedness.

The purpose of the "listing book" is two-fold. It furnishes the auditor with the amount to be charged to accounts receivable and credited to the revenue of the department, and also serves as a means of quickly indentifying the unpaid items. The first of these functions would be just as well served by an adding machine slip and with much less labor. The second would be equally well

benefit of the city should come directly to the terasurer, who is the responsible financial officer of the corporation.

Applications for Service Connection and for Turning on Supply.

The procedure incident to receiving and granting these applications is satisfactory.

Meter Reading.

Consumers' meters in the gas department are read monthly. The city of Richmond is divided into four districts and the months have been divided into four periods, one for each of the four districts. District number one is billed on the first of the month, district number two on the eighth, district number three on the sixteenth, and district number four on the twenty-third. The reading of meters in the four districts in this manner provides for an even distribution of the work and also favorably affects the work of collection at the city treasurer's office. The hand books used by the meter renders provide space for consecutive monthly readings for a period of several years for each meter. This practice is open to the objection previously stated in connection with the water department in that it allows meter readers to make a very accurate estimate of the consumer's consumption for the month without going near the meter itself. It would appear to be better for the meter reader to be furnished monthly with a list of meters and addresses only, so that he would be compelled to visit the consumers' premises and inspect the meter before being able to enter in his hand book the amount of the monthly consumption.

Inspection.

The inspection service supplied by the gas department is very thorough. As previously stated, this inspection begins with the erection of the building and is continuous even after service is being supplied. The policy of the superintendent of supplying expert inspection service covering fixtures on the consumers' premises is the cause of considerable expense to the department but it provides an opportunity of making a closer inspection than would otherwise be possible and greatly adds to the convenience and usefulness of the service to the public. All inspectors' reports are carefully followed up and violations and abuses promptly corrected under penalty of discontinuance of service.

Billing.

In connection with the methods of billing and of recording data concerning consumers in the gas department, the same criticism may be made as was set forth above with respect to the corresponding functions of the water department. The gas bill "listing book" now requires a considerable expenditure of labor which could be saved if more scientific methods were adopted. The form of the gas bill should also be changed so as to encourage payment by check in order to facilitate the work in the collecting offices. and at the same time provide the customer with a receipt and without expense to the city.

Coal Given Free.

It was stated that the gas department sometimes gives coal to indigent persons. The cost of coal thus given away should be recorded in the accounts if accurate operating statements of the gas plant are to be prepared.

Complaints.

Complaints are received at the office of the inspector of gas by telephone. letter or in person and generally cover such subjects as excessive bills, leaks, requests for refunds, rebates and miscellaneous matters. On receipt of complaints, an order is issued to the deputy inspectors directing them to investigate the facts and report thereon, which reports furnish the basis for subsequent adjustments.

Electric Department.

The electric department, while authorized by charter to sell current for commercial purposes. is restricted, by ordinance, to municipal uses only, for which reason there are, in the strictest sense, no administrative offices. The superintendent of the electric department has the assistance of a draftsman and a clerk. By virtue of his office he is also the city electrician and is in charge of the department of electric inspection of the city government. Approximately one-fourth of his time is devoted to this latter work. and a corresponding division of his salary between the two departments supervised is made by the city. In the statement of the accounts hereinafter set up, the expense of this inspection bureau is included in the total expense of the electrical department.

Consolidation of the Three Utilities.

From the foregoing discussion it will be noted that the city of Richmond is maintaining three distinct departments, there being a separate organization for each of its public utility services. Whereever the nature of the services of two of these departments are at all similar, the departmental organization and the duties of the employees are also similar. This fact, together with the somewhat similar character of the work to be performed for the three departments, indicates that for the purpose of greatly improving the service and of effecting substantial economies these three departments should be consolidated into a single organization, having charge of the three services.

Stated in a very condensed form, the present administrative organization of the above departments, together with the annual salary payments, may be shown as follows:

Water department—
1 Superintendent ....$	3,000.00	
1 Chief clerk	1,500.00	
23 Inspectors, clerks, messengers, etc.	23,140.00	
		$27,640.00

Gas department—
1 Superintendent ....$	4,000.00	
1 General bookkeeper	1,650.00	
1 Chief inspector of gas......	2,500.00	
18 Deputy inspectors of gas...	21,600.00	
		29,750.00

Electric department—
1 Superintendent ....$	2,700.00	
2 Clerks	2,400.00	
		5,100.00

Total general office payroll.	$62,490.00

Note.—The amount shown for the superintendent of the electric department represents that portion of his salary which is chargeable to the electric department because of his supervision of the electric plant.

An outline for the organization of such departments when consolidated, readily suggests itself from the above. The new department should be under the direction of a single commissioner, who should be an experienced and well qualified executive, and responsible directly to the mayor. Such commissioner should be assisted by superintendents in direct charge of the plant operations. There should be but one chief clerk in charge of all the office work, and a re-organization of the employees and re-assignment of their duties so as to make possible one department for the reading of meters, one department for the rendering of bills, one department for complaints, etc. To bring about this simplicity of organization a radical re-arrangement of the present office staffs would be necessary, but such step should be taken to the end that the administrative work of the Richmond municipally owned utilities would be carried out with the efficiency, dispatch and economy now shown for similar work by privately owned utilities operating two or more utility services in large cities.

The detailed plan of such combined organization should provide for the elimination of one chief clerk, one bookkeeper, fourteen clerks and possibly one superintendent, the closing of the South Richmond office, the discontinuance of district offices and the opening of more commodious offices for the new staff arrangement. The elimination of one superintendent is contingent on the possibility of combining the two hydraulic plants under a single head. Since this latter subject is more properly a part of the engineering survey the matter is merely referred to in this part of the report. It is possible, however, to state that the work of the combined department could be cared for by the following organization and with a substantial saving to the public as well as greatly improving the efficiency of the employees:

1 Commissioner of utilities	$ 5,000.00
3 Superintendents	9,700.00
1 Chief clerk	3,000.00
27 General employees as clerks, meter readers, billing clerks	32,400.00
Total general office salaries	$ 50,100.00

The annual saving made possible by such consolidation would be $12,390. This amount would be reduced somewhat by the substitution of a clerk in place of the present bookkeeper, but would be further increased in the event of the elimination of one of the superintendents.

The advantages growing out of the consolidation of the present departments in addition to the annual saving are numerous. Under such an arrangement there would be but a single appropriation from the city to the utility departments, the amount of such appropriation being based on estimates carefully prepared under the direction of the commissioner and showing in detail the requirement of each service, which estimates would be prepared with due regard to the necessities and the harmonious development of the property as a whole. Under the present organization it is the practice of each utility department to ask for an appropriation from the administrative board without regard to the needs of the other departments, resulting either in compromises of requests which should possibly be allowed for in giving unduly large sums to that department which best presented its case. Under a single executive it would also be possible to carry out campaigns for the promotion of business along uniform lines and designed to correct inconsistencies in the present service developments considered in their entirety. Uniform rules and regulations could likewise be prescribed which would cover all of such public utility services throughout the city.

The present form of organization naturally leads to the development of inconsistencies in policies and practices, of which a large number now exist. For example, the water utility collects its rates in advance, while the gas utility collects after service has been rendered. No statements for inter-departmental service are issued by the electric department which is, however, producing a valuable service for the benefit of certain other municipal departments. Again, the gas department requires a deposit from customers in certain cases, while the water department requires no deposit. Gas is sold under a uniform rate schedule, while water is sold at both flat rates and meter rates under a schedule which is discriminatory and obsolete in form. The water and gas departments both have minimum bill provisions, but the former collects its minimum bill with each meter reading, while the latter makes adjustment for the minimum charge only on an annual basis. The gas department inspects and maintains with efficiency its service up to the point of consumption on the customers' premises, while the water department merely cares for the service to the customers' meter.

The public in its dealings with the utility departments is now subjected to many delays and inconveniences which would be corrected by a consolidation of the departments. At present, a customer for service must visit two offices in order to adjust a complaint. or for the purpose of requesting a change in the place of his service. or in making application for the connection of service. These matters are of considerable importance during the moving season of the year when the number of changes, claims and complaints are very numerous. A single office in which all these matters could be adjusted under uniform rules would add greatly to the appreciation of the service by the public and would eliminate many criticisms and complaints which frequently delay the progress of the departments' work and try the patience of employees and public alike.

In connection with the consolidation of the three departments there should be a revision of the city ordinances which in certain instances have been outgrown by the developing utility properties. The practice of prescribing office duties and routines and also of fixing the number of employees by ordinances, interferes with the management of the property. because it removes the power to exercise a proper judgment and discretion according to the facts and conditions as they arise. It would be better to confer on the department head broad and general duties with a fixed responsibility to proper authorities, but leaving to such official sufficient freedom of action to bring about in an efficient and expeditious manner the service conditions and financial results expected of good management.

II—EXAMINATION OF ACCOUNTS.

The Accounts in General.

A study of the operating accounts of the three utilities was attempted. but with little success since no adequate records are maintained covering their revenues and expenses. Only in the gas department is any attempt being made to keep the records in accordance with a standard classification of accounts and this attempt is not entirely successful because the accounts are kept partly on a cash basis.

Two of the utilities have been in service for over sixty-five years and there are no records of the cost of their properties. The electric plant was completed less than six years ago. and a complete record of its cost is available. According to the data obtainable from such records as are now available, the present book values of the properties of the three utility plants as of December 31, 1916, are as follows:

Water utility $3,864,674.28
Gas utility 1,554,493.78
Electric utility 642,499.48

Total $6,061,667.54

To the above book value should be added the amount of depreciation credited to the cost of the electric plant during four years, amounting to $86,540.60. With this addition, the total cost of the properties, including the value placed on the real estate and the riparian rights of the electric plant, becomes $6,148,208.14. The real estate and riparian rights of the electric plant are included in the department's book valuation at $200,000. An analysis of the original cost of securing this property shows that the actual cost was approximately $57,803. If this amount is inserted in place of the valuation of $200,000, the total cost of the electric plant appears to be $586,843.08.

There was no analysis of the expense of the water department available prior to 1916. The department kept no such record and its annual reports do not show the detailed and classified expenses of operation. The other two utilities, however, have kept detailed analysis of expenses for a period of years, and, in the case of the gas department, the analysis of its operating expenses is published in the annual reports.

Since much of the available data pertaining to the operating expenses of the different utilities consisted of memoranda rather than actual accounting records, expense statements were compiled for each department, including such adjustments as were necessary to bring the statements to a correct accounting basis. These statements covering the operations of the year ending December 31, 1916, are included in this report and are appended at the close of this section.

Water Department.

In analyzing the revenues and expenses of this department, it was found that no provision had been made for a portion of certain general expenses incurred for the joint benefit of the city and the water utility. These joint expenses consist of the collector's salary, and the city attorney's salary and the expenditure for rent, light and heat. The amount required to cover these three items chargeable against the water department was estimated by the special accountant of the administrative board as follows:

Collector's salary ....$ 1,500.00
Legal expense 500.00
Rent, light and heat 1,000.00
_____
Total ....$ 3,000.00

To the other general expenses was added the sum of $56,916, to cover the estimated amount of taxes lost to the city through its ownership of the water plant. This sum was arrived at by computing the tax at 1 1-2 per cent. on the book value of the plant at the beginning of the year 1916. Nothing was added to the operating expenses to cover uncollectible bills, although the city council, by ordinance, has at various times relieved the delinquent tax collector of the responsibility of collecting certain accounts in arrears and has ordered them written off the books of the city. It was noted that the revenue of the water department included an item representing the value of water given to churches, charities, etc. This item being in the nature of a donation, has been considered as an item of general expense. The pumping expense was increased by the sum of $14,192.90 to cover the cost of electrical power supplied by the electric plant. This amount was determined by analyzing the cost of production in the electric department and was substituted for the cost, as determined by the latter department amounting to $11,431.75.

The total expenses of the water department for the year 1916 as above adjusted, aggregated $242,863.47. This sum, when deducted from the operating revenues leaves an operating profit of $187,039.25 before allowing for fixed charges and for depreciation.

There was added to the operating revenue the sum of $36,575, by which amount an analysis showed the estimate of the water department covering hydrant rental should be increased. The fixed charges for the department were estimated at 5 per cent. on the par value of the water bonds to cover interest and sinking fund requirements and 1 per cent. of the average property for the year to cover depreciation. From the total of these two items there was deducted the amount of the annual sinking fund requirement, since to make a charge against the revenue both for sinking fund purposes and for depreciation would be equivalent to a duplication. The total of the fixed charges for the year amounted to $124,215.30, leaving as net income $62,823.95.

In addition to the interest allowed on the bonds a further charge of 4 per cent. was made to cover interest on the amount invested in the property in excess of the par value of the bonds. This interest charge for the year is $68,606.97, and when deducted from the net income for that year shows a deficit from operation of $5,843.02.

Gas Department.

The statement of revenue and expenses for the gas department required no adjustment, except for the item of taxes. In order to show the expenses of this department on a basis corresponding to that used for the water and electric departments, provision was made in the accounts for taxes at the rate of 1 1-2 per cent. on the book cost of the property as of December 31, 1915. The taxes on this basis amounted to $22,274.09. Including this item of expense, the total operating expense of the department for the year 1916 aggregated $299,504.87, and the operating profit $232,364.30.

The fixed charges of the gas department were determined by computing the interest and sinking fund requirements at 5 per cent. on the par value of the bonds outstanding and depreciation at the rate of 2 per cent. on the average property for the year. The deduction of the sinking fund in order to avoid duplication in the depreciation charge was made in the manner described in connection with the water department accounts, and interest was computed at 4 per cent. on the cost of the property in excess of the par value of the bonds now outstanding and chargeable to the gas department. After making the above allowances, a surplus accrues to the credit of the gas department for the year's operations. amounting to $139,790.22.

Because of the effect which estimated future expenses have upon the recommendations herewith submitted, reference is made to the increased cost of production, which will be occasioned by changes in the cost of coal and oil. A new contract for gas oil entered into in 1917 calls for delivery at 7.36 cents per gallon, as compared with 3.44 cents per gallon for delivery under the contract which obtained for 1916. For gas coal, prices have advanced from $2.52 to $4.70 per ton, and for steam coal the advance has been from $2.75 to $5.10 per ton. On the basis of the 1916 output, these changes in prices will result in the following increases in gas manufacturing costs:

Increased cost of oil ....$ 85,890.14
Increased cost of gas coal 45,482.58
Increased cost of steam coal 7,708.12
_____
Total ....$ 139,080.84

Had the above increased costs prevailed throughout 1916, the unit operating cost of production for the year would have been increased to approximately 50 cents per thousand cubic feet made, and the entire surplus from operation would have been absorbed.

Since other price increases will no doubt occur if the present economic conditions continue for some years, and since the department is required by ordinance to charge rates sufficiently high to cover all costs of service, including fixed charged on the entire investment in the gas system, additional sources of revenue must be sought through rate increases or otherwise, or the cost of production must be reduced through changes in the present method of gas manufacture. In the latter direction the possibility of decreasing the heating value of the gas should be given consideration. The present tendency on the part of the public is to permit a reduction in the heating value of the gas below the standard generally adopted ten years ago, and to eliminate entirely the candle-power standard. At the present time the department delivers gas which tests over 600 B. T. U. The manufacture of gas testing 565 B. T. U. is now considered good operating practice. From the best estimates obtainable the adoption of this standard heating value would result in a saving of approximately one-seventh of the present expenditure for oil. From a monetary standpoint this saving would have amounted to approximately $22,600 for the year 1916. This change would also harmonize with the present recommendations of the department superintendent for the construction of a new coke oven plant. In order to make such change a department rule or an ordinance providing for the discontinuance of the present flat flame burners and the substitution of mantles, would have to be adopted. From information gathered in the office of the gas department it appears that only about 10 per cent. of the present consumers have flat flame burners on their premises. The removal of these burners could be facilitated by a demonstration of the advantages of mantle lighting and by giving a certain number to consumers at cost or even less than cost. While the advisability of a reduction in the B. T. U. requirements in Richmond was not investigated as a part of this survey, it is known that such a reduction would be in conformity with present tendencies in many large cities throughout the country.

Electric Department.

The operating expenses of the electric plant for 1916, before allowing for depreciation and other fixed charges, were $49,955.24. This amount was determined by adding to the direct expenses shown by the department records an allowance for legal expense, rent, light and heat, and taxes as follows:

Legal expense ....$	250.00
Rent, heat and light	500.00
Taxes	9,637.47
Total ....$	10,387.47

The cost of inspection amounting to $6,525.82, which represents the expense of the office of the city electrician, has been included in the total expenses of the plant. There was deducted from the cost of production the sum of $14,192.90, which represents the cost of power furnished to the water department and which amount has been included in the adjusted expenses of that department described above.

The fixed charges of the electric department were arrived at in the same manner as for the water department. The interest and sinking fund requirement was computed at 5 per cent. on the par value of the bonds outstanding during the year 1916, and the depreciation allowance was estimated at 3 1-2 per cent. on the average property for the year, which was determined for this purpose by eliminating the book value of real estate and riparian rights, and substituting therefor the actual cost of such property. The book value was further adjusted by recharging the amounts previously credited to plant for depreciation, and the allowance for depreciation for 1916 was then computed on such result, after deducting the cost of real estate. The allowance for sinking fund purposes computed at 1 per cent. on the par value of the bonds was eliminated as explained above. To the total fixed charges as thus determined, there was added interest at 4 per cent. on the cost of the plant in excess of the par value of the bonds to the end that the fixed charges for the year would include interest on the total investment. The total operating expenses and fixed charges for the year 1916, as thus adjusted amounted to $92,988.46.

The electric plant takes no credit in its accounts for power supplied the city, and except for the sum of $7,503.13 actually transferred by the auditor to the credit of the electric department in payment for light in public buildings, no accounting is made for inter-departmental service. The statement of the electric department therefor covers only the operating expenses and the fixed charges as explained above.

In the aggregate the expenses of the three departments do not appear to be unreasonable. The determination of the reasonableness of the separate items of expense is rendered difficult by the fact that the water and electric departments do not keep their accounts in accordanc with any standard classification.

In the case of the gas utility the following unit costs obtain:

Total cost of production. 26.2c per M cubic feet made.
Distribution expense:
Service expense. $1.08 per customer.
Consumers' premises expense. $0.32 per customer.
Distribution pumping, $42.20 per mile of main.
Maintenance of mains and services, $43.70 per mile of main.
Maintenance of meters, 19.4c per meter.
Setting and removing meters, 25.6c per meter.
Sales expense (including meter reading, inspection and collection. $1.67 per customer.

Except for the item of sales expense per customer, none of the above unit costs appear to be unreasonable, and recommendations are made in this survey designed to reduce the charges to this account.

For the purpose of establishing the reasonableness of the operating expenses of the electric department as a whole, and also the cost of supplying the various services now furnished by that utility. a distribution was made of the direct operating expenses and fixed charges to the classes of service in which such costs were incurred. The following table shows, in condensed form, the direct expenses and fixed charges of this utility distributed over the pumping. street lighting and building lighting services:

Classification	Total Expense	Amount Chargeable to Pumping Service	Amount Chargeable to Street Lighting Service	Amount Chargeable to Lighting of Buildings
Production	$ 21,981 87	$ 6,770 41	$13,958 49	$1,252 97
Distribution	22,447 03	....	22,059 14	387 89
Gen'l Miscellaneous	3,555 95	206 82	3,299 55	49 58
Taxes	9,637 47	1,455 26	7,729 25	452 96
Depreciation	19,559 50	2,215 88	16,389 72	953 90
Interest	23,473 72	3,544 53	18,825 92	1 103 27
Total	$100,655 54*	$14,192 90	$82,262 07	$4 200 57
Total kilowatt-hours supplied to each service	5,610,591	1 459 810†	3,932 656†	218 125
Cost per kilowatt-hr in cents.............	1 79	0 97	2 09	1 93

*Excludes expense of electrical inspection.
†Switchboard measurement

In making the above apportionment, production expenses were divided between the various services mentioned on the combined basis of the maximum loads of these services on the plant, and their yearly consumption. The distribution expenses were in most cases directly assignable to either the street lighting or public building lighting services, but where this was not possible, an apportionment was made. The general expenses were distributed on the percentage basis resulting from the apportionment of the production and distribution expenses. The fixed charges, including taxes, depreciation and interest on that part of the investment which is represented by the land, buildings, plant equipment, and riparian rights, were apportioned on the same basis as the operating expenses under production expense. The investment in the distribution system was in most cases directly assignable to either the street lighting or public lighting services, thus permitting the apportionment of fixed charges on this part of the investment on the same basis.

The average cost of all energy at the point of consumption was 1.79 cents per kilowatt-hour. The unit costs per kilowatt-hour consumed by the various services, as determined by the apportionment were as follows:

Pumping service ....0.97 cents
Street lighting service ....2.09 cents
Public building service ....1.93 cents

The energy used for pumping is delivered at the switchboard of the electric plant. The distributing lines to the water plant are a part of the water works investment, which fact accounts to some extent for the comparatively low unit cost of energy used in this service.

By a re-distribution of the expense items, including fixed charges as shown in the foregoing apportionment, it is possible to determine the cost of generating and distributing energy during 1916. Such an apportionment has been made and is summarized below:

	Total Cost	Cost per Kilowatt-hour Consumed in Cents.
Cost of service production ....$	46,653.65	.83
Cost of service distribution ..	54,001.89	.96
Total ....$	100,655.54	1.79

This distribution of expense shows that the unit cost of current delivered at the plant switchboard was 0.83 cents. This unit cost of generating energy will be found to be about normal when consideration is given to the fact that it is possible for the electric department to regulate to a considerable extent the electric power pumping demands at the time street lighting service is being rendered and that the demands of the latter service do not fluctuate materially. The entire analysis shows that the unit cost of energy production and distribution for the year 1916 compares favorably with the average electric plant in other cities operating under similar conditions and circumstances.

In case the city of Richmond desired to purchase electric energy from a private company, in lieu of generating its own requirements, it could not materially reduce the total expenses of the present plant as shown above because the investment in the undertaking has already been made and this fact necessarily means that all expenses attendant upon such investment must be provided for annually. Practically the only expenses which would be reduced under an arrangement to purchase current would be the annual operating and maintenance expenses of the power plant. Even this possible decrease in expense would be lessened to some extent if energy were purchased at the switchboard of the power plant, because it would then be necessary to pay the expenses incident to operating such power plant as a sub-station. The fixed charges, such as taxes, depreciation, and interest on the entire investment in the municipal plant would have to be met, regardless of whether current was purchased or generated.

The cost of operating and maintaining the power plant is shown above to amount to $21,981.87. This expense is equivalent to 0.39 cents per kilowatt-hour. The balance of the total expenses, $78,673.67, equivalent to 1.40 cents per kilowatt-hour generated, would continue under an arrangement to purchase the energy now required by the city.

The fact that the total electric light and power service for the city of Richmond is supplied by two plants, one municipally owned and the other privately owned, must necessarily lead to some duplication of investment and for that reason every effort should be made in the future to avoid further duplications. All future demands on the part of the city for an increased supply of electrical energy, which demands would require an increased investment in the municipal plant, should be carefully analyzed to ascertain whether or not such additional service could be obtained more economically from the private plant. Further investments in the city's plant should be made only in the event that energy cannot be obtained elsewhere on a more economical basis.

Statements showing the operating revenue and expenses of the water, gas and electric utilities for the year ended December 31, 1916, follow:

MUNICIPAL WATER UTILITY.

OPERATING REVENUE AND EXPENSES FOR YEAR ENDED DECEMBER 31, 1916.

Operating Revenue.

Water rents	$ 327,503.21
Delinquent bills	1,576.38
Fractional bills	9,628.06
Builders' permits	209.55
Miscellaneous sales	4.474.12
Gross operating revenue	343,391.32
Refunds	2,590.49
Net operating revenue	340,800.83
Water supplied city (in addition to $9,886.00 included in water rents) for which no transfer of fund was made	83,259.87
Water given to Charity, Churches, etc.	5,842.02
Total	$ 429,902.72

Operating Expenses.

Settling basins:

Labor	$ 9,275.65
Repairs	1,705.89
Coagulant	30.299.41
Sundries	1,379.93
Total settling basins	42,660.88

Pumping:

Labor	11.441.35
Repairs	2,231.60
Sundries	1,076.89
Fuel	554.43
Miscellaneous	16.66
Total	15,320.93
Cost of electric power, estimated by electric department)	14.192.90
Total pumping	29,513.83

Storage of water:
Salaries 4,707.75
Repairs 7.55
Sundries 272.15
                                                   ─────────
          Total storage of water 4,987.45

Mains and services:
Labor 35,334.10
Repairs and renewals 773.62
Contracts, paving, etc. 1,665.62
                                                   ─────────
        . Total mains and services 37,773.34

General:
Administrative expense:
Salaries 28,160.99
Stationery and printing 1,390.97
Sundries 1,928.12
                                                   ─────────
          Total administrative 31,480.08

Storehouse expense
Salaries 3,497.31
Supplies and expenses 2,764.61
Bulk supplies 21,200.93
                                                   ─────────
          Total storehouse expense 27,462.85

Automobile expense:
Gasoline 900.00
Tires 437.98
Repairs and supplies 1,633.94
Storage, cleaning and insurance 255.10
                                                   ─────────
          Total automobile expense 3,227.02

Miscellaneous:
Taxes estimated at 1 1-2 per cent. on $3,794,400.. 56,916.00
Legal expenses (estimated by special accountant)   500.00
Rent, light and heat (estimated by special ac-
     countant) 1,000.00

Collector's salary (estimated by special accountant) 1,500.00
Free water 5,842.02

Total miscellaneous 65,758.02

Total general 127,927.97
Total Operating Expenses ....$ 242,863.47

Operating Profit ....$ 187,039.25

Fixed charges:
Interest and sinking fund on $2,148,000.00 water
bonds at 5 per cent. ....$ 107,400.00
Depreciation at 1 per cent. on $3,829,530.00...... 38,295.30

Less sinking fund provision of 1 per cent. on bonds. 21,480.00

Total fixed charges ....$ 124,215.30

Net income ....$ 62,823.95
Interest on excess cost of plant over par value of
bonds at 4 per cent. ....$ 68,666.97

Net deficit for year ....$ 5,843.02

MUNICIPAL GAS UTILITY.

OPERATING REVENUE AND EXPENSES FOR YEAR ENDED DECEMBER 31, 1916.

Operating Revenue.

Sales of gas	$ 514,733.65
Delinquent gas bills	1,760.27
Penalties on gas bills	3,780.90
Municipal street lighting	11,054.80
Miscellaneous sales of gas	604.24
Total operating revenue	$ 531,933.86
Refunds	64.69
Net operating revenue	$ 531,869.17

Operating Expenses.

Coal gas production:
Labor:

Supervision and production labor	$ 35,431.19
Purification labor	2,027.67

Manufacturing material:

Boiler fuel	3,043.33
Gas coal	49,254.75
Purification supplies	805.71
Production supplies and expenses	1,906.82
Maintenance of buildings and apparatus	9,035.94
Total coal gas production	101,505.41

Residuals:

Ammoniacal liquor sold	2,458.33
Coke used in plant and sold	35,025.15
Tar sold	7,499.44
Sundries	740.84
Total residuals	$ 45,723.76
Net coal gas production	$ 55,781.65

Water gas production:
  Labor:
    Supervision and production labor ....\$ 22,929.53
    Purification labor 1,013.83
  Manufacturing material:
    Boiler fuel 6,086.33
    Generator fuel 29,874.90
    Oil 74,448.93
    Purification supplies 1,611.43
    Production supplies and expenses 2,068.27
  Maintenance of buildings and apparatus..........   2,340.57

        Total water gas production ....\$ 140,283.79

Residuals:
    Tar sold ....\$ 8,171.90
    Sundries 740.10

        Total residuals ....\$ 8,912.00

        Net water gas production ....\$ 131,371.79

        Total production ....\$ 187,153.44

Distribution:
  Supervision ....\$ 1,500.00
  Service expense 17,058.44
  Distribution pumping 6,637.50
  Maintenance of mains and services.............   6,863.63
  Maintenance of meters 3,258.94
  Setting and removing meters 4,309.59

        Total distribution 39,628.16

Utilization:
  Consumers' premises expense 5,008.00
  Street lighting expense 10,880.00

        Total utilization 15,888.00

General:
  Officers' salaries 6,499.84
  Clerks' salaries 8,400.00
  Meter readers' and inspectors' salaries...........   13,500.00

Collection expenses	2,000.00
Office expense including rent	3,567.90
Legal expense .:..............................	500.00
Insurance	93.50
Taxes estimated at 1 1-2 per cent. on $1,484,939.34..	22,274.09
Total general	56,835.33
Total Operating Expenses ....$	299,504.87
Operating Profit ....$	232,364.30

Fixed charges:

Interest and sinking fund at 5 per cent. on $833,-618.00 bonds ....$	41,680.90
Depreciation estimated at 2 per cent on $1,519,716.56	30,394.33
Less sinking fund provision of 1 per cent. on bonds.	8,336.18
Total fixed charges ....$	63,739.05
Net income ....$	168,625.25
Interest on excess cost of plant over par value of bonds at 4 per cent. ....$	28,835.03
Surplus for year ....$	139,790.22

MUNICIPAL ELECTRIC UTILITY.

OPERATING REVENUE AND EXPENSES FOR YEAR ENDED DECEMBER 31, 1916.

Operating Revenue.

(Plant does not sell commercial current).

Operating Expenses.

Production:

Payroll	$ 15,944.20
Fuel	4,708.68
Supplies	290.23
Tools	121.49
Repairs to building and machinery	736.84
Miscellaneous	180.43
Total production	21,981.87
Less current supplied to water department	14,192.90
Net production	7,788.97

Distribution:

Payroll	10,626.78
Automobile and truck expense	1,436.47
Arc lamp supplies	3,505.35
Incandescent lamp supplies	4,557.79
Line supplies	333.74
Tools	620.05
Teams	558.67
Repairs	80.04
Miscellaneous	728.14
Total distribution	22,447.03

General and miscellaneous:

Rented lights	2,139.38
Office expenses	393.97
General expenses	272.60
Legal expenses estimated	250.00
Rent, light and heat	500.00

Taxes estimated at 1 1-2 per cent. on $642,498.47...	9,637.47
Inspection	6,525.82
Total general and miscellaneous........$	19,719.24
Total Operating Expenses ....$	49,955.24

Fixed charges:

Interest and sinking fund on $310,000 bonds at 5 per cent. ....$	15,500.00
Depreciation at 2 1-2 per cent. on $558,843........	19,559.50
Less sinking fund provision of 1 per cent. on bonds.	3,100.00
Interest on excess cost of plant over par value of bonds at 4 per cent.	11,073.72
Total fixed charges ....$	43,033.22
Total expenses and fixed charges........$	92,088.46

III—EXAMINATION OF RATES.

Scope of Inquiry.

The study of the rates charged by each of the departments for utility service included an analysis of the consumers' accounts in the water and gas departments and a study of present and possible future development in the case of the gas utility. Since the electric department does not supply service to commercial consumers it was unnecessary to make an examination of those factors on which its rates would be based. As a result of the facts disclosed by the analyses and the information obtained covering the customer development, certain conclusions may be stated with respect to the rates now in force.

Water Department.

The water department renders service at various rates. In general, these rates may be classified into those applying to flat rate service and those applying to meter rate service, the latter covering both private and public consumption of water. The former class, called "ordinance rates," are shown below:

	Per Year
Bakeries, each ....$	12.00
Boarding schools, each	25.00

Blacksmith shop—one forge	4.00
Each additional forge	2.00
Buggies, wagons etc. kept for hire or in livery, ea.	1.50
Bricks laid, per 1,000	.05
Barber shop—one chair	6.00
Each additional chair	1.50
Billiard room, etc., with water fixtures convenient	12.00
Billiard room, etc., without water fixtures convenient	5.00
Barroom, each (with a faucet)	15.00
Each additional faucet	3.00
Beer pump, each	3.00
Barrooms, each (without a faucet)	10.00
Carpenter, paint shops, etc., each	5.00
Coach or wagon shop	15.00
Candy factory	10.00
Cows, each	1.00
Closet trough, or sink closet, per lineal foot......	1.50
Currier shops, each	37.00
Dwelling house, one hydrant...................	4.00
Dwelling house, one hydrant, one closet..........	8.00
Additional faucets, each	1.50
Dyeing establishment, exclusive of steam boiler..	22.00
Daily newspaper printing office	20.00
Families (over a store), one hydrant, each.......	3.00
Fountains—each 1-16 inch jet	6.00
Fountains—each 1-8 inch jet	10.00
Fountains—each 1-4 inch jet	20.00
Fountains—each 3-8 inch jet	30.00
Fountains—each 1-2 inch jet	50.00
Fountains—each 3-4 inch jet	80.00
Fountains—soda or mineral water—each........	10.00
Green grocery and fish stand, each.............	5.00
Hotel or house of private entertainment.........	5.00
And for each bedroom (used or not)	1.00
Baths and water closets same as public rates.	
Hacks, carriages, hearses, omnibuses, etc., each...	4.50
Horses or mules, each	1.25
Hose sprinkling, including yard and sidewalk, each lot of thirty feet front or less	3.50
Each additional foot over 30 feet front..........	.05

Hose sprinkling, including yard, sidewalk and one-
half of road bed, each 30 feet front or less.... 8.00
Each additional foot over 30 feet front.......... .08
No nozzle to be more than 1-8 inch orifice.
Yard or street sprinkling not to exceed 3 hours per
day for any one lot. Lawn sprinklers or
jets will be charged fountain rates. Locomo-
tives using city water, special rates.
Livery stables—each stall (used or not) .... .75
Lager beer, porter or soda bottling establishments,
one table 20.00
   Each additional table 10.00
Manufacturing mills, each 45.00
Mule or wagon lot 30.00
Milk depot or dairy 10.00
Office 4.50
Printing offices, each 10.00
   Printing offices using motors, special or water rates.
Private boarding house 5.00
And for each bedroom (used or not) 1.00
   Water closets and baths same as families.
Private bathtubs, each 3.50
Public bathtubs, each 9.00
Private water closets 3.00
Each additional water closet on premises........ 2.00
Public water closets, each 6.00
Private urinals, each 1.50
Public urinals, each ....$5.00 to 10.00
Private schools, each 5.00
Private carriages or buggies, each.............. 1.50
Public greenhouse or flower garden 25.00
Public greenhouse or conservatory 5.00
Public laundry 20.00
Public hall—with water fixtures accessible...... 10.00
Public hall—with water fixtures inaccessible..... 5.00
Photograph gallery 15.00
Plastering, per 100 square yards .... .10
Restaurants, each 15.00
Rectifying establishments 45.00
Railroad depots, each 100.00

Rolling mill, foundry, machine shop, factory, or stemmery, etc., where no more than 15 hands are employed 15.00
For each additional employee over fifteen....... .30
Store 10.00
Shop 5.00
Snack house or lunch counter 10.00
Spike machine, each 40.00
Storage warehouse, each 10.00
Soap factory ...:........................... 10.00
Stable, where wagons, drays or carts are kept for hire, for each horse or mule.................. 1.25
Stationary steam engine—for each estimated horse power boiler from one to ten................. 5.00
For each estimated horse power of boiler from ten to forty ....:.................. 3.00
For each estimated horse power of boiler over 40. 2.50
Street sprinkling—each cart of 250 gallons—per month 18.00
Or special rates.
Stone laid, per cubic yard..................... .02
Tobacco manufactory—for each employee........ .30
No charge per annum to be less than............ 15.00
Theater, opera house, etc., each 30.00
Warehouse—wholesale tobacco, etc. 30.00

Approximately 20 per cent of the total number of consumers are billed under flat rates, these rates varying, as will be noted, according to the number and kind of fixtures on the premises in the case of a domestic consumer and according to the kind of business carried on and the estimated amount of water consumed for various uses in the case of commercial consumers.

The city ordinances provide for the following general meter rates to be applied quarterly:

For 3,000 cubic feet or less—11 cents per 100 cubic feet.
From 3,100 to 4,000 cu. feet, inclusive, 10.5 cents per 100 cu. feet
From 4,100 to 4,500 cu. feet, inclusive, 10.0 cents per 100 cu. feet
From 4,600 to 5,000 cu. feet, inclusive, 9.9 cents per 100 cu. feet
From 5,100 to 5,500 cu. feet, inclusive, 9.8 cents per 100 cu. feet
From 5,600 to 6,000 cu. feet, inclusive, 9.7 cents per 100 cu. feet
From 6,100 to 6,500 cu. feet, inclusive, 9.6 cents per 100 cu. feet

From 6,600 to 7,000 cu. feet, inclusive, 9.5 cents per 100 cu. feet
From 7,100 to 7,500 cu. feet, inclusive, 9.4 cents per 100 cu. feet
From 7,600 to 8,000 cu. feet, inclusive, 9.3 cents per 100 cu. feet
From 8,100 to 8,500 cu. feet, inclusive, 9.2 cents per 100 cu. feet
From 8,600 to 9,000 cu. feet, inclusive, 9.1 cents per 100 cu. feet
From 9,100 to 9,500 cu. feet, inclusive, 9.0 cents per 100 cu. feet
From 9,600 to 10,000 cu. feet, inclusive, 8.9 cents per 100 cu. feet
From 10,000 to 10,500 cu. feet, inclusive, 8.8 cents per 100 cu. feet
From 10,600 to 11,000 cu. feet, inclusive, 8.7 cents per 100 cu. feet
From 11,100 to 11,500 cu. feet, inclusive, 8.6 cents per 100 cu. feet
From 11,600 to 12,000 cu. feet, inclusive, 8.5 cents per 100 cu. feet
From 12,100 to 12,500 cu. feet, inclusive, 8.4 cents per 100 cu. feet
From 12,600 to 13,000 cu. feet, inclusive, 8.3 cents per 100 cu. feet
From 13,100 to 13,500 cu. feet, inclusive, 8.2 cents per 100 cu. feet
From 13,600 to 14,000 cu. feet, inclusive, 8.1 cents per 100 cu. feet
From 14,100 to 14,500 cu. feet, inclusive, 8.0 cents per 100 cu. feet
From 14,600 to 15,000 cu. feet, inclusive, 7.9 cents per 100 cu. feet
From 15,100 to 15,500 cu. feet, inclusive, 7.8 cents per 100 cu. feet
From 15,600 to 16,000 cu. feet, inclusive, 7.7 cents per 100 cu. feet
From 16,100 to 16,500 cu. feet, inclusive, 7.6 cents per 100 cu. feet
From 16,600 to 17,000 cu. feet, inclusive, 7.5 cents per 100 cu. feet
From 17,100 to 17,500 cu. feet, inclusive, 7.4 cents per 100 cu. feet
From 17,600 to 18,000 cu. feet, inclusive, 7.3 cents per 100 cu. feet
From 18,100 to 18,500 cu. feet, inclusive, 7.2 cents per 100 cu. feet
From 18,600 to 19,000 cu. feet, inclusive, 7.1 cents per 100 cu. feet
From 19,100 to 19,500 cu. feet, inclusive, 7.0 cents per 100 cu. feet
From 19,600 to 20,000 cu. feet, inclusive, 6.9 cents per 100 cu. feet
From 20,100 to 20,500 cu. feet, inclusive, 6.8 cents per 100 cu. feet
From 20,600 to 21,000 cu. feet, inclusive, 6.7 cents per 100 cu. feet
From 21,000 to 21,500 cu. feet, inclusive, 6.6 cents per 100 cu. feet
From 21,600 to 22,000 cu. feet, inclusive, 6.5 cents per 100 cu. feet
From 22,100 to 23,000 cu. feet, inclusive, 6.4 cents per 100 cu. feet
From 23,100 to 24,000 cu. feet, inclusive, 6.3 cents per 100 cu. feet
From 24,100 to 25,000 cu. feet, inclusive, 6.2 cents per 100 cu. feet
From 25,100 to 26,000 cu. feet, inclusive, 6.1 cents per 100 cu. feet
From 26,100 to 27,000 cu. feet, inclusive, 6.0 cents per 100 cu. feet
From 27,100 to 28,000 cu. feet, inclusive, 5.9 cents per 100 cu. feet
From 28,100 to 29,000 cu. feet, inclusive, 5.8 cents per 100 cu. feet
From 29,100 to 30,000 cu. feet, inclusive, 5.7 cents per 100 cu. feet
From 30,100 to 31,000 cu. feet, inclusive, 5.6 cents per 100 cu. feet
From 31,100 to 32,000 cu. feet, inclusive, 5.5 cents per 100 cu. feet

From 32,100 to 33,500 cu. feet, inclusive, 5.4 cents per 100 cu. feet
From 32,600 to 35,000 cu. feet. inclusive, 5.3 cents per 100 cu. feet
From 35,100 to 36,500 cu. feet. inclusive, 5.2 cents per 100 cu. feet
From 36,600 to 38,000 cu. feet. inclusive, 5.1 cents per 100 cu. feet
From 38,100 to 39,500 cu. feet, inclusive, 5.0 cents per 100 cu. feet
From 39,600 to 41,000 cu. feet. inclusive, 4.9 cents per 100 cu. feet
From 41,100 to 42,500 cu. feet. inclusive, 4.8 cents per 100 cu. feet
From 42,600 to 44,000 cu. feet, inclusive. 4.7 cents per 100 cu. feet
From 44,100 to 45,500 cu. feet. inclusive, 4.6 cents per 100 cu. feet
From 45,600 to 47,000 cu. feet, inclusive. 4.5 cents per 100 cu. feet.
From 47,100 to 48,500 cu. feet. inclusive, 4.4 cents per 100 cu. feet
From 48,600 to 50,000 cu. feet. inclusive. 4.3 cents per 100 cu. feet
From 50,100 to 51,500 cu. feet, inclusive. 4.2 cents per 100 cu. feet
From 51,600 to 53,000 cu. feet, inclusive, 4.1 cents per 100 cu. feet
From 53,100 to 54,500 cu. feet. inclusive. 4.0 cents per 100 cu. feet
From 54,600 to 56,000 cu. feet. inclusive. 3.9 cents per 100 cu. feet
From 56,100 to 58,900 cu. feet, inclusive. 3.8 cents per 100 cu. feet
59,000 cubic feet and over, 3.75 cents per 100 cubic feet.

The application of these meter rates is limited in the case of the domestic user by minimum bill provisions varying according to the fixtures installed on the premises and also according to the number of consumers receiving service through the same meter. The ordinance provides that for all premises having one or more hydrants or faucets the minimum charge shall be $4 per year and for premises having one or more hydrants, faucets and closets or other fixtures, the minimum charge shall be $8 per year. These minimum bill provisions do not apply in the case of commercial and industrial consumers. The minimum charges which are payable in advance, entitle the consumer without extra charge to 10 cubic feet and 20 cubic feet of water per day, respectively. For all consumption in excess of this amount the meter rates given above are applied at the end of the quarter. The practical effect of this rule is to require the domestic consumer to pay for more water at the initial or maximum rate before receiving the benefit of the lower steps in the schedule than is the case with the commercial or industrial consumer. A domestic consumer paying a fixed minimum at $8 per year is required to take more than 4,800 cubic feet of water per quarter before receiving a lower rate than 11 cents per 100 cubic feet, while a commercial or industrial consumer secures the advantage of a rate lower than 11 cents when his consumption exceeds 3,000 cubic feet.

Aside from the above meter rates, special concessions are given to public hospitals, charitable institutions and churches, and to the American Locomotive Works. The institutions and churches pay at the rate of 3.75 cents per 100 cubic feet, while the American Locomotive Company is billed at 2.5 per 100 cubic feet. Free use of water is provided in the case of assemblies, "of whatever denomination, and used for religious services or public worship," and for use in cemeteries. The superintendent is allowed to grant free water permits or make special reductions in the minimum rate to indigent persons. Consumers living outside of the city limits are billed at the rate of 23.5 cents per 100 cubic feet.

An examination of the consumer records for flat rate service shows that these rates apply largely to the poorest class of domestic consumers, although there are a considerable number of commercial and industrial consumers who are billed at those rates.

A study of the metered water consumption and billings for the last quarter of 1916 was made by the water department at the request of the administrative board. This study shows that of a total of 22,656 billings, 16,879, or about 75 per cent. of the total, were only for amounts represented by the minimum bills. The remainder, or about 25 per cent. of the total, were rendered to consumers paying in excess of the minimum charge. The number of bills was taken from the above study and is shown in summary form below:

	Number of Bills Rendered.	Per Cent.
Minimum bill consumers	16,879	74.5
Consumers using water in excess of minimum	5,724	25.2
Charitable institutions	38	.2
Non-resident consumers	15	.1
Total	22,656	100.0

The minimum bill consumers are shown in the water department compilation to be distributed as follows:

Quarterly Minimum Rates.	Number of Billings.	Per Cent.
$ 0.75	275	1.6
. 1.00	294	1.7
2.00	16,029	95.0
3.00	65	.4
4.00	184	1.1
5.00	6)	
6.00	12)	
8.00	2)	
10.00	1}	.2
12.00	7)	
12.50	2)	
14.00	1)	
0.11	1)	
Total.........	16,879	100.0

The quarterly minimum of 75 cents shown above applied to indigent persons, while the minimum charges in excess of $2.00 apply to premises where more than one consumer secures water from the same service pipe. The compilation shows that of the 75 per cent. of the total number of bills which were rendered under the minimum bill provisions of the ordinance, 95 per cent. were made out to consumers paying $2.00 per quarter.

A summary of the number of billings and the consumption of those domestic and commercial consumers who use water in excess of the amount allowed under the minimum bills and of the commercial, industrial and other consumers who receive service under the meter rates and also to whom the minimum bill provisions do not apply, is given below:

Classification of Consumers.	Number of Billings.	Consumption in Cu. Ft.
Domestic and commercial:		
$ 0.75 minimum per quarter and excess.	31	94,100
1.00 minimum per quarter and excess.	32	98,400
2.00 minimum per quarter and excess.	5,452	23,920,600
3.00 minimum per quarter and excess.	5	29,900
4.00 minimum per quarter and excess.	40	303,400
5.00 minimum per quarter and excess.	1	5,200
6.00 minimum per quarter and excess.	7	83,200
8.00 minimum per quarter and excess.	2	30,200
12.00 minimum per quarter and excess.	5	115,600
16.00 minimum per quarter and excess.	2	101,500
Total domestic and commercial......	5,577	24,782,100
Industrial and miscellaneous:		
Industrial	147	7,364,100
Non-resident	15	118,200
Charitable institutions, etc.	38	623,400
Total industrial and miscellaneous...	200	8,105,700
Grand total	5,777	32,887,800

The above summary shows that by far the largest percentage of the total number of billings occurs in the domestic and commercial group under the sub-divisional group of $2.00 minimum per quarter and excess. While this class of consumers also consumes the largest amount of water, there is a considerable amount used by the comparatively few large industrial consumers.

For the purpose of further analyzing these statistics another summary has been made showing the number of billings and the amount of consumption by rate groups. Since the meter rates are many in number, the table included below shows this information for rate groups only:

Range of Rates In Cents Per 100 Cu. Ft.	Number of Billings.	Per Cent.	Consumption In Cu. Ft.	Per Cent.
11	4,664	80.8	12,589,000	38.2
10 to 10.9	318	5.5	1,762,700	5.4
9 to 9.9	374	6.5	3,059,800	9.3
8 to 8.9	98	1.7	1,319,300	4.0
7 to 7.9	54	.9	998,500	3.0
6 to 6.9	66	1.1	1,629,400	4.9
5 to 5.9	46	.8	1,544,100	4.7
4 to 4.9	23	.4	1,080,700	3.3
3.75 to 3.9	80	1.4	7,419,900	22.6
2.5 American Loc. Co.	1)		742,800	2.3
23.5 Non-residents	15}	.9	118,200	.4
3.75 Charitable Inst....	28)		623,400	1.9
	5,777	100.0	32,887,800	100.0

The above table shows that a large percentage of the consumers using water in excess of the amount measured by the minimum charge pay for the same at the 11 cent rate. From the point of view of consumption, however, only about 38 per cent. is paid for at this rate. The larger consumers, such as industrial establishments, consume relatively more water and pay correspondingly lower average rates.

Due to the fact that the meter rates are applied differently to domestic and to industrial consumers an analysis has been prepared for the last quarter of 1916 showing the distribution of consumption and billings according to various consumption groups. The consumption and billings of charitable institutions has been eliminated from this analysis. The information referred to is shown in the following table, the data of which pertains only to consumers paying more than the minimum bill:

Consumption Classification.	Number of Billings.	Per Cent.	Consumption In Cubic Ft.	Per Cent.
0 to 5,000 cu. ft.	4,733	82.5	12,867,800	39.8
5,100 to 10,000 cu. ft.	582	10.1	3,968,900	12.3
10,100 to 15,000 cu. ft.	134	2.3	1,618,200	5.0
15,100 to 20,000 cu. ft.	60	1.1	1,041,500	3.2
20,100 to 25,000 cu. ft.	52	.9	1,182,500	3.7
25,100 to 30,000 cu. ft.	37	.6	1,007,400	3.1
30,100 to 40,000 cu. ft.	38	.7	1,305,000	4.0
40,100 to 50,000 cu. ft.	16	.3	693,600	2.2
50,100 to 60,000 cu. ft.	22	.4	1,229,100	3.8
60,100 to 70,000 cu. ft.	18	.3	1,175,200	3.6
70,100 to 75,000 cu. ft.	3)		219,300	.7
75,100 to 80,000 cu. ft.	2)		152,700	.5
80,100 to 90,000 cu. ft.	15)		1,254,900	3.9
90,100 to 100,000 cu. ft.	3)		287,500	.9
100,100 to 150,000 cu. ft.	20}	.8	2,254,200	7.0
150,100 to 200,000 cu. ft.	1)		157,500	.5
200,100 to 300,000 cu. ft.	1)		211,900	.7
All over 300,000 cu. ft.	2)		1,637,200	5.1
Total	5,739	100.0	32,264,400	100.0

From the above table it appears that over 80 per cent of the billings analyzed were for consumptions of less than 5,000 cubic feet per quarter, while only approximately 40 per cent of the total consumption was represented by this classification grouping.

Since the study upon which the analyses shown above are based obtains for one-quarter of the year, only some allowance must be made for the seasonal variation in consumption. An examination of the consumer records of the department shows that such variation is apt to be irregular in the case of the large consumers and quite the opposite in the case of domestic consumers. Without a record of the total annual consumption, which the department does not at present keep. it is impossible to determine with accuracy the influence of such seasonal variations upon the percentage distribution of the billings and consumption. Based upon an examination of the records of over 2,000 consumers for a full year period it appears that the maximum allowance for consumption variation would not materially affect the percentage distribution shown in the above tables.

The foregoing discussion relates to flat rates and meter rates for domestic, commercial and industrial uses of water. For public and charitable uses the department makes an estimate of the amount of revenue which would be derived were the regular meter rates applied and includes this, except in certain cases provided for by ordinance, as memorandum information in its annual report. For fire protection service this memorandum account provides rentals at $25 per hydrant per year.

Radical changes should be made in the rates charged for service by the water department. Comments on the undesirable nature of flat rates for water are unnecessary. Such rates lead to waste of water, especially among domestic consumers, and for commercial consumers there is yet to be found a reliable basis for estimating the maximum consumption upon which a reasonable flat rate could be based. The water department has recognized the desirability of universal metered service, but the number of flat rate consumers which can be transferred annually to the meter basis is limited, since by far the greater part of the yearly appropriation for new meters is required for the construction made necessary by the taking on of additional consumers. A systematic policy of elimination of all flat rate service should be adopted by the department.

The present meter rates are not only too numerous, but are also discriminatory and obsolete in form. As will be noted from the schedule, there are at the present time 64 of these meter rates in force, each rate depending upon quantity consumed for its assessment. The application of these quantity rates is different in the case of domestic and commercial, and industrial consumers, the former class being precluded to a considerable extent from securing the advantages of the lower steps in the meter rate schedule by the interpretation which the water department has given to the minimum bill provision in the ordinance. It is also possible at present for a consumer to secure a smaller aggregate bill by increasing his consumption and in this respect the rate schedule leads to waste of water, but in justice to the department it must be stated that it was for the purpose of minimizing this recognized incentive to waste that the numerous steps in the present schedule and the system of monthly inspections were adopted.

Rate schedules of the regressive type in the application of which the range of consumption determines a uniform rate to be assessed for the entire amount of service used are now generally considered by public utility commissions as unreasonably discriminatory. This incentive to waste the service has been recognized by the utilities themselves and such schedules of the type mentioned as are still in force are rapidly being discontinued.

As a substitute for the present meter rate schedule there should be adopted a schedule of the increment type which provides for the payment for service through each rate step, thus preserving the incentive to make free use of the service by the earning of a lower average rate for increased consumption, but at the same time eliminating the objectionable waste feature of schedules such as are now in force. The billings and consumption as shown above have been analyzed to determine the application of an increment rate to the water consumers in Richmond. This analysis by increment steps follows:

Classification of Consumption.	Number of Cubic Feet To Be Billed At Each Increment Step.	Per Cent of Total
First 5,000 cubic feet....	17,897,800	55.5
Next 5,000 cubic feet....	3,178,900	9.8
Next 5,000 cubic feet....	1,728,200	5.3
Next 5,000 cubic feet....	1,291,500	4.0
Next 5,000 cubic feet....	1,032,500	3.2
Next 5,000 cubic feet....	787,400	2.4
Next 10,000 cubic feet....	1,195,000	3.7
Next 10,000 cubic feet....	923,600	2.9
Next 10,000 cubic feet....	779,100	2.4
Next 10,000 cubic feet....	565,200	1.8
Next 5,000 cubic feet....	229,300	.7
Next 5,000 cubic feet....	212,700	.7
Next 10,000 cubic feet....	324,900	1.0
Next 10,000 cubic feet....	257,500	.8
Next 50,000 cubic feet....	454,200	1.4
Next 50,000 cubic feet....	157,590	.5
Next 100,000 cubic feet....	211,900	.7
Over 300,000 cubic feet....	1,037,200	3.2
Total	32,264,400	100.0

This compilation excludes sales to charitable and similar institutions, but includes such sales for the non-resident consumer class. It shows that about 55 per cent. of the consumption in any increment schedule would be paid for at the rate obtaining for the first 5,000 cubic feet. The succeeding increment steps show much smaller percentages of total consumption to be included within their range.

Before determining upon the number of steps to be included in any increment rate schedule, the maximum and minimum rates. and the extent to which detailed classification is desirable should be decided upon. These matters are of considerable importance in the case of the Richmond water department, because of the numerous meter rates now in force and because of the large differential between the maximum and minimum rate assessed. The present rates for consumers living in Richmond range from 11 cents per 100 cubic feet to 2.5 cents for the same quantity. while the non-resident rate is 23.5 cents per 100 cubic feet.

The application of the maximum rate is at present limited by the assessment of the minimum bill. Where the minimum bill is applied to consumptions. which at the 11 cent rate would bring about a monthly charge less than such minimum, the maximum rate per 100 cubic feet of water used is automatically increased. For example, a customer having a fixed minimum bill of $2 per quarter and consuming on the average only 1,000 cubic feet per quarter pays in effect a rate of 20 cents per 100 cubic feet. At the 11 cent or maximum rate this customer would only pay $1.10 per quarter. The application of the principle of a minimum bill and a maximum rate in the manner indicated is not to be considered as objectionable. It is merely noted for the purpose of showing the effect which the established minimum bill has upon the maximum rate which should be adopted. At the present time such a large proportion of the total number of consumers pay a fixed minimum bill of $2 that it would appear that either a slight reduction or increase in the maximum rate would not appreciably affect their monthly bills. The minimum bill and maximum rate should be so balanced in their application to water consumers that a free but not wasteful use of the water would be encouraged.

Since such a large proportion of the total consumers pay no more than the minimum bill per quarter. the question immediately arises as to its reasonableness. While there are a number of minimum bills in cities throughout the country. which are as high or even higher than those assessed in Richmond. there are also a greater number which are considerably lower. From the public policy point of view it would seem desirable for the department to direct all future energy toward the reduction of the minimum bill.

The minimum rate of an increment schedule for a water plant operated by hydraulic and electric power as this plant is. should be determined by the reduced costs which are occasioned by the large consumption of those customers, the nature of whose use with respect to demand and quantity entitles them to low average rates. Since the expenses of the water department are largely made up of fixed charges it follows that the output cost of supplying additional consumption must be small.

From a study of these conditions at Richmond it appears desirable to slightly decrease the present maximum rate. to reduce the minimum bill. and to provide for a small increase in the minimum rate.

In order to illustrate the above matters more concretely. an increment schedule incorporating the above principles is applied below to the consumption of all consumers who, on the basis of the analysis mentioned, used more water than the allowance under the minimum bills. This schedule is to be considered merely as illustrative, the consumption figures on which it is based not having been checked against the records: .

SCHEDULE	Number of Cubic Feet	Revenue Derived
First 20.000 cu. ft per quarter at 10c per 100 cu. ft.........	24.096.400	$24.096.40
Next 20.000 " " at 8c " "	3.014.800	2.411 92
Next 20 000 " " at 6c " "	1.702.700	1.021 62
Next 40.000 " " at 4 5c. " "	1.589.600	715 32
Over 100.000 " " at 3c. " "	1.860 600	558 24
Total....	32.264.400	$28 808 50

This schedule would increase the present revenue of the water department and would thus furnish some basis for a small reduction in the minimum bill. The schedule also has the advantage of simplicity. In connection with the adoption of a schedule of this character it would be advisable to apply the rates to both domestic and industrial consumers alike, and to discontinue the present practice of collecting the minimum bill in advance.

Gas Department.

In the gas department a uniform meter rate of 80 cents per 1.000 cubic feet is now applied, a reduction in rates of 10 cents per 1.000 cubic feet having been made in 1916. The records of the department show that for the last year the average heating value of the gas delivered at this rate was 609.8 B. T. U.. and the average illuminating power of the gas was 19.86 candles. In addition to the uniform meter rate referred to an annual minimum bill provision has been adopted by the department, which minimum requirement is graduated according to the size of the meter in the manner shown below:

3 light meter	2,500 cubic feet per annum
5 light meter	3,000 cubic feet per annum
10 light meter	4,000 cubic feet per annum
20 light meter	5,000 cubic feet per annum
30 light meter	6,000 cubic feet per annum
45 light meter	8,000 cubic feet per annum
60 light meter	10,000 cubic feet per annum
100 light meter	15,000 cubic feet per · annum
200 light meter	30,000 cubic feet per annum
500 light meter	68,000 cubic feet per annum

From an examination of the consumer records of the gas department covering two out of a total of four districts, and extending over two typical months of the year a percentage distribution of billings and consumption was arrived at. This distribution when applied ti the total consumption for the year, shows the following results:

Consumption Classification.	Number of Billings.	Per Cent.	Consumption In Cu Ft.	Per Cent.
0 to 1,000 cu. ft.	27,010	14.4	2,552,500	.4
1,100 to 2,000 cu. ft.	35,076	18.7	49,135,500	7.7
2,100 to 3,000 cu. ft.	35,076	18.7	77,851,100	12.2
3,100 to 4,000 cu. ft.	28,886	15.4	89,337,300	14.0
4,100 to 5,000 cu. ft.	20,633	11.0	82,318,000	12.9
5,100 to 6,000 cu. ft.	13,318	7.1	63,174,200	9.9
6,100 to 7,000 cu. ft.	7,690	4.1	45,306,800	7.1
7,100 to 8,000 cu. ft.	5,252	2.8	35,734,900	5.6
8,100 to 9,000 cu. ft.	3,751	2.0	28,715,600	4.5
9,100 to 10,000 cu. ft.	2,438	1.3	21,696,200	3.4
10,100 to 15,000 cu. ft.	4,877	2.6	51,049,900	8.0
15,100 to 20,000 cu. ft.	1,688	.9	24,886,800	3.9
20,100 to 25,000 cu. ft.	563	.3	10,210,000	1.6
25,100 to 50,000 cu. ft.	750	.4	22,972,500	3.6
50,100 to 75,000 cu. ft.)			14,676,800	2.3
75,100 to 100,000 cu. ft. }	564	.3	4,466,900	.7
100,100 to 200,000 cu. ft.)			11,486,200	1.8
All over 200,000 cu. ft.)			2,552,500	.4
Total	187,572	100.00	638,123,700	100.0

The above table shows that less than 5 per cent. of the total number of billings are for consumption of more than 10,000 cubic feet per month. On the other hand, about 22 per cent. of the gas sold is represented by this small percentage of billings. The billings for less than 5,000 cubic feet of gas per month make up 78 per cent. of the total number, while only 47 per cent. of the total consumption is sold to consumers represented by such billings. The relation of the average consumption per meter reading (3,400 cubic feet) to this distribution indicates that among the domestic or residence consumers, a liberal use of gas service has been made. The present rate is no doubt responsible in large measure for the high average consumption in the case of these consumers.

In order to determine more fully the relative development of the gas sales in Richmond a comparison has been made between such development and that in other cities in which gas utilities are operating under somewhat similar conditions. The following comparison is given:

	Meters per Mile of Main	Sales per Meter in Cubic Feet.	Sales per Mile of Main in Cu. Feet.	Inhabitants (White) per Meter	Inhabitants (White) per Mile of Main	Sales per Inhabitant (White) in Cubic Feet.
Atlanta	111	36,900	4,090 000	5 23	580	7,050
Baltimore	159	31,700	5,050,000	4 57	713	6,960
Birmingham	63	31,300	1,980,000	9 79	600	3,170
Memphis	88	26,000	2 280 000	5 72	504	4 550
New Orleans	87	33,400	2 880,000	8 65	744	3 840
Washington	117	43,400	5,060,000	4 10	476	10,500
Average of above	117	34,900	4,060 000	5 80	620	6,570
Richmond	111	39,200	4 370 000	5 92	660	6,620

The statistics of white population in the above table were determined by estimates based on the census conclusions for 1913. The comparative statistics show the present development of the Richmond gas utility and serve as an index to the possibility for future business expansion. The number of meters per mile of main and the number of cubic feet sold per mile of main show the extent of which the service in the aggregate is used; the number of cubic feet sold per meter and per inhabitant shows the extent to which the average individual consumer utilizes the service; the number of inhabitants per meter and per mile of main shows the extent to which the utility has made the service available. All of these factors must be taken into consideration in order to determine whether the development of the business is normal or otherwise. From the data given above, it appears that the Richmond gas development compares favorably with that of other large southern cities. Some improvement by solicitation and by rate differentiation could be made in the number of consumers, the amount of the unit sales, and the extent of the distribution system, but such suggestions are meant for the future and are not intended to reflect on the present state of development.

The department has pursued the policy of determining the advisability of making specific distribution system extensions by the probable revenue which would be derived from such extensions, and it has recently inaugurated the policy of soliciting the public for the purpose of securing the maximum number of consumers on the existing distribution systems. In order to secure the most economical operation of a gas system and the lowest rates for service the continuance of these policies should be encouraged.

The matters mentioned above have considerable bearing on the question of rates. Uniform meter rates have been generally applied by gas utilities for a number of years, but at the present time the tendency is toward a differential rate, customarily of the increment type. The effect of a uniform meter rate is to stimulate consumption among the smaller users of the service while the larger users are deprived of that incentive to use service over and above their minimum requirements, which an increment schedule provides. The granting of a lower rate for additional increments of consumption is justified economically on the ground that the greater the gas sales the lower the unit cost, and consequently lower rates are made possible. By substituting an increment rate for the present uniform rate and by continuing the present policy of the department, relative to the solicitation of gas consumers along the existing mains, it is believed that the sales per unit of distribution system can be increased without material additions to the present investment. Whether the increased sales which would result from the introduction of an increment rate would be large cannot be predicted without making a survey of the possible commercial and industrial uses for gas in Richmond, but no effort should be spared to secure greater average consumption, which development would be greatly stimulated by the adoption of the form of rate mentioned.

From the consumer analysis, which was made, the following distribution of consumption by increment steps is obtained:

Increment Steps In Cubic Feet per Month		Distribution of Consumption by Increment Groups	Per Cent of Total
First	1,000	139,749,200	21.9
Next	1,000	124,434,100	19.5
Next	1,000	93,166,100	14.6
Next	1,000	65,088,600	10.2
Next	1,000	44,030,500	6.9
Next	1,000	28,077,400	4.4
Next	1,000	21,058,100	3.3
Next	1,000	15,315,000	2.4
Next	1,000	11,486,200	1.8
Next	1,000	8,295,600	1.3
Next	5,000	23,610,600	3.7
Next	5,000	10,848,100	1.7
Next	5,000	6,381,200	1.0
Next	25,000	16,591,200	2.6
Next	25,000	7,657,500	1.2
Next	25,000	3,828,700	.6
Next	100,000	5,743,100	.9
Over	200,000	12,762,500	2.0
Total		638,237,100	100.0

If the present rate of 80 cents per 1,000 cubic feet is to be retained as a maximum rate, and if increased costs because of increased prices are taken into consideration, the minimum rate under an increment schedule cannot be less than 50 cents per 1,000 feet in accordance with the above table, approximately 85 per cent of the consumption would be paid for at this rate. Progressively lower rates on additional increments down to 50 cents per 1,000 cubic feet would not materially decrease the total revenues of the department.

The present minimum bill policy of the department should be changed from an annual to a monthly basis. Under the present provisions a consumer paying the minimum bill secures considerable service for less than its cost to the department. Further, due to the present penalties imposd for failure to pay promptly and also to the policy of the department not to render bills for consumptions of less than 1,000 cubic feet, many consumers find it necessary to inquire at the department office why they have failed to receive their monthly statements. In order to obviate the necessity for such inquiries a statement should be rendered to each consumer monthly whether such consumer uses less than the minimum allowance or more than this allowance. A minimum bill of 50 cents a consumer per month would increase the revenue of the department from $7,000 to $10,000 per year. A minimum rate varying with the size of the meter installation is in some respects more desirable than flat monthly minimum and could be made to yield about the same revenue as shown above.

Electric Department.

The electric utility has no schedule of rates, since it does not sell energy to commercial consumers. The charge of 3 cents per kilowatt-hour used in the various city departments is more in the nature of an insurance against waste than a measure of the cost of the service rendered. No rate has been established for service to the water department or for street lighting. In order to show the operating results of the electric department from year to year it would be advisable to establish rates for all service rendered. The amount of operating profit accruing to the department when properly determined would then be an index to its efficiency.

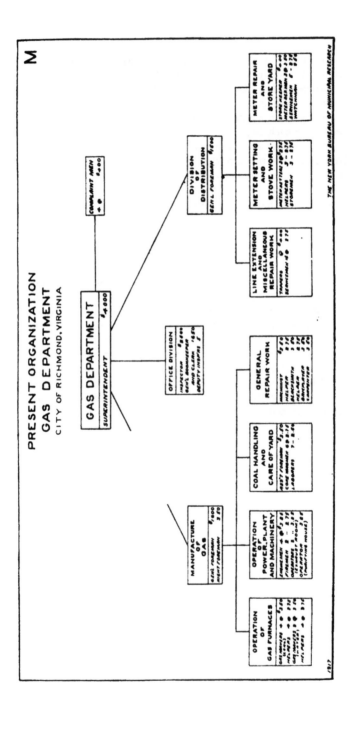

PRESENT ORGANIZATION
GAS DEPARTMENT
CITY OF RICHMOND, VIRGINIA

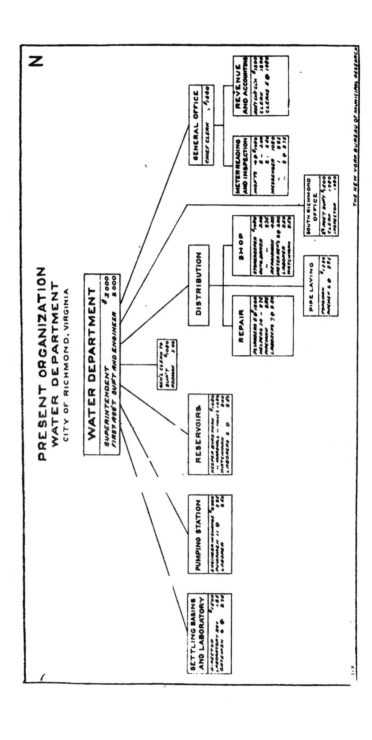

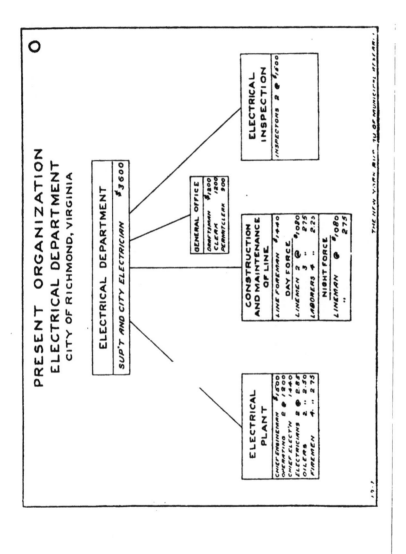

PRESENT ORGANIZATION
ELECTRICAL DEPARTMENT
CITY OF RICHMOND, VIRGINIA

ELECTRICAL DEPARTMENT $3600

SUPT AND CITY ELECTRICIAN

ELECTRICAL INSPECTION

INSPECTORS 2 @ $1,600

GENERAL OFFICE
DRAFTSMAN $1,200
CLERK 1200
PERMIT CLERK 900

CONSTRUCTION AND MAINTENANCE OF LINE

LINE FOREMAN $1,440

DAY FORCE
LINEMEN 2 @ $1,080
3 " 275
LABORERS 4 " 2.25

NIGHT FORCE
LINEMAN @ $1,080
" 275

ELECTRICAL PLANT

CHIEF ENGINEMAN $1,500
OPERATING 2 @ 1,200
CHIEF ELECT'N 1,440
ELECTRICIANS 2 @ 2.85
OILERS 2 " 2.50
FIREMEN 4 " 2.75

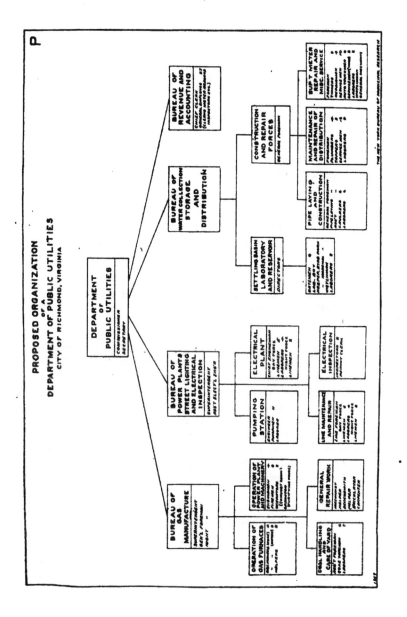

PROPOSED ORGANIZATION
of a
DEPARTMENT OF PUBLIC UTILITIES
CITY OF RICHMOND, VIRGINIA

IV—ENGINEERING.

Water Department.

The organization of the water department (shown in **the** accompanying chart) is divided functionally as follows:

> Settling basins and laboratory.
> Pumping Station.
> Reservoirs.
> Distribution.
> General Office.

South Richmond Water Works Department.

At the time of the annexation of South Richmond in 1913, the city took over the private water works serving that area and certain employees formerly connected with it. Since that time a' independent office of the department has been maintained in South Richmond with the following organization:

> Second assistant superintendent, $125 per month.
> Clerk, $90 per month.
> Inspector, $90 per month.

The work of the second assistant superintendent is concerned principally with maintenance and distribution on the south side of the city and the making and carrying on of main line extensions. The clerk and inspector keep records and render the miscellaneous service included in connection with the reading of meters and collection of revenues. The actual supervision of the distribution system and its needs is exercised by the first assistant superintendent and engineer of the department, and the needs of South Richmond in this matter do not justify additional supervision. A similar condition exists with respect to the work of the clerk and inspector in this office.

It is recommended that the office be discontinued and the position of second assistant superintendent be abolished.

Settling Basins and Laboratory.

The city of Richmond derives its water supply from the James River, a concrete diversion dam being constructed at the lower end of Williams' Island, Korah, Virginia. At the intake the water passes through gates to two settling basins, each with an approximate capacity of 75,000,000 gallons. The bottom of these basins is lined with concrete, while the banks are of rip-rap construction. They have not been cleaned, however, since their construction, and at the present time the capacity actually available for domestic use is only about 66 2-3 per cent of their capacity, due to the large amount of mud and silt which has accumulated in them during freshets in the river.

The Condition at Intake.

The conditions at the intake are not conducive to securing a satisfactory supply. Currents in the river adjacent to that structure tend to form sand bars and the lack of flow has resulted in a considerable growth of algae and other micro-organisms. The water has a distinctly unpleasant taste which can be attributed largely to these causes. Apparently the only means of correcting this condition is to secure a supply from a point farther upstream and it is understood that surveys have been made and plans prepared for the construction of intake works and a concrete conduit from Bosher's dam, a point seven miles above the present intake. This improvement is one that is greatly needed and funds should be provided for carrying it out at as early a date as possible.

Treatment Works.

At certain times of the year the water of the James River is high in turbidity, making it necessary to treat it with alum in order to remove the matter held in suspension. The raw water passes from the settling basins to alum tanks.

Alum Tanks.

The alum solution is prepared in two alum tanks each with a capacity of about 5,000 gallons. The alum is hoisted in barrels to a loading platform by means of a hand-operated chain hoist, and dumped into the tanks by hand. The tanks are filled with water from a six-inch line from the pumping station, although a 7 H. P. gasoline engine operating a centrifugal pump is provided for emergency use. A crude device is used for stirring the solutions and considerable difficulty is experienced in securing uniformity in the mixture. At the time the inspection was made the gates of the coagulation basins were leaking and the general condition of the settling basins' banks and grounds showed need of maintenance

Coagulation Basins.

The coagulation basins have a rated capacity of **fourteen and fifteen** million gallons each, but at the time inspection was made the available capacity was placed at eleven and a half and twelve and a half million gallons, respectively, for the two basins, due to the precipitated material and silt in the bottom.

Good practice demands that basins such as these should be cleaned at least once during each three months, and these basins have not been cleaned sinc October, 1916. Neglect to provide funds for work of this character is reflected in the poor quality of the water supplied to the citizens.

While this report was being prepared the water in the coagulation basins was found to be in such condition as to require immediate action, and the cleaning of the basins was authorized by the administrative board.

Purification Treatment.

The settled water passes from the coagulation basins to a 42 inch concrete conduit, at the upper end of which is provided apparatus for chlorinating the supply. The equipment for this purpose consists of two Wallace & Tierman units, one being held in reserve. The apparatus is automatic in operation, being equipped with intensifier and compensating valve, thus insuring a fairly uniform flow.

Organization.

The force employed at the settling basins includes:

> Director of settling basins and laboratory, $1.500.
> Laboratory boy at $1.25 per day.
> Six gatemen at $2.75 per day.

The director of the settling basin is also the chemist and bacteriologist in charge of the laboratory. In addition to his work at the settling basins he makes periodic inspections of the watershed to a point twenty-two miles above the intake works.

The gatemen are employed in operating the gates at the treatment works, in the preparation of the alum solution, and on miscellaneous work about the plant. They work twenty-four hour shifts, three men to a shift, every day in the year. This is a very undesirable practice and should be discontinued.

Laboratory.

The laboratory is well equipped for making the necessary chemical and bacteriological examinations of the water supply. Samples of the raw and treated water are tested daily; the latter include samples from the reservoir at Byrd Park and a point on the distribution system. The chemical tests are made for turbidity, color, alkalinity, the presence of carbon dioxide and also the oxygen content. Periodic tests are also made to determine the presence of sulphate, the latter serving as a means of indicating the presence of trade waste. The customary bacterial analyses are made of all samples taken.

The condition of the water at the time of survey was particularly bad, due to excessive rainfall and high turbidity, so it would be unfair to make such conditions the basis for any general statement. Nevertheless, the city of Richmond must be brought to a realization that its present water supply is unsafe. Bacillus coli is present in practically all the raw water, and to a very considerable extent in spite of the chlorine treatment presumptive tests indicate its presence in the clear water. Such conditions constitute a distinct hazard to the community.

The presence of this bacillus indicates the contamination of the water supply and the possible presence in that supply of the bacilli of typhoid and other intestinal diseases. The experience of many cities throughout the country has shown that where bacillus coli is present in the water supply, the most satisfactory manner of relieving the conditions is by mechanical filtration of the water subsequent to its coagulation treatment. In the case of Richmond the importance of this cannot be over-emphasized if the welfare of the community is to be adequately safeguarded, and steps should be taken at as early a date as possible to provide funds for the construction of the necessary mechanical filter plant.

Clear Water Conduit.

The clear water passes through a 42-inch concrete conduit from the treatment works to the pumping station. This conduit is located adjacent to the Chesapeake & Ohio railroad right of way and for the greater portion of its length is without protective covering of any kind. At certain points there is considerable hazard of injury to this conduit from possible freight wreck or other cause.

The expense involved of rip-rapping the bank at these points sufficiently to provide a protective mat would not be excessive and it is urged that this work be authorized at as early a date as possible. The mere fact that in the event of a break in the conduit the pumping station might pump directly from the canal into the mains is not particularly reassuring when it is conceded that practically all the raw water in the canal is contaminated with bacillus coli.

Pumping Station.

The pumping station is operated partly by water power taken from the James River and Kanawha Canal and partly by electric current obtained from the city lighting plant.

Water Power Pumping Equipment.

The pumping equipment includes three Poole pumps, each operated by Leffel undershot 160 H. P. turbines. The rated capacity of each unit is 3,000,000 gallons per day, but under present conditions their output is somewhat greater.

In connection with the water power equipment there is an auxiliary steam plant consisting of two Babcock & Wilcox boilers supplying steam to a 200 H. P. S. Morgan Smith engine with Lombardy governor, and in addition there is a 200 H. P. General Electric Company's A C generator for generating electric current.

Electric Pumping Units.

The electric pumping units which are located in a separate building include 2 Westinghouse 200 H.P. 3,500,00 volt 60 cycle 3-phase, A C induction motors, operated at 880 r. p. m. direct connected to Jeansville Iron Works' three stage pumps with capacity of 2,000 gallons per minute when operated against 290 foot head. These pumps have ten inch sections with sixteen inch discharge. Each pump has a rated capacity of three million gallons per day.

These two units supply water to the high service section of the distribution system. A contract has been awarded for a Cameron pump with capacity of five million gallons per day to be used as a booster on the high service system.

In addition, there are four other units, each comprising a 200 H. P. Western Electric induction motor of the same type as previously noted, direct connected to a De Laval two stage centrifugal pumps, each with a capacity of 4,000,000 gallons per day pumping against a 50 foot head, these pumps having twelve inch suctions and twelve inch discharge. Independent Venturi meters are placed on each line. There are also three transformers designed to increase the voltage from 2,300 to 3,500 volts when the generator at the water power station is operated.

This pumping plant includes a machine shop and blacksmith shop. The equipment is adequate for all ordinary repairs.

Pumping Plant Organization.

The organization at the pumping plant includes:

> Engineer in charge, $2,000.
> 11 pump men, at $3.25 per day.
> 1 laborer, at $2.50 per day.

In addition to operating the machinery about the plant, the pump men are employed in miscellaneous construction and repair work and in the care of the grounds. They work twenty-four hour shifts, five men to the shift, one pump man who is a superannuated employee and the laborer about the plant being employed on the day shift alone.

The policy followed with respect to hours of employment of the force at the pumping plant and the character of the force is open to criticism. The operation of a plant such as the one under consideration is, under ordinary conditions, of such a purely routine character as to minimize the force required to operate it. It is recommended that the employment of men on twenty-four hour shifts be discontinued and that the plant be operated on two ten-hour shifts, the shifts at the hydraulic and electric pump houses to overlap so as to permit one pump man to cover the intervening four-hour shift at each plant. The force required under normal operating conditions would include:

> 5 pump men at $3.25 per day.
> 3 laborers, at $2.50 per day, day shift.

Compared with present operating conditions which include continuous employment every day in the year, the proposed organization would effect a saving of approximately $5,900. Provision should be made, however, for rest day and vacations for the men, and this would increase the cost for labor approximately 15 per cent., thus reducing the possible annual saving to approximately $4,500.

It should be noted that while the administration of this plant is nominally under the superintendent of water, the actual responsibility for the operation of all electrical equipment is vested in the superintendent of the lighting plant.

In connection with the operation of the pumping plant, attention is called to the desirability of maintaining a uniform pumping rate in place of varying it, as at present, in order to maintain a constant head at the Byrd Park reservoir. If this constant rate were maintained, it would simplify the operation of the congulation basin and treatment works, and secure a better quality of water through longer sedimentation.

Condition of Plant and Grounds.

The general condition of the buildings and grounds at the pumping plant is commendable. Considerable skill has been exercised in beautifying and improving the grounds which are adjacent to a park boulevard of the city.

Records and Reports.

There is no satisfactory control exercised in the matter of records and reports over the operation of this plant. The actual amount of water pumped at the electrical plant is determined from the Venturi meter charts by the engineer in charge of the plant. At the water power plant the amount pumped is determined by periodic measurements of the speed at which the pumps are operating. No tests are made to determine the efficiency of the plant operation, an arbitrary allowance being made for slippage. There is no record kept of the cost of repairs at the plant.

The existing laxity in the above respect is open to serious criticism. Complete records of the operation of the plant and the nature and cost of repairs should be kept. In order to accomplish this suitable reporting forms should be prepared and an adequate control system devised.

There appears to be no justification for a continuation of the present anomalous division of responsibility over the operation of the plant between the superintendent of water and the superintendent of the electric plant. It is recommended that the entire operation of the pumping plant be placed under the supervision of the superintendent of the electric department.

Undeveloped Power at Pumping Station.

It should be noted that there is available at the pumping plant in addition to the water used to operate the water-driven pumps, undeveloped power amounting to approximately 850 H. P. Consideration should be given to the future development of this available power for pumping purposes, but there does not appear to be any necessity for such action at present.

Division of Storage and Distribution.

The distribution system includes three separate services, termed high, intermediate and low service. Each of these services supplies water to a definite area of the city, but they are all connected up to permit supplying water from each of the higher services to the lower ones, if desired.

High Service.

The high service is supplied from a standpipe with a capacity of 4,000,000 gallons, located in Byrd Park athletic field. This service supplies the west end of the city, which is a residential district of from 30,000 to 35,000 population. At the time of the survey the structural work of the standpipe was badly in need of painting. There are evidences of progressive deterioration in the steel work and the general condition of the structure requires immediate attention. It is important to note in this connection that as far back as 1913 the superintendent of the city water works called attention to the need for painting the structure. Failure to provide funds for maintenance of this character is evidence of false economy that cannot be too severely criticized.

Intermediate Service.

The intermediate service is supplied from the Byrd Park reservoir. This reservoir comprises two rectangular basins with a total capacity of about 46,000,000 gallons. It supplies water to the major portion of the city, including a population of approximately 88,000. The reservoir and grounds surrounding it are well kept up. The force employed includes:

> 1 keeper, salary $90 per month.
> 1 laborer, $2.50 per day.
> 1 night watchman, salary $70 per month.

Low Service.

The low service is supplied from Marshall reservoir, which has a storage capacity of 10,000,000 gallons. The area supplied from this reservoir includes the lower section of the city, consisting largely of manufacturing and low class, congested residential districts, and a part of South Richmond.

There is considerable question as to the desirability of continuing the operation of this reservoir as a part of the distribution system. The area which derives its supply from this reservoir could be equally well served by the intermediate service, and without the loss of head which exists at present. Furthermore, the storage capacity of the Marshall reservoir is not sufficient to constitute a factor in the reserve water supply of the city. It is suggested that consideration be given to the matter of abandoning the Marshall reservoir and either selling the property it now occupies or utilizing it for some other purpose.

Force Employed at Marshall Reservoir.

The force employed at this reservoir includes:

1 keeper. who receives $90 per month and a house.
1 laborer at $2.50 per day.

Attention is called to the obvious discrepancy between the compensation received by the keeper of Marshall reservoir and the one at Byrd Park reservoir. The duties of the keeper at Byrd Park reservoir are decidedly more arduous than those required of the keeper of Marshall reservoir. If this reservoir is to be continued in service, the keeper should be called upon either to pay a fair rental to the city for the occupancy of the house located on the reservoir grounds. or else his compensation should be fixed with due regard to the value of this perquisite received by him.

Furthermore, the extent of the work involved in the care of the grounds and attending to the routine duties connected with Marshall reservoir do not justify the continuous employment of a laborer at this place. It is recommended that provision be made for temporary employment not over six months of the year to make such repairs as are required. and aid in the maintenance of the grounds.

Adequacy of the Distribution System.

The present distribution system supplying water to the city of Richmond is defective in the following respects:

An insufficient number of large supply mains exist both from the pumping plant and from Byrd Park reservoir.

Inadequate Size of Service Lines in Certain Sections of the City.

As a result of these conditions the available pressures and supply of water for fire purposes is entirely inadequate. An in-

\vestigation of hydrant pressures at various points in the city disclosed pressures as low as fifteen pounds at the hydrant. At such points where one outlet of the nearest adjacent hydrant was opened. the discharge a each hydant was insufficient to supply the ordinary type of fire engine, thus precluding the use of more than one line of hose from these hydrants in the event of fire.

It is not intended to intimate that such conditions prevail throughout the entire city, nor is it wise in the scope of this report to enter into a detailed discussion of them or to make specific recommendations in respect to the necessary construction to correct them. It should be emphasized, however, that conditions such as have been noted exist to a sufficient degree throughout the city to constitute a serious fire hazard to the community.

Contributing Causes for Existing Condition.

The two factors which have most seriously affected the work of water department in connection with the development of the distribution system, and which have largely contributed to the present unsatisfactory conditions, are:

Lack of a well defined program of extension work.
Inadequacy of funds for new construction.

The present water supply distribution system of Richmond, like many other cities of this country, is the result of haphazard expansion to meet the rapidly increasing demands of the community rather than the development of a well defined scheme for furnishing an adequate supply to the city as a whole. As a result, the city now faces the necessity of laying a considerable mileage of large water mains to serve as the basis for a co-ordinated system adequate to serve the city even for the immediate future. The complexity of the problem has been increased by reason of the recent acquisition of the outlying districts of the city by annexation and the necessity for tying in the present distribution eystems in those districts with the system serving the rest of the city.

Recommended Policy.

In view of the conditions noted. it is essential that the city government take the following action:

1—Authorize the preparation of plans and estimates of cost of a water distribution system adequate to serve the entire city. In this connection it is urged that the water department secure the co-operation of the city engineer's department in that work.

2—The preparation of a work program. Such a program should indicate the amount to be expended each year to extend possibly over several years.

Obviously the successful carrying out of any plan designed to secure a safe and adequate water supply for the city of Richmond will depend upon the appropriation of adequate funds. Such funds should be provided either out of a bond issue or by setting aside a definite percentage of the city's tax levy each year, rather than by leaving the amount to be appropriated annually for water supply purposes to the administrative board as at present. Furthermore, after a definite plan of improvement has been decided upon, deviation from this plan or diversion of funds provided for carrying it out should not be permitted except in the case of emergency affecting the whole city's interest.

Division of Construction and Maintnance.

The division of construction and maintenance is concerned with the construction of all extensions to the distribution system, the placing of house connections, the making of repairs to the distribution system and all work incidental to the setting, testing and repairing of meters. The headquarters of the force connected with this division are located at Canal and Madison streets, where the water department maintains a storeyard and meter repair shop. The division forces include:

Pipe-laying force.
Repair force.
Storeyard and meter testing force.

Organization of Pipe-Laying Force.

All pipe-laying incidental to making extensions to the water distribution system is done by city forces. The necessary excavation and back filling of trenches in connection with that work is carried out under an annual contract entered into by the city for that class of work. At the time the study of the water department was made the pipe-laying force included:

1 foreman, $110 per month.
7 pipemen, $2.85 per day.

No laborers are permanently connected with this force, but are hired as needed. One pipe man is employed practically in the inspection of and making minor repairs to valves and fire hydrants on the distribution system. This latter practice is commendable. The pipe-laying force is also employed in making repairs of breaks in the distribution system.

During the first six months of 1917, water main extension was curtailed owing to lack of funds provided for this class of work. Up to July 31st there were laid in six different localities 18,435 feet of pipe, principally twelve inch and below. At the time the study of the department was made the pipe-laying force was principally engaged in taking up and relaying six inch pipe that had been replaced by pipe of a large size. Obviously the demands of this amount of work would not justify the continuous employment of a force of the size noted, augmented as it would be from time to time by additional laborers. No specific recommendations are made, however, relating to the reduction of the force, as it is felt that it is not excessive to meet normal needs of the city in the matter of water main extension. and also due to the advantages that accrue to the city from maintaining a relatively permanent organization for pipe-laying work.

In this connection it is desired to call attention to the duplication of force and equipment existing in the departments of water and gas in the matter of pipe-laying and repair work, and consideration is given elsewhere in this report to economies that could be effected by a central administration of those activities.

Pipe-Laying Policy.

Water mains are laid when practicable six feet south and west of the center line of the street and at a minimum depth of three feet below the surface.

There is no shop or field testing of pipe and specials. These are delivered on the job by the contractor, and there is no pressure testing of a line before being put into service. This latter practice is open to criticism. While the extent of pipe-laying done by the city would probably not justify the employment of a special inspector at the shop. yet there should be a careful physical inspection made of pipe and specials as they arrive on the job before placing them in the ground and a separate pressure test should be made of the sections of water main laid before the line is put into service.

The policy is followed of requiring all pipe lines to be laid in a street before any permanent pavement is constructed. When water mains are laid, taps are placed to serve the property abutting on the street, and the necessary house connections are carried to the curbline where a valve and meter box are installed. When connection is made with the house, the plumber making the connection for the householder is required to carry his pipe to the valve box in an open trench and the work is inspected by the city plumber to ensure its conformity with the city's requirements governing that class of work.

Lead Pipe for House Connections.

Under a city ordinance all house connections from the water mains are required to be of lead pipe with brass fittings. The policy of requiring the exclusive use of lead pipe for work of this character is at least questionable on account of the excessive cost involved. Consideration should be given to use of galvanized iron pipe on work of this character. Only where conditions exist that are likely to cause rapid deterioration of the latter material, as for example, where the pipe is to be laid in cinder filled ground, the use of lead pipe is justifiable.

Method of Defraying Cost of House Connection Work.

In all house connections involving the use of pipe up to and including one inch in diameter, the city furnishes the necessary tap and brass fittings and all labor, while the consumer is required to pay for the lead pipe. In cases where the pipe used ranges in size from one inch to ten inches the city furnishes the labor necessary to do the work while the consumer is required to pay for all material used including the tap. In all work involving the use of pipe in excess of two inches in diameter, and on all separate fire services, the consumer pays for the entire cost of the work. This cost constitutes a lien on the property affected and must be paid by the consumer before water is turned on the premises served.

The above procedure is not based on any scientific apportionment of cost, and in many cases is distinctly inequitable. The expense incidental to furnishing special or extraordinary service should be borne by the consumer receiving such service, but there should be no discrimination, such as exists at present, in the matter of expense to consumers receiving the same quality of service. Probably the most satisfactory and equitable method of apportioning the expense involved in connection with the construction of

ordinary house connection immediately before the improvement of
any street is by including this expense in the assessment made on
the property benefited. As this procedure is not feasible under
present conditions in Richmond, it is recommended that the entire
expense of making house connections with water mains on any
street be borne by the property collectively benefited and that this
expense be equitably apportioned in accordance with the character
of the service received.

Water Meters.

According to the report of the superintendent of the city water works there were 23,651 meters in service in the city of Richmond on January 1, 1917. This constituted approximately 80 per
cent of the total service in the city. Of these meters 22,068 are
owned by the city and 1,583 by private citizens. The policy is
followed of furnishing all meters in service lines up to and including one inch in diameter to the consumer without charge. The
consumer is required to pay for all meters in lines above 1 inch in
size. Meters are tested and repaired upon request from the consumer, no charge being made for this service. No rental is charged for the use of city owned meters.

The policy of discrimination between consumers in the matter
of ownership of meters according to the size of the meter is open
to criticism. The city should preferably own all meters on its
service lines. Furthermore, these meters should not be furnished
to the consumer without charge, but on an annual rental basis, the
rental charge to include capital and depreciation charges and overhead expense for testing and ordinary repairs to and maintenance
of meters. Where damage to the meter is due to negligence on the
part of the consumer, he should be required to bear the expense
involved in repairing the same.

Organization of Repair Force.

The forces employed in connection with the miscellaneous repair and installation work of the water supply distribution system, at the time the inspection of the department was made, included the following:

> 5 plumbers, $105 per month.
> 14 helpers, $2.75 per day.
> 7 regular laborers, $2.50 per day.

The repair gangs, each under a plumber as foreman, are distributed geographically throughout the city. One plumber designated as foreman of plumbers reports at headquarters each morning and receives orders concerning the work for the day. Instructions are then transmitted by telephone to the other gang foremen and subsequently each foreman is handed an order slip relating to work in his district. These orders are made out by the assistant superintendent on blank forms with a duplicate stub, the back containing the stub being retained in the office. At the end of each day the orders are returned to the assistant superintendent with a record of the character of the work, number of men employed, and the materials used.

The form employed is crude and the control exercised is purely a personal one and inadequate. The form, however, could be readily modified so as to provide for the recording of essential data, and adequate control over the work could be developed by the use of carbon copies supplemented by suitable methods of filing and follow-up. This is important, as the information returned by the foreman on these assignment slips constitutes the basis for billing the consumer for the cost of the work where special connections are made for any purpose.

The repair gangs are not provided with transportation facilities of any kind other than push carts for carrying tools and equipment. Material required on the work are delivered on the job by one of the two motor trucks kept at the storeyard of the department. The organization of the force employed on this work and the character of the equipment provided are discussed later in this report.

Organization of Forces at Store Yard and Repair Shop.

The force employed at the store yard at the time the inspection of the department was made included the following:

1 Storekeeper, $90 per month.
1 Laborer assisting storekeeper, $2.50 per day.
1 Motor truck operator, $3.00 per day.
1 Motor truck operator, $2.75 per day.
1 Watchman, at night, $2.50 per day.
1 Foreman of meter repairs, $4.00 per day.
2 meter repair men, $3.00 per day.

Storehouse and Yard.

The storekeeper is in general charge of the department store-yard. A small stock of pipe and valves is kept at the yard, together with water meters and miscellaneous supplies. Accommodations are also provided for the two motor trucks maintained by the department. These include:

1 Alco 2 ton truck.
1 Sanford 1 ton truck.

The general condition of the yard and storehouse is commendable.

Control of Material in Stores.

The storekeeper keeps a stores ledger which at the time of the inspection was fairly up to date, and makes periodic reports to the assistant superintendent in regard to supplies on hand. There is decided laxity in the control exercised over the withdrawal of supplies from the yard for repair work and the subsequent return of unused supplies to the yard. There is a marked need for stores control over the entire maintenance and repair work of the department.

Meter Repair Shop.

The meter repair forces are employed in collecting and replacing meters requiring repair and testing and in carrying on the necessary shop work in connection with their testing and repair. Lists of meters requiring attention, giving information as to type and location, are transmitted daily from the central office. Upon receiving this information the meter repair men start out with the required number of meters to replace those reported as defective and bring the disabled meters back to the shop for repair. The men are provided with push carts for transporting the meters and tools required. One of the motor trucks is used to a limited extent on this work in transporting men and push carts to the locality in which they intend to work during the day.

Criticism of Repair Administration.

The entire administration of the repair work of the water department is open to criticism in the following respects:

1—The distribution of gangs and the number of men employed.
2—Inadequacy of transportation equipment.

Distribution of Gangs.

The distribution of repair gangs according to arbitrary geographical lines in a city like Richmond in place of assigning them on the basis of work needs is indefensible. A very considerable portion of the work of these gangs is concerned with making house connections with new buildings and obviously this work is not uniformly distributed over the city. Also the number of men employed appears to be considerably in excess of the work requirements. It is difficult with the data available to determine the amount of work done by the repair forces of the department, but attention is called to the number of taps placed during any period of time as being a fair basis for judgment in respect to its magnitude.

During 1916, according to the report of the superintendent of the water department, there were 1,318 taps placed in the main city and 150 in South Richmond, making a total of 1,468 for the entire city. It is understood that the force engaged in repair work during that year was somewhat in excess of the present force. Assuming 303 working days and five gangs, we have 1,515 working days, or rather less than an average of one tap placed per working day. While it is appreciated that under peculiarly difficult conditions such work may require more than a day for its completion, it is maintained that such conditions are the exception rather than the rule, and that such an average is way below what can reasonably be expected of properly equipped repair gangs. It is also appreciated that other work than making taps is occasionally required of these repair gangs.

However, it is maintained that with adequate transportation facilities and co-ordination of work and forces employed the demand of the city in the matter of repair and maintenance of its water supply distribution system can be met adequately by a repair force materially less than the one at present employed.

It is therefore recommended that the repair force of the department, if it is to be retained as a separate department, be reorganized to include:

1 general repair foreman, $110 per month.
2 gang foremen, $105 per month.
9 helpers, $2.75 per day (303 days).
6 regular laborers, $2.50 per day (303 days).

The general repair foreman should be a plum
actively supervise the work of a gang in the field ?
He should also be responsible, under the assistant
for the general direction and planning of house c
other work of the repair force.

In considering the above organization it shoul
the present pipe-laying force which is in excess ?
needs of the department constitutes a reserve for
called upon in an emergency.

Methods of Transportation.

The repair forces should be equipped with no?
automobile trucks, either a Ford or its equivalent.
be equipped with the necessary tools and suppli
emergency work. The present one ton Sanford t
dispensed with and the Alco two ton truck retain
hauling, to be used not only for the water depart
for the gas works or other departments as needed
trucks of this character for the distribution of su?
cellaneous small hauling is distinctly uneconomica
the use of push carts for the daily repair men shou
ed. The work of picking up and delivering meters ?
by one of the small trucks in the department. It s
ble to do this by intelligent co-ordination of the n
pair work and of the meter work of the departmen

Assuming that the replacement of the Sanford
by a Ford truck or its equivalent involves no addi
ture and ignoring any economies that may result
economical operation of the latter, the only additio
volved will be the acquisition of one Ford truck an?
This will amount to approximately the following:

1 Ford truck, plus freight, etc....$400.00
Carrying charge 6 per cent.......
Depreciation 20 per cent ....
Operating cost—first year........

It is possible that the needs of the work will
of three Ford trucks, and in that event the additio?
volved will amount to $888.00.

Resulting Economies.

Against this expenditure, on the basis of the proposed organization, there will be a reduction in personal service required of approximately $7,406, or a net saving of $6,518. In this connection it is desired to call attention to the likelihood that considerable additional economies could be effected by a centralization of the forces concerned with pipe-laying and repair work in the water and gas departments. This matter is discussed elsewhere in the report in the chapter relating to the proposed department of water supply, gas and electricity.

Gas Department.

Department Organization.

The organization of the gas department includes the following divisions:

> Manufacturing division.
> Distribution division.
> Revenue and accounting division.

The distribution of the forces employed in the various divisions is shown in the accompanying organization chart.

Manufacturing Division.

The Richmond gas works has a manufacturing capacity of about 3,500,000 to 3,900,000 cubic feet of gas in twenty-four hours, this capacity being based on the continuous operation of all the operating units.

The works includes a coal gas plant, capable of producing 1,400,00 cubic feet per twenty-four hours, and a water gas plant with a capacity of 2,500,000 cubic feet during the same period of time.

Coal Gas plant.

The coal gas plant consists of twenty regenerative benches of nine units each. The entire plant is in duplicate, ten benches being operated at one time while the other ten are shut down for relining or making such repairs as are necessary. This plant is equipped with coal charging and drawing machines and a coke conveyor for handling the coke after it is drawn from the retorts.

Water Gas Plant.

The water gas plant consists of one 10 feet and ten 7 feet United Gas Improvement Company water gas sets of six units each, with their accessories, including washers, scrubbers and condensers.

Miscellaneous Auxiliary Equipment.

The plant is equipped with the usual pumps and exhausters. The purifiers are of the Chollar type, two being used for coal gas and three for water gas.

The exhausters are of the most approved type of design with rope connections, manufactured by the P. H. and F. M. Rotts Company. Other equipment includes two 60 H. P. ball engines, and two Ingersoll-Rand air compressors.

Tar Extractor.

The water gas plant is equipped with a T. & A. tar extractor with a capacity of 4,000,000 cubic feet in twenty-four hours. The superintendent of the gas works has recommended the installation of similar equipment at the coal gas plant. The cost of such an installation is not excessive and its value in securing a better quality of gas in addition to the commercial value of the tar exhausted fully justifies the proposed expenditure.

Boiler Plant.

The boiler equipment at the gas works includes three batteries of Heinie water tube boilers of ten units each serving the water gas plant, and two horizontal boilers serving the coal gas plant. The entire plant has a capacity of 1,054 boiler horsepower.

Coal Storage.

The coal yard has a storage capacity of 1,000 tons. There are three coal storage bins supplied from the yard by hydraulic lifts. The main bin, which has a capacity of 700 tons, is of steel construction and is equipped with two 35 ton C. W. Hunt coal crushers. The small bins which are supplied from the larger one furnish the charging machines at the coal gas plant.

This capacity is not adequate to meet the rapidly increasing production demands. The present tracks should be enlarged and extended and a modern telephone system installed at as early a date as possible.

Gas Holders.

There are two gas holders at the plant, one a relief holder with a capacity of 100,000 cubic feet, and the other a storage holder with a capacity of 600,000 cubic feet. The gas from each plant is measured separately, a 14 feet Hinman drum meter being used to measure the water gas, while the coal gas is measured by a meter of the rotary type. The latter, according to the superintendent of the gas works, is not giving satisfactory service, and should be replaced with more modern equipment.

General Condition of Plant.

The general condition of the gas plant is excellent, both in respect to the character of equipment and the maintenance. Attention should be given, however, to the need for increasing the capacity of the plant to meet the increasing consumption. In this connection careful consideration should be given to the recommendations of the superintendent of the gas works in respect to the installation of the most improved type of coal gas plant with vertical benches, as a means towards reducing the cost of manufacturing gas in Richmond.

Gas Works Organization.

The operation of the gas works is under the supervision of a general foreman, who receives an annual salary of $1,600. During the night shift a night foreman, who receives $3.50 per day, is in charge of the plant. The distribution of the forces working under the direction of the general foreman is shown in the accompanying chart, grouped according to the following activities:

Operation of gas furnaces.
Operation of power plant and machinery.
Coal handling and care of yard.
General repair work.

Operation of Gas Plants.

The force engaged in operating the coal and water gas plants include:

4 coal gas makers, $3.50 per day.
4 coal gas makers' helpers, $2.75 per day.
2 water gas makers, $3.50 per day.
4 water gas makers helpers, $2.75 per day.

This force is employed on twelve hour shifts every day in the year, the shifts alternating weekly.

Operation of Power Plant.

The force engaged in the operation of the power plant and other machinery at the gas works includes:

4 engine men, $3.25 per day.
2 firemen, $2.75 per day.
2 exhaust room operators, $3.25 per day.
1 purifying house operator, $3.25 per day.

These men likewise work twelve hour shifts during the entire year. In the case of the purifying house operator, whose duties are mainly concerned with the pumping of condensation drips about the plant and the care of the purifying house equipment, the position is only filled during the day shift.

Coal handling and General Care of Yard.

The force engaged in handling coal, ashes and coke and the general care of the yard includes:

1 assistant foreman, $3.50 per day.
6 coke yard men, $2.75 per day.
7 yard laborers, $2.50 per day.

employed on day shifts alone six days in the week except in an emergency.

Three coal handlers at $2.50 per day are employed during day shifts during the entire year.

General Repair Work.

In addition to the operating force at the gas works, there is a general repair force of skilled mechanics. This force which is employed during the week days on day shifts except in the case of emergency, includes:

One machinist, $3.50 per day
One machinist helper, $2.75 per day
One blacksmith, $3.50 per day
One blacksmith helper, $2.75 per day
One bricklayer, $3.50 per day
One carpenter, $3.50 per day.

The needs of a plant of this character justify the employment of such a force.

Superannuated Employees.

There are ten superannuated employees connected with th gas works organization, each of whom receives $30 per month, and one man, a cripple injured in the discharge of his duties, who receives $2.50 per day.

Adequacy of Present Organization.

Under the existing working conditions the present force at the gas works appears to be adequate without being excessive.

Division of Distribution.

The work of the division of distribution is concerned with the making of all repairs and extensions to the distribution system, the installation and repair of meters, and the rendering of miscellaneous services to the consumer. The headquarters of the division are at the storeyard and meter repair shop of the department. The work connected with the division of distribution is carried on under the direction of a general foreman who receives an annual salary of $1,500. The forces working under his direction may be grouped according to the following classes of work:

> Extension to distribution system and making house connections.
> Installation and repair of meters.
> Stove work.
> Store yard and miscellaneous service.
> Maintenance of West End holder.

Main Line Extension and House Connections.

The work of the division includes all pipe laying in connection with the extension of main lines and the making of house connections and miscellaneous repair work. The working force is divided into four gangs distributed geographically about the city, each gang consisting of from five to six service men working under a tapper as gang foreman.

Methods of Conducting Work.

On main line extension work all trench excavation is done under an annual contract, the pipe is delivered on the job and the gas department forces are merely concerned with the laying and testing of the pipe and supervision over the back-filling of the trench.

These men do not report to headquarters daily, but receive instructions concerning the work from the general foreman. In connection with the repair and house connection work, supplies are delivered from the store yard to the various gangs by a two ton Alco truck owned by the department. In case of emergency work when the truck is absent from the yard, it is customary to use one of the motor wagons for the delivery of supplies. The field gangs are equipped with push carts, in which they transport tools and supplies from job to job.

Defects in Present System.

The same criticism applies to the policy followed in handling the repair and construction forces in the gas department as is noted for the water department, namely:

> The geographical distribution of repair gangs.
> The inadequacy of transportation facilities.

It is doubtful at least if there is any justification for the permanent assignment of repair gangs to any specific territory. Distribution of forces should be primarily based on work requirements, and if the work of the gas department repair forces were properly co-ordinated, it should be possible to secure a more effective and economical handling of the work than exists at present. Obviously the matter of adequate transportation facilities has an important bearing on the securing of satisfactory results. The use of push carts by repair gangs should be discontinued, and these gangs should be provided with motor transportation, preferably Ford trucks or their equivalent, these trucks to be equipped with tools and supplies for the work.

The extent of the transportation required for the repair work of the gas department is considered in connection with the personal service needs of the department in the matter of repair and construction forces.

The two departments of gas and water present analagous problems in the matter of their pipe-laying and repair work. The handling of these classes of work separately by the above departments involves a duplication of forces and equipment that entails unnecessary expense. This is particularly in evidence in the matter of pipe-laying. In 1916 the gas department laid 25,143 feet of

gas mainly four and six inches in diameter. This work could just
as well have been done by the pipe-laying forces connected with
the water department, and probably without requiring any material
increase in those forces. It is recommended that, in the future,
responsibility for all pipe-laying work for the department of gas
and water be centralized in one properly equipped pipe-laying
force.

The force and equipment required to serve the gas and water
departments in the matter of repair and construction work are
considered later in the report in connection with a proposed centralization of the departments of water supply, gas and electricity.

Meter Setting and Repairs.

The city owns all gas meters. These are furnished to the consumer and kept in repair without charge. The force concerned
with the installation and repair of meters includes:

> 3 meter setters, each receiving $2.75 per day.
> 3 service men assisting meter setters—same rate of pay.
> 3 tinners and meter repair men, $3.50 per day.

The meter setters and assistants are responsible for all work
done in connection with the setting or removal of gas meters, and
also investigate complaints relating to stoppage, gas leaks, etc.,
and make the necessary repairs. Each of these meter setting gangs
is provided with a horse and wagon.

The meter repair men are mainly employed in the testing and
repair of meters returned to the repair shop of the gas department.
In addition they are occasionally called upon to do miscellaneous
repair work requiring the employment of tinners.

The force concerned with making connections with meter and
similar work should be supplied with motor transportation in place
of the present horse drawn equipment. The work of these forces
should also be co-ordinated with the other repair work of the gas
department in order to secure an effective use of the transportation facilities of the department and an efficient distribution of
the repair force.

Stove Setters and Helpers.

A special force of men including four stove setters and their
assistants are engaged in making all connections to gas ranges,
water heaters, etc. These men are not provided with transporta-

tion facilities. This force appears to be in excess of that required for this particular phase of repair work. Stove work is largely periodic, being influenced by people changing their residence. During 1916 there were 3,593 stoves connected. This would give an average of less than three stoves connected per day per gang.

Recommended Repair Force for Gas Department.

It is felt that the most economical and effective results in the matter of repair and construction work in the department of water supply, gas and elecricity would be received by centralizing their forces at a single headquarters. and also place certain of the activities of these departments under a single jurisdiction. In the event that this matter should not receive serious consideration by the city government, it is desired to point out certain changes in the organization of the repair and construction forces of the gas department on the assumption that these forces will continue to be independent. The proposed organization is predicated. however, on the centralization of pipe-laying work of the city in a single force working under the jurisdiction of the department of water.

It is recommended first that the repair force be organized into four gangs, each working under a gang foreman. One of these gangs would be concerned with the general care of meters and meter connections, independent of shop repair of meters. The other three gangs would be employed in general maintenance and repair of the distribution system, and in rendering miscellaneous service to the consumer, including making connections with stoves.

The personnel suggested as adequate for this work would include the following:

- 4 gang foremen, $1,200.
   22 service men at $2.75 per day. This force to include men assigned to operate motor trucks. This would effect a saving in personal service of approximately $6,666 a year.

Transportation facilities for the repair force should include in addition to the two ton truck at present maintained by the department—

   3 Ford trucks or their equivalent.
   1 Ford runabout for general foreman of repairs.

This equipment should be ample for all transportation needs of the gas department and if provided it should be possible to dispense with five of the seven horses now maintained by the department. The approximate annual expense for the motor equipment would amount to the following:

Esimated Cost of Additional Motor Equipment.

Capital charge 6 per cent on cost of three Ford trucks and one Ford runabout, $1,450 plus freight, $1,500 ....$	90.00
Depreciation 35 per cent	507.50
Operating cost—estimated	1,300.00
Total ....$	1,897.50
Credit cost of maintenance of five horses and wagons, $20 per month..................	1,200.00
Net additional cost ....$	697.50

On the above basis it is estimated that a net saving of approximately $6,000 a year can be effected in the cost of handling the repair work in the gas department.

Control of Repair Work.

All orders relating to the work of the repair forces are sent from the central office to the repair shop headquarters. These orders are issued in duplicate, a copy being sent to the general foreman. This copy constitutes a job order to the men doing the work and upon its completion the copy is returned to the general foreman with the significant information concerning the work done. A special form is employed for meter repair work. The general foreman keeps in close touch with all extension and repair work on the distribution system. He is provided with a horse and buggy for this work.

The type of forms used for this purpose and the procedure followed are inadequate to effect a proper control over the field work. A multiple copy loose-leaf form should be adopted with adequate procedure for follow-up and subsequent filing.

Records of Repair Work.

The general foreman in charge of repair work keeps a job card record of all repair and extension work. This record in-

cludes information in respect to location of work and of labor,
material and hauling. The general foreman also keeps miscellaneous records relating to the re-setting of meters and other repair
work. The keeping of these records by the foreman takes up time
that could well be devoted to a supervision over the work in the
field. The information they contain should be transmitted direct
to the general office by suitable reports.

Store Yard.

A small stock of general supplies required for repair work and
a supply of meters are kept at the store yard of the gas department. These supplies are in charge of a storekeeper who receives
$4.00 per day and is on duty twelve hours in the day every day in
the year. In the absence of the foreman, he is in charge of the
yard, receives complaints or orders for repairs and takes appropriate action concerning them.

Store Records.

The storekeeper submits to the foreman a daily report of the
supplies received and issued from the stores. He also keeps a
store ledger which is posted monthly. No special form is employed in recording the issuance of supplies from stores and the only
control exercised over supplies returned to store is by a periodic
checking up of the latter. An inventory of supplies in the store
yard is taken annually. The general condition of the store yard
is satisfactory, but there is a laxity in the control exercised over
the care of supplies that is open to criticism.

What the city needs is a central store yard, preferably to supply all city departments, but at least one to serve the departments
of water supply, gas and electricity.

Other Force at Store Yard.

The regular force at the store yard also includes two service
men, each of whom receives $2.75 per day. These men are em-
ployed principally on the "drip wagon" used in pumping condensation water from the distribution system. There are also two
service men at $2.75 per day employed in operating the two ton
automobile truck owned by the department. This truck is used
for heavy hauling about one-third of the time it is in use. One
service man acting as hostler and stableman is in charge of the
seven horses stabled at the storage yard. A watchman is on duty
from 6 P. M. to 6 A. M. during the entire year.

Force at West End Gas Holder.

The foreman in charge of the distribution system and repair yard of the gas department is also responsible for the maintenance and operation of the west end gas holder. This holder, which has a capacity of two million cubic feet, furnishes the supply for the entire west end of the city. Three so-called "pressure men" are employed at this holder. One man is employed during the day shift of twelve hours and two men are on the night shift. Each of these men receives $3.60 per day. They are on duty throughout the year. Their duties include the operation of the valves and control apparatus and the general care of the tank and grounds.

Special Repair Force.

In addition to the repair forces of the gas department reporting directly to the general foreman in charge of the distribution system, there are four gasfitters, each of whom receives $4.00 per day, who report directly to the superintendent of the gas department. The work of these men is concerned mainly with correcting faulty conditions in respect to piping gas connections.

It should be observed that all of the services previously noted, which are rendered by the gas department to the consumer and which necessitate the employment of a very large force, are given without charge. While it is appreciated that the results of this service are to the advantage of the city, to some extent in securing adequate installations and bettering the service to the consumer, it would appear that a certain proportion of the expense involved should be borne by the individual consumer benefited rather than by the city at large.

When it is considered that the mere labor cost of certain of the service rendered, excluding the making of house connections and the repair of meters, amounted to approximately $16,200 for the year 1916, one may get some idea of the extent of this service. That certain of the expense should have been charged against the consumer appears to be unquestioned. For example, the service rendered by the force of gas fitters or complaint men who report directly to the superintendent of the gas department and which costs the city upwards of $5,000 annually, is of such a character as to directly benefit the property of the consumer.

It is urged that consideration be given to the establishment by council of standards of workmanship in the matter of gas piping, fixtures, etc., and that the superintendent of the gas department be empowered to charge a reasonable fee for making any changes in the gas-piping system or connections in a consumer's building in order to make such installation conform to the requirements of the city.

City Electrical Department.

Organization.

The organization of the electrical department (shown in an accompanying chart) may be roughly divided into the following divisions:

> Operation of plant.
> Construction and maintenance of line.
> Inspection and control of electric installations.
> General office.

The administrative head of this department is known as the superintendent of the electric plant and city electrician. He receives a salary of $3,600 a year and is appointed by the administrative head for a term of two years. He not only has supervision over the operation of the electric plant, but also over the electrical equipment and operation of the water works pumping station.

Electric Plant.

The electric plant is located on the James River about two miles below the pump works. It was built in 1910 at an expenditure of approximately $225,000. The value of the real estate involved represents an additional amount of approximately $200,000. The plant is hydro-electric with auxiliary steam equipment. The main units are four S. Morgan Smith turbines rated at 660 H. P. working under a 17 foot head, direct connected to four General Electric A-C generators with rated capacity of 375 K.W. operated at 4,000 volts. Each unit is equipped with a Lombardy governor.

The auxiliary steam equipment includes two Babcock and Wilcox hand-fired boilers, rated capacity of 400 H. P., supplying steam to two General Electric steam turbines with a rated capacity of 750 K.W. There are also two Cameron boiler feed pumps, with an Alberger type of condenser, and two General Electric exciter sets. At the time the inspection of the plant was made, construction was under way to provide for the accommodation of an additional steam unit with a capacity of 1500 K.W. for which a contract has been awarded. The street lighting equipment includes the usual type of switchboard together with seventeen 100-light constant current transformers.

Organization of Plant Forces.

The organization at the electric plant includes:

1 Chief engineer, $1,500.
2 Operating engineers, $1,200 each.
1 Chief electrician, $1,440.
2 Electricians, $2.85 per day.
2 Oilers, $2.50 per day.
4 Firemen, $2.75 per day.
Laborers as needed.

At certain seasons laborers are required to remove ice and leaves from the trash racks and to do miscellaneous repair work. The normal force of the plant does not include any laborers.

The chief engineer is in direct charge of the plant and of all men employed there. The chief electrician exercises supervsion over the operation of the switchboard and also is responsible for the condition of the electrical equipment.

The duties of the other employees are those pertaining to such positions as are indicated. The work of the plant is divided into two 10-hour shifts, the chief operator and chief electrician being personally responsible for 4-hour shifts and the time of the other men overlaps in such a way as to provide an adequate force on each shift.

The plant is kept in good condition.

Construction and Maintenance of Line.

The work of this division is concerned with the construction of all extensions to the street lighting system and in making all repairs and changes in that system.

Organization of Line Forces.

The organization employed in line work comprises a day force and a night force. At the time the inspection was made these forces were distributed as follows:

Day Force.

1 Foreman lineman. $120 per month.
2 Linemen. $90 per month.

3 Linemen, $2.75 per day.
    (These men are not permanently employed.)
4 Laborers, $2.25 per day.
    (These men are virtually linemen helpers and as such
    their present compensation is entirely inadequate.)

Night Force.
    1 Trouble lineman, $90 per month.
    1 Trouble lineman, $2.75 per day.

This latter force is concerned with replacing lights, correcting other line trouble or making emergency repairs to the line during the night.

In addition to the above forces there are two employees connected with the electrical department known as lampmen, one of whom receives $2.75 per day and the other $2.60 per day. These men were formerly concerned with the repair and maintenance of arc lamps, but since the latter have been entirely replaced with nitrogen lamps, there is no further need for work of this character. The lampmen are at present assigned to the care and replacement of all glassware and the repair and maintenance of the ornamental lighting system along Broad street. The extent of this work does not appear to justify the continuous employment of two men, but the general repair work of the department justifies the employment of one of these incumbents on that class of work.

Department Storeroom.
    The headquarters of the forces concerned with the extension and maintenance of line are at the department storeroom. A reserve supply of lamps and miscellaneous tools and supplies are kept at this storeroom, but there is no provision for housing department equipment. The city pays a rental of $600 per year for the premises occupied.

Transportation Facilities.
    The maintenance and construction forces of the electrical department are provided with the following transportation facilities:

    2 Single horses and wagons.
    1 Ford truck.
        (A second Ford truck has been ordered for the department, but has not yet been received.)

The two horses and wagons are housed at the street cleaning department's stables when not in use, but the Ford truck is kept standing in front of the storeroom ready for emergency work at all times. When the needs of the work require heavy hauling, as for example, in the hauling of poles, this work is done by hired teams or trucks. With two Ford trucks available at all times it should be possible to eliminate the two horses and wagons at present used by the department forces.

While the necessity for a central headquarters for the construction and maintenance forces of the electrical department is not questioned, consideration should be given to the practicability of combining such headquarters with those of the repair forces connected with the water and gas works. This is particularly desirable in view of the necessity for having the emergency trucks available at all times and the lack of provision under present conditions for housing them.

Furthermore, it should be noted that no storekeeper is assigned to the care of department supplies, the control over these supplies being a more or less casual one exercised by the foreman of linemen. This is undesirable, although the needs of the department in this matter would not justify the continuous employment of a storekeeper. However, the present undesirable features would be obviated by centralizing the stores of the three departments of water, gas and electricity in a single storehouse under a competent storekeeper with an adequate system and procedure for the control of stores. An additional advantage that would result from centralizing the repair forces of the city is in the matter of transportation facilities. There are at present in the three departments noted sufficient motor trucks to handle all the heavy hauling required by these departments if that work were properly co-ordinated.

Handling of Complaints Relating to Line Trouble.

Complaints of outages or other trouble with the line are received either at the central office, the electric plant or the storeroom. Upon receipt at either of the other two places they are immediately telephoned to the storeroom where they are recorded in a loose-leaf form of blotter. Information in respect to the nature of the complaint and its location is either given directly to the lineman or foreman or else transmitted to him by telephone, and these men subsequently report to the superintendent of the department as to the action taken to correct it. The present control over this work is a personal one and inadequate. A modification in this procedure automatically insuring a follow-up on the complaint, together with a change in the design of the form used should be installed in order to secure better control.

Division of Inspection.

The principal work in the division of inspection consists in the examination of plans for all interior electrical installation and the subsequent inspection of those installations to ascertain if they conform to the regulations. The latter are practically indentical with the 1915 regulations of the National Board of Fire Underwriters. The work of this division also includes attendance at all important fires and the conducting of investigations of an electrical nature when ordered by the city electrician or the administrative board. This work constitutes practically the only fire prevention work carried on by the city.

Organization of Inspection Division.

The organization of the division of inspection includes two inspectors, each of whom receives an annual salary of $1,500. These inspectors are supplied with automobile runabouts which are kept in private garages. The latter is an undesirable practice, as it tends to a use of the machine for other than city business. City owned automobiles should be housed preferably at some central headquarters where adequate control can be exercised over their use. Obviously, if a central storehouse and yard were provided it would be feasible to furnish accommodations for such equipment.

Control of Electrical Inspection.

The control of electrical inspection both in the matter of making inspections and enforcing the requirements of the code is good, except that the present force is inadequate. It should be noted also that while care is given to the inspection of interior electrical installations, no definite provision is made for the inspection of outside construction where the hazard to the community under certain conditions may be greater than in the case of interior construction. Aside from a periodic checking up of construction work along the line by a draughtsman no attention is paid to this all-important matter. In this connection, it should be noted that while the city derives a revenue of approximately $26,000 a year from exterior electrical construction of various kinds, it fails to provide for inspection of this construction.

It is urged that the city government provide funds to employ the necessary service required to make such inspections.

Possible Revenue from Electrical Inspections.

It should be noted that no fee is charged for electrical inspections made by the department. This policy is at least questionable and against the interests of the city. The service rendered to the individual householder and the public at large in making inspections of interior electrical installations is one that, if not given by the city, would be required by the fire underwriters as a prerequisite to placing insurance. Also, if made by them, it would be at the expense of the householder. It is maintained that the expense involved in making electrical inspections constitutes a legitimate charge against the property inspected, and it is urgel that the city government take the necessary action to establish a scale of charges for this service similar to those prevailing in Chicago and Detroit. If this were done it would increase the city revenues by approximately $6,000 and make the division of inspection practically self-supporting.

As an example of the existing hazard to the community from electrical construction, it is important to note that the city government has consented to the construction of a high-voltage feed line within the city limits against the protest of the superintendent of the electric plant. This policy is open to severe criticism, and should be discontinued.

General Office Division.

The organization of the general office division of the electrical department includes the following:

1 Draughtsman, $1,200.
1 General clerk, $1,200.
1 Permit clerk, $900.

The duties of the draughtsman include the preparation of all plans required in connection with line extension or repair, general checking up of outside work, and the making of miscellaneous inspections under the direction of the city electrician. The title of the position is inconsistent with the duties required, which are essentially of an engineering character.

The general clerical work of the department which includes the keeping of miscellaneous records, is carried on by the clerk, while the permit clerk is concerned with the issuance and control of all permits relating to electrical installations throughout the city.

Permits For Electrical Work.

All work involving the construction or change of any existing wires or poles or the installation of interior fixtures or electrical apparatus is carried on subject to a permit issued by the electrical department. In the case of interior work, upon receipt of an application, which is submitted on a standard form, the application is first examined to see that all details affecting the construction are given and that the licensed contractor who is to undertake the job is in good standing. If the application meets all requirements, it is then given an application number and recorded on a log sheet provided for this purpose. A permit is then issued by the permit clerk in quadruplicate, a color scheme being used to identify the various copies.

One copy is temporarily filed according to the serial number in a drawer devoted to that purpose, the second copy is filed in the inspector's book in which the work called for is located according to the serial number of the permit, the third copy is filed in a book file of uncompleted jobs according to the serial number of the permit, and the fourth copy is given to the applicant.

Essentially the same procedure is followed with respect to the issuance of all permits, whether for the removal or for the joint use of poles, or the installation of wires, cables and other electrical apparatus. In the case of applications for the location of new poles, the approval of the application by the administrative board is required before the permit is issued.

The office procedure in this matter and the control exercised over the work, which is automatic, are commendable.

Miscellaneous Records.

In addition to the issuance of permits in the office a very comprehensive set of records is kept as affecting both the distribution line of the department and other electrical installations throughout the city. These include a card history of lamps containing complete information in respect to the life of the lamps. This is particularly valuable as indicating the behavior of the lamps of different capacity under service.

Adequacy of Street Lighting System.

At the present time the streets in approximately 86 per cent of the area of the city are furnished with electric lights. The un-lighted areas are in those sections of the city recently acquired by annexation, and funds have not been available up to the present to make the extensions required to serve those areas. These lights are all nitrogen lamps, the arc lamps having been replaced recently by the former.   ,

In general. the lighting of the streets in Richmond is adequate. It is desired, however, to call attention to the conditions in the matter of lighting on two main residential streets of the city. namely, Monument Avenue and Franklin street. The lighting of these streets is entirely inadequate, although they are main arteries of traffic. The inadequacy of the street lighting in these districts is due to action on the part of the city government in acceding to the requests of residents along those streets in respect to the location and intensity of the street lights. This action was taken against the protests of the superintendent of the electrical department. The policy of allowing the selfish personal desires of a few individuals to outweigh the needs and welfare of the community in as important a matter as lighting of streets cannot be too severely criticized. It is urged that the city government take the necessary action to secure adequate lighting facilities for Monument Avenue and Franklin street of the interests of the community are to be properly safeguarded in this respect.

Proposed Department of Public Utilities.

The present duplication of plant and organization in the departments of gas anl water supply of the city of Richmond. both in the matter of revenue and accounting and in the conduct of the pipe-laying and repair work of these departments, makes it desirable to develop an organization centralizing the administration of these activities and thereby eliminating waste. The division of responsibility between the water supply and electricity departments in the supervision of the pumping plant is also in many respects undesirable.

In view of these facts it is suggested that consideration be given to a centralization of the three departments mentioned in a single department to be known as the department of public utilities. A tentative outline of the organization of such a department predicated on the recommendations contained in this report is shown in the accompanying chart.

Proposed Organization of Department.

The main division of such a department would include:

> Bureau of gas manufacture.
> Bureau of power plants, street lighting and electrical inspection.
> Bureau of water collection, storage and distribution.
> Bureau of revenue and accounting.

The administrative head of the department would be a commissioner. The bureau of water collection, storage and distribution would be under the supervision of an engineer. the bureau of revenue and accounting would be under the supervision of a chief clerk, and the bureaus of gas manufacture and power plants would each be under a superintendent.

Obviously under the proposed organization there would be no change from present conditions in connection with the new bureau of gas manufacture and in the case of the bureau of power plants and street lighting the only change would be to place entire instead of partial responsibility for the operation of the pumping plant in the head of the bureau with some possible modification in the handling of the clerical and accounting work in that office.

Economies to Be Effected.

The main justification for any such centralization of the departments would lie in the economies that would be effected and in the increased efficiency of administration. The two principal bureaus in which it would be possible to effect economies over the present cost of administration are the bureau of water collection. storage and distribution anl the bureau of revenue and accounting.

Proposed Bureau of Water Collection, Storage and Distribution.

The forces engaged in the construction, repair and maintenance of the distribution systems of the departments of water supply and gas, and the forces concerned with rendering miscellaneous service to the public, together with their transportation equipment provided for them, are presented in the following tabulation:

Repair and Service Forces.

Water Department.

1 foreman pipe laying	$ 2,320.00
7 pipe men, $2.85 per lay, 303 days	6,044.85
5 plumbers, $105 per month	6,300.00
14 helpers, $2.75 per day, 303 days	11,665.50
7 regular laborers, $2.50 per day. 303 days	5,302.50
1 storekeeper	1,080.00
1 auto truck operator. $3 per day, 303 days	909.00
1 auto truck operator, $2.75 per day, 303 days	833.25
1 laborer assisting storekeeper, $2.50 per day 303 days	757.50
1 watchman, $2.50 per day, 365 days	912.50
1 foreman of meter repairs, $4 per day, 303 ds	1,212.00
2 meter repair men, $3 per day, 303 days	1,818.00
Total	$38,155.10

Equipment.

1 Alco two ton truck
1 Sanford two ton truck

Gas Department.

1 general foreman	$ 1,500.00
4 tappers, $4 per day. 303 days	4,848.00
15 service men. $2.75 per day, 303 days	12,498.75
3 meter repair men, $3.50 per day, 303 days	3,161.50
6 meter setters and helpers, $2.75 per day, 303 days	4,999.50
1 storekeeper, $4 per day. 365 days	1,460.00
7 stove men, $2.75 per day, 303 days	5,832.75
2 auto truck men. $2.75 per day, 303 days	1,666.50
1 stable man, $2.75 per day, 303 days	833.25
2 service men, 2.75 per day (drip wagon) 303 days	1,666.50
1 watchman, $2.50 per day, 365 days	912.50
Total	$39,399.25

Equipment.

1 Alco two ton truck
5 horses and wagons
1 pump wagon and horse.

It will be seen from the above figures that the city pays more than $77,000 annually for personal service alone in carrying on pipe-laying and repair work in the departments of water and gas and in rendering miscellaneous services to the consumer. It is evident from a comparison of the forces in these departments that a considerable duplication exists both in respect to personal service and equipment that should be obviated by a centralization of plant and organization.

Obviously certain of the work done by the repair forces of the departments of water and gas is of such a character, particularly in the matter of rendering service to the consumer, as to require separate forces. At the same time it should be possible by a co-ordination of this work and providing suitable transportation equipment to effect a reduction in the present forces assigned to it without in any way impairing its efficiency.

The organization proposed for the division of collection, storage and distribution is predicated on the physical centralization of the maintenance forces in the three departments of water supply, gas and electricity. Obviously the character of the maintenance and repair work of the department of electricity and the requirements of that department in the matter of organization are in no way comparable with the maintenance and repair work of the departments of water supply and gas. Hence the only benefit that would accrue to the city from a physical centralization of the maintenance and repair forces of the former department with those of the latter would be in providing a central storehouse and adequate housing for department equipment. In this connection it should be noted that the department of electricty at present maintains a storehouse for which the city pays a rental of $600 per year. No provision exists at this storehouse for housing department equipment which includes the following:

2 Ford trucks used on repair work

2 horses and wagons—at present kept in street cleaning department stables.

2 runabouts used by inspectors and kept in private garages.

Analysis of Proposed Forces and Equipment for Maintenance.

The following tentative organization is submitted as adequate to meet the ordinary needs of the departments of gas and water supply in the matter of pipe-laying and maintenance. Obviously the proposed distribution of forces should be considered with due regarl to the transportation facilities provided for the work. It will be noted that the titles used and compensation suggested vary considerably from those prevailing at present:

Force and Equipment Requirel for Pipe-Laying anl Repair Work in Department of Public Utilities.

Force.

General foreman ....$ 1,800
Pipe-laying foreman 1,500
Pipe-laying assistant foreman 1,200
6 caulkers, pipe men at $3 per day............. 5,454
6 laborers, $2.50 per day 4,545
                                              ─────────
                                               $14,499

Equipment.

Ford runabout.
1 Also 2 ton truck.
1 Sanford 1 ton truck.

There are at present in the two departments under consideration:

2 two ton Alco trucks.
1 one ton Sanford truck.

These trucks are used for miscellaneous hauling, the one in the gas department being in use only about one-third of the time on heavy hauling. The proposed equipment should be adequate to serve all ordinary needs of the departments of water supply, gas and electricity, in the matter of pipe-laying work and other heavy hauling. The third truck should be assigned to the city engineer's office for use by the maintenance bureau of that office.

Proposed Force and Equipment on House Repair Work and House Connections.

Force.

Foreman of repairs ....$ 1,500
4 plumbers (gang foreman) $105 per month...... 5,040
3 tappers, $4 per day 3,636
16 service men (skilled laborers) at $2.75 per day:. 13,332
                                              ─────────
                                               $23,508

Equipment.

Two Ford trucks equipped with repair tools and miscellaneous supplies should be at all times available for use by the repair gangs in the field.

A third Ford truck completely equippel should be kept at the yard for emergency work. These machines to be operated by service men.

At the present time there are 9 gangs in the field, 5 in the water department and 4 in the gas department doing miscellaneous repair work and making house connections. The gangs are distributed geographically and are provided with no transportation equipment other than push carts. The geographical distribution of repair gangs in Richmond is of questionable policy. Forces should be distributed according to work demands rather than specifically assigned to serve certain districts. The force suggested and the equipment recommended should be adequate to carry on the normal repairs and house connection work of the department.

Meter Repair Work.

Force Required for Meter Repair Work.

Meter repair foreman	$1,200.00
2 meter repair men (tinners) $3.50 per day.....	2,121.00
2 meter repair men (water meters) $3 per day..	1,818.00
The above force on shop work.	
10 service men on meter and stove work, $2.75 ..	8,332.50
2 auto truck men, $3 per day	1,818.00
1 storekeeper	1,500.00
2 service men at yard, $2.75 per day..........	1,666.50
2 laborers at yard, $2.50 per day..............	1,515.00
1 watchman	960.00
1 general mechanician in charge of auto equipment	1,200.00
	$22,131.00

1 Ford truck replacing three horses and wagons.
1 Ford truck in reserve.
Miscellaneous needs. 2 horses.

On the basis of the proposed organization the estimated cost of carrying on the work of pipe-laying, repair work and miscel-

laneous service in the matter of personal service is $60,138 as com-
pared with $77.554.35 under present conditions. Adding 10 per
cent to the estimated cost to provide for vacations, etc,. we have
$66,151 which should be entirely adequate to meet the ordinary
needs of the work under consideration and would effect an annual
saving of approximately $11,000.

Transportation Facilities Required.

There are at present 3 automobile trucks and 7 horses and wagons used by the departments of water supply and gas. It should
be borne in mind that the 2 Ford trucks owned by the department
of electricity will be located at the proposed central yard, thus
constituting a reserve for emergency work that has not been included. In order to provide for the transportation needs of a
combined department it is proposed to purchase 5 Ford trucks and
a Ford runabout and dispense with 5 of the horses and wagons and
1 of the auto trucks An analysis of the estimated cost of the proposed transportation facilities is shown in the accompanying table.

Estimated Cost of Transportation Facilities.

Capital charge of 6 per cent in cost of 5 Ford trucks
and a Ford runabout $2,200 plus freight $2,250. .$ 135
Depreciation 35 per cent   770
Operating cost 1,950
                                               ———————
                                                 $2,855

Crediting cost of maintenance of 5 horses and
    wagons at $20 per month $1,200
Credit 1 Alco 2 ton truck 1,000 2,200
                                               ———————
    Net additional cost .... $ 655

On the above basis it will be seen that the esimated increased
annual cost of the proposed transportation facilities over the present ones amounts to approximately $655. It should be noted, how-
ever, that the facilities provided are exceedingly liberal and no
account is taken of possible economies through eliminating the necessity for hiring teams to do heavy hauling as is the practice at
present n the electrical department. It is urged that the city government give serious consideration to some such centralization of
the repair forces of the departments of water supply, gas and elec-

tricity as is recommended in this report, as a means towards securing a more economical and effective administration of those activities than exist at present.

Additional Economies of Administration. •

In addition to the economies that could be effected in the matter of construction, maintenance and repair work by a centralization of the administration of the departments of water supply, gas and electricity, a considerable saving would also result in the administration of the clerical and accounting activities of those departments. An analysis of the present organization concerned with the latter activities and the work methods employed in operating them, together with recommendations in respect to their centralization and its resulting advantages, are contained in the section of this report prepared by Hagenah and Erickson, so no further discussion thereof is necessary at this point.

It should be noted, however, that the amount of the economies possible in the matter of accounting, clerical and office work alone is estimated at upwards of $12,300. It will then be seen that the total saving in personal service that can be secured from a centralization of the departments of water supply, gas and electricity amounts to approximately $23,300 per year. Deducting the estimated additional expenditures required for adequate transportation facilities there results a net saving of approximately $22,635 per year.

In addition to the financial benefits to be derived from a centralization of the administration of the departments of water supply, gas and electricity of Richmond there are numerous other advantages discussed elsewhere in this report that will accrue to the city from such centralization that make it extremely desirable for the city government to give prompt and serious consideration to the matter of bringing it about.

Standardization of Salaries and Wages

STANDARDIZATION OF SALARIES AND WAGES.

Summary of Conditions Found and General Recommendations.

Defective Appointment Methods.

The conditions of employment in the service of the city of Richmond show many of the same characteristic evils that are to be found in public employment in other cities where a thorough system of civil service control has not been established. Appointments are made without publicity or open competitive examination. There are no established entrance requirements of training and experience even for technical positions. Salaries are fixed arbitrarily without relation to any definite standards of compensation and without provision for advancement in salary or promotion to positions of higher responsibility. Vacancies may be filled without public announcement that the position is open and without any attempt to secure the best qualified person available. Certain positions are filled by direct appointment of the administrative board which fixes the salaries for all employees under its jurisdiction. Other appointments are made by the mayor as authorized in the city charter, and minor appointments are frequently left to department heads. There is at present not even a central roster of all the city employees anywhere in the administrative offices of the government.

Permanency of Employment.

There is not, however, the frequent "turnover" in personnel that is so common where civil service is lacking, but, on the contrary, a tendency toward long and fairly secure tenure of office is evident. Fortunately, there exists in the community a certain respect for public service, and this has enabled the city to secure a higher type of employee than is usually found where "civil service" regulations are lacking.

Can Obtain Benefits of "Civil Service."

In a city as large as Richmond it is clearly desirable that there should be a single agency for the recruiting of employees and uniform methods for advancing and promoting employees. Such uniformity can only be secured through a central employment agency. It is not recommended at this time that a new and independent civil service commission be established, because it is possible to obtain the benefits of "civil service" with little or no additional expense. This can be accomplished simply by extending the functions of an agency which already exists—the public employment bureau commission—to include the recruiting, promotion and keeping of records of municipal employees. It is therefore recommended that the following functions be added to the present duties of the public employment bureau commission:

1—Current maintenance of a roster of all city employees. This roster should indicate the dates of original appointment, transfer, resignation, increase in salary, promotion, address, etc. It should include the original salary and the various steps in salary increases and salary promotions. It should include also the service record of each employee. All this information can be codified.

2—Holding of examinations for entrance into the city service. These examinations, excepting in the case of laborer positions and hospital positions, should include public advertisement stating the nature of the position to be filled, salary range, requirements and the subjects and dates of examination. The subjects should consist of an experience paper, physical, oral, written or other practical test. It is not necessary at the present time that written examinations be held for all positions. The physical examination should be held by physicians designated by the health department. Appropriate standards should be set up by the commission according to the nature of the position to be filled. The requirements should be definitized by the commission as experience dictates. The rating of experience and of the oral or practical examinations should be made by two members of the commission and a representative of the department or departments chiefly concerned in the examination. As a result of each examination a list should be prepared of candidates in the order of standing in the examination. Three names should be certified for each appointment. Candidates should be permitted to decline appointments temporarily under certain conditions to be fixed by the commission. In the case of laborer positions and positions in hospitals only a physical and oral examination should be held. For these positions an oral examination could be held by the secretary of the commission. Those who pass the examination should be listed according to the date of their registration. In this case also three names should be certified for appointment.

3—The submission of lists of those eligible for promotion. These lists should be made up as follows:

Service records should be maintained for each employee in the city service. These records should consist of the semi-annual submission by heads of departments on a form to be devised by the commission, a statement indicating that the work of the employee for the preceding six months has been far above standard, above standard, standard, below standard, or far below standard, with an explanation of the reason for the rating. Percentages of 100, 90, 80, 70, 60, respectively, should be allotted to the above factors The ratings should be originally made by the immediate superior of the person rated. They should then be reviewed by a personnel board consisting in each department or group of departments of the heads of the largest divisions therein. All employees should have the right to see their records. Employees should have a right to appeal to the personnel board of the department and from the decision of this board to the public employment bureau commission. When promotion examinations are to take place, the service records of all employees who are declared eligible should be averaged for the preceding two years. This average should be given a weight of 8 on a scale of 10. A weight of 2 should be given to seniority which should be computed as follows:

Beginning with 70 per cent, 3 per cent should be added for each six months of service up to a maximum of 100 per cent for five years of service.

4—The preparation of a simple procedure governing the work of the commission with regard to the functions above outlined, together with simple rules governing transfers, reinstatements, dismissals, eligibility for examinations, etc.

5—The annual submission as a part of the budget estimates of the service records of all employees for whom increases in salary are requested.

Basis of Classification.

The employees of the city of Richmond are herein classified in the form of (1) grand divisions called services, (2) divisions of service called groups, and (3) grades within groups. The following are the definitions of these terms:

1—The term "service" is used to designate the broadest convenient division of related offices and employments, determined irrespective of the legal class to which they belong.

2—The term "group" is used to designate a subdivision of a service established for the purpose of distinguishing the work or duties generally performed in the same profession, votation, trade or calling, etc.

3—The term "grade" is used to designate a subdivision of a group distinguishing the specific quality of work or duties to be performed by individual officers or employees and an appropriate range of salary, the dstinctions between grades being based upon clearly discernible differences in the importance, difficulty, responsibility, and value of the work.

Such a classification is a necessary first-step toward comparing and standardizing the several hundred employments of the city. The next step is the determination of proper salary ranges for each sub-classification. The complete classification and salary ranges as recommended for adoption are shown in a key chart herewith.

Explanation of Service.

The services which have been adopted do not represent the only possible divisions of employments, but they seem to be those which are best suited to the needs of Richmond. It wll be seen that the theory of standardization is that the divisions are along functional rather than departmental lines, although it was not possible to mainain this distinction in all cases:

The execuive service includes only the functions of elective officers and certain executive heads of departments for whom no regulations governing appointment are recommended.

The professional service includes only the recognized professional employments requiring such high qualifications of professional training and experience as clearly differentiates them from employments in the subprofessional service.

The subprofessional service includes positions as assistants to members of the professions, such as draftsmen, laboratory assistants, etc., who should have an opportunity to graduate into the professional ranks, but should not be classified or paid on a professional basis.

The investigational service includes the higher type of examining and investigational work in public charitable and social work.

The recreational service includes only positions as recreation instructors and other miscellaneous instructors.

The clerical service is practically self-explanatory. The word "clerical" is a very comprehensive term, and under it are included all kinds of office work not requiring particular training and skill of the kinds set forth in the other services.

The inspectional service includes health, building, public works, and other inspections involving observation and inquiry of a more routine and stereotyped nature than that included in the investigational service.

The custodial service includes work or the supervision of work closely related to laboring work, but of a character involving the custody of public property, such as the work of caretakers, janitors, watchmen, storekeepers, etc., and of their supervisors.

The institutional service is another service which is not entirely functional. It includes in general all positions in institutions other than those involving professional work, from helpers and artisans up to and including lay administrators. A helper in an institution who receives maintenance may be doing work very similar to that of a laborer or skilled laborer in other departments, but the condition of employment and salary are so different from those of employees in other departments as to constitute for purposes of classification a separate and distinct kind of employment.

The protective service includes the forces of the police and fire departments.

The street cleaning service is created because it affords a more convenient and practical classification for employees of that department. It is true that the duties of the rank and file of the street cleaning department are very similar to those of laborers and that the duties of the police are similar to those of inspectors, investigators and watchmen, but these forces have peculiar identities and duties of their own, and no purpose could be served by classifying them otherwise than separately.

The skilled trades service includes the recognized skilled trades mostly unionized trades. and in addition helpers in the skilled trades, the supervision of skilled workers and a few classes of technical employees such as signal operators '(fire alarm) and employees of the gas plant, who have been placed in this service because the work is more closely related to the skilled trades than to any other class of employment in the city service.

The unskilled service includes positions as laborers, park workers, hostlers, cleaners and supervisors of laborers, in general, employments requiring physical strength or the ability to supervise physical workers.

Basis of Rates of Compensation.

In determining the rates of compensation inquiries were made of leading corporations, such as public utility corporations, private hospitals, business and banking houses in the city of Richmond and in other places where work and living conditions were thought to be comparable. Inquiries were also made to determine the rates of compensation in other city and state governments, especially where scientific methods have been employed to determine salaries. It has been found unwise to use rates paid in other government units without careful consideration of differences in local conditions and methods adopted in fixing rates. There are of course numerous positions in the city service not found in private employment or differing from positions with the same or related titles in private employment in so many essentials that comparison in salary are often of apparent rather than real value. The fixation of their compensation by comparison with private employment without regard to their peculiar duties would be unfair and inaccurate.

There are in connection with certain positions, conditions of location, housing, long hours and surroundings which have had a direct bearing upon the rates of compensation finally recommended. This is especially true in the case of institutional employees. The remote location of institutions, the unpleasant character of inmates and patients, bad physical conditions, overcrowding, undesirable associates in dormitories and rooms naturally influence properly qualified and respectable persons to refuse to enter and remain in the institutional service. On the other hand, there are employees in institutions, such as male helpers and artisans, who will render satisfactory service at rates considerably lower than those received by persons performing similar work in private employments and even in other branches of the city service. For example, there are persons who have some skill and experience in carpentry and other skilled trades, but who on account of age, lack of ambition and other causes, are willing to accept employment at low salaries in institutions where they will receive maintenance.

The rate of pay to institutional employees in Richmond are, however, extremely low. Such rates as $180 and $120 per year with maintenance are unjustiffable except for former patients of the Tuberculosis Hospital, who are able to perform regular duties but wish to remain in the institutions, or similar cases in the City Home. They cannot be economical because only the least competent and most shiftless persons can be secured at such pay.

Where maintenance, including both meals and lodging, is a part of the compensation received it is valued herein at approximately $240 per annum in determining the proper salary rates. Persons performing the same duties but not receiving maintenance should in general receive about this much additional salary. There are a number of positions in the institutions of Richmond the incumbents of which get one or more meals, or partial maintenance. When it amounts to only one meal per day it has usually been ignored, but in a few cases the rateswere adjusted to fit a situation of partial maintenance that was likely to be permanent.

Basis of Determination of Titles.

In standardizing salary rates in this report the change of many titles is also suggested. The new standard titles have been determined in accordance with the following principles:

1—Titles have been made descriptive of duties. Long titles have been avoided.
2—Titles have been made generic wherever possible, such as chief clerk, clerk, assistant clerk, junior clerk, or engineer, assistant engineer, junior engineer.

Where specialized titles are required, they have been created by adding descriptive words after the generic title. For example, if a specialized position requiring the services of a physician and surgeon to look after all sickness or injury to firemen or policemen is to be created, the title should be physician (fire and police) and not fire and police surgeon. In thi way in all but a few cases the title will immediately identify the rank and grade of an employee and the specialized field in which he is qualified will be indicated by a word or words in brackets.

Long Hours and Sunday Work.

One of the most serious evils in Richmond's public employment service is the comparatively large amount of continuous service—365 days a year either on twelve or twenty-four hour shifts. Regardless of the cost of substituting three eight-hour shifts where necessary and employing extra help to allow each man one day of rest in seven, the present practice cannot be too strongly condemned. Private industry has long since learned that such a condition of employment is not only inhuman but uneconomical in the long run. The only industries that continue to employ men twelve hours a day every day in the year are those that prefer to "scrap" their men as they would machinery and that are branded as exploiters throughout the civilized world.

City Should Be Model Employer.

It is to be assumed that the city of Richmond wishes, as far as it is financially able, to be a model employer. The city should therefore not only maintain standard conditions as to hours of labor, days of rest and physical conditions of safety and comfort, but in those employments in which private corporations generally pay inadequate salaries, the city should pay adequately. The city should under no circumstances pay less than a living wage. A part of the administration of standardized personal service should be the periodical investigation of the cost of living in the community to determine whether heads of families in the city service were receiving in any case wages or salaries which do not conform with such prinicples.

Advantage of Range of Salary Over a Fixed Rate in the City Service.

The experience of the most progressive private corporations and governments in this and other countries indicates that even if it is possible to determine exactly the value of a particular position, it is nevertheless preferable to establish a range of salary with a minimum compensation somewhat below and a maximum somewhat above the exact value. This range of salary reflects the fact that in many cases an employee enters a position with relatively little experience and that through application and experience over a considerable period of time his usefulness increases to its maximum value. Advancement within this range of salary from the minimum to the maximum is held out as an incentive to efficient service. In the case of a classification of city employments, in which a number of positions of similar but not identical value must necessarily be placed in the same grade, it is absolutely essential that there should be a range of salary fixed for the grade, the minimum of which should be a proper minimum for the least important position in the grade and the maximum of which should be a proper maximum for the most important position in the grade. In the lower grades, all positions are usually worth from the minimum to the maximum compensation, assuming that the quality and quantity of service rendered by the incumbents are up to standard. However, in the higher grades, where positions within the same grade frequently differ in importance and value irrespective of the efficiency of the incumbents, the maximum rate and in some cases the initial rate must be determined upon the basis of a specific appraisal of the value of the position in question. In certain cases an exception to the general rule of a range of salary has been made and flat rates have been established, notably in the skilled trades.

The Need for an Adequate Pension System.

There is at present no provision for retiring superannuated employees except a resolution passed by the council on April 23, 1915, establishing a "Superannuated or Infirm Employees Fund" and authorizing the administrative board to re-employ former employees of the street cleaning and other departments "who have served the city for not less than ten years continuously and been laid off by reason of their age or other infirmity" at a compensation of one dollar and fifty cents per day each, the expenditures for this purpose to be charged to the special fund. This scheme, which is not rigidly adhered to, is entirely inadequate and should not be considered a satisfactory substitute for a pension system. It is recommended that a special committee including representatives of the city employees be appointed by the council to make a study of pension systems and be given funds, to secure the assistance of some person who is familiar with the operation of scientific pension systems in this country and abroad with instructions to report and make detailed recommendations within a year's time.

Principles Which Should Govern Amount of Increases.

The regulations recommended for governing amount of each increase within the respective salary ranges are embodied in the following table:

Salaries up to $1,200, advances of $24, 30, 36, 48 or 60.
Salaries from $1,200 to 1,800, advances of $120.
Salaries from $1,800 to 2,400, advances of $·80
Salaries from $2,400 to 3,600, advances of $240.
Salaries from $3,600 to 4,800, advances of $300.

The following general principles determine the amount of increase, whether $24, 30, 36, or 60, in salaries up to $1,200:

1—$24 increases per annum should be applied in the case of positions involving manual labor of the simplest character in the lowest grades of the unskilled, skilled trades, institutional and street cleaning services, such as laborer, cleaner, institutional helper and sweeper.

2—$30 increases should be applied in positions in the institutional service involving domestic or handicraft work, such as cook and hospital attendant.

3—$36 increases should be applied in the case of positions in the lowest grades of the custodial service involving work requiring ability and responsibility somewhat above that required in ordinary manual labor, but not ranking with the skilled trades in these respects, such as caretaker, elevator operator, etc.

4—$60 increases should be applied in the case of the following positions:

    a—Positions in the lower grades of the professional, subprofessional, investigational, recreational, clerical, and inspectional services.

    b—Positions in the skilled trades service to which annual salaries are attached, involving work in recognized skilled trades and similar employments, such as signal operator (fire alarm), motor driver, etc.

    c—Positions as foreman in the unskilled and street cleaning services.

It has been found necessary to make certain exceptions to regulations governing amount of increases, namely, where there is a rate of $1,140, $1,740, $2,340, the increase appropriate to the range immediately above has been applied. Therefore, the next rate after $1,140 is $1,260, after $1,740 is $1,920, after $2,340 is $2,580. The next rate after $2,280 is $2,460, unless the increase involves promotion to a higher grade, in which case the next rate is $2,520.

In the case of a higher grade involving initially much greater responsibilities and much more important duties than any in the grade below, the minimum salary rate for the higher grade has been placed above the amount fixed by the general rule. For example, the maximum salary for a deputy collector of taxes in grade 1 is $1,560, while the minimum salary for collector of delinquent taxes in grade 2 is $3,000.

Below $1,200, $120 increases are applied in some cases, for example, where the city is employing professional men who cannot be expected to remain long within a grade at a low salary rate. The first grade in the engineer group is an example of this kind of exception.

One hundred-twenty dollars are also applied in some cases where a considerable period of apprenticeship is required before entrance into the grade, and a $60 increase would not be adequate; and the maximum rate represents the proper salary at the end of two or three years' experience in the city service, as in grade 1 of the bookkeeper group.

Above $1,200, $60 increases are applied in some cases, for example, where it is expected that employees will remain within a grade for a long time, and an increase of $120 is thought to be too large.

The rates for internes and pupil nurses are not in the nature of a salary, but a stipend to provide for personal needs beyond the bare maintenance they receive.

KEY CHART

SHOWING CLASSIFICATION AND SALARY RANGES RECOMMENDED FOR ADOPTION AS STANDARD

Service		Group		Number of Grades	Salary Range	Examples
Title	Code Symbol	Title	Code Symbol			
Executive	X	Elective executive	E	1	$1,920-2,250	Mayor, treasurer.
					1,740-1,920	City clerk, auditor, city attorney.
Professional	O	Appointive executive	A	1	1,920-2,220	Special accountant.
		Accountant	A	1	1,920-2,220	Director of settling basins.
				1	1,020-1,200	Chemist and bacteriologist.
		Chemist and bacteriologist	B	1	1,020-1,200	Junior engineer.
		Engineer	E	2	1,600-2,100	Assistant engineer.
				3	2,110-2,550	Chief building inspector.
					2,340-3,040	Senior assistant engineer.
				4	3,420-4,800	Engineer, assistant (civil) (electrical) (mechanical).
		Lawyer	L	1	2,400-3,300	Assistant city attorney.
		Nurse	N	1	640- 720*	Nurse.
					710- 930	Field nurse.
				2	790- 3 00*	Chief nurse.
					1,020-1,200	Supervising field nurse.
				3	1,020-1,140*	Supt. of nurses in large hospital or entire supervision of small hospital.
		Physician		4	1,500-1,560	General superintendent of nurses.
				1	160- 300*	Medical interne.
				2	720-1,060*	Assistant physician (hospital).
				3	390	Physician (dispensary).
					(part time)	
					480- 720	Physician (field).
					(part time)	
					1,620-1 9.0	Physician (fire and police).
					(part time)	
				4	2,250-2 760	Physician (medical inspector).
Sub-professional	P	Draftsman	D	1	3,400-3,900	Chief health officer.
		Instrumentman	I	1	930-1,440	Draftsman.
		Junior interne	I	1	90-1,200	Instrumentman.
		Laboratory assistant	B	1	60*	Junior interne.
					2 0- 610	Laboratory apprentice.
		Probationer in office	P	1	95- 120*	Pupil nurse.
		Pupil nurse	N	1	1,140-1,440	Probationer in office.
Investigational	V	Recreation instructor or	R	1	720- 900	Recreation instructor, recreation instructor (swimming).
Recreational	E				$1 per session	Pianist.
				2	960-1 140	Recreation supervisor.
				3	1,200-1,620	Director of recreation.

maintenance (without maintenance add about $240 per annum).

Service		Group		Number of Grades	Salary Range	Examples
Title	Code Symbol	Title	Code Symbol			
Clerical	C	Bookkeeper	B	1 / 2 / 3	840-1,200 / 1,320-1,540 / 1,640-2,100	Junior bookkeeper. / Bookkeeper. / Chief bookkeeper.
		Clerk	C	2 / 3 / 4 / 5	380- 540 / 720- 900 / 1,020-1,320 / 1,440-1,560 / 1,680-1,800	Junior clerk. / Assistant clerk, junior stenographic clerk. / Clerk, assistant stenographic clerk. / Stenographic clerk. / Chief clerk. / Secretary.
		Court clerk	K	1	1,200-1,800	Court clerk, acting court clerk. / Acting court clerk (juvenile and domestic relations court).
		Employment agent	E	1	900-1,360	Employment agent.
		Revenue officer	R	2 / 3	1,200-1,540 / 1,560-2,160 / 1,200-1,560 / 3,000-3,500	Superintendent (public employment bureau). / Cashier, deputy collector of taxes. / Collector of city taxes, collector of delinquent taxes. / City treasurer.
Inspectional		Inspector of buildings	B	1 / 2 / 3	1,200-1,560 / 1,680-1,900 / 2,240-3,100	Building inspector, bldg. inspector (electricity) (plumbing). / Senior building inspector (plumbing). / Chief building inspector.
		Health inspector	H	2	1,040-1,350 / 1,440-1,800 / 1,560-2,100	Health inspector. / Supervising health inspector (food) (sanitation). / Supervising health inspector (milk).
		Inspector of meters	T	1	960-1,140	Inspector of meters.
		Inspector of public works	P	1	1,080-1,320	Inspector of public works.
Custodial	K	Caretaker	C	1	780- 924	Caretaker. / Custodian (reservoir).
		Court and legislative attendant	K	1	960-1,200	Bailiff (civil court) (police court), first deputy (hustings court), deputy (hustings court) (court attendant).
		Dockmaster	D	1	1,200-1,560	Dockmaster.
		Elevator operator	E	1	792- 900	Elevator operator.
		Storekeeper	S	1	960-1,210	Storekeeper.
		Watchman	W	1	720- 792 (excl. of Sundays) 816- 888 (every day.)	Watchman.
Institutional		Culinary worker	Q	1	480- 780* / 380- 420* / 240- 330*	Baker. / Cook A. / Cook B.
		Helper	H	1 / 2 / 3	120- 150* / 288- 360* / 216- 312* / 390- 480*	Junior institutional helper. / Institutional helper A. / Institutional helper B, seamstress. / Sr. institutional helper.

*With maintenance (without maintenance add about $240 per annum).

Service		Group		Number of Grades	Salary Range	Examples
Title	Code Symbol	Title	Code Symbol			
		Hospital attendant	A	1	300- 450*	Hospital attendant.
		Institutional clerk	C	1	360- 540*	Assistant institutional clerk.
				2	600- 780*	Institutional clerk.
		Institutional supervisor	S	1	600- 780*	Matron, housekeeper.
					780- 960*	Steward.
				2	1,440-1,680*	Lay superintendent.
		Correction officer	O	1	840-1,080	Correction officer.
					600- 780*	Matron Juvenile Detention Home.
				2	720- 900	Police matron.
					1,200-1,440	Warden.
					840-1,320	Correction matron.
Street cleaning		Refuse collector and street cleaner	K	1	816- 888(1)	Driver, hostler.
					792- 864(2)	Stableman, sweeper.
		Refuse disposer	D	2	990-1,080	Stable foreman (refuse collection), (street cleaning).
				2	792- 864(2)	Disposal plant operator.
		Supervisor	S	2	1,200-1,560	Foreman disposal plant.
				1	1,080	District superintendent.
					990-2,580	Superintendent (department street cleaning).
Skilled		Builder	B	1	$3.50 per day	Bricklayer.
		Electrical worker	E	1	960-1,080(3)	Lineman, signal operator (police).
					1,020-1,140	Electrical switchboard operator, signal operator (fire alarm).
				2	720- 840(2)	Groundman, lampman.
				3	1,200-1,440	Foreman (fireman) (electrician).
					1,620-2,100	Superintendent of fire alarm and police signal system.
		Engineman	G	1	948- 888	Fireman, oiler.
				2	1,020-1,320	Engineman, engineman (steam roller).
					1,140-1,320	Engineman (gas plant), (electric plant).
				3	1,440-1,920	Chief engineman.
		Journeyman's helper	J	1	$2.75 per day	Helper to blacksmith, machinist, plumber, tapper, etc.
		Marine engineman	N	1	814- 864(1)	Marine fireman.
				2	1,080-1,440 (every day)	Marine engineman.
					1,020-1,320 (excl. of Sunday)	Marine engineman.
		Marine officer	O	1	600-1,020	Mate.
				2	1,320-1,560	Captain.

*With maintenance (without maintenance add about $240 per annum).
(1) Per diem rate for temporary service $2.50
(2) Per diem rate for temporary service 2.50
(3) Per diem rate for temporary service 2.70

Service		Group		Number of Grades	Salary Range	Examples
Title	Code Symbol	Title	Code Symbol			
		Mechanic	K	1	$2.85 per day 3.10 per day 4.00 per day 900- 960 1,020-1,200	Caulker. Machinist, tinner, gas meter repairer. Topper, machinist (automobile). Mechanic (meter repair). Foreman mechanic (meter repair).
		Metal worker	M	2	$3.50 per day (4)	Blacksmith.
		Motor driver	X	1	840-1,140	Motor driver, motor driver (ambulance), (patrol), (a re t cleaning).
		Plumber	P	1	$4.50 per day (4)	Plumber.
		Woodworker	W	1	1,080-1,200(5)	Carpenter, dock builder, machine woodworker, pattern maker, ship carpenter, wheelwright, etc.
		Miscellaneous skilled worker	Z	1	1,020-1,080(6) (every day) 840- 888(6) (excl. of Sundays)	Skilled laborer (gas plant), (gas service). Skilled laborer (gas plant). (gas service).
Unskilled				2	1,140-1,320 (every day)	General mechanic (gas plant). (pumping station).
		Cleaner	C	3 1	1,440-1,680 720- 792 (men 7 hrs.) (7) 600- 720 (women 7 hr) (7) 276- 372 (women 3 hrs) (8)	General foreman (gas plant). Janitor in city hall, cleaning only portion of building, sweepers in public, extra janitors in armory, etc. Janitor in city hall, cleaning only portion of building, sweepers in public market, extra janitors in armory, etc. Janitor in city hall, cleaning only portion of building, sweepers in public market, extra janitors in armory, etc
		Hostler and driver	H	1	816- 888(3)	Hostler.
		Park worker	P	1 2 3	$2 70 $2.90 per day 1,020-1,200 1,800-2,340	Gardener. Arboriculturist, park foreman, cemetery foreman. Superintendent of parks.
		Laborer	L	3 1	792- 864(9) 900-1,200(10)	Laborer. Foreman (in charge of ordinary labor gangs). Foreman (in charge of large gang incl. skilled laborers).
		Miscellaneous laborer	Z	2	1,140-1,680 720- 744 828- 900	General foreman. Dog catcher. Pound keeper.

(4) Or prevailing rate.
(5) Temporary hourly compensation .... $.50
(6) Per diem rate for temporary service 2.75
(7) Temporary hourly compensation .... .28
(8) Temporary hourly compensation .... .20
(9) Per diem rate for temporary service 2.50-2.80
(10) Per diem rate for temporary service 3.00-4.00

STANDARDIZATION OF EXISTING POSITIONS AND APPRAISAL OF SALARY RATES
(EXCLUSIVE OF UNIFORMED POLICE AND FIRE FORCES)

(NOTE—In appraising the present duties of the city's employees the aim has been to fit the compensation to normal conditions. Existing conditions are not normal and financially they may become more acute as the war continues. To work out in advance a schedule of compensation which will meet the changing conditions of war times is both impossible and impracticable.

It is also to be noted that no appraisal has been made of the uniformed forces of the police and fire departments, because no basis exists for such an appraisal. The compensation which should be paid policemen and firemen is largely a matter of opinion. There is nothing in the commercial world with which to make comparison. The salary rates of the police and fire departments vary somewhat as between cities, but there is nothing to prove that any particular city is paying the correct rates.)

Number of Positions	Present Title	Present Salary	Proposed Title	Code Reference	Appraised Salary Range
			City Council		
	City clerk	$3,000	City clerk	XA	$2,400
	Sergeant-at-arms	2,000	Sergeant-at-arms	KK1	900–1,200
	Clerk council committee	2,400	Should be merged with office of city clerk		
			Mayor's Office		
	Mayor	$5,000	Mayor	XE	5,000
	Secretary	3,000	Secretary	CC6	1,800–2,160
			Legal Department		
	City attorney	5,000	City attorney	XA	5,000
	Assistant attorney	3,000	Assistant city attorney	OL1	2,400–3,380
	Clerk and stenographer	1,500	Stenographic clerk	CC4	1,440–1,560
	Stenographer	900	Junior stenographic clerk	CC2	720–900
			City Treasurer		
	City treasurer	5,040	City treasurer	XE	1,680–2,160
	Clerk	2,500	Chief bookkeeper	CB3	1,200–1,560
	Clerks	1,600	Cashier	CR1	840–1,200
	Clerk	900	Junior bookkeeper	CB1	720–900
	Clerk	720	Assistant clerk	CC2	1,200–1,560
	Deputy	1,500	Cashier	CR1	
			City Auditor		
	City Auditor	3,600	City auditor	XA	3,600
	Clerk	1,800	Chief bookkeeper	CB3	1,680–2,160
	Clerk	1,200	Bookkeeper	CB2	1,320–1,560
	Clerk	1,200	Clerk	CC	1,090–1,380
	Checking clerk	1,020	Clerk	CC3	1,090–1,38
	Clerk and stenographer	1,000	Assistant stenographic clerk	CC3	1,090–1,380

Number of Positions	Present Title	Present Salary	Proposed Title	Code Reference	Appraised Salary Range
	Special Accountant				
	Accountant	2,000	Special accountant	OA1	1,920-2,280
	Assessment clerk	1,350	Clerk	CC3	1,020-1,380
	Collection of Taxes				
	City collector	3,600	City collector	CR2	3,600
	Deputy city collector	1,800	Assistant city collector	CR1	1,200-1,560
	Assistant city collector	1,500	Clerk	CC3	1,020-1,380
	Assistant city collector	1,320	Assistant city collector	CR1	1,020-1,560
	Clerks	1,020	Clerk	CC3	1,020-1,380
	Collection of Delinquent Taxes				
	Delinquent tax collector	3,600	Deputy city collector	CR2	3,000
	Deputy delinquent tax collector	1,500	Assistant city collector	CR1	1,200-1,560
	Special delinquent tax collector				(15% of amount collected)
	Court and Juries **(Exclusive of State Courts)**				
	Civil court clerk	1,800	Court clerk	CK1	1,200-1,800
	Bailiff	1,080	Court attendant	KK1	960-1,200
	Police court clerk	1,200	Court clerk	GK1	1,200-1,800
	Bailiff	1,095	Court attendant	KK1	960-1,200
	Bailiff	1,000	Court attendant	KK1	960-1,200
	City Jail				
	Chief deputy at jail	1,320	Warden	NO2	1,200-1,440
	Chief deputy at Hastings court	1,320	No appraisal		
	Deputy, Hastings court	1,020	No appraisal		
	Deputy, city jail	1,020	Correction officer	NO1	840-1,080
	Deputies and guards	720	Correction officer	NO1	840-1,080
	Matron	600	Correction matron	NO2	840-1,320
	Visiting physician	500	Physician	OP3	No change recommended
	Resident physician	600	Assistant physician	OP2	720-1,080

*The present position of matron at the jail, which is part-time only, is appraised under this title with a salary for full-time service, as recommended in the report on the ..ty jail.

Number of Positions	Present Title	Present Salary	Proposed Title	Code Reference	Appraised Salary Range
	Juvenile Court				
	Probation officer No. 1	1,200	Probation officer	VP1	1,140–1,440
	Probation officer No. 2	1,000	Probation officer	VP1	1,140–1,440
	Clerk	720	Acting clerk (Juvenile Domestic Relation) court	CK1	1,200–1,500
	Detention Home (White)				
	Matron (white detention home)	480	Matron (Juvenile detention)	NO1	480– 720*
	Custodian	40wm	Caretaker	KC1	540– 684*
	Cook	144wm	Institutional helper	NH2	216– 312*
	Detention Home (Colored)				
	Superintendent (Colored detention home)	480	Caretaker (Juvenile detention home)	KC1	540– 684*
	Helper	180*	Matron	NO1	600– 780*
	*With maintenance (without maintenance add $240).				
	Employment Bureau				
	Manager	1,500	Superintendent (public employment bureau)	CB2	1,560–2,160
	Clerk	900	Employment agent	CE1	900–1,380
	Assistant clerk	$2.25 per day	Employment agent	CE1	900–1,380
	Police (civilian Employees)				
	Lineman	900	Lineman	TE1	900–1,080
	Mechanician	1,200	Mechanist (automobile)	TK1	4.00 per day
	Matron	720	Matron (police)	NO1	720– 900
	Patrol central office operator	900	Signal operator (police)	TE1	900–1,080
6	Janitors	780	Caretaker	KC1	780– 924
2	Janitresses	240	Cleaner	UC1	Not less than 3 hours per diem 276–372
	Hostler	780	Hostler	UH1	816– 888
4	Chauffeurs	1,020	Motor driver (patrol)	TX1	840–1,140
3	Probation officers	1,212	Probation officer	VP1	1,140–1,440

Number of Positions	Present Title	Present Salary	Proposed Title	Code Reference	Appraised salary Range
			Fire Alarm		
	Superintendent	$1,449.12	Superintendent of fire alarm and police signal systems	TE3	1,620-2,100
	Assistant superintendent	1,209.60	Foreman lineman	TE2	1,260-1,440
	Operators and inspectors	1,102.56	Signal operator (fire alarm)	TE1	960-1,140
	Lineman and inspector	945.12	Lineman	TE1	960-1,080
	Lineman		Lineman	TE1	960-1,080
			Administrative Board—Employees		
	Chief clerk	$2,400	Secretary	CC6	$1,860-2,100
	Assistant clerk	1,500	Clerk	CC3	1,020-1,380
	Filing clerk	1,200	Clerk	CC3	1,020-1,380
	Chauffeur and mechanic	1,080	Motor driver	TX1	840-1,140
	Paymaster	2,100	Bookkeeper	CB3	1,680-2,100
	Stenographer and assistant clerk	1,500	Stenographic clerk	CC4	1,440-1,560
	Assistant paymaster	1,500	Janitor bookkeeper	CB2	1,320-1,560
	Printer	600	Position unnecessary		
			Building Department		
	Building inspector	3,600	Chief building inspector	OF3	2,160-2,880
	Deputy building inspectors	1,500	Building inspector	IB1	1,200-1,560
	Special deputy building inspector	1,200	Building inspector	IB1	1,200-1,560
	City hall —engineer	1,350	Engineman	TG2	1,020-1,320
2	Firemen	900	Fireman	TG1	840-888
3	Elevator man	900	Elevator operator	KE1	792-900
7	Janitors	780	Cleaner	UC1	720-792
2	Watchmen	840	Watchmen	KW1	816-888
	Janitor (chancery court)	168	Cleaner	UC1	720-792
	Custodian (Howitzer's armory)	840	Caretaker	KC1	780-924
	Custodian (auditorium)	900	Caretaker	KC1	780-924
	Custodian (Blue's armory)	840	Caretaker	KC1	780-924
	Custodian (First Regiment armory)	840	Caretaker	KC1	780-924
	Janitor	2.50 p d	Cleaner	UC1	720-792
	Janitor	2 25 p d	Cleaner	UC1	720-705
	Janitor (South Richmond offices)	5 40	Cleaner	UC1	720-792
			Electrical Department		
	Superintendent of electrical plant and city electrician	3,600	Engineer (electrical)	OF4	3,420-4,800

Number of Positions	Present Title	Present Salary	Proposed Title	Code Reference	Appraised Salary Range
			Electrical Inspection		
	Chief inspector	1,540	Building inspector (electricity)	IB1	1,200–1,560
	Electrical inspector	1,540	Building inspector (electricity)	IB1	1,260–1,560
	Permit clerk	960	Clerk	CC3	1,020–1,380
			Electric Lighting		
	Chief clerk	$1,200	Chief clerk	CC5	$1,080–1,560
	Chief engineer	1,500	Chief engineman	TG3	1,440–1,920
	Draughtsman	1,200	Junior engineer	CF1	1,020–1,380
	Chief electrician	1,440	Foreman electrician	TI-2	1,500–1,440 (345 days)
	Engineers	1,200	Engineman	TG2	1,140–1,320
	Electricians	2.50 p.d.	Switchboard operator	TE1	1,200–1,440 (315 days)
2	Oilers	2.50 p.d.	Oiler	TG1	840–888
2	Firemen	2.75 p.d.	Fireman	TG1	840–888
2	Foreman linemen	1,440	Foreman linemen	TI2	1,260–1,440
2	Linemen	1,080	Lineman	TI2	960–1,040
4	Linemen	1,080	Lineman	TI1	720–840
2	Laborers	2.70 p.d.	Ground man	TI1	960–1,040
3	Trouble linemen	2.25 p.d.	Lineman	TI1	900–1,060
2	Trouble linemen	1,080	Lineman	TI1	900–1,060
4	Lamp man	2.70 p.d.	Lamp men	TI1	720–840
	Lamp man	2.60 p.d.	Lamp men	TE1	720–840
			Department of Health		
	Chief health officer	3,200	Chief health officer	GP4	3,600–4,560
	Medical inspector	2,400	Physician (medical inspector)	GP3	2,280–2,760
	Bacteriologist	2,400	Chemist and bacteriologist	CB1	1,920–2,280
	Registrar of vital statistics	1,320	Chief clerk	CC5	1,680–1,800
	Clerk	1,080	Clerk	CC3	1,020–1,380
	Stenographer	780	Junior stenographic clerk	CC2	720–960
	Fumigator	1,000	Health inspector	II1	970–1,200
	Plumbing inspector	1,650	Sanitary inspector (plumbing)	II2	1,080–1,080
	Assistant plumbing inspector	1,290	Building inspector (plumbing and sanitation)	jI1	1,200–1,410
	Food inspector	1,290	Supervising health inspector (food)	II1	1,440–1,560
7	Assistant food inspector	1,080	Health inspector	II1	900–1,200
6	Chief sanitary inspector	1,290	Supervising health inspector (sanitation)	II2	1,440–1,800
	Physicians to p. or.	780	Health inspector	II1	9 (–1,500
			Physician (field)	OI3	840–720
					(part time)
	Dairy inspector	1,800	Supervising health inspector (milk)	II2	1,560–2,100
	Assistant dairy inspector	1,080	Health inspector	II1	960–1,270
	Laboratory helper	600	Laboratory apprentice	BB1	240–630

Number of Positions	Present Title	Present Salary	Proposed Title	Code Reference	Appraised Salary Range
	Department of Health—Continued				
	Chief infantile nurse	900	Supervising field nurse	CN2	1,020–1,200
	Office boy	420	Junior clerk	CC1	360– 540
	Guard	480	Senior institutional helper	NH3	390– 480
					(with maintenance)
	Smallpox nurse		Nurse	ON1	660– 720
					(with maintenance)
	Assistant infantile nurses	780	Nurse (field)	ON1	780–900
	Physician (tuberculosis dispensary)	360	Physician (dispensary)	OP3	360 (part time)
			Street Cleaning		
	Superintendent	2,000	Superintendent (S. C. D.)	SS2	1,980–2,640
	Assistant superintendents	1,200	District superintendent	SS1	1,200–1,560
	Clerk	1,200	Clerk	CC3	1,020–1,320
	Assistant clerk	900	Assistant clerk	CC2	720– 900
	Chauffeur	2.75 p d	Motor driver (S. C. D.)	TX1	840–1,140
	Truck chauffeur	2.50 p d	Motor driver (truck)	TX1	840–1,140
	Chauffeur	2.50 p d	Motor driver	TX1	840–1,140
	Stable foreman	900	Stable foreman	SK2	960–1,080
2	Foremen (Ash and truck)	2.62½ p d	Foreman (refuse collection)	SK2	960–1,080
	Foremen (garbage collection)	2.62½ p d	Foreman (refuse collection)	SK2	960–1,080
2	Foremen (Sweeping)	2.62½ p d	Foreman (street cleaning)	SK2	960–1,080
	Inspector	2.50 p d		SK1	Position unnecessary
3	Hostlers	2.50 p d	Hostler	UH1	816– 888
105	Drivers	2.50 p d	Driver	SK1	816– 888
6	Stablemen	2.50 p d	Stableman	SK1	816– 888
60	Patrol and sweepers	2.50 p d	Sweeper	SK1	816– 888
38	Ash and trash collectors	2.50 p d	Laborer	UL1	792– 864
	Man	2.50 p d	Stable fireman	SK2	960–1,080
	Foreman crematory	2.75 p d	Foreman (disposal plant)	SD2	960–1,000
2	Pound master	900	Pound keeper	UZ2	828– 900
	Dog catchers	720	Dog catcher	UZ1	720– 744
			Engineer's Department		
	City Engineer	4,800	Engineer	OE4	3,420–4,800
	Chief clerk	2,000	Chief clerk	CC5	1,680–1,870
	Assessor of damages	1,500	Draftsman	PD1	960–1,440
	First assistant engineer	2,700	Senior Assistant engineer	OE3	2,340–3,060
	Second assistant engineer	2,460	Senior Assistant engineer	OE3	2,340–3,060
	General inspector	1,200	Inspector of public works	IP1	1,080–3,320
	7th Assistant engineer	1,590	Assistant engineer	OF2	1,500–2,160
	Foreman (Sewer)	900	Foreman	U12	900–1,200

Engineer's Department—Continued

Number of Positions	Present Title	Present Salary	Proposed Title	Code Reference	Appraised Salary Range
	Assistant chief clerk	1,500	Stenographic clerk	CC3	1,020-1,380
	Inspector-office manager	1,200	Clerk	CC3	1,020-1,260
	Assistant Engineer-computor draftsman	2,000	Assistant engineer	OE2	1,500-2,160
	Inspector-rodman	3.25 per day extra for over-time			
	Inspector (temporary)	1,200	Inspector of public works	IP1	1,060-1,320
	Inspector (temporary)	1,200	Inspector of public works	IP1	1,060-1,320
	Inspector (temporary)	1,200	Inspector of public works	IP1	1,060-1,320
	Inspector	1,200	Inspector of public works	IP1	1,060-1,320
	3rd assistant engineer	1,750	Assistant engineer	OE2	1,500-2,160
	Bridge watchmen	750	Watchman	AW1	(unnecessary)
	4th assistant engineer	1,750	Assistant engineer	OE2	1,500-2,160
	Inspector	1,200	Inspector of public works	IP1	1,060-1,320
	Rodmen-inspector	1,200	Instrumentman	BI1	900-1,200
	5th Assistant engineer	1,500	Assistant engineer	OE2	1,500-2,160
	Hostler	2.50 per diem		SK1	charge to street cleaning
	6th assistant engineer (annexed territory)	1,500	Assistant engineer	OE2	1,500-2,160
	Assistant engineer	1,800	Assistant engineer	OE2	1,500-2,160
	Chief of party	1,500	Junior engineer	OE1	1,020-1,380
	Draughtsman	1,500	Draftsman	BD1	960-1,440
	Chief draughtsman	1,600	Draftsman	BI1	960-1,440
	Instrumentman	1,200	Instrumentman	BD1	960-1,200
	Draftsmen	1,800	Draftsmen	BD1	960-1,440
	Title examiner		Title examiner	BX1	Position unnecessary
	Rodman (Sur. annex. ter.)	2.50 p. d.	Laborer	UL1	799-864
	Axeman	2.50 p. d.	Laborer	UL1	799-864
	Chairman	2.50 p. d.	Laborer	UL1	799-864
	Dockmaster	1,500	Dockmaster	KD1	1,200-1,680
	Captain and Supt. Tug and Dredge	1,500	Captain	TO2	1,320-1,620
	Engineer (tug)	1,020	Marine engineman	TN2	1,080-1,440 (365 days)
					1,020-1,320 (313 days)
	Mate	960	Mate	TO1	990-1,020
	Fireman	720	Marine fireman	TN1	814-864
	Pipe tender	720	Laborer	UL1	792-864
	Night and Sunday man	720	Watchman	KW1	720-792
	Engineer of dredge	1,200	Marine engineer	TN2	1,060-1,440 (365 days)
					1,020-1,320 (313 days)
	Fireman	720	Marine fireman	TN1	814-864
	Dipper tender	720	Laborer	UL1	792-864
	Deckhand	660	Laborer	UL1	792-864
	Deckhand-assistant fireman	720	Laborer	UL1	792-864

Engineer's Department—Parks and Grounds

Number of Positions	Present Title	Present Salary	Proposed Title	Code Reference	Appraised Salary Range
8	Assistant superintendent parks and grounds	$2,000	Park superintendent	UP3	$1,800–2,340
	Park keeper (also janitor at Hustings court which pay $35 of salary)	1,020	Park foreman	UP2	1,020–1,200
4	Foreman	1,020	Foreman	UP2	1,020–1,200
21	Laborer	960	Laborer	UL1	900–1,200
	Extra men (temporary)	2.50 p. d.	Laborer	UP2	792– 864
	City nurseryman	2.25 p. d.	Arboriculturist	UP2	1,020–1,200 (with house)
2	Laborers in nursery	900	Gardener	UP1	2.70–2.90 p. d
3	Cemetery keeper	1,200	Cemetery foreman	UP2	1,020–1,200
	Cemetery keeper	900	Cemetery foreman	UP2	1,020–1,200
14	Laborers in cemetery	2.50 p. d.	Laborer	UI1	792– 864
4	Laborer in cemetery	2.25 p. d.	Laborer	UI1	792– 864
	Assistant superintendent playgrounds	1,200	Director of recreation	ER3	1,260–1,620
4	Directors (playgrounds)	$80 month	Recreation supervisors	ER2	960–1,140
5	Assistant directors	70 month	Recreation instructor	ER1	720– 900
	Caretaker	40 month	Caretaker	KC1	780– 924
	Pianist	25 month	Recreation instructor	ER1	?
2	Pianist	15 month	Pianist	ER1	$1 per session
	Director	50 month	Recreation instructor	ER1	720– 900
	Director	70 month	Recreation supervisor	ER2	960–1,140
	Assistant director	50 month	Recreation instructor	ER1	720–1,140
2	Caretaker	60 month	Caretaker	KC1	780– 924
	Caretaker (part time)	30 month	Caretaker	ER1	?
2	Extra workers (part time)	25 month	Recreation instructor	kC1	?
	Caretaker (part time)	10 month	Caretaker	ER1	?
2	Caretaker (part time)	15 month	Caretaker	KC1	?
	Director	25 month	Recreation instructor	ER1	720– 900
	Director	75 month	Recreation instructor	ER1	720– 900
	Life guard	75 month	Recreation instructor	ER1	720– 900

Virginia Hospital

Number of Positions	Present Title	Present Salary	Proposed Title	Code Reference	Appraised Salary Range
	Superintendent	$1,500	Medical superintendent	OP3	1,020–1,140*
	Assistant superintendent	1,080	Superintendent of nurses	ON3	780– 900*
	Night supervisor	780	Chief nurse	ON2	780– 900*
	Superintendent, operating room	780	Chief nurse	ON2	780– 900*
	Superintendent nurses	780	Superintendent of nurses	ON3	1,020–1,140*
	Housekeeper	720	Matron	NO1	600– 780*
	Graduate nurse	660			
28	Pupil nurses	108	Pupil nurses	BN1	$8–10 per month
	Chief interns	720	Assistant physician (hospital)	OP2	720–1,080*

*With maintenance (without maintenance add $2.40)

Number of Positions	Present Title	Present Salary	Proposed Title	Code Reference	Appraised Salary Range

Virginia Hospital—Continued

Number of Positions	Present Title	Present Salary	Proposed Title	Code Reference	Appraised Salary Range
6	Internes	60	Medical internes	OP1	180– 200*
	Engineer	900	Engineman	eTG2	1,020–1,320
1	Night telephone operator	600	Assistant institutional clerk	NC1	360– 540*
1	Day telephone operator	900	Assistant institutional clerk	NC1	360– 540*
	Clerk	900	Institutional clerk	NC2	600– 780*
	Seamstress	180	Seamstress	NH2 (B)	216– 312*
	Cook	420	Cook A	NQ1 (A)	300– 420*
	Assistant cook	240	Cook B	NQ1 (B)	240– 330*
	Assistant cook	180	Institutional helper	NH2B	216– 312*
2	Orderlie	240	Institutional helper A	NH2A	288– 360*
3	Orderlies	300	Institutional helper A	NH2A	288– 360*
2	Dishwashers	180	Institutional helper B	NH2B	216– 312*
1	Orderly	360	Institutional helper A	NH2(A)	288– 360*
1	Fireman	360	Institutional helper A	NH2 (A)	288– 360*
2	Kitchen helpers	180	Institutional helper B	NH2 (A)	216– 312*
6	Maids	240	Institutional helper A	NH2 (b)	288– 360*
	Elevator man	240	Institutional helper A	NH2A	288– 360*
	Helper (to engineer)	240	Institutional helper A	NH2A	288– 360*

*Utility man.

*With maintenance (without maintenance add $240).

Pine Camp Hospital

Number of Positions	Present Title	Present Salary	Proposed Title	Code Reference	Appraised Salary Range
1	Superintendent	$1,080	Superintendent of nurses	ON3	$1,020–1,140*
1	Ward nurse	750	Nurse	ON1	640– 720*
1	Ward nurse	360	Hospital attendant	NA1	300– 480*
1	Ward nurse	300	Hospital attendant	NA1	300– 480*
1	Ward nurse	120	Junior institutional helper	NH1	120– 150*
1	Orderly	336	Institutional helper A	NH2-A	288– 360*
1	Night orderly	450	Hospital attendant	NA1	300– 480*
1	Orderly	360	Institutional helper A	NH2-A	288– 360*
1	Laborer	420	Senior institutional helper	NH3	360– 480*
1	Cook	360	Cook A	NQ1-A	360– 420*
1	Waiter	336	Institutional helper A	NH2-A	288– 360*
1	Waiter	336	Institutional helper A	NH2-A	288– 360*
1	Dish washer	216	Institutional helper B	NH2-B	216– 312*
1	House Maid	168	Hospital attendant	NA1	300– 480*
1	Night Nurse	300	Hospital attendant	NA1	300– 450*
	Interne	720	Assistant Physician (hospital)	(iP2)	720– 900*

Number of Positions	Present Title	Present Salary	Proposed Title	Code Reference	Appraised Salary Range
	Markets				
	First market:				
	Weighmaster	900	Assistant clerk	CC2	720- 900
3	Clerk	900	Clerk	CC3	1,020-1,380
	Sweepers	2.15 p. d.	Cleaner	UC1	720- 792
	Second Market:				
2	Clerk	900	Clerk	CC3	1,020-1,380
	Sweepers	2.15 p. d.	Cleaner	UC1	720- 792
	*With maintenance (without maintenance add $240).				
	City Home				
	Superintendent	$1,500	Day superintendent	N82	$1,440-1,680*
	Steward	1,300	Steward	N81	780- 900
					(with full maintenance)
	Engineer	1,080	Engineer	TG2	1,020-1,320*
	Matron (white department)	720	Matron	N81	600- 784*
	Matron (colored department)	720	Matron	N81	600- 784*
	Day clerk	600	Assistant institutional clerk	NC1	360- 540*
	Night clerk (colored department)	480	Semi-institutional helper	NH3	390- 480*
	Baker	720	Baker	NQ1	480- 780*
	Cook (white department)	240	Cook	NQ1B	240- 330*
	Wagon driver	240	Institutional helper A	NH2A	288- 360*
	Laundress	240	Institutional helper B	NH2B	216- 312*
	Night watchman (white department)	300	Institutional helper A	NH2A	288- 360*
	Internes	720	Junior medical interne	BP1	60- ...
3	Cook (officers' table)	120	Cook B	NQ1B	240- 330*
	Superintendent—nurse	780	Chief nurse	CN2	780- 900*
2	Nurse (old men's ward, white)	240	Hospital attendant	NA1	300- 450*
	Nurse (old women's ward, white)	240	Hospital attendant	NA1	300- 450*
2	Nurse (old women's ward, colored)	120	Hospital attendant	NA1	300- 450*
	Nurse (old men's ward, colored)	240	Hospital attendant	NA1	300- 450*
	Nurse (graduate, t. b. wards)	360	Nurse	ON1	660- 720*
3	Nurse (colored hospital)	240	Pupil nurse		Contract with Richmond College Hospital
3	Nurse (colored t. b. wards)	240	Pupil nurse		Contract with Richmond College Hospital
2	Orderly (colored hospital)	240	Institutional helper A	NH2A	288- 360*
	Cook (colored department)	180	Cook	NQ1B	240- 330*
	Emergency nurse	180	Salary on contract basis—no appraisal		
	General utility man	360	Institutional helper A	NH2A	288- 360*
	Clerk (for outside poor)	600	Superannuated Employee—no appraisal		
2	Chauffeur	1,080	Motor driver (ambulance)	TX1	1,140
	*With maintenance (without maintenance add $240).				

Virginia Hospital—Continued

Number of Positions	Present Title	Present Salary	Proposed Title	Code Reference	Appraised Salary Range
6	Interne	60	Medical interne	OP1	180– 300*
1	Engineer	900	Engineer	eTG2	1,020–1,320
1	Night telephone operator	600	Assistant institutional clerk	NC1	360– 540*
1	Day telephone operator	600	Assistant institutional clerk	NC1	360– 540*
1	Clerk	900	Institutional clerk	NC2	600– 780*
	Seamstress	180	Seamstress	NH2 (B)	216– 312*
	Cook	420	Cook A	NQ1 (A)	360– 420*
	Assistant cook	240	Cook B	NQ1 (B)	240– 330*
	Assistant cook	180	Institutional helper A	NH2B	216– 312*
2	Orderlies	240	Institutional helper A	NH2A	288– 360*
3	Orderlies	300	Institutional helper A	NH2A	288– 360*
2	Dishwashers	180	Institutional helper B	NH2B	216– 312*
1	Orderly	360	Institutional helper A	NH2A	288– 360*
	Floorman	300	Institutional helper A	NH2(A)	288– 360*
1	Kitchen helpers	240	Institutional helper A	NH2 (A)	288– 360*
1	Maids	180	Institutional helper B	NH2 (b)	216– 312*
2	Elevator man	240	Institutional helper A	NH2A	288– 360*
6	Helper (to engineer)	240	Institutional helper A	NH2A	288– 360*
	Utility man		Institutional helper A	NH2A	288– 360*

*With maintenance (without maintenance add $240).

Pine Camp Hospital

Number of Positions	Present Title	Present Salary	Proposed Title	Code Reference	Appraised Salary Range
1	Superintendent	$1,080	Superintendent of nurses	ON3	$1,020–1,140*
1	Ward nurse	780	Nurse	ON1	660– 720*
1	Ward nurse	360	Hospital attendant	NA1	300– 460*
1	Ward nurse	300	Hospital attendant	NA1	300– 460*
1	Ward nurse	120	Junior institutional helper	NH1	120– 150*
1	Orderly	335	Hospital attendant	NH2-A	288– 360*
1	Night orderly	430	Hospital attendant	NA1	300– 460*
1	Orderly	390	Institutional helper A	NH2-A	288– 360*
1	Laborer	420	Senior institutional helper	NH3	360– 480*
1	Cook	360	Cook A	NQ1-A	360– 420*
1	Writer	335	Institutional helper A	NH2-A	288– 360*
1	Waiter	335	Institutional helper A	NH2-A	263– 360*
1	Dish washer	216	Institutional helper A	NH2-A	278– 360*
1	House Maid	108	Institutional helper B	NH2-B	216– 312*
1	Night Nurse	300	Hospital attendant	NA1	300– 460*
1	Interne	720	Assistant at Physician (hospital)	(P2)	780– ,000*

Number of Positions	Present Title	Present Salary	Proposed Title	Code Reference	Appraised Salary Range
	Markets				
	First market:				
	Weighmaster	900	Assistant clerk	CC2	720- 900
	Clerk	900	Clerk	CC3	1,020-1,380
3	Sweepers	2 15 p. d.	Cleaner	UC1	720- 792
	Second Market:				
	Clerk	900	Clerk	CC3	1,020-1,380
2	Sweepers	2 15 p. d.	Cleaner	UC1	720- 792

*With maintenance (without maintenance add $240).

Number of Positions	Present Title	Present Salary	Proposed Title	Code Reference	Appraised Salary Range
	City Home				
	Superintendent	$1,500	Day superintendent	N82	$1,440-1,680*
	Steward	1,200	Steward	N81	780- 960
					(with full maintenance)
	Engineer	1,080	Engineer	TG2	1,020-1,320*
	Matron (white department)	720	Matron	N81	600- 784*
	Matron (colored department)	720	Matron	N81	600- 784*
	Day clerk	600	Assistant institutional clerk	NC1	300- 440*
	Night clerk (colored department)	480	Semi-institutional helper	NH3	300- 480*
	Baker	720	Baker	NQ1	480- 780*
	Cook (white department)	720	Cook	NQ1B	480- 780*
	Wagon driver	240	Institutional helper A	NH2A	240- 330*
	Laundress	340	Institutional helper B	NH3B	288- 360*
	Night watchman (white department)	300	Institutional helper A	NH3A	216- 312*
3	Interne	720	Junior medical interne	BP1	288- 360*
	Cook (officers' table)	120	Cook B	NQ1B	60- *
	Superintendent—nurses	780	Chief nurse	CN2	780- 900*
2	Nurse (old men's ward, white)	240	Hospital attendant	NA1	300- 450*
	Nurse (old women's ward, white)	240	Hospital attendant	NA1	300- 450*
2	Nurse (old women's ward, colored)	120	Hospital attendant	NA1	300- 450*
	Nurse (old men's ward, colored)	240	Hospital attendant	NA1	300- 450*
3	Nurse graduate, t. b. wards	800	Nurse	ON1	660- 720*
3	Nurse (colored hospital)	240	Pupil nurse		Contract with Richmond College Hospital
3	Nurse (colored t. b. wards)	240	Pupil nurse		Contract with Richmond College Hospital
2	Orderly (colored hospital)	240	Institutional helper A	NH2A	288- 360*
	Cook (colored department)	180	Cook	NQ1B	240- 330*
	Emergency nurse	180	Salary on contract basis—no appraisal		
	General utility man	360	Institutional helper A	NH2A	288- 360*
	Clerk (for outside poor)	600	Superannuated Employee—no appraisal		
2	Chauffeur	1,080	Motor driver (ambulance)	TX1	1,140

*With maintenance (without maintenance add $240).

Gas Department

Number of Positions	Present Title	Present Salary	Proposed Title	Code Reference	Appraised Salary Range
	Superintendent	$4,000	Engineer	OE4	$3,420-4,800
	Inspector of gas	2,500	Chief clerk	CC3	1,080-1,800
2	Water gas engineers	3.25 p. d	Engineman (gas plant)	TG2	1,140-1,320
2	Engineers	3.25 p. d	Engineman (gas plant)	TG2	1,140-1,320
2	Foreman	2.75 p. d	Foreman	TG1	840-888
19	Service men	2.50 p. d	Tapper's helper	TJ1	2.75 per diem
	Watchman		Watchman	KW1	816-828
4	General bookkeeper and clerk	1,680	Bookkeeper	CB2	1,320-1,560
	Gas fitters	4.00 p. d	Plumber	TP1	4.50 p. d. or $1,260 yr
	Storekeeper	4.00 p. d.	Storekeeper	KS1	960-1,200
	Machinist	3.50 p. d.	Machinist	TK1	3.50 per day
3	Machinist's helper	2.75 p. d.	Machinist's helper	TJI	2.75 per day
	Tinners and meter repair man	3.50 p. d	Tinner (gas meter repair)	TK1	3.50 per day
4	Main and service men	4.00 p. d.	Tapper	TK1	4.00 per day
11	Deputy inspectors of gas	1,200	Inspector of meters	ITI	960-1,140
5	Deputy inspectors of gas		Assistant clerks	CC2	720-900
	Bricklayer	3.50 p. d	Bricklayer	TB1	3.50 per day
	Blacksmith	3.50 p. d.	Blacksmith	TM1	3.50 per day
	Blacksmith's helper	2.50 p. d.	Blacksmith's helper	TJ1	2.75 per day
	Night foreman	3.50 p. d.	General mechanic (gas plant)	TZ2	1,140-1,320
	General foreman	1,600	General foreman (gas plant)	TZ3	1,440-1,680
2	Service men	2.75 p. d.	Motor driver (truck)	TX1	840-1,140
	Service man	2.75 p. d.	Skilled laborer (gas service)	TZ1	1,440-1,680
	Foreman—upper gas works	1,500	General foreman	UL3	900-1,200
	Assistant foreman	3.50 p. d.	Foreman	UL2	1,020-1,080
3	Meter setter	2.75 p. d.	Skilled laborer (gas service)	TZ1	1,020-1,080
6	Service men	2.75 p. d.	Skilled laborer (gas service)	TZ1	1,020-1,080
4	Stove setters	2.75 p. d.	Skilled laborer (gas service)	TZ1	1,020-1,080
4	Water gas maker helpers	2.75 p. d.	Skilled laborer (gas plant)	TZ1	840-888
2	Coal gas maker helpers	2.75 p. d.	Skilled laborer (gas plant)	TZ1	840-888
7	A-brollers	2.50 p. d.	Laborer	UL1	792-864
3	Yard and coal shed men	2.50 p. d.	Laborer	UL1	792-864
3	Coal stoker	2.50 p. d.	Laborer	UL1	792-864
2	Substitutes		Laborer	UL1	792-864
2	Coke standa		Laborer	UL1	792-864
	Service men (drip wagons)	2.75 p. d	Skilled laborer (gas service)	TZ1	1,020-1,080
2	Carpenter	2.75 p. d	Carpenter	TW1	1,080-1,200
4	Water gas makers	3.50 p. d.	General mechanic (gas plant)	TZ3	1,140-1,320
2	Coal gas makers	3.50 p. d.	General mechanic (gas plant)	TZ2	1,140-1,320
	Exhauster room men	3.25 p. d.	General mechanic (gas plant)	TZ2	1,140-1,320
	Purifying house man	2.00 p. d.	General mechanic (gas plant)	TV2	1,140-1,320
3	Pressure men	3.00 p. d.	General mechanic (gas plant)	TV2	1,140-1,250
	Superannuated employees	360 year			Pension
	Superannuated employee	2.50 p. d			Pension

Water Department

Number of Positions	Present Title	Present Salary	Proposed Title	Code Reference	Appraised Salary Range
	Superintendent	$3,000	Director of settling basins	XA1	$1,740–1,020
	Director of settling basins and laboratory	1,500	Senior assistant engineer	OB1	2,340–3,060
	First assistant superintendent	2,000	Assistant clerk	OE3	720–
4	Clerk	1,080	Assistant clerk	CC2	720– 900
	Inspector	1,080	Clerk	CC2	720– 900
2	Clerks	1,200	Clerk	CC3	1,020–1,380
	Assistant chief clerk	1,200	Clerk	CC3	1,020–1,380
	Chief clerk	1,500	Chief clerk	CC3	1,680–1,800
	Clerk to superintendent	1,080	Assistant stenographic clerk	CC3	1,020–1,380
3	Messengers	2.75 p. d	Inspector of meters	IT1	960–1,140
7	Inspector (meter repair)	2.85 p. d	Inspector of meters	IT1	960–1,140
	Messenger	1,080	Inspector of meters	IT1	960–1,140
	Storekeeper	1,080	Storekeeper	KS1	960–1,200
	General repair man	4.00 p. d.	Foreman mechanic (meter repair)	TK2	1,020–1,200
	2nd assistant superintendent	1,500	Foreman	U L2	1,140–1,320
	Foreman	1,320	Foreman	U L2	900–1,200
	Meter repairer	3.00 p. d	Mechanic (meter repair)	TK1	900– 960
	Pipeman	2.85 p. d.	Caulker	TK1	3 85 per day
	Keeper—reservoir with house	1,080	Custodian (reservoir)	KC1	900–1,020
	Keeper—reservoir with house	1,080	Custodian (reservoir)	KC1	900–1,020
	Watchman	2.50 p d	Watchman	KW1	816– 888
	Watchman	840	Watchman	KW1	816– 888
	Inspector	1,080	Inspector of meters	IT1	960–1,140
10	Pumpman	3.25 p. d.	General mechanic (pumping station)	T22	1,140–1,320
5	Plumber	1,260	Plumber	TP1	1,250 per yr or 4.50 p d.
14	Plumber's helper	2.75 p. d.		TJ1	2.75 per day
	Driver	2.75 p d.		TX1	840–1,140
	Chauffeur	3.00 p d		TX1	840–1,140
	Laboratory boy	1.25 p. d		BB1	240– 600
	Rodman	3.00 p d		BD1	960–1,440
	Engineer in charge	2,000	Chief engineman	TG3	1,440–1,920
11	Laborers	2.50 p d	Laborer	UL1	792– 964
16	Gateman	2.75 p d	Laborer	UL1	792– 964